GLASNOST

An Anthology of Russian Literature under Gorbachev

Edited by
Helena Goscilo & Byron Lindsey

Ardis, Ann Arbor

Glasnost: An Anthology of Russian Literature under Gorbachev
Edited by Helena Goscilo & Byron Lindsey
Copyright © 1990 by Ardis Publishers
All rights reserved under International and Pan-American Copyright Conventions.
Printed in the United Stated of America

Ardis Publishers
2901 Heatherway
Ann Arbor, MI 48104

Library of Congress Cataloging-in-Publication Data

Glasnost: An Anthology of Russian Literature under Gorbachev/
edited by Helena Goscilo & Byron Lindsey
p. cm.
Translated from Russian.
Contents: Old Hasan's pipe / Fazil Iskander — Our crowd / Lyudmila
Petrushevskaya — Rough weather / Anatoly Genatulin — Left behind / Vladimir
Makanin — Captain Dikshtein / Mikhail Kuraev — The parakeet & Anna's body /
Viktor Erofeev — Night / Tatyana Tolstaya — The visit / Nikolai Shmelev —
Dreams from the top berth / Valery Popov — Anna Petrovna / Alexander
Golovin.

ISBN 0-87501-070-9 (alk. paper).
1. Russian prose literature—20th century—Translations into English. 2. English
prose literature—20th century—Translations from Russian. 3. Glasnost—Fiction.
4. Soviet Union—Politics and government—1985—Fiction. I. Goscilo, Helena,
1945- . II. Lindsey, Byron.
PG3276.L58 1990
891.78'440808 — dc20   89-18525
                                                                 CIP

C ONTENTS

FROM THE EDITORS   vii

Helena Goscilo INTRODUCTION   xv

Lyudmila Petrushevskaya OUR CROWD   3

Fazil Iskander OLD HASAN'S PIPE   25

Mikhail Kuraev CAPTAIN DIKSHTEIN   59

Tatyana Tolstaya NIGHT   187

Vladimir Makanin LEFT BEHIND   195

Nikolai Shmelyov THE VISIT   271

Valery Popov DREAMS FROM THE TOP BERTH   293

Anatoly Genatulin ROUGH WEATHER   303

Viktor Erofeyev THE PARAKEET   367

ANNA'S BODY   379

Alexander Golovin ANNA PETROVNA   383

ABOUT THE AUTHORS   455

FROM THE EDITORS

In an essay for the *New York Review of Books* entitled "What Is Modern?" (1965), Paul de Man justly observed: "Precisely because they have an appearance of impersonality about them, encyclopedias or anthologies can be among the most subjective of documents." Awareness of that paradox might reduce the likelihood of subjectivity, but does not guarantee its elimination. Moreover, the criteria of balance and inclusiveness that one logically adopts in the service of objectivity invariably run the risk of generating their own contradictory principles of selection. Thus a text chosen primarily for its topicality, for example, may not meet the criterion of artistic merit, which in turn dictated the inclusion of other items. That problem is magnified x-fold when one seeks to compile an anthology of glasnost fiction, for the bulk of Soviet literature debuting in the last four years suffers from large infusions of journalism and unmediated historical recuperation. Yet novels bulging with semi-digested historical data, nakedly ideological argumentation, and all the devices of political exposé, such as Anatoly Rybakov's *Children of the Arbat* and Vasily Grossman's *Life and Fate*, are precisely the works singled out by the Soviet intelligentsia as vital to their current situation. For most readers in the Soviet Union they exemplify glasnost literature. We have endeavored, therefore, to assemble a collection that encompasses the diversity of current Soviet prose, yet at the same time retains its orientation and emphases, without compromising literary quality.

Although space limitations automatically precluded any translations of novels, the anthology contains several sizable novellas. The rationale for such a decision is compelling: both at home and abroad, novellas have generally created a greater stir than stories; some authors (e.g., Vladimir Makanin), define their talent in this genre, and others (e.g., Mikhail Kuraev) had not produced anything else at the time we were determining the contents of the anthology; and the venturesome but isolated recent experiments with modernist techniques have been conducted mainly in novellas. Apart from their inherent interest, the four in this anthology suggest the variety of contemporary fiction. Thus the nuanced intellectual retrospection of Alexander Golovin's *Anna Petrovna* contrasts markedly with Anatoly Genatulin's straightforward, largely external, chronological depiction of brute life on a Bashkir collective farm (*Rough Weather*). Thematic and stylistic differences likewise distinguish Makanin's *Left Behind* and Mikhail Kuraev's *Captain Dikshtein* both from the other two novellas and from each other, even though Makanin and Kuraev share an almost obsessive preoccupation with time and history. Similarly, the seven stories, in which oral elements and first-person point of view preponderate, range over a wide terrain: from the good-natured topical satire by Popov, through Petrushevskaya's acidic indictment of the intelligentsia's depravity, to Tolstaya's affective poetic evocation of mental illness.

Although all of the entries in the collection were published in 1987 or 1988, the direct pertinence of quintessential "glasnost issues" is more perceptible in some cases than others. History, for example, plays a role in the works of Kuraev, Golovin, Shmelyov and Makanin. It also figures in Iskander's story, to which, moreover, ethnic identity is critical. The narrative by Genatulin spotlights the deplorable living conditions in Russia's backwaters. Moral issues are addressed in the majority of texts, whether in the form of general corruption, as in Popov and Shmelyov, or sexual laxity and physical violence, as in Iskander, Petrushevskaya, Shmelyov, and Erofeyev, or in less easily definable ethical categories, as in Golovin, Makanin, and Kuraev. Even Tolstaya's masterpiece of anomalous interiorization could be placed in the context of recent Soviet admissions that mentally handicapped individuals actually exist in the USSR.

The omission of certain authors requires a few words of explanation. Texts, not authors, were our chief consideration. When copyright to specific works by Sergei Kaledin, Viktor Konetsky, Anatoly Pristavkin, Evgeny Popov, Anatoly Kim, Bulat Okudzhava, and Andrei Bitov originally slated for the anthology proved unavailable, we did not substitute other, less exciting items from their recent publications. Instead, we reinstated narratives of comparable quality that had tempted us earlier but that we had provisionally rejected on account of space. Even so, the unmanageable proportions of the anthology have forced us to split it into two volumes. Authors represented in the second volume include Boris Ekimov, Daniil Granin, Alexander Ivanchenko, Vyacheslav Kondratyev, Vitaly Moskalenko, Boris Pyetsukh, Leonid Shorokhov, Natalya Sukhanova, Vladimir Tendryakov, and Yury Trifonov.

The sketches of the authors at the end of the volume summarize the basic facts of their personal and professional biographies. In the conviction that literature is not hermetically sealed off from other forms of human experience, the first part of the Introduction supplies an overview of the historical and cultural context in which Soviet authors have produced their work. That picture is intended as a general background that charts significant developments, dominant trends, and crucial conflicts. Those who conceive of literature as a discrete entity need not be detained by these pages, proceeding instead to the second part of the Introduction, which focuses more narrowly on literary matters, or to the texts themselves.

The popular or non-specialist system of transliteration, slightly modified, is used throughout. Bibliographical data likely to be consulted only by those with a command of Russian, however, follow the Library of Congress system.

** ** **

This anthology is the brainchild of my co-editor Byron Lindsey. I became its stepmother at Byron's invitation in the summer of 1988, when we tentatively christened the newborn *The Glasnost Reader*. We chose the texts together on the basis of a preliminary list drawn up by Byron and we apportioned the subsequent editing work as equitably as the demands of our respective schedules over the last eighteen months or so have allowed. Both editors have checked the translations, which in most cases underwent further editing at Ardis. Final decisions regarding the make-up of the volume rested with Ardis.

Extending thanks to institutions and individuals may seem a conventional exercise, but it is partially redeemed from formula, I hope, by the sincerity of my gratitude: among institutions, IREX, which awarded me a Senior Scholar Grant that financed an educational spring in Moscow under the auspices of the Soviet Academy (1988); the Kennan Institute, which, in addition to a Reseach Scholarship, provided me with an excellent research assistant, Rebecca Epstein, and with an environment conducive to the completion of my share in the project (1989-90). I am also indebted to the following: our translators for their patience, perseverance, and sheer hard work; Byron for things too varied to enumerate; Elena Trubilova for her hours spent in the Lenin Library, and Natalya Ivanova, not only for an illuminating interview in Moscow, but also for her superb intuition and critical gifts—many of her assessments and recommendations steered us in rewarding directions; Svetlana Mikhailova, formerly of VAAP, for her resourcefulness and trust; Vladimir Padunov and Nancy Condee for stimulating conversations, numerous forms of collegial and friendly support, and more specifically, for first acquainting me with Viktor Erofeyev's latest fiction; Mark Altshuller for his readiness to combine wine-drinking with consultation about neologisms, barbarisms, and other recondite -isms; Mary Ann Szporluk at Ardis for her umpiring and editorial skills, her steadfastness, and her ability to stay tranquil in the midst of chaos; Ellendea Proffer and Ronald Meyer at Ardis for their epic aid; Carol Erickson at IREX for unfailing efficiency and cheer; Donald Barton Johnson, a fellow scholar at the Kennan Institute, for casting an experienced critical eye on the Introduction; and, as always, Brittain Smith, for generously putting my prose before his cons. Finally, last but most: loving gratitude to Walter Arndt, whose poetic gift for friendship matches his genius for poetic transformations.

Washington, D. C.   *Helena Goscilo*
January 1990

** ** **

> *The transition to gold currency is the
> business of the future, and in the province of
> culture what lies before us is the replacement
> of temporary ideas—of paper banknotes—
> with the gold coinage of the European
> humanistic tradition; the magnificent
> florins of humanism will ring once again,
> not against the archaelogist's spade, but
> when the moment comes, they will recognize
> their own day and resound like the jingling
> coins of common currency passing from
> hand to hand.*
>
> *Osip Mandelstam (1923)*

Have Mandelstam's "magnificent florins" returned to currency in Russia?
Do we hear the true, golden ring of humanism again in Russian literature?
More than anything else, this collection lets the reader apply his own critical judgment to these questions. Descriptive reports of the new or the
rediscovered are never as satisfactory as the direct experience of seeing
them for oneself: my belief that the act of reading is the first critical step
led me to the idea of an anthology in English translation. A wide readership can create a broad dialogue, and dialogue was my conceptual goal.

"Return" is a word encountered frequently in discussions of this period
in Russian literature because suppressed masterpieces (e.g., Andrei
Platonov's *Foundation Pit*, Mikhail Bulgakov's *Heart of a Dog*) and writ-
ers banned categorically and completely (Evgeny Zamyatin, Vladimir
Nabokov) or forced into exile and forbidden (Joseph Brodsky, Alexander
Solzhenitsyn) have all been returned—printed for the first time in the
Soviet Union. Both historical factuality and free discussion have returned
more or less on their own along with a freedom to choose one's own style
and mode of expression—realistic, modernistic, or sui generis eclectic.
Often timid, tentative, and self-conscious, the dismantling of previous
taboos has, nevertheless, been steady and persistent, and this movement
toward freedom continues in all aspects of thought and culture in the
Soviet Union. But the very scope of the process of retrieval has created a
diffusion of directions and a mixture of voices often at odds with each
other. This speaks persuasively for the diversity of the period, and while
the traditional role of Russian literature as a St. George primed to take on
all national dragons stands maybe a bit diminished, it no doubt augurs
well for the development of a democratic society. Contemporary Russian
writers have had to compete for attention, publication space, and readership with historians, economists, sociologists, and—in an especially uneven

match–with the great, excoriated writers of the past and present generations in exile whose works have been "returned."

During the first surge of the readable in 1986-88, we sought out the
fresh, independent and authentic voices in the shorter fictional genres of
novella and short story. Literary quality is seldom homogeneous in form,
style, or philosophical and social viewpoint, and in a period of renewal and
rediscovery, this may be especially true. But also, literature is a composite
of esthetic and moral values, and so its evaluative criteria are perforce subjective if not outright personal. My initial selective procedure was consciously subjective and was guided by the radically outspoken, reform-
minded critics such as Natalya Ivanova, Igor Dedkov, Tatyana Ivanova,
and Igor Zolotussky. Conversations with Helena Goscilo led to necessary
modifications or reinforcements in my preferences, and of course she
brought her own choices to the collection. While we tried for balance and
diversity in style, theme, and generation—keeping in mind the distinction
between newly published writers and long established ones now taking
benefit of the relaxed conditions of glasnost—we did not give any special
considerations to those writers associated with the nationalistic, politically
conservative and xenophobic ideas espoused by the journals *Nash Sovremennik* and *Moskva*. The omission of Sergei Kaledin and Evgeny Popov
from our roster of writers was a major disappointment: their merit by all
the above criteria could not—try as you may—overcome the copyright
obligations made for them elsewhere by VAAP, the Soviet Union's copyright bureau.

** ** **

Paternal analogies seem altogether fitting when a project of such genetic
complexity and extended gestation as this one finally goes forth into the
world. Helena Goscilo has been far too modest, however, in making herself this offspring's stepmother. With my occasional departures to other
commitments—including those to my own natural children and especially
my year's sojourn in the Soviet Union which caused me to neglect this literary embryo at a crucial stage—if either of us can be viewed as the distant
stepparent, I am the one. And if Helena began as a godmother concerned
for the project's spiritual integrity (it was she who christened the nameless
as *The Glasnost Anthology*), she soon became a full and equal partner in its
realization. Her devotion to the project was a given; her seemingly endless

resources of warmth and humor during times of stress were simply a gift for which I am grateful.

Vyacheslav Davidenko, professor of English at the Institute of Foreign Languages in Alma-Ata, Kazakhstan, USSR, and visiting professor of Russian at the University of New Mexico during 1989-90, compared some of the original texts with the translations. His superb command of linguistic alternatives has made an inestimable contribution in skirting pitfalls and probing for accuracy in my share of the editing.

Our super colleague-translators deserve the primary credit for the realization of this collective endeavor. Without their talented work and cooperative spirit the anthology would not exist.

I owe some other special thanks: to Professor Maurice Friedberg, who in his NEH Seminar first provided the stimulus to begin and then the steady encouragment to continue; to the Summer Research Laboratory of the Russian and East European Studies Center at the University of Illinois-Champaign-Urbana for the necessary research support and particularly to the ever resourceful staff of its Slavic Library; to the United States Information Agency and the Council for International Exchange of Scholars for the Fulbright year of experience in Alma-Ata and Moscow; and always to Tania for everything.

Albuquerque, New Mexico   *Byron Lindsey*
March, 1990

INTRODUCTION
A NATION IN SEARCH OF ITS AUTHORS

I

GLASNOST CONTEXTS

> *"History is past politics, and politics is present history."*
>
> John Robert Seeley

> *"To articulate the past historically does not mean to recognize it 'the way it really was.'"*
>
> Walter Benjamin

At present the twin stars of chaos and uncertainty preside over the Soviet political and cultural scene. Amidst the tumultuous conflicts, paradoxes and anomalies proliferating under Gorbachev's seemingly ever-accelerating policy of glasnost, perhaps the single imperative uniting the intellectual segment of Russian society is the concerted drive to repossess and reconstruct the nation's history. In recuperating the past, Russians seek a clarification of—indeed, a justification for—the present, as well as potential guideposts or caveats for the future. Edmund Burke's dictum, that "You can never plan the future by the past," would encounter scant sympathy in the Soviet Union today, where the majority endorse George

Santayana's axiom: "Those who cannot remember the past are condemned to repeat it." While the Soviet economy, increasingly lagging behind political reforms, lurches from one disaster to another, historians, sociologists, journalists, literati, film directors, and others determinedly struggle to fill in what Academician Dmitri Likhachev—People's Deputy, specialist in Old Russian literature, and newly appointed chairman of the board of the Soviet Cultural Foundation—at the Eighth Writers' Congress (1986) called the "blank spots" of their recorded heritage. Memory and moral judgment, the two faculties routinely manipulated and devalued by Soviet dogma, have become the principal requisites for the by now familiar processes of "archeological discovery," exposé, revision, rehabilitation, and repatriation. The assumption underlying this arduous activity is that truth, like Sleeping Beauty, has been lying in some repository, awaiting discovery; embraced by the advocates of glasnost, truth will awaken like the virginal princess roused by the prince's kiss. And the insatiable appetite, not only of professional historians, but of the Russian populace at large, for hitherto inaccessible information about seventy years of Soviet history evidences that the majority wish to attend that delayed awakening.

Facts about the purges and concentration camps, collectivization and famine, Soviet-Polish relations, persecution of non-Russian nationalities, and other experiences and events long ignored, denied, or suppressed in official versions of the past, but now unearthed through documents and witness accounts, inundate the press. Throughout 1987 Soviet journals and newspapers essentially communicated information that had long been known to the West, and posthumously repatriated the works and restored the reputations of writers who generations earlier had been executed, exiled, or pressured into emigration or suicide: Nikolai Gumilyov, Osip Mandelstam, Marina Tsvetaeva, Isaak Babel, Ivan Bunin, Evgeny Zamyatin, as well as the idealist thinkers Nikolai Berdyaev, Pavel Florinsky, and Ivan Ilyin. As glasnost gained boldness and momentum, various members of the intelligentsia who had been expelled from the Party were readmitted (e.g., in 1988, the Marxist historian Roy Medvedev, expelled in 1969 for writing *Let History Judge*, which, ironically, has become an influential text); works by emigre writers still (or until recently, like Vladimir Nabokov) living abroad suddenly saw Soviet publication (Joseph Brodsky, Vasily Aksyonov, Vladimir Voinovich, Sasha Sokolov, and later, Alexander Solzhenitsyn); and the Soviet media began disseminating completely new data unfamiliar to Westerners, particularly about Stalin, though certain sections of the Communist Party Archives still remain closed even to Georgy Smirnov, the director of the Party's Central Committee Institute of Marxist-Leninism. As myriad revelations accumulate, long-standing orthodox interpretations of former periods undergo radical revision or wholesale rejection; idols topple, while controversial political and cultural leaders earlier strategically omitted from historical accounts or dismissed as ideological enemies are recast in a markedly different light and their works finally printed. Of all the reversals abounding in this comprehensive process of reassessment, undoubtedly the most radical is the turnabout in the public image of Joseph Stalin.

As in his years of glory, so during his days of disgrace, Stalin dominates the stage of history's drama. Those formerly unmentionable excesses that are synonymous with the Stalinist era—repressions and executions, the camps, anti-Semitic campaigns, the wholesale deportation of minorities, the Lysenko scandal—have become a mainstay not only of current essays, articles and more substantive studies, but also of fiction, drama, and film. Indeed, works treating the volatile topic of Stalin and Stalinist practices have sparked more excitement and impassioned controversy than any others: apart from Solzhenitsyn's writings, such original fiction as Anatoly Rybakov's *Children of the Arbat* (wr. 1960s, pd. 1987), Daniil Granin's *The Bison* (1987), Vladimir Dudintsev's *White Robes* (1987), Vasily Grossman's *Life and Fate* (1988), Anatoly Pristavkin's *A Golden Cloud Spent the Night* (1987) and Yury Trifonov's unfinished *Disappearance* (1987), Boris Mozhaev's *Peasant Men and Women* (wr. 1978-80, pd. 1987); such films as Tenghiz Abuladze's *Repentance* (1987), and several documentaries. The last category includes *Soviet Power* (1988), which examines the Solovki camp (in the old Russian monastery on the Solovki Islands in the White Sea), the most famous of the early camps in the Soviet Gulag system so painstakingly described by Solzhenitsyn in *Gulag Archipelago*; also Leningrad producer Vinogradov's *D. Likhachev: I Recall* (1988), which recounts Academician Likhachev's imprisonment in Solovki and his sense, upon his release and return to Leningrad in the 1930s, that the entire country had metamorphosed into a vast labor camp throttled by terror and denunciations; and Igor Belyaev's televised two-hour *Trial* (1988), in which Vladimir Tikhonov, a member of the Soviet Academy of Agricultural Sciences, reveals facts shattering for the average Russian: (1) that 15 million peasants were unjustly repressed as kulaks during Stalin's forced collectivization of Soviet agriculture in the early 1930s, a pointless sacrifice because the first year of the war with Germany destroyed the industry built at their expense, (2) that contrary to the long-standing myth that Stalin led Russians to victory in the war, Stalin's poor judgment and actions encouraged Hitler's invasion of the Soviet Union, and (3) that during the Stalin terror, in 1937 alone 40,000 army officers perished, including 80 percent of Russia's top military leadership. Equally chilling corrections of previously underestimated numbers have been provided by Roy Medvedev and acknowledged by the government. Medvedev's claim, first published in the monthly *Argumenty i fakty* (1989) edited by V. A. Starkov, that Stalin's purges resulted in the deaths of 40 million people, only a few months later became official when a new school textbook on Soviet history incorporated it among its revised statistics.

Extensive debates on the issue raised by Tikhonov of Stalin's role in the second world war have centered on the secret protocol of the non-aggression Molotov-Ribbentrop Pact of August 23, 1939. During 1987 and 1988 the key question was the authenticity of the protocol, which established Soviet and German spheres of influence in Eastern Europe and the Baltic. While, with a fine disregard for logic, officials and conservative historians denied simultaneously both the authenticity and the existence of the protocol, Konstantin Simonov's memoirs (pub. 1988), and the historians Roy Medvedev, Yury Afanasyev, and V. Kulish affirmed the contrary. Their position has steadily gained ground, and, partly under the pressure of unremitting ethnic unrest in the Baltic states and Eastern Europe, the Soviet government has begun to recognize the protocol as authentic.

A pattern of gradually broadening admission by the authorities may be observed also in the touchy issue of Katyn that has surfaced in the course of Gorbachev's de-Stalinization campaign. In 1940 Soviet security police killed thousands of captured Polish soldiers at Katyn forest, near Smolensk, but shifted blame for the mass murder on to the Germans. Although the joint commission of Soviet and Polish historians charged with clarifying the murky areas in the history of relations between the two countries has made little progress in definitively establishing responsibility for the Katyn massacre, items in the Soviet press leave few doubts regarding the culpability of Stalin's NKVD forces. It is doubtless only a matter of time before the Soviets abandon their lengthy policy of camouflage regarding their culpability in the affair.

As a consequence of highly publicized analyses of such historical phenomena as the Molotov-Ribbentrop Pact, Katyn, and Stalin's role in World War II, practically all of the remarkable attributes that for half a century aureoled Stalin's image have been thoroughly discredited for some, though by no means all, segments of the intelligentsia. The repercussions have been extravagant, if to some extent foreseeable.

Since the dialectical structure of Soviet mythmaking dictates that dispossession in one quarter entails restitution in another, the overthrow of entrenched historical icons like Stalin enables the transformation of erstwhile villains into victims of his injustice if not into full-fledged political heroes. Beneficiaries of Stalin's loss of reputation include Leon Trotsky, a main organizer of the October Revolution of 1917, founder of the Red Army, and Stalin's chief rival in the 1920s, who after Lenin's death was expelled from the Party, deported, sentenced to death *in absentia* at the three Moscow show trials (1936-38), and assassinated in Mexico in 1940. Of all those who fell (fatally) out of Stalin's political favor, Trotsky alone still provokes vehement disagreement, makes many uneasy, and awaits total official rehabilitation. The minority representing a more unorthodox viewpoint on Trotsky are the historians Medvedev and Viktor Danilov, as well as Yury Afanasyev, Rector of Moscow's Institute of Historical Archives. Partly owing to Afanasyev's efforts, Trotsky is slowly and incrementally being restored to respectability, as evidenced by the publication of a number of his articles (1989). The posthumous reputation of other Bolshevik leaders liquidated by Stalin has been dealt with more leniently: In 1988 the USSR Supreme Court exonerated Nikolai Bukharin, whom many since 1987 consider a genuine but unrecognized alternative to Stalin in the 20s. As such, Bukharin recently has attracted favorable attention from the media and intelligentsia mainly because of his ideas on the Soviet economy, his preference for gradual collectivization and industrialization, his opposition to repressive measures as a standard enforcement of policy, and his friendship with writers like Boris Pasternak and Osip Mandelstam. Other rehabilitated Politburo members who fell victim to Stalin's purges include Lev Kamenev, Grigory Zinoviev, Alexei Rykov, Mikhail Tomsky (who committed suicide), and all of the defendants in the trials but Genrikh Yagoda (head of the secret police). Moreover, a Politburo Commission on the repressions of the 1930s, 1940s, and early 1950s reinstated Bukharin and Rykov to membership in the Communist Party and confirmed Tomsky's Party membership. Reversals of this kind have freed authors from the obligation to present these figures as criminals or to omit all mention of them in literary works—the only options that formerly enjoyed official sanction. Hence Mikhail Kuraev in his novel *Captain Dikshtein* (1987) can refer neutrally or with irony to Trotsky instead of casting him in the role of turncoat mandated by pre-perestroika Soviet ideology.

The *volte face* regarding Stalin and the victims of his terror has required some major adjustments in thinking. Perhaps no reappraisal, however, has shaken popular faith in Soviet history and its heroes more fundamentally than the aspersions cast since 1988 on the hitherto unassailable Lenin. Lenin's traditional image in Russian eyes as inviolable authority in all matters of state, Gorbachev's strategy of self-legitimization as a direct descendant of Lenin's untarnished heritage, and the widespread habit among commentators of contrasting Stalin's violation of socialist ideology with Lenin's rigorous adherence to inspiring revolutionary ideals make the recent perspective on Lenin's precepts and activities nothing short of blasphemous. As a rule Soviet censors delete any critical references to Lenin, as happened even recently when *Druzhba narodov* serialized Nabokov's memoirs *Speak, Memory* and *Knizhnoe obozrenie* published Brodsky's Nobel Lecture. Even such liberal, informed supporters of perestroika and glasnost as Afanasyev advocate a return to Lenin's legacy. A series of plays by Mikhail Shatrov (especially *The Peace of Brest-Litovsk* [wr. 1962, pub. 1987] and *Onward, Onward, Onward* [pub. 1988]), which explore the connection between Leninist principles and the subsequent course of Russian history conclude that those who followed Lenin or lacked his fervent commitment to the revolutionary cause polluted the pure fount of Leninism. While probing the nature and the consequences of the 1917 October Revolution, *Onward, Onward, Onward* demythologizes standard Soviet models of historical processes, above all the notion of inevitability. Owing to its confrontation of painful questions, the play proved a *succès de scandale* that inspired protests from several historians. It also elicited what many interpreted as an anti-perestroika campaign orchestrated by then Party ideologist Yegor Ligachev—an outraged and outrageous letter by the Leningrad teacher Nina Andreyeva that appeared in the newspaper *Sovetskaya Rossiya* (March 1988), accusing Shatrov of debasing Soviet achievements. Yet Shatrov's play is comparatively temperate insofar as it subscribes to the sacrosanct national myth of Lenin's rectitude—both moral and political.

Until the second phase of glasnost the mystique of Lenin's omniscience and infallibility was inscribed in the Soviet political tradition. For more than half a century Lenin represented an absolute against which other, lesser beings could be measured. Apostates have materialized recently, however, as scholars have started delving into the origins of Stalinism in a more thoughtful and sophisticated fashion. On Russian soil, the economic journalist Vasily Selyunin ("Roots," *Novy mir*, 1988) was the first not only to trace the sources of Stalin's terror and his suppression of the New Economic Policy (NEP) to Lenin's policy of War Communism, but also to hold Lenin's conservative insistence on monopoly responsible for strangling democratic forces. Selyunin's ideas resonate in the philosopher Alexander Tsipko's article "The Roots of Stalinism" (*Nauka i zhizn*, 1988), which faults the very Leninist-Marxist concepts on which the Bolsheviks built the new Soviet society. An article in *Pravda* (1988) written by Gennady Bordyugov and Vladimir Kozlov of the Institute of Marxism-Leninism advances the same hypothesis: that Stalin's "command-administrative system" dates back to Lenin and grew naturally out of Leninist principles. Publications by such scholars as Sergei Andreyev

(*Neva*, 1989) Igor Klyamkin, (*Novy mir*, 1989), and Roy Medvedev (*Let History Judge*, 2nd ed., 1989) hold Lenin's moral relativism and justification of means by ends accountable for much that earlier was blamed exclusively on Stalin. In like vein, the film *Soviet Power* shows that not Stalin, but the Bolsheviks established the Solovki camp—a revelation that is confirmed in numbing detail in Solzhenitsyn's *Gulag Archipelago* and Vasily Grossman's *Forever Flowing*, both published in the Soviet Union in 1989. If the plans tentatively broached by the Soviet press (1988) to make public the unexpurgated versions of Lenin's censored writings, which have languished in closed archives, come to fruition, then the vicious, cynical aspects of Lenin's domestic and foreign policies doubtless will further diminish the fanatical esteem he has enjoyed in the USSR for decades. Complete derogation of Lenin's image and his philosophy will leave Soviets with little to believe in or salvage from over 70 years of their history.

Whatever the skepticism of Gorbachev's detractors, the fact remains, then, that a wide spectrum of politico-historical concerns that were either taboo for years or subject to heavy censorship have become the topics of heated arguments and extensive literary treatment. These new areas of inquiry and dissent include Stalin and Stalinism, Lenin, the Revolution, War Communism, Russo-Polish and Russo-Baltic relations, Party loyalty and Party activity, World War II and patriotism. In light of countless profound reevaluations it comes as no surprise that Soviet historians and teachers have finally articulated (1986) what Westerners have long contended: that the profusion of falsifications in all Soviet history textbooks impugns their credibility in general. Accordingly, new textbooks are being issued with a view to their usefulness as educational and reference tools instead of venues for propaganda. Furthermore, jettisoning decades-old habits, Soviets have started acknowledging the merits of Western scholarship on Soviet history and culture—a development that has led to a plethora of collaborative projects that will inevitably alter future Soviet publications.

Additional symptoms of political change include the formation of diverse groups, especially the popular front organizations, a decrease in the power of the Party, authentic elections involving multiple candidates, and a broad-based awareness of national identity that that has spread rapidly, fostered in part by such proponents of reform as Academician Likhachev and Igor Dedkov. Articles by these and other commentators in *Druzhba narodov* and *Kommunist* have promoted national self-expression, championing diversification of ethnic traits as essential to an environment's balance and health.

Views such as theirs have enhanced, to some extent, the lot of minorities in the Soviet Union, as evident in improved conditions for Jewish cultural life: a rabbinical school and a kosher restaurant have opened in Moscow, as have organizations built around Jewish religious and cultural institutions; Tallin now has a permanent Jewish cultural center; and in several republics synagogues long used as institutes, warehouses, etc., are being restored to their original function. Many expect the reported growth in religious activity to spread further, as popular mistrust of other aspects of Soviet life and traditions intensifies. Admittedly, desecration of graves, chiefly in Jewish cemeteries, has taken place in Leningrad, Moscow, and elsewhere, which suggests aggressive hostility to Jews and possibly a more random violent resentment against "the system" that finds release in vandalism. Increased religious tolerance in general, however, attests to a revival of respect for spiritual values. Indeed, Gorbachev himself has made overtures to the Russian Orthodox Church and has spoken favorably of the role religion fulfills in contemporary society.

Unexpected developments in the system of official rewards and recognition offer less sweeping but nonetheless eloquent testimony of change. A striking example is the unorthodox choice of recipients of State prizes in 1988, none of whom belong to manistream socialist art: in prose, Dudintsev's *White Robes* and Pristavkin's *A Golden Cloud Spent the Night*; in literary criticism, Lidiya Ginzburg, the venerable Leningrad scholar who has written widely on the poets Mandelstam, Anna Akhmatova, and Boris Pasternak—all victims of official disfavor at some juncture in their careers; in film, German's *Road Checks*, the Latvian Juris Podnieks' *Is It Easy To Be Young?*; and in architecture, the Georgian memorial to the victims of Stalin by sculptor Georgy Ochiauri and the architects Vladimir Aleksi-Meskhishvili, Otar Litanishvili, and Kiazo Nakhutsishvili.

Not only controversial political issues, but social ills unacknowledged for decades and introduced into literature timidly, if at all, now receive extensive coverage in the media and dominate the thematics of Russian fiction. An article of 1987 in *Pravda* by the outspoken sociologist Tatyana Zaslavskaya lambasted the Soviet government for not admitting the existence of, or releasing statistics pertaining to, social problems in the country. That trend has reversed. Official data are plentiful and, as in the United States, present a dismaying picture that reflects and may well exacerbate the country's spiritual, moral, economic and ecological crisis. According to statistics made public in 1988, there are 120,000 drug addicts in the Soviet Union and the polluted air in over a hundred cities presents a health hazard. Current fiction has been quick to explore in some detail many of the defects cited in the press: crime, corruption, and opportunism (Viktor Astafyev's *A Sad Detective Story* [1986], Nikolai

Shmelyov's "The Visit," Valery Popov's "Dreams On the Top Berth," Leonid Shorokhov's *Volodka Osvod*, Eldar Ryazanov's film *Forgotten Melody for Flute* [1987]); absence of spiritual values (Chingiz Aitmatov's *The Executioner's Block* [1986], Gennady Golovin's *Anna Petrovna* [1987]); moral bankruptcy, especially on the part of the intelligentsia (Lyudmila Petrushevskaya's "Our Crowd" [1988]); betrayal on all fronts— of values, groups, and individuals (Trifonov's "A Short Stay in the Torture Chamber"); prostitution and sexual dissoluteness in general ("The Visit," "Our Crowd"); disaffection among the young generation (Juris Podnieks' film *Is It Easy To Be Young?* [1986]); physical violence and brutality *(A Sad Detective Story*, Vitaly Moskalenko's "Wild Beach," [1987], Valentin Rasputin's *The Fire* [1985], Viktor Erofeyev's "The Parakeet"); the backwardness of rural life (Anatoly Genatulin's *Rough Weather* [1987]); alcoholism (*Rough Weather*, "Our Crowd") and drug addiction (Rashid Nugmanov's film *The Needle*); the plight of the "fringe" elements; widespread pollution and the threat of ecological disaster (most works by Aitmatov, Valentin Rasputin, and sundry representatives of Village Prose).

Until Gorbachev's accession to power, official policy pronounced these dilemmas endemic to the decadent West but unimaginable in a socialist milieu. Now officials generally admit, for instance, that thousands of organized criminal groups operate throughout the Soviet Union and that crime in 1989 increased by 34 percent over 1988. Many attribute part of the rise to the anti-alcohol campaign, the spread of co-ops, the deteriorating economic conditions, and the scarcity of goods. While apartment burglaries are skyrocketing, policemen are killed in Leningrad, gun battles take place in the Moscow streets, and youth gangs terrorize cities, the number of arrests, indictments and convictions has decreased appreciably, as a consequence, in part, of perestroika's emphasis on humaneness, professionalism, and respect for due process of law on the part of law enforcement agencies. Here, as in other spheres, Gorbachev's reforms are impaled on a two-horned dilemma that leaves him vulnerable to criticism from many quarters: for the sake of liberalization, control and suppression must be reduced; greater liberty, however, means greater likelihood of rampant lawlessness. For the first time in Soviet history citizens voice fear not of government repression, but of violence from fellow citizens. Most liberals laud the government's public disclosure that crime, suicide, and youth problems exist in the Soviet Union and the innovative measures it has adopted to combat them. Conservatives, however, perceive both as symptomatic of an ignominious strategy to erode Russians' national identity and pride, and to defame their country in the eyes of the world. The very possibility of such contradictory opinions openly co-existing in the

Soviet Union suggests how rapidly aspects of Soviet thought have under-
gone transformation.

* * *

Nihil est ab omni
Parte beatum.
Horace

It would seem, then, that under glasnost Russians have acquired a measure of autonomy and freedom of speech. At official meetings and
roundtable discussions, in informal conversations, and in the journals,
magazines, and newspapers that have become the major forum for unin-
hibited debate and dissent, the pluralism urged by Afanasyev, Likhachev,
Vitaly Korotich, and others appears to be at work. Andrei Sakharov publicly criticized Gorbachev to his face and deputies have contradicted the
president without reprisal. Both *Ogonyok* and *Moscow News* have printed
conversations with leading intellectuals who frankly or implicitly challenge
virtually the entire range of Russian opinion, e.g., Venedikt Erofeyev, who
declares that "everything happening in Russia is irretrievable" and finds
today's Russian fiction unremarkable. Throughout 1988, two rival Soviet
TV talk shows called "Views" and "Before and After Midnight" compet-
ed for audiences in quintessentially American fashion by presenting such
provocative issues as the war in Afghanistan, poverty in the USSR, and
organized crime. Unflattering comparisons of Russia with other countries
have become commonplace in the media, while ritualistic condemnation
of the West, capitalism, religion, and their adherents has practically disappeared. Glavlit, the official censorship agency notorious for its former
stranglehold on all printed matter, nowadays reportedly instructs its censors (still assigned to all Soviet publications) to ignore ideological dogma
and focus on state and military secrets.

Why, then, do commentators like Andrei Sinyavsky, Lev Kopelev
(*Ogonyok*, No. 1989, 46) and Alexander Yanov feel apprehensive at several aspects of the conditions unwittingly ushered in by glasnost or emerg-
ing as an unforeseen consequence of the "new freedom"? Because Soviet
society—especially during the last year, which witnessed the gradual,
involuntary slackening of Gorbachev's grip on the unpredictable forces
unleashed by his own reforms—has become increasingly politicized and
polarized. And because the relaxation of age-old controls that allows conflicting views to coexist has permitted potentially alarming tendencies to
surface more strongly. Two cardinal questions repeatedly posed throughout the massive retrieval of bygone years recall the interrogative titles of

two classic nineteenth-century novels that programmatically appealed to Russians' civic conscience: Herzen's *Who Is to Blame?* and Chernyshevsky's *What Is to Be Done?* During the present epidemic of recrimination and restitution, these questions have acquired unprecedented weight, and the current permissiveness toward self-expression after such prolonged muzzling has encouraged Russians to respond with a veritable torrent of writing that gives an answer of sorts. That oblique answer may be roughly summed up as *J'Accuse!*—the title, appropriately enough, of Emile Zola's epistolary defense of Dreyfus in one of the most infamous nineteenth-century cases of anti-Semitism.

Whatever its other motivations, anti-Semitism, as well as the growing ethnic unrest in several republics, largely springs from the need to find a scapegoat, an "other" onto whom one may transfer fears and affix blame. Today in the Soviet Union anti-Semitism manifests itself in crude propaganda, including leaflets that threaten Jews in the major cities with physical violence. Anti-Semitic sentiments have been vented in varying degrees by the most radical representatives of the conservative nationalist movement. That highly vocal movement, which equates Gorbachev's policy of modernization with materialism and corruption, loosely unites such otherwise dissimilar figures as the Village Prose writers Valentin Rasputin, Vasily Belov, and Viktor Astafyev (who, as editor of *Pravda*, constitutes an influential voice); the chauvinistic, racist *Pamyat* (Memory) group under Dmitry Vasilyev, which resembles the prerevolutionary pogromist organization called the Union of the Russian People, credits the existence of a Jewish-Masonic conspiracy, boasts an active membership of 20,000 in Moscow, and has high-level backing, possibly from the KGB; scholars like Vadim Kozhinov and Sergei Vikulov, the editor of *Nash sovremennik*, which, together with *Moskva* and the youth-oriented *Molodaya gvardiya*, represents anti-perestroika sentiments in the "thick" journals; the theater critic Mark Lyubomudrov, reportedly expelled in 1988 from the Theater Workers' Union for his anti-Semitism; and an expanding number of powerful individuals and closely-knit groups.

In an atmosphere of disorder and bleak material deprivation, when ethnic unrest and crime seem to be undermining the country's central institutions and overturning all norms, these Russophiles yearn for a return to a largely mythical, purely Russian (in some cases, monarchical), more stable past, with its Orthodoxy, observance of ritual, indigenous folk art, tight family structure, and exclusion of "foreign" elements. The extremists among the nationalists would like to see the country purged of those factions which they blame for Russia's present woes: intellectuals influenced by Western ideas, minorities, and above all—Jews. Although some

Slavists have expressed qualms about the legitimacy of reading the Village Prose authors' fiction through the prism of their interviews and essays, it is difficult to dissociate Astafyev's rankly racist essay "Gudgeon Fishing in Georgia" (1986 in *Nash sovremennik*) and his vitriolic, anti-Semitic exchange with the historian Natan Eidelman (*Sintaksis*, 1987) from his use of the derogatory neologism "Jew-kids" in his depressing fictional portrayal of Russian provincial mores (*A Sad Detective Story*). Similarly, Rasputin's apocalyptic depiction of Russia's moral indifference and decay in his novella *Fire* takes on ominous overtones in light of his chauvinistic interview and article (*Literaturnaya gazeta* and *Nash sovremennik* in 1988). Rasputin's aberrational thinking regarding Jews finds full expression in a statement of his cited in Bill Keller's excellent article in *The New York Times Magazine* (28 January 1990): "I think today the Jews here should feel responsible for the sin of having carried out the Revolution, and for the shape that it took. They should feel responsible for the terror [. . .] that existed during the Revolution and especially after the Revolution. They played a large role, and their guilt is great. Both for the killing of God, and for that. In this country those are Jewish sins." Belov's misogynistic novel *Everything's Ahead*, Viktor Ivanov's *Judgment Day* (*Nash sovremennik*, 1988), and Igor Shafarevich's article "Russophobia" (*Nash sovremennik*, 1989) all make little attempt to disguise a kindred anti-Semitic bias. Through an identical scapegoat strategy, according to the reformist historian Viktor Danilov, local party leaders and conservative historians ascribe the tragedy of collectivization to the Jews: Trotsky and Lazar Kaganovich. Orthodox religious nationalists especially are not likely to forget Kaganovich's demolition of a Moscow cathedral for the sake of a swimming pool.

While some nationalists disclaim prejudice and emphasize their dedication to the preservation of cultural and historical monuments, ecology, and the resurrection of native Russian traditions, others (e.g., Andreyeva, Stadnyuk, the novelist Vladimir Luchutin) evince unambiguous pro-Stalinist leanings. The group *Otechestvo* (Fatherland, founded in 1989), in fact, has been justly characterized as an organization uniting nationalists with anti-reform conservatives from the Soviet military and the ranks of the neo-Stalinists. Although Soviet scholars who caution against throwing all nationalists into a single anti-Semitic, neo-Stalinist pile provide a corrective to those liberals who oversimplify through crude generalization, one cannot overlook the almost hysterical anti-Semitism of the nationalists who distort or ignore undisputed facts so as to find Jews accountable for Russia's travails. In the face of all logic, for example, Vadim Kozhinov lays at Trotsky's door the destruction of Moscow's churches in 1934, even though Trotsky went into exile in 1929 (*Moskva*, 1986); the editor of *Molodaya gvardiya* also ascribes to Trotsky the popularity of Mandelstam's and Pasternak's poetry (Mandelstam was Jewish, Pasternak partly Jewish); and an issue of *Nash sovremennik* (1988) ran an article by Kuzmin that not only assaulted Trotsky, but also implied that Yury Afanasyev, who has agitated for Trotsky's rehabilitation, is a member of the Judeo-Masonic conspiracy against the Russian nation (*Nash sovremennik*, 1988). Although Soviet authorities traditionally have fostered anti-Semitism—despite Article 52 of the Constitution, which guarantees citizens the right to profess any religion—Gorbachev has discouraged its extremist manifestations, which have also drawn objections from liberal intellectuals like Evgeny Evtushenko, appalled by the parallels between today's Soviet anti-Semites and their Nazi counterparts under Hitler.

The alarming wave of anti-Semitism, in fact, is frequently difficult to separate from the current propagation of a Stalin cult. Danilov has noted that precisely those functionaries who blame the Jews for collectivization (which the nationalist faction considers the worst crime of the Soviet regime) laud Stalin for his purportedly merciful restraint of the most zealous activists in the campaign. And both *Ogonyok* and *Moscow News* have shown video tapes of veterans and random citizens, including women, who convene regular meetings to celebrate Stalin's memory, reminisce nostalgically about his unequalled charisma and effectiveness as a man of action, and keep his name and heritage alive. Even as revelations about Stalin's atrocities mount, many revere Stalin as the epitome of the strong leader.

The sharp conflict between liberal supporters of Gorbachev's reforms and the conservative opposition that some alarmists have labeled a "civil war" has been waged vehemently in the press. Ideological adversaries for the most part have affiliated themselves with publications that more or less share their convictions. Fiction, articles, and letters reflecting liberal values have predominated in the thick journals *Novy mir* under Sergei Zalygin, *Druzhba narodov* under Sergei Burazdin, *Znamya* under Grigory Baklanov, *Neva*, and *Yunost* under Andrei Dementyev, and in the literary weekly newspaper *Literaturnaya gazeta* (during 1989 under Yury Voronov) and *Sovetskaya kultura*. Conservative forces have found an outlet in *Nash sovremennik*, *Molodaya gvardiya*, and *Moskva* under Mikhail Alexeyev, as well as the nationalist papers *Sovetskaya Rossiya* and *Literaturnaya Rossiya*. The multi-lingual weekly newspaper *Moscow News*, with a readership of 250,000 (after its revolutionary improvement by Yegor Yakovlev, chief editor since 1986), and above all the outspoken illustrated weekly *Ogonyok* under Vitaly Korotich's editorship since 1986, with a circulation of 3,083,000, have deservedly acquired a reputation as the most uncompromising and active champions of openness and pluralism. Unlike their nationalist opponents, Yakovlev and Korotich as a matter of principle have encouraged disagreement among reformists and have published widely differing views on every imaginable topic. Because *Moscow News* was conceived with a foreign audience in mind (its English edition dates from 1930, the Russian one, only since 1980), has a substantially smaller audience, and thus carries less impact with Russians, conservatives have concentrated their anti-glasnost dissatisfactions on *Ogonyok* and its editor, despite Gorbachev's personal defense of both. Among the recent spate of abuse heaped on Korotich's head the collective letter published in *Pravda* in January 1989, signed by Astafyev, Belov, Rasputin, Alexeyev, Vikulov, Pyotr Proskurin, and the film director Sergei Bondarchuk, allegedly ousted from the leadership of the progressive Cinematographers' Union in the 1986 elections for his role in Andrei Tarkovsky's persecution, has evoked a storm of indignation among the liberal intelligentsia. Denouncing *Ogonyok* for dragging Russia's spiritual values into the mire, the signatories in fact were repudiating, as they have frequently done in the course of 1988-89, Korotich's sustained exposure of Stalinism, anti-Semitism, Party privileges, and those speaking for their perpetuation today.

Analogous partisan loyalties divide the various Unions, whose meetings provide occasions for acrimonious assaults on avatars of opposing factions. Since its radical reorganization in 1986, the Cinematographers' Union under Elem Klimov and Andrei Smirnov's chairmanship has sought dialogue with the West and taken a firm pro-reformist stand on controversial developments. A parallel transformation occurred in the theater world with the formation of the Union of Theater Workers (1986). It adopted a statute that safeguards against infiltration by self-seeking bureaucrats, set limits on Union personnel's terms in office, ensured a high degree of artistic autonomy, and assumed financial responsibility for its own activities. Experimental groups and theater studios (such as the small but talented Chelovek, which has had extraordinary success in its staging of Petrushevskaya's play *Cinzano*) now handle their repertoire and budget themselves. By contrast, the ossified Artists' Union and the USSR Academy of Arts, in a country with only one museum of modern art (in Armenia!), are strongholds of conservativism motivated by material self-interest. Admittedly, since 1986, Soviets have held exhibitions of previously proscribed artists, predominantly avant-gardists like Marc Chagall, Vasily Kandinsky, Kazimir Malevich, Lyubov Popova, Natalya Goncharova, Mikhail Larionov, and Vladimir Tatlin. And while the nationalist painter Ilya Glazunov's popularity with the public has dwindled, non-conformist

artists like Ilya Kabakov, Boris Zhutovsky, Erik Bulatov, and Dmitry Prigov
have attracted sizable audiences. The Union and the Academy, however,
not only control exhibitions, art scholarship, and the purchase and sale of
artworks, but categorically resist modernist innovation. Moreover, nasty
internal skirmishes over finances and perquisites have resulted in mutual
charges of abuse of power among members who have no intention of surrendering their prerogatives so as to accommodate an influx of younger,
less conventional artists. These establishment monopolists have much in
common with the comparatively small (2,500 members) but creaky
Composers' Union headed by the troglodytic People's Deputy Tikhon
Khrennikov, and the vociferous top leaders in the considerably larger and
more powerful Russian Writers' Union, particularly Yury Bondarev and
Union Board Chairman Sergei Mikhalkov, as demonstrated at various ses-
sions since 1986. Their aversion to everything equated with glasnost was
couched in such rancorous terms at a meeting of the secretariat of the
board in Ryazan (1988) that *Kommunist* ran an editorial criticizing the
speeches as anti-democratic, anti-Western, and, by implication, anti-
Semitic. Moreover, the Union's most influential members now advocate
excluding the Leningrad chapter of the organization for its purported
domination by Jews.

That much of the resistance to change derives not only from ideological convictions, but also from practical considerations was argued com-
pellingly by the writer Natalya Ilina in an article printed by *Ogonyok* in
1988. Enumerating the cynical self-serving practices still entrenched in
publishing houses, Ilina demonstrates how frequent publication and success in Soviet literature have no relationship to artistry. Self-promotion, as
well as exploitation of ghost writers and a network of quid pro quos, has
perpetuated the careers of men manifestly devoid of creative talent and,
apparently, of genuine interest in literature. They revere the muse of expe-
diency.

Under these circumstances, it is unsurprising that writers, artists and
thinkers have taken the initiative of launching independent periodicals
(e.g., *Glasnost* under the editorship of the political ex-prisoner Sergei
Grigoryants, the literary publication *Epsilon-Salon*, and the cinema journal *Cine-fantom*), banding in groups such as the artists' Hermitage and
the writers' April, and creating professional organizations administered
along drastically different lines, such as the PEN Center in Moscow, with
Rybakov as president, Andrei Bitov and Andrei Voznesensky as vice-presi-
dents, and an executive committee comprised of Bella Akhmadulina,
Sergei Kaledin, A. Kurchatkin, Vladimir Lakshin, Bulat Okudzhava, Evgeny
Popov, and Tatyana Tolstaya. Cooperatives of artists and theater workers,

an entirely original phenomenon in the Soviet Union, mount exhibits, sell their paintings, and stage shows independently of unions, and external financing or prescriptions. And the popular culture created or coordinated in the streets by Soviet youth, of course, presents such a radical departure from both institutionalized and newly-evolving Soviet standards as to warrant separate analysis.

Three years after his historic, optimistic proclamation of glasnost as a prerequisite for the implementation of vital transformations in Soviet society, Gorbachev appears caught between two extremes that leave him squarely in the middle. Wedged in between diehard conservatives who attribute all of Russia's innumerable current ills to the new thinking on the one hand, and the more radical contingent of reformers who are impatient with his moderate approach to critical needs, Gorbachev must negotiate his way through a minefield of hopes, resentments, fears, and possibly unrealistic expectations. A survey conducted in late 1989 among Russians from all social strata revealed that 17 percent of the population support Gorbachev's policies as pursued at their present rate, whereas 71 percent believe they should move faster; 5 percent advocate a return to pre-perestroika strategies (*Moscow News*, January 1990). Unreserved endorsement, in other words, comes from a minority, while outright antagonists, though less numerous, occupy seats of power. The prevailing ferment in the Soviet Union suggests not so much pluralism as volatile tension.

II

GLASNOST TEXTS

*Tous les genres sont bons hors le genre
ennuyeux.*

Voltaire

*The historian, essentially, wants more doc-
uments than he can really use; the dramatist
only wants more liberties than he can really
take.*

Henry James

In the context of these complex and contradictory developments, what
constitutes the major trends in current Soviet literature? How may one
characterize the fiction published under the aegis of glasnost? The first
problem is one of definition, for the elastic and imprecise rubric "glasnost
literature" encompasses at least five dissimilar and largely incompatible
categories: (1) the "archeological" fund—literature belonging to earlier
eras but banned until now primarily on "ideological" grounds (e.g.,
Zamyatin's *We*, Bulgakov's *Heart of a Dog*); (2) more recent works,
whose successful or attempted publication resulted in the author's public
vilification, imprisonment, or expulsion (e.g., Vladimir Voinovich's *The
Life and Extraordinary Adventures of Private Ivan Chonkin*, Solzhenitsyn's and Sinyavsky's writings) and works of approximately the
same period that circulated only unofficially in Russia, but saw Western
publication unaccompanied by scandal (Venedikt Erofeyev's *Moscow to the
End of the Line*, Andrei Bitov's *Pushkin House*); (3) manuscripts "kept in
the drawer"—written in the 1960s, 70s, and early 80s that were rejected
or not even submitted for possible publication by authors who simply
bided their time (e.g., Rybakov's *Children of the Arbat* and Dudintsev's
White Robes); (4) current fiction by writers who thrived throughout the
stagnation (*zastoi*) of the Brezhnev years, but who now have leaped on
the careening bandwagon of thinly-veiled journalism in support of glasnost; and (5) works by authors whose debut or belated discovery happens
to have coincided with glasnost or proved useful to its advocates, but
whose vision of the world evolved prior to glasnost, even if the publication of their works did not (e.g., Tatyana Tolstaya, Viktor Erofeyev).

The majority of Soviet readers frankly favor the first three categories, to
which the thick journals (the chief purveyors of literature in the USSR)
likewise give priority. The titillation of biting into formerly forbidden fruit

(about the only fruit available in Soviet markets) undoubtedly accounts in part for this taste, though few would recognize or admit the mechanism at work here. Baklanov, the editor of *Znamya*—a standard-bearer in the tireless purveyance of reclaimed materials—asserts that pre-perestroika fiction by the likes of Boris Pilnyak (1894-1937), Varlam Shalamov (1907-82), Vasily Grossman (1905-64), and Vladimir Tendryakov (1923-84) overshadows new submissions: "There are still no contemporary books equal to the importance of the current period of change" (*Moscow News*, 1988). A cursory glance through recent issues of Russian periodicals confirms that such an estimate is not peculiar to Baklanov alone. Alla Latynina, a prolific centrist literary critic, has echoed that sentiment: "Literature of the past has become today's literature" (*Moscow News*, 1989). Others concur. To what extent, however, does this privileging of a recovered legacy edge out potentially gifted newcomers? One must invest inordinate trust in the taste and judgment of editors like Baklanov not to challenge both his sweeping claim and his editorial decisions. Is that trust warranted? What standards does Baklanov apply to candidates for publication? Clearly, ideological rather than aesthetic ones. However impressive in their high-minded censure of ethical misconduct, virtually all of the glasnost "block-busters" (*Children of the Arbat*, *Life and Fate* and *Forever Flowing*, *White Robes*, Daniil Granin's *The Bison*, as well as Chingiz Aitmatov's more recent *The Executioner's Block*) have come from clumsy and often artless, if well-meaning, pens. Wooden dialogue, characters that fail to come alive, interminable harangues, shaky transitions and faltering command of viewpoint, in fact, substantially compromise their status as artistic creations. Yet their phenomenal success evidences that what Soviet editors (and, apparently, the public) esteem above all else nowadays is topical exposé, publicistic statements that, *mutatis mutandis*, still operate stylistically within the dispiriting framework of social realism or "poor man's realism." In that respect, Sinyavsky's shrewd remark that Soviet literature has entered the Solzhenitsyn era is a genuine aperçu, substantiated, moreover, by Vyacheslav Kondratyev's admission that in the Soviet Union "today Solzhenitsyn is perhaps the only writer who has been accepted by everyone" (*Moscow News*, 1989). Belated semi-journalistic unmasking of the past or invectives against the present, masquerading as literature, now verge on a new orthodoxy—a new social, if not socialist, realism—and as befits Soviet orthodoxy, find voice in a prose that bears the stamp of the period and its exigencies rather than of the artist.

Yet very few Soviet or, for that matter, Western critics have expressed qualms about the effect of journalism on the fiction most closely identified with glasnost. Isolated exceptions include (implicitly, at least) the writer Venedikt Erofeyev, the Slavist Nora Buks, and particularly Natalya Ivanova, whose principled commitment to openness has not blunted her aesthetic sensitivity. As early as 1986 she drew attention to how noticeably the artistic level of fiction has suffered from massive infusions of journalistic features—precisely those features that writers like Ales Adamovich recommend as the sole means of elaborating the "superprose" (*sverkhproza*) that can answer the needs, and be commensurate with the realities, of Soviet society today. Ideology and social relevance, the hallmarks of socialist realism, remain the imperatives of Soviet literature, though now reoriented in accordance with the devaluation of former truths and truisms and the concomitant valorization of erstwhile heterodoxy.

In that sense and others, some of the touted changes in new literature and its publication are more apparent than real. Perhaps censorship more than any other facet of the "literary process" discloses how at this stage in history musty old wine can still get decanted into vaunted new bottles. As Michael Massing (*New York Review of Books*, 1989) discovered during recent interviews with press personnel, although Party leaders still monitor all newspapers, the censorship function long monopolized by the state is gradually being transferred into the hands of individual editors. In addition to the authors themselves, who have internalized decades-old prohibitions, individuals at all levels of the publishing process now censor works. Prudery regarding sex, violence, various unglamorous bodily functions, profanities and obscenities still causes texts to be bowdlerized, though now on a more random basis, depending on the tastes of those who exercise their editorial privileges. These are exercised most noticeably in the thick journals, which reach an appreciably broader audience than the collections published in book form, typically in insufficient runs to satisfy the demands of Russian readers. The fate of Venedikt Erofeyev's *Moscow to the End of the Line*, written in 1969, circulated in manuscript form in 1970 in the Soviet Union, then published in its entirety without excisions in Paris, demonstrates how Soviet puritanism leads to startling idiosyncrasies in the system. When the weekly *Nedelya* printed a chapter from the novella in September 1988, it expunged a humorous passage that satirically linked Russians with homosexuality and the Arab-Israeli conflict. Moreover, even when the novel was reprinted in the journal tellingly entitled *Sobriety and Culture* purists removed vocabulary that Russians presumably would find offensive, substituting ellipses for several "unprintable words."

Public response to Lyudmila Petrushevskaya's story "Our Crowd" and to Viktor Erofeyev's readings from his fiction indicates that a society reared on palliatives and "supervised," expurgated texts may not yet be ready to cope with unsanitized prose. According to Petrushevskaya's own comments and the letters that bombarded *Novy mir*, "Our Crowd" offended many and earned her enemies among the very intelligentsia which purportedly is the strongest supporter of glasnost. Analogous complaints have sounded against the violence, preoccupation with physiological matters, and profusion of verbal impieties that comprise the authorial signature of Viktor Erofeyev.

However unpropitious the current circumstances, in compliance with the unfathomable dynamics of artistic creativity, original talents have materialized in the last few years (our 5th category of glasnost literature). Some, like Vladimir Makanin, have gained prominence rather late in their careers, while others have attracted a following with the publication of their first work, e.g., Mikhail Kuraev with *Captain Dikshtein* (1987). Whereas the rise of certain authors (like Tolstaya, who began writing in 1983) has been meteoric, others, like Petrushevskaya have struggled for twenty years to attain recognition, or, as in the case of Alexander Ivanchenko (*The Technology of Safety I*, 1988), access to print. In its technically novel treatment of any and all aspects of life, the "new" prose has revived the modernist tradition long stifled by prescriptive Stalinist aesthetics, and thus may more appropriately be characterized as "renewed" or "renovative." A grain of truth may be buried under the mountain of abuse heaped by Dmitry Urnov on this "alternative," or, as he pseudo-ingenuously labels it, "bad" prose (*Literaturnaya gazeta*, February 1989): part of its appeal for Soviet readers (trained to read literature as encoded political statement) may, indeed, reside in the involuntary frisson produced by texts glamorized through prohibition. More likely, however, the intelligentsia welcomes "alternative prose" not because of its piquancy, but as a promising liberation from hoary formulas—a chance for writers to pursue flights of individual imagination instead of adhering to collective stereotypes.

Radical differences in authorship, subject and manner notwithstanding, the novellas and short stories, if not the novels, by the period's most gifted prosaists share a number of refreshing tendencies: a more subtle or original perspective on familiar phenomena; a focus on the inner world of human experience, with the external defamiliarized or relegated to the periphery; attentiveness to the stylistic, rather than the ideological, aspects of prose; scrambling of temporal and spatial categories; a propensity for irony and fantasy; a post-modernist explosion of intertextuality; enriched vocabulary and a generally freer approach to language. The heterogeneous, unaffiliated group associated with this trend—Tolstaya, Erofeyev, Kuraev, Valery Popov, Vyacheslav Pyetsukh, Alexander Ivanchenko, Evgeny

Popov, Sergei Kaledin, the Viktor Konetsky of "Cat-Strangler Silver" (1987) and Andrei Bitov, especially in "Pushkin's Photograph (1799-2099)" (1987)—has closer parallels to Vladimir Nabokov, Sasha Sokolov, and the writers of the 1920s than to immediate Soviet predecessors. Most seem to have imbibed, at creative (re)birth, Sinyavsky's prophetic intuition (*What Is Socialist Realism?* [wr. 1956]) that the future of Russian literature lies in an absurd, fantastic, phantasmagoric art of hypotheses instead of Purpose.

Kuraev's *Captain Dikshtein* splendidly illustrates how artistic complexity can vouchsafe a more nuanced treatment of a subject that seems doomed to simplification in the hands of overt polemicists. *Captain Dikshtein* comprises a lengthy "historical" account of the Kronstadt uprising, set within a short fictional frame. This insurrection against Communist rule by the Kronstadt naval base, which had been a major supporter of the October Revolution, has long remained a forbidden chapter of Soviet history. Kuraev's literary debut broke the stubborn silence on this volatile topic. Playful, digressive, and self-reflexively ironic in tone, Kuraev's text nonetheless offers a serious meditation on the nature and meaning of history. For Kuraev, the master narrative of history has disintegrated. A temporal sequence neither guarantees nor implies a teleological ordering, for history consists of random phenomena that become organized into a meaningful design only through subsequent perspective. According to this destabilized view of history, historical "facts" cannot exist independently of their later, constellating representation. Hence Kuraev's predilection for diverse, often contradictory points of view on historical events, which, however, are highly particularized. If that technique communicates the accidental nature of history, Kuraev's self-conscious mode of narration in the framing portions of the novella likewise underscores how a constructed perspective determines the fictional organization of materials. Whereas Rybakov, Grossman, Solzhenitsyn, and other practitioners of historical retrieval credit both the necessity and the possibility of learning the Truth about the past, Kuraev confronts the truism that the past is not marked by simple facticity or continuity, but by rupture, breaks in identity, changes in name, and gaps in narration. Russia, like Kuraev's protagonist Igor Ivanovich, underwent a fantastic series of transformations—in name, government, culture, and identity—accompanied by equally fantastic explanations of these metamorphoses. Thus the novella's subtitle of "a fantastic narrative" refers less to Kuraev's fictional mode, which evokes Gogol and Dostoevsky, than to the course of Russia's history, which Kuraev conceives in Tolstoyan terms. Kuraev's originality consists not only in perceiving contingency where others have claimed inevitability, but in revealing how the contingent and fantastic constitute so-called history.

Temporality and perception, sequence and causality, ends and beginnings—and the zigzags connecting and separating them—likewise fascinate Makanin and Bitov, who share a reputation as difficult, intellectual writers. The artist's relationship to history, the need for cultural continuity, and the processes shaping the individual psyche are minutely explored in their highly self-conscious narratives, complicated by the interplay of layered spatial and temporal planes, multiple perspectives, and a knotted, looped, and loosened narrative thread. In Makanin's case, calculatedly enigmatic references to events or characters, intense efforts to situate oneself in relationship to times past, present, and future, in tandem with a complex interaction between two or more plotlines, heighten both the formal sophistication and the interest of his works in the late 1970s and 1980s. Such recent publications as *A Man and a Woman* (1987), *The Loss* (1987), and *Left Behind* (1987) reflect the refinement in his perpetual concern with forging meaningful links between manifestations of one's various selves within closely examined moral and cultural contexts. *Left Behind* exemplifies Makanin's penchant for interweaving several plot lines and ostensibly unrelated characters for brief but highly revealing moments at irregular junctures in the narrative. Like Bitov, Makanin seeks continuity in change and integration within dissolution, in a style that places rigorous demands on the reader. Bitov, especially, presupposes a reader with an instant recall of the entire span of Russian literature, whether in his endlessly intertextualized novel *Pushkin House* or in the superb story that could function as its epilogue: "Pushkin's Photograph (1799-2099)" (1987). There, the science-fiction convention of time travel literalizes Bitov's matrix metaphor for tracing cultural origins as he continues his profound and often hilarious pursuit of Russia's supreme cultural icon: Pushkin. Although Makanin's transgressions against an unbroken linear structure are less colorful than Bitov's, his deliberate omissions and unexplained juxtapositions force the reader to perform the very jointure that he urges in the name of humanism, yet eschews narratively: for example, in *The Loss* and especially in *Left Behind*. Both authors share Kuraev's passionate interest in process and his skepticism regarding History as an inert body of interconnected facts awaiting reclamation.

The necessarily subjective nature of memory also finds poignant expression in Golovin's *Anna Petrovna*, made into a film for television almost immediately upon publication that aired in June 1989. *Patience and Hope*, the title of Golovin's first collection of novellas (1988), attend the lessons that his slowly dying protagonist, Anna Petrovna, has learned from her long life, which she resuscitates in kaleidoscopic fragments through recollections, dreams and fantasies in the course of the narrative. This flutter of incessantly shifting, haphazard impressions ranging over six decades skillfully simulates the associative processes of memory, dream, and semiconscious reflection. The collective images transmit a palpable sense of an intensely rich life, one illuminated by Anna Petrovna's generous responsiveness to everyday occurrences, to small details, atmosphere, visual stimuli, and human needs. Those familiar with recent Russian history will be tempted to read Golovin's delicate portrait of the refined yet resilient protagonist as a homage to an entire generation of real-life heroines: women with Anna Petrovna's sensitivity and spiritual resources—some now dead, others in their eighties, but still working—who under often inhuman conditions, in poverty, isolation, and sickness, have made the preservation of Russian culture their life's work: for example, Nadezhda Mandelstam, Emma Gershtein, Lidiya Ginzburg, I. Grekova, Natalya Baranskaya.

Golovin's collage technique, which enables him to slip unobtrusively in and out of psychological and physical states in a succession of temporal frames, allows Anna Petrovna's life to speak through her thoughts and reminiscences, without omniscient authorial intervention. This use of *erlebte Rede/style indirect libre*, of first-person narrative (both of which sometimes teeter on stream of consciousness), and of multi-voiced narrative reflects the decentering or dissolution of authoritative perspective prevalent in alternative prose. Freedom from dogmatic pronouncements or a single, unified center of consciousness that labors to orient readers' responses according to authorial convictions marks the fiction of Iskander, Valery Popov, Bitov, Petrushevskaya, Erofeyev, Tolstaya, recent Makanin, and Shmelyov. In Iskander's and Popov's satires, the dissociation of author from narrator displaces onto the latter any political and social criticism, which may be ascribed more to his personal idiosyncrasies than to objective conditions. It also confers a certain legitimacy on the lively oral delivery—full of colorful slang, regional proverbs, and other individualized peculiarities of speech—favored by contemporary narrative.

In his self-perpetuating cycle of stories devoted to Abkhazia, Iskander's sardonic references to repressive aspects of Russian history that the establishment has ignored or denied for decades, as well as the inflammatory issue of minorities and nationalities, made publication of his Sandro cycle unlikely in the Soviet Union until the late 1980s. Parodying the genre of the picaresque, with its morally questionable protagonist, its exposure of a cross-section of society, its ironic tone, episodic structure, and linguistic diversity, Iskander's often tall tales, typified by "Old Hasan's Pipe" (1987), recreate Abkhazia's patriarchal village life. Iskander captures its contradic-

tions, its poetic heights and depths, in vivid, mythic colors that contrast
dramatically with the more somber, subdued hues of Soviet urban prose.
Bold, elemental characters whose lives celebrate physical energy, like
Hajarat in "Old Hasan's Pipe," are inseparable from their immediate natural environment, which Iskander renders with lyricism and sensitivity.
Their specific biographies, nonetheless, pose universal moral dilemmas
that underscore the primacy of experience, honor, loyalty, and integrity in
human existence. Under Iskander's sly and sometimes rollicking humor
resides a serious concern with ethical values no less profound than that
found in the solemn and dogmatic exposé prose that abounds under glasnost.

While the prolific Leningrad satirist Valery Popov on first glance appears
to lampoon social ills, in fact the majority of his fiction explores his major
theme of happiness. For unabashedly pursuing that theme in such quintessentially Popovian stories as "Paradise" and "A Big Success" (reprinted
in the collection *A New Scheherazade*, 1988), he was accused by the influential arch-conservative critic-scholar Feliks Kuznetsov of a "neo-hedo-
nistic" philosophy. As Vladimir Novikov has argued, however, it would be
more accurate to characterize Popov as an eudaemonist, one who defines
moral obligation by reference to personal well-being through a life governed by reason. "Dreams from the Top Berth" illustrates precisely the
absence of reason in the circumstances of everyday Soviet life: the conditions under which the protagonist takes what should have been a rather
mundane train ride pile one irrational absurdity upon another in a topsy-
turvy world that ultimately makes minimal human comfort the pinnacle
of one's dreams. Like Petrushevskaya and Shmelyov, Popov spotlights the
illogicalities, passions, and degradations that are inseparable from contemporary Soviet existence, but the lightness of his touch, his sheer joy in
language, and his ability to approach chaos with humor set him apart and
align him with earlier satirists like Ilf and Petrov.

Humor, by contrast, has virtually no place in the prose of either
Shmelyov or Anatoly Genatulin. Devoid of glamorization and poetry, the
fiction of Shmelyov, who has gained prominence as an economist under
Gorbachev, has an empirical foundation. It squarely and unadornedly
tackles some of the issues that have emerged full force during glasnost: the
relations of past to present, moral compromise, the consequences of a
purely pragmatic philosophy, and the seductive ease of self-deception.
The majority of his stories, like "The Visit" and "The Case of the Fur
Coat," treat the contemporary urbanite's attempts to attain a comfortable
niche in the world around him. Usually the process entails material temp-
tations, erroneous decisions, disillusionment in others or the self, and

some form of self-confrontation. Middle-aged men predominate as protagonists in Shmelyov's cast of characters. Watershed events in their lives frequently trigger reminiscences of earlier days, which accounts for the somewhat retrospective cast to his fiction. Although Shmelyov's straightforward narratives lack the formal complexity intrinsic to alternative prose, they nonetheless share the latter's elimination of unmediated authorial commentary. Although "The Visit" addresses the topical questions of prostitution (and touches on incest, which until recently would have been unthinkable in Soviet literature), professional corruption, the amoral network of exchanged favors that rules so much of Soviet society, and the disintegration of family ties, it eschews lurid detail, focusing instead on the psychology of the protagonist, which Shmelyov deftly unfolds through quasi-direct discourse.

A native of Bashkiria, Genatulin, despite his rather conventional style, merits attention for his novella *Rough Weather*, which belongs to the growing body of current fiction depicting the lesser-known "minority" areas of the Soviet Union. Its grim picture of the melancholy inefficiency, tragic ignorance, and lack of moral coherence on a modern day Bashkir collective farm provides an eloquent index of the unimaginable discrepancy between Soviet cities and the countryside. Like much of the farm's antiquated machinery and its farming methods, the mentality of the area's inhabitants belongs to the Middle Ages. Amassing detail upon detail, Genatulin shows the fatal consequences of backward thinking, sloth, alcoholism, child neglect, bribery and theft. The tragic events of the narrative, with its accumulation of minutely recorded realia, contrasts with the dark poetry that Genatulin brings to his extensive descriptions of the area's forest as experienced by a terrified five-year-old child. Verging occasionally on folkloric renditions of ominous settings, those passages are rendered all the more memorable by the almost documentary manner that Genatulin favors throughout the narrative. Whatever exoticism attaches to the names of the novella's cast of characters (Gulnara, Faizulla, Marziya) drowns in the unrelieved black and gray of the atmosphere and events that Genatulin unflinchingly records without any overt moralizing.

Authorial attitudes and allegiances, which are trumpeted forth in both standard Soviet fiction and the exposé branch of glasnost literature, are challengingly elusive in alternative prose. With her customary astuteness, Natalya Ivanova has remarked on the emergence of a new genre in Soviet literature—"discourse" or "the word" (*slovo*), which subsumes the disparate contents of a work under the overarching monological *profession de foi* that the author cannot resist conveying unambiguously. That mode is exemplified by Astafyev's *Sad Detective Story* and Belov's *Everything's*

Ahead. By contrast, the multiple perspectives, unexpected shifts in tone and lexical levels, startling juxtapositions, and frequent compression of material in alternative fiction tend to dialogize or obscure even tentatively implied values and hierarchies. Whereas monologists wishing to "speak out" conceive of text as soapboxes to be mounted, dialogists strive to distance themselves from their works. And the warmly amiable humor of Iskander and Valery Popov, like Petrushevskaya's mordant wit, Tolstaya's deflective irony, and Erofeyev's macabre funniness in the midst of monstrositites, all help to achieve that distance.

An exploitation of narrative techniques pioneered by Dostoevsky similarly heightens the complexity of alternative fiction. For example, Kuraev's second novella, entitled *Night Patrol* (*Novy mir*, 1988, No. 12), reaps the advantages of first-person narrative in a Dostoevskian key as it recreates the past from a dialogized perspective. Like the compulsive chatter and rationalizations of Dostoevsky's Underground Man, the discursive ruminations of the protagonist Polubolotov, a former executioner of "enemies of the people," reveal more than he realizes. No explicit recriminations on the author's part could communicate as starkly as Polubolotov's self-presentation the sheer horror of his activities and of his imperviousness to that horror. A similar effect is achieved in Erofeyev's and Petrushevskaya's stories, which has prompted several commentators who equate explicitness with presence to assume that no moral standards obtain in their fictional universe.

Indeed, the narrator and central figure in Erofeyev's "The Parakeet" likewise enjoys, in all senses, the profession of executioner. A hair-raising account of how he and his henchmen interrogated, tortured, and drove to suicide the son of the man to whom the story's events are related, the narrative consists entirely of the official murderer's monologue, which usurps and internalizes all other voices. Since the oral delivery has an addressee as an implied interlocutor, the torturer engages in constant objections, parries, assurances, and the like. This orgy of rhetorical devices, full of vulgarisms, political slogans and clichés, elevated diction, blended with a clinical, cold-blooded catalogue of such inhumane, revolting acts as tearing off the son's testicles, coalesces into a chilling image of the unspeakable torments to which humans subject one another, though it could be read more narrowly as a parable of the civil terrorism practiced in Soviet prisons and camps. The rapid swings in tone and the various clashing voices discernible in an externally monological text owe an incalculable debt to Dostoevsky's *Notes from Underground* and Albert Camus's *The Fall*.

A deliberate echo of the Underground Man's confession that he is "a nasty man, a sick man" opens Petrushevskaya's "Our Crowd," which closes with the narrator's insistence on her own cleverness. At several junctures, however, the phenomena described by the narrator herself call that emphasized cleverness into question. Her gritty, mocking litany of the personal betrayals and compromises, the dissoluteness, and the vicious games enacted by a group of "friends" from the intelligentsia—customarily viewed as the conscience of Soviet society—derives its impact primarily from Petrushevskaya's skillful manipulation of her ambiguous reporting persona. The highly condensed narrative scatters tangential references to grim social and historical occurrences—hostile invasions, imprisonment in camps, persecution of "refuseniks," widespread groundless police surveillance, and political meddling in research—throughout a vitriolic portrayal of the maimed milieu in which she has spent her entire adulthood. That the narrator herself is not exempt from either the base motives or the self-deluded posturing that she ridicules in the group's members may be deduced from the uneven rhythms of her unwittingly self-revelatory monologue, with its mixture of occlusion and logorrhea. Indeed, the onset of the blindness that is an early symptom of her fatal disease serves a metaphoric function in the story. On one hand, it connotes her Teiresias-like gift for detecting others' concealed desires, grasping the hidden significance of immediate circumstances, and to some extent predicting their eventual outcome. On the other hand, it simultaneously transfers to the physical plane her weightiest psychological failing: an incapacity to subject her own psyche and behavior to the merciless scrutiny that she brings to bear on others. Petrushevskaya's well-known penchant for chatty first-person narration, observable in her technique as a playwright, is chiefly motivated by her protagonists' conflicting impulses and strategies of survival. Like Erofeyev and Tolstaya, Petrushevskaya takes scrupulous care to withhold her authorial voice and unmediated judgment from her fictional texts, which camouflage the essential with the incidental.

In addition to sophisticated narrative stratagems, a major factor contributing to the complexity and exuberance of alternative prose is its densely intertextual nature. Whether one defines intertextuality à la Roland Barthes—as relevant presuppositions sedimented in the past as a "mirage of citations" that prove evasive and insubstantial as soon as one attempts to grasp them—or à la Julia Kristeva, as a consciously ironic play of discourse that derives its very identity from a wholesale but non-committal appropriation of existent discourses, the prose of Erofeyev, Tolstaya, and to a lesser extent, Bitov, Petrushevskaya, and Boris Pyetsukh (e.g., in his *The New Moscow Philosophy*) teems with intertexts. A comparison of Tendryakov's "Donna Anna" with Erofeyev's "Anna's Body, or the End of the Russian Avant Garde" clarifies not only the distinction between simple citation and intertextuality, respectively, but also the vast conceptual divide separating current authorial practices from more traditional Soviet writing. Alexander Blok's poem "The Steps of the Commendatore" (1912) supplies the title and the lines cited in Tendryakov's story by the protagonist narrator, who directs readers to the poetic source by asking a fellow soldier, Galchevsky, whether he likes Blok (from whose poem *The Scythians* [1918] Galchevsky subsequently recites a quatrain). Given the hyperbolic nationalism of *The Scythians* and the centrality of betrayal and retribution in Blok's lyrical version of a fraught moment from the Don Juan legend, the two quotations serve chiefly to underscore Tendryakov's concern with the perils of unreflecting jingoism and the nature of treason, both subsumed by his focal theme of moral responsibility. The quotations are grafted onto a text that would lose relatively little by their omission. By contrast, the very foundation of Erofeyev's story, its distinctive structure and rhythm, would disintegrate were its many Annas and the Blokian refrain of "Anna! Anna! Anna!" eliminated. Any meaning attaching to Erofeyev's narrative hinges on all the Annas evoked by the unidentified allusions accumulated within the few pages that dramatize a comic tragedy of love, treachery, and retribution: Blok's/Mozart's violated Donna Anna; the eighteenth-century Empress Anna Ioanna, who reneged on a contract; the Anna of Tolstoy's *Anna Karenina*, with its appositely vengeful Biblical epigraph; Anna Akhmatova, justly admired for her superb love lyrics and her scholarship on Pushkin's treatment of the Don Juan legend; and Chekhov's several lovelorn Annas—whether in the guise of a "Lady with a Dog" or "Anna on the Neck" (the latter citation from Chekhov's story being a paronomastic reference to the medal the Tsarist government awarded for state service). Erofeyev's Anna culminates not only two centuries of Russian heroines ruled by passion, but synecdochically reviews the very culture that produced them. The interstices in this network of allusions are filled by additional cultural metonyms in the form of truncated, enigmatic references: from French art, Borges, the Eiffel Tower, the Leaning Tower of Pisa, the Caucasus, and Women's Day, to traditional subjects of still life canvases, and the folkloric literalization of cannibalistic metaphor. The bared device of the climactic finale reveals the loving "murderess" Anna as Erofeyev's creative alter ego. Just as she performs the ultimate act of possession by swallowing the object of her love/hatred ("the other"), so Erofeyev asserts and nurtures his own authorial self through his nihilistic assimilation of "other" sources. In other words, intertexts comprise the building blocks of Erofeyev's self-reflexive narratives.

Tolstaya's luxuriously poetic prose likewise installs and subverts concepts, cultural myths, literary styles and the very act of narration through ironic intertextuality. Recontextualized citations from multiple sources—poetry and prose, folklore, songs, slogans and popular clichés—proliferate in her fiction. By embedding this panoply of voices in dialogue, description, commentary on plot developments and characters, Tolstaya synecdochically packs mini-worlds so tightly into her prose that some readers feel overwhelmed by the wealth of verbal color and variety. In "The Okkervil River," for instance, Tolstaya orchestrates an extraordinarily sophisticated interplay among a seemingly endless array of voices from Pushkin, Lermontov, Gogol, and Blok; unfurls a series of extended, ornate metaphors that stretch into paragraphs; slides with lightning speed from scrupulously particularized fantasy into fantastic reality, from comic ridicule to elevated lyricism; collapses and expands time, and anchors her plot in irreconcilable paradox. "Night," Tolstaya's personal favorite among her stories, depicts a retarded adult whose affliction communicates itself above all in his relationship to language. Arrested at a child's level of mental development, he interprets the surrounding world in cosmic-mythic terms, as a dark forest teeming with unfathomable forces and populated by mysterious, threatening creatures from whom the sole haven is his bulky tower of a mother. Here, as elsewhere, Tolstaya's authorial manner rather than her matter seduces the reader. The sensual pleasure of reading her trope-saturated prose—which, in addition to its assonances and onomatopoeia, falls into rhythmic patterns that invite poetic scansion—matches the considerable intellectual challenge of understanding it. Of all contemporary prose, Tolstaya's is probably furthest removed both from canonical Soviet style and from the journalistic novels of glasnost.

However innovative and unconventional Tolstaya and other representatives of alternative literature may be, they nonetheless subscribe to a mainstream cultural myth: that of Pushkin as supreme poet. It is no accident that Alexei Petrovich, the mentally retarded adult in Tolstaya's "Night" who cannot use the bathroom and eat breakfast without his mother's supervision, nevertheless knows Pushkin and wishes to imitate him; that Igor Odoevtsev in Bitov's "Pushkin's Photograph (1799-2099)" follows the example of his forefather Lev Odoevtsev (of *Pushkin House*) in endeavoring to "capture" Pushkin's life (with the aid of futuristic technology and a camera), and has at his fingertips detailed recall of the minutia of the poet's official biography; and that Iskander has incorporated Pushkin into several short works and his *Eugene Onegin* into "Old Hasan's Pipe." Almost two hundred years after his death Pushkin as both man and artist continues to inspire a plethora of fictions. Current disillusionment in the credibility of virtually every former political idol has boosted Russians' long-standing trust and admiration for authors of fiction as repositories of truth. Perceived as both fountainhead and peak of the national modern literary tradition, Pushkin for countless Russians is synonymous with Russian poetry and in that capacity enjoys tropological status. A fleeting mention of his name suffices to conjure up an artistic ideal and the aggregate of inestimable human virtues associated with his mythic persona. That universal veneration accounts for the vituperation unleashed by Sinyavsky's *Strolls with Pushkin*. Sinyavsky's demythologizing separation of man from artist, which enabled him to laud Pushkin's poetic gift, yet at the same time point to his human weaknesses, for many Soviets was tantamount to desecration. The uproar demonstrated that ambivalence and bifocal vision have yet to establish a foothold in the unilinear approach of many Soviets, who resist not only political, but also philosophical and artistic pluralism.

Writers like Tolstaya, Bitov, Kuraev, both Erofeyevs, and Pyetsukh, whose imagination constantly entertains myriad options, bring an ironic consciousness even to their most prized tropes. Their receptivity to manifold phenomena, which threatens institutionalized monolithic constructs, is at the heart of alternative prose in general. Like post-modernism in the West, that prose calls for decentering, detachment in the midst of involvement, and skepticism of closed systems; it installs unresolved contradictions and raises questions to which only provisional and contextually determined answers are posited. Its basic premises about the role and nature of literature, in other words, run counter to the assumptions apparently ingrained in the majority of Soviet intellectuals, including editors of mainstream publications, literary and social commentators, and influential leaders in the professional unions. At this stage, alternative fiction is competing for a place in an overcrowded cultural forum more absorbed with investigative journalism than stylistically sophisticated art. Once the stream of retrieved materials runs dry, as it inevitably must, perhaps the role of alternative prose in contemporary Russian fiction will undergo reassessment and its rich potential will gain wider recognition.

Creative habits that have been molded by monolithic ideology do not disappear overnight, and to expect sudden masterpieces from experienced writers who have operated by accommodation or through the adoption of an oppositional stance (two sides of the same coin) is utterly unrealistic. To hope for an original, independent Russian literature within the Soviet Union, then, is to place one's faith in writers whose prose does not march in tune with glasnost, but which bows to the dictates of an inner vision. Dudintsev's *Not By Bread Alone* (1956) and Ilya Ehrenburg's *The Thaw* (1955), the equivalents during the post-Stalinist Thaw of today's exemplary glasnost novels, also captivated readers for extra-literary reasons. Their fate suggests that fiction steeped in journalism or written "to the occasion" may confer temporary glory but ultimately dooms its authors to membership in a passing parade. Alternative fiction, as its name implies, offers an alternative through its commitment to aesthetic principles instead of overtly political causes. Without rejecting the moral engagement of glasnost exposé literature, alternative prose registers its subversiveness or opposition through indirect means. Its statements are endlessly mediated, for it presupposes a readership attuned to subtlety and indirection. In a more narrow sense, of course, the aberrational development of Soviet cultural and political history has insured that formal complexity in and of itself be tantamount to political heterodoxy. The vitality, playfulness, robust jousting with language, flouting of expectation, fracture of linearity, and imaginative handling of voice that are the hallmarks of alternative prose translate its concern for history, ethics, and tenable values into aesthetically integrated, intellectually exciting texts that require considerable effort on the part of a reader who may be more accustomed to emotional identification with or, according to Lev Tolstoy's scenario, moral "infection" by an author's more directly articulated position. Even proponents of the current notion that no discourse is innocent of ideology would not deny that whereas some discourses are naive and clumsy, others are skillfully elaborated and make greater demands on a reader's education, sensitivity, and hermeneutic skills. In that regard, today's alternative prose in Soviet Russia not only impresses by its independence, freshness, and technical mastery, but also validates any optimism about the future of Russian fiction.

Washington, D. C.   *Helena Goscilo*
January 1990

Recommended readings for those interested in literature under glasnost: Volume XXVIII, No. 4 of *Michigan Quarterly Review* (Fall 1989), entitled *Perestroika and Soviet Culture*; *The New Soviet Prose* (New York: Abbeville Press, 1989); Vol. XXI, Nos. 3/4 of *Studies in Comparative Communism* (Autumn/Winter 1988); and pertinent issues of *Radio Liberty Research Bulletin* published during the last four years, from which the above Introduction has benefited.

GLASNOST

LYUDMILA PETRUSHEVSKAYA
OUR CROWD

I'm a hard, harsh person, always with a smile on my full rosy lips and a sneer for everyone. For instance, we'll be sitting at Marisha's. People get together at Marisha's on Fridays, they come one and all, and if someone doesn't come, it means either their family or their family situation doesn't let them, or they're just not let into Marisha's apartment, either by Marisha herself or by the whole furious company, just like for a long time they didn't let in Andrei, who, when drunk, punched our Serge in the eye, and our Serge is sacred, he's our pride and joy; for instance, a long time ago he calculated the principle of flight for UFO's. He calculated it just like that on the back of the sketchpad his genius daughter uses for drawing. I saw these calculations, then brazenly examined them in full view of everyone. I didn't understand a thing, it was all nonsense, artificial constructions, based on some theoretical Hub of the Universe. In short, it was beyond my understanding, and I'm very smart. What I don't understand just doesn't exist. So Serge made a mistake with his theoretical Hub of the Universe, for it was a long time since he'd read the literature, relying instead on intuition, and you've got to read the literature. He discovered a new principle of operation in a locomotive, with seventy percent efficiency, something really fantastic again. They started parading him everywhere with this principle, sending him back and forth, to a Kapitsa seminar, to Academician Fram and Academician Livanovich. Livanovich came to his senses first and pointed out the original source for all this; the principle had been discovered a hundred years ago and was described in a popular style in small print on page such-and-such in a university textbook, where the efficiency turned out to be reduced to thirty-six percent, and the result was zilch. There was a fuss anyway, they created a new department under Livanovich, and made our Serge its head, even without a degree. Our crowd understood completely and rejoiced, while Serge took a long, serious look at his life, wondering whether those were the values he needed, and he decided they weren't. He decided he'd better stay where he was in the Institute for Oceanic Research, and everyone was in shock again: he'd given up a career for the sake of liberty and freedom, in the Institute for Oceanic Research he was simply a run-of-the-mill junior researcher, he had complete freedom there and was on the verge of an ocean expedition that had been planned long ago, with stops in Vancouver, Boston, Hong Kong, and Montreal. Half a year of sea and sun. Fine, he chose freedom, and there, in the department of his brainchild with thirty-six percent efficiency, they'd already hired a staff and made a mediocre assistant professor its head; all the regular positions were filled, and they started working at a snail's pace, going over to the snackbar, taking business trips, or sitting around smoking. They would come to consult with Serge, or rather, they came at the beginning, twice. Marisha laughed, saying that they no longer knew who was who in the Institute for Oceanic Research, for all the time people kept dragging off some Serge, a junior scientist, from under their noses for consultations. But that stopped soon afterwards and they settled down; it wasn't a simple matter, after all, it wasn't a matter of principle, but of a different technology for the sake of which they had to do away with existing production; electricity wasn't needed, everything was going back to the age of steam, everything was a load of useless crap. So at first instead of progress, everything basically went to hell, as usual. And all this was being pushed through by a single five-person department; one of our acquaintances, Lenka Marchukaite, got set up there as a lab worker, and she came and brought the comforting news that the assistant professor was about to have an illegitimate child, that the girl's parents were writing a letter about him, he was totally out of it at work, yelling on the telephone, this all in one room, and there wasn't even any talk of power engineering. In the meantime they were preparing an official request for a proficiency-testing joiner's bench, to be delivered in the basement of the institute for three hours during the night shift. But that liberty and freedom turned out much worse for Serge; when the time came for him to fill out the forms for his expedition, he wrote on a form that he was non-Party, whereas when he'd joined the Institute for Oceanic Research he'd written on a form that he was a member of the All-Union Leninist Komsomol. They compared both statements, and discovered that he'd quit the ranks of the Komsomol independently, hadn't even registered in the Komsomol organization in the Institute for Oceanic Research, and so hadn't paid membership dues for many years, and it turned out that neither dues nor anything could fix that now, and the Institute review committee didn't let him go to the ocean. All this we learned from that same Andrei-the-Apostate when he arrived, and we let him drink vodka with all of us, and he said in an outburst that nobody was to tell him anything, for he'd become a stool pigeon so as to be included in the expedition, but he was obliged to inform only on board, he didn't hire out on dry land. And indeed Andrei did leave for the ocean, whereas Serge sat there gloomily, though he'd been given complete freedom. The whole institute went to the ocean, while he and a small staff of women who worked in the lab administered the departure, registration, and reception of expeditions in Leningrad. This happened a long time ago, however, and now the days were over when Serge and Marisha agonized jointly over Serge's future and held steadfast; the days of understanding were over for good, and the devil knows what had come, but every Friday we regularly arrived, as if magnetized, at the house on Stulina Street and drank all night. We—that's Serge and Marisha, the hosts with two rooms; and in the other room, to the sounds of the tape recorder and bursts of laughter, would be sleeping their daughter Sonya, a child who'd been brought up with a firm hand, a talented, original beauty of a girl, who's my relative now, if you can imagine that, but I'm getting ahead of myself. Marisha and Serge are also my relatives now, although that's the funny result of our whole life and is a simple case of incest, as Tanya expressed it when she attended the wedding of my husband Kolya and Serge's wife Marisha, but I'll get to that later.

At first, then, it was like this: Serge and Marisha, their daughter in the other room, I in my superfluousness, my husband Kolya—Serge's faithful, devoted friend; Andrei-the-Stoolpigeon, first with one wife, Anyuta, then with various other women, then with the constant Nadya; also, Zhora, who's half-Jewish on his mother's side, which nobody besides me ever mentioned, as if that were a vice of his: once Marisha, our divinity, decided to praise our plain-looking Zhora and said that Zhora had large eyes—what color were they? Everybody spoke up, some said yellow, others light brown, and I said Jewish, and for some reason everyone got embarrassed and Andrei, my eternal enemy, snorted. And Kolya slapped Zhora on the shoulder. But strictly speaking, what had I said? I'd said the truth. To continue: our Tanya was always there, a Valkyrie six feet tall, with long blond

hair, extremely white teeth that she brushed maniacally three times a day
for twenty minutes (spend an hour on them and your teeth will be white
as snow, too), and with extremely large gray-blue eyes, a beauty, a favorite
of Serge's, who sometimes would stroke her hair after he'd had loads to
drink, and nobody understood anything; Marisha would be sitting there
as if nothing was going on, and I'd be sitting there too and would say to
Lenka Marchukaite: "Why aren't you dancing? Dance with my husband
Kolya," in response to which everyone laughed crudely, but that was
already at the sunset of our shared life.

Lenka Marchukaite would be there too, a very pretty girl with a D-cup
bust and long, light brown hair, a real luxury item, twenty years old. At
first Lenka behaved like a crook, which she actually was when she worked
in a record store. She wormed her way into Marisha's confidence by
telling her about her tough life, then she hit her up for twenty rubles and
ignored the debt completely for a while, and then disappeared, to return
with her four front teeth missing, gave back the twenty rubles ("There,
you see?" said Marisha triumphantly), and said that she'd been in the hospital, where they'd sentenced her to be childless for life. Marisha loved her
even more after that, Lenka practically lived at her house, though she slept
elsewhere, but without those teeth she was different, no longer a luxury
piece. With Serge's help Lenka got set up as a lab worker in his thirty-six
percent department, had new teeth put in, and married Oleg, a Jewish
boy-dissident who turned out to be the son of the famous cosmetician
Eva Lazarevna, and for a time Lenka was our scout of sorts in this incredibly rich family, and she'd laugh as she told us about Eva's bedroom and
her closets, each of which could support you in dollars for a lifetime, and
she'd also tell us what gifts Eva gave her; Eva spoiled Lenka and said that
her skin was a natural treasure. Lenka's skin was indeed naturally delicate,
unusually so, white flesh and red blood making for a fantastic combination even at different times of the day, just like a sunset or a sunrise, and
her lips were always red as blood. All children have skin like that; my
Alyoshka, for example. But Lenka didn't take care of herself, hung out at
various joints like a floozie, didn't think she was worth much, and finally
announced that her Oleg was leaving for the States with his whole family,
via Vienna, but she wasn't going. And she didn't; she divorced him and
started to distinguish herself by the fact that every time she entered a
house she'd right away sit down in the lap of one of the men and would
feel great, while our poor boys—my Kolya, for example, or Andrei-the-
Stoolpigeon, or Zhora—would smirk wryly. The only one in whose lap
she didn't dare sit was Serge; Serge was sacred, and moreover, Marisha,
whom Lenka worshiped, was right there, and Lenka couldn't make fun of

Marisha the way she made fun of all of us and of Andrei-the-Stoolpigeon's young wife, who flushed and went out into the kitchen when Lenka, without meaning anything by it, plunked herself down in Andrei's lap. This wife, Nadya, was even younger than Lenka, she was actually eighteen years old, but you could take her for fifteen, she was thin, slender, red-haired and depraved, but looked like a schoolgirl, she was all Andrei could hook, since thanks to the blabbing of his legal wife Anyuta, he'd been long known to be totally impotent and needing nothing. Depraved as Nadya was, when she got married, she became a typical housewife; every time this nymphet opened her maw she'd sing the same tune: she'd cooked such and such, Andrei would drink, but she'd stop him from drinking more, they'd bought such and such. The only thing she retained of her depravity and degeneracy was her false eye, which would slide out of its orbit during some awkward movements and pop out onto her cheek like a soft-boiled egg. This must have been an awful sight, but Andrei made a fuss over it, drove Nadya, who held her eye in her hand, to the hospital, and there they set the eye back in, and on those nights, I think, Andrei had his supreme moments. With his former wife, Anyuta, too, Andrei lived for the sake of the exciting moments of her attacks, when he would drive her, wrapped in a blanket, from hospital to hospital in an ambulance, until it turned out that her illness, so-called poison, was, to put it more simply, barrenness. This poison of Anyuta's was going around in our crowd, and the seal of doom lay on Anyuta and Andrei. We all already had children, Zhora had three, I had Alyosha, and all I had to do was not show up for two weeks at Serge and Marisha's for the news to spread that I was giving birth in a delivery ward: that's how they made fun of my figure. Tanya had a son famous for having had the nickname of Cat's Mummy as an infant. Andrei and Anyuta couldn't have children, though, and we felt sorry for them, for it's kind of absurd to live without children and it wasn't the thing to live like that, the cool thing to do, after all, was to have children, mess about with porridge and kindergarten, and on Friday night suddenly feel like real people and let loose for all you were worth, to the point of even having the people opposite on Stulina Street call the police. Anyuta and Andrei were doomed until suddenly one day Anyuta unexpectedly gave birth to a daughter, almost without having changed at all! There was universal rejoicing, the night of the delivery Andrei brought Serge two bottles of vodka, they called up my Kolya and drank all night, and Andrei said that he'd call his daughter Marisha in Marisha's honor. Marisha was affected unpleasantly by the honor, but she couldn't do anything—you can't forbid something like that—and the sponger Andrei called his daughter Marisha. But with that the celebration and also the family romance ended, and Andrei must have abandoned his conjugal duties for a long time, whereas Anyuta, on the contrary, suddenly felt that she was just like other women and, like them, she stopped having attacks, and in that connection in the course of her year-long maternity leave she started inviting over more and more new male friends, whereupon Andrei went to sea in his capacity as stool pigeon, and upon his return home found a whole swarm of acquaintances apparently attracted by Anyuta's single status—Anyuta, who'd formerly been poisonous. Andrei found a new romance in his situation as an abandoned husband, and romantically started bringing choice girls to Serge and Marisha's, but Lenka Marchukaite brazenly kept sitting on his lap as if affixing a seal on his loins, which, having done their job, had exhausted themselves. This was her way of joking and mocking him.

She also sat on my Kolya's lap once. Kolya, who was thin and kind, was literally crushed by Lenka's weight both physically and morally, he hadn't expected such a turn of events and he just kept his hands at a distance and repeatedly cast imploring glances at Marisha, but Marisha abruptly turned away and started talking to Zhora, and right then I started to understand something. I started to understand that Lenka had made a blunder, and I said:

"Lenka, you've made a blunder. Marisha is jealous of you on account of my husband."

Lenka twisted her mug unconcernedly and continued sitting on Kolya, who wilted completely, like a plucked stem. It was then, I think, that Marisha started cooling toward Lenka, which led to Lenka Marchukaite's gradual disappearance, especially when she finally gave birth to a dead baby, but that was already after. Right then everyone reacted by starting to fuss rather exaggeratedly: Tanya clinked glasses with Serge, and Zhora, who was pouring, passed some drinks to the burdened Kolya and the cold Marisha, while Andrei gallantly began speaking with his fool Nadyusha, who gazed triumphantly at me, the wife of a crushed husband.

Lenka Marchukaite never dared sit on Zhora's lap, however, that wasn't safe, for Zhora, like many small men, demonstrated constant arousal and loved everybody—Marisha, Tanya, and even Lenka, and Lenka, who was cold through and through, would be taking the risk of provoking Zhora into attempted rape in everyone's presence, as had already happened once with a lady of Andryusha's who'd pretended to be terribly passionate while dancing with Zhora; but you couldn't do that with Zhora, and when the music ended Zhora simply grabbed his strapping lady under the arms and dragged her into the next room as if oblivious, and as we knew all too well, no one was sleeping in the next room that night; Marisha and

Serge's daughter was at her grandmother's. Zhora managed to throw the half-crazed lady down on Sonechka's small bed, but Serge and Andrei came in and, smiling involuntarily, dragged Zhora away, while the alarmed lady straightened her dress, which had ridden up in the course of events. The incident provoked wild laughter the entire night, but besides that, everybody except the lady, who was an outsider, knew that this was a game, that Zhora had been playing the bon vivant and libertine since his student days, though in fact he spent his nights writing a doctoral dissertation for his wife and would get up to take care of his three children, and it was only on Fridays that he adopted the guise of a lion and pursued ladies until morning.

But careful Lenka, who could also play sexual games with phenomenal coldbloodedness, wouldn't risk provoking Zhora into his usual role, that would be too much, two performances, and it would make some kind of ending obligatory: Lenka would sit down, Zhora would instantly start pawing her and so on, whereas Lenka didn't like that, just as essentially Zhora didn't either. However, Lenka Marchukaite came and went according to the way Marisha wanted things; one moment she was there and the next she'd disappeared, and now whenever I mention her out loud in front of everybody, it sounds like my usual tactlessness.

Everything's got kind of confused in my memory in connection with recent events in my life, namely in connection with the fact that I've started going blind. Is it ten or fifteen years since those Fridays started? Is it the Czech, Polish, Chinese, or Yugoslavian events that have rolled by? Such and such trials took place, then the trials of the people who'd protested the results of the first trials, then the trials of the people who'd collected money for the families of prisoners in the camps—all that flashed by. Sometimes a stray bird from other, contiguous spheres of human activity would fly in; at one point the district policeman Valera, an arrogant, stubborn man who knew the art of self-defense, got into the habit of attending our Fridays. On Fridays the door to the apartment wasn't closed; just three steps up from the sidewalk, and you'd be at the door; the first time he came, he asked everybody for their papers in connection with a complaint from the tenants of the house opposite on Stulina Street about excessive noise from 11 P.M. all the way until 5 A.M. Valera meticulously checked everybody's papers, or more precisely checked whether anyone was carrying theirs, because it turned out that none of the boys had their passports. He didn't check the girls', which afterwards made us think that Valera was looking for somebody, and all next week everybody kept calling everyone else, excited and nervous; everybody was dreadfully disturbed, frightened, and at fever pitch. Danger, in fact, had invaded our quiet abode, in which the only sound had been a tape recorder, and we found ourselves at the center of events on account of Valera and his checking our papers. By the following Friday everybody definitely assumed that Valera was looking for Lyovka, the American Russian who'd been living with an expired visa for a whole year, wandering around various private apartments and hangouts, and hanging around not because he didn't wish to return to the States, but simply because he'd missed the deadline; they told him that according to our laws, he'd have to serve a term for that, and it was then that he started hiding out, and everybody would greet him with shouts and laughter, but I didn't once see him at Marisha's, though Lyovka the American did occasionally spend the night on the floor at Marisha's neighbors, who were suspect company, consisting of two perpetual female students who weren't registered as permanent residents in Moscow, and their roommates, who were of different races, and, as the students told the story, once, when Lyovka came to borrow a ruble, he ended up spending the night with Rimma, a government minister's daughter who was a sophomore in the journalism department. After that Lyovka the American disappeared without a trace, but Rimma didn't hold it against him and now, people said, she in turn was wandering around various hangouts looking for Lyovka, to whom she'd given everything, in the Russian sense. People said that since then Lyovka hadn't spent a night on Stulina Street and so Valera had come for nothing.

Valera came again, however, at five past eleven; he came to turn off the tape recorder, and the tape recorder was turned off and we sat drinking in silence. Valera sat there too, with unfathomable intentions: either he had decided to wait until Lyovka came, or he just had to destroy the very foundation of our harmless company, so he just sat and wouldn't leave. Marisha, who had enthusiastically convinced everybody that all people are interesting—she always had people, whom she picked up at railroad stations, spending the night at her place, a woman with a paralyzed one-year-old girl who'd come to the pediatrics institute for a consultation without having permission for hospitalization had lived there for a month—Marisha found the key first and started to act as though Valera was an unhappy and lonely person. After all, they didn't turn away any strangers from this house, only it was rare that anyone ventured to foist himself on them. Marisha and then Serge started talking excitedly with Valera on various topics, gave him a glass of dry wine, and passed him the black bread and cheese, the only things that were on the table, and Valera didn't evade a single question and didn't once feel any pricks to his self-esteem. So, for example, Serge asked:

"What did you do, join the police to get a resident permit?"

"I already had that before," answered Valera.

"So why are you on the force?"

"It's a rough district," answered Valera, "I know the art of self-defense, I'm an expert, but because of a shoulder injury I couldn't get a second-class rating while I was still in the army. If you get caught in a hold you can't break in self-defense, then you've got to signal by making a sound."

"What kind of sound?"

"Forgive the expression, even a cough or passing gas will do, so they won't break your arm."

I immediately asked how it was possible to pass gas on order.

Valera answered that he hadn't had time to give a loud signal and his arm had been pulled out of its socket, so now he had a third-class rating. Then, without taking a breath, Valera expounded his viewpoint on the existing order of things and on the fact that soon everything would change and everything would be the way it had been under Stalin, and under Stalin there'd been real order.

To cut a long story short, we spent the entire evening in sociological analyses of Valera's image and finally either he turned out to be more resourceful, or our common role was too passive, but instead of the usual barrage of standard questions, which we'd repeated more than once with such stray birds as the prostitutes whom Andrei had brought, or with the people who got interested in the music and stopped at the window on quiet Stulina Street and started a conversation with us through the window and finally climbed into the room by the same route and were then obliged to answer a whole series of questions—this time it ended differently. Without concretely referring to his professional duties, Valera lectured us loudly for a full hour on how things had been under Stalin, and nobody particularly contradicted him, everyone was evidently afraid of provocation, was afraid of expressing their views—in front of a representative of authority, and in general that wasn't the thing to do in our crowd— to express your views. How childish it was to shout about your views, especially in front of the idiot Valera, a slippery customer we didn't know who had arrived with unknown intentions and was sitting at the poor round table in Marisha and Serge's impoverished room.

At twelve everyone got up, utterly mortified, and left, but not Valera. Either Valera had nowhere to spend his night duty, or he had a specific assignment, but he sat at Marisha and Serge's till morning, and Serge spoke out, and later Marisha passed on to the masses by phone that this was the most interesting person Serge had met in the last four years, but that was his defensive formula and nothing more. Serge took Valera on all

by himself, for Marisha left to sleep on the floor in Sonechka's room, and
Serge, like a man, stayed and drank herbal tea with Valera, a whole pot of
the diuretic, during which Valera didn't once go to the toilet, and left only
when his stint of duty was over. Evidently Valera didn't want to leave his
observation post for a single second and he performed a feat of restraint.
Serge, on his part, didn't leave either, for fear of a search in his absence.

Be that as it may, that Friday was a Friday of torture, and we all sat feeling out of sorts. Lenka Marchukaite didn't once sit down on anyone's lap,
especially Valera's, nor did Zhora shout "Virgins!" even once through the
window to the schoolgirls who passed by; only I kept asking how specialists in self-defense learn to signal by making sounds—was it by an act of
will or by eating special foods? This topic was enough for me for the
whole evening, since the one thing Valera avoided was precisely this transmission of signals. He'd wince and evade the topic, and didn't return once
to those signal sounds, and, like everyone else, he took a dislike to me,
instantly and forever. But he didn't have a leg to stand on, for the offensive word which I kept repeating at every chance evidently doesn't appear
on the unpublished list of the words you get sent to jail for fifteen days for
uttering in public, especially since Valera himself uttered it first. And I was
the only one to butt into the intellectual discussion which Serge launched
with the help of leading questions, hoping to rise, anyway, to the position
of a mocking observer of real-life phenomena, for which real-life phenomenon Valera could be taken, but Valera didn't give a damn about
Serge's paternal questions, and stopped at nothing and said things that
were dangerous for his job situation regarding the fact that a lot of people
understood a lot of things and our bunch didn't have much longer to play
around and the boss was coming.

"Still," I butted in, "Where do they teach you to pass gas? But I see
you didn't learn how to do it because you couldn't pass it in time and
didn't make second-class."

"The army's got such guys, such a technical staff," continued Valera,
"Their hands have such technical skill. Everything's in their hands, they're
sharp guys, and they've got something upstairs, too."

Serge asked him, for example, whether he often had to do night duty
and where he had a room. Marisha, in her usual tone of kindness and sympathy, asked Valera whether he was married and whether he had children.
Our Valkyrie Tanya, our beauty, merely kept neighing with laughter and
commenting under her breath, as she leaned over her glass, on Valera's
particularly colorful remarks, and she kept turning to Zhora all the time as
if giving him support in this difficult situation, in which he, someone half-
Jewish, had shown Valera his passport (he was the only one to have his

passport this time), which Valera had read aloud: "Georgy Alexandrovich Perevoshchikov, Russian."

Yes, during this second visit of his, Valera asked to see the men's passports again, and again checked Serge's passport and again didn't get either Andrei's or my Kolya's, or that of the outsider who wandered into this dangerous party by chance—the Christian Zilberman, who rarely visited Moscow and was terribly frightened and showed his old student ID instead of his passport, the very student ID with which he always got a discount on train tickets. Valera took the ID from Zilberman and simply put it in his pocket, while Zilberman loudly asked where the toilet was and then cut out. Although at first Valera had threatened to take Zilberman away and to go so far as to make him prove his identity, he made no move to follow him, while we all stood around and worried about how poor Zilberman would be frightened and shaking now, and how in addition to his present situation he'd find himself in a situation he couldn't wriggle out of. But Valera evidently didn't need Zilberman.

I was interested in how Andrei-the-Stoolpigeon would behave, but Andrei also behaved carefully and with discretion. As soon as the tape recorder was switched off, Andrei lost the chance to dance with the person of his choice; he usually danced only when the fancy struck him and sometimes didn't dance at all, and his wife Nadya, who by now verged on a caricature of the typical housewife, even though she looked like a depraved adolescent, would also sit then like a statue and be jealous after the fact—so now Andrei sat down beside his Nadya. Nadya's father was an up-and-coming colonel, and Nadya interpreted all statements made by Valera, a member of the junior personnel, through the prism of Valera's response to Serge's question about rank. Asked which rank he'd been given, Valera said that he'd been given the rank of lieutenant right away, though a lot of people hadn't wanted him to be given it. Nadya alone immediately got the feel of the situation, started pacing back and forth, took Andrei off to call some Irochka, then led Andrei away for good, and Valera didn't react at all. It's possible that if we'd all left he'd have stayed anyway, for that was his beat—but possibly not.

Kolya and I didn't splurge on a taxi this time, but managed to catch a bus after we left the subway and arrived home like normal people and discovered that at 1:30 A.M. Alyoshka wasn't asleep, but was sitting like a zombie in front of the television, when nothing was on. This was the first time we'd returned from our Friday gathering at night instead of in the morning, and we saw that Alyoshka was also celebrating the night in his own way, and when I was putting him to bed he said that he was afraid of sleeping alone and was afraid of turning out the light. In fact, the lights were on everywhere, and yet Alyoshka hadn't been afraid earlier, but then, his grandfather had been around earlier, whereas recently his grandfather—my father—had died, and my mother had died three months before that; in a single winter I'd lost both parents, with mother dying of the same kidney disease that some time ago had begun to show up in me and which starts with blindness. Be that as it may, I discovered that Alyoshka was afraid of sleeping when nobody was home. Apparently his grandparents' ghosts rose before him, my father and mother had brought him up, pampered and raised him, and now Alyoshka was left completely alone, if you took into account that I would die soon, while my kind Kolya, who was quiet in company but bored at home, or started yelling disgracefully at Alyoshka whenever the latter ate with us—Kolya apparently was planning to leave me, planning to leave me for none other than Marisha.

I already said that many years had flown over our peaceful Friday nest. Andrei in the meantime had turned from a gold-haired young Paris into a father, an abandoned husband, a stool pigeon on an expedition ship, then a legal husband again and the possessor of a good cooperative apartment, which the colonel bought for Nadya, and finally, into an alcoholic; he still loved only Marisha, as he'd done all his life beginning with his student days, and Marisha knew and appreciated that, whereas all the other ladies in his life were simply substitutes. And the best number in Andrei's program were the dances with Marisha, one or two sacred dances a year.

Zhora also grew up from a mischief-making student into a modest, indigent senior researcher sporting the cheapest shirt and dark-gray pants, the father of three children, a future academician and laureate without any pretensions, but the one thing that always remained constant in his innermost core was his love for Marisha, who had always loved only Serge and no one else.

To go on, my Kolya also worshiped and loved Marisha; they had all become unhinged on account of Marisha as early as their first year at the institute, and this game continued until Serge, who won the beautiful Marisha and lived with her, suddenly found himself a lady love whom he'd known since schoolboy days, and once during a New Year's celebration, when everybody had had a lot to drink and we were playing charades, he said, "I'm off to call my lady love," and everyone was thunderstruck, for if the men loved Marisha and considered Serge the one and only real human being, then we all loved Marisha and Serge above all. Serge was always on everyone's lips, though he himself spoke little; it was Marisha who'd elevated him, who loved him adoringly, like a mother, perhaps, or a comrade-in-arms, revering his every word and gesture because once, long ago, when they were still freshmen, when Serge, among others, fell in love with her and proposed marriage and was sleeping with her, she left him, rented a room with some Jean, and succumbing to an erotic attraction, renounced Serge's first, pure love. Then Jean left her, and she herself came of her own free will to Serge, having now rejected forever the idea of an erotic love on the side, and she herself proposed marriage to him, they got married, and sometimes Marisha in a paroxysm of sacred ecstasy would blurt out that Serge was really a crystal glass. Now I would tell her not to sleep with a crystal glass, it wouldn't work out in any case, and if it did, you'd get cut. But at that time we all lived on hikes and campfires, drank dry wine, were ironic about everything, and didn't go near the subject of sex, because we were too young and didn't know what lay ahead of us; the only thing that disturbed everyone in the area of sex was that I had a white swimsuit that showed everything, and the group amused itself at my expense all it could; this happened when we were all living in tents somewhere on the seashore, and the subject of sex also came up when Zhora complained that there wasn't a toilet and that it was hard to do your business in the sea. The rest of the time that very same Zhora would shout that females on vacation needed a good abortion center, while Andrei romantically would walk more than six kilometers to date tubercular girls from the sanatorium at dances in the town of Simeiz, and Serge persistently kept trying to spear fish while he scuba dived and realized his virility this way, while at night I heard a rhythmic thumping coming from their tent, but Marisha was a restless creature with fire in her eyes all her life, and that said nothing good about Serge's abilities, and the boys were all raring to go for Marisha and, it seems, wanted to collectively fill the gap, but couldn't make any headway. As a matter of fact, this sexual fire that consumed Marisha, the priestess of love, combined with her inaccessibility, is what allowed our whole company to last for such a long time, for another person's love is infectious, that's already been proved. We, the girls, loved Serge and at the same time loved Marisha too, suffered along with her and, like her, were torn, but in our own way—on the one hand, loving Serge and dreaming of displacing Marisha, but on the other, being incapable of doing that because of our sympathy for Marisha, because of our love and compassion for her. In short, everything was taken up with Marisha and Serge's indivisible love and the non-realizability of their love, and everybody took it for the real thing. And Serge, the only one with full rights, was furious. This ulcer burst open once, though not completely, when in the midst of the usual harmless sexual conversations at table— these were the conversations of pure people, and thus capable of speaking about anything—when the conversation shifted to *Sexual Pathology*, a book by a Polish author. This was something quite new for our whole society, in which everybody until then had lived as if their case were unique, which they shouldn't examine themselves or reveal to anyone else. The new wave of enlightenment touched even our crowd, however, and I said:

"Someone was telling me about the book *Sexual Pathology* and there the sexual act is divided into stages: husband and wife keep arousing each other. As it turns out, you've got to stroke the partner's earlobe first, Serge! It turns out that's an erogenous zone!"

Everybody froze and Serge said there and then that he had extremely negative feelings towards me and started spluttering and shouting, but what did I care; having hit a bull's eye, I sat like a stone.

But all that was before Serge found himself a lady love who lived on his childhood street, before he met his youthful erotic dream, now a plump brunette, as several informed individuals reported, and before Valera the policeman started coming regularly to the apartment on Stulina Street and fighting for silence from eleven till seven in the morning, and this also happened before I gradually discovered that I was going blind and definitely before I saw that Marisha was jealous of Lenka Marchukaite on account of my Kolya.

So all the knots unraveled in a flash: Serge stopped spending nights at home, the Fridays were all dropped, and the same kinds of Fridays started in a safe place, in Tanya the Valkyrie's room, even though that involved the participation of her adolescent son, who was jealous of absolutely everybody on account of his mother. Later we isolated the adolescent, sending him to spend Friday nights with little Sonechka on Stulina Street, in which connection I observed that it was good for children to sleep with each other, but, as usual, nobody paid any attention to me, though I was telling the truth.

In general, a wave of turbulent events rolled in during the periods between Fridays: Marisha's father, who visited her one day on Stulina Street, died that same evening when he was hit by a car when walking in an unauthorized place on the same street, and furthermore, as the postmortem showed, he died in an intoxicated state, for Marisha's father had had a lot to drink with Serge before going home. Everything came together in this dreadful accident: the fact that Marisha's father wanted a man-to-man discussion with Serge about why he was leaving Marisha, and the fact that this conversation took place in the evening, when Sonechka wasn't yet asleep, and Marisha and Serge had been hiding from Sonechka the fact that Serge didn't spend his nights at home; Serge would only go to the other woman after he'd tenderly tucked Sonechka into bed, and it so happened that in the morning Sonya always got up for school when Serge was already on his way to work, and after work, from six to nine, Serge stayed on duty at his daughter's side, studied music with her, wrote fairy tales with her—and it was precisely during one of those unctuous periods that Marisha's distressed father barged in; he himself, incidentally, had been living a long time with a second family, and had a lot of unfortunate experience and a twenty-year-old son. Marisha's father drank, pointlessly said God knows what, and also pointlessly died under a car right there, on the doorstep of his daughter's house on Stulina Street in the quiet of the evening at nine-thirty.

During that same period my mother quietly slipped away; she'd dwindled from 176 pounds to 60, dying courageously and cheering up everybody, including me, and at the very end the doctors set out to find a nonexistent abscess inside her, opened her up, accidently sewed her intestine to her peritoneum and left her to die with an open wound the size of a fist, and when they wheeled her out to us, dead, ripped up, and then sewn up any which way right up to the chin, and with this hole in her stomach, I found it inconceivable that a thing like that could possibly happen to a person, and I started thinking that this wasn't my mother, that my mother was someplace else. Kolya had no part in all these proceedings; we'd been officially divorced then for five years, only neither of us had paid for the divorce, we'd agreed simply to live together like husband and wife without making any claims, and we were living together like everyone else when suddenly it turned out that he'd gone and paid for a divorce and after the funeral he quite sensibly suggested that I should also pay, and I did. Then my father died, utterly crushed by grief, an easy and lucky death from a heart attack in his sleep, so that when I got up to cover Alyoshka with his blanket during the night, I saw that Dad wasn't breathing. I went back to bed, and lay there till morning, when I saw Alyoshka off to school, then Dad to the hospital morgue.

But all this was between Fridays, and I'd missed several of the Fridays, and a month later it was Easter and I invited everyone to come again, like every year, to Kolya's and my place. Once a year at Easter we all used to get together at Kolya's and my place, I would cook a lot of food with Mom and Dad, then Mom and Dad would take Alyoshka and go off to our garden plot, which was more than an hour and a half's ride away, so as to burn the fallen leaves, clean up the cabin, and plant something, and they'd also spend the night there, in the unheated cabin, giving my guests the opportunity to eat, drink, and live it up the whole night. And this time everything was just the same, and so that everything would be just the same, I told Alyoshka that he was to go alone to the garden plot and spend the night there. There was no other possibility; he was already grown-up, seven years old, and knew the way perfectly well, and I also

warned him not to come back and ring at the door under any circumstances. And off he went, a solitary wanderer, and it so happened that just
that Sunday morning he and I had been at his grandparents' graves; it was
his first time at the cemetery and he'd carried water in buckets for me and
we'd planted daisies on the graves. From here on he was going to have to
start a new life, and we had a quick lunch of bread with sausage, cheese
and tea—from the stuff that was supposed to be for the holiday meal, and
Alyosha set off for the garden without a break, while I started making the
dough for the cabbage pies; I didn't have much money now. A cabbage
pie, pies with Mother's jam, potato salad, egg with onion, minced beet
with mayonnaise, a little bit of cheese, and sausage—they'd gobble it all
up anyway. And a bottle of vodka. As a matter of fact, I didn't earn much,
I couldn't expect anything from Kolya, he'd practically moved in with his
parents, and on the rare occasions when he was around he'd shout at
Alyosha that he didn't eat properly, didn't hiccup properly, didn't sit
properly, and dropped crumbs on the floor, and in conclusion he'd yell
that Alyosha watched TV all the time and was growing up into hell knows
what, without reading anything or drawing anything on his own, nothing.
This impotent shouting was a shout of envy on account of Sonechka, who
sang, composed music, was enrolled in Gnessin's Music School, for which
the competition was one opening for three hundred applicants, who'd
read a lot from the age of two and wrote her own poems and fairy tales.
Kolya ultimately loved Alyosha, but he'd have loved him much more if the
child had been talented and good-looking, brilliant at his studies and
strong in his relations with his schoolmates. Then Kolya would have loved
him much more, but as it was, he saw himself in him and got mad, especially when Alyosha was eating. Alyosha had rather bad teeth; when he
was seven the front ones still hadn't grown in completely, Alyosha still
hadn't adjusted to his orphaned state after his grandparents' death, and he
ate absentmindedly, took big bites and didn't chew, letting crumbs and
drops fall on his pants, and was constantly spilling everything, and to top
it off, he started wetting his bed. Kolya shot out of our family nest like a
cork, I think, so as not to see his son drenched in urine, his thin legs shivering in his wet shorts. The first time Kolya was awakened by Alyosha's
crying and saw this disgrace, he walloped Alyosha right across the cheek
and Alyosha lightly tumbled back onto his wet, sour-smelling bed, but he
didn't cry much, for he actually felt relieved that he'd been punished. I
just grinned and left and went to work, leaving them to sort it all out.
That day I was having my retina examined, which showed the beginnings
of the inherited disease that my mother had died of. To be more precise,
the doctor didn't make a definitive diagnosis, but she did prescribe the

same drops mother had taken, and she scheduled the same analyses. Now
it was all starting with me, things were in such a state that I couldn't have
cared less that Alyosha was wetting his bed and Kolya had hit him. New
horizons were opening before me—I won't say what kind—and I started
taking measures. Kolya left, and I returned home to find his clothes gone;
he'd nobly left everything else, you have to give him that. And here Easter
had rolled around, and I baked pies, pulled out the table, spread a table-
cloth on it, set out the plates, little glasses, salads, sausage and cheese,
bread, there were even a few apples, a gift from a friend of my mother's
who'd brought some painted eggs and a bag of rare spring apples, I took
part of it all to the cemetery, and sprinkled bits of everything onto a little
board for the birds, and Alyosha and I also ate some. I remember that
people were standing inside the fences of the grave plots around us, talking excitedly, drinking in the fresh air and eating; to this day we've kept
the tradition of Easter picnics in the cemeteries when everything seems to
have finally worked out fine in the long run, the dead lie there nicely, people drink to them, the graves are neat, the air is fresh, nobody is forgotten
and nothing is forgotten, and it will be the same with everybody, everything will pass and end just as peacefully and happily, with paper flowers,
photographs on ceramic, birds in the air, and painted eggs right there in
the earth. Alyosha got over his fear, I think, and planted daisy seedlings in
the earth with me more and more confidently; the soil in our Lyublino is
clean and sandy, I had my parents cremated, so only the urns with the
ashes stood deep in the ground, there was nothing to be scared of, it was
all over, and Alyosha ran and watered what needed to be watered. Then
we went and washed our hands and ate the eggs, bread, and apples, and
put away the leftovers and crumbled them up, just like all the numerous
visitors to the other graves. And on the way home, on the bus and the
subway, although everybody was high, they were somehow friendly and
kind-natured, as if they'd peered into life beyond the grave and seen the
fresh air and plastic flowers there and had drunk to all this in unison.

   So, alone and free that evening, I finally saw my annual guests arrive, a
bit embarrassed, but all present, each and every one, for Marisha, being a
very brave woman and of noble blood, couldn't not come, and the rest
came thanks to her, and Serge was also there, and my now already former
husband Kolya with exactly the same wretched teeth as Alyosha. Kolya
arrived and headed for the kitchen to unpack everything they'd brought,
and they'd brought boiled potatoes sprinkled with dill, and pickles, and
also a lot of wine, enough for the whole night. And why shouldn't they let
go when they're in someone else's empty apartment and moreover there
was a ticklish situation, namely, how I'd react to the arrival of my newly-

wed relatives, Kolya and Marisha, since they'd just got married yesterday, that's the way it was, and Serge was there too, a little more impatient than usual to start drinking; he and Zhora immediately started celebrating everything that had happened. There'd been no trace of Lenka Marchukaite for a long time now; they said that she'd been seen walking somewhere, her chest covered with a warm scarf, and someone saw her in the subway after the birth of her dead baby, but she didn't complain, her only complaint being that her breasts were swollen with milk. So Andrei-the-Stoolpigeon put on a record, his under-age Nadya once again started playing at being a housewife and told me how much alimony Andrei was paying and how there was no point in his even writing a dissertation because everything would go to alimony payments. And when would they end? In fourteen years, when Nadya would hit thirty-three, and only then would it be possible to have a baby of her own. Tanya the Valkyrie came in, her teeth and eyes flashing radiantly, and I asked her whether they'd put Sonechka and her boy together, it would be more convenient for them together, and in reply to this, Tanya as always gave a soft neigh of laughter, showing still more of her incredibly big teeth, whereas Marisha got angry, unlike other years when I had asked: "Just what are they up to?"

"Just *that*!" replied the radiant Tanya.

"It's fine for you, you've got a boy, but it's worse for Marisha, Marisha, have you already taught Sonechka to take precautions?"

"Don't worry, I have," replied Marisha and joined in Tanya's soft neigh of laughter, although I'd told the honest truth, as I usually did.

"What's the matter?" asked Nadya, one of whose eyes was just about ready to fall out of its orbit.

"Nadya," I said, "Is it true that you have a false eye?"

"She's always like that," beaming Tanya said to poor Nadya.

And Andrei-the-Stoolpigeon put in his two cents worth:

"I have extremely negative feelings toward you!" he announced, recalling Serge's formulation, but I paid no attention to Andrei-the-Stoolpigeon.

Serge and Zhora came in from the kitchen, already high, and my Kolya emerged from our former bedroom, I didn't know what he'd been doing there.

"Kolya, were you able to pick out the better sheets for yourself?" I asked, and realized that I'd hit the nail on the head.

Kolya shook his head and twisted his finger at his temple, and because of this remark he didn't take a single piece of bed linen during this visit, thanks to my perspicacity.

"Marisha, do you have something to sleep on with my husband? I gather you gave some of your sheets to Serge. But my sheets are all faded;

last time Kolya decided to wash the whites for the first time in his life, and he threw them into boiling water and boiled all the stains on the sheets, so they show through like clouds."

They all burst into friendly, pleased laughter at that and sat down at the table. My role had been played, and Serge played his role next, starting to argue with Zhora, inarticulately, vaguely, and nasally, about the general field theory of some Ryabikin, during which Serge attacked Ryabikin furiously, while Zhora defended him indulgently and then gave in as if reluctantly and agreed, and for the first time we caught a glimpse of the unsuccessful, thwarted scientist in Serge, whereas in the downtrodden Zhora you could see for the first time a hint of a rising luminary of science, for there's no better indicator of personal success than indulgence toward others in your field.

"When are you defending your doctoral dissertation, Zhora?" I asked him, guessing, and he took the bait and instantly replied that the preliminary session was on Tuesday, but he'd have to wait his turn for the defense.

Everybody fell silent for a moment, then started drinking. Everyone drank himself into oblivion. Andrei-the-Stoolpigeon suddenly started complaining about the district executive committee, which wouldn't give them a three-room apartment for two, whereas Nadya's dad had become a general and was creating an uproar, bombarding Nadya with one gift after another, and a car was in the works and also a three-room co-op apartment if only Nadya would enroll in school instead of having a baby.

"But I want a baby," said Nadya stubbornly, but nobody picked up on the topic.

In short, the conversation at the table didn't get off the ground; Kolya and Marisha were having a quiet exchange, I knew about what—about his taking his remaining things right now and about where he should store those things while they were exchanging Marisha's apartment for a room for Serge and a two-room apartment so that Sonechka would have a place to herself to study her violin music and Serge would have a place to live with the brunette, and my husband would have a place to live with Marisha. But perhaps they were whispering that it would be better to give me their two-room apartment and to move into my three-room one and to start exchanging it.

"Marisha, how do you like being in my apartment?" I asked. "Perhaps you can move in here and Alyosha and I can live where you tell us to? Alyosha and I don't need much, you take our household stuff."

"Fool," said Andrei loudly, "Stupid fool! Marishka's only concern is not to take anything from her, you fool!"

"But why not, take them!" I said. "I don't need much for myself, and

Alyosha's going to an orphanage, I'm already making arrangements and taking care of it. In the town of Borovsk."

"Come on!" said Kolya, "You're kidding."

"Let's leave. To sit through this performance is really...," said Andrei-the-Stoolpigeon and even started getting up decisively together with his Nadya, but the others didn't stir, it was important to them to see the trial through to the end.

"I'm arranging to place him in an orphanage, see, here's the application," I said, and without getting up I got the application and the forms that were filled out from behind the glass of the bookshelf.

Kolya took them to look at and then tore them up.

"Brazen fool," said Andrei.

I settled back in my chair.

"Drink, eat, I'll bring in the jam and cabbage pies in just a second."

"Okay," said Serge, and they started drinking again.

Andrei put on a record, and Serge went up to his wife-no-longer Marisha and invited her to dance. Marisha blushed, and how nice it was to see her cast a furtive glance in my direction, mine for some reason, and no one else's! "So I've become a yardstick for people's consciences now," I muttered, setting the cabbage pies on the table.

Everything got really going at this point, the celebration of their love was complete, everybody was yelling in unison and singing—having a really good time—and Kolya, who was left with nothing to do, came up to me and asked:

"Where's Alyosha?"

"I don't know, out for a walk," I said.

"But it's already after midnight!" said Kolya and went out into the entrance hall.

Although I made no move to stop him, he didn't start getting dressed to leave, but turned off into the bathroom on the way and stayed there for a long time, and in the meantime Marisha felt sick: she'd had too much to drink and the best thing she could think of was to lean out of the kitchen window and bring up her bill of fare right onto the wall, as we found out the following day from what the maintenance man told us after he arrived.

Now it was pies, cigarette butts, pillaged salads, apple halves and cores, bottles under the couch, Nadya sobbing violently and holding her eye, and Andrei holding Marisha in his arms and dancing with her—they enacted the same famous annual one-act show when Marisha got to feeling better, but Nadya was seeing it for the first time in her life and was so frightened by the whole business that her eye almost fell out.

Then Andrei got ready to leave and sternly got Nadya ready, for the subway would stop running soon, Serge and Zhora were happily putting on their coats, when Kolya came out of the bathroom and, not thinking too clearly, lay down on the couch, but Zhora got him up and led him out, with joyful Tanya marching behind them, and I finally opened the door for all of them, and they all saw Alyosha, who was sitting asleep on the stairs.

I leaped out, dragged him upright, and with a wild shout of "What are you doing? Why are you here?!" I struck him across the face so that blood started flowing from the child's nose, and not being fully awake yet, he began to choke. I started hitting him blindly, and they threw themselves at me, grabbed my arms, pushed me inside, and slammed the door shut, and someone held the door for a long time while I kept banging, and you could hear someone sobbing and Nadya shouting, "I'll kill her with my bare hands! Lord! What a monster!"

And Kolya shouted as he went down the stairs:

"Alyoshka! Alyoshka! That's it! I'm taking you away! That's it! Wherever the hell it might be—anywhere'd be better. Just not here! What scum!"

I locked the sliding bolt. My calculations had been perfect. Not one of them could bear to see a child's blood; they could calmly slice each other into pieces, but a child—children were something sacred to them.

I stole into the kitchen and looked out the window just above Marisha's half-smeared-off beets. I didn't have long to wait. The whole group tumbled out of the front door. Kolya was carrying Alyosha! It was a triumphant communal procession. They were all exchanging excited remarks and waiting for somebody. The last one to come out was Andrei, so, therefore, he had been the one holding the door. When he came out last, covering their flank, Nadya greeted him with a shout: "She should lose her mother's rights, that's what!" Everybody was at his best. Marisha was fussing over Alyosha with a handkerchief. Their drunken voices carried far through the neighborhood. They even took a cab! Kolya carrying Alyoshka, and Marisha supporting them, stumbled as they got into the back seat, and Zhora got in the front. Apparently Zhora was going to pay, I thought, right as always, and it's on the way for Zhora, he always takes cabs anyway. That's okay, they'll make it.

They won't take me to court, they're not that kind of people. They'll hide Alyoshka from me. They'll surround him with attention. Andrei-the-Stoolpigeon and his childless wife will romantically love Alyoshka longer than all the others. Tanya will take Alyoshka to the beach for the summer.

The Kolya who took Alyosha in his arms is no longer the Kolya who'd hit a seven-year-old child flat across the face only because he'd wet himself. Marisha will also love and feel sorry for little Alyosha with his rotten teeth, who hasn't shown the slightest bit of talent. And Zhora, who'll be rich in the future, will throw something his way from his means and bounties, and the next thing you'll know, he'll get Alyosha into an institute. Serge is something else—a person who's basically unromantic, a dry person, cynical and mistrustful; but he'll end up living together with the only being he really loves, with Sonechka, his crazy love for her leading him down crooked paths, back streets, and dark basements, until he finally realizes it completely, drops all women, and lives for the sake of his one and only, whom he himself fathered. Such things have happened before and will happen again. Now that's going to be a predicament and an occupation for my small crowd of friends, but it won't happen soon, it'll be in eight years, and in those years Alyosha will have time to gain strength, intelligence, and everything he needs. I've already arranged his fate at a very cheap price. Otherwise after my death he'd have gone from one boarding school to another and would have had a hard time being received as a visitor in his father's own home. When I sent him off to our garden plot, I simply didn't give him the key to the cabin there, and he was forced to come back, but I'd forbidden him to knock on the door, and I'd already taught him at his age to understand when something was forbidden. And the whole child-beating scene, which didn't cost me much effort, gave a push to the long, new romantic tradition in my orphan Alyosha's life with his noble, new foster-parents, who'll forget their own interests, but will watch over his. That's how I calculated it all, and that's the way it will be. And what's also good is that this whole group family will live in Alyosha's apartment, in his home, and not he in theirs, that's also splendid, since I'll be setting off very soon on the road of my forefathers. Alyosha, I think, will visit me on the first day of Easter, that's what I mentally agreed to with him, showing him the way and the day. I think he'll figure it out, he's a very perceptive boy, and there among the painted eggs, among the plastic wreaths and the rumpled, drunken, kind crowd he'll forgive me for not having let him say good-bye, and for hitting him on the face instead of blessing him. But it's better this way—for everybody. I'm smart, I understand things.

1979

Translated by Helena Goscilo

Originally published in *Novyi Mir*, January 1988.

FAZIL ISKANDER
OLD HASAN'S PIPE

Why do you sing your flute-like
martial song, dear Bullfinch?
G. R. Derzhavin

Light is the water of the heavens. And water—the light of the earth. O, waterfall of roaring light!

Hasan, an old shepherd from Chegem, and I were sitting in a blooming alpine meadow. It was a hot summer day. Directly in front of us a waterfall burst forth from a high granite cliff and fell in many streams. Striking ledges on the wall, some of the streams intertwined and untwined on their journey downward. The main channel fell unobstructed, without touching a single ledge. The ledges may once have been in its way, but it had dislodged them through persistent effort. Now the channel descended freely and slowly, as though fearing its own incredible power, and restrained itself in flight, which made it appear all the more powerful.

The roar of the waterfall, washing away the residual debris of life's bustling sounds, quieted my soul. A waterfall is a mighty current in nature's circulation that has been exposed on the earth's surface by chance. We are calmed as we watch it and listen to its great, wet sound. Here is another source of rejuvenation! The earth's health is our health!

Nature offers us her wisdom without forcing it upon us. But we thick-headed humans require marching orders to heed it.

The earth's health is our health! Even the goats understood this and grazed together, pressing close to the waterfall, where the lush alpine grass, bilberry bushes and holly were sprinkled with an ozone of spray, making them look appetizing even to the human eye—at least to my hungry eye. I was tempted to munch on that lush salad with the goats, but unlike them, salting it a little as I went. A matchbox of salt was left in my backpack.

This excursion into the mountains had been arranged by Tengiz, Uncle Sandro's favorite. He had taken me to his friends in Svanetia to show me mountain-goat hunting. We spent the night in the home of his friend Vano, a sturdy, gloomy fellow. When he wasn't hunting, Vano also worked in the village as a school teacher.

In the ascetic decor of the Svan house I was surprised by the luxury of the beds we were given: fluffy pillows, warm, light blankets, soft mattresses and fresh sheets that smelled of sunshine.

Later, after I had seen for myself that Svans are the most tireless walkers on earth, I realized that the luxury and comfort of their beds is unconscious self-compensation for their lengthy expeditions and nights spent on a felt cloak spread under the glaciers.

In the same way, a Chegem plowman, resting in the shade of a walnut tree at noon, might not seem to notice a sparkling glass of spring water offered to him: unhurriedly, with fitting deliberation, he would finish speaking to his companion and then, perhaps, reach for the glass, but suddenly he might remember that he should clarify what he'd said or hear out a reply and you'd see his hand stop near the extended glass.

Even after finally taking it, on occasion he would silently dump it out, not even condescending to explain the reasons (one thing being clear—the proper procedure had not been followed), and the woman standing with the pitcher would rinse the glass again in almost mystical trepidation, perhaps even in silent exultation (aren't they wonderful!), refill it with water and offer it once more without complaint, knowing that both the sparkling cleanliness of the glass and the fresh spring water, as well as the luxury of his capricious act, were nobly justified by those strong, bare legs in rolled-up jodhpurs, blackened to the ankle with freshly turned earth that was ready to bear fruit. Blessed be the breadwinner!

We set out the next morning at daybreak. There were four of us: our host, his neighbor (an old hunter), Tengiz and I. About two hours later we really did come across the trail of a mountain goat, or goats, if as experienced border violators (actually we were the ones violating borders) they walked in each other's tracks. Long-legged Tengiz and the old Svan pulled ahead of us, but Vano was forced to slow down in order to stay near me.

Several hours later we were already crunching across blinding glacial snow. My companions kept on walking. I was so tired that I even contemplated stopping them with gunshots. In the air, of course.

The invisible goat continued to leave increasingly brazen, but by no means fresher, tracks. The more tired I got, the more I naturally wondered who was going faster, the goat or us? If the goat was, then there was no reason to hurry. At the very least we could have stopped and talked about what to do next. But no, they kept on walking.

On the glacial snow our catch added two sets of droppings to the scanty information of its tracks. I reasoned that if we ascertained the temperature difference between the first and second droppings and divided the distance between them by it, we could determine the goat's speed.

Unfortunately, a very sensitive thermometer was needed to ascertain that difference and we didn't have any thermometer with us.

There was nothing left to do but console myself with the thought that the goat really did exist and its stomach was in good working order. But the thought didn't console me in the least. I finally so lost hope of catching the goat that I asked Vano, who was walking in front of me, "How can you be sure we're moving faster than the goat?"

I can swear by Mohammed's remains the tone of my voice was not shrill. Vano stopped dead for a few seconds without turning. I realized that I had said something utterly tactless. Then he looked back, gave me the once over in a long glance and walked on without saying a word. Mountain men are truly the most reserved people in the world!

I sensed that hunting in the high mountains was not subject to the arithmetical logic of the valleys, but to the laws of higher mathematics, perhaps even to the theory of relativity. I had long realized that I had done nothing to deserve a luxurious Svan bed. Trips like this ought to be prepared for, not discussed in coffee houses by the sea.

A while later I noticed that Vano, who was walking about thirty meters in front of me, stepped over an obstacle without stopping. There even appeared to be a certain demonstrative ease in his movements.

I reached the spot and saw a bottomless crevice in the snow. An invisible stream gurgled in its depths. I needed to take a big step, but that invisible stream gurgling far below caused me to hesitate. Yes, I hesitated, but I remind the reader of a mitigating circumstance—the stream was invisible.

I decided that I could make the step across that devilish crevice only if I tossed across my rifle, which would otherwise certainly drag me down with it. As soon as I had taken the rifle from my shoulder, my companion looked back. I don't know if he understood why I had taken it off, but from the look on his face I knew there was no way I could throw it across the crevice. That would be a complete ethical disaster.

Apparently for a Svan, a rifle was an armed banner to be held high over-head not only when jumping a crevice, but also when falling into it. What if he thought he'd caught me in the shameful act of shooting myself in the foot? It was hard to understand completely just what the look on his face meant. Then his lips parted slowly in a granite smile that, with crafty hos-pitality, invited me to come toward him. I realized this was his revenge for my careless question. Any expedition is the enemy of skepticism—some-thing I frequently learn the hard way.

I stepped over and we moved on. We walked and walked until Tengiz finally waved to us from a distance. Something had happened up ahead. Judging by Tengiz and the old Svan's stooping figures, they had captured the exhausted goat. Not surprising after so much trouble. However, the idea of taking it alive had never been discussed, at least not out loud. We drew closer and saw that Tengiz and the old Svan had left the tracks we had been following and, off to the side, were digging a dead goat out of the snow.

It lay under a high cliff, from which it had obviously fallen, and thus had plunged so deeply into the snow. As it turned out, only the tip of one horn had been sticking out and the old Svan had spied it.

The goat had been killed by an unknown hunter in unknown times. The only thing we could be sure of after digging it out was that it had been killed by a firearm. As I figured, it could have been killed two months or two centuries ago. Firearms could hardly have appeared in Svanetia before that.

As soon as our friends started to skin it, a carrion crow began circling overhead, not without a certain restrained solemnity. It was odd—a moment before there had only been deserted blue sky, deserted icy peaks, and now the bird was right there.

The goat's meat smelled a little strong, but it hadn't spoiled. It was well preserved for being two centuries old. The glacier's refrigerator was in good working order. Having prepared the meat, our friends rightly decided that the intestinal tract of this goat had completely exhausted its usefulness and threw it away.

I raised my head again and looked at the crow. With some difficulty it held on for one more circle, then quickly and efficiently flapping its wings, obviously flew off to summon its companions.

After finishing with the carcass, our friends carefully laid out the hide and, to my surprise, began to pack the meat and internal organs back into it. They did this with an air of conscious purpose, as though recalling an anatomical chart of the parts' natural arrangement. At first I decided that this was an homage to an ancient pagan cult—the victim is given a symbolic last chance to revive itself and escape.

Then I realized that the whole thing was much simpler. The meat and organs are placed in the hide with such primal accuracy for ease of carrying. Apparently, the Svans had long ago noticed that nature has arranged our internal organs with sensible compactness, the way an experienced shepherd does the load on the back of a pack animal. So that nothing rubs, sways or gets in the way.

As I watched them work, I easily grasped why our hearts are on the left side. Because our right hand, as the more vigorous and therefore the more restless, would often disturb its even rhythm. Besides that, in any attack it is easier to defend the left side with the right hand. (The reader may stop for a moment and practice.)

The essential thing about the peaceful gesture of shaking hands with the right hand is that, for both parties simultaneously, the most powerful weapon of aggression is disengaged while the humanistic glands that fill the body with a pleasant warmth are engaged. Obviously, the firmer the handshake, the more abundantly the humanistic juices flow and the better a person feels. That's why a handshake is usually accompanied by mutual smiles and nods, which confirm that the juices are being properly secreted.

True, we can't ignore cases when the abundant secretion of the humanistic glands is feigned. Sometimes we see two people caught in a handshake, convulsively pumping each other's hand and feeling that their humanistic glands just won't kick in. Poor things! In the same way the alcoholic tries to shake the last drops from an empty bottle, and the immortal Charlie Chaplin shook the policeman's hand.

So, we have determined that the heart is on the left side to be farther from the overactive right hand, whose movements often do not harmonize with the heart's activity. But what about southpaws? This sad medical discovery follows: other things being equal, a lefthander's heart should wear out more quickly.

This is where the mind can lead you if you don't participate in cutting and gathering goat meat, yet know for certain that you'll take part in the subsequent feast. If, on the other hand, you observe the preparation of the meat, knowing that you won't participate in its subsequent consumption, completely different conclusions follow—harsh ones about social class.

We finally descended a little lower, where there were some trees and we could build a fire. Sunset was drawing near.

Night in the mountains under an open sky, in the campfire's house of light, harbors, as they said in the old days, ineffable delights. Darkness makes the most natural walls for a dwelling, so a house of light is the coziest in the world. The space we are able to illuminate in the darkness is indeed our natural home. Perhaps this is the fairest allocation of living space in the world. Apparently, that's how it was intended from the start, but much got distorted later on.

For a while longer I improvised freely on the theme of the house of light without leaving its walls. Generally speaking, it's easy to improvise to the sound of grilling shashlyk.

Then we settled down to supper. I don't know how those Siberian huskies felt when, if you believe the papers, they devoured the million-year-old meat of woolly mammoths that had been dug up from the permafrost, but all of my companions and I enjoyed eating that hot, tender shashlyk with its gentle hint of alpine, aristocratic decay.

I realized that a hunt like this, without a single shot fired, was more to my liking. You just walk through the mountains and look in other people's refrigerators. One should be just as watchful at the foot of steep precipices as one is under fruit trees.

We slept on cloaks next to the fire. It was then I felt several defects in the house of light. The part of my body that faced the campfire was red-hot. At the same time the other part of my body, the side facing the glaciers, turned into a small moraine, but thawed rather quickly when flipped toward the fire.

No doubt it would be fine sleeping by a fire on top of the glaciers if someone would turn you evenly like meat on a spit. Asking our gracious hosts to do this was out of the question. Especially since they themselves added further worry to my already troubled repose. The fact is, both Svans would suddenly whoop in their sleep, leap up and grab for their rifles.

With gun in hand, each of them would look around half-blindly, as though he had come too quickly from the twilight of dreams into the house of light. Then, reassured, he would lie back down, or stir up the embers of the fire, and then settle down comfortably with his rifle in his arms.

Judging by the number of times he leaped up, the younger man went after the goat more often than the older one. Once they went after it at the same time. Then I realized that perhaps it didn't have anything to do with goats, but with the ancient instinct of a warlike people. Perhaps they

were subconsciously jolted from their sleep because outsiders with guns—
that is, Tengiz and I—were lying nearby, next to the fire.

I decided that at future stops, if, of course, I survived this night, I
would simply let them keep my weapon. Or, on the other hand, perhaps
hold theirs until morning.

Anyway, it's unpleasant when you're by a fire in the mountains at night
and your companion whoops in his sleep, wakes up and immediately grabs
for his rifle. The problem is knowing how to act—whether you should let
out a loud, peaceful snore or put your hand on your own rifle, as if to say,
"I'm watching and waiting to see what happens next."

The morning was beautiful if only because it came. Over steaming
shashlyk I learned from our friends that some shepherds from Chegem
were staying not far from there, a half day's journey away. The name of
old Hasan came up. Suddenly a half-forgotten memory stung me with
strange, incomprehensible excitement.

"Isn't that the Hasan who plays the song of Hajarat Kiahba on his
pipe?" I asked.

"Oh yes," nodded the old Svan, "but he doesn't play anymore, now he
tells the outlaw's story."

When I was very young, a shepherd's pipe could sometimes be heard
on the green hill above my grandfather's house. It always blew the same
manly, piercingly sad melody. It was a folk song about Hajarat Kiahba, the
famous outlaw.

"Quiet, Hasan is playing!" one of the women would cry suddenly,
most often Aunt Nutsa, Uncle Kyazym's wife.

Old Hasan would play for a long, long time and then the melody would
fade and die away. The shepherd and his goats had gone somewhere else.

I noticed that when Hasan played, the women's faces became thoughtfully tender, while the men seemed embarrassed and detached.

"What is he after?" one of them would say mournfully. "Our hoes have
worn us out long ago."

Even then, as a child, I was secretly amused by this quaint folk dema-
goguery. I knew they were all working the same as usual and not knocking
themselves out while weeding the corn or tobacco.

"He's letting out his feelings. His father was a friend of Hajarat's,"
someone recalled.

"Doesn't he have anything better to do?" someone else added with
annoyance. "Bringing back Tsar Nicholas' time. . . ."

"Hush up!" Aunt Nutsa would cut him off with an abruptness that was
uncharacteristic of mountain women when speaking to men.

Hasan lived on the other side of Chegem and showed up near Grand-father's house very rarely. Even more rarely did his appearances coincide with the midday rest of the peasants who worked in some nearby field and so had dropped by the yard of the Big House.

Sometimes no one paid any attention to his pipe, but if they did listen, I had the impression the same conversation repeated itself, and it even seemed that Aunt Nutsa would twist her spindle with the same irritation and say, "Hush up!"

Today I realize that this conversation could never have been repeated word for word, but then, in my childhood, it seemed that everything was repeated to the point of delicious agony. Not only were the words repeated, but also the feeling that when those words had been spoken before I had felt then, too, that everything was repeated to the point of that same deli-cious agony. The memory of a memory harked back to an unknown pro-tomemory.

Hasan was considered an eccentric by Chegem standards. The chief marks of his eccentricity were his pipe, natural in the hands of a teenager, but not in those of an elderly shepherd; his extraordinary physical cleanli-ness; but most of all, the fact that he always referred to his wife as "the smart one." There may have been other things, but I've forgotten them now.

Of course, the men of Chegem sometimes called their wives "the smart one" too, but when they did, they meant the exact opposite. It was unseemly to reveal a wife's intelligence publicly, if indeed it existed (said with a smile); better in public to put her head on your knees and check her scalp for lice.

So at all their gatherings the people of Chegem didn't miss a chance to poke fun at Hasan, presenting him with some ostensibly profitable but mind-boggling deal.

"No, no, I've got to talk it over with the smart one," Hasan usually answered, evoking general laughter, to which he paid not the slightest attention. But sometimes he quickly exposed the false advantageousness of the mind-boggling transaction with the same plain straightforwardness and without his wife, and everyone laughed in an even friendlier way, for nothing makes people laugh more than a joker who's been made a fool of.

His neatness and extraordinary physical cleanliness also elicited inex-haustible jokes and surprise. Sometimes all the roads would be out, but he would appear at the village council or a home where a banquet was to be held without so much as a speck of dirt even on his shoes.

"How could you have come by the Upper Chegem Road?" people asked in amazement. "Maybe you flew?"

"Oh, I jumped from rock to rock," answered Hasan with an embarrassed smile, wiping his rawhide boots on the grass before going into the house. On occasion he simply detoured around a road that was too muddy, not minding a few extra kilometers' walk along some unexplored pathway.

That's how I remembered Hasan, looking at the porch with embarrassment yet at the same time with a secret obstinacy, cleaning his shoes or boots on the grass for a long time, now and again turning his head and glancing at his shining soles, from which he continued to wipe the dirt he alone could see. Tall, wiry, and somewhat frail for a peasant, he had big blue eyes and for some reason seemed like an old man to me even then. What was he like now?

Of course, I knew the story of Hajarat Kiahba as well as children did back then. We loved it and took pride in it, but the song that poured from Hasan's pipe gave the impression of something incomprehensible and even bitter. An impression of wrongdoing? But what wrongdoing? The very same song was beautiful when sung by our men at the table after dinner, and it seemed that if the occasion arose any one of them could be just like Hajarat. Then what was old Hasan trying to say with his pipe?

All of this surfaced now and I suddenly had an irresistible urge to see him. Several years before I had gone up to see our shepherds, but he hadn't been there.

"How do you get to their camp?" I asked the old Svan.

"What?" Tengiz was surprised. "Have you forgotten why we came?"

I didn't say a word.

"You go down this hollow," Vano cut in with unexpected cheerfulness before the old Svan could answer, "and you'll see a path. Follow it. By noon you'll run into a waterfall. He always grazes his goats there. Just don't turn off anywhere, keep going and going and going right along that path."

I had the feeling he enjoyed repeating the verb that would separate me from him. I'll say it again: there's no one more reserved than mountain men! The desire for revenge keeps well in the refrigerator of reserve. I know that from my own experience.

Together Tengiz and the Svans once again began to pack the meat into the long-suffering goat hide, from which it had been removed twice the previous day. They did this with the same life-giving, surgical diligence as before: at times halting a second for consultation, as though, unconcerned by missing parts and the completely eaten liver, they were trying precisely to recall and restore its primal condition.

They intended to bury the poor goat in the snow again so the meat wouldn't spoil before they returned from the hunt.

I said good-bye to my companions and threw my half-empty backpack over my shoulder, feeling a double sense of relief. Now no one would leap up in the middle of the night and grab for a rifle, looking around half-blindly. I can't stand it when people grab their guns first and then look around half-blindly. They should wipe their eyes, then look around and grab for their guns if they need to. Tengiz had hinted that I might meet a bear, so he wouldn't have to lug around my rifle as well as his own, but I didn't believe that was any more likely than meeting the Abominable Snowman.

"You can bury it in the snow with the goat," I said and added jokingly, "then if you happen to die, when hunters of the post-atomic age dig up your goat, they'll know what kind of barbaric weapon it was killed with."

"Enough of your fooling around," said Tengiz, taking my rifle. "Stay with the shepherds about three days. I'll come over..."

Vano translated my words for the old Svan and even showed him with gestures where I had intended to hide the rifle. Although the old Svan understood Russian relatively well, from his point of view it seemed the idea of burying the rifle in the snow inside a dead goat (perhaps in exchange for the liver we had eaten?) was such sacrilegious nonsense that it was easier for him to believe he had misinterpreted what I had said.

But Vano explained in a rapid eagle-like squawk that there was no other way to take my words. He clearly went on to say that I had been impudent enough to ask who was moving faster, the goat or us hunters, and despite that, the tongue of this low mountain dweller (my tongue, that is) hadn't withered.

Once he had started, there was no stopping him. He told how I had stood next to the gap in the ice, deciding how to get rid of my rifle. To make things perfectly clear, Vano went so far as to take his own rifle from his shoulder and pretend to push it into an invisible crevice. For some reason such a pacifistic interpretation of my gesture hadn't occurred to me. I had wanted to throw the rifle away, but wary Vano had turned around just in time—under his gaze I had pulled my hand back, and since there was nothing else to do, stepped over the crevice.

Squawk, squawk, squawk and the old Svan's astonished clucking in response. As he told the story, Vano looked at me more and more warmly, as though beginning to understand the excusable reasons for my strange behavior. Then he looked at me again and started to imitate the rapid, labored breathing of a tired person, or so I thought. Both Svans burst out laughing for some reason.

Then I realized that he wasn't imitating fatigue, but simply explaining that certain low mountain dwellers disregard the customs of the high mountains not from any desire to be insulting, but from the slight idiocy that comes over them at the sight of glaciers, although it is supposedly from lack of oxygen.

That must have been how Vano explained certain quirks of my Endurian* behavior to the old Svan. Alas, everything in this world is relative, including Endurianism. Both Svans were in a much better mood. After I had said good-bye and started to descend the steep slope, which was covered with loose rock, Vano shouted after me, "If you see a bear cub, don't go after it!"

"Why not?" I asked, looking back.

"Because its mother will catch you!"

A mountain joke. Both Svans laughed. The scree of stones behind me stirred.

I was in high spirits during my hike through the alpine meadows.

I remembered a story by our immortal Abesolomon Nartovich. Back in the days when he had an important post, he was escorting a German delegation that had been brought up to the alpine meadows for some reason. It may have been done to demonstrate the unquestionable superiority of peaceful means—a friendly delegation easily achieved what the Edelweiss Divisions could not. In the region of Otkhara, his guests marveled at the distant white stream of a waterfall that had suddenly come into view.

"That's how our shepherds transport milk," said Abesolomon Nartovich, freely translating majestic natural phenomena into the grandeur of human accomplishments. "There is a processing plant below."

This statement was a surprise not only to the guests, but to our interpreter as well. Of course, he had taken tourists around the area before, but this was his first time with Abesolomon Nartovich. Fortunately, the processing plant wasn't visible beyond the tall fir trees, but the way the interpreter paled was. However, we must suppose that, mentally leaping to the top of the waterfall and managing to note the countless, fat herds grazing beyond the ridge, he rose to the task, although not without paying a price.

"That's what we decided," continued Abesolomon Nartovich, "to keep the pipes from spoiling the scenery. It's inexpensive and beautiful."

His guests all nodded, quite touched by Abesolomon Nartovich's ecological concern, while one sensitive German woman gave the interpreter a tablet for his heart.

---

*Enduria is a fictitious district in eastern Abkhazia. See Iskander's novel *Sandro of Chegem*.

"The mountains are no place for high-strung people." Abesolomon Nartovich tossed this offhand remark in his direction and went on to tell the myth-loving Germans the folk legend of an extinct tribe of mountain dwarfs, the Atsans.

One might get the mistaken impression that Abesolomon Nartovich always indulged in fantasy. Nothing of the sort. If certain phenomena in life or nature were sufficiently colorful in and of themselves, he left them in their primal state. But if they weren't, or, particularly in the area of the economy, they smacked of a depressing squalor that was harmful to the well-being of the people, he confidently put into play his rich, colorful palette, on which at one time, in a sequence that can no longer be determined, rainbows and swine had been squeezed.

Now Abesolomon Nartovich has been gradually demoted to the level of chief agronomist for a valley sovkhoz which he used to protect with much ado from the top. The so-called irony of history is apparent here: when Potemkin fell from favor, he was named chief agronomist of a Potemkin village. But the banquets Abesolomon Nartovich used to throw! And the guests! Is it worth describing? Oh, if only one could! But who cares now? Oh, the times we live in, as the Chegemians used to say!

About three hours later I was resting near a mossy boulder and admiring the bluish-green patterns of the lichen on its surface. Suddenly part of the pattern came to life, and rising in flight, turned into a greenish-blue butterfly that had been completely camouflaged on the boulder. After fluttering for a while near the spots of lichen, which it seemed to have woven, the butterfly floated away.

I had the distinct impression that it wasn't Darwin who had noticed similar phenomena and invented his theory, but rather the butterfly who had learned Darwinism like an A student and adapted itself to his laws. When it rose from the blue-green pattern and fluttered nearby, I felt a flash of joy fly out of me to meet it. Another butterfly.

I will try here to analyze not Darwin's teachings, of which I have only the vaguest ideas from grade school, but the nature of my own joy. This is an organism I know fairly well. In a sense, I know it even better than Darwin knew the animals he studied. This organism transmits its sensations to me by itself, which is something that can't be said of Darwin's animals, especially the ones that have long been extinct.

So what was it that caused my feeling of joy? The existence of a certain rational principle in nature? Undoubtedly. But I wasn't happy just because for millions of years all the other butterflies around this boulder were, let's say, eaten by birds, while this particular one managed to adapt itself and survive to the present. This would be a strange pleasure for a human. More likely, people would mourn the butterflies that had perished heroically on the lichen-covered ladder of evolution.

"To take on the surrounding spots or nobly to defend one's own color? That is the question," as Hamlet would say.

Another doubt exists. Let's reduce the fraction to make the experiment simpler: the earth is a boulder. Its inhabitants are butterflies and birds. Eternal struggle for existence and adaptation on both sides. As the butterfly took on the spots of the lichen, why didn't the bird's vision develop in parallel? Why didn't it equip itself with evolutionary glasses and begin to remove the false spots on the lichen with precise pecks? Why did it refuse to struggle with this crafty butterfly, and looking around half-blindly (a familiar scene), fly off to other meadow planets in search of less artfully colored butterflies?

Everything here is accidental, and most accidental of all is the belief that the butterfly landed on the lichen by the law of unconscious camouflaging. The butterfly landed on the boulder by chance, and by chance I saw it the very moment it flew away. The only thing not accidental was my feeling of joy.

So let's return to this precise sensation. The joy was actually there and I knew what had caused it. The amazing similarity of the blue-green butterfly to the blue-green pattern on the lichen had uplifted me as a poetic symbol of the kinship of all living things and the oneness of our ultimate goal. This means that I, as a human being, have within me a desire for the kinship of all living things, even though it is continually outraged by the hostility among living things. But if I had no inclination to believe in the kinship of living things, there would also be no outrage over the hostility, only a sense of natural adaptation.

The blue-green butterfly that flew up from the blue-green lichen did not beget my butterfly of joy, but only gave it the signal to rise from my soul, where until then it had been as imperceptible as the first butterfly on the boulder. A desire for the oneness of all living things exists within humans just as does joy at the sight of a child or the sun, no matter how much they may bore us at times.

In the chaos of world egoism people get worn down, become depressed and involuntarily ask themselves, "Is there really a common goal?" "There is, there is!" flashes the butterfly, communicating with the lichen in their common language of color. The spiritual uplift I experienced from this poetic proof is as objective to me as a mathematical formula.

In fact, this method of proof has saved me many times. Once I had the nerve to argue with a friendly biologist who maintained that life on earth had begun by chance. He knew and loved literature, a fact that I used to my advantage.

"Tell me," I asked ingratiatingly, "does the structure of a living cell differ much from a dead one?"

"There's an incredible difference!" he exclaimed with the fervor of a man who has a practical knowledge of this difference.

"About as much as the mind of a brilliant poet differs from that of a hack writer?"

"Much more!" he exclaimed with even greater fervor.

"Do you imagine," I asked, "that a hack could write two brilliant lines in his entire life?"

"In principle, yes," he said after a moment's thought.

"What about four?" I asked.

"I suppose that's possible," he agreed, deciding this assumption was no threat to science. "What do you think?"

"Of course," I agreed, "it can happen. In your opinion, could the hack write twelve brilliant lines?"

"No," he said, sensing an imminent trap, but not knowing quite where to expect it, "that's probably not possible."

"Think about it," I reassured him, "thousands of years pass, millions of hacks come and go, and one of them accidentally stumbles onto twelve brilliant lines, even though after that the glow of his feeble mind is extinguished forever."

"That might be possible," he agreed reluctantly and added, "if it isn't a psychiatric mistake to consider him a hack in the first place."

"It isn't!" I exclaimed with glee. "It isn't and can't be a mistake! Can you imagine that millions and millions of years pass, billions of hacks come and go, and one of them finally writes *Eugene Onegin*?"

"Never!" he cried, hurt by this slight to his beloved literature.

"That's what I'm talking about," I said and we clinked glasses in a sign of mutual agreement.

I reached the waterfall by midday or even a little earlier. The shepherd Hasan sat on a green knoll, past which the stream born of the waterfall merrily ran. He was sitting on a cloak he had spread out. I said hello and he stood up to greet me.

So there were old Hasan and I in a blooming alpine meadow. He truly was an old man now, lean and erect. Clean rubber boots, military jodhpurs, a gray wool shirt pulled tight by a narrow belt. Gray hair cut short, a slightly hooked nose and big blue eyes filled with fresh sorrow.

He was terribly glad to hear that I spoke Abkhazian; his eyes gleamed with awkward, almost girlish pleasure. Apparently he didn't expect a traveller from Svanetia to speak Abkhazian. His happiness turned to exultation when he learned that we were both from Chegem, and on top of that, it turned out that in the early twenties my uncle from the city had helped him through the courts recover his favorite one-eared mare from a horse thief. I'll make this story of his brief so that later, when he talks about more important things, we can hear him out in full.

"Her ear, you see, was bitten off by my own mule. As you probably know, the mules around here are extremely fond of the little ones. My mule believed that the mare hadn't defended her foal well enough when some wolves attacked. Believed, nothing! That's the way that mare was! So the mule took off half her ear. But I loved that mare anyway, half-ear and all. One day some people said, 'Hasan, a horse thief from Dranda is getting the best of you! He's always on your mare.' I went to his place and saw that it was my horse. He wouldn't give it back. He hauled out witnesses and said, 'It was a wolf that took half her ear off.' You'd think we were born in the woods and didn't know that when a wolf jumps a mare, it goes for the throat, not the ear.

"The next time I rode over on the mule, to show the village court that the mule's bite fit exactly with the edge of my mare's torn ear. But in those days the court wouldn't even look at the mule's teeth. You think it's only today that people take bribes? They took 'em back then too! That thief bought off the elder.

"And the city court, no matter how hard I tried, no matter how many times I went to Kengursk and Mukhus, just laughed and wouldn't take up the case. It was too petty from their point of view. Petty for them, but I was fit to be tied. Things dragged on for two and a half years and I spent so much money on it that I could have bought three horses with ears like rabbits. But for the sake of truth, for the sake of fairness and honesty, I wanted to get that horse thief into court. But I couldn't. Then the mule died and there wasn't anything to compare with the tooth marks on my mare's ear, even though no one was very interested in matching up his incisors with her ear when he was alive.

"So my case had become hopelessly tangled when your mother married a man from the city and Kyazym introduced me to your uncle, the lawyer. And he, God bless him, unraveled the whole thing, down to the last thread. In court he showed that the mare was mine, put all the witnesses to shame, and even proved that the mare had been in foal when the thief took her, so he had to throw in a yearling as well."

Old Hasan finished his story: "He put his heart into it, your uncle did. They don't make them like that any more. Lawyers today are too self-satisfied. I'll never forget him! It's a shame you didn't know him, God bless his soul!"

Old Hasan was wrong on that count, but I didn't try to correct him. I remembered Uncle Samad well. In my time he was already an incorrigible alcoholic and his practice amounted to no more than writing petitions for illiterate peasants in the coffee house or bazaar. They paid him in kind and he came home drunk every night. Then he disappeared, as many people did in those days—not a single letter or postcard from him. Evidently his life just snapped, together with the alcoholic thread by which it had hung.

I felt as though a warm rain had fallen on my soul. I had never met his friends, much less his clients, and suddenly, in such an unlikely place, I meet a man who all his life had been grateful to my unfortunate uncle.

"What's driven you over here?" old Hasan asked in his shepherd's language.

I told him. Upon hearing the name of Hajarat Kiahba, he gave a start and a passionate fire flashed in his eyes, sparked perhaps by the memory of my uncle. As he told the story, at times he would shout, trying to overcome not so much the noise of the waterfall, as I thought at first, but our human deafness.

"I'll tell you the story of Hajarat Kiahba, his heroism and his torments as they really were. You're our flesh and blood, you should know the truth. Nowadays many people prettify his life, but that's indecent. The bad things in his life didn't come from him, but from other people— sometimes even his relatives. When they prettify Hajarat's life, they're really trying to make themselves look better. Because they're ashamed— and they've got reason to be ashamed.

"Hajarat was a distant relative of ours on my mother's side. The first time I met him, he was already an outlaw. The first time I met him, I was a sturdy boy of about ten. I could already drive twenty or thirty goats from the pen, graze them in the woods until they were full, and come home in the evening without losing a single goat or getting myself lost.

"That was five years before the Big Snow and eight years before the first war with the Germans. The Big Snow covered Abkhazia to the rooftops—only chimneys melted through and stuck out. The Big Snow meant that the war with the Germans was coming.

"But we didn't know anything back then. We didn't even know how to say the word 'German' right. We said 'Gelmans'. It took another German war to straighten us out. When the wounded started coming home, we realized 'Gelmans' was wrong—it's 'Germans.' Why should we have cared?

Hardly any of our boys came back. Still, we were ashamed of mispronouncing the enemy's name, so we started saying 'Germans.'

"Hajarat was a pure-blooded peasant. He lived in Eshery. At the time we lived in Achandary. You'll understand why we moved to Chegem if you listen to my story.

"In those days a rich prince of the Dziapshba family lived in Eshery. His name was Omar. Omar was the same age as Hajarat. No, he was about three or four years older. Why do I think so? Because for a long time Omar didn't even notice Hajarat, but when Hajarat grew up Omar began to envy him.

"While Hajarat was a boy, Omar always came in first in the village games. Then one day Hajarat surpassed him. Omar was strong. Hajarat was even stronger. But Omar was a head taller, so he could toss a stone farther.

"I have to tell it the way it was. Hajarat was good-looking but he wasn't especially tall. He was like a snow leopard. Before the Big Snow you could find leopards in our forests. They say they all went to Azerbaidzhan after that. They say the oil heats the ground there, but I don't know, I've never been there.

"So, Omar was first at shot put and Hajarat at all the rest: horse racing, shooting, jumping, fighting on horseback.

"There was so much strength in Hajarat's flint knees that he could jump onto a horse's back from a dead start without touching it. Not onto a Cossack horse, though—they're much taller than ours. He could jump onto one of our Abkhazian mountain horses. I'm telling it the way it was.

"There was so much strength in his flint knees that he couldn't squat down and milk a cow or a goat. His strength would push him up and he'd stand with an empty pail. The strong of this world often end up with empty milk pails.

"He loved farm work. But he didn't like to sit with a pail at all. He would stand up and toss it aside. On the other hand, when he plowed he'd leave his ox behind, he had so much strength in his arms. He loved to plow. But he didn't like to milk goats and cows, no sirree! In those days the women here in Abkhazia rarely milked the livestock. Now they do, if there's anything to milk.

"There was someone at Hajarat's place to milk the cows and goats. He had two sisters. Words can't describe how much they loved him. And he loved them just as much. Hajarat's father and mother had died by then, so only his sisters were left at home. And at Omar's house only his mother, the princess, was left.

"That's how things were when it started. Omar kept picking on

Hajarat out of envy. Envy is a black blindfold on the eyes of reason. Hajarat kept himself under control. He had to—he was thinking of his sisters. If he got killed, his sisters would die of grief. If he killed the prince, he'd become an outlaw and they'd be left alone. Even back then that clan of princes was considered overly fierce.

"But Omar wouldn't let up. Calm down, Omar! Hajarat was that way by nature. I can't grab that waterfall and turn it back, can I? That's how nature created it! Accept it! Mind your own business! But no, Omar kept picking on Hajarat.

"One day two of Hajarat's relatives came over. One by the name of Akuzba, the other by the name of Ahba. They were servants in the prince's house.

" 'Hajarat,' they said, 'the prince wants you to give him your horse. In return you can have any horse in his herd or money.'

" 'You know I wouldn't sell my horse.'

"Not long before his death, his father had driven the horse in from Cherkessia when it was still a foal. Hajarat had broken it in himself and kept it in memory of his father. It was a good horse. But the prince didn't realize that when Hajarat toppled both him and his horse as they fought on horseback, it wasn't because of the horse but because of the rider. And you have to know how to spur a good horse on! Hajarat knew how to do it. Haughty Omar didn't understand that.

" 'We know, but that's what the prince told us to say.'

" 'So tell him what I say!'

" 'We're afraid to go back empty-handed.'

" 'You're afraid of him, but not me?'

" 'Yes.'

" 'Go tell him what I said.'

"The two stood around for a minute and left. Hajarat got to thinking. He realized that now the prince would never let up on him. Omar would either cast a spell on the horse, or send horse thieves after it, or something else. Hajarat wasn't afraid for himself, but he was for his sisters. What would happen to them if he tangled with the prince and became an outlaw?

"A couple of days later the two relatives returned.

" 'Please, Hajarat, for God's sake give in! The prince is furious. He's ready to give you any amount of money and any of the horses in his herd. Take it! Otherwise, even if you live, we're done for. After all, we are your relatives!'

"Hajarat gave in and sold the horse for one hundred gold rubles. The prince promised the money in a month. But when his relatives had led the horse from the stable, Hajarat realized that his life was empty now. He was restless and couldn't sleep at night. Hajarat got so attached to things! Whether it was a horse, or a dog, or a person—they touched his heart. That's what finished him in the end!

"A month passed and there wasn't a word from the prince or any money. Hajarat endured this for three more days, and on the fourth he filled his pocket with cartridges, shoved his Smith and Wesson (the name for the pistol of Tsar Nicholas' day) into his belt and appeared at the prince's house. The servants rushed around the courtyard.

" 'Call Omar!'

" 'He went to Mukhus!'

" 'Where's my horse?'

" 'He's riding it. He said he'd be back today.'

" 'Where is the princess?'

" 'She's sleeping.'

" 'Wake her!'

" 'How can we wake the princess?' said the one standing nearest him. 'She's a princess and can get up whenever she wants.'

"Hajarat grabbed him by the shoulder and shoved him to the ground!

" 'Wake her up!'

"The servant went to wake her.

"The princess appeared on the veranda in just a nightgown, with a Persian blanket pulled around her like a horse cloth.

" 'Who's making all the noise out here?'

" 'Open your eyes and you'll see!' answered Hajarat. 'My patience has run out.'

" 'So what if I do see you? What do you want?'

" 'Your son begged for my horse, didn't he? Where's the money he promised?'

" 'What do you need money for, shepherd? Take any horse from the herd and go in peace.'

" 'Hand over the money you promised or return my horse—or you'll be tying that horse on your son's grave!'

"The princess threw off the Persian blanket.

" 'If a little man like you,' she cried, 'can kill my Omar, he has it coming to him! When he returns you'll grovel at his feet. Now get out of here!'

"Hajarat turned and headed for the Gumista River—the direction Omar would come from. Back then the banks of the Gumista were covered with boxwood forests. They've since grown bare. Hajarat hid there and waited. About two hours went by before Omar appeared on Hajarat's horse. He forded the Gumista and had just come up onto the bank when Hajarat grabbed the horse's bridle.

" 'Where's my money?'

" 'What good will money do you, Hajarat? Take any horse from my herd and we'll call it even!'

" 'Get off the horse!' He held the bridle more tightly.

"Omar struck Hajarat on the face as hard as he could with his whip. He expected him to fall. But Hajarat pulled Omar off the horse and they both tumbled to the ground. First one would get the upper hand, then the other. Hajarat was weak from lack of sleep. The horse, sensing that things were bad, quietly slipped down the path.

"Others nearby heard their cries, but no one was man enough to come between them. Finally the prince was on top of Hajarat and began to strangle him. Hajarat, who was choking by now, managed to pull the pistol from his belt and fire. Omar fell to the ground dead.

"Hajarat stood up, put the body in order, wrapped it in his own coat so wild animals wouldn't eat it, and returned to the prince's house. The place was in a commotion—the horse had returned home without a rider.

" 'Princess,' shouted Hajarat, 'your son lies on the banks of the Gumista! Go fetch him, or dogs will eat him!'

"With these words he walked through the village in broad daylight and hid in the forest. But he didn't go far. He watched from a tree to see what they would do. He didn't know what to expect from the prince's relatives and servants. Omar's family had a habit of burning their enemies' houses. Not that they worshiped the god of fire—they simply loved arson.

"From a distance Hajarat saw the prince's relatives gather and head toward his house with their servants. But he was much closer than they were. He bounded out of the forest and ran into the house next door to his. One of the princess' maids lived there with her husband. Hajarat went to the attic, tore apart the shingles and watched the people walking toward his house. There were several princes among them and a lot of servants. The maid whose house he was in carried a can of kerosene.

"What could he do? Hajarat decided to shoot at the princes and servants when they got close enough. But the peasants of Eshery came out to meet the arsonists and stopped them.

" 'Don't disgrace our village with arson,' they said. 'We give you our word that we'll catch Hajarat ourselves and turn him over to the law.'

"The people were buzzing like a swarm of angry bees. Omar's relatives retreated in the face of their anger. The habit of burning their enemies' houses was very deep-seated, but this time they backed down. Suddenly one of the princess' relatives, who happened to be in Eshery by chance, said in a shrill voice, 'Let's go calm the princess. I'll be the one to tighten the noose around his neck myself.'

"Not only was he a pip-squeak, but he had bad eyes to boot. As he talked, he wiped his eyes because they were always running. No one had ever heard of him before. He turned out to be a clerk of the court. He had studied in Tbilisi and Moscow and now worked in the Mukhus court. As it turned out, there was a lot more to that pip-squeak than met the eye, but nobody knew it then.

"And so everybody left, deciding to get at Hajarat through the villagers or the police and Cossacks. Everyone turned back except the maid with the can of kerosene, who went home. She knew the habits of the prince's family. She figured they wouldn't be able to resist, couldn't stop themselves, and would come back to burn Hajarat's house. When they did, the kerosene would be handy. She'd take it to them.

"When she got to her door, she found it was locked from the inside. She couldn't understand what was going on. Then Hajarat, who had already come down from the attic, opened the door a crack and dragged her into the house. She, of course, was petrified.

"'So you're the one, neighbor, who was about to burn my house?'

"She didn't say a word.

"'Answer me!'

"No reply. Hajarat grabbed her by her braided hair and threw her against the wall.

"'The princess ordered me to!'

"Hajarat snatched up the can and doused her with kerosene. He took matches from his pocket and rattled the box near her ear.

"'Should I set you on fire, princess' bitch?'

"She fell to her knees, pleading with him. Of course, Hajarat had no intention of setting her on fire, but he was putting a scare into her for the future.

"'Go tell the princess,' he said, 'that I'll burn her and light my cigarette from her ashes if one hair falls from my sisters' heads or flames lick so much as the fence around my house! I did what I promised to her son. And I'll do what I promise to her too. Let them catch me and kill me if they can, but my sisters are to be left out of it. Go!'

"Hajarat went into the forest and the maid, reeking of kerosene, ran to her mistress. She told her how the monster Hajarat had almost set her on fire and how he'd promised to burn the princess and light a cigarette from her ashes if anything happened to his sisters or his house. The princess realized that Hajarat was master of his word. Now she not only didn't urge people to burn down Hajarat's house, but from time to time she shooed Omar's relatives away from kerosene and smoldering logs.

"Of course, spies kept an eye on Hajarat's house, hoping to catch him when he came to visit his sisters. Several months passed until the night came when Hajarat decided to go home. He knew, of course, that the house could be watched and so he picked the most moonless night.

"He jumped over the back fence that was away from the front gate and, holding his pistol at the ready, crept quietly toward the house. At that moment two men wrapped in cloaks were guarding the gate. One of them was his relative, Akuzba, the very same servant of the prince who had convinced him to sell his horse in the first place. The other was a relative of Omar's whose last name was Emukhvari.

"Right then Akuzba decided to have a smoke. He struck a match and had just brought it up to his cigarette when Hajarat fired, hitting him in the mouth. He died on the spot. The other guard took off into the night. Hajarat fired as best he could and hit him in the leg. He screamed and fell. Hajarat ran to him. Wounded, without his rifle, the guard was trying to crawl away. Hajarat picked up the rifle, yanked the bolt out of it and handed it back.

" 'Hobble on this. You can bear the sad tidings for that spy. After all, he was my relative.'

"Emukhvari hobbled off into the darkness. Hajarat went over to the dead man, straightened his arms and legs, closed his eyes and wrapped him in his cloak so the animals wouldn't eat the body. The people who had been awakened by the shots had already started calling out to one another.

"Next he went in to his sisters, poor frightened little chamois, hugged and kissed them, comforted them ('You have nothing to fear while I'm alive!'), and disappeared into the night.

"And so Hajarat's fame warmed the hearts of the people of Abkhazia: the police simply couldn't catch him. The spirits of the people rose, while the mustaches of the arrogant princes drooped. Even the Cossacks were a bit quieter. Before that, if someone committed a crime and fled into the woods, Cossacks were sent to his relatives' homes. They'd live there for as long as the authorities assigned them. Execution of orders, they called it! Eat, Cossack! Drink, Cossack! Enjoy yourself, Cossack!

"If there were several relatives in the village, Cossacks were assigned to all of them. If there was only one, they descended on him. With Hajarat around, the Cossacks were a little more orderly. If in the past they said to the master of the house 'Kill a bull!', now they would say 'Slaughter a sheep!' That's the difference one man can make if he's a hero!

"The life of an outlaw in the woods isn't easy. Loneliness is the worst thing. There was a Greek merchant living in Eshery— I've forgotten his name, damn it! He had a young son who became attached to Hajarat. He went off with him sometimes, wandering through the mountains and forests after him like a puppy. Sometimes he took Hajarat home to have something to eat and to rest.

"The princess found out. Omar's relatives got excited: we'll burn that infidel's house to the ground! Today some folk still believe the family worshiped the god of fire. People who worship the fire god keep a prayer anvil at home. No one ever saw one of those in their house. They didn't worship the god of fire, they mocked him because they loved arson.

"To make a long story short, the princess kept the relatives away from fire this time too. She remembered well what Hajarat had said. She secretly talked with the merchant and promised him five hundred rubles in gold to set the police on Hajarat's trail. But the merchant wouldn't admit a thing: 'I haven't concealed Hajarat, and if my son spends some time away from home, it's because he's enjoying himself in the coffee houses of the city, as a young Greek should when his father has money.'

"But then that snake of a clerk came crawling out. He started asking around about where the merchant was from, where his family lived and who they were. He learned that the merchant's younger brother lived in Kengursk. But the brothers hadn't seen each other for thirty years. He had to ask why.

"The clerk went to Kengursk and found out from the brother that the merchant had forged his father's will thirty years earlier and taken almost all his property after he died. The younger brother was too ashamed to complain to the law, but after that wouldn't let his older brother into the house.

"The clerk rustled through the official papers and found it was all true. He went to the merchant with this information and broke him down. The five hundred rubles in gold combined with the forged will to break him. He promised to let the right person know when Hajarat came to his house.

"One night Hajarat came home with the son. They had something to eat and drink and went out to spend the night in the corncrib. When he stayed with the merchant, Hajarat never slept in the house. He slept in that corncrib. It stood on high pilings in a corn field next to the forest. It was easier to defend, and with luck, he could make an escape if he had to.

"They had already bedded down when the boy's mother came out.

"'Son,' she said, 'you need to wash up. I've heated the water.'

"The son climbed down and followed his mother, and Hajarat went to sleep, as always, holding a pistol on his chest. In the meantime the merchant got the word out and the police came and surrounded the corn field. Achyrba was with them. Have you heard of him? He had finished off a lot of outlaws. He was the most courageous of the police, as Hajarat was among the outlaws.

"'Hey, Hajarat,' he yelled, 'you're surrounded! Give up, or we'll see what kind of man you are.'

"Hajarat leaped up at the sound of his voice.

"'Here's the kind of man I am,' he shouted and fired a shot in the direction of the voice. But he missed. That policeman was as sly as a fox. He knew Hajarat's tricks. Even before he had finished yelling, he jumped aside, so that the bullet was a second too late.

"Well, then came thunder and lightning, shots split the night. Hajarat, seeing where the shots were coming from, jumped out of the corncrib and ran through the corn, returning fire. His coat caught on the thorns of the dogwood bushes on the other side of the fence, but he leaped out of it and tumbled into the woods.

"The police were so frightened that they thought he had hidden in the dogwood bushes. They shredded his coat with bullets, but when they got closer they saw it was empty. That's how the rumors got started about Hajarat having a charm against bullets. The police started the rumors themselves. They were ashamed to admit they had kept shooting at an empty coat.

"And so Hajarat got away again. That's when he started showing up at our place in Achandary. We lived a short distance outside the village and sometimes he came to our house, usually at night, but occasionally during the day.

"Sometimes his mood was as black as a storm cloud and he shuddered at every noise. One night he was washing his hands on the veranda before supper. I was pouring water for him. He held his pistol in one hand and put the other under the stream, his eyes sweeping the darkness. Then he put the pistol in the other hand and put the free one under the water.

"'Why do you come here if you don't trust us?' Father joked.

"'This is the only thing I trust now,' said Hajarat, nodding at his pistol.

"But on occasion he was easygoing, cheerful. Completely different. He came to us one warm day in August. Father laid a goat skin in the shade of a quince tree as Hajarat had asked him to. He lay down and went to sleep. The road was clearly visible for a long way on either side of our house. I sat on the fence, watching in case anybody suspicious came along. Father slaughtered a lamb and mother prepared dinner while Hajarat slept.

"He slept as long as he wanted, then sat up on the hide and lit a cigarette. He sat there and smoked. Just then the wind had to blow and a huge quince fell from the tree and hit him on the head. Hajarat collapsed onto the hide. Then he raised his head, swearing, laughing and rubbing the spot where he'd been hit. He reached for the fallen quince, took out his knife and began to eat it, peeling off the skin. At dinner he kept making jokes whenever he thought about that quince.

"'Don't tell my enemies,' he laughed. 'They couldn't stop me with bombs, the next thing you know they'll be throwing quinces at me.'

"He gave Father a hard time.

"'Admit that you cut the stem of that quince and laid the goat skin under it on purpose so you could turn me over to the authorities.'

"Father laughed it off. Now when I remember that day, I think it must have been the happiest one in Hajarat's life. He made a lot of jokes about his head and that quince. And we had a good laugh along with him!

"He was clever and quick-witted, Hajarat was! One time Father and I were coming down from the alpine meadows with several shepherds. It was a hot day. In one place there was a nest of wild bees in the cliff above the path. Because of the heat the honey ran through a crack and dripped onto the path.

"Father warned me not to taste it. He fashioned a smoker out of some rotten wood and climbed up the cliff. Wild honey like that had to be boiled before you could eat it. Father dug out the hives with his knife and filled two goat-skin bags. He lowered them to us on a rope, then climbed down. I got the smaller bag, he took the other himself and we continued down the mountain. It got hotter and hotter. I pulled off my shirt and adjusted the bag on my bare back so that it would be cooler walking.

"About two hours later I felt sick. My head was splitting, my stomach was upset, I was dying. I lay down on the grass. Father began to worry. The shepherds cut some branches to make a stretcher and carry me down. As luck would have it, Hajarat was watching us from a distance above. He didn't know who we were, but he always approached common folk in the mountains. He wasn't afraid of anything. He realized that something was wrong and came down. Then he recognized us.

"'Did you eat any of the honey?' he asked right off.

"'No, not at all,' the shepherds said, 'he was just carrying it in this bag!'

"'Why is his shirt strapped to it?'

"'It's hot. He took it off along the way.'

"'That's the problem! The wild honey soaked through the skin of the bag and into his body. He's been poisoned. Give him some sour milk. He'll be fine!'

"They fed me sour milk. I lay quietly and my head cleared. We went on. Father had worked with bees his whole life and didn't know that wild honey could poison you through your skin. But Hajarat knew what was wrong right away!

"Yes, Hajarat. . . . He missed farm work so much that sometimes he'd come to our place in the summer, grab a hoe at night and weed the corn until morning. I think that's why people suspected us. Someone going by our house must have noticed that the corn wasn't weeded in the evening, and suddenly in the morning it was. They wondered how that had happened. Our people don't work at night. They don't even work that hard during the day. Armenians are a different story, to be honest.

"I think that's how it got to the village elder. He talked with Father several times, but Father said, 'No, Hajarat hasn't been at my house!' But of course, the elder must have told the clerk that Hajarat had been to our place. And the clerk began to weave a web around our relatives to find a weak link that would let him get Father.

"Of course the relatives knew Hajarat visited—we couldn't hide it— and they kept their mouths shut. But we didn't realize what was going on. Father only knew that the clerk had bought off the Greek with the princess' money. What he didn't know was that the clerk was already sniffing out our place.

"Oh, yes! I forgot to tell you how Hajarat got even with that merchant. I'm getting old! Hajarat, of course, found out about the whole thing, grabbed the son, took him into the forest and had someone he trusted deliver a message to the merchant: 'I taught your son to be a man and you sold my life for five hundred rubles. Bring the money to me at the Anchar Slope. I'm going to eat your money and wipe myself with it. If you bring the police, you'll never see your son.'

"Do you know the Anchar Slope? It's on the road to Kaman Peak. Maybe they've renamed it on today's maps, but we'll call it by the name our grandfathers used: Anchar Slope.

"There was nothing left for the old merchant to do but get the money and go. He gave up the gold and brought back his son. Hajarat didn't hurt anybody, but went back into the forest cursing human greed."

...Only old Hasan's voice and the great roar of the waterfall. The goats were feeding in the grass, occasionally coming across tall, slender bilberry bushes. They stood on their hind legs to nibble at the bushes, resting their front hooves on bent branches. From time to time their forelegs would slip off a branch, and just as they started to slip the goats would hurry to grab the leaves and get them into their mouths quickly, before their forelegs left the branch. They continued to chew as they slid to the ground—with heads raised they would look at the bush, trying to gauge whether it was worth clambering up again. After deciding, sometimes they clambered back up, but sometimes shook their heads as if to say "It's not worth bothering!" and went on to a new bush.

They say goats have stripped Greece and Asia Minor. Thank God, we aren't faced with that threat. A topic for discussion: goats and civilization.

A dozen or so sheep grazed there, sticking their noses into the grass as though sniffing it diligently before snipping it off with their teeth. They would stay near the flock of goats, who would drive them away if they got too close: sheep are too low in rank! The sheep would move off, but then follow the flock again with submissive stubbornness.

To the left of the waterfall, on an emerald slope lightly gilded with blooming primrose, appeared a man driving an airy cloud of kids in front of him. The cloud spread out and crept merrily up the green hill. The man walked with a steady gait, carrying a long thick branch on one shoulder and supporting it with an axe across the other. It was Kunta.

Coming down the slope was Bardusha, gripping the reins of a horse. I recognized his tall, upright figure immediately. The horse was loaded down with sacks. He appeared headed for Chegem with a shipment of fresh cheese. He entered the oncoming cloud of kids, moving as though sweeping them aside. When he reached Kunta, he stopped and talked to him, pointing up the hill from time to time. As he listened, Kunta stood the branch on end to give his shoulder a rest. I could see it was a dead fir tree.

The men parted. Kunta carefully hoisted the long branch onto his shoulder and began to climb the hill. Bardusha and his horse disappeared behind a knoll.

The goats slowly started down the slope next to the waterfall and approached a large boulder. The old bellwether with powerful triumphal horns, yellow beard and tufts of the same yellowed wool hanging from his sides was the first to scramble onto the boulder. He climbed to the top, looked around importantly and lay down. The flock followed.

There was only the roar of the waterfall and old Hasan's voice.

"Yes, I often met Hajarat in the woods when I was a boy, in the days when he used to visit us. He would warn me if he was planning to come to our house that night. Then sometimes he'd say, 'Go on, throw me a walnut switch.'

"I'd break off a walnut branch and tear all the leaves off except one on the end. I'd toss it into the air as hard as I could, and when it began to fall back to earth, Hajarat would shoot at the leaf. He usually fired twice. If he only hit it once he'd say, 'I'm a bad shot today.'

"Time passed and they simply couldn't catch Hajarat. The spirits of the people rose and the spirits of the clerks and princes fell. When people were treated badly by those in power, they would say, 'I'll go complain to Hajarat.'

"Envoys came looking for him and they found him. Hajarat would snarl in the mountains, and in the valley a letter would fall from the hands of some thieving clerk. That's what Hajarat had become! They simply couldn't catch him, but it was also hard for Hajarat to be in the mountains by himself. A person can't get by without other people. Even if you get a speck of dust in your eye, you need someone else to get it out.

"Hajarat became friends with three outlaws and they lived in a cave near Bzyb Peak. They wandered all over Abkhazia, but lived in this cave.

"Once one of them went to visit his own village. As it happened, old Bad Eyes—the clerk—had found a way to get to him. I don't know what chink he found to crawl into his soul. I didn't know then and I don't want to make up anything now. Maybe he promised to close the cases of the three outlaws if they brought Hajarat into Mukhus dead or alive.

"The outlaw returned and agreed with the others to pounce on Hajarat that night and take him dead or alive. But Hajarat smelled trouble. He realized the three of them had already distanced themselves from him and thrown in together. That was fine. Hajarat could smell the stench they gave off, but they didn't realize it. Rotten people don't know how bad they smell.

"That night he lay down in his spot and pretended to go to sleep. He had decided to wait and catch them with weapons in their hands. They were frightened, of course, even though this dirty business had been their idea. He heard them whispering, whispering. The fire burned and they whispered. Then they stopped whispering and picked up their guns. Hajarat leaped up. There was nowhere to hide their weapons now. Hajarat had always slept with a gun in his hand, but now he was specially prepared.

"'Hajarat,' said the strongest of the outlaws, 'there are three of us. Better give up!'

"'Right,' said Hajarat, 'I'll kill three and you'll kill one.'

"Then something happened that no one has ever heard of before or since! They sat like that, three steps apart, for five days and five nights. Since there were three outlaws, one of them could take a nap, stir the fire or give his friends something to nibble on, but Hajarat couldn't do a thing. He later told us that by the third day he had figured out how to fall asleep for a second and wake up again without their noticing. They had hoped to starve him out, but in the end their plans went sour.

"At dawn on the sixth day, they backed out of the cave and disappeared forever. Maybe they went to Mingrelia. At the time Hajarat was too tired to go after them and he never saw them again.

"The village elder kept after Father. 'Go talk to the court clerk. Otherwise things will end badly.'

"'I don't have anything to say,' Father answered, 'and if he comes around here, I'll set the dogs on him. Tell him that!'

"So they knew Hajarat had been to our place. But no one could stand up in court and say, 'Yes, he was there, I saw him.' However, old Bad Eyes kept sniffing around our relatives until he finally got what he wanted from a relative of ours named Badra.

"This was his story: Badra had been a widower his whole life, but he had one son and he loved him so much he wouldn't let a speck of dust settle on him. One day Badra was walking through a thicket of ferns looking for his horse. At the same time a local widow was looking for her calf in those ferns. She was young and strong and the ferns crackled under her feet.

"Badra joked, 'Where are you dragging your treasure to through these ferns?'

"If she had lowered her head or even smiled properly and walked on, nothing would have happened. But no! She laughed! He realized that she would let him. They sinned and it went on for many years.

"Badra's son grew up, knowing nothing about the affair, and fell in love with the widow's daughter. You can see how strange it turned out, can't you? Apparently their stock was drawn to each other.

"No matter how much the father tried to talk him out of it, no matter what he did, the son married her. Badra had left the widow a long time before that, but what happened goes against our laws: the father had slept with the mother of the girl his son married.

"The couple was living well and the girl was soon due to have a baby. That's when old Bad Eyes sniffed the story out and sent his man to Badra: 'Either you talk to me about Hajarat or I'll talk to your son about incest!'

"Badra got scared. But he was an honest man. He warned Father.

"'I'll disgrace both of us,' he told Father, 'I'm no match for old Four Eyes. If my son hears about this, he'll shoot himself. I'm telling you now, I'll do anything for my son—I'll tell Four Eyes everything I know. You'd better think of something before it's too late!'

"That very night Father made his decision. That very night, without saying a word to anybody, we left and moved to Chegem. Back then Chegem was as unspoiled as that meadow under the waterfall.

"A peasant house wasn't cluttered up with things then like it is now. Televisions, chests of drawers, couches—a plague on them, damn them. We didn't know those things then. We put our household goods on the horses, the livestock ahead, and set out. We've lived in Chegem ever since.

"The clerk left Badra alone after that. He had hoped to make Father talk by making Badra suffer, but when Father disappeared, he didn't need Badra anymore.

"Time passed and they simply couldn't catch Hajarat. I've already said how hard it is on a person alone. Forgetting past injuries, Hajarat became friends with a certain outlaw. They ate together, slept side by side and ran from their pursuers together. The brother of the outlaw had been arrested and exiled to Siberia. He was an outlaw too.

"One time they—Hajarat and this outlaw—came across a house high in the mountains. As it happened, an old Abkhaz lived there with his spinster daughter. He had cleared a space in the forest, planted corn and kept bees. I used to know his name, but I've forgotten now, damn it!

"Hajarat liked the place—not a soul around, woods too thick to cut through, ravines too deep to cross. The old man had lived there for fifteen years and no one knew about it. Sometimes he went down the mountain, but nobody ever came up."

From beyond the ridge a helicopter plunged down almost directly over the waterfall. For a second the din of its motor drowned out the water's roar, and madly spinning its huge, grubby blades, falling into and climbing out of air pockets, it sawed its way over the alpine meadows and dropped down behind the northern ridge.

Old Hasan followed it with his usual calm gaze and said, "That monster sees everything from the air. Last year it found the last of the New Athos monks near the Pskhu mountains in the thickest part of the woods. A person can't make it in the forest without a fire. And a fire can't make it without smoke. Found 'em because of the smoke. Took them all away by helicopter, brought them to the city and let them go. The authorities don't like it when you hide from them. Like us shepherds—graze where we can see you!

"There weren't any helicopters back then, so it was possible to hide out. Hajarat and his friend began to visit the old man. They couldn't go home. Our people couldn't cross the Caucasus and live with foreigners either. Now they live everywhere, but they couldn't back then.

"If he had known there'd be a revolution and the government would be stood on its head, maybe he would have waited things out somewhere in the Kuban. But he didn't. Now some people would like to think that he knew everything: revolution, constitution, whatever! All he knew was execution of orders, like the rest of us. He didn't know revolution constitution. He was a simple man and decided to marry the old man's daughter.

"'So,' Hajarat told the old man, 'you know who I am, like the rest of Abkhazia. I want to marry your daughter. I'll come once a week, wash up, change and rest. I have money, I have property, and if I'm killed, everything is yours. And I'll help out around the place as long as I'm alive. What do you say?'

"The old fellow was frightened, but what could he say to a man like Hajarat?

"'Ask her,' he said. 'She can marry you if she wants to.'

"He asked.

"She lowered her head. 'If someone like you finds me attractive,' she said, 'I agree.'

"So Hajarat became her husband. Of course, there was no wedding and no guests. Only his outlaw friend knew about the marriage. And so they lived. Poor Hajarat became very attached to her. After all, she was a woman and it was a home. Like an old stick in the garden suddenly sprouting leaves in the spring, she grew young and rosy.

"Now the clerk sat in Mukhus and sent his spies around to various villages. Of course, he sniffed out which outlaw Hajarat had befriended. This outlaw had a wife and he would secretly come home to visit her. One time old Bad Eyes went to her and persuaded her to help him meet with her husband.

"'If your husband gives me a hand with some business,' he said, 'I'll get him back for you.'

"The wife was overjoyed. She was tired of living without her husband. She arranged the meeting and the clerk said to the outlaw, 'Your brother's in Siberia. It's a big place—a man might not find his way home. I want Hajarat dead or alive. I'll see to it that your brother returns and I'll close your case.'

"The outlaw thought hard, but not for long.

"'He won't give himself up alive to anyone.'

"'Then kill him.'

"'I can't,' answered the outlaw. 'But try this fellow.'

"So he told the clerk about the old man and his house in the mountains. The clerk hadn't known a thing about it.

"'Who is this old man?' the clerk asked, pleased. 'Where is he from? Who are his relatives? Why does he live so far from everyone?'

"The outlaw told him everything he knew. When people sit around a campfire in the mountains by themselves, they'll say a lot they wouldn't say down in the valley.

"Fifteen years earlier Cossacks had been quartered in the village where the old man lived. Execution of orders! One day the old man and his daughter had gone into the woods to gather wild pears to make vodka. He shook down one tree, his daughter started to gather the pears, and he went off to find another. Suddenly he heard her scream. He came running and saw that a drunken Cossack had fallen upon his daughter to violate her. The old man killed him with an axe and dragged him into the bushes. The other Cossacks were in the village, drinking and carrying on. Execution of orders! The old man was terrified. He had only his wife and daughter. He was short on relatives. During the night he gathered their belongings and left for the mountains before the Cossacks could find their comrade's body. He knew the mountains well. Later his wife died and he remained there with his daughter.

"'Good,' said the clerk, 'I'll find the old man. But don't say a word about our meeting. I'll do everything I promised your wife.'

"So they parted, and the clerk finally went after the old man. Of course, the old man was no goat, he didn't stay in the mountains all the time. Sometimes he came down. That's how they met.

"'I know everything about you,' the clerk said. 'You're from this village. You're a little short on relatives. You live with your daughter in the mountains. And I know why you live there. I know you've harbored two outlaws in your home. One of them is the state criminal Hajarat Kiahba. We've been looking for him for many years. Before long Cossacks will surround your house. Hajarat, as you know, won't give himself up alive. That means the Cossacks will kill you in the skirmish and burn down your house. There's only one way out—kill Hajarat!'

"See what a devil that clerk was? He told what he knew, but didn't mention that the old man's daughter was Hajarat's wife. Why not? Because he was afraid the old man would be ashamed of betraying his son-in-law.

"The old man gave it a lot of thought and then said, 'Fine!'

"'Do you want a gun?'

"'No, I'll use an axe.'

"'Right,' said the clerk, 'you can handle that.'

"Some time passed and then Hajarat met the outlaw in the woods. They went to the old man's place. The outlaw already knew the old man had plans to kill Hajarat. Hajarat sensed the emotional distance between them. Hajarat thought that the outlaw had been bought off or somehow intimidated. So he began to question him, hoping he would break down and give himself away. But the outlaw wouldn't answer. Hajarat didn't suspect the old man: he had grown close to him, gotten attached.

"They had dinner at the old man's. Then the outlaw said,

"'You're home, Hajarat. I want to go home too. If I leave now, I'll be there by morning. Let's meet back here in three days.'

"He left. Hajarat was tired and went to bed. His wife lay down beside him. He went to sleep. After a while his wife poked him, but he didn't wake up. He was sound asleep. She rose, got dressed and went out to her father.

"'Go ahead, Father!'

"The old man picked up his axe and approached the bed. These days some peasants have two-story houses, but who had heard of them back then? Certainly not that old man in the woods. In his house there was one room divided by a curtain. He slept in one half, Hajarat and his daughter in the other.

"The old man threw the curtain aside, stood by the bed and raised the axe as high as he could to chop off Hajarat's head, but the blade got caught in the curtain. The old man couldn't stop the axe and the edge grazed the side of Hajarat's head, almost cutting off his ear, which hung just by the lobe.

"'Ouch!' cried Hajarat, and grabbing his pistol from under the pillow, flew into the air. The old man didn't have time to raise the axe again. A shot rang out and he fell.

"'Father!' shouted the daughter. 'That bandit has killed you!'

"Hajarat became wide awake then, and realizing why she was dressed and not in bed, shot at her. But he missed. The woman ran out the door. Hajarat went after her, holding his ear, blood gushing. They circled the house twice. Little did they know that the old man wasn't dead, just wounded in the stomach. He crawled out of the house, axe in hand, and when Hajarat ran by, threw it at his legs from where he lay. The axe cut the tendons in Hajarat's right leg. He collapsed, but got up again and finished the old man off.

"The woman fled into the woods, and Hajarat, bleeding, leaning on a stick, made it to the village of Otkhara by morning. A family he was friends with lived there—the Garps. Good, pure-blooded peasants. They took Hajarat in like a brother, stopped the bleeding with herbs, washed his wounds, gave him something to drink and put him in a clean bed. They did everything that could be done.

"Hajarat, however, was tired of betrayal. He knew that if the old man had promised to kill him that night, the police would come to collect the body in the morning. They wouldn't have any trouble following the trail of blood to the Garps' house. He realized that perhaps even these fine people might break down and betray him. You need to know this to understand what he did next.

"'My friends,' he said, 'I'll never forget how decently you've treated me. But leave me now. I'm tired.'

"They supposed he wanted to go to sleep and began to leave the room.

"The father, who was the last to leave, heard him say, 'Let's part friends.'

"He decided that Hajarat was mumbling in his sleep. He didn't know that Hajarat intended to go to sleep forever. A minute later a shot was heard from the room. They ran in to find him lying dead, shot through the head. So, my son, we didn't protect him well enough. He lifted the spirits of the people, but then, he was just a man, wasn't he? Didn't his spirits need lifting too? We like to blame it on others, but his own people betrayed him! That's what finally broke him. I know there were admirable men like my father—and people even better than him, but the traitors won out in the end.

"'Let's part friends!'—with those words the best man among us departed. It would make a stone cry to think of it. If we're worth anything as a people, we'll remind our grandchildren, great-grandchildren and great-great-grandchildren of our shame. Let it burn on! If we forget, we will be forgotten! If you don't heed your own shortcomings, who can you reproach?"

Old Hasan stopped. The raging sheaf of the waterfall continued to plunge from its incredible height, covering us with a damp mist, the smell of wet rocks, and the light, unobtrusive breath of eternity. The goats on the large flat boulder were as white as patches of snow. Under the boulder, their heads thrust into the shade, the sheep lay in swooning poses of sacrifice.

"Let's go have something to eat," said old Hasan, getting up. "These goats aren't going anywhere."

We stood up. He picked up his cloak, shook it out carefully and just as carefully folded it, as though preparing for a long journey.

"You're coming back, aren't you?" I asked.

"Of course I am," he answered, nestling the folded cloak under his arm. "Where else would I go? There's livestock around, though. They might track it up."

We headed for the shepherds' camp.

Translated by Joseph Kiegel

Originally published in *Oktiabr'*, April 1987.

MIKHAIL KURAEV
CAPTAIN DIKSHTEIN

A FANTASTIC NARRATIVE

From the Sevastopol *they're firing,*
Too short and too wide!
And cadets keep on diving
Beneath the ice, beneath the ice.
Popular song, 1921

But then, what a backwoods and what a nook!
N. V. Gogol, *Dead Souls, II*

On January 27, 196–, in the town of Gatchina, in the house on the corner of Chkalov and Socialist Streets, on the second floor, in apartment number eight, in a corner room already filled with grayish morning mist, the dream was leaving Igor Ivanovich Dikshtein.

He hadn't awakened yet, but the objects and figures that had filled the fragile haze of his dream began to assume weight, settling in a place where you could no longer make things out or bring them nearer. The morning pushed into his dream with its unconditional concreteness.

Even before he opened his eyes, Igor Ivanovich realized that he was waking up. His first thought was how not to start thinking about anything, otherwise it would all be over—he'd wake up. Dreams attracted Igor Ivanovich with their special light construction of a world.

Igor Ivanovich himself could hardly have explained at all clearly this forceful attraction of dreams, where life was no less queer than it was for him when he was awake, but where all the fateful intricacies of people and events, in contrast to those in life, had only one happy ending—awakening. His inability to explain this came not from his secretive character or from being tongue-tied, but rather because he wasn't in the habit that you and I share, perhaps, of not dwelling on the question "why?" when you are successful or when luck and happiness just seem to come by themselves. Endless questions usually arise in precisely the opposite situation. But in contrast to most people, even when fate dealt him a blow, Igor Ivanovich never asked the banal question "why?" directed at some unknown being. He knew exactly why.

One can only suppose that without being aware of it, Igor Ivanovich was attracted to dreams because of his secret power over the unpredictable world hidden in the most remote and tiny cranny of his watchful consciousness; and this power changed falling into flying, the horror of a dreamed execution was dissolved, upon waking, into the happiest feeling of resurrection, if not immortality. Even love wasn't miserable, but easy— and shame, pain, grief—all these were subordinate to the merciful will of the vigilant guardian angel who stood watch at the boundary line.

So now, too, he stood at the very edge of the precipice and tried to lean forward, realizing through the most remote cranny of his waking consciousness that nothing terrible and irreparable would happen anyway. He wanted to have a good look, to see the bottom, but he was thwarted by slender living things, bare twigs or perhaps roots growing out of the impenetrable depths. His feet were still touching firm ground, but someone was pulling him down harder and harder; he felt that he was hanging above the abyss. Nevertheless, he felt suffocated by fear. Suddenly his chest felt spacious and cold, the precipice opening beneath him penetrated him, pierced him, and his heart sank, but the emptiness became solid, and his inhalation, familiar as an old trick, made him weightless, and soon he was hovering above the abyss and falling slowly, tense with expectation.

As he fell, pierced by this endless fall, he didn't think about the fact that there was a bottom to the abyss, but tried to get a look at a large bird falling alongside him, tumbling head first, then turning sideways, twisting in a most surprising fashion, and because of this Igor Ivanovich couldn't examine or identify it, although the whole time it seemed to him that he knew this bird. And the question didn't arise as to why the bird didn't spread its wings and why these wings didn't hold it up, although once in a while they'd flap around like wide rustling curtains, but would immediately give way, making the bird turn over so strangely.

...The pine was motionless, it stood at the edge of the precipice that wasn't really a precipice but simply the edge of a pond, and this pond looked familiar.

Igor Ivanovich didn't notice that his right eyelid had opened a fraction by itself, and he started to peer hazily through his eyelashes at the picture hanging by the foot of the bed. As soon as Igor Ivanovich realized this, he immediately squeezed his eyes shut, but this overly energetic movement caused the dream to disappear.

He stayed still in order to slip back to where the bird was, to restore everything to its former state, but the abyss was settling quietly in his chest, and even his closed eyes couldn't keep back the day that was invading Igor Ivanovich's body from all sides.

Well then, so be it.

He didn't need to open his eyes to see and sense the bright morning silence in the room that had gotten cold during the night, to see the doubled-shelved veneered sideboard of classic pre-war design with a mirror in the central recess, something like a rectangular grotto in which there stood a cup from the court service of Emperor Paul's reign with the imperial monogram and a painted plaster sailor with an accordion, also the cupboard, the table, six unmatched chairs, including two sturdy Viennese ones, and the doormat woven of colored rags, the burned-out Moskvich radio with two channels in the place of honor by the window, the flower in a rectangular container beside the radio, its wide shiny leaves hiding the icon of Saint Nicholas the Sailor in the corner.

Everything was still and quiet, as at a parade a moment before the starting signal: "Attention!"

It was quiet in the kitchen—so Nastya must be peeling potatoes or had gone to get kerosene.

Igor Ivanovich sank into contemplation of the sideboard without opening his eyes.

This was really something. Quite something. He'd gotten it from his eldest daughter Valentina, who was on the verge of throwing it out at a time when you could easily get thirty rubles for it, or twenty-five at the worst. If you stood there a little longer, persistently, you could easily get thirty. That's too much? Well, okay. That's with delivery! Even to Kolpany. I'll borrow Pavel's cart and it'll be no problem. Why, it's as light as a feather. And with the cart it's a breeze. There! You want it, you give me three tenners and it's all yours. Will that hurt? You can't afford it? Oh, you like it, don't you? See, it's got this mirror...

Igor Ivanovich was already asleep again and was selling the sideboard at the bazaar in freezing weather.

To those who didn't know Igor Ivanovich personally and to those who to this day have never heard of him, these daydreams about thirty rubles for such a piece of junk with two legs missing, with dark cracks on the veneered sides and on the little doors that had resulted from earlier efforts to give the sideboard the look of mahogany by using manganese on it, not to speak of the cracked back, but who cares about the back if it can't be seen anyway—so then, these greedy dreams could really present Igor Ivanovich as a fantastic hero, but only in the most ordinary and least flattering sense.

How remote all these hasty suppositions are from the real— the truly real—Igor Ivanovich.

So as not to confuse the reader who's giving up a small part of his life—also unfortunately not eternal—for me and Igor Ivanovich, it should be pointed out that Igor Ivanovich at this moment is that inhabitant of the town of Gatchina who's been bald since age thirty-five (just like King Henry III of England, a fact Igor Ivanovich did not even suspect), who's sprawled in a relaxed position under a red quilt in a white duvet, in an oversized metal bed built at the very beginning of the century in a well-known Petersburg factory that subsequently was converted to the production of airplanes. Here he is, in a state of nature, known to almost the entire Chkalov Street, completely unadorned, unless you count as adornments the neat little bows of tape at his ankles which evidence his love of order rather than his former inclination to stylishness.

The clearcut thought that there had been no point, after all, in Valentina's throwing away such a thing brought Igor Ivanovich back to reality; he still hadn't opened his eyes and hadn't noticed his transition from the dream.

The thought that he had carried over from his dream absorbed him completely. Selling the sideboard, going to Valentina's, and just like that, without taking off his coat—bang!—slapping thirty rubles down on the table. Here, take it and don't throw things like that around. So they don't need a sideboard. And do they need this polished piece of junk! Even if it was made at the Gatchina factory, so what? Who cares about the polish if it doesn't even have a mirror. But this one's got one. You can shave if you want, or comb your hair, straighten your collar, your tie... It's true that it's not very convenient to look at yourself, the mirror's recessed and it's a bit dark, but so what! What kind of ass would think of shaving in front of a sideboard?

Only a man can know that state of exalted bliss which comes from dispensing nonchalant generosity and casual charity, which elevate the soul and mind to heights of true freedom and divine wisdom.

CAPTAIN DIKSHTEIN 63

Yes, you could also give back the thirty rubles just to feel, in the fullest sense, like a father who has experienced life and understands something about it, and knows how to live!

In the kitchen a knife clanked as it fell into the sink, and the faucet grunted.

Igor Ivanovich grew tense. Was the water going to run? When there was a strong frost the water pipes froze, but there didn't seem to be any frost yet... The hissing changed to a belly grumble. All the pipes in the house began to rumble. They shook as if wanting to throw off the confining shell of the dwelling that stuck to them. The tension mounted. The pipes shook hollowly, choking on something or fighting against a superior will. In his mind's eye Igor Ivanovich could see the three-inch basement vent oozing with grease and he knew what to do if it happened again... But after sputtering three times, the faucet grunted, spat once or twice and then began to hiss reassuringly.

The water came pouring out in an even stream as if nothing was the matter.

Igor Ivanovich opened his eyes quickly and easily.

He immediately saw the wall clock beside the picture. Actually he didn't see the clock itself, but the hands showing thirteen minutes to three. "Hey," Igor Ivanovich grinned at the smirking face of the clock and shifted from examining the hands to observing the pendulum. A regular pace, a businesslike sound, nothing unnecessary, just as it should be. The clock was running...

Igor Ivanovich didn't use this clock to tell time, although he spared no effort to maintain its faltering movement.

Six years earlier the clock began to stop and it took quite a bit of effort to restart it. The clock worked only in one position, not vertical at all, but leaning slightly to the left. Then when it was wound up, a weekly procedure, the clock would get nudged just enough from its ideal position so that it wouldn't run anymore. And then enormous patience and great respect for Paul Bourré were required, as well as the conviction that the clock would perhaps still serve for several generations, so that one wouldn't regret the time and effort needed over a day or two—or three—to push the stopped pendulum and to help the clock find that single convenient position which allowed the clock to continue its work.

That time, five years earlier, Igor Ivanovich took the clock to the repair shop. The repairman turned out to be serious, attentive and unhurried. After examining it carefully he refused payment. "There's nothing here to fix," said the repairman. "This was a good clock. But nothing lasts forever and this one is finished." If he had spoken differently, with too much sympathy or condescendingly or carelessly, Igor Ivanovich would definitely have started arguing or, if worse came to worse, he would have taken the clock to Leningrad. While the repairman was talking he touched the clock with one hand and looked past Igor Ivanovich as though talking about himself.

The repairman was old, Igor Ivanovich wasn't young, and the clock had grown old, too.

After returning from the repair shop Igor Ivanovich hung the clock in its old place, mostly to hide the spot on the faded wallpaper, but it started ticking and ran superbly for two or three months, cheering Igor Ivanovich with its immortality. Then it began stopping again, but Igor Ivanovich was implacable; he wouldn't allow it to die and it kept on running, telling some kind of special time of its own. And it wasn't important if it told the correct time or not, the important thing was that it ran at all.

But, let's be completely frank. Igor Ivanovich simply couldn't go to sleep when the clock stopped, he would eventually fall asleep, of course, but it was distressing and sad to be immersed in this motionless, soundless darkness. A few times he woke up when the clock had stopped in the night and right then and there tried to start it up again. "Don't be crazy," said Nastya and dropped back to sleep.

Inside Igor Ivanovich there had imperceptibly formed not exactly a thought or conviction but almost a foreboding that death is when time stops, and perhaps this is why he took such care of the clock.

For two months now the clock had been running perfectly. Gone was even the light jingling of the spring that used to inspire a certain anxiety in Igor Ivanovich. The pendulum filled the room with a soft clicking sound, as though a horse were stepping on the cobblestones outside the window, going on its endless way, calm and dignified. Tick tock, tick tock.

Since he had stopped telling time by this clock, Igor Ivanovich moved it to where it was less prominent and where it would be easier to get to in the night; and really, why gawk at the clock if it was obvious anyway that it was now half past nine at the latest.

"Nastya, I'm getting up," shouted Igor Ivanovich, rolling over on his side and starting to tuck in his blanket for warmth.

"Kolya's supposed to come today," shouted Nastya from the kitchen.

"Do you think I forgot," shouted Igor Ivanovich who had actually forgotten that Nikolai was coming, and threw off his blanket.

For a second his long body in underpants and shirt lay motionless on the bed, getting used to the cold, but after a minute he started waving his arms, changing this into a motion distantly related to gymnastics. In all this tumult of short-lasting body movements one could only distinguish two flappings of the arms, once to the side, once together, and then he smartly pulled on his pants.

I suppose that each person who knew Igor Ivanovich Dikshtein personally has a *moral obligation* to preserve from oblivion the features of this man who factually didn't exist; this would actually constitute an attractive fantastic element in any narration about him. And this observation isn't intended as a reproach to the literary and artistic authorities of those days for their remarkable blindness in not preserving a single sketch from life of Igor Ivanovich. And it is, of course, not a reproach to the dogma of a canonical type of hero who provides the bulk of our literature and painting. Igor Ivanovich doesn't intend to push anyone out or to assume anyone's place. Having only once in his life assumed someone else's place, so to speak, he never again pushed anyone out, never made any claims and, strictly speaking, didn't occupy any space at all.

Actually, why should a man who, it might turn out, didn't even exist suddenly claim anyone's attention? Or aren't there any heroes around? Or is the author completely...

No, Igor Ivanovich wasn't just anybody, no, not just anybody...

Judge for yourself: except for a single secret that he himself had almost forgotten toward the end of his life, he was remarkably open in his fervor, sincerity and integrity.

So what if his emotions occupied, frankly, a very small space, and his sincerity concerned things that didn't excite anyone else's interest, and no one ever tried to bribe him. So what? Do sincerity, fervor and integrity really lose their value because of this, or does it make it easier for us to find a man in whom these three qualities were joined together so successfully? I wouldn't be acting against my conscience if I added to this honesty, goodness, frankness and an acute sense of justice. Perhaps this is still not enough to attract us to a hero who isn't of the canonical type?

But most of all it's the memory of the *quiet chroniclers* that moves me to this labor—those who stay silent and wait, and later, when they are convinced that unconcerned forgetfulness reigns, they begin to compose the fate of the dead man, report suspicious rumors and information about him, or, worst of all, erase him altogether from history.

"Nastya, I think that we should slaughter a rabbit today, the one with the ear," uttered Igor Ivanovich with remarkable ease, behind which one could barely discern considerable mental stress, as he looked around the kitchen nonchalantly. It's well known that Igor Ivanovich had six rabbits, not ten.

While Nastya is getting ready to answer, we might note that Igor Ivanovich knew the whole rabbit business quite well and only lack of space prevented him from expanding the business: his animals were hardly ever ill, and they bred well. He could also skin them and process the hide better than most. Only one moment in rabbit breeding, indicated by the little word "slaughter" was beyond his ability. We may recall the very first time when Nastya said, "You should slaughter that old gray one." Igor Ivanovich froze for a second and then answered Nastya distinctly, looking sternly at her: "That isn't in my nature." "That gray one" and all the others—both gray and white ones—were killed by the neighbor Efimov or someone else.

Nastya looked attentively at Igor Ivanovich standing there with his hands in his pants pockets, and she attributed this sudden suggestion to his uneven character.

If all eyes looked like Anastasia Petrovna's, there would be much more human kindness and truth in our life!

Everybody remembers how in 1942 five people were taking shelter in her 20 square meters of living space in Cherepovets. Then her cousin, miraculously evacuated from Leningrad with her two children—who already had one foot in the grave—descended on her. For almost two years the guests occupied not only the entire bed but also three places at the table. Then the young and eternally hungry Valentina and Evgenia rebelled. Then there sounded forth the historic words, spoken simply and uncompromisingly by Anastasia Petrovna: "If anyone doesn't like it in my house, I won't keep him here."

Her own children didn't like it, and she didn't keep them.

"Maybe he's not going to have dinner with us."

"Why not?" Igor Ivanovich gave a start. "He has to be in court at one. How long will that last? Until dinner, then he'll come. I'm surprised at you..."

Nastya was used to Igor Ivanovich's asserting his worldly wisdom with either surprise or resentment, depending on his mood.

"I'll make mushroom soup. He loves it. We'll open a can of stew for the main course. He's skinny, let him have some fun still," added Nastya, without transition now referring to the rabbit with the ear.

Igor Ivanovich hadn't counted on stew, so he decided to reply as generously.

"Do we have any empty bottles to turn in? I'd like some beer for dinner, especially with the stew. That would be nice."

"You know yourself that there aren't any," said Nastya calmly, pouring water into a saucepan. "Wash out the oil and turn them in."

"I'm telling you that they won't take them," Igor Ivanovich said, continuing a long-standing argument.

"Don't talk nonsense, they're normal half-liter bottles like port wine, why shouldn't they take them? Tear off the labels, that's all."

"Do we have kerosene?"

"Yes, I got some."

"So why didn't you wake me up?"

"You were sleeping so well. And since I woke up at seven, and couldn't go back to sleep... Your color isn't good."

"I must stop staying up late at night," said Igor Ivanovich, snorting over the sink. "Let's make it a rule: at ten—taps. Otherwise the morning is lost. The best time of the day."

Nastya was used to these fits of imposing order and she just sighed. Igor Ivanovich was drying himself with a waffle-weave towel, so he didn't hear the sigh.

Five dusty bottles were standing under the sink.

The sink was of the antediluvian kind installed in homely Petersburg kitchens, not with the very earliest water pipes but perhaps with the second oldest ones, when all artists everywhere were enchanted by lilies, sedgegrass, seaweed, swamp and lake vegetation, and emaciated naked women with flowing hair. Now it's hard to know what used to be the name for the washtub underneath the faucet before the appearance of these iron basins cast in a corrugated pattern, wide above and narrow below. Most likely it was those basins that gave the generic name "scallop" to all subsequent objects with an analogous purpose. This scalloped basin looked like a large crater and wasn't very convenient, but it didn't seem possible to replace it since it was located near the door, and to put in its place a modern rectangular, enameled little trough (Nastya's dream) would mean to block the already narrow entrance to the small, triangular kitchen which had somehow resulted from one of the numerous and extensive renovations of this rather uncomfortable house.

The reader, of course, has absolutely no interest in watching Igor Ivanovich deliberating how best to remove the dried-up oil from those opaque and sticky bottles. The reader does, on the other hand, expect a speedy explanation of how Nastya, the eldest daughter in her family—who, as everybody knows, used to live with her sisters and parents in a fine apart-

ment on Old Peterhof canal near Obvodny Canal, a stone's throw from
the Triangle factory and very near the famous Narva Gate—how Nastya
had ended up in this awkward little apartment in Gatchina with three
smallish rooms shaped like lopsided triangles. Actually there were two triangles: the entrance with the toilet, and the kitchen, while the living room
was more like a distorted trapezoid.

The one in the best position to tell about this move is the head of
Militia Station No. 13 in the former Kolomenskaya district, Grishka
Bushuev. But he died just about the first day of the war, which caused the
sharp-tongued youngest daughter, Evgenia, to say straight out to Lyuska
Bushuev, when she visited her childhood apartment after the war: "That
was God's punishment!" "Zhenya, please, I really wouldn't know. Only
don't speak ill of the dead." Which was all that Lyuska Bushuev, a widow
with three children, could think of to say.

After he had become head of Station No. 13, Grishka continued to live
poorly somewhere near the Moscow Terminal on Ligovka, or maybe on
Kursk Street. But he remembered the apartment at Old Peterhof from the
time when he was still a police operative and went on requisitions, and
when by 1935 he had settled in with the new order and enjoyed an authority which opened up great possibilities, he remained faithful to his dream
and easily finished off the exploiter who had made his nest right by the
Narva Gate.

An amazing male Irish setter moved in along with Grishka. Grishka
called him Nero, clearly arguing with someone. The dog was strikingly
handsome and no doubt purebred. It even seemed that he himself knew
the high quality and value of his genealogy, and so when Grishka took him
out in the yard to do his business and gave commands (apparently to
impress the residents) like "Nero, fetch," then Nero just smiled with his
carefree, cheerful face and didn't fetch. These outings with the dog, calculated to have a strong psychological effect with a certain political accent,
were sometimes undercut by Lyuska, who was right nearby, leaning out
the window of the roomy kitchen on the third floor and announcing to
the entire courtyard: "Grisha, hey, come and eat your potatoes with linseed oil!"

Grishka would get furious and obscenely curse his wife and Nero, too.

In all probability his aesthetic sense indicated to Grisha a certain dishar-
mony: Nero's tamer shouldn't be tempted by potatoes with linseed oil.
How many times had he told Lyuska: "Keep your lack of culture to yourself. Look how people are laughing at you. It's the class enemy that's
laughing at you."

The capitalists and landowners, swept out of Petrograd-Leningrad, would be pretty surprised if they could see within their ranks on the garbage dump of history Pyotr Pavlovich and his wife, their two grown daughters, their son-in-law Igor Ivanovich and three grandchildren.

The concept of Yezhovshchina* has, one would think, been sufficiently illuminated and exhaustively described in the relevant literature; this concept sheds light on numerous subjects lying beside the road of history and if anything needs additional research, then it would be only "Bushuevshchina," that is "Yezhovshchina" within the boundaries of one separate militia district.

So, Nastya's father, Pyotr Pavlovich, who was well-respected in the Kolomenskaya district, walked around until 1935 in a derby hat, had a mustache with amazing points, loved tight-fitting coats, and considered himself a manufacturer, inasmuch as he referred to his establishment by the harsh name of "louse-scratching factory," either because of some inexplicable pride, or in order to please his democratic clientele. The barbershop on Obvodny Canal remained in good standing and was left to Pyotr Pavlovich in a sort of sublet from the Health Inspection Department, where he continued to work for two years immediately after Soviet power was established.

Pyotr Pavlovich suffered because of his work force. And that work force was, as we know, Petka Kudryavkin, nephew of the nurse Tatyana Yakovlevna, also named Kudryavkin. He had been taken on as an "errand boy," not from the village Zaluchie, where Tatyana Yakovlevna came from, but from the little-known village of Leshchin. He had been hired long before.

But in 1934, when Pyotr Pavlovich tossed the snow-white cape over the shoulders of his client in the barbershop on Obvodny Canal and shouted out his habitual, "Boy, get the water," it was no longer Petka who brought the water. At that time an old woman was working as the "boy"... In view of our chosen genre, this fact is completely natural, and what's more, if such a fact couldn't be found anywhere in history, then we would have to invent it in the interests of the genre—in order to achieve a more entertaining and fantastic result.

So, in the guise of an errand "boy" Pyotr Pavlovich's middle-aged wife enters onto the stage of history. She was already a grandmother at this

---

*Nikolai Yezhov, nicknamed "the bloodthirsty dwarf." He headed the NKVD from September 1936 to January 1939. During this period, known as "the Yezhovshchina," over 3 million people were killed and many more arrested by the NKVD.

time, and her entrance would have been a total success if she hadn't confused her boss, by continuously using Pyotr's nickname, and saying, "I'm
coming, dear Petenka,* I'm coming," to the great dissatisfaction of Pyotr
Pavlovich, who had a name to maintain.

Petka Kudryavkin, who was by this time working as a master barber,
was disinclined to call the "boy" and, telling the client something amusing, flew into the back room where the hardworking Olya bore all the
rear-guard maintenance of the barbershop on her gaunt, but still strong
shoulders.

And this is when Bushuev brought down Pyotr Pavlovich and put in
Petka Kudryavkin.

...And how could one explain to the Cheka troika in the few minutes
provided that, for Pyotr Pavlovich, Petka Kudryavkin was compensation
for the son God hadn't given him, that Petka was Pyotr Pavlovich's pet
and dandy, that to Petka much was allowed, forgiven and forgotten, that
Pyotr Pavlovich, who had during his long life trained quite a few high-
class master barbers, was proud of Petka.

No, at that turbulent period the Cheka troika had neither the power
nor the time to listen to all these petty bourgeois tales about class peace
between a bunch of exploiters and the exploited masses. Bushuev's punitive hand liberated from hostile elements Petya, the barbershop on Obvodny
Canal and the apartment above the barbershop.

So is this how Nastya and Igor Ivanovich ended up in Gatchina?

Oh no, such a hasty assumption can arise only once on the rectilinear
paths of historical consciousness, or perhaps twice—if imagination is lack-
ing.

We won't speed up history, it has already happened and it can never
become different no matter how many times it is rewritten. We will not
hurry, if only out of respect for those who did not have and will not have
any other life than the one they were given.

However, if you are in a hurry, take a look at the end and we can say
good-bye.

But even unhurried histories sometimes acquire an amazing tempo.

In twenty-four hours, actually rather hurriedly, and actually without
having time to collect himself, Pyotr got rid of the Singer sewing machine
on which the handy Olga Alexeevna used to do all the sewing for her family, barely having time to sell everything he could as fast as he could and
for a song, and after numerous quarrels and mutual accusations the dumb-
founded Pyotr Pavlovich and his family managed to load their things and

---

*Petenka is a diminutive for Pyotr and Petka, so both are called this.

set off to their destination, the town of Cherepovets. Only after the war could the decimated family minus Pyotr Pavlovich and Olga Alexeevna make their way to Gatchina, following the older sister Valentina, who worked through the war near Cherepovets in a rear unit involved in repairing army weapons. At the end of the war this unit was apparently relocated closer to Leningrad, and Valentina, a labor union organizer and shockworker, was the first to gain a foothold in Gatchina and later brought the others there.

But what about Igor Ivanovich?

Why haven't we seen his face or heard his raspy voice during these stormy events that shook the family?

Igor Ivanovich behaved extremely sensibly and circumspectly, not often the case with him, but here he wasn't thinking of himself, since he knew that if Bushuev should try to get at Pyotr Pavlovich not through Petka but through his son-in-law, that is, himself, then the family might be sent off considerably farther than Cherepovets.

It is possible that Igor Ivanovich will disappear a few more times from the pages of this fantastic narrative, drop out of sight during even more important events, but this is not because these events do not concern him: quite the contrary—he will disappear or drop out of sight only to assume the place assigned to him in world history.

The bottles were washed unhurriedly and carefully. The entire procedure, no matter how Igor Ivanovich tried to prolong it, was over quickly, in half an hour or so. It wasn't just that Nastya thought that the bottles would be accepted and had conveyed this to Igor Ivanovich, although it must be said that he came to believe this profoundly and fully, but that while scraping, shaking, washing, sniffing, and examining the glass against the light, he was seized by the wonderful idea that he was making money, not much, but still money, and this gave him a sense of being involved in something serious and worthwhile even when fussing around with kerosene and greasy dishwater. Igor Ivanovich was a good worker: he could sew a pretty good rabbit-fur cap, he could line slippers and build a shed, he was a roofer, and to some extent, a porter, he led a mandolin class at the Raznoprom Union, where he also did other jobs, he repaired shoes, but didn't like to, he could saw wood and even liked chopping it, but whenever the uncertainty of his pay gnawed at his heart, which was unhealthy anyway, it took away some of the pleasure of the work. Perhaps it was for just this reason that he was always glad to take on any job with fixed pay: what was important here wasn't the profit but the mental harmony and peace derived from the clear understanding of his future. So, even while fussing with the bottles, he wasn't thinking about the concrete twelve kopecks but rather about money in general, and about the beer which he would drink with pleasure, but mostly he was thinking about the beer which would embellish his dinner. In his mind Igor Ivanovich all but delivered a pretty decent lecture on the benefits of beer in general—and with dinner in particular—but he stopped himself in time and directed his imagination in another direction.

Maybe he should get a bucket of beer? He'd get more than in bottles...

But this treacherous thought was immediately brushed aside with all the ruthlessness of a man who knows the price of timidity. And it wasn't a problem of finding and washing a bucket to carry it in, but just that the whole idea of a good dinner somehow got undermined, perverted and distorted. To deprive himself of the pleasure of easily picking off the cap with its dented edge, of seeing the foamy head in the glass, of enjoying the lively taste of the light beverage that made your head spin just like the springtime air when it smells of ice and snow... And as for the dinner table, it is one thing to have three bottles, or maybe only two, but altogether another to have a bucket...

Perhaps one might at this point suspect Igor Ivanovich of innocent cunning. Perhaps he had on purpose gotten this silly, preposterous idea about a bucket of draft beer only so that he could crush it once and for all—and then with all kinds of details affirm the only correct and—above all—utterly beautiful idea of bottled beer for dinner.

After Igor Ivanovich had quickly drunk his tea, eaten his roll and put on his coat, he discovered that his shopping bag was missing, the bag he usually took back bottles in, the little yellow net bag.

"So take this bag," Nastya said and pulled out a bag sewn like so many things in their home—the cloth on the round table, the curtain over the door into the room, the cover on the chest—from an old worn-out plush curtain that Igor Ivanovich had obtained at the Raznoprom Union Club.

"What? You want me to look like a bumpkin? Look, where's the yellow net bag?"

"God knows, I haven't seen it for a long time, just take this one."

"Great! This is something new. I'm supposed to take the bottles in a potato bag?! Nothing's in its place here. Is it really that hard? When you bring home the bag, unpack the things and hang it up. Look, here's a nail just for it. Is it really that hard?"

It's easy to imagine how moralists of various orientations will pounce on Igor Ivanovich to expose the moral vulnerability of his attempts to locate precisely the yellow net bag. Let him look, let him look! Only blind pride could prevent one from seeing in his searching a search for and affirmation of order, this highest good, the highest master of the world to which formerly even the gods were subordinated. And since I know that the net bag is lying in the pocket of the kerosene jacket (he himself put it there) I'm not going to interrupt his search, for the philosophical and ontological meaning of his action is much higher than its everyday meaning.

"A tidy cook is better than a chef," said Igor Ivanovich, softening his sharp pronouncement with a smile while looking in the nooks and crannies of the kitchen.

Nastya calmly moved from the primus-stove to the sink and from the sink to the kitchen table.

Igor Ivanovich pressed on:

"Tidiness isn't only putting things in order. For May Day and Easter we have it orderly too. Tidiness is not just cleaning up but maintaining order, it is when it's always neat, that's what ..."

Igor Ivanovich Dikshtein himself could have put his signature to these aphorisms with both hands, not the Dikshtein we have been discussing so far but the one whose acquaintance we will make in the near future. But Anastasia Petrovna had heard all these variations on the theme of neatness and order a hundred times and therefore turned a deaf ear for the hundred and first time.

"I'm afraid I won't manage on the primus. You might carry in a couple of little logs. I'll have to light the stove."

"Hey, here I'm leaving, and now it's take off your coat, put on the padded jacket, and out to the shed you go ... Where were you earlier? Did I refuse? You keep changing your mind, now it's something new again, now it's go to the shed..."

It was actually quite easy for Igor Ivanovich to change his coat and bring in the firewood, and the realization that Nastya would herself bring in two logs at a time even crept into his breast and made him feel ashamed; he could even see how her heavy body swayed as she climbed up to the second floor on these stupid stairs, but to agree was still harder, even impossible. Today firewood, yesterday kerosene, tomorrow something else, the day after something else again... There ought to be some kind of order finally. Igor Ivanovich didn't admit even to himself that he was rejecting the pleasure of changing his coat.

An outsider wouldn't understand the profound meaning of this changing of clothes but would interpret it rather superficially, and Igor Ivanovich himself hadn't even once reflected on the pleasure he experienced when changing his coat for the padded jacket or the kerosene jacket. It wasn't that he liked the padded jacket more than the coat, but the very ability to change his clothes in spite of his never having acquired a single new item of outer clothing since he got married and not having had any made for himself—the very ability to change coats was like a step in the direction of a kind of life where a person is surrounded by lots of necessary objects that have been invented and made just for his convenience. The energy provided by nature for the transmission of positive emotions in connection with the acquisition of new things or the making of new clothes in Igor Ivanovich found an outlet in the quest for and recognition of merit in every separate item of his diverse clothing.

The padded jacket, the regular jacket and the coat—each item accentuated in its own way the strict proportions of his lean figure and in a way directed it toward specific accomplishments and actions. Each of Igor Ivanovich's three articles of outdoor clothing was distinctive not only by its style and material, but primarily by the degree of wornness, and only secondarily by its different accompanying details. The padded jacket, for instance, which was of better quality than the jacket and coat—apart from the tiny hole which had appeared the devil knows how beside the left outside pocket—had an inside pocket, a neatly sewed-on piece of dark blue satin. Igor Ivanovich had never had occasion to use this pocket, but when he wore the padded coat he was aware of the presence of the pocket and knew that a pocket was always useful, it could suddenly come in very handy. And another story from long ago bound Igor Ivanovich to this padded coat with tender sympathy. Once he put it on to go outside to help Vasily Dmitrievich build a proper dovecote; Nastya saw his thin face with deep vertical wrinkles in his sunken cheeks, his high forehead extending into an extensive bald area, his concentrated inward look, and the stern crease of his narrow lips, she saw all this and said, "You really are my professor of sour cabbage soup."

He understood that she was trying to cover the fact that his appearance impressed her greatly with this joke, and almost every time he put on the padded jacket he hoped to hear that "professor" again. And although Nastya didn't say anything like that again, he would wager his head that he had heard it more than once, praise the Lord.

The regular jacket had other qualities. In addition to the fact that it had been remodeled from a black navy coat and carried many memories, it was also a work of skill and intense imagination. This jacket was also an answer to those two of little faith, Nastya and Valentina, who insisted that it was impossible to make something useful out of that old coat that didn't really have a patch of good cloth left on it. The jacket now had a strict purpose: it was worn to go for kerosene and in the autumn to work in the garden plot, since the plot was next to the highway and you had to look decent in public.

Two years earlier Igor Ivanovich had been struck by the fact that the coat, which had in its turn been altered for him many years ago from the spring coat belonging to Vladimir Orefievich, Nastya's brother-in-law, looked so worn-out and impossible. After that, he wouldn't put it on for half a year; at that time, by the way, the jacket hadn't been appointed to kerosene jacket yet. But after the toppled primus stove gave the final name to the jacket and he had nothing to wear for good, Igor Ivanovich again put on the coat and was amazed because it no longer gave that discouraging impression of being totally impossible, as it had before. "What a stupid whim, why haven't I been wearing it?" Igor Ivanovich kept wondering.

So now this happy situation had come about, which made it possible for him to change his clothes and which provided him the complete satisfaction of having to make a choice before each new circumstance.

It will probably never be possible to explain satisfactorily why, when he put on that particular coat, Igor Ivanovich also put on a certain facial expression which you could only call a readiness to ward off insults. Something in his face made him look almost proud and even slightly defiant, and observant people might notice that when wearing this particular coat Igor Ivanovich was especially sparing with words.

But before following Igor Ivanovich down Chkalov Street and then at once left on Gorky Street, watching him greeting acquaintances reservedly and slightly more ceremoniously than usual, we must return to his exit from the apartment, otherwise neither his progress to the container return center, nor his purchase of the beer will be fully understood.

While Igor Ivanovich was looking for the yellow net bag it seemed to him that if only he found it, he could show Nastya how you really could make a minor but very useful improvement in the housekeeping routine without extra words or fuss. Yes, yes, turning in the bottles and going to the store, all this would be very simple, not at all difficult if you didn't turn it into a major event. And no need for extra talk. You'd take the net from the place where it belonged, put on a coat, and after fifteen or twenty minutes you'd be home again. That's all. But no...

In the end, Igor Ivanovich discovered the net in the pocket of the kerosene jacket. Ten minutes before he stuck his hand into this pocket, bunched up the net in his fist and quickly transferred it to his coat pocket, he was already suspecting that it might turn out to be there, but he drove this thought out of his mind as well as he could and looked for the net even in the dish cabinet in their room, grumbling that because of such a trifle you had to rummage through the whole apartment.

Once his coat was on, it turned out that he wouldn't be able to go out independently and efficiently. He had to ask Nastya for money. For this reason he started to shine his shoes after he had his coat on and was chased out by Nastya to the landing outside the front door. Then Igor Ivanovich took his thick winter cap, decided to brush it off too, but went out on the landing on his own.

Nastya's lack of understanding might seem to an outside observer like craftiness, even refined craftiness, but only to an outside observer and not at all to Igor Ivanovich. He knew that in the morning especially Nastya had to make the most careful calculations about all the circumstances of the coming day, and as she was stirring in the sauce pan or regulating the flame on the primus, she was barely paying attention to her movements but was tensely and with concentration calculating the combinations of their life, ordering them in a temporal sequence, attributing to each action a degree of importance and an amount of effort needed to overcome the complicating circumstances. Igor Ivanovich joked that this mental work was "political economics," but in his mind he respected it; he often grumbled because of her proposed decisions, but inasmuch as he himself could never suggest anything worthwhile, in the end he accepted Nastya's program both for the coming hours and for the following years. Nastya was the oldest among her sisters and Pyotr Pavlovich used to lovingly call her "little elephant" because of her good sense and calm disposition. If Igor Ivanovich ever remembered this nickname, it was just during these moments of "political economics" when she didn't notice that she was being stared at, and she didn't sense how much he enjoyed looking at her at that moment. Her gray hair, with its steely shine, was firmly held down by a comb but didn't stay slicked flat, a look Igor Ivanovich didn't like, but retained its whimsical and irrepressible curl, and her still thick, luxuriant helmet of hair reminded Igor Ivanovich of a plowed field lightly covered by the first pure snow. Her large features were motionless as though preserving the peace necessary for the internal concentration on her difficult mental work. Igor Ivanovich knew that Nastya could even answer questions in this state or ask about some minor thing without breaking the thread of her main reflections.

"Will you give me something?" asked Igor Ivanovich, examining himself in the large crooked mirror fragment above the sink.

Nastya wiped off her hands and took out her handbag, counted through all her cash and handed over fifty-seven kopecks.

Igor Ivanovich gave Nastya a peck on the cheek that earned him a smile, a light poke in the chest and a "drunkard," after which he started toward the door for the third time this morning.

"Why did you stick the bottles in your pockets?" asked Nastya.

"Well, never mind, it isn't far," said Igor Ivanovich lightly and shut the door carefully.

The landing on the second floor in front of the entrance to the two apartments was the same size as the command bridge of some kind of puny torpedo boat. Enclosed by a railing, it enabled one to overlook a very wide area which apparently had at one time been utilized more rationally. The staircase down clung to the wall like a ladder for three flights of stairs, occupying very little space since it was rather narrow. Above the street door there were two windows at the level of the second floor, on an empty wall. Apparently at one time there had been a room there, but how it had been propped up without any support under it was incomprehensible. Why, in a house with cramped little rooms cut up over and over again dozens of times and, finally, to the great joy of the tenants, joined into separate little apartments with similar conveniences, why did there remain so much extra space? Was it possible that a humanity-loving architect proposed to build in the near future not just one, but two elevators in this house—one for passengers and one for deliveries—since there was room enough for both? They had failed to widen the stairs for reasons unknown to Igor Ivanovich. When a visitor came in from the street for the first time and saw the landing up above with the entrances to the two apartments, he didn't even notice the stairs leading to this landing, but experienced a momentary bewilderment, since the railing on the stairs and the surrounding walls were both painted bright green and blended together to the untrained eye.

Then the guest's eyes would fasten upon the two vertical beams directed upwards to where the upper landing opened up, looking like a balcony, and the perplexed traveler would begin to wonder about the purpose of this balcony and at this point it would involuntarily occur to him that, although not very wide, the three flights of stairs running along the wall provided the only actual access to the upper living quarters. But the perplexity of the curious stranger didn't cease at this point. The space opening before him was so very considerable that the question involuntarily arose as to where the living area was located, because the two-story house, covered with boards, standing with its corner at the intersection of two streets, didn't give the impression of a building with such a spacious vestibule. And the fact that there wasn't any of the usual household junk in this entry hall only strengthened the impression that no one lived there.

As he went out onto the landing, Igor Ivanovich flattened with a mechanical movement the sharp lapels of his coat, which hung like fangs above

two rows of almost identical big black buttons. At one time, in the style of
the forties, the sharp triangular lapels proudly stuck up like the ears of a
young rabbit. In all probability the tailor made some kind of engineering
miscalculation—the flowers of fashion fade quickly—and the sharp tusks
of the lapels at first stuck out from the chest, then slowly started to turn
down. At that point the coat was transferred from Vladimir Orefievich to
Igor Ivanovich. Essentially, the small movement, intended to give the
lapels a vertical position, was useless, since after three minutes the tusks
again resumed their aggressive appearance, but Igor Ivanovich had made
it a rule not to pay any attention to his appearance once he'd finished
dressing, and permitted what little negligence might appear subsequently.
It doesn't at all become a man to be too smooth and, as they say, have all
his buttons buttoned.

Igor Ivanovich himself didn't notice that his lack of stiffness had turned
into a rule, a habit, and sometimes even led to minor misunderstandings.
Once in a while Nastya even had to indicate to Igor Ivanovich the need to
pay attention to those buttons which needed to be taken notice of even in
the most informal dress.

After Igor Ivanovich had already gone out onto the porch, the door
upstairs opened and Nastya shouted after him:

"Gosha,* get some cigarettes!.."

Igor Ivanovich didn't turn around and didn't acknowledge that he had
heard, since he might not have.

On the street Igor Ivanovich was concentrated and restrained, businesslike and sparing with words, collected and purposeful, emphatically
laconic in his answers to questions about his own health and that of Anastasia
Petrovna.

Having forgotten to put the bottles into the net while on the stairs, he
decided not to bother with it at all, seeing that the walk was only five minutes long.

Yermolai Pavlovich's wife, who didn't miss a single historic event, lived
in number five on the first floor and came out in front of Igor Ivanovich
just as he stepped out into the yard. As soon as she saw three bottles in his
hands and two sticking out of his pockets, Yermolai Pavlovich's wife, who
knew Igor Ivanovich to be an exceptionally tidy man, was ready to bom-
bard him with questions but she knew, or rather felt, something in Igor
Ivanovich which didn't permit her to treat him like she did everybody

---

*Diminutive for Igor.

else. In connection with this last observation there is a certain need to linger a little over Yermolai Pavlovich's wife, who, incidentally, didn't give a brass farthing for her fourth husband.

There needs to be at least some kind of justification for the introduction into this fantastic narrative of Yermolai Pavlovich's wife who, if she served as a model, would only be suitable for monumental sculpture or at least for monumental painting.

Let us say straight out that if Yermolai Pavlovich's wife could explain the feelings that governed her few aspirations in life, we would receive the most interesting evidence of the power over people which Igor Ivanovich possessed without even guessing it.

Yermolai Pavlovich's wife was a bulky and simple woman who, as everybody knows, deeply despised all her husbands, and Yermolai Pavlovich was no lucky exception. When she listened to his discourses, which were as a rule not devoid of common sense and simplicity of expression, she would invariably grunt, shrug her shoulders, make some kind of farewell gesture with her hand and, turning away her rather large face, she would say *à part*, "Lie some more!" However, it was noticeable that during Yermolai Pavlovich's conversations with Igor Ivanovich about things that weren't accessible to her mind, blinded as it was by pride, she didn't butt in or hush up her husband—on the contrary, it was as though she received what her husband said into her consciousness, nodding in agreement. And there was no other power in the world that could overwhelm Yermolai Pavlovich's wife with her exclamations, her waving arms, her drawn-out screeching, so unexpected in such a large person, and the way she narrowed her eyes and squeezed her thin lips together into various shapes. The shattering power of her sighs, groans, whimpers, and ability to despise people in the most diverse ways was felt even by the Germans billeted in her house on Volodarskaya Street during the occupation; not only did they not permit themselves any excesses, but when they left they warned her that they would burn the house down and suggested that she get ready to put out the fire; to appease their conscience before Germany the great, they felt obliged to sprinkle kerosene on a corner and touch it with a torch for formality's sake, and without looking back they slunk off to the houses across the street, where there is now a new marketplace, and indeed they skillfully burned them down without noticing that the future wife of Yermolai Petrovich used an old door mat to beat down the flames before they had time to spread. And here is a strange thing: only in the presence of Igor Ivanovich did this woman, who recognized no limits, listen more than speak, restrain herself from gestures and sighs, and in order not to seem like a fool during an intelligent conversation, manage to slip in a couple of words, smiling sweetly and addressing Igor Ivanovich exclusively: "Who are you and what can I eat you with?"*

This silly saying, which she delivered regularly only because she didn't know anything more appropriate, always made a strong impression on Igor Ivanovich: he instantly became tense, he tossed his head, and distinct deep vertical lines appeared on his hollow cheeks which made a hidden strength discernible in his face; he waited for more, but Yermolai Pavlovich's wife was satisfied with the effect she had achieved and just smiled, playfully threatening him with her little finger. Yermolai Pavlovich shook his head accusingly and immediately tried to steer the conversation onto rabbits, which, after years of friendship with Igor Ivanovich, he had become become very skilled at slaughtering. Yermolai Pavlovich's last name was Efimov.

"I put Yermolai in line for cabbage," said Yermolai Pavlovich's wife instead of "hello"—"you need any?"

"Thank you. Nikolai is coming. I can't." There was a note of sympathy in Igor Ivanovich's voice, as though he had been asked for help, instead of offered a favor.

"Then we could get you some," his monumental neighbor shouted after him.

"Ask Nastya, I'm in a hurry," shouted back Igor Ivanovich, half turning around.

Now, it really was a five-or-ten minute walk. We must use this short time for two things: to give the reader the minimal information about Igor Ivanovich's fantastic fate, and, naturally, to examine through the prism of history the city of Gatchina where the hero is presently domiciled.

Igor Ivanovich's place of birth was Zagorsk, which from approximately the middle of the fourteenth century until the current, twentieth century was called Sergiev Posad after its founder, until 1919, when the city was known as Sergiev; in 1930 it was renamed for Vladimir Mikhailovich Zagorsky, the well-known revolutionary and secretary of the Moscow Party Committee, whose life was cut short at the hands of the counter-revolution in the stormy year of 1919. When Igor Ivanovich heard that Sergiev was to be renamed Zagorsk he approved of it, as he also, incidentally, approved of changing the name of Trotsk to Krasnogvardeisk in 1929, although he didn't imagine that he would have to live out his

---

* A rhyme in Russian.

remaining days and years in Krasnogvardeisk, which in fact changed its name once more to the original name of Gatchina. For the sake of completeness we must note that even if Igor Ivanovich had known that V. M. Zagorsky's real name was actually Lubotsky, he would have accepted even this circumstance with approval.

Igor Ivanovich's childhood in the family of a railroad employee who had advanced along the difficult path from switchman on the station Novy Vileisk on the Libavo-Romen railroad to luggage checker at the Sergiev station on the Moscow-Yaroslavl railroad abounded in extremely ordinary events. From his mother, a kind and illiterate woman, Igor Ivanovich inherited an ear for music, and with help from the psalm reader's bow, which was used to beat him if he made mistakes when singing alto in the church choir, he achieved a fine understanding of various musical elements, which enabled him to learn to play the mandolin without difficulty.

Igor Ivanovich's father also had an ear for music, and considering himself to be a Muscovite rather than a resident of Sergiev, on major holidays—in contrast to those Muscovites who sought grace in Sergiev—he thought it was absolutely necessary to hear the service in one of the distinguished cathedrals of Moscow. Once on Maundy Thursday during Holy Week he had squeezed in under the tall vaults of the Christ the Savior Church on Volkhonka, and the baggage checker, who had properly fasted, heard the famous trio of Chaliapin, Sobinov and Nezhdanova all together. One might say that all of Moscow had come out and gathered together to hear "The Good Thief." After communion, anytime he felt his heart moved, and without regard to the church calendar, he would intone: "The good thi-i-ief..." "At the first hour..." his mother, who loved to sing, would chime in at once and with a glance invite her son to join in. "Glo-o-ory to Go-o-od" the adolescent alto voice found itself a spot in the harmony, and the whole family together grieved in their hearts over someone else's suffering, forgetting their own, and for a short moment the family was carried from their own house, which in size hardly exceeded the smallest Russian bathhouses, to the base of three crosses where a cruel and partly unjust execution was in progress.

Close observance of the vanity of church life had deprived Igor Ivanovich of any poetic feeling for ancient legends, and the presence in Sergiev during almost the entire year of a large multitude of cripples and beggars fruitlessly hoping for a miracle deprived Igor Ivanovich also of pragmatic religious belief; the only thing that connected him with the world of the unknown and the beautiful, like dreams and hope, was music. The memory of the family singing about the repentant thief seemed to him many years later like a warm ray shining from a receding and generally cold distance.

A guardian of conservative traditions, Ivan Ivanovich's father saw science and education chiefly as a means of getting away from heavy and dirty work. Life offered numerous examples confirming the truth of his point of view at the dawn of our century, but even more at its end, as a result of the flourishing of scientific institutions, general literacy and the entry onto the historical arena of a great number of amazing personalities of doubtful education but who nevertheless possessed one important and invaluable asset—the power to direct the destiny of a large number of people. It is true that Igor Ivanovich's father didn't have to look far—there were some examples in the immediate vicinity and the first and best example was his younger brother Vasil, who realized all his dreams and, in addition, obtained the post of stationmaster at Koshary. In a predominantly peasant country where progress in easing the heaviest farm labor and in the production of food lags behind science, which progresses by giant steps, the position of Igor Ivanovich's father, considered by many smart alecks to be rather stupid, should be recognized as deserving attention if only to explain the short progress along the road to enlightenment made by Igor Ivanovich himself.

In his childhood Igor Ivanovich once did something—it was a minor incident, but it remains completely unsolved to this day. Although all the participants of this event died before Igor Ivanovich, he related this incident once in a while without making corrections or adding any details, as though he might be caught incriminating someone.

His sister Vera was three or four months old at the time. His mother went out somewhere with the girl in her arms and gave the boy a silver half-ruble so that he wouldn't get bored. The boy played with the coin in the small front room, but spent more time looking out the window than playing. On the floor there was a basin with slops for the piglet. The boy kept tossing the coin in the air and catching it until the ill-fated toy fell into the basin. Igor Ivanovich distinctly remembered his fright. His mother came back and asked where the coin was.

"I don't know, it fell."

And so he kept saying, "I don't know" both before and after his father came home.

His father, who got a salary of twelve rubles and ten kopecks, took the loss of the fifty kopecks very much to heart.

Igor Ivanovich watched his parents look all over the floor and move everything that could be moved away from the walls, but naturally they didn't find anything.

The basin was taken out to the pig.

Just before going to sleep, when his mother came to make the sign of the cross over him for the night, he confessed.

They went out to the pigsty but the slop basin was already sitting there clean.

Igor Ivanovich told this episode from his childhood more often than any other but nobody ever thought of wondering about the reason for this particular attachment. You might even notice that Igor Ivanovich remembered this event not only when people were talking about various losses and disappearances or about how people reject money because of some higher idea, but that this incident floated to the surface mainly when people started talking about that inexplicable and mysterious something that surrounds man and even exists inside man himself. In all likelihood Igor Ivanovich was sometimes forced to remind himself that fate itself had, so to speak, prepared him to be a man capable of inexplicable deeds.

...The crunching sound accompanying Igor Ivanovich as his shiny boots stepped on the trampled snow imparted a categorical decisiveness not only to this movement but also to his feelings. In this crunching there was the clarity and exactitude of the flute whistling from Emperor Paul's regiment, which started and guided the soldiers marching on the palace parade ground. In Igor Ivanovich's quick pace there was the openness of a person who clearly realizes his goals and abilities, a person who can't imagine a life different from how it appears to him in its everyday concreteness. Those who have read Tacitus and have watched Igor Ivanovich's stride may recall that haste has the appearance of fear, while moderate slowness looks like confidence. I venture to affirm decisively that not only, yes, fear, which had in fact once nested in Igor Ivanovich's heart, well, not only had fear evaporated and flown away never to return, but not even the nest remained, nor the place where in earlier times the nest itself took up a rather large space, as they say, from head to toe. So his rapid walk, looking like haste, should be explained only by the quality of his footgear, which wasn't intended for freezing weather.

The snow crunched distinctly and monotonously beneath Igor Ivanovich's light boots.

It was the stride of a real man.

And the crunching of the snow was proper and decisive; a woman would throw herself at a man who could walk like that, forgetting and abandoning everything else in the world. Igor Ivanovich had in mind a beautiful woman with sorrowful eyes, expressing mute vulnerability and hope. It is as clear as two times two is four that the beautiful woman, tired

out by offers of all kinds of emotions and love, believes only what she herself can find, and she is searching, searching, searching, looking everywhere with hope in her eyes. She needs an independent and decisive man.
And what could express the worth of a man better than his stride? Nothing.
A glance of blue lightning flashed from under a lilac-colored little cap in
the direction of Igor Ivanovich and a tender murmur of gratitude rumbled in his chest; in his state of concentration Igor Ivanovich didn't notice
that it was only the neighbor's daughter greeting him, Marseillaise Nikonovna's older daughter, whom we won't meet, but Marseillaise Nikonovna will come up further on. Thus, singed by lilac lightning, Igor Ivanovich chuckled silently—why aren't I twenty-five years old?— forgetting
that it was just at the age of twenty-five that he was cast into the abyss of
trouble which had the most fantastic consequences for the rest of his life.

Igor Ivanovich walked past the one-story little houses on low stone
foundations. The windows looked out onto the street and were placed at
chest level of someone of average height, and therefore, the despairing residents had hung up homemade signs on the walls requesting passers-by not
to stop in front of the windows or look inside. It is possible that not all the
authors of these plaintive and sometimes stern posters suspected that in
Gatchina there is a long tradition of *looking in people's windows,* as opposed
to Kishinev, where it is done exclusively for the purpose of philandering.

The little town of Gatchina is located on a sort of island that rises up in
the middle of a damp swampy lowland. The slightly elevated higher part is
occupied by the imperial palace and the cavalry barracks attached to it,
while the vast northeastern part, gradually turning into swamp, was set
aside for the townspeople to build on.

High society and the aristocracy from the capital spontaneously shunned
this place as though some kind of evil omen hung over it; which is perhaps
why Gatchina, in contrast to Tsarskoe Selo, Pavlovsk and Peterhof, had
the gloomy appearance of a minor provincial town.

None of the buildings in Gatchina go together, in which fact the
esteemed historiographers see not so much the richness of imagination on
the part of the builders and houseowners as the diversity of poverty. There
was a much stronger similarity among the interiors of the citizens' dwellings
where the furniture, dishes and decor—consisting of homemade rugs,
embroidery and houseplants—served as an indication of domestic comfort and civil well-being.

His Majesty Nicholas I received Gatchina as his property from his dear
departed mother, and loved to stay here every autumn in true patriarchal
style. But his summer visits seemed more like warlike raids when the

sovereign, filled with martial ardor after successful maneuvers at Krasnoe Selo, came out to Gatchina at the head of the cuirassiers, covered with dust and glory. He held a review on the parade ground in front of the palace and arranged for the housing of the family members who came with him, but himself galloped off to Kolpino, where his tent was put up near the little church, where he ate supper all alone and cooled down after his martial exercises. And even in the absence of the emperor the Head Table, set after the maneuvers, and the Family Table, and especially the Gentlemen's Table, could feel sharply the inflexible spirit, decisiveness and will of the new master of the palace.

In the fall, in contrast, His Majesty was at peace and filled with good-will: he bothered no one and he even liked the local inhabitants to treat him with that trust and love that characterizes relations between children and their father.

The simplicity of their relations went so far that the inhabitants weren't prohibited from looking in through the windows of the palace when the imperial family was sitting down to dinner or tea or were spending the time in conversations and entertainments in the style of *European luxury*.

In his concern for the proper organization and external attractiveness of the town, His Majesty dispatched to Gatchina a notebook with draw-ings representing facades to be used for the residential structures and instructions to build on foundations no lower than three and a half feet. One concludes that before these instructions the windows of the resi-dences were even closer to the ground. Not only didn't the prescribed height prevent the residents of the structures from surveying the street and the passers-by, but the passers-by were in their turn able to observe the interiors of the residences, satisfying the need nowadays referred to as information hunger.

Although Gatchina served as Emperor Nicholas I's residence for very short intervals of time, the circumstances of the imperial visits were such that the town always had to be ready to receive the august guests, and these circumstances imparted life and energy to the city.

However, as the chronicles testify, the graces which the tsar from time to time showered on the town did little to enable the town to move along the paths of progressive development.

By the time of the events described here, the town had long forgotten about the tension produced by the possibility of imperial inspections, those restless times had receded into the distant and not-so-distant past, and the *Kammerfurier*'s* journals and the other journals with articles

---

*A court official of the 6th rank who kept a journal recording court ceremonies and events.

entitled "Kerensky in Gatchina" were turning into dust in the archives. The People's Theater in the Palace of Culture hadn't opened yet and hardly anyone could remember the performances and divertissements by French theatrical companies or the plays performed at court by highly placed personages and members of the imperial family with the participation of the sovereigns themselves. By the way, the chiming bells of the palace towers were lost during the war and the twice-renamed town—which was Trotsk for a short time, then for slightly longer Krasnogvardeisk—then again received its original name, and, thanks to the advantages of living in a quiet province, the town consoled itself with the idea that life there was "no worse than elsewhere."

The highway from the Smolensk Gate in the south to the Ingeburg Gate in the north divided Gatchina into two unequal parts, and if the area to the left of the road leading to the capital could correctly be called historic, where all the significant buildings and events are noted and described by historians and the minor events were punctually noted in the *Kammerfurier*'s journal, then the area to the right of the road, occupied by the town itself, can equally correctly be seen as on the side roads of history, where for the most part there reigns a passive and contemplative attitude to historical reality, not described by anyone.

The very highway dividing the town bears the marks of historical movement; first it was called the Kiev Road, then it became the Great Prospect, after that the Prospect of Emperor Paul I, and in the last segment of history it finally became the October 25th Prospect. To the left all was unique and inimitable: the palace, from the outside reminiscent of a military fortress, whose stern exterior appearance contrasted with the refined luxury of the interior accoutrements, the vast park which, with its ponds, lakes, bridges, foot-bridges, terraces, the Sylvia Grove, the Menagerie, and its own fleet and artillery, had no equals; the round threshing-barn with a crenellated tower, the *Connetable*'s quarters, even the barracks, ordinary cuirassiers' barracks, shone with the names of the architects Bazhenov, Brenna and Starov. At the same time the structures, events and names in the right hand part of the town, vast and gloomy, forcibly reminded one of that classical Russian city in which you can ride for three years without ever reaching the border. So can we consider the changing of the Constable Department with a watchtower to the Department of the Interior a worthy historical event, and the changing of Constable Street to Revolution Alley? Few people nowadays know the name of Kuzmin, the architect who built the Peter-and-Paul Cathedral at the

intersection of Malogatchinskaya and Boulevard Streets, since the most
memorable page of his biography was probably his ten-day stay in prison
by order of the sovereign for exceeding the estimate approved for making
icons and wall paintings in the cathedral. The city's inhabitants are proud
of the house of the famous artist, ethnographer, and caricaturist Shcherbov
in the whimsical architecture of which hardly anyone would recognize the
hand of the architect Krichinsky, who was at that time engaged in the construction of the Principal Mosque in Petersburg...

   We can further scrape together a rather short list of composers and
writers who in their search for peace and solitude fled to this backwater so
near the capital. But what Russian city that had stood and endured on this
unstable ground for a couple of centuries would not have acquired its own
Kuzmin, or taken pride in its own Shcherbov, or mentioned with respect
five or six celebrities who, on their way to immortality, had once or twice
rested under its dusty linden trees?

   And yet, Gatchina is incomparable! Where else could you find a place
where side by side, close to each other but on opposite sides of the narrow
highway, clocks ran differently, showing different time! On the left the
bells of history struck with a measured imperial pace, while to the right
the fine sands of destiny kept right on pouring through the silent clocks of
eternity...

   But did Gatchina really have a history?! Its own history, and not the
history of the whims of its innumerable proprietors? What did he want to
convey, that first man lost in the abyss of time—yes, there really was a first
man!—who for some reason named the lake Khotchino? Did he give it
some thought? Or did he toss it off as a joke as he was freezing or languishing from heat, or feeling sentimental or furious, was he old or young?
God knows! He has rotted and left us the puzzling word as a reproach to
our pride, to our ability to understand and explain everything. What did
the Novgorod scribe think, or did he think at all as he diligently entered
into the cadasters for the Votskaya section of the Novgorod lands in the
final year of the fifteenth century, the village of Khotchino by the Khotchino
lake among the other grand ducal volosts, villages and settlements in the
Dyatlinsky churchyard? The little village also seems to have belonged to
Novgorod, but then Emperor Peter I deeded "the poor Finnish farmstead" Gatchina to his sister as a gift. From that time on Gatchina was
passed from hand to hand along with all its male and female souls of the
adjoining twenty villages, with all the lands, fields, fallow lands, meadows,
woods, moss-covered bogs and common pastures. And among the many

who thought of Gatchina as their very own there were distinguished men, for instance, Kurakin, privy councillor, and Prince Boris Alexandrovich; there was the fortunate stepson of Baltic Germans, Archduke Blumentrost, adopted by a fatherland that had no special liking for its own sons; this ownerless land then went as a reward to a court steward, then reverted to the treasury for debts, only to become a gift to the thirty-five-year-old general-ensign and cavalier, Grigory Orlov, a great hunting enthusiast. The Empress Catherine II often donned the uniform of the Infantry Guards and, drawn by a feeling of friendship, she desired to absent herself from Tsarskoe Selo and go to the Gatchina farmstead to visit the "Gatchina landowner" accompanied by a small suite. Exhausted from the journey, the Empress would partake of dinner with her gracious host and after the meal she was pleased to stroll a little around the lake, amuse herself at cards with the courtiers in the gallery, not forgetting to have supper at the usual hour with the personages in her accompanying suite. Gatchina was also offered as a gift to that great champion of kindness and justice, Jean-Jacques Rousseau. It is hard to say what turned the French enlightener away from the temptation to become a landed proprietor and slaveowner at Gatchina, but it couldn't have been the healthy air, the amazing water and the knolls surrounding the lakes, forming pleasant nooks for walks and daydreaming, as the generous Empress-donor described it. Presumably the deciding factor was the truthful Empress' communication that the "local inhabitants understand neither English nor French, let alone Greek and Latin." As it happens, there has been no noticeable progress among the local population in this respect during the last two centuries. After the Empress' favorite, Grigory Orlov, had gone to find his repose in the Lord, the forgetful little mother at once gave this castle and property, erected by the assassins of Peter III, to the victim's son, her ill-fated heir, Paul Petrovich. Being a practical man and always expecting the worst, the heir appreciated above all the distance of the castle from the little mother's eyes, the fastness of its walls, and the possibility of finally building on this fickle ground a firm and solid nest in the German style. The dexterous servants of the muses fashioned, as best they could, the historical foundations according to the whims of the current owner, managing to read the very word "Gatchina" as German and to affirm its discovery in the refined verses: "...and this is Gatchina's fair duty, outside and inside full of beauty."* In agreement with the wishes of the Emperor, and thanks to the talents of the rather rough Brenna and the imitative Lvov, Gatchina came to look

---

*Author's note: An attempt to present "Gatchina" as a German derivative—*hat Schönes,* or "has beauty."

like a small German town. Rathaus, hospital, public school, post office, church, army orphanage, glass and porcelain factory, weaving factory, hatter, a fulling mill, and as if straight out of an illustration to a German fairy tale, the Priory Palace with a pointed spire on an octagonal tower—all this gave the village, raised to the rank of town, a new design and appearance; where the former appearance disappeared to and whether anyone grieved over its loss is not known. The decorations of the palace, capable of satisfying the most sensitive tastes of the true art lover, and the beautifully arranged and adorned park were combined in a most unexpected manner with a disregard for the everyday conveniences of life. Just take the staircase, for instance, narrow and steeply winding, connecting Paul's rooms in the palace with the interior chambers of Maria Fyodorovna. Historians are amazed to this day: "how could the Empress and her daughters, the Grand Duchesses, and the Ladies-in-waiting, all dressed in ceremonial Russian clothes," climb up this stairway on those days when for some reason the royal procession went from the lower floor to the upper, and then from the throne room to the formal chambers?

Gatchina's heyday with its civic improvement and military might came during the difficult thirteen years of an "exercise in patience" by its tempestuous owner, who was doomed to wear the mask of an obedient, appreciative son, for many years endlessly tormenting his soul with the thought of the crown which his mother had stolen, and finding support for his hopes and an outlet for his passions in endless military exercises and games. The all-powerful and almighty master of the throne whose momentary caprice and passing fancy could determine the fate of numerous people was tortured by his inability to live his own life; he moved back and forth among *his own* three palaces at Pavlovsk, Gatchina and Kamenny Island in Petersburg, but nowhere did he feel quite like himself, that is, like a benefactor, a peacemaker, an enlightened and just father to his peoples.... Where, then, can the people be if even his own children had immediately been removed from their parent by Her Majesty—his mother—and placed under her guardianship and upbringing.

He, too, has vanished, suffocated with the silent consent of his son, on the camp bed; beside his Wellington boots, as though in his last palace, the strongest, most reliable and richest one, he had just broken camp in his tireless and aimless wanderings.

So the remarkable castle remained in Gatchina, splendid scenery for a senseless show performed no one knows why or for whom.

Gatchina, Gatchina, whose misery are you? whose happiness?

Just like the steep, overhanging shores of the river Slavyanka which revealed the compressed history of the earth, you are lying there thrown open before all, like a forgotten book on the side of the road, "a city without a county" of the royal ministry, where the mayor is the Emperor himself! Where better than here does the great empire reveal its secret essence, where, but here, can you see the threads, invisible elsewhere, joining the highest point situated, maybe, on the top of the cross adorning the crown, with an indistinguishable point somewhere on the worn-out soles of the humblest subject of the empire? Where, better than here, were played out and maybe are being played out even today fantastically impossible stories which are capable of astounding those people who haven't yet unlearned or lost the ability of being amazed to the bottom of their hearts, regardless of their having long since become used to a life where every manifestation and detail is explained?

At the time of the events described here the city was living through its possibly most favorable period as far as the diverse and versatile development of a network of bottle collection points is concerned. It is worth mentioning that at this time the word combination "salon for the collection of glass containers" couldn't have even occurred in the brains of our domestic Jules Vernes. On the contrary, the ban against receiving empty glass bottles in the same place where filled ones were sold forced the bottle collectors to seek shelter in the most unlikely buildings, parts of buildings, and buildings five minutes away from being ruins.

Omitted from Intourist's travel itinerary, the town had with a great effort extricated itself from the desperate misfortune, the bottomless pit into which it had been cast by the German invasion.

Incidentally, among the first buildings to be restored and opened to visitors was the "Pavilion of Venus" on the "Island of Love" in the Gatchina park. The occupiers who had slogged to Gatchina, risking their lives, in the early forties of this century, did not spare the works of their former fellow countryman Mettenleiter, who had become an Academician in Russia in the art of "genre painting in the Flemish manner" and who painted an 80-meter-long ceiling entitled "Triumph of Venus" in the pavilion of the same name. The court painter's countrymen used the frolicking cupids on the ceiling for target practice with their loud parabellum pistols; they hadn't had enough of the pleasures of bachelor life in the active army, so they riddled Juno, the patroness of marriage, with bullets, and since they hadn't quenched their desire to see Venus in all her nakedness, they shot the tender Horae, the goddess' servants, who were holding her veil, and then demonstrated their courage and fearlessness by slaughtering with well-aimed bullets a rabbit which, as everybody knows, is a symbol of timidity... They stole the mirrors in the embrasures between the enormous weightless windows but were unable to steal the marble vases with fountains that were fixed to the floor, so they simply broke them, apparently with their rifle butts... All these details became the property of history only because the "Pavilion of Venus" itself, built entirely of wood and covered with a light wicker trellis, capable of instantly going up in smoke from any cigarette butt carelessly crushed in a corner, remained standing in contrast to a large number of stone palaces, tens of pavilions and residences and hundreds of monuments and obelisks, all constructed from much stronger materials.

The destroyed buildings, which incidentally included the palace, were not so much rebuilt as adapted for public use, to house both people and institutions. The wounds, even though treated hurriedly with the strength and means available, remained wounds. The most characteristic element of the buildings which were neither artistic nor historical treasures became the additions attached alongside, on top and in front—an amazing symbiosis of stone-and-timber constructions, as a result of which a plank shed had been affixed to what was formerly a hotel, built in a style with Italian pretensions, and it was hard at times to distinguish a dwelling from a warehouse and a warehouse from a dwelling.

The sad monuments to hastily knocked-together post-war life had become dilapidated by the mid-sixties and demanded decisive new efforts in order to maintain minimal living conditions, and since they presented a danger to the residents, they were accordingly vacated, and this offered a very rich and varied choice to the agents who ran glass collection points. We recall that some kind of collection point existed for two years even in a rather nasty movie theater, described in its day by Kuprin but which is in our time closed and destined for immediate demolition.

The house to which Igor Ivanovich was headed gave an unfinished impression. Its smooth two-story walls with windows like eyesockets without eyebrows still awaited, it seemed, some minor finishing strokes before it would acquire its face. But for some unfathomable reason there were no provisions for giving the house a face. Most likely because it had been moved from the street to a back lot, to an empty place surrounded by squat storehouses of well-laid bricks, two-story sheds of planks and smaller sheds built of the most unexpected materials: doors and bodies of cars, small pieces of flatcars and metal sheeting, but mostly of bits of planks and tar paper.

The smooth wall with the two rows of windows that seemed carved out with a razor in grayish cardboard was broken by a small entrance with two steps leading to the third window from the right, which had from necessity been changed temporarily into a door. Straight from the street you came into a room through which you could go directly into the kitchen—between the kitchen and the room there used to be something like a vestibule, but to make it more convenient they had removed one wall completely and moved the other almost up to the street entrance. The walls retained traces of the destroyed dwelling in the form of spots from pictures and photographs on the faded wallpaper, a piece of cardboard from a loose-leaf calendar, a bedraggled round stove and an ancient empire armchair with a leg missing, but nevertheless upholstered in tapestry, even though the fabric was all ripped up.

This drastic remodeling had created a small entrance hall that could accommodate five or six persons with their bottles, and an extensive area filled with wooden crates.

The house had been vacated two years earlier, but prematurely, as it turned out, because in the fall of last year permission to rent out a part of its premises for temporary use was given.

Igor Ivanovich walked up to the entrance where at the most ten people were shifting from foot to foot in the freezing cold. After reading the sign fastened to the door he acknowledged the group with a nod of his head and an indistinct sound, something like "good day." After hearing something equally indistinct in reply, he asked clearly:

"Been gone long?"

"She left with Vitka," said some lady shrilly.

Igor Ivanovich calculated quickly: the assistants were named Shurka and Kostya, the shop manager was named Viktor Pavlovich, but he was never called Vitka, so therefore she must have left with her son. She might have gone either to the doctors' clinic or she might have been called to the school. Everybody knew Anka: she wouldn't be held up at either place, she wouldn't be long.

Igor Ivanovich took his place in line, patiently stamping his feet in the cold and huddling himself into his clothes to preserve his body heat better. "Did she leave long ago?" Igor Ivanovich asked, but the question dissolved in the freezing air, the silence broken only by the noise of snow being crunched, as the people returning bottles shifted from foot to foot.

"So young and drunk already," said a girl with three bottles, watching how two fellows were walking.

One was wearing an unbuttoned padded pea jacket of military cut with a sloppy bedraggled old scarf that didn't cover his bare red neck, and enormous felt boots so big that it seemed you could wear them even over normal boots. The fellow stopped and greeted the company with a happy smile.

The second one went directly to the notice on the door. In each hand he firmly held a pair of bottles by their thick necks with his fingers red from the cold, and they shone lustrously like ice-covered firebrands after a winter fire.

"A bust?" said the one in the pea jacket, still smiling, both asking a question and stating a fact. The unexpected obstacle had ruined his plans but hadn't yet spoiled his good mood.

The one reading the notice started to pull at the door.

The fellow was sturdy and the door shook dangerously, threatening to fall outwards along with the door frame, and if it did, it occurred to Igor Ivanovich, Anka would be closed for at least a week.

"You guys, don't bother anything here. Just stand in line like you're supposed to, and there's no point in fooling around. There!" proclaimed Igor Ivanovich, not even looking at the guys, but instead seeking support from the line.

"Gramps," said the happy fellow, convinced that it was possible to get along with anyone in the world since anyone could understand their situation, "See, we don't have enough for a 'Faust Patron,'" he said and shook the heavy bottles.

"And do you think we turn them in for bread, or what?" said a little guy, sticking his face out from his raised collar.

Everybody laughed, the fellows too; only Igor Ivanovich didn't laugh because he was preparing for serious business.

"Hey, Ma," said the happy one, "are you going to stand here?"

"Of course!"

"Turn in ours, too... It's all the same to you!"

"What am I—your collection point?" said the woman with three bottles in a net. "Everyone stands in line, you have to, too."

"We can't, people are waiting for us," the other one quickly came to his aid.

"Drunks just like yourselves are waiting for you, but I left my children at home," said the gregarious matron.

The happy one turned gloomy, searched along the line as though choosing someone he could talk to. Everyone looked somewhere past him.

"Peo-ple..." the fellow grinned maliciously, looked at the bottles, and swinging sharply, clanked first one, then the other against the wall.

"Now stop acting like hooligans!" said Igor Ivanovich threateningly.

"It's OK, gramps, hang on," the fellow said and placed the four large bottles beside his boots. "Alik, give me yours." And he added two more. "Here, pops, hand them in like you're supposed to, buy like you're supposed to. Don't freeze your nose off!"

The fellows strode off briskly.

With such boots and a padded pea jacket, thought Igor Ivanovich, you would be able to stand here half the day.

"Take the bottles, take them... look how they tossed them," said the gregarious woman.

"See, they get drunk, and then they get on their own nerves and others' too," said the woman with three bottles.

"Are you going to take the bottles?" once again the little guy peeped out from his collar.

Snakes were writhing in Igor Ivanovich's mind.

"Six times seventeen... more than a ruble... I put them in their place, called them to order, but to pick up the bottles now... I probably should take them, but so as not to lower myself... I have to get the net out... More than a ruble, why that's three more beers. Three plus three, six bottles of beer, but why get so much beer, better to get something more substantial..."

If Igor Ivanovich had stood ten or fifteen minutes longer beside these ill-fated bottles, getting used to them, getting used to thinking about them, then he could have most likely moved these lawful trophies into his net with a natural-looking, unhurried motion, but at that moment the one in the collar peeked out again.

"Are you going to take them?" And he took one bottle in his hand as though he meant to look to see if the neck was chipped or if there was something in it. "No, it's a normal bottle." And he put it in his bag, which he had pulled out of his pocket specially for this. "This will come in handy."

Then he took a second bottle and for propriety's sake he also started to examine it.

Igor Ivanovich kicked the bottle beside him and it spun around on the trampled snow.

"They set them up here!" Igor Ivanovich took a step to the side.

"They're just right for me," said the little guy, and no longer examining each one of them, he gathered up the rest and ran over for the one Igor Ivanovich kicked away.

"See what a smart aleck," said the woman with the three bottles. "Did they give them to you, huh?"

"I asked the comrade, he didn't want them, but they're just what I need... They're perfectly good bottles," he grunted and sank back into his raised collar.

There was nothing left for the women to do but to exchange condemning and ironic smiles about the pushy guy.

The street was cold and empty, a typical morning.

Not only was Igor Ivanovich afraid of the cold, but he was even afraid that someone might notice this fear.

"Nice frost," he said unexpectedly to everyone's surprise, addressing no one in particular, and then fell silent, energetically wiggling his toes inside his boots.

A famous polar explorer, probably Amundsen, contended that cold and frost are the only things that humans can't get used to, and if he could have stood right now beside Igor Ivanovich and could have understood Russian, he would certainly have been highly interested in the announcement so unexpectedly coming from a man in a cap and light boots. In this connection it's necessary to digress once again in order to finally direct the narrative firmly into its fantastic channel.

The city of Kronstadt, located on the flat and low-lying island of Kotlin, must be recognized as a propitious place for the staging of a fantastic story, along with Zagorsk and Gatchina. To be sure, no one is surprised when reading official accounts of the events that took place on this island that the facts seem enigmatic from the point of view of ordinary perception.

It is reliably known that 3000 sailors and 1500 soldiers took part in the armed uprising of September 1905,* but when this spontaneous revolutionary uprising was suppressed, 4000 sailors and 800 soldiers were arrested, of whom ten were sent into exile and 67 were rewarded with prison terms.

Much more enigmatic and inexplicable from the point of view of the practical sciences are the traces left in official publications by the bloody mutiny of 1921. The military historians of the future will be more than a little surprised to find that among those who attacked a first-class naval fortress from the ice fields—open to the winds, where you could only find cover behind the corpse of a comrade who had fallen before you—the

---

*There were two rebellions in Kronstadt during this period: one in September-October 1905; the second in July 1906.

losses were very modest—527 men, while among the defenders of the fortress twice as many fell in the course of the assault; a sense of satisfaction is also aroused by the assertion that among the attackers only one in ten was wounded. From the point of view of mercy and the love of mankind this information is very comforting, but completely unnecessary questions immediately arise. Namely, didn't Tyulenev's brigade lose exactly half of its complement during the first hours of the fighting? And a brigade consists of a minimum of three regiments. Does that mean that Reiter's brigade, which was the first to burst onto the Petrograd dock at Kronstadt, wasn't depleted by one-third during 20 minutes of battle? Does that mean that the Nevelskoi Regiment didn't fall at the Italian Pond? Or that the cadets of the Brigade school, thrown in to cover the retreat of the drained and defeated Nevelskoi troops, weren't killed to the last man? Or that the commander of the bleeding Consolidated Division, digging in on the eastern edge of the island, didn't report that it wasn't humanly possible to hold on, but that by retreating they could avoid total annihilation? And why is it that only Petrograders remember that on March 8 the young commander of the Seventh Army threw 3000 selfless Red cadets into the attack on a fortress with a garrison of 30,000, and how on their way to the stronghold the cadets took icebound and inaccessible forts with bayonets and grenades, how they somehow came bursting into the town and in the town they fought and fell without thinking of glory, or thinking of how historians, afraid of catching colds and trouble at work, because of ideas of a higher order, would consider that their death and loss of blood hadn't taken place.

The Kronstadt mutiny, unlike the July uprising in Kronstadt in 1906, is still patiently awaiting its historian.

The events of February and March 1921 were reflected strangely in the contradictory and surprising reports about them. It all started with everyone trying to forget these events. A five-volume history—in a substantial dark red binding, decorated with portraits and pictures lovingly covered with shrouds of lacy onion-skin paper, and even including a Red Guard armband—illuminates at length the entire Civil War all the way until its end in 1922, but its vellum pages contain neither a narrative nor even a mention of the mutiny which, in Vladimir Ilych Lenin's opinion, represented a greater danger for the Soviet power "than Denikin, Yudenich and Kolchak together."* Even the memoirs of the participants in the event,

---

* Generals of the White Army.

which have partially come down to us, came out sometimes missing a beginning, sometimes missing an end, and sometimes completely missing a middle. The memoirists, some of whom had never set eyes on each other, seem as though by agreement to become mute and victims of amnesia as soon as the story touched on details excluded from the boundaries of history. Certain historical personages who were at the forefront during the Revolution and the Civil War and who also played some role in the Kronstadt events, suddenly disappear as though they had fallen through the ice along with the hundreds of nameless Red Guards and cadets who attacked the impregnable naval fortress at night during a blizzard. Even the rounded-off count of victims on either side, where the numbers end in two or three zeros, arouses not only sadness about the disdain for those tens, not to speak of the units, but also exposes the historians and statisticians to rebuke for their haste to reach completely correct conclusions while omitting details and particulars...

So where are you to look for fantastic heroes and fantastic events if not in the black holes of history, which, one must assume, swallowed more than one careless, curious man who dared look over the edge! Exactly here, where life is compressed into super-dense matter, where cities freeze in the glow of fires, where the bowels of snow-covered battleships burn from desperation, where bandages and blood are indissolubly baked and caked together, where horses, unused to flight, hover over the ice, rearing on their hind legs in the sky from the explosions, becoming the last things seen by the fighter who has gone mad from the rumble and the roar, shielded from death by a mother's prayer and a white robe given out before the attack; where, if not here, among the panting steam-engine and the arrogant armored cars, sniffing the spring air with the blunt snouts of their machine guns, where, if not here, where we were born, should we not all gather, we who remember, who saw, who know... to toss a handful of earth and go our silent ways...

The results from the uprising of 1906 are clear at least: 1417 persons convicted, 36 executed. However, it's significantly more complicated with the mutiny, though one thing may be asserted with authority: the mutiny of March 18 was crushed, and Igor Ivanovich Dikshtein was executed on March 21. The reader expects an immediate explanation and assurances that Igor Ivanovich's death was accidental, not at all necessary and, as it were, not quite death, and although there obviously is some small basis for such an opinion, one has to remember the mutiny, so furious and bloody, and the cruel and merciless fighting on both sides in order not to be misled about death during war. One might call life during a war accidental, but death—not at all.

Between the events of July 1906 and February 1921 one cannot overlook the mutiny of the mobilized sailors in Petrograd on October 14, 1918, which was in a social and political sense the precursor of the Kronstadt rebellion of 1921. On the one hand, the mobilized sailors couldn't yet free themselves from their peasant feelings and carried within them the dissatisfaction of the kulak and middle peasant masses with the politics of the dictatorship of the proletariat, but on the other hand, according to the cogent remark of the commissar of the Baltic Fleet, "all the counter-revolutionary blackheads hadn't been squeezed out" yet from among the mass of sailors themselves. And the slogans then were the same as they were two and a half years later at Kronstadt—"Free Soviets," "Down with Commissarocracy," and the like, and the instigators were the same: Leftist Social Revolutionaries, maximalists, anarchy. The experience in the spring with the liquidation of such attitudes in the mortar division of the fleet made it completely clear that it would probably be necessary to resort to revolutionary repression in order to remold the mobilized sailors.

But they managed without that. The constant misfortune of the Left SR's was their inability to estimate their chances for victory and their desire to make a big splash as fast as possible.

The mutiny clanked its weapons, but on the 14th they went out to demonstrate, leaving their arms in the barracks, and they refused to go without an orchestra. As is well known, the crew of the Second Fleet was located next to the Mariinsky Theater, and that is where the sailors went to get an orchestra right in the middle of a performance of *The Barber of Seville:* the performances used to start early in the day. They apologized and politely explained to the audience and the conductor their purpose for mobilizing the orchestra and asked the musicians to go outside and line up with their instruments. The strings and the harp were told not to bother, they stressed the winds, but a snag developed with the percussion. The principal big drum, the pride and joy of any orchestra, turned out to be solidly anchored in the orchestra pit. First they tried to remove it nicely, then they started to apply force and all this during the whistling and hooting of the politically backward public, the majority of whom was petty and middle bourgeoisie. It was especially insulting for the sailors to hear the shouts with the addition of "Bolsheviks" and "Commissars," but it wasn't possible to explain to the audience that they were going to march with the drum precisely against the Bolsheviks and Commissars. In the end the percussionist of the orchestra, the man who had suffered most, promised to extract the same sound from the medium drum as he would have from the large one. They had to agree to this compromise since it turned out to be impossible to tear the big drum away from the theater without significant damage to both.

At the Nikolaevsky Bridge the demonstrating mutineers had already been frightened by an accidental salvo of rifles, and they became confused and started back toward the barracks.

Igor Ivanovich heard this story when the crew of the battleship *Sevastopol* was passing a resolution demanding of the Commissars of the Baltic Fleet "a strict investigation of these elements" and asked that they not stop "at anything, even if they had to remove several dozen men from the midst of the mobilized forces."

In 1921 it started almost the same way in Kronstadt, only it didn't continue or end the same way.

The row continued through February; the sailors from the ice-locked vessels got bored with the inactivity and the meetings and had nothing else to do but calculate how complete or how short the rations were, to observe the slipshod work of the quartermaster in charge of supplies, and to carry on endless conversations about their villages, the land, free trade, the long drawn-out mobilization, and the anti-profiteer detachments assigned to catch anyone bringing food into the city to trade.

With dull faces they loafed around on the dirty, dingy ships and didn't even clear off the snow for weeks on end. Interest in politics and in literature was fading by the day despite the abundance of lecturers who gladly came to the ships for payment in food. They went unwillingly to lectures on political topics and, therefore, hardly any of that kind were held. The Political Section's program of lectures for soldiers and sailors included such subjects as "The Origin of Man," "Italian Painting," "Greek Sculpture," and "The Stone Age." For some reason there was much demand among the sailors for a lecture about a totally landlocked country— "Customs and Life in Austria." But as a rule, even if thirty or forty men got together in the messroom to listen to some lecturer or other, it all came around to the same endless questions about land, free trade and the anti-profiteer detachments.

Refusal to obey orders became almost commonplace on the ships and a slack attitude toward their duties also became noticeable among Party members. The issue of furloughs caused ferment among the crew, which was expressed in the independently convoked regimental meetings at which the crew refused the alloted five percent of furloughs; they demanded more. The sailors wanted to have it out in person with the Fleet commander and his deputies and demanded the convocation of a brigade-wide conference.

Yes, this was no longer the same navy or the same *Sevastopol* that had unanimously passed a resolution against the dissatisfied new recruits and adroitly shelled the mutinous *Krasnaya Gorka* fort in the fall of 1919.

To replace the revolutionary sailors, scattered on all fronts from the Ukraine to Siberia, came a raw mass of peasants who were tired of "War Communism" and ready to explode from any spark. And at this time also the Judas Trotsky, as the historians testify, "shipped to Kronstadt many of his people from the provinces where kulak uprisings were widespread."

By 1921 Kronstadt was like a badly guarded and maintained powder magazine.

On February 28, the senior clerk on the *Petropavlovsk* pushed through a resolution in favor of "Soviets without Communists." Men went over to the other battleship, since both ships were standing along the sea-wall in the harbor of Ust-Rogatka. On the *Sevastopol* a general meeting supported the resolution.

Delegates were sent to Petrograd to find out the cause of unrest in factories and plants, and at the same time to test the mood on the *Poltava* and the *Gangut*, which were docked at the Baltic Shipyards in the city, out of commission, but still formally a part of the First Brigade of battleships.

Many generally considered that the whole row originated on the battleships, and therefore they later went over the *Petropavlovsk* and the *Sevastopol* with a fine toothcomb. As far as the *Gangut* and the *Poltava* were concerned, they can thank the twenty-six-year-old, non-Party member commander of the Communist detachment on the Petrograd Naval Base, Misha Kruchinsky, who, without his belt or gun, went up on deck of the battleship, which was frozen fast in the Neva's ice. On the ship the mood was one of terrible excitement, kept at boiling point just then by the success of the Kronstadt rebels who had easily repulsed the first assault. What he told the crew of the *Gangut*, who were shouting angrily and brandishing their weapons, and the delegates from the *Poltava*, no one can tell any more, but after a two-hour meeting both crews found it best to hand over their weapons and ammunition and to leave the ships. Cadets from Petrograd were posted as guards on the decks of the empty dreadnoughts. Evidently quite a few people must have prayed for Kruchinsky's health, since he went through two wars, joined the party in 1942, and lived to a ripe old age.

The news about the *Gangut* and the *Poltava* instantly reached everyone and knocked the breath out of the Kronstadt agitators, who had been asserting that sailors don't turn on each other and who had depended firmly on the twelve-inch guns of the battleships being held to the temples of the city.

...Everything in this history consisted, as it were, of two completely opposing halves, just like weather in the changeover from winter to spring—frost and thaw, puddles and snowstorms. Here is the brigade of battleships—split in half, there are two powers at Kronstadt—and the troops in both the Petrograd garrison and the fortress waver back and forth, even the Bolshevik party cell at Kronstadt broke in two—one for the mutineers and the other categorically against them. And there is nothing more to say about the *Sevastopol*; evidently since its birth the ship had been predestined to have two fates: two names, two wars, two fleets, two hearts—one of coal and one of oil... Only in her declining years, after the long life given her by a kindly fate, when the glass lampshades and light bulbs on the lower deck would break with a crash when the main battery was fired, paint and insulation rained down, and the rusty supports for the lockers that had served out their time fell out from the bulkheads, did the battleship once again regain her original name, changed back to the *Sevastopol* from the *Paris Commune* before being decommissioned (now from the Black Sea fleet) and scrapped for metal.

Still, it is much harder to investigate and describe the fate of a single man than the history of a state, a city or a famous ship.

In spite of the obscurity concealing the origins of Igor Ivanovich and people like him, it is possible to establish something, but only with the greatest effort. However, in the information brought to light, for the most part certainly reliable, there may be one or two inaccuracies which simply can't be checked. In order to reduce the chance for error to a minimum, it is necessary to resort to the time-tested method of writing extensive biographies both of ancient and not so ancient heroes about whom nothing at all is known—or almost nothing. One collects grains of trustworthy details preserved by the grateful memory of mankind and generous chance, and one submerges oneself in an abundance of circumstantial information—about the epoch, weather, fashions, rumors, geological and sociological processes—drawn from earlier editions that have been checked, thanks to which the one or two invented details in the hero's biography begin to look more or less plausible.

...While still in Helsingfors on October 28, 1917, Igor Ivanovich read the speech by Trotsky, the chairman of the Petrograd Soviet, in the newspaper *News of the Kronstadt Soviet of Workers' and Soldiers' Deputies*,*

---

* *Izvestiia Kronshtadtskogo Soveta rabochikh i soldatskikh deputatov.* Later referred to as *Izvestiya.*

about the installation of the new power and the new victory of the lower classes over the upper, which had been unusually bloodless, unusually successful; aware now that the establishment of a dictatorship places the lower above the upper, he could clearly see his own place in this struggle—namely in the middle. He definitely had no use for the benefits brought by the overthrow of the Provisional Government. He didn't need land, he didn't care to own the factories and plants, the freedom which had begun on March 1, 1917, was more than enough for him, it could even be reduced a little, and as for the war, it wasn't particularly burdensome for the navy, and the idea of an immediate peace seemed to him so unrealistic, that it appeared to be merely a tactical slogan of the Bolsheviks.

Igor Ivanovich Dikshtein was one of the "black marine-guards," those who had not finished their training, a short-statured non-commissioned officer from among the students who had ended up in the navy during the war. He had a sparse and, consequently, untidy-looking little beard, glasses with silver frames, and a quiet command: the hold of the No. 2 turret of the main battery. Having effortlessly learned all the rules of the maintenance, care and storage of ammunition, he diligently "nursed" the ammunition with Germanic precision, often earning the approval of the senior artillerist of the *Sevastopol*, Gaitsuk, whose death will be described below. After the peace of Brest-Litovsk many officers and warrant officers of the old army and navy were cashiered, receiving tickets for furlough with the following text: "...Discharged until recall, to return to original status." Igor Ivanovich was in no hurry to return to his "original status"; in Petrograd there was hunger, and according to the information that was so widely discussed at endless meetings and discussions in the non-commissioned officers' ward-room, the coming year, 1921, didn't promise any relief. The substantial Red Navy ration deserves detailed description, since the workers in Petrograd didn't receive half as much: one and a half to two pounds of bread, a quarter pound of meat, a quarter pound of fish, a quarter pound of cereal, 60-80 grams of sugar—and all this per day. It's true that many had a desire to eat bread or something else even after just finishing a navy meal. The basic quantity was supplied regularly and without interruption according to wintertime norms, but the food allowance wasn't always of good quality. Instead of cereal they were often given frozen potatoes, and there wasn't enough fat and sugar...

His mother and younger brother had died of hunger in 1919 in the cramped apartment on the fifth floor of an old house on Petropavlovsk Street in Petrograd, which is why the problem of survival became Ivan Ivanovich's single main aim. He could foresee, he could calculate, but more and more often some not unexpected chain of events already under-way somehow destroyed his apparently well-calculated designs...

At first all went according to his calculations.

Anticipating mobilization, Igor Ivanovich went as a volunteer, which gave him perfectly obvious advantages, the right to choose a branch of the service and even a specialty. At the same time his joining the navy eased the situation of his family, which lived on his father's small pension. He chose the safest place on the ship—the shell magazine, and he was right, because even at a time when all duties on board had slackened and there was no order left, the ammunition keepers enjoyed undisputed authority. The duty details were allotted on a democratic basis, the watches were kept miserably, the snow lay uncleared on the decks, the ice wasn't hacked off, but the artillery watch guarding the hold and responsible for the con-dition of the ammunition and the water supply system, for firefighting and flooding of the magazine were given strict orders and they did their job conscientiously. Even the densest country sailor boy soon understood what it meant when the cartridge chambers were defective and the pow-der magazines were in a mess.

Igor Ivanovich didn't intend to spend his whole life in the navy; he wanted to survive all these unpleasant things, finish his education and live the solid and secure life of a Russian engineer. Therefore, he avoided any kind of political activity, called himself a sympathizer but didn't specify with whom, and in his heart he didn't condemn the crews of the *Aurora,* which had sworn allegiance to the Provisional Government on practically the day after the unsuccessful July rising, and then frightened that same government with a blank shot from behind Nikolaevsky Bridge during the night when the Winter Palace was taken by the Bolsheviks.

It would be absolutely untrue to assume that at the time when all of the people were supposedly ready to rally round a single great goal, when the thirst for freedom was on everybody's lips and their hearts were filled with a desire to forge ahead, it was only Igor Ivanovich Dikshtein in his central section below the turret where the shells were stored, among the shelves, caissons, and storage containers with whose help the shells were loaded on carts and moved to assembly tables—that only he didn't feel a thirst for freedom and a desire to forge ahead. Of course he felt this, but only for a very short time, and after certain events that followed one another, liter-ally one day after the other, and both times right in front of his eyes, Igor Ivanovich became reserved and preferred not to speak aloud either of his thirst or of efforts to forge freedom.

In accordance with battle orders, in the winter of 1917 both fleets of battleships were anchored off Helsingfors.

On March 2, the day after they had received the news that the autocracy had fallen, Rear Admiral Nebolsin was killed. And on March 4, when
Admiral Nepenin, who was arrested because he refused to resign the
Supreme Command of the Baltic Fleet without an order from the Provisional Government, was taken away from the Helsingfors Harbor, they
shot him right by the gate in full view of the crowd.

Both events were referred to in the newspapers as incidents and no one
had to answer for them, which is what struck Igor Ivanovich most of all.

Igor Ivanovich locked himself in below three armored decks and with
even greater diligence looked after the "Westinghouse-Leblanc" air-con-
ditioning system, which provided a temperature of 15-20 degrees centi-
grade in his automatically regulated magazine. With the utmost attention
he took care of his 300 wards, which were spun by brass driving bands and
had all sorts of armor-piercing and ballistic points. Like a diligent first
sergeant of ammunition he strictly inspected the hermetic seals on the
cases containing the bagged charges of powdered nitroglycerin in magnificent combustible silk; checked that the ammunition carriers moved easily
as they turned on a spherical strap, checked the functioning of the small
hoists for the 60-kilo charges, and fussed over the rubber rollers in the
projectile cradles that protected the fuses and the driving band of the 400-
kilo shells.

Finding himself in Petrograd in February 1921, Igor Ivanovich at once
felt the striking similarity to the events four years earlier, although the
number of people in the city had noticeably decreased.

...It wasn't even that it had decreased, but you might say that the city
had been depopulated; from the 2.5 million inhabitants in 1916 there
remained only one third—fewer than 800,000. The working class, the support of the revolution, had been dispersed as well, you could barely find
90,000 of them—a fifth as many as in 1916, and it was no longer composed of the same people—now it was whoever might want to avoid being
drafted into the army by working in the factories or just out to get a
worker's ration card. The lack of manpower was replaced by Red Army
conscript laborers—army units that received work orders instead of their
long-awaited demobilization. Citizens were brought in from 37 provinces
as conscripted and mobilized labor, only no one could really count them,
since they ran away if they could, just like the first builders of Petersburg.
They also concealed their trades and, in general, after the victorious end of
the war, they simply didn't wish to live far from home in barracks under
semi-military discipline. These conscripted workers worked like they lived—
and they lived badly, as far as living conditions and food and clothing went.

At the Eighth All-Russian Congress of Soviets, Trotsky, who was responsible for transport, assured the country that the coming winter "doesn't threaten us with destruction, doesn't threaten us with the total paralysis that we might have expected by mid-winter." It's hard to say what the optimism of the leader was based on, but the paralysis approached before winter reached its mid-point.

However, economic difficulties concealed the political crisis, which had already surfaced in the speeches of the peasants at that same Eighth Congress of Soviets. "...Everything is fine," said a cunning delegate with the usual peasant resignation, "it's only that the land's ours but the grain's yours; the water's ours but the fish's yours; the forest's ours but the wood's yours..." For this reason the peasants unwillingly participated both in timber cutting and in supplying the city with provisions. Having freed the poorest peasantry from forced requisitions, the authorities started to call not individual peasants but entire villages to account for delayed and inadequate fulfillment of the quotas for food and firewood imposed by the People's Committee for Supplies, and this provoked opposition from the backward masses.

In January Petrograd received a third as much fuel and firewood as planned, and in February only a quarter. The winter was a hard one, freezing cold and with big snowdrifts. The stony center of the city began to heat itself by using the wooden outskirts. One hundred and seventy-five buildings were razed and the 165 cords of wood obtained in this way were distributed equitably: two thirds went to the population and one third to heat institutions. In February, 50 more structures were condemned to be torn down. Understanding that this resource was, like all others, limited, the Petrograd Soviet published a decree explaining to the citizens that the *tearing down of buildings* could only be undertaken with the permission of the Council of National Economy.

Although the harvest in 1920 wasn't bad, the trains with provisions crawled toward the city at an average speed of 89 kilometers per day, sometimes only 34 kilometers per day. Food spoiled on the way, eggs arrived rotten from Siberia and potatoes froze on the way and arrived inedible.

On February 15 not one train with provisions made it to the city. There was no grain reserve, that is, there was, but only for a day or two and only if it was distributed in half rations. And so it was during all of March.

In January the specially formed Commission for Supplying the Capitals under the Council of Labor and Defense decreased the rations of bread by one third for ten days, giving out two days' rations every three days. This decision applied not only to Moscow and Petrograd but also to the Ivanovo-Voznesensky region and Kronstadt. However, upon the expiration of the stipulated period, the Petrograd Soviet was forced to announce the reduction of bread norms for some citizens, and for others the special food rations were cancelled.

Without fuel, without food, without qualified workers interested in working, you can't produce much, and 93 enterprises had to be closed down and not just any, but ones like the Putilovets, Lessner, Treugolnik, Franco-Russian, Baranovsky and Längenzippen plants. There were 27,000 people without work, one third of the workers remaining in Petrograd, but during the emergency stoppage the government guaranteed for all the right to receive rations and average wages calculated on the basis of piecework plus bonuses. In order somehow to retain the workers' vanguard in Petrograd, orders were published for them to report to work every day for registration. The newspaper *Petrogradskaya Pravda* reported on the resourceful tobacco workers who, after the prohibition against using electric energy, started up manual machines and in this way employed 125 men, while 200 men worked on finishing the articles and another 428 started to clear away the snow and bring in raw material. Attempts to use electricity even for a short period at the closed-down enterprises were cut short at the outset, because 150 plants continued working at full capacity, although it is true that "slowdowns" crippled the work. This word "slowdown" was on everyone's tongue and appeared quite often in print and in official documents, though it didn't make it into any dictionary and one can only guess that the new usage replaced the terms "labor unrest" and "strike," which had outlived their usefulness.

Anxiety and dissatisfaction reigned in the city. Exhaustion—terrible exhaustion, inhuman exhaustion—nourished the gloomy mood of the people who had beaten the White Guards, banished the interventionists, endured all deprivations and adversity, starved, froze, and survived typhus and cholera, people who had waited three years for peace and had been hoping for an immediate improvement in their life.

First a shop at the Baltic plant would stop work; then the workers at Laundry No. 1 would refuse to unload firewood... The workers who previously had spared no effort in the defense of Soviet power now began to present demands to it, their mood was being manifested mainly in their demand that the population should be satisfactorily supplied with food, but there were also demands of a different kind: the workers at the Dyumo plant demanded to be given soap and an authorization for public baths.

The Provincial Party Committee of Petrograd sensed all the tension of the moment, and at a meeting at the end of February these prophetic words were spoken: "We have come to the moment when demonstrations might occur."

Demonstrations began at the end of February.

In the editorial entitled "Hands Off!" *Petrogradskaya Pravda* openly admitted that counter-revolutionary agitators had "succeeded in causing slowdowns at the plants." They caused slowdowns at the Arsenal and the Trubochny plants, at the Laferme tobacco factory, at the Baltic plant, at the First Nevsky thread factory—it isn't possible to list them all. The "slowdowners" demonstrated in the city with demands that those arrested be set free; they disarmed the guards, taking away not only their rifles but also their cartridges. Red Cadets dispersed the crowd without using their weapons, but some shots came from the crowd and injured one cadet.

Just as in February 1917, there was open agitation against the government and, just as then, the same problems, including the absence of fuel and food, were blamed on the government, which was now the Bolsheviks; just as then, a motley crowd gathered in front of the barracks and army schools, testing the mood of those who had weapons; in the factories and plants spontaneous meetings were taking place, in the same way attempts flared up to disarm now this, now that guard, and if in February 1917 the Junkers were the pillars of support for the government, then this time the heroes of the day were the staunch and militant Red Cadets. Their appeals to the Petrograd workers were filled with threats of decisive action, and their statement that "yesterday we didn't fire a single shot, but tomorrow we may no longer distinguish the innocent from the guilty, the honest but misled toiler from the dishonest provocateur and scoundrel" resembled the appeasement efforts of a shaky government.

From word of mouth it was reliably reported that Zinoviev, who headed the recently formed Committee for the Defense of Petrograd, had moved it into the Peter-and-Paul Fortress. This measure corroborated reports that a revolt would break out in Petrograd any day now.

The Committee for the Defense immediately released the appeal "Beware of spies! Death to spies!" The newspapers explained: "It is a well-known fact that England, France, Poland and others have their spies in Petrograd... The Military Council proposes through the Commissions of Struggle against Counter-revolution to take immediate measures to uncover all espionage organizations and to arrest those who are spreading evil rumors and sowing panic and confusion."

The Bureau of the Petrograd Party Committee put on the day's agenda the specific question: "Measures to be taken tomorrow in connection with mutiny in the factories." The session was long and stormy and finished in total darkness, since the supply of electricity had run out. In accordance with the resolutions of the Bureau, Cheka troikas were formed in local districts, special mission units were re-established, and Party members were mobilized. A curfew was imposed for 11 p.m.; in any case walking in the street was unsafe since street lighting no longer existed. Theaters of an "unserious nature" were to be closed, and at "serious" theaters the start of performances was moved from seven to six in the evening.

The biggest icebreaker in the world, the *Yermak,* cut the city in two halves several times a day by breaking up the sled tracks across the Neva and the foot paths worn by citizens, mercilessly blowing smoke out through its two gigantic straight smokestacks in front of the few pedestrians roaming along the empty embankments. The bridges were raised for the entire night, which was normally never done in winter, and cadets in full fighting gear marched along the streets with songs and bands, inspiring courage and confidence in those who needed it and warning the enemy: "No tricks!" Wires from the field telephones snaked through the streets and gave the city the appearance of a battle front.

Petrograd remained gloomy and empty, armored cars loomed *as though forgotten* at the crossings of the main streets. The faces of the populace bore the stamp of exhaustion and confusion.

The desperate appeals of the Petrograd Soviet and the Provincial Party Committee to the working class who had come out in the street—"Back to work! Back to work!"—drowned in the united chorus of Socialist Revolutionaries, Mensheviks and mixed anti-government people calling for the Bolsheviks to be removed from power and thrown out of the Soviets. The proclamations of the Anarchists urged people to "overthrow the autocracy of the Communists."

Handbills also turned up with reminders of the Constituent Assembly: "We know who is afraid of the Constituent Assembly. They will not be allowed to rob and will have to answer before the people's representatives for their deceit, robbery, and all their other crimes. Down with the hateful Communists! Down with Soviet power! Long live the Constituent Assembly!" Here it was difficult to figure out who had a hand in it—maybe the Socialist Revolutionaries, maybe the Constitutional Democrats. But the hand of the deacon of the Luga cathedral was visible in the homemade posters put up all over Luga: "Rejoice and celebrate—soon the White liberators will come!"—the district Revolutionary Troika recognized that without difficulty. On the whole it was comparatively peaceful in the outlying Petrograd areas; the population was even getting used to the wandering bands of 20 to 30 deserters, the peasants established a roster for housing them—for the responsibility of receiving and then sending these armed and hungry gangs on their way. In the Rozhdestvensky and Gatchina precincts posters appeared: "Long live the Constituent Assembly!" but there were no notable peasant outbursts, unless you count the misunderstanding over the hay in the Smerdovsky precinct.

On February 24, martial law was imposed on the city, and a few days later a state of siege was declared.

The Petrograd Soviet passed a resolution to demobilize the army labor detachments and all citizens brought to the city as conscript labor, they all received two weeks' wages and a free ticket home. In this way part of the most dissatisfied and, therefore, the most explosive elements were removed from the city.

Unstable and unreliable troops, who were beginning to ferment, especially the navy units, were immediately sent out of Petrograd on three troop trains to the Caucasus and the Black Sea.

Cadets faithful to the Bolsheviks and special units stood guard at the buildings of the local Soviets and protected the Party Committees, telephone stations, railroad stations, bridges and major thoroughfares of the city. Patrols of cadets caught counter-revolutionaries and their accomplices and sent them to be dealt with by the merciless revolutionary troikas.

Holding meetings and the presence of outsiders were banned on the ships and in the institutions of the Baltic Fleet; those who were observed carrying out agitation were subject to arrest, and in case of resistance force was ordered.

The Petrograd Party organization was maximally mobilized to repulse the mutineers and to uphold order.

In Oranienbaum a requirement that the populace provide transport was imposed and carried out calmly and in an orderly fashion as more and more troops, equipment and ammunition were brought to the shore.

The railroad workers' behavior was beyond praise; however, they may have been afraid of mobilization.

It was typical that the "spontaneous" assemblies and meetings were attended exclusively by non-Party elements; it was precisely the non-Party people who claimed that the Communists were to be blamed for all the current difficulties, although at that point it was already easy to understand "for whose mill these wolves in sheep's clothing were bringing grist," as a historian would so cogently say later.

And again a thirst for "freedom" appeared on many lips.

When Igor Ivanovich first embarked on the *Sevastopol,* in the beginning of the summer of 1916, he hesitated to tread on her, to take his first step on her top deck, swabbed to the color of yellow amber, as smooth as a table top from bow to stern.

The sun, shining brightly, was blindingly reflected in the brass, chrome and bronze parts of various machinery, handrails, gangways, speaking tubes and portholes; all this metallic grandeur seemed to be newly cast and forged and the metal, shining like fire, seemed to be still hot.

Later on Igor Ivanovich began to notice that the closer freedom came, the more the bronze and chrome tarnished and the more the deck somehow gradually developed the dismal appearance of a provincial town's sidewalk. Igor Ivanovich was convinced that this dirt came to the ship not from the visiting delegations and agitators, not from the commissions and delegates who were constantly testing and shaping the mood of the battleship's crew, but that it crept out directly from the depths of the ship itself. This was inevitable, just as inevitable as the messy appearance of any broken or negligently maintained mechanism in which some pipe inevitably drips, dirty black lubricating oil oozes out of a broken packing, and a flange that's not turned all the way causes a leak.

Uncertainty and forced inactivity depressed and demoralized the men.

The strongest response caused by the unrest was felt by the crew in the hold and the stokers who were stationed at the battleship's 25 boilers; the most heard, the most unnoticed, they crawled upwards to forge freedom—noisy, implacable, harsh, vociferous. Looking at them, Igor Ivanovich thought that freedom or not, someone had to stay in the dank hold all the same, someone had to be roasted by the fire-breathing furnace and drink the tepid water from the teapot suspended on a string.

A fellow with a scalplock came to his mind, one of the "specters," painted and drawn all over with tattoos just like a gazebo in a city park; he was sitting surrounded by his mates from the No. 3 boiler in the sun by the stern funnel and singing softly, accompanying himself on a mandolin:

> In the midst of a rye field I was born
> to the slave of tyrant masters.
> Great woe lay in store
> for the child's innocent heart.

Igor Ivanovich noticed the long clever face of the stoker, his strapping figure and rather good ear, and his appearance somehow didn't go with the accusing-orphan words of the popular song.

Igor Ivanovich's observation, although fleeting, was correct, but how could he have known that the singer wasn't really born in a field of rye, but in a normal railroad worker's family and that he had inherited his fine ear for music from his mother, an illiterate woman who remembered many songs and refrains? On the other hand, Igor Ivanovich knew for certain that one square meter of the furnace-bar in the Yarrow boilers used on the battleship consumed 200 kilos of coal per hour, and consequently he always looked upon the stokers with sympathy.

As if overhearing Igor Ivanovich's thoughts about the orphan's song, the scalplock interrupted it in mid-word and started to play something piercingly tender, apparently improvising as he went along.

The thin vibrating sound of the mandolin, like a titmouse that had accidentally flown in under a shipyard roof, dashed above the deck between the structures towering in the sky, among the gun turrets and the enormous smoke stacks, supported on the outside by ribs.

The stoker, who was pursing his lips importantly, would nod his head without noticing anyone near him, and then bend his ear down as though he couldn't hear the strings, which sounded trusting and open under his claw, corroded by coal. And the thin, vulnerable sound filled one's heart with self-pity and longing for one's woman and child, for the forest, the field, for solid land where it befits a man to live instead of huddled together shut up in the stifling belly of a floating fortress.

On March 1, on Anchor Square—by then renamed Revolution Square—Igor Ivanovich and this man from the No. 3 boiler happened to stand next to each other.

March 1 turned out to be the noisiest day in the history of Kronstadt. On the square in front of the cathedral people were walking around alone and in groups—there were workers from the steamship wharf, the electrical plant and the shops, women and teenagers—almost ten thousand people had gathered, half the city and garrison.

In contrast to the majority of the units, both the officers and the crews of the *Petropavlovsk* and the *Sevastopol* came to the meeting organized in ranks with music but, true, without flags. The motley crowd near the rostrum yielded before the neat columns of sailors from the battleships. It was their precision and the perfect position they held that helped turn the meeting in the intended direction.

Company columns of the *Sevastopol's* crew re-formed, and the artillery and the stokers ended up side by side; Igor Ivanovich cast a glance at the scalplock and tried to place his face, but without the mandolin, without the tattoos covering his body, even his back, he couldn't recognize him and didn't especially try, having gotten used to the fact that the crew he met off ship all seemed quite familiar, but who they were and where they were from was hard, sometimes even impossible, to remember.

Comrade Kalinin, chairman of the All-Russian Central Executive Committee, mounted the rostrum. He had come to the square on a light sled over the ice of the gulf. He came without security guards and guides, straight from the door of the political division of the 187th Detached Rifle Brigade at Oranienbaum.

He had come to speak with the sailors and was greeted with applause. They were waiting to see which way he would turn, but when he started the same old Bolshevik song, they wouldn't let him talk. Petrichenko,* his coat unbuttoned, waved his sailor's hat and interrupted Kalinin, saying let's hear instead the delegates who went to Petrograd to find out the reasons for the unrest in the factories and plants. He gave the podium to the anarchist Shustov, a sailor on the *Petropavlovsk*. According to him, people in Petrograd were just waiting for an uprising at Kronstadt and had put all their hopes on it.

Using this, Petrichenko came up with a resolution: freedom for the leftist socialist parties and free elections of "new Soviets," and went as far as setting free those arrested for counter-revolutionary activities and removing the anti-profiteering detachments that combatted speculation and profiteering.

The battleship had the decisive word here, too.

Then Kalinin could stand it no longer and gave a sharp speech, warning that history wouldn't forget or forgive this shameful action, and that future generations would curse the sailors of Kronstadt. Further, he said that starting that very day the Petrograd Council of Labor and Defense would withdraw the anti-profiteer detachments from the entire province and would allow free deliveries of provisions to the city... But it was too late, they didn't believe him anymore.

The scalplock for some reason wiped his fingers on his pea jacket and unhurriedly, paying no attention to the fact that the crowd was roaring, stuck four fingers in his mouth, rolled his eyes as he got his fingers in place and gave out a sound as sharp as the whistle of a whip.

...The sturdy health that came from his mother and the staunch prejudices concerning education that came from his father had led the tall fellow with the scalplock to enlist in the navy and become a stoker at the No. 3 boiler of the battleship *Sevastopol*. This fellow from Sergiev Posad, near Moscow, which had only become a city in 1919, had imagined himself immediately chewing the ribbon of his sailor's cap and strolling through the streets and avenues of Petrograd as "the pride and beauty of the Revolution" in the firm hope that during the coming hungry years he could put the burden of his food and military clothing on the shoulders of

---

*A senior clerk on the battleship *Petropavlovsk*, who became a leading member of Kronstadt's Provisional Revolutionary Committee.

the Commissary. He'd been charmed by the tales about the Baltic Fleet and the romantic image of sailors in bell-bottoms who, with a slightly rolling and threatening walk, ply the fairways of world history. How could he have expected to find himself surrounded by boorish peasants dressed in shabby, second-hand navy uniforms. The endless conversations—in the stoker room, on the crew deck, and wherever crowds gathered—about land, forced requisitions, and the harsh new regime in no way corresponded with what the new recruit had expected to see and hear on the ships of the revolutionary Baltic Fleet. Therefore, when the unrest broke out, with endless meetings, resolutions and protests, the sailor with a scalplock seemed to wake up. He didn't miss a single noisy meeting and whistled amazingly loudly with four fingers.

On the orders of the battleship brigade staff one hundred men were sent daily to Petrograd to unload firewood and to clear the snow off the tracks near the Nikolaevsky railroad station. No volunteers could be found and the brigade HQ warned all commanders and commissars that if the order wasn't carried out, they would be "put to justice before a revolutionary tribunal," but the scalplock was not against going to town one more time and was even eager to do so. The colder the boilers on the *Sevastopol* grew and the worse the winter cold became, the brighter the flame of love for a barber's elder daughter grew in the stoker's heart.

After finishing his work at the railroad station he didn't hurry back to Oranienbaum with his mates, but after changing into a new uniform jacket, and decorating himself with a well-pressed ship's ensign, he set off to his fiancée's, looking slightly mysterious and excited. He always grabbed an armload of wood for them, and his pockets were usually bulging pleasantly with a pound or two of millet, consequently he felt confident in the house of his future father-in-law. He let drop a few words to suggest that he personally didn't wish to accept this life but would pretty soon take some decisive steps. To seem more important he asked the papa whether the battleships *Poltava* and *Gangut* from his brigade were still anchored in the Neva. The barber got confused and just twitched the bars of his mustache, but his clever wife, who always believed in the best, consoled her future son-in-law: "Where could they go before spring? They'll stay there, of course." And the fiancée laughed so that the sailor's heart raced, as it did when he saw her for the first time behind the enormous crystal-clear window of the barber's establishment. Stressing the fact that one half of the battleships were anchored off the city and the other half were under steam in Kronstadt, the future son-in-law let it be understood that this distribution of forces corresponded to some important design of his—the son-in-law's—own. Silence ensued.

The conversation got noticeably livelier when they started talking about the new life, how the city's population had dwindled, and how the conscripted workers only ate up the bread and started slowdowns.

With the impassiveness of a society person reporting news from the other hemisphere, Olga Alexeevna mentioned that a pound of bread cost only 370 rubles in September, but now was already at 1,515. And, actually, the subject was abstract, since the family was completely unable to pay that kind of money for bread. In March they were asking 2,625 rubles a pound, but this price, also, could feed only curiosity. The scalplock pointed out the significance of wages, but Pyotr Pavlovich, who knew how to count kopecks, made a few simple calculations, converting the pay rate of the proletarians in 1920, amounting to many thousands, to the value current in 1913, and then the current monthly wages seemed quite humble, somewhere between 16 and 21 kopecks a month.

Then the sailor declared that money was a holdover from the past, that it had already irretrievably lost its significance, and emphasized the cost-free distributions, and here it was impossible for Pyotr Pavlovich to come back with anything. Since 1920 food had been given out free for coupons, at the end of 1920 city transport, communal services and baths had also become free, and now they had even stopped charging rent. It might be War Communism, but it was still Communism.

Pyotr Pavlovich agreed and remarked reasonably that it was both correct and wise to assign the population to public dining rooms, in view of the habits of our fellow countrymen, because if they handed out the miserly rations all at once, then the comrades would eat it up all at once and might not go to work anyway, but this way, according to the Petrograd Commune, 600,000 people, almost the entire population of the city, were fed more or less regularly.

Nastya related that for the purpose of economizing on fuel the holidays would be extended, and since the 19th and the 22nd January were red-letter days on the calendar, a resolution would be passed proclaiming from January 19 to 22—the whole work week—a holiday.

As an active participant in the political activists' collective at the Sanitation and Hygiene Department, Nastya knew the holiday program planned for all five days. At this point she recalled that Comrade Agulyansky, secretary of the committee organizing the celebrations of the third anniversary of the February Revolution, was going to receive from the Council of Trade Unions one pair of shoes, four pairs of socks and twelve buttons, the buttons being in place of the coat and hat he had requested. Laughing, Nastya told how many signatures—and from whom!—Comrade Agulyansky had to collect and how at every point, in every office, the coat and hat underwent a miraculous transformation, at first combining into a winter overcoat, then dividing into a three-piece suit, the suit then shrank to a waistcoat, the waistcoat turned into a set of underwear, but the underwear wasn't available, and he had to accept twelve buttons.

The sailor was gazing admiringly at Nastya and could hear only her laughter and see her even white teeth and the curl which was bouncing and dancing by her ear. The future in-laws treated the scalplock attentively and seriously, having already seen how people who were earlier considered ignorant and insignificant had suddenly become part of "the vanguard." What could be said about this? Nothing. He was awfully impatient, the enamored stoker, and amused his fiancée with his earnestness: he wanted as quickly as possible to take the path outlined on many banners. Since he was a "nobody," he had lately been living with the exciting presentiment that he would become "everything." The Bolsheviks were a pretty good example. They had been "nobodies" and just look, one, two, three, and they were kings. They had given the orders, commissared the country, and enough, now let somebody else have a chance...

And now his soul was hovering above the seething crowd, intoxicated either with its own power or from a sense of impunity.

Commissar of the Baltic Fleet, Kuzmin, who had sensed the tense mood a day earlier, couldn't believe that it was going to turn into an uprising, and he tried to cough out a speech about the military traditions of Kronstadt, but he wasn't allowed to speak. "Have you forgotten how they shot every tenth man on the northern front?!" they shouted from the crowd. It was subsequently proven that Kuzmin hadn't participated in the "decimations," but he defended himself from this reproach in a peculiar way, screaming to the accusers that he had shot traitors to the cause of the working class and would do so again, and in his place another man would have shot every fifth man instead of every tenth.

Without thinking the scalplock screamed, "Down with him," and to make it more convincing he stuck his fingers, formed in a circle, in his mouth and produced a whistle as piercing as a needle. Igor Ivanovich, on the other hand, started thinking. He always felt ill at ease when people bragged about killing out of conviction. He saw how the tall thin Kuzmin in a long cavalry overcoat scorched the crowd with the gloomy stare of his deep-set eyes, how he sucked in his hollow cheeks, how he opened and closed his straight mouth, which seemed never to have known a smile, how he waved his sleeve with a very wide cuff: he saw all this but couldn't hear or understand a single word.

"Remember," shouted the fearless Kuzmin to the crowd of many thousands, "remember that you can talk about your needs, about what needs to be reformed, but reform doesn't mean starting an uprising! Remember that Kronstadt, with all its ships and artillery, no matter how formidable, is only a dot on the map of Soviet Russia!"

"You shot a lot of people—that's enough!" "Don't you threaten us, we've seen your kind!" "Away with him." "Down with him!"

All kinds of scum like the prison commandant were already shoving toward the rostrum with hysterical speeches against the Communists.

Igor Ivanovich was paying absolutely no attention to the scalplock from the No. 3 boiler who covered his frozen ears with his hands, grinned, shouted something, and whistled so that it rang in the ears of those standing near him. The place was swarming with people who were grinning, whistling and screaming...

Yes, here they should have gotten used to each other, or perhaps have become better acquainted before they were caught up in a common disaster, while their hearts were open—the scalplock's heart was wide open and Igor Ivanovich's open a crack, more open than at other moments in his short life; if they had only stepped on each other's feet, pushed each other, even inadvertently, looked each other in the eye and remembered... But there's nothing stupider than to suggest various paths along which history could have developed in the distant past, especially at a time when even its current path isn't influenced in any way even by a great many people who not only read but also write.

This is the time to point out that although the scalplock, as opposed to Igor Ivanovich, was both stately and tall, and his mustache, unlike the scanty beard of the ammunition custodian, was thick, there was nevertheless more similarity between them than might appear at first glance.

The similarity lay in the fact that the one with the mandolin didn't understand anything, although he thought that he understood everything and was filled to bursting with enthusiasm. And Igor Ivanovich simply didn't understand anything period, although he sensed with his semitechnical mind that behind the visible part of the events there was some mechanism hidden from him, the function of which he could neither calculate nor compute, and therefore he was, as always, far removed from stormy emotions.

Generally speaking, in the No. 3 boiler room complete clarity reigned as far as the future path of history under the leadership of the recently formed Kronstadt Revolutionary Committee, the "Revkom," which had chosen the *Sevastopol* as its base of operations because of its safety. Such nearness to power relieved the conscience of doubt and the heart of hesitation.

Kronstadt was curious about the situation on the *Gangut* and the *Poltava*, which were wintering in Petrograd, but on the battleships they were curious about Kronstadt. On March 1 two delegates left the *Poltava* for Kotlin; one didn't return, vanishing God knows where, and the other didn't notice the events that were rocking the island on that day because he was nursing a grudge in his heart: "Let their meetings be damned, they didn't even offer me a meal, the devils!"

The news that they were unable to learn from the offended delegate became known from the political agitators who had gone to Petrograd. Actually, there weren't all that many who went, maybe 200, so the fortress preserved its strength, all the more since none of the agitators returned. Special patrol units caught the sailors attempting to take thousands of handbills to Petrograd with the "resolution" of the mutinous fortress. The mutineers themselves demonstrated their democracy, their lack of fear of the ideologically defeated enemy and their total faith in the justice of their cause by publishing without comment in their own *Izvestiya* the text of the 20,000 handbills dropped onto the island from airplanes, guaranteeing life and amnesty to the rebels only on the condition of immediate and unconditional surrender.

Petrograd got ready in earnest for decisive events.

A circular from the Political Department required that all more or less "major misunderstandings occurring among the crew" should be reported to the security section of the Political Department.

For the most part the dispatches reported a lukewarm attitude toward Soviet power and a bad one toward the Bolshevik party. From the *Pobeditel* it was reported that: "Among the crew there is ferment because of the events, but it is not spilling over in either direction." So that the uncertain mood of the sailors would not swing to the other side, they took control of the guns on the ships wintering in Petrograd, furlough and shore leave were cancelled for the Communists, the Communists were given arms and on many ships martial law was declared. These decisions were received with nervousness on the vessel *Samoyed* and the destroyer *Kapitan Izylmetev.* On the destroyer *Ussuriets,* the minesweepers of the first division and the icebreaker *Avans,* these events were correctly interpreted. It was also quiet on the harbor ship *Vodolei II,* where the conversations, judging from the dispatches, mostly concerned the predominance of Jews in government institutions. An interesting slogan was devised on the dispatch-boat *Krechet*: "Long live only the power of the Soviets!" Everyone could understand that behind that short little word "only" stood the removal of the dictatorship of the proletariat and the leading role of the Communists, that is, the main points of the Kronstadt program.

The sailor Tan-Fabian, a participant in the famous meeting at Kronstadt on March 1, was especially active in the icebreaker-rescue detachment stationed in Petrograd. On icebreakers of the same type, the *Truvor* and the *Ogon*, he succeeded in having the "resolution" passed with the overwhelming support of the Communists even though on the *Ogon* three Communists voted against and four non-Party members abstained. As Ten-Fabian later admitted under interrogation, in order to put an end to any vacillation he told them that on March 10 the *Sevastopol* and *Petropavlovsk* would pound the Smolny with their main guns. The crews of the icebreaker *Avans* and the rescue ship *Erei* weren't impressed by this and they refused even to put the "resolution" to a vote.

It later came out that of the numerous crews on the Petrograd naval base, only the two icebreakers and one auxiliary ship accepted the "Kronstadt Resolution." It is true that after the successful repulsion of the first attack the Kronstadt mutineers were almost able to bring the crew of the *Yermak* over to their side in the hopes of breaking up the ice around the island and making the fortress inaccessible to infantry. The crew of the *Yermak* was removed, the boilers were extinguished, and a guard consisting of trusted Party members and sailors was posted on board.

On that same day, immediately after the victorious meeting, the war commissars were removed from command on the battleships.

The arrests began.

On the night of March 2 the telephone operator at the Kronstadt area communications center, a member of the mutinous Revolutionary Committee, called "comrade chairman," in the old way, and a deputy of Petrichenko, dispatched a telegram to all units and institutions: "Copy to all Kronstadt sentries... In Kronstadt at the present time the Communist Party has been removed from power and a Provisional Revolutionary Committee is in charge. Non-Party comrades! We ask you to take the government in your hands for the time being and watch the Communists and their activities closely, and check all conversations so that there are no conspiracies anywhere... Elected representative of the Kronstadt area command, Yakovenko." Subsequently Yakovenko became the commissar of the Revolutionary Committee attached to the Defense Staff of Kronstadt, where he supervised cooperation between the engineers and officers.

But the numerous attempts of the Revolutionary Committee to control the anarchists and criminals were not successful, the latter even offered armed resistance, and disorder kept breaking out in the fortress. All sorts of scum, waving slogans about freedom, more and more openly embarked upon the road of self-government and total anarchy.

The power that had been grasped with such ease only a few days earlier now started drop by drop to seep through the fingers of the Revolutionary Committee.

A note with the ironic title "On Communist Foundations" in the *Izvestiya* of the Kronstadt Revolutionary Committee reported: "Since the temporarily arrested Communists do not need footwear now, these have been removed from them in the number of 280 pairs and sent to be distributed to the detachments of troops defending the approaches to Kronstadt. The Communists have instead been issued bast sandals. This is how it should be."

Actually, in place of their removed boots, the prisoners were promised torn-up greatcoats so that they could sew "bast shoes" for themselves from the coats, but in fact they didn't get any coats. It was a good thing that one of them had galoshes so that they could take turns moving over the stone floors of the prison in these galoshes.

Of the 26,687 men of the non-commissioned and political personnel on the Kronstadt base there were 1,650 members and candidate members of the Party, plus 600 more persons in the civilian Party organization of Kronstadt. These are, of course, large figures, but only a handful had been members before 1917 and more than half was a mass of peasants who had joined the Party in September of 1920, during the "Party week," before which, during that same month, 27.6 percent had been purged from the military Party organization in Kronstadt. The new Party rank-and-file began to talk with resentment about the "higher-ups" and "lower-downs" in the Party. In order to stop the talking, POBALT* issued an order on December 11, 1920, to all the heads of political departments to immediately carry out simultaneous replacement of 25 percent of the commissars, moving them "down" and replacing them with people from among the Party collectives. This was called a "shake-up" of the command structure.

The day before these events, the head of the Navy Political Section, Batis, telegraphed to the center: "Especial dissatisfaction within the navy does not exist. The influence of Right Social Revolutionaries and Mensheviks is negligible."

In the meantime, resignations from the Party and the decline of Party discipline reached their highest level in January and February. Instances were observed in which sailors refused to speak to the political instructors and had the same answer for all questions: "What business is it of yours?" and that was it for the conversation. The Party membership cards of the sailors who were leaving the Party were brought to the political department not by the responsible secretaries, but by rank and file party members in bundles; no one was summoned to the Party Commission, and the political department didn't even ask questions about the situation in the

---

*The Political Department of the Baltic Fleet.

Party cells. The head of statistics barely had time to give daily summaries to POBALT. And what was altogether amazing was that all applications to leave the Party had the same reason given: "Because of religious convictions." Either grace had descended upon the naval base or the second coming of John of Kronstadt was directly observable from the battleships.

From the point of view of the contemporary development of progress and science, such an argument may appear as only a naive trick that could easily be seen through, but one only needs to look at the situation from a historical point of view for the picture to appear somewhat different.

The invented stories about the miracles performed by Father John Sergiev were so numerous and convincing that not only ignorant folk but also zealots of the faith were forced to recognize divine characteristics in the illustrious pastor, and Porfiriya Ivanovna Kiseleva, who had devoted herself body and soul to the glory of John and his followers, was exalted and honored as the Holy Mother of God. Despite the fact that after the death of John of Kronstadt in 1908 the Synod proclaimed that the teaching of John's followers was heresy and blasphemy, just remember how even many years after both wars members of his sect came to prostrate themselves at the basement window of the Scientific Land Improvement Institute, which was housed in the former John Sursky Convent, on Karpovka across from Textileworkers Street, formerly Charity Street; this is where the vault had been placed with the grave of the Kronstadt miracle worker who had been especially revered by the family of Emperor Alexander III.

At first the meeting hit the Bolsheviks, and terror and repression began. Active participants and accomplices in the mutiny seized the members of the Special Section* and the Revolutionary tribunal.

One hundred and fifty men were thrown into the hold of the *Petropavlovsk*, 60—on the *Sevastopol,* and 300 Party members were sent to the Kronstadt prison for interrogation.

The post-mutiny re-registration rolls of the Kronstadt organization of the Bolshevik Party showed that 135 persons had become involved in illegal activities and had carried out underground work. They were not able to break even those under interrogation; in one of the common cells the prisoners organized a prison newspaper which energetically explained the meaning of the events at Kronstadt. Despite the cruel threats and repressions, the Communists risked their lives to communicate with the deluded sailors, and later, already at the time of the assault, there were efforts to set up communications with the Party organization in the Seventh Army, which was advancing toward Kronstadt.

---

*A forerunner of the KGB in military units.

———

In response to the arrest of Communists in Kronstadt on March 5 the national newspaper *Izvestiya* reported the taking of hostages in Petrograd—adult family members of the generals and officers who had actively participated in the rebellion—and other suspicious persons already under arrest were declared hostages.

On March 2, under cover of night, many active Party workers, led by the commissar of the Kronstadt fortress Comrade Gromov as well as the entire Party School, consisting of 100 men with rifles, machine guns and ammunition, decided to leave the fortress. They left in an orderly manner, prepared to fight. Near the Second Artillery Division they saw drivers harnessing horses to drive off somewhere. A decision was made immediately: the machine guns and ammunition were loaded, and all 165 men left through the Citadel Gate and headed for Oranienbaum across the ice.

Incidentally, the mass shootings in Oranienbaum that the rebels would have liked and that they reported in their paper *Izvestiya* didn't take place. For example, in the First Navy Air Division, which had voted in favor of the Kronstadt Resolution, only 115 men were arrested—about half of the personnel—but only five of them, with the division commander Kolesov at their head, were executed in strict adherence to the sentence of the Revolutionary Tribunal, and 110 men soon returned to their unit and later even fought well in the Seventh Army, pounding the mutineers from the air.

The faltering Communists who remained in the fortress formed a "Provisional Bureau of the Kronstadt Communist Party Organization," which issued a declaration supporting the mutineers' "Revolutionary Committee" and all its measures.

The last to be thrown into prison for interrogation were the sailors from the tug *Tosno*, which was breaking the ice around the battleships. Both dreadnoughts were docked together, getting in each other's way when firing, and the seawall in turn got in their way. But the vessels couldn't be pulled out onto the open roadstead; the tug broke the ice, but the ice broke its propellers, and when the main shaft of its engine broke, the Revolutionary Committee deemed this entire demonstration to be pure sabotage, and threw the sailors in prison, but the battleships remained idle.

In order not to lose face in the eyes of the country and hoping for support, the mutineers explained by radio to the proletarians of all countries that they weren't commanded by White officers and that they weren't in communication with foreign powers. But after just a few days the "proletarians of all countries" could see how General Kozlovsky* was gaining more and more power and the lack of reserve provisions in the fortress compelled them to start negotiations with the Americans about possible deliveries. The American Red Cross depots in Finland had 3.6 million pounds of flour, tens of thousands of pounds of dried milk, fat, sugar, dried vegetables and more than 5,000 pounds of powdered eggs. Only Finland, treasuring her independence, refused major involvement, and about 14,000 pounds of food arrived on the island. Two days before the suppression of the mutiny the Kronstadt soldiers, sailors, and workers with top priorities received a quarter pound of bread or a half pound of rusks each, and one can of meat per every four men; instead of bread and rusks, the rest of the population received one pound of oats per day.

On March 7, after the last warning of the government had been rejected, the fort Krasnaya Gorka, just recently pacified by the guns of the *Petropavlovsk, Andrei Pervozvanny* and the cruiser *Oleg,* opened fire on the mutineers.

The artillery barrage of Kronstadt was practically without consequences, since the firing was rather "general" in the absence of maps of the city and the forts, although such maps were available at the army headquarters.

The *Sevastopol* fired in reply.

As to who should open fire, this was decided more or less by itself; the exemplary state of the artillery magazine in the No. 2 turret of the First Artillery division, that is, the main battery, was well known. Windows were broken in the buildings near the harbor from the deafening reports, upsetting the residents and persuading them of the rightfulness of the cause and the invincibility of the fortress.

Igor Ivanovich was convinced that the opening of fire, the main work of a battleship, always began precisely in his section in the lower shell magazine. Therefore, after the announcement of battle alarm when everybody was running to battle stations to test the mechanisms, shouting in turn, "Ready to fire" to the turret commander, Igor Ivanovich was always the last to give his report, not allowing even a second's pause that could cause a reproach for delay in reporting.

Those who have served in the army know the value of those details that seem negligible from the civilian point of view—like bell bottoms that are just a little too tight or too wide, a pea jacket that is a little short or maybe

---

*General A. N. Kozlovsky was a former Tsarist general who was the military specialist in charge of artillery at the Kronstadt Fortress. He would play a major role in the rebellion and, as the only former White General at Kronstadt, was useful for Bolshevik propaganda.

longish, or the razor sharp edge of a sailor's hat. In these expressions of one's personal will, initiative and taste, strictly limited by regulations and the commander's eye, flickers the personality thirsting for its separate, special fate, unlike that of any other, after having become a number in a military unit, reduced to the common denominator through oath, regulation and uniform. But what are mere pea jackets and sailors' hats? There are people who have won for themselves the right to have their own voice in military reports and who in time have become legendary in the regiments, batteries and ships. Igor Ivanovich was already on his way to becoming a legend; he was almost permitted an intonation that wasn't quite according to regulation, but was his own when giving his report on the state of the battle readiness of the ammunition store. From the azimuth gunlayer to the No. 1 gun crew (on ships the turret gun crew, on land the emplacement gun crew) they reported: "Ready to fire." Only Igor Ivanovich invariably reported, either over the communications system and heard by the whole turret, or on the telephone directly to the commander: "The shell magazines are ready *to open fire*." After firing or practice, the turret commander as a rule remarked to Dikshtein in a friendly way, in public, "You, Dikshtein, like to hold long conversations when reporting. What is that again—'to open fi-i-ire.' That's a whole speech, you know." Igor Ivanovich smiled slightly and said smartly, "No excuse, sir." But if the next time he were to dare to report according to regulations, "Ready to fire," he would certainly distress both his commander and the entire turret; these long speeches from the magazine were sort of the specialty of the No. 2 turret, its distinctive coloration, its signature and even its talisman. Once while firing during an inspection by representatives from fleet headquarters, Igor Ivanovich reported the regulation way so as not to let down his superiors. And on that day the No. 2 turret performed worse than the rest: they misfired three times in a row, the galvanic circuit failed, the galvanic primers had to be replaced by percussion primers, in a word—it couldn't have been worse. And every last man in the turret was convinced that all this was because Igor Ivanovich's non-regulation rooster's crow hadn't been heard before the firing and for this reason no one gave the galvanizers and gun crew any trouble, or scolded or cursed at them, but instead they were all cold to Igor Ivanovich for a week because they thought that he'd simply lost his nerve.

In reality, Igor Ivanovich's duty consisted of making sure that not a single shell under his supervision, either outwardly or in fact, differed from the ideal one which existed in the instructions and in the imagination of the ordnance authorities, and which had no distinctive marks and peculiarities such as nicks, scratches, or specks, either in the metal or in the paint. But, nevertheless, Igor Ivanovich could, as part of his job, not only separate and distinguish among shells of the same type, but he even gave names to some of them, which, it's true, weren't notable for their variety: Piglet, Little Boar, Baby Hog, Porky, and so forth, a fact that he never admitted to anyone.

The path of the shell that Igor Ivanovich could see was short: grasped by a ratchet wheel mechanism, it rocked for an instant in a metal claw, the hulking, half-ton thing, almost as big as a man, was placed on a cart to be brought by the feeder to the ammunition wagons, which were situated at the conveyor tube. Igor Ivanovich could not see the ammunition wagon, but he mentally followed the shell to the loading section and from there directly to the turret on the loading chute in front of the yawning breech of the gun.

When they were firing single salvos with only one gun and there was little work down below, as he heard the roar, Igor Ivanovich allowed himself to be carried along the given angle of elevation along with the shell toward its approximate, or precise, goal. With a full charge a shell of the main battery would remain in flight up to 80 seconds, that is, more than a minute, and during these long moments Igor Ivanovich could see in his mind's eye both the tiny scratches known only to him on the heated body of the projectile, and simultaneously from the height of 200 or 300 meters (depending on the angle of elevation) he could survey the sea, shore, clouds, ground, all that the shell itself would see if it had eyes and the ability to admire its flight.

Now that the No. 2 turret was firing from all three guns, because it was impossible to fire from the No. 3 and No. 4 turrets, Igor Ivanovich didn't even have a second to make his aerial excursions, even though the way to Krasnaya Gorka was both short and familiar. Instead of soaring above the bay in his imagination he was drenched in sweat in the lower artillery hold.

When darkness set in both sides ceased firing.

On the night of the 8th, during a snowstorm, the forces of the Red Cadets attempted to attack the fortress from across the ice. Two battalions of the special forces regiment were even able to get into the city chiefly thanks to stealth and surprise, but they were swept out by the insurgents, and the destructive canister fire from the forts prevented the reserves from approaching. Many cadets lay dead on the ice, and under the ice, and in the city.

Many attribute the failure of the first attempt to take the fortress by storm to insufficient political preparation of the attack, as if the cadets, with their rifles ready and carrying Lemon fragmentation grenades, were going to a political debate. The "debate" was preceded by two days of artillery preparation.

Trotsky, who had arrived in Petrograd at the beginning of the mutiny, impatiently demanded that they attack, convinced that the mutineers would "show the white flag" as soon as fire was opened on the fortress. On March 7 the Northern group of troops fired 2,435 shells on the fortress and forts, but even the additional 2,724 shells fired on March 8 failed to convince anyone. There were just a few six-inch shells—only 85—the rest were all three-inch ones... Aerial reconnaissance showed that the shells had landed short and it wasn't possible to see any destruction, either in the city or on the ships.

The artillery worked quite ineffectively in conditions of bad visibility, and merely disclosed the intentions of the command and in effect warned the mutineers of possible attack.

Of course, the political work couldn't be considered ideal but why count on the morale and political constancy of the troops when the rein-forcements, which arrived the day before to that same 501st Rogozhsky Regiment, were completely untrained, and when immediately before the attack they had to be taught basic handling of the rifles and how to fire?

The command had a rather dim concept of the strength and weakness of the opposing side, and, for that matter, of their own army; in fact, besides the battalions of Red Cadets, ready to fight selflessly and to the death, there were unreliable regiments; for instance the 561st of the 187th Brigade, consisting, almost to a man, of demoralized elements, captured Denikin* troops and former Makhno** men. The tribunal of the Petrograd military district had warned beforehand about the weak fighting ability of the regiment. And so it happened that at the beginning of the operation the Second Battalion refused to enter the attack. The Communist element tried, of course, to convince the fighters and some-how they succeeded in making them go out onto the ice of the Finnish Gulf. A wide sector of the attack was assigned to the regiment: the num-bered batteries in the south, Fort Milyutin, and the strike on Kronstadt from the south. But communication between the battalions was practi-cally non-existent, so that the Third Battalion went in the direction of the No. 1 and No. 2 Southern Batteries by itself. To ensure better control of the unreliable mass of soldiers, the battalion was led over the ice in a col-umn, and only when they were shot at from the forts did they spread out

---

* General Denikin was a leader of the White Army during the Civil War.
** Nestor Makhno was a Ukrainian rebel leader who professed anarchy.

in a chain. They waited for the Second Company, lagging far behind, then they went to the left of the batteries to Fort Milyutin, where red flags waved to them. Forty paces from the fort they saw the machine guns the mutineers had put out, and heard the proposal to surrender. Everyone surrendered except the commissar of the battalion and four Red Army soldiers who decided to turn back, and on their way they forced back the Seventh Company, which was also on its way to surrender.

There were instances of refusing to enter the attack from among the cadet units as well.

In his account of the situation in the Northern battle sector, Commissar Uglanov reported the mood of disaster and hopelessness to the Petrograd District Committee as well as the fact that vacillation continued even on the morning of March 8—the day of the attack. Consequently, at first only the Communists and the more courageous of the non-Party comrades entered the attack.

The personal leadership and encouragement of the attackers by high-ranking Party workers and the most prominent military officers helped persuade the cadets to attack.

They occupied the No. 7 Fort, the one nearest Lisy Nos, but were soon forced to leave it because of the loss of morale resulting from the concentration of twelve-inch artillery fire on the No. 7 Fort from the other forts and the ships. The No. 7 Fort was by this time disarmed, and there was no way to return the fire.

Uglanov reported honestly to Trotsky, Lashevich and Avrov that it wasn't "feasible to rally the troops and attack the forts a second time."

If there was no order in the regiment of special forces, where two hours were wasted in composing inspired appeals, causing them to break the schedule for going out on the ice instead of efficiently carrying out the battle orders, then what could be expected from that Third United Battalion of the 12th Rifle Reserve Regiment which had refused outright to attack on the night of March 7? Instead of carrying out the order amicably, the Red Army soldiers started to chant: "Give us food, bread, and overcoats!" It turned out that they hadn't gotten dinner on March 6 and had remained hungry the whole next day. Then the regimental commissar's assistant gave a firm promise to deliver some food by the morning of March 8. Exactly one half of the soldiers had no overcoats. In the end, after prolonged discussion and much persuasion, the battalion went on the attack.

Food arrived only on March 9.

In Martyshkino the brigade school of the Junior Commanding Staff (93rd Rifle Brigades, 11th Division) didn't follow orders. When these

cadets arrived at the battle zone of the 95th Regiment and the commander appeared, the Red Army soldiers started to shout: "Why were we
forced to come here?" The command "Attention!" did not pacify them. It
was necessary to resort to punitive measures and to remove the most conspicuously disobedient Red Army men. Only after these measures and
extensive Party educational work among the masses was the cadet school
brought to order. And as early as the second offensive against Kronstadt,
many Red soldiers fought heroically and received battle decorations.

The work of the Revolutionary Military Tribunals had a great educational influence on the Red Army soldiers. The Tribunals reacted energetically to all unhealthy phenomena. They gave the malicious troublemakers
and provocateurs what they deserved. The sentences quickly became
known to the masses of the Red Army soldiers. The most important sentences were printed as leaflets. The political workers would gather the Red
Army soldiers, read the sentences aloud and analyze them on the spot,
explaining that the tribunals divided the offenders into the malicious, the
misled and the just plain stupid. The Red Army soldiers usually approved
of the punishments imposed by the Tribunal.

When the women found out that wounded Red Army soldiers had
been left on the ice after the first attack, they implored the Revolutionary
Troika to give them a chance to remove the wounded from near the walls
of Kronstadt; the continuous artillery fire didn't stop them...

The only "trophy" of the first assault was Vershinin, who was captured
on the ice; he was a member of the Kronstadt "Revolutionary Committee"
and a *Sevastopol* sailor from the draft of 1916.

The tragic fighting on March 8 was reported neither in the central
press nor in the Petrograd newspapers; only on March 9 did the presidium
of the Tenth Congress of the Russian Communist Party (Bolsheviks) consider it appropriate and necessary to give relevant explanations to the
members of the congress. They learned of the real situation only from
Trotsky, who arrived in Moscow on March 10.

"The partridges are biting back," joked the Kronstadt defenders, drunk
with their own success. They had in mind Zinoviev's appeal as chairman
of the Petrograd Committee for Defense, in which he promised to shoot
all the Kronstadt rebels "like partridges."

Tired from his hard work Igor Ivanovich was in no hurry to rejoice and
even avoided the gratitude of the Revolutionary Committee. He remembered well that at the end of 1919, when it seemed even to him that Lenin
had no chance of holding out, events suddenly reversed themselves com-

pletely. And now Igor Ivanovich adjusted his thoughts about the future of the incomprehensible, inexplicable, but completely real power of the Bolsheviks, which seemed to come from nowhere. But even though the Geisler fire control system can take into account the movement of the target during the trajectory of the projectile, the movement of the hull in the sea, the wind and temperature, and therefore, also the density of the air at different elevations, and allows the exact prediction of the result, this adjustment for the inexplicable deprived Igor Ivanovich of any confidence whatsoever in the final results of his own remote calculations.

When the former battleship commander Vilken arrived on the *Sevastopol* from Finland (historians have proven that he was an English spy) and started to reward the lower ranks with silver rubles, like Suvorov after Izmail, Igor Ivanovich didn't emerge from his hole under the turret, pleading the need to perform pressing tasks after the recent firing. He sent all the sailors up to the deck and stayed there alone, and, putting away the ammunition and arms supply journals, did nothing.

The personnel was lined up. Vilken walked around the formation and at the tactful suggestions of the senior artillery officer and the company commanders, he shook hands with those who were to be rewarded and handed them a ruble. The scalplock from the No. 3 boiler hadn't been proposed for a reward by anyone, since the power of the battleship had at that time been supplied only by the No. 1 and No. 4 boilers. But the scalplock's dashing and bold look appealed to Vilken and he placed a heavy silver coin in the stoker's grimy hand.

To complete the picture let us note that at this very time Vasya Shaldo, recruited from the Petrograd Criminal Investigation Department, was hanging around the military harbor, after leaving the horse thieves of Petrograd to the mercy of fate, and was busy pinpointing the exact mooring places of the battleships. The *Sevastopol* was held fast by the stern to the pier at Ust-Rogatka, but the hull of the *Petropavlovsk* had been moved forward. Vasya estimated possible angles of bombardment.

Igor Ivanovich sat staring at the rivets, round as the caps of young mushrooms, supporting the storage racks; his internal gaze didn't encompass the events which had shaken Kotlin Island and the forts nearby, nor did it extend to Petrograd, but even within the confines of his own ship there were enough reasons for doubt and uncertainty.

The nature of these doubts could be explained by the fact that Igor Ivanovich constantly found similarities between the methods and means employed by the opposing sides. It was precisely in this spirit that events continued to develop up until the very last day.

The Bolsheviks and Communists remaining on the battleship after March 3 hadn't yet been completely deprived of their freedom of movement, unlike the arrested commissar of the ship, Comrade Turka, and they immediately decided to blow up the battleship. Through channels known only to himself, Igor Ivanovich had found out that the hold specialists Arkady Maidanov, Pavel Yanochkin, Ivan Osokin and Andrei Turo were busily making preparations for this. They wanted to place blasting charges in his area of command as well, because they had reasonably decided that it would be easiest to destroy the battleship through the magazine of the main battery. Igor Ivanovich began to convince the comrades that it would really be better to scuttle the battleship by opening the Kingston valves after moving it out to deeper water, because if it exploded by the seawall, then an enormous number of people would certainly suffer, and as an example he told them about the explosion of the battleship *Empress Maria* on the roadways outside Sevastopol. For example, it was practically impossible to calculate where the turret would fly and on whom it would fall, but it was certain that it would indeed fly a long distance. These arguments seemed suspicious to Maidanov, in fact Igor Ivanovich himself with his obstinate lack of political feeling seemed suspicious, and so the specialists from the hold set off in search of more trustworthy allies for their cause.

On the 17th, in the daytime, when the fortress was thundering, repulsing the second assault, the idea of blowing up the *Sevastopol* surfaced once again, but this time to prevent the Bolsheviks from getting it. Now the officers took charge of it. The mine officer Bylin-Kolosovsky also decided to place blasting charges in the model magazine of the No. 2 turret for the additional reason that while the battleship was shaking from its firing on the attackers, many mechanical failures in the No. 2 turret suddenly cropped up: first the galvanic circuit went out, and as soon as it was repaired, the rotating mechanism of the turret got stuck, then the 30-horsepower motor of the azimuth layer burned out and it was necessary to use the combined strength of ten men to turn the turret at the speed of a tortoise, then something got stuck in the hoist—in a word, the shells were not brought up and hardly anything was fired.

The trouble in the artillery area on the day of the second attack was worse than ever. In the fifth, seventh and ninth anti-mine platoons, one gun after the next went out of commission, naturally not without help from the gunner of the tenth regiment, Stepan Alexeev. During the second attack the crew in the hold was ordered to list seven degrees to be able to fire more effectively on Trotsky, who was approaching across the ice, but for some reason the seven degrees, already entered in the automatic control system, couldn't be achieved precisely, instead they got either more or less.

The senior artillery commander, Gaitsuk himself, together with the senior mechanic Kozlov, dashed up to check the listing.

Everyone remembers that Gaitsuk came to a bad end.

After setting up his seven degrees and with his last words cursing at the hold specialists, he flew up to the bridge of the conning tower to his six-meter range finder to direct the fire. Which is where someone from the navy picked him off with a rifle; the bridge with the range-finder was open on all sides.

The first shot hit him in the leg, which was like a warning, but in spite of his wound Gaitsuk didn't leave the bridge but continued to command, convinced that both his fate and that of Russia were being decided precisely where the *Sevastopol's* shells were bursting. Nevertheless he was then killed by a second shot. The bullet hit him in the mouth. Artillerist Mazurov took over the command. Hiding in the armored cocoon of the conning tower, leaving only the range finder operator and galvanizers on the bridge, he kept firing until evening, until 6 p.m., that is, until the fortress command became convinced that it wasn't possible to combat the attack with artillery alone but that they must arm the crews with rifles and lead the sailors out onto the ice.

Igor Ivanovich saw and heard, but mainly felt, that almost every command, almost every order and disposition, either wasn't carried out at all or was carried out somewhat ambiguously. Then there was the arrest of the battleship commissar, Turka. But what kind of arrest was it if no sooner than Commander Karpinsky had given the order to go ashore than Comrade Turka, who was under arrest, ran up to the top deck and explained to the command what to do and where to go, and along with the other agitators, detained the sailors on the ship and created a split among the crew. And by 10 p.m. Comrade Turka himself had already organized two detachments to defeat the rebels, occupy the city and establish order.

The action of the second detachment under the command of Comrade Petrov was particularly successful. Turka, who remained on the ship, regularly received reports: they had been shot at by someone on the seawall, they had managed to reach Lenin Prospect, they were under machine-gun fire near Engineers' Bridge, they had occupied the People's House where the Revolutionary Committee was located and disarmed the guards consisting of workers and militia posted by the Revolutionary Committee. At 11:30 p.m. provisional power had already been established and a proclamation to this effect was issued.

To complete the description of the events it is necessary to go back in time to three and a half hours earlier on board the *Sevastopol*, where, for unknown reasons, a fire had broken out in the third furnace hold. The commissar, Comrade Turka, at once undertook decisive measures, the first of which was to set free the arrested senior mechanic, Kozlov, to direct the men in extinguishing the fire. The crewmen in the hold distinguished themselves by their energetic work and put out the fire which didn't last more than half an hour.

Igor Ivanovich's education enabled him to discern the striking similarity between the events of the 9th of Thermidor, 1794, in Paris and the events of early March in Kronstadt. In the conspiracy against the Jacobins, as Igor Ivanovich recalled more or less clearly, both the right and the left joined forces. He forgot Collot d'Herbois but remembered Billaud-Varenne, both of whom, as we know, represented the Jacobins on the left; Danton's supporters from the right, the Girondists, Chaumette's supporters and the Hébertists united with them, and it is worth noting that this whole motley coalition was supported by those without party affiliation, that is the *Marais*, the swamp. In the same way the Socialist Revolutionaries and the Mensheviks (right), the Constitutional Democrats (Kadets) and Maximalists (left), the Monarchists (extreme right) and the anarchists (extreme left) appeared in the role of non-affiliated participants in the Kronstadt events. The former had united in order to overturn the dictatorship of the Jacobins, and the latter in order to overthrow the dictatorship of the Communists.

On the day following the 9th of Thermidor, those to the right took the upper hand and started to liquidate the Revolution. Something similar also began at Kronstadt when it became clear that the Revolutionary Committee (left) would play the role of screen for and appendage to the Defense Headquarters (right).

However, there is no point in regretting that Igor Ivanovich didn't think of comparing these two events; the Thermidoreans were, after all, completely successful in suppressing the Jacobins, and their coalition turned out to be indestructible. And even an illusory faith in victory of the mutineers might have taken Igor Ivanovich far, far away, first to Finland, and then even further.

The scalplocked sailor from the No. 3 boiler-room, who had twice listened to lectures by starving historians in the non-commissioned officers' ward-room, might, in principle, have been able to draw a parallel if he had remembered the names of the parties or even their political orientation. But during both the first and the second lectures on the history of the

Great French Revolution he was thinking more about the elegant simplicity of the guillotine. Being basically not a malicious man, he thought of
how lucky Nicholas II and his family had been, since they were, after all,
shot and not decapitated. He was amazed at the barbarity of the French
when he heard that the invention of the tender-hearted Dr. Guillotin was
even to this day performing medieval executions.

These brief details from the history of the staggering events during the
French Revolution aren't offered here so that the reading public should
recognize the author as an attentive reader of old journals. These digres-
sions are necessary in order to explain why the battleship *Petropavlovsk*
was renamed *Marat* after the March events. The renaming of the *Sevastopol*
to the *Paris Commune* doesn't require any explanation, since the storm-
ing of the mutinous fortress took place, as everybody knows, during the
fiftieth anniversary of the Paris Commune. According to the newspaper,
the Kronstadt Revolutionary Committee refused to commemorate this
bicentennial anniversary. The suppression of the mutiny occurred on
March 18 precisely, and therefore it was reasonable and edifying to name
the subjugated battleship precisely the *Paris Commune* and nothing else.
    But in reality, historical analogies illuminate little in the life around us,
but serve for the most part to entertain *beauties thirsting for enlightenment* and bear witness not so much to the education of the historian as to
his ability to look impressive; for simple mortals historical analogies are
nothing more than a consolation, as if to say, well, we're not the first it's
happened to... In order not to assume the entire responsibility for what
has been said, I would like to quote that most objective idealist, Georg
Wilhelm Friedrich Hegel, who could find something reasonable in literally everything. So, even he, after having studied all of history to the end,
sadly turned the last page and wrote: "Experience and history teach us
that peoples and governments have never learned anything from history
and have not acted in accordance with the precepts which might have
been derived from history." And this disturbing situation can be explained
by the fact that if one so desires, one can always without difficulty find
some kind of reason or circumstance which supposedly prevents people in
present-day conditions from benefiting from an intelligent example or a
good lesson from history.

Since the time when Joshua son of Nun stormed the proud towers of
Jericho, which had stood immovable for ages beside the entrance to Canaan,
it has been well known that only those weak in spirit rely on the strength
of walls.

Since those biblical times it has been understood that an irregular army going into battle under the command of twelve sheiks from different tribes is just an unstable mass, subject to anarchistic moods, and does not represent a real military force in any way.

Both three thousand years ago and today only a regular army under the command of a single leader has a chance of victory, one can find countless examples in history of how the authority of an army leader became the source of strength uniting a nation.

Among those who were entrenched at Kronstadt there wasn't and couldn't have been a leader able to halt the sun in the sky, and darkness was the only armor capable of protecting the soldiers ready to walk across the unstable ice fields to attack the forts, to attack the inaccessible fortress.

However, an unprecedented attack on the naval fortress by infantry from the ice had also been undertaken by the Swedish general, Maidel, in January of 1705. They launched the attack in a freezing cold snowstorm but lost their way in the storm and weren't able to find their Rychert, Rissert, Retusari, or as it was called on German maps, Ketlingen, otherwise who knows how much more blood would have fertilized the ground on the uninhabited gloomy island named Kotlin.

The first admiral in the history of Russia, Fyodor Matveevich Apraksin, launched an attack from the ice with much greater success. For six days, also in the middle of March, he led a siege corps of 13,000 men across the ice from Kronstadt to Vyborg covering 130 kilometers, blockaded and took the fortress, magnificent for those times, thereby adding "with God's help" this strip to the marshy Izhorsk lands "of our forefathers and fathers," given away at one time by the feeble Mikhail Romanov* "in my name and that of my descendants," a very important border area...

But what sense is there in picking the bones of history if you can't find the answer to the simplest question there: why is it that a fantastic fate is given to certain people or, for example, certain towns, and not to others?

...March 16 and 17 were decisive for the fate of the mutineers.

The morning of the 16th was clear and sunny. The snow on the ground was getting soggy and was dissolving in the calm and sunny warm weather. The air had a spring fragrance, it was light, saturated with ozone and it seemed that if you were to breathe deeply and hold your breath, you could rise off the ground and almost hover without touching the snow with your feet.

---

*Young Mikhail Romanov was named tsar in 1613. His descendants ruled until 1917.

In such weather it's impossible to believe that the boundless sky enveloping the earth is empty and dead, and to a religious man it seems quite possible that if your eyes were sharper and if you only knew where to look, you'd see the gates to the heavenly kingdom, the angels, and the apostle with the keys.

At the very edge of the sparkling white plain, hatched with the even lines of the forts set into the ice, Kotlin stood out, ghostly and unreal, with the steep domes of the Naval Cathedral, the factory smokestacks, the harbor cranes, the barracks and the ships' masts.

Both the sky and the vast snow fields surrounding the forts and the fortress were clean and deserted.

The attack started from the sky.

The airplanes, clumsy and rattling, which had until now been harmlessly dumping leaflets on Kotlin, started bombing the ships and the harbor on March 16.

The bombing raids on the fortress and the ships were mostly of a demonstrative character inasmuch as a bomb weighing less than a ton couldn't inflict noticeable harm on the besieged.

From overhead the nearest railroad stations, packed with troop trains, were clearly visible.

Oranienbaum, Old Peterhof, New Peterhof, Ligovo and Martyshkino were filled with constantly arriving forces, equipment and artillery.

Five armored trains and mobile armored detachments were waiting under cover, and they had already assumed their battle positions with the muzzles of their weapons pointing to the sea.

Regiments and battalions were occupying their starting positions. The narrow streets of Oranienbaum were crowded with columns of soldiers moving in different directions; people were cursing at each other not at all as if they would have to go shoulder to shoulder toward death in a few hours.

They were readying and delivering the assault gear to the shore—to those places selected for the entrance of the troops onto the ice: they collected poles, boards and wooden ladders for crossing cracks and open water.

There was no more room for the newly arriving troops to squeeze onto the narrow strip of shore; the 81st brigade arriving at Gatchina was prevented from disembarking and was soon turned back altogether and dispatched to the lower Volga to put down mutinous bands there.

Just as the airplanes constantly circling above the ships and the island couldn't see the Lower Volga, they also couldn't see the faces of the soldiers, exhausted from chronic lack of food, nor could they see their tattered uniforms, nor their ruined, completely useless footwear. Also not visible from above was the fact that the soldiers, unable to remember the time when they had last received their full food rations, to their own surprise received two pounds of bread each with a hot meal and fat, and as a result of the confusion and commotion in moving from one station to the next, they contrived to receive their daily ration two or three times.

Twenty-five airplanes, defying the unorganized shooting, which splattered the smooth whitish-blue sky with buds of explosions, sprayed the ships and piers with their machine guns and dropped 300 bombs. One fell right on the deck of the *Petropavlovsk.*

At two o'clock in the afternoon the artillery started roaring at the mutineers as though intoning a prayer for the dead.

Kronstadt struck back fiercely. It seemed that the entire island shook from each salvo of the battleships.

Toward evening it got warmer and the hollow, double rumble of 300 gun barrels, which all day had shaken both sky and earth, gradually started to quiet down as though drowning in the fog that came floating in over the ice.

The ice was steaming and light whitish puffs of smoke were rising to the cool bright sky.

The fog was lying low and from the command point on the south shore the tops of the forts and the helmet-shaped dome of the Kronstadt Naval Cathedral could be seen, sticking out like islands in the unstable, sleepily swirling shroud.

The spacious premises prepared for receiving the wounded in the largest buildings on both shores of the gulf were still standing empty.

Institutions for children in the zone where the front was had been evacuated and the hospital at Razliv station had been moved to underground premises.

The commander of the Western front, a man of firm character who had celebrated his twenty-eighth birthday exactly two months earlier, squinted with his left eye and examined through his brass spyglass the forts, the fortress and the fires burning where shells had hit their targets. The spyglass had been given to him in 1919 after the capture of Omsk, as a gift from the Bolshevik astronomer Pavel Karlovich Shternberg, who had taught a course in astronomy at Moscow University. Now personally commanding the newly reformed Seventh Army and with all the armed forces in the Petrograd district and the Baltic Fleet under his command "in all respects," the commander of the Western front held in his hands all the strings of military action against the mutineers.

The army commander was indignant: they were shooting badly, the effectiveness of the firing was lower than all expectations, although the entire artillery was gathered into one concentrated force on the narrow strip of land between Martyshkino and Malaya Izhora. For six hours running, five heavy divisions and the sections E, S, and M from the special-purpose heavy artillery divisions of the main reserve, supported by 100 medium caliber guns, had fruitlessly hammered Kronstadt, spending half of the ammunition reserves available in the batteries, and the ammunition reserves were enormous. The fortress replied forcefully and accurately.

In Petrograd windows rattled.

Toward night the sky became overcast with high, fast-moving clouds, which in spite of the absence of wind, were flying in from somewhere beyond the edge of the sky either in order to provide majestic but simple decorations—or to conceal from the tender spring stars the bloody tragedy which was getting ready to be played out.

At midnight the infantry regiments began to descend on the ice which was eroding and groaning beneath their feet.

The rescue station was blazing like a luxurious bonfire. It had been lit by the well-aimed fire of the mutineers. The places indicated with markers where the 237th Minsk Regiment and the 235th Nevel Regiment of the famous 27th Omsk Division were to go onto the ice were brightly lit by the high flames of the dry wood burning in a hot, crackling fire... Changing the decamouflaged zone was now impossible due to the congestion of troops and the just completed redistribution of the 80th Brigade. Exactly at 4:15, 15 minutes later than the time specified in the battle order, both regiments started to descend onto the ice.

The living, fluttering bristle of bayonets over the backs of the soldiers reflected the red flashes of the station burning down and seemed to be already stained with blood.

The ice exuded a tomb-like cold and it was horrible to step on it with the water squishing under the snow, but there was no way of postponing it: on the 12th, the day of St. Vasily "the Dripper," a spring storm had blown through, sprinkling the ice with the first light rain, and ahead was the day of St. Alexei "the Warm," when the ice would already be melting away.

They went onto the ice in columns, taking a risk both in regard to the enemy and in regard to the unreliable state of the ice, but since the command was uncertain of the mood of the soldiers, they had figured that a fighting man feels calmer in a column than in a line, and it is also easier to direct and maneuver a column than a line.

In the *Red Chronicles* it is written that "never in all the years of the Civil War was the Red Army soldier as well outfitted and as well fed as at the battle of Kronstadt." This is correct as far as food and clothing are concerned, but they weren't really successful in solving the problem of footgear. Some of the Red soldiers were marching on the wet ice and snow in swollen felt boots; there were even fighting men in bast shoes. On the other hand, each Red soldier had 100-150 rounds of ammunition this time, as opposed to the three or four clips of cartridges and a few fragmentation grenades they each had at the time of the first attack.

One third of the delegates to the Tenth Congress of the Bolshevik Party, meeting in Moscow during these same days, left the session for Petrograd to take part in putting down the mutiny.

The wavering elements in the Kronstadt mutiny carried within their motley mass little certainty, clarity or structure.

They were opposed by a comparatively small but monolithic and invincible organization. The staunchest and most inflexible fighters, the flower of the Party, its vanguard and leaders, secretaries of the Central Committee and the Central Control Committee, members of the Revolutionary War Committee, secretaries of the district committees, chairmen of the executive committees, commanders and commissars of divisions and regiments, journalists and writers all went down onto the ice on the Finnish Gulf as rank and file soldiers, having become the bearers of a united and inflexible will.

This extreme, unbelievable and desperate measure could only be understood by those who realized the full danger of a petty bourgeois counter-revolution in a country where the proletariat constituted a minority.

The fate of the Revolution was being decided on the soft melting ice surrounding the smallish low-lying island, blocking the entrance to the shallow gulf.

Swallowed up in the darkness of night, the columns went farther and farther out from the shore. The 300 delegates to the Party Congress walked along with the ranks of the fighters, indistinguishable from them, inspiring decisiveness and firmness in the advancing army by their example of personal bravery and the spirit of self-sacrifice.

The bluish-white spokes of light passing through the high clouds by search lights on the ships and in the fortress came down and searched over the icy surface of the gulf like the hands of a blind person, seeking victims for their as yet silent cannons and machine guns.

In the hushed fortress they were expecting an attack.

Behind the clouds the blindingly icy eye of the moon was sliding, moving against the wind; the thick impenetrable sky in the confusion of flying clouds was impassive and silent.

The leading ranks of the columns were crunching on the new ice formed on top of melted snow, and behind them the only noise was the champing sound of hundreds of feet in the liquid, mushy snow.

Behind each column stretched telephone cables, not a single one of which would survive, nor would the telephone operators who were sent to locate the breaks and to re-establish contact.

The infantry fell on the ice, cut down by the dull beam of the search light, but it had hardly moved to the side before the fighters got up without a command and walked on in their soaked, white camouflage cloaks, which stuck to their legs, dissolving into the fog at a distance of 600 paces.

It would have been possible to avoid falling in the wet snow, it would have been possible to avoid falling in the water that had oozed through to the top of the ice, if they had only known that the search lights couldn't illuminate anything further away than 200-300 paces from the defenders of the fortress, because the blinding beam, shining blue like the steel of a good blade, struck the fog like a solid wall.

It was only on the morning of the attack that the forces in Fort No. 6 to the north and No. 2 to the south discovered the attackers practically beneath their walls.

Surviving witnesses would tell of the *profound impression* made by the rumble of the guns, the roar of the explosions, the piles of torn-up wet ice, the stones that fell from the sky after being ripped from the bottom of the shallow water by the exploding heavy shells; they would tell how their mouths went dry and their ears kept ringing for a long time from the searing whine of the lighter shells hitting the ice and ricocheting away in search of bloody victims...

The ice shuddered and broke, forming stretches of open water and ice holes.

The columns turned into lines, and nothing could hold back any longer the furious onslaught of the infantry soldiers who knew that if they survived at all it would only be there, on the island.

Neither the fortress walls, nor the barbed wire with electrical current, nor the land mines throwing the attackers up in the air along with the ice, nor the all-destructive fire of the 12-inch guns, capable of shattering dreadnoughts and cities, could hold back the foot soldiers in their bloody cloaks and black faces, deaf from the crash of gun fire and rifle shots, as they walked with fixed bayonets right into hell.

At first only a few were wounded; after the ordnance explosions, they went down under the ice along with the living and the killed. The aerial bursts of the exploding "shimoza" shells struck them on the head and laid out those killed in almost perfect concentric circles. Encountering machine gun fire, the troops began to suffer casualties—both killed and wounded.

At ten in the morning the fighting was rumbling throughout the harbor and streets of Kronstadt.

The enemy, chased into the stone casements, couldn't be reached, the majority of the hand grenades didn't explode, the artillery, confused because there weren't enough signal flares of the right colors, started to hit forts which had already been taken; the attackers quickly retreated with their losses, only to start all over again three hours later.

With a swift attack the Mints Regiment drove off the enemy and seized Fort Pavel. In spite of heavy machine-gun fire, especially on the right flank from the walls of Kabotazhny Harbor, the Nevel troops cut through the wire entanglements by the water's edge and while suffering losses, seized the city ramparts, burst into the city and engaged in protracted fighting on Citadel and Saidash Streets. The Mints troops rushed along Alexandrov Street and Northern Boulevard...

By the time the number of killed and wounded in both regiments included 90 percent of the officers, control of the fighting was basically lost.

The wounded regiments began to retreat in their bloody cloaks.

What was left of the Brigade School was thrown in to close the right flank of the departing Nevel troops.

The School fought splendidly and was wiped out completely.

The retreating soldiers were met by horse sleds with provisions, ammunition and empty sleds for the wounded; the horses were concealed in enormous covers sewn from army sheets with the indelible stamps of hospitals, clinics, and regimental storehouses on them. They appeared to be dressed up to participate in some kind of carnival.

They managed to gather together the survivors from the Nevel and Mints Regiments who had reached the south shore; and they were formed into two incomplete battalions near the smoking ruins of the rescue station and transferred to the operative reserve of the Southern Group's Commander. Three hours later, not yet recovered, nor having had time to understand where they were, they were once again thrown into battle to save the broken United Division from being routed by pressure from the counterattacking mutineers pushing them toward the Petrograd Harbor.

The echo of artillery thunder rolled between the walls of the houses, and fires were blazing; the buildings, cleared of rebels, as if coming back to life, hit the attackers in the back with a dagger of machine-gun fire, and the surviving foot soldiers turned around once again to storm a broken-down house with gaping holes on all sides.

The situation of the units which had burst into the city was unstable. The commanders saw that the units were melting away due to loss of men, and could not attack successfully, let alone keep what they had taken.

The machine-guns were of enormous service to the attackers, especially in the street fighting, and the same can be said about the machine-guns of their opponents, which inflicted huge losses on the attackers. The mutineers had easily established positions on balconies which were convenient for enfilade fire on the streets. It was hard for the attackers to eliminate such firing points without field artillery. When he subsequently gave a theoretical interpretation of practical experience, the commander of the Seventh Army pointed, with reason, to the artillery and armored forces as the principal means for putting down mutinies in cities.

But here the street battles were still being run badly, the troops were dispersed into small groups, which in the absence of junior officers were practically on their own; such groups were easily destroyed. Scattered around the unfamiliar city, the Red Army soldiers grabbed their holsters whenever they caught sight of an officer: "Hey, Commander, command us!" The troops suffered great losses because of the muddle, the mix-up of the units and, most importantly, the impossibility of establishing command. The casualties among the command officers exceeded 50 percent, in certain units they reached as high as 90 percent.

Under pressure from the counterattacking mutineers, units of the United Division started to stream back toward the Petrograd dock in disorder and it was here that the leader of the United Division, Comrade Dybenko, stumbled onto a platoon from the Fifth Company of students from the United Higher Military School of the Western Front; they were reserves and had arrived on orders of unknown origin. Each of the soldiers at once received orders to fight his way from the pier into the city and assume command of the groups of Red Army soldiers who had been left without commanding officers. After this lucky development the division chief himself went up to every soldier who looked like an officer and asked whether he was from the Military School...

Before telephone communication was broken off, command headquarters had ordered everyone to act energetically and to hold on to the occupied places no matter what, regardless of losses. There was no one who could re-establish contact, due to injuries, there were no telephone operators, and any reserves had already been thrown onto the wobbly ice, which shook under the feet of the attackers.

Mutineers in automobiles were moving the units of sailors with machine-guns who had mowed down the groups breaking into the city.

Remains of the debilitated units stretched toward the southern shore near Martyshkino and the Kronstadt colony.

By five in the afternoon the mutineers had pushed back the attackers from the city, but the latter held on to the fortifications in the harbors and nestled close to the edge of the ice.

The commander of the United Division, the main attacking force of the Southern Group, reported to the higher command his lack of confidence in success and raised the possibility of abandoning the city. The command immediately threw into the fire two regiments of the 79th Brigade that had been gathered into incomplete battalions, and with Battle Order No. 541 they recalled the division commander, Comrade Dybenko, and the military commissar, Comrade Voroshilov, for rest in Oranienburg. It proved to be impossible to carry out this order since the division staff headquarters was located directly in the firing zone, nearly surrounded by a large organized group of mutineers. Comrade Voroshilov ran out from the staff headquarters and, in the thick of the whistling of bullets, he personally gathered up soldiers and organized the defense...

This was the hour of desperation and maximum application of force from both sides. And again, just like the Prince's troops had come from behind the Raven's Rock on Lake Peipus* and the Zasechny regiment at the field of Kulikovo,** to the aid of the infantry that had been dislodged from the fortress across the ice came the cavalry from Martyshkino to slash and hack with their saber blades the sailors who were drunk with the specter of victory.

The strength of the attackers was exhausted, there was nobody who could take prisoners, occupy the battleships that had announced their surrender and take over the schools of mines and machinery, there were no forces left even to pursue the fleeing mutineers.

At the end of the day on March 17 after finding out that their "leaders" had gone to Finland, the mutineers started giving themselves up.

By this time there were fewer victors than defeated on the island.

---

*   Peipus, the Estonian name for Lake Chud, where Alexander Nevsky battled in 1242.
** The Battle of Kulikovo took place in 1380 between Dmitri Donskoi and Mamai.

After the battleships had announced by radio that they were ready to lay down their arms, a painful, incomprehensible period began on board the *Sevastopol*, the time of the first and second watch from midnight until morning. In the city fighting was still rumbling, Fort Rif was resisting desperately—covering the escape of the "leaders" who had promised real freedom, real soviets, amnesty, demobilization and regular rations, but the gray giants, the icebound dreadnoughts, seemed to be asleep, indifferent and abandoned.

Those who felt guilty set out for Finland, others, on the threshold of a new fate, took a bath and put on clean underwear if they had it, and some even tried to clean the deck which hadn't been washed for ten days.

It is striking that many, not only those who remained but even those who had fled to Finland, regarded the entire event as personal, a family affair, a quarrel among relatives; even the ringleader of the mutiny, Stepan Petrichenko, repented and returned to Soviet Russia in the mid-twenties after a short stay in Czechoslovakia.

The following morning at eleven, the cadets, worn out from the attack, started to climb the admiral's ladder at the stern boarding area, passing by the port holes of the commander's lounge on board the *Sevastopol*.

All the guards at the cabins with the arrested officers were replaced by cadets, the cadets posted guards at the conning-tower, on the bridge, in the companion-way, by the main engine and at the shut and locked turrets of the main battery.

"What heroes!" the Navy men said with a swagger, trying to retain their self-respect as they encountered the cadets.

"The heroes stayed on the ice and are lying by the forts." The victors were reserved and stern.

Pitiful, guilty, hungry, just yesterday intoxicated with the flattering epithets "pride and beauty of the Revolution," and "hope of freedom," but today called bell-bottoms, Georgie, or Ivan-Navy, the sailors tried to engage the cadets in conversation, but the latter hadn't recovered yet from the horror of the night's attack: they hadn't gotten over the death of their comrades and didn't have any idea which of their friends had survived and which hadn't, and they didn't feel like talking. It was strange to see soldiers' greatcoats on board a battleship, on the deck and by the gangways beside the sleepy and apathetic sailors, who were hanging around waiting for their fate, having suddenly become passengers on their own ship. If these same people as recently as two weeks ago, marching in straight columns on Revolution Square, had seemed like a monolithic, invincible force, then now they were like chaotically discarded parts of a machine which no longer existed, each part still continued its senseless spinning only from inertia, still continued to move inside the space defined by the armored hull of the ship.

Soon after lunch a transport unit of 20 scraggy peasant horses, harnessed to sleds, pulled up on the ice not far from the stern. They had been mobilized on orders of the rear staff commander of the Southern group, Comrade Shtykgold. A commanding officer in a pointed cloth helmet and wearing felt boots with galoshes broke away from the Red Army men accompanying the transport unit. The officer ordered the guard by the stairway to summon a certain Raspopov. Raspopov came up from the depths of the ship rather quickly. The officer took ten steps toward the hull through the snow, mashed down by the thaw, and shouted to Raspopov a request to let him have 50 or so men to work on the ice.

Right by the fourth turret they started to line up the first men they saw.

"Give me some artillery men! Let them look at their work!" shouted the officer, watching Raspopov's efforts.

Security men made out lists of those who were drawn up in formation, and the detachment went down on the ice.

In a column four men wide, accompanied by a convoy riding beside them on sleds, the sailors moved in a large arc toward the Petrograd Gate.

The heavy navy shoes soaked through after a hundred paces, and the sleds' runners left ruts behind them which quickly swelled with water. The horses were slipping and the whole train moved slowly. The sailors, stepping in the water, looked with envy at the sleds, each one with a driver and a soldier with a rifle, and continued to slosh through the loose, wet snow.

At first they walked around several enormous black ice holes; in the first hole the sailors saw a camouflage cloak turning around slowly with the sleeves sticking out—it had lost its owner and now seemed to be looking at him in the impenetrable darkness beneath the ice. In some places the planks and wooden ladders with which the attackers had advanced over wide cracks and open stretches of water had been left lying. In the iceholes broken ice floated, colored here and there with dark brown spots— hay from a sled that had gone down under the ice, bits of wreckage, trash...

In the snowy soup, trampled by a thousand feet, lay guns, clothes— greatcoats, some jackets, torn and bloody camouflage cloaks—then, more planks, newspapers, bandoliers, and machine-gun ammunition belts with unspent cartridges. Here and there you could see people calmly collecting and stacking arms in one place, but even with the arrival of the sailors and cart drivers on this enormous snowy expanse stretching from the barbed wire entanglements by the shore to the forts which were hanging ghost-like in the unstable damp air, there were fewer living than dead.

North of the Petrograd Gate, just at the assault line of the 32nd Brigade of the 11th Division, the chief of the convoy gave orders to halt.

"Your assignment," without any preliminaries said the man in charge who wore a Budyonny* cap, "is to collect our comrades who have laid down their lives in the fight against the hydra of counter-revolution! Bring them over to the sleds—that is your assignment. The weapons of the fallen fighters aren't your assignment. Any man who takes a gun in his hand will be shot by the convoy without warning."

When they began to fan out over the ice, one of the sailors saw a rifle under his feet and picked it up. Immediately a shot rang out. The sailor didn't even understand that it was aimed at him but had missed. He stood there holding by its sling a rifle with the bayonet knocked to the side from hitting the ice and looked without comprehension at the soldier who had shot at him. The latter cocked his gun and was about to shoot again, but hesitated.

"To hell with it! He'll shoot from fright!" shouted one of the prisoners.

The sailor spat emphatically and tossed the rifle to the side.

During the two attacks so many people had been killed that it was impossible to bury each in a separate grave. In the streets of Kronstadt alone 500 corpses were picked up. In the fortress workshop axes and hammers were banging all day, putting together common coffins two meters wide.

The sailors divided into twos, since it wasn't feasible to pick up and drag the bodies alone.

Igor Ivanovich and the scalplocked sailor from the No. 3 boiler didn't work as a team and didn't even notice each other, like everyone else, they just did their gloomy work silently, as if alone. Silence was the thing most suited to this work, even the convoy drivers spoke to each other in an undertone.

The snow and ice, just like brittle, weak paper, still preserved a record of the recent events.

Here is a man lying alone, holding in his outstretched hand a cap with the cotton plume torn off by a stray bullet.

---

* Budyonny cap, named for the Civil War hero Semyon Budyonny.

And these were felled by a successful machine-gun blast, four of them cut down as by a scythe, but with one difference—one tried to crawl and did manage to crawl a little way, but the others died where they fell.

Here a well-aimed canister shot had come bashing down and over here a mine had apparently broken through the ice and carried a few soldiers with it since the edges of the five-meter-wide hole was so generously smeared with reddish brown.

Near the wire entanglements, which were almost at the edge of the shore, there were especially many dead: they lay not only in the snow but also on stakes, in the hammocks of barbed wire, on the rocks and behind the rocks...

Those who were now floundering through the heavy wet snow, stacking on the sleds corpses, frozen in the last movement of their life, unbending, swelling from each other, those whose only concern now was to load as many as possible on each sled (there were only a few sleds and so many to be taken away), only a few hours ago during the first and second watch, when the battleship was out of the battle and captured, these men had been hanging around the decks, languishing in the crew's quarters and on watch, incessantly and, for the most part, separately constructing a strong hold of their personal innocence or smallest possible guilt, in anticipation of the necessity of soon having to answer questions—not the howl of a hundred mouths, but each one separately and for himself.

Never do people, not even the most dissimilar ones, seem so like one another as in that moment when they separate themselves from everybody, from the whole world, and become absorbed in their thoughts, in erecting in their imagination a fortress of their righteousness or well-being. Here all laws governing human destiny recede, losing their force and right, and only Charity, Justice and Luck come forward together, helping each other. For the human soul is made like this: when hope doesn't find any support or help from anything anywhere, when the ultimate disaster, too terrible even to mention either aloud or to yourself, is approaching, depriving you of will and strength, then the soul's last resort remains faith in miracles. The price of miracles had fallen drastically on the public market, and therefore, each person was thinking of a miracle just for himself, as though afraid that there might not be enough of this rare grace for everyone.

Igor Ivanovich Dikshtein wasn't counting on a miracle and since he knew for certain that the mutinous crew wouldn't be left on the battleship, he had purposely dressed a little warmer, stuffed the most necessary things in his pockets and put on the sturdy boots which had been awaiting their moment.

After the work on the ice was finished, the officer in the pointed helmet started rushing around the higher command asking what to do with his men. The owners of the emaciated little horses, who had worked with all their might, staggering and slipping through the whole long March day until dark, were also complaining. Finally, the commanding officer succeeded in scheduling his men for interrogation out of order as it were, by tempting the higher-ups with the possibility of quickly sending this command off to the shore at Martyshkino, where the horses had been mobilized for transport duty. The commanding officer was concerned for his totally exhausted soldiers, thinking it was one thing to trudge in a convoy for ten kilometers on the ice along with the arrested men but another thing to ride beside them in the sleds.

Igor Ivanovich answered the questions clearly and without fuss: "I didn't leave my battle station because I could be of use to the Revolution there. Yes, the turret was firing. Only they hadn't removed the Radutovsky base fuse from the safety catch, they hadn't set it at the first or second delay. Therefore there was no damage at all from such firing. Who can confirm it? The entire turret." He said this confidently, knowing that he was throwing a life preserver to the entire turret.

The final question seemed strange. "Do you have any money? Show it!" He showed it. They quickly searched him, ordered him to pick up the money and—"Next."

It was the scalplock's turn. When they heard that he was from the No. 3 boiler-room they looked at each other and their first and last question was, "Do you have any money? Show it!" He showed it. Among the bills and coins glittered the heavy silver disk of Vilken's ruble.

They took the ruble, and—"Next!"

And no more questions, although the scalplocked sailor had, like everyone else, as it happens, prepared a story which it would have been interesting to hear, namely that if it hadn't been for him... However, they wouldn't listen...

The sailors, who had gotten frozen during the day on the ice, had barely warmed up during the brief interrogation, when once more they were slopping through the soft snow accompanied by guards on sleds. It would have been shorter to go straight, to Oranienbaum, but they turned left to Martyshkino, evidently according to instructions.

They arrived in Martyshkino in the middle of the night. They were led to a tall wooden barn not far from the station and handed over to the local commandant or perhaps some sort of Army command— actually no one cared about this for the moment. The barn was solid and dry with a plank floor, the walls, rafters and floor were covered with flour frost—there had apparently been bran here, and possibly some kind of fodder, but now the premises were empty and retained only the dry, satisfying smell of flour. At first it seemed downright warm in there but that was only after being outside; after half an hour it was obvious that the temperature in the barn hardly differed from outside.

Those who still had some strength left took off their shoes and boots, squeezed out their footcloths, rubbed their frozen feet, cursing to warm themselves up. The pea jackets, damp from the day's work, had stiffened in the wind into a crust on the walk from Kronstadt and didn't give any warmth. The men lay down in the corners, along the walls, and beside each other, overcome with exhaustion, hunger and cold.

Someone, invisible in the dark, announced loudly:

"Mates, we mustn't sleep, no one will be able to straighten out in the morning, we will all freeze to death! If you go to sleep, it's curtains! Mates, hold out until morning... we've endured worse."

It was hard to imagine where this invisible man got his strength, his common sense and his capacity to think for his mates. He walked around, chatted, swore, kicked those who had lain down on the floor... After lazily grumbling at him a bit, each man understood that if he did go to sleep he might not wake up, but for some reason it seemed to each man that this wouldn't happen to him.

Then he suddenly got an idea and started to sing: "The snowstorm was howling, the rain was roaring..." Those who understood what the singing was for, that it would help break the sleep of death, started to join in.

The guard pricked up his ears: singing in the middle of the night was suspicious. From the slanting roof of the barn the heavy layer of snow that had partially melted during the day came flying down with a rustling sound and hit the ground with a soft thud. At that moment a shot rang out: the guard had fired from fright. The singing stopped, the shot had awakened even those who were dozing.

The sentry came running, waving his Mauser, and five more cadets with rifles accompanied him.

The guard wasn't about to mention the snow but said they had been singing.

"They should've sung earlier," mused the sentry, who left one more cadet as guard, had a cigarette, and left.

At about five in the morning light started to filter in through the cracks of the barn door.

The song leader who had quieted down was the first to awaken. Cursing softly, he started to shake the sleeping men. Those he was able to wake up recognized him as the commander of the fourth platoon, a member of the ship's Revolutionary Committee. He seemed to feel that he was in command here, too, and hadn't given up his responsibilities. There were two who didn't wake up, they had gone to sleep forever, having in their imagination warmed themselves with that last warmth which comes to a man who is freezing to death.

The scalplock sat hugging his knees with his hands stuck into the sleeves of his short pea jacket.

It was so cold in the barn that it seemed you'd get warmer if you went outside in the snow.

Cold penetrated his entire body. Actually there didn't seem to be a body any longer, all that remained was a light suspension of frost in which everything was dissolved, he couldn't feel himself anymore, he couldn't remember anything, nor think, nor wait. All night and half the day he wavered between dream and reality, for a second or sometimes for several minutes sinking into oblivion, then again waking up from an icy burn. The pain in his feet had changed into a dull, nagging heaviness, he could no longer pull his hands apart, and only the sharp pain in his heart, as though a sharp piece of ice had fallen under his pea jacket and wouldn't melt, made him feel life in himself. As soon as the heart let go, he had no other sensation, and he slipped away somewhere as though there was nothing in him but frozen air. He didn't even know for sure whether he was lying, sitting, or suspended.

In the morning they had still tried to cause trouble; those who still had some strength left knocked on the door, demanding bread and tobacco, but now it had become quiet in the barn as though everyone in there had died.

Beyond the walls the life of the victors was bubbling. Singing "Yermak," a company of cadets marched by, sled runners crunched, drivers shouted, orders and laughter could be heard, people called to each other asking what had happened to their friends and chance acquaintances. From the station not far away you could hear steam whistles and the clanking of buffers when trains moved.

They started to call out names. People somehow straightened themselves up and dragged themselves toward the exit where a convoy was waiting.

When they called out the second group of five men, they called for a Semidenko or perhaps a Semirenko six times.

"He's asleep," said the song leader.

"Wake him up!"ordered the cadet from the door.

"Wake him up yourself. There he is," said the song leader, pointing.

The cadet left the rifle outside the door and walked into the barn. He went up to this Semirenko or Semidenko who was lying on the floor, grabbed him by the jacket and tugged. He lifted from the floor a body which retained the shape of a curled-up sleeping man. He let go and the head hit the wooden floor with a soft thud. Then he grabbed the song leader by the shoulder and pushed him toward the door. He didn't resist.

At the end of the day they were given frozen bread and warm water. The food aroused hope that no more names would be called, and for half an hour the scalplocked sailor felt as if he could see the light of freedom, but then he once again dissolved in frost.

In the morning the door opened and five names were called.

He could clearly hear his name, his last, first and middle names. These words, these three words were pronounced, it seemed to him, louder than the rest, louder than last night's shot. He shuddered and made a movement as though to stand up. His body would not move. He once again strained to overcome this icy weightlessness, tried to make that incomprehensible mental effort thanks to which it is sometimes possible to break off a bad dream, wake up and turn over on the other side, punch the pillow and plunge into a new dream world. His last name sounded again and again. With his awakening consciousness he understood that this was the last thing that would be demanded of him and he even got frightened that he wouldn't be able to obey this last command; he pressed himself, his breath failed. The icy air was insurmountably solid. He once again tried to get up, he wanted to cry out for them to wait for him, but only moved his head with his mouth half-open under his frost-covered mustache.

"Aha," said the cadet by the entrance and walked into the barn without letting the rifle out of his hand, looked around, saw the good boots on Igor Ivanovich Dikshtein's feet and pulled him toward the exit.

The rest of his life, those last hours which he was granted because of some unknown delay, Igor Ivanovich Dikshtein lived in an inconceivable, never before experienced, enormous and feverish awareness of life. His consciousness, deprived of time to make his usual thorough deliberations, could simultaneously encompass both what had happened, what he had seen and what he had experienced. And all at once he came to the final conclusion, the final reality, that he would never again return to what had happened, to what he had experienced and to what he had seen around him.

The man who had taken a liking to Igor Ivanovich's boots disappeared. They were led around from place to place for a long time, first joined up with someone, then again separated, were kept once more in some barn half filled with logs, and finally given over to new people, to a new guard...

The first thought, which at once forced Igor Ivanovich's consciousness to wake up and work at maximum effort as soon as the soldier's hand grabbed him by the shoulder, was—why?.. how do they know?.. who?.. The answer came instantly, just as the receipt pops out of a National cash register when the cashier turns the handle and the machine answers with a cheerful ringing.

The journal! The journal... The journal!!! He could see the journal of the turret section, the journal kept in ideal order, perhaps exemplary, not only for the brigade of battleships but also for the entire fleet,... the journal in which he, Igor Ivanovich Dikshtein himself, with his own hand, feeling that familiar sensation of satisfaction with a job well done, had for two entire weeks been writing his own sentence and had sealed it with his signature.

He at once dismissed the journal from his mind because he couldn't live stuck on something irreparable. But his life, over which he slid in a feverish mental glance, seemed a long series of fatal, irreparable mistakes... Everything had been a mistake—the fact that he hadn't gone over to the *Poltava,* that he hadn't let himself be arrested by those who were preparing to blow up the battleship, it also seemed to have been a mistake not to go to Finland as Kolosovsky had suggested, but the biggest mistake suddenly turned out to be his joining the navy and even his technical education, in consequence of which he had got the job with the ammunition. Whatever detail cropped up in his memory, it immediately acquired the aspect of a terrible and irreparable mistake. But worst of all was the realization that his whole life—all of it, as it turned out—had been given to Igor Ivanovich so that he could take just one step to the side, just one step, and none of *this* would have happened...

He walked along the icy road in the last group of the condemned, while around him the many-voiced, populous life of the victors bubbled and boiled from success. The houses, the columns of soldiers, the trees in the park, Kronstadt, which briefly appeared on the horizon—he saw and perceived all this as something both familiar and alien: *there* everything went its course, there was no room *there* either for his presence, or his participation. He walked like a man who was finally leaving a foreign city, a foreign planet where all was habitual, familiar to the tiniest detail, but senseless and alien. He had to leave, go back to himself, somewhere to the forgotten places that had been effaced from his memory, but that he knew about... He tried to see, to remember this distant forgotten place, but the cold kept him from it. His body seemed to have become hard, rigid, impenetrable from the cold... The convoys at first ordered them to put their hands behind their backs, but later they didn't pay attention when the sailors, hunched over from cold and sadness, stuck their hands in the sleeves of the pea jackets and under their arm pits.

Igor Ivanovich slipped. In a second he pulled out his hands which were stuck in his sleeves, by habit he grabbed his glasses that were about to fly off with one hand, the other he flapped in a funny way, trying to hold on to the damp spring air in order to remain standing on the earth that was slipping away from under his feet.

"Watch out, you'll break your glasses," one of the escorts walking beside him said with concern.

These were the last human words spoken directly to Igor Ivanovich in this world; he didn't reply.

The escorts fenced off Igor Ivanovich from all the rest of life with their rifles, the fixed bayonets pointing downwards, they separated him from the whole earth, from the enormous, bottomless blueness of the sky edged with gold near the cold sun, from life, united and moving according to rules and laws which hadn't been revealed to him. This incomprehensible life was now speeding away into its endless springs and winters, by itself now, without Igor Ivanovich.

...Three bullets entered the soft body of the mutinous non-commissioned officer together; one went through his arm, one lodged in his stomach and only the third stopped the beating of his heart, which was trembling and thirsting for a miracle, thirsting for the impossible. Igor Ivanovich felt no pain and fell into the snow, already dead.

Properly speaking, Soviet power had no claims on Igor Ivanovich Dikshtein, and the scalplocked sailor who had walked to the Arkhangelsk area in the spring was now riding in a train, amazing the summer passengers with the variety of blue pictures on his badly emaciated body; unfortunately the pictures didn't look their best—as if they were drawn on crumpled sheets of paper. He was going not to Petrograd, not to Anastasia Petrovna—Nastya—his still unwedded wife, but instead, to be on the safe side, to his mother in Moscow, where she had moved from Sergiev after the death of his father. She had sold the house and settled on Shabolovka Street and had been able to find a job nearby at a factory where they made official government paper (Goznak); at the time, this was considered to be a stroke of luck. Nastya was also sent for and she arrived with Valentina, who was born on one of the first days of July.

Nastya reasoned soberly: during the Revolution many people took new names, both first and last names. Now when the whole world around them was being renamed, when Tsarevokokshaisk, for instance, became Krasnokokshaisk, and Nevsky Prospect in Petrograd became October 25th Prospect, when they had abolished internal passports—that "rotten remnant of the police regime, an instrument for control and persecution," many citizens, even some in their Kolomenskaya district, had decided to begin a new life under a new sign. She mentioned numerous examples—four just from the agitation collective "The Red Kettle" at the city Department of Sanitation and Hygiene, where right up to Valentina's birth Nastya had been performing with her younger sister, pouring the boiling water of satire on dirt in all its forms and manifestations. Apropos, Sasha Smolyanchikov from the agit-collective had officially become Ferdinand Lasalle, Petka Govorukhin was too shy to call himself Trotsky directly and had modestly changed his name to Lev Bronstein. Konstantin Vedernikov kept his first name but thought up a unique last name, Klarazetkin, and it was all right, people were amazed for a couple of weeks but then got used to it. Therefore the appearance on Staropeterhof Lane of the previously unknown Igor Ivanovich Dikshtein couldn't attract the attention either of the authorities or of the few acquaintances and neighbors who knew about the on-again, off-again romance between Nastya and the sailor from the *Sevastopol*. But those who remembered the original name of Nastya's husband were given a very unoriginal and therefore quite convincing version: he had changed his name to immortalize the memory of the never-to-be-forgotten hero who had so early burned to death in the fire of the Revolution—without going into details.

During the long journey on foot to the Arkhangelsk area the scalplocked sailor from the No. 3 boiler-room became close friends with the former clerk from the Tenth Company of Torpedoes. The latter, in his turn, had sometimes pitched in for the clerk of the First Company, that is, of the main battery, and he retained in his memory valuable information which he shared for his and the others' benefit during the exhausting journey. For bread, tobacco, sugar, a dry corner in a leaky barn and other important creature comforts, the clerk helped people—and not only from the *Sevastopol*—to prepare themselves for the serious discussions ahead at their destination.

The scalplock learned the main thing: to answer all questions as briefly as possible, if possible with one word, and without details, emphasizing what everybody knows or what can be verified, and citing dead men as witnesses. From what little the clerk could remember about the first sergeant of ammunition for the No. 2 turret, they constructed a simple and beautiful life story: he descended from Russified Germans from Estonia, which was, incidentally, an amazingly correct guess. He was born and lived on the island of Ezel (check this if you can: after the war Ezel was no longer part of Russia). His father was a businessman who traded on the stock exchange; for political reasons he broke with his family and after the peace of Brest-Litovsk he stopped corresponding with them. The scalplocked sailor had been to the turret of the main battery several times during emergencies when they received and unloaded ammunition, so there was no difficulty in establishing the basic points of "his" job.

During the three or four days' march to Kargopol they were able to get hold of some home-brewed vodka. After the clerk had freely partaken of it, he saw himself surrounded by honor and respect, he saw his fellow walkers' concern and love for him grow right before his eyes, and he became so brave that he foolishly started to brag: "I am already the godfather of about forty fellows, I might get a big reward from the authorities..." This joke was the end of him. Igor Ivanovich was inseparable from his savior, but once after a day's rest when he returned from the field kitchen with a small tidbit he found his "godfather" with his head covered, already dead. The "godsons" who had suffocated him were there to watch how Igor Ivanovich would react.

Igor Ivanovich didn't refrain from rebuking them: "You can't take a joke," he said, looking over the "godsons," but after that he behaved correctly.

At the evening roll call they reported the clerk's passing away. The event wasn't unique, and the convoy didn't try to discern any particular meaning in it. All was noted down and buried according to proper procedures.

That most dangerous thing for which the stoker from the No. 3 boiler had prepared himself—the conversation at their destination—turned out to be simple and painless.

There were three interviewers. The one who sat in the middle and asked more questions than the others made a sinister impression. His head, as naked as a peeled hard-boiled egg, was unnaturally white and even looked soft, he had thick light brown eyebrows and an obviously dyed black brush of a mustache, in addition to a slit-like thin mouth with no lips and a gruff voice, all of which promised no good. The man sitting to his left was dressed as if on purpose in a civilian jacket and tried to indicate in every way that his participation in these conversations was almost accidental, since it didn't correspond to his rank, position, weight and status. He was ironic and condescending, not so much with the changing interlocutors as with his own colleagues, stressing in this way their different status. To this end he directed his questions mostly to the one with the naked skull, addressing him familiarly: "What if he's lying?" "How you gonna check it?" "Hey, listen, let's go on to the next one. I'm hungry," and more of the same.

The third man was sweating over the minutes, and refrained from questions, since any question would inevitably increase the amount of writing.

The conversation was preceded by various formalities including photographing, during which process Igor Ivanovich Dikshtein obtained a new face. In a thin folder under the heading "Case No. ..." Igor Ivanovich's life was reproduced in the fictional version of the clerk from the Ninth Company in a most laconic account.

But the most fantastic feature of the events described above was the fact that after being separated from its original bearer, the name didn't transfer to its new owner as a revolutionary pseudonym but, on the contrary, pulled him away from himself, as it were. In the combination of a new face with a new name, features and characteristics of a new person resulted, who had nothing in common with either the stoker from the No. 3 boiler or the first sergeant in charge of ammunition for the No. 2 turret of the main battery.

Similar stories have happened since biblical times. After Saul took the name of Paul, he became, as we know, a strikingly different person, essentially as do all monastics, hermits, lay brothers and monks who abandon their former lives along with their former names.

For the scalplocked sailor originally it was only the thought of self-preservation that caused him to reflect on how he could conform to his new appellation, then he began to think more often about the previous owner of his name, and since the only person he could, without danger, discuss Igor Ivanovich with, the clerk of the Ninth Regiment, was no longer among the living, he had to be content with his own fantasies. His fellow prisoners in the barracks suddenly noticed that Igor Ivanovich, who had earlier been so willing to sing the malicious ditties and plaintive songs then especially popular among sailors, suddenly started to change his repertoire. He took up his mandolin less and less, and was seen more often taking guitar lessons from the warrant officer, Verbitsky. He became more demanding of himself and, most striking of all, he rebuked both non-commissioned and warrant officers several times for allowing themselves to go to seed in anticipation of their doom.

He easily refrained from habits which one might have thought had penetrated him as indelibly as the tattoo. For example, emptying his glass neatly, he used to let out three or four elaborate gasps so that his comrades could easily imagine how the invigorating flame dashed down, burning his insides in its search for its single predestined place. The scalplock had learned this mannerism from the first sergeant of the No. 4 boiler, whom the men would go over to watch as he "partook." As early as the funeral feast for the "godfather" Igor Ivanovich had sensed that there was no point in trying to cheer up this company, and later he simply decided that there was no reason for a respectable person to make such a spectacle of himself. On the other hand, he would now sternly interrupt the man on mess duty: "Your tea, Barkalov, stinks like a dog." "You should have ordered coffee," the melancholy Barkalov retorted. Others remained silent or bit back without spite, but no one dared send him to the devil because they could sense in Igor Ivanovich an explosive force that was always ready to go off.

When Igor Ivanovich happened to hear his last name, or rather Dikshtein's last name, he responded almost instantly, as if afraid that someone might answer before he could.

You couldn't say that the scalplocked sailor's sociable manner had changed completely. Just like any other person who plays the mandolin, guitar, accordion, or balalaika, he attracted people—generally speaking, there aren't that many wistful people in the world who play music for themselves alone. At the same time his behavior had become a little less open, not as noisy and cocky as before. He became sharp in his opinions, even categorical, and looked around guardedly.

During the first month after arriving he had a fair amount of leisure and starting up his imagination, he made himself into a petty officer and even tried to create for himself the mannerisms of the obstinate offspring of a stock-market entrepreneur from the island of Ezel. His ideas of the style and manners of such people were so vague that at times he felt like a man who had unexpectedly been informed that he was of noble descent, and he began to conform to his high rank to the best of his imagination.

However, at first Igor Ivanovich was convinced that he wouldn't continue playing this assumed role for long, that it was more like a game, like an interlude... He clearly remembered his own birth name, both first and last, and he knew that for him they would have the ring of a sentence. Not only did he expect exposure, he was even ready for it and understood that this game couldn't go on for too long...

But observing the audience of non-commissioned and warrant officers, all of whom were in this together, he came to an unexpected conclusion—one with which, I'm sure, psychologists and sociologists might have disagreed, if there had been any around at the time. On the way to their assigned place Igor Ivanovich observed how the signs by which people were distinguished on the ships and in Kronstadt forts were lost, how the importance of rank and duty was lost, although a short time earlier these things had given weight and strength to each man, and he decided that freedom makes people different and oppression makes them alike—whether oppression by fear, hunger, cold or violence.

Once a warm ray of hope touched Igor Ivanovich's heart when he heard the news that all at once, noisily and conspicuously, the heads were rolling of those who directed the attack on Kronstadt—those who had led regiments and divisions, posted guns, and fired up the hearts of the half-shod and half-clothed soldiers. As he read in the newspapers about the fate of Putna, Dybenko, Tukhachevsky, Rukhimovich, Bubnov, Kuzmin,* and others, Igor Ivanovich suddenly started to feel again like the "pride and joy...," his chest swelled and he was ready to tell everything that he had thought and heard about them earlier. It was just that the word "Kronstadt" for some reason never slipped out anywhere, and the wise Anastasia Petrovna who had already gotten used to the new Igor Ivanovich, restrained the impetuous stoker simply and easily: "Didn't they drag you around enough, do you want more?" Each time for some reason Igor Ivanovich remembered a head, soft and bare like a peeled hard-boiled egg, and he calmed down.

And the more relentlessly and ruthlessly the struggle went on against the counter-revolution which, as the years went by, took on the guise of anarcho-syndicalism, or right opportunism, or leftism, or Trotskyism, or workers' opposition, or the trial unmasking the Industrial Party or the Shakhtinsk affair and the endless multitude of forms and shapes of "wreckers," the more clearly the understanding grew in one's consciousness that the only way for a person to be spared, to survive, to save his family and friends, was to be exactly like Igor Ivanovich Dikshtein, against whom Soviet power had, as we know, no grievance.

Oh, Igor Ivanovich! If he had only suspected how much pain and difficulty he was adopting along with his new first name and patronymic and sonorous last name, he might never have accepted life itself with this weight eternally lying heavy on his heart.

Without intending to, he had acquired a role he had to play without interruption for his whole life—of a man he didn't actually even know. His imagination pictured him in different ways but only one thing remained constant—the unknown Igor Ivanovich was always—perhaps because he remembered those wire-framed glasses—smarter, more serious, noble and honest than the scalplocked stoker from No. 3 boiler room.

* All executed during the show trials and purges of the officer corps in the late 30s.

Experiencing sincere feelings of guilt before the trusting reader, I must admit that history hasn't preserved all of the very likely most interesting details of the long and laborious road to recreating a true likeness of Igor Ivanovich Dikshtein. Long-suffering history has been burdened enough with inventions and fantasies.

Condemned to seeking all human strength within himself, the scalplock created a saving image for himself on his own; but, of course, nothing elevates the soul like a talent for solitude.

...It is known that after just two or three years everyone sensed that an aversion to falsehood had become Igor Ivanovich's strongest passion, he had started to consider specifically this the most vile and unforgivable sin. Apparently sensing how truth suffered in this life and keeping in mind his own guilt before truth provided Igor Ivanovich with an unshakable loyalty to a new oath and he followed it unflinchingly, only the truth he had to deal with was minor and his heart, ready to serve honor, one could say was set on idle.

Igor Ivanovich's remark concerning the "nice frost" didn't go unnoticed and served as the impetus for a new wave of conversation in the line.

"You didn't forget your drawers, did you?" asked a nondescript man, looking all the time at the snow, the houses and the road as though expecting to see something funny any minute. His question was so simpleminded that it would have been tactless to suspect him of indecency.

"I-I did put 'em o-on," drawled a woman on the steps indifferently, as if to suggest that when combating the cold, all measures were relative.

"It looks like the oven door will freeze stuck again!" And he looked around victoriously.

In the line people smiled politely.

"Oh, you just know everything!" the woman with three bottles said tongue-in-cheek.

"No one knows everything," the nondescript man said with the dignity of true modesty.

"It's damn freezing!"

"Ten below they announced, and tonight it'll be minus 20."

"During the Finnish War it was 40 below—down to 54 below."

"No, it wasn't any 54 below."

"Yes, it was, on the gulf; I was there myself. We were just moving tanks over to Kokkola, then half of us ended up in the hospital, some for frozen noses, some for fingers, some for an ear, but mostly feet..."

"Here comes Anna Prokofievna!"

A woman was approaching the line. She was wearing felt boots and a frayed white cloak like a camouflage one, with washed-out yellow spots. Naturally, she wore the cloak over a quilted jacket, and the quilted jacket, perhaps, over a coat, all of which gave her figure a monumental shape and inspired a certain authority.

"Are you last in line?" asked Anna Prokofievna. "Tell people not to get behind you. I don't have any money. Maybe there isn't even enough for you."

The first half of the line here noted the happy turn of fortune that had come their way.

"I don't accept jars," Anna Prokofievna tossed out as she walked up to the porch, more or less to the elderly owner of two large bags with crystal-clear jars sticking out of them.

"So where, then?"

"Hand them in wherever you want," said Anna Prokofievna firmly, and opened the door,

They started to console the sufferer, suggesting various addresses where maybe they took jars, or at least used to.

"Never mind, I have some bottles, too, under the jars!" cheerfully shouted the person who was standing firm against the blows of fate.

There was hardly anyone in the line who wasn't experiencing the warm joy of success. The sufferer because he had bottles, too, and the rest because they had managed to get in line before Anna Prokofievna's stern warning came. The right to return empty glass containers and receive either nine or twelve kopecks seems like a trifling one, but if you deprive someone of this right or make it complicated for him to use it, then at once a slight taste of bitterness and vexation is added to the joyful savoring of life. It's just that man is constructed in the very worst possible way: the happiness he gets when he manages to return his bottles easily is, like many other kinds of happiness, transitory, it doesn't leave an impression and doesn't light up even a single additional hour of his life, but everyday difficulties and burdens are capable of poisoning the entire day. And this continual blind game with fate engenders excitement in some, in others an enterprising effort worthy of admiration, and in still others, a dull resignation and an unvoiced, unspoken resentment.

Sorting, counting and placing the bottles in crates, Anna Prokofievna wasn't silent for a moment, but was continuing a speech, the beginning of which the first person in line had heard and the end of which was obviously intended for those who would come after the renewal of her gold reserves, which was now running out, as she had frankly admitted.

"Vitka came home from school, he was kicked out of class. He said that they won't let him back in until his mother comes. What can one do?"

Money—clink—and the next customer.

"Wouldn't you go? You have to. After all, he's my kid... No, we can't accept Hungarian bottles... Like it or not, you have to go..."

Money—clink—and the next customer.

"He started sticking his drawing compass in the nose of a kid called Ivliev or something. Either during math or botany... My memory's gone, I don't remember. He and this Ivliev sit together, see. He must've really asked for it—to stick the compass up his nose! I think it's the teachers' own fault if the children aren't interested in their classes."

Each customer received his portion of Vitka's story: Vitka who suffered because he had no father, and his mother was busy taking care of their home and working, because he had mean teachers, bad friends and was dumb himself.

"They call the parents to school, but they oughta be ashamed of themselves."

Igor Ivanovich waited for her to put the previous bottles into the crates.

"You should punish him," said Igor Ivanovich as he put up his oil bottles.

"Who asked you!" retorted Anna Prokofievna, staring suspiciously at the bottles.

Igor Ivanovich got tense and ready.

Coins clinked down on the table. While he was picking up the copper and silver coins, putting them in his pocket and walking out, he heard:

"Punish, punish... What kind of life does Vitka have with me? He has a lousy life with me."

Outside in the street Igor Ivanovich felt victorious.

Yes, say what you like, but if you could have found fault with the bottles, if it had been possible to find anything wrong with them, then Anka wouldn't have taken them, she definitely wouldn't have taken them. This was fine work, no cause for complaint, no fault to find here, the bottles were washed just like they should be. No less important was still another reason for his sense of victory: the bottles which those impudent clouts had left, the "bombs" at 17 kopecks, the ones the fast little guy had grabbed right out from under Igor Ivanovich's feet, Anka had not accepted. She had said, "I don't accept bombs..." Let him just run around. Igor Ivanovich even smiled, although his little smile was turned inward instead of outward. There you are!

Stepping firmly with his slightly warmed-up feet, Igor Ivanovich turned toward the grocery store, although it was possible to buy a half-pint closer to home, but the grocery store was somehow nicer.

———

Those who have read the prominent French philosopher Charles Louis Montesquieu attentively would find it easy to notice certain characteristic traits which accompanied Igor Ivanovich through the major part of his life, which did not desert him even during the bottle expedition, as he stood in line in the frost, and possibly not even while striding toward the grocery store.

Let's agree that "man of honor" is a title—the highest badge of human virtue which can only be attained if one is prepared to give up even life itself, not only its blessings.

Living something like a borrowed life which didn't wholly belong to him and being ready to return it under certain conditions, Igor Ivanovich was deprived of the main obstacle which prevents the majority from being men of honor, namely placing one's own rules higher than those pre-scribed him by the despotism of life.

The understandable feeling of guilt regarding the ammunition store petty officer who had dissolved in the last frost of March forced Igor Ivanovich even unconsciously to observe the code of honor and never to lower himself to such actions to which a noble scion of successful mer-chants from the island of Ezel wouldn't easily have consented.

At the cashier's window in the grocery store there was a hitch. Having briskly ordered a small bottle of vodka and a pack of *Sever* cigarettes, Igor Ivanovich discovered that except for one ruble and 24 kopecks he didn't have any more coins at all in his pocket. Those 37 kopecks which he had really counted on had probably been left behind in the kerosene jacket. He had to be firm with the cashier and instead get her to issue a chit for beer.

One way or the other it didn't work out.

They didn't have any *Zhiguli* beer and he only had enough for two bottles of *Moskva*. But it was too late to retreat, he couldn't very well march all the way home for those coins in the kerosene jacket...

This incident pretty much upset Igor Ivanovich. Since morning he had been living with the thought of how nice everything would be, and now he was already getting irritated both at this *Moskva* beer and at the pack of *Severs*. The fact was that but for Nastya's order, which he could actually pretend not to have heard, he could have had three bottles after all. After all, he could have bought cigarettes separately in the little shop by the bathhouse, but he should have thought of this earlier and when he was faced with the necessity of making a new decision right at the cashier's, he instinctively defended himself against everything he might have to hear if he asked the cashier for his money back.

He didn't feel like going home.

Once again all the petty misunderstandings, each of which in essence does not even deserve to be remembered, forced Igor Ivanovich to feel the border separating his life from the life he considered to be the real one.

In that other, real life everything was reminiscent of the strict clarity of a children's book—its correctness, simplicity, convenience, and above all the absence of numerous unexpected and ever-present annoying details.

That clear, simple life was somewhere nearby, sometimes he could even observe it.

At the bakery when he was thinking about buying an expensive loaf that he liked a lot instead of two French rolls and a loaf of plain bread, he heard somebody next to him, in the pastry department, say "No, no, don't give me any *bouchées,* they're heavy. Two doughnuts, please, a couple of *baisers,* and two Alexanders, and you select the rest." This was a chapter from the kind of life where a person arrives at the railroad station half an hour before the train departs, goes to the ticket office and asks for a ticket: "First-class sleeper, please. If possible, the lower bunk. Thank you very much." Then, right in the compartment, he drinks strong hot tea with crackers or a couple of sandwiches bought from the hawkers, and goes to sleep on the fragrant crisp sheets, laid out by a smiling conductor. During the day he dines in the restaurant car, and at the station where he gets off, a porter in a white apron and cap carries his light suitcase and convenient traveling bag to a taxi. In all probability this fortunate first-class passenger would proceed to a hotel where he would immediately get a room with a bath, but even in his daydreams Igor Ivanovich would leave this pet of fortune at this point and would remain instead with the porters in white aprons, who in actual historical reality had thrashed Igor Ivanovich to within an inch of his life. They beat him to protect their jobs at all three stations—Moscow, Vitebsk and Warsaw—where Igor Ivanovich had arrived from Gatchina in the difficult years of 1949 and 1950 in order to make some extra money. Rather quickly, after two, or at the most, three days, the porters recognized a competitor in this tall and very thin man who looked almost like an intellectual. Igor Ivanovich knew that they had the strength of the collective on their side and that his kind was doomed, so he changed stations, worked only for an evening or two, but this didn't help. The only thing he could do to protect himself from further insults was to avoid using the public toilets at the railroad stations where, as a rule, the porters would carry out their sentence on people like Igor Ivanovich. Each time they beat him, it happened outside. A couple of times they tried to take his money but, thank God, after two times in prison, he had learned to hide it on himself. But it wasn't the reprisals performed by jealous professionals that were the most noteworthy of Dikshtein's railroad-station adventures. Rather often something almost worse happened—he would carry luggage, they would thank him...and pay nothing, and he was never able even once to ask for payment. The safest thing was to find clients at the streetcar stop. At first Igor Ivanovich picked out respectable people, older people who looked intelligent, women with kids. "Are you going to the train?" Igor Ivanovich would approach travelers who were getting off the streetcar. "Let me help you." "Are you going to the station, too? Oh, thank you." And taking him simply for a kind fellow traveler, they would be embarrassed to offer him money. After several such episodes Igor Ivanovich began to pick out simpler people; no misunderstandings usually occurred then. But nevertheless, Igor Ivanovich's respectable appearance sometimes gave people the wrong impression...

The outfit he wore for his railroad-station business caused Igor Ivanovich quite a bit of concern. Any of his shirts worn under his suit jacket might, to put it mildly, scare off clients, for they clashed with his image as an intellectual and carefree innocent traveler without luggage, so, therefore, when he went to the station, Igor Ivanovich wore a snowy white knit scarf under his jacket which admirably hid the absence of a shirt. But to prevent this small defect in his wardrobe from being discovered, Igor Ivanovich had to be extra careful; it was hard to keep the heavy and smooth material in place and avoid exposing the undershirt hidden beneath it, which, by the way, was always clean and had all its buttons.

It was at the stations that he saw how people left glasses with cognac, plates with half-eaten salmon sandwiches or even whole half-chickens—maybe it was a little tough. But even when he was ready to drop from hunger, even alone among these plates in the night buffet restaurant, he never permitted himself this final step.

Of the heaviest things which Igor Ivanovich had to carry, he was most afraid of suitcases with meat. As a rule they looked rather small, more often than not ordinary wooden suitcases bound with rope for insurance, but they were as heavy as lead. Once when he picked up such a suitcase at the streetcar stop he instantly felt a sharp hook catch in his heart. He immediately got out a thick strap that he kept concealed, and threw the suitcase onto his back, forfeiting his respectable appearance, but the hook still stayed in his heart and under certain conditions and during awkward movements it would make itself felt, sometimes frequently, other times at long intervals.

Even suitcases with books weren't as heavy as the meat deliveries going from well-supplied Leningrad to the unfed provinces.

And it must be said that Igor Ivanovich's aspirations to a better life, more suitable to his sonorous name, were almost unwittingly manifested in a pedantic attention to detail, in an ability to find a strict hierarchy of qualities in simple everyday circumstances, and he always preferred the best. So now, after considering the fact that he still had 11 kopecks, even more, left, he didn't immediately turn right after leaving the store, though he could see straight from the door that there was hardly any line at all outside the nearest beer stall, but set off instead in the direction of the market, to the Flatiron.

This haven for the thirsty was so cleverly named, not thanks to the refined fantasy of its patrons, but rather thanks to the inscrutable progress of permanent architecture which had given the building an appearance the well-chosen word precisely described.

Say what you like, most people drink beer in a rather mindless way...

A German? What about a German?... Well, he sits keeping watch over his bottle all evening and rewards himself for his diligence and thoroughness with very small sips spaced out at such long intervals that you might think the meaning and pleasure of sitting with a bottle consisted of these intervals, this non-drinking. For a German beer is either a means of killing time or a way of spending time. This was all alien to Igor Ivanovich.

Not being noted for greed or for love of luxury, Igor Ivanovich was able to transform beer drinking into a subtle and profound enjoyment.

Almost every one of us has in his life seen people drink beer, but far from every one has had the fortune to see a man who *knows how* to drink beer—those lucky enough to have known Igor Ivanovich personally can say unflinchingly that they did know such a man!..

Who else drank beer so beautifully! So cleverly! So lightly, openly, without embarrassment, hardly even noticing either the mug in his hand or the slowly diminishing life-giving drink...

Go and stand for an hour or two by a beer stand, look around, listen... It's the rare man who can maintain between himself and the beer that natural, unaffected distance which keeps the consumption of beer from becoming a commonplace quenching of thirst, or on the contrary, some kind of event; how many people constantly glance first down, then sideways into their mugs, contemplating the lowering level, and with such a grimace that it seems they aren't the person actually sipping but rather some old codger, and how many put aside the mug altogether or place it so that they barely touch it with their elbow and then fool around with some kind of papyrus-colored little fish, consisting for the most part of skin and desiccated fragile bones; while doing this they also manage to crane their necks and read something in a spread-out old newspaper, and only after they pick off some more or less substantial piece of fish remains do they hurry to wash it down with a sip of beer, as if they were taking medicine; and how many empty a mug in three swallows and then rush toward the little window, pushing aside their fellow citizens and asserting their right to a go-to-the-head-of-the-line happiness without showing any unusual honorary medals or a wounded veteran's certificate, but using the password understood by all: "Give me another!"

Not many have chanced to see how aristocrats drink beer, and there's no certainty that Igor Ivanovich had ever seen that kind of picture... How, then? How, dammit, did he develop this refined, casual, light manner of handling beer? Oh, there were times when fortune smiled on Igor Ivanovich with a generous face and without fearing the future he could allow himself to drink three or five or however many mugs of beer his heart desired. And wherever did he learn that beer isn't vodka and that one shouldn't get drunk on it, that one can allow oneself six mugs only during a serious conversation and not in just any company, but with Shamil, for instance, a man of similar age and ideas, or perhaps with Yermolai Pavlovich, but with whom else would be hard to say.

The art of a man who knows how to drink beer is revealed in his first sip.

If he can bring the mug to his mouth, move his wide-open eyes about, and still have time to blink, too, I assure you he understands nothing about beer!.. Take a look at Igor Ivanovich right now: after holding the mug at chin level for a suitable period of time, as though he had even forgotten about it, he lifts it to his lips with a quick, hardly noticeable movement, touching the brim like a clarinetist or expert bassoonist touches the reed before the intended sounds are extracted from the instrument raised to his lips, and then only after the instrument is finally ready... Can the performance proceed now, do you think? No, one must, of course, also prepare oneself! Igor Ivanovich takes a tiny, the tiniest sip—this is like a gesture of acquaintance, a mutual greeting and exploration. And then the larynx, which had completely dried out while he stood in line, is rinsed, a cool and fresh sigh has filled his lungs, all senses have received the necessary information about the beverage's obvious quality and pungency, the instrument is ready, the player is ready, it can begin...

Igor Ivanovich drank down half the mug with his first swallow.

...It was like a first real kiss, deep and long: you lose your breath, your heart acquires a new rhythm, it turns the head, it makes the world around you a little different than it was before, and it seems that everything is still to come, because after the first big swallow a new reckoning begins, the used-up page is turned over and a new, clean one is opened upon which there will be no blots and the marks will be entered according to a strict and meaningful system; the first swallow always washed all of life's minor vexations from Igor Ivanovich's soul, and perhaps the fact that he always had more than enough of them was the reason his swallow was so substantial.

With what a sweet weakness Igor Ivanovich lowered his hand with the half-empty mug, all the way down, as a duellist lowers his hand after a shot. Many who saw this gesture for the first time actually became afraid that Igor Ivanovich had decided to pour out the remaining half mug on the ground, but it only looked that way, Igor Ivanovich didn't let the mug tilt, he looked at his neighbor, looked at his drinking partner, looked at the world with a soul filled with lightness and freedom, with a soul elevated by quenched desire, and his hand began to gain strength and slowly rose, coming to a stop at his chest, alongside his soul, if that really is located between the lungs and the diaphragm...

Denied his sip of beer, Igor Ivanovich's life would have been much dimmer, both in the sense of color and in the sense of the nuances of his mental condition.

During the last five or six years especially, one could see definite signs in Igor Ivanovich of fastidiousness, a strict meticulousness and even an ability to lose interest in an object instantly if it wasn't marked by some sign of superiority compared to other objects of its kind.

Specifically, Igor Ivanovich was a firm opponent of those who drink beer in winter, even if it has been warmed up, at a stall right on the street. He was convinced that only a lack of culture and a foolish hurry could force people to go to such extremes; at the Flatiron, even though there were no tables, at least there was in front of the counter a space of about 45 square feet and an eight-inch shelf along the walls.

Nor can we pass over still another circumstance which confirms Igor Ivanovich's absolute aversion to lies. He was irritated by the hypocrisy of the sign "Beer—Soda Water" on the little street stalls where the only "water" available was for washing the mugs. By contrast, the Flatiron bore the enviably straightforward name "Beer—Beer."

The first person Igor Ivanovich noticed was Shamil—not counting two drivers in quilted jackets, which smelled of oil, who were washing down with beer some food set out on a newspaper.

On the narrow green shelf nailed along the wall and level with Shamil's chest stood a mug of beer which he had just started to drink. Shamil himself looked like a man who had forgotten about the mug next to him and was evidently deciding where to turn next. Still thinking about the main thing, Shamil slapped his pockets and found a pack of *Zvezdochkas*. Nina, who was pouring the beer and looking like she had dropped in just for a minute and was staying only because the patrons didn't have the tact to notice how bored she was with the whole thing—how right now she needed to be doing something else more important—shook her finger at Shamil.

Shamil suddenly remembered, nodded toward the sign "No smoking" and grinned guiltily. To show his repentance graphically he slapped his forehead and wanted to make some other grand gesture, but no one was looking at him any more.

There was a special rule about smoking in the Flatiron. Before 4:30, before people showed up in the establishment directly from the day shift, Nina strictly watched that the stated rule was obeyed, but after 4:30 it was no longer Nina but the patrons themselves who watched the observance of etiquette regarding smoking. One had to smoke hiding the cigarette in one hand and carefully shooing away the smoke with the other hand, and although the tobacco smoke was hanging from floor to ceiling by 7:30, filling the entire premises like smooth thick batting, in different corners one could see men who were ritually waving their hands at head level.

Igor Ivanovich received his tiny little mug of beer and walked over to the wall farthest from Shamil.

"Are you carrying coals to Newcastle—a samovar to Tula?" shouted Shamil, nodding to the bottles of beer in Igor Ivanovich's net bag.

Igor Ivanovich, acting as though he had just noticed Shamil, smiled and walked over to him.

"I'm really in a hurry," said Igor Ivanovich. "It's one of those days. I thought I'd just swallow some beer on the run."

Shamil held out his hand, but Igor Ivanovich's hands were full. In one there was the net bag and in the other a mug, and there was nothing left to do but to make the gesture a surgeon makes as he is preparing for an operation—to stick out his elbow as a greeting. Shamil squeezed the elbow with his five fingers.

Although the two friends were most probably of the same age, it had somehow come about that Igor Ivanovich was considered the older, perhaps simply because he stood three centimeters taller than Shamil's fur hat.

"I keep meaning to come and see you," said Shamil, "it's time to get a new fur hat."

This statement must be duly appreciated because Shamil after all was a genuine Tatar and in his mind he was of course dreaming of lambskin.

To a discernible degree Shamil's fur hat was Igor Ivanovich's pride. Five years ago Igor Ivanovich had constructed it from his own rabbits. When Igor Ivanovich had occasion to sell a rabbit or a skin, he always made sure to mention that they were especially good for fur hats and that he could provide the address of a man who had his fur hats sewn exclusively by him, Igor Ivanovich.

"I have one with a great ear... I'm sure you'd like it. It doesn't even need to be dyed." Igor Ivanovich took a small swallow and in gratitude for the pleasant conversational start he added, "Only not today. I'm in a hurry. My nephew from Leningrad is coming. I just picked up some beer."

Knocking with his wooden leg, Mishka Bandaletov entered the Flatiron. He was a real rascal, an old fox, capable of drinking a half-pint of vodka through one nostril for your amusement and, of course, at your expense. Understanding his special status in the town, he never recognized anyone first and never said hello to anyone first. And if the citizens of Gatchina themselves hadn't noticed and said hello to him, he could have lived that way, too, like a passenger who had arrived at an unfamiliar place for the first time. This guise of pride and dignity allowed him to address those very same people using words he might have read in some old book, or more likely had heard at the movies: "Don't let a noble man perish..." He didn't insist on friendship and didn't remind anyone of acquaintance, thereby showing a true nobility of soul, protecting his drinking partner from any demeaning equality, and therefore it was a rare day when Mishka wasn't already drunk by noon. Three knocks of his wooden leg on the floor, and Bandaletov stood before the drivers who were eating. Hearing the suggestion about saving a noble man, the drivers considered it best to curse at the supplicant, not from stinginess but out of a feeling of security and reluctance to participate in some kind of incomprehensible performance. Bandaletov bent his chin down sharply and the next second he jerked his head like an obedient aide-de-camp who had received clear orders for further action. He at once turned around and after carefully and deftly taking two steps, he stood before the friends. Bandaletov's noble soul would not disown acquaintance with Igor Ivanovich and Shamil.

"I wouldn't dare to interrupt the conversation of the smartest citizens of Gatchina," Mishka announced clearly.

Igor Ivanovich was glad that he still had seven kopecks left and he immediately tossed them into the outstretched palm. Shamil gave him 18 kopecks. Thanking the donors with the same aide-de-camp bow, Mishka turned on his wooden axis and quit the Flatiron.

"Your nephew likes *Moskva* beer?" inquired Shamil, nodding in the direction of the net bag.

"What do you think? I wasted half the morning looking for it."

"That's good beer, I've drunk it. You and I have drunk it. On May Day they were selling it from a truck. They always sell expensive beer from trucks."

"Look what's happened to my hands." Igor Ivanovich put down the mug and held out a hand. "See, it won't stretch out all the way, only to here."

The fourth finger on the cracked and scratched brown claw did in fact assume an unusual position.

"You should try a calendula compress."

"I don't believe in homeopathy. Take offense if you like, but that's how it is..." Igor Ivanovich moved closer and announced confidentially, "It's the Buryats who thought it up, so it helps them."

Shamil thought about it, then remembering something, smiled and said:

"Academician Pavlov wasn't a Buryat, I believe, but he was treated only by homeopaths."

"They did him in with their pills."

"It wasn't the pills—it was his wife..."

"His wife? But he buried her."

"By the way, science denies that Academician Pavlov believed in God."

"And where was your science when he was worshipping at Znamensky Church on Vosstanie Square? They didn't tear down Znamensky Church as long as Academician Pavlov was alive."

"I heard, on the radio, on the program "Atheists' Corner..."

"I don't need the radio when I myself... actually not me, but Nastya...her younger sister lived on Goncharnaya Street and used to go to Znamensky Church... So go listen to your radio..." His conviction that he was right prevented him from finding the necessary words.

"Marco Polo, the Venetian traveller, generally considered Russia to be a Chinese province...and called it Tataria. But that was a mistake!.."

"So there's no need to repeat nonsense... Marco Polo!"

"I only meant to say that great men make great mistakes."

"That's right. Because around each man there are lots of yes-men and they'll pick up any nonsense and repeat it!.."

Igor Ivanovich paused significantly and took a sip of his beer with pleasure, examining Shamil's face as though it were an inanimate object.

Except for a squeezed-in section near the temples, Shamil's face would have been completely round, and since the shape wasn't quite round, one was left with the impression of something incomplete or slightly irregular. For just this reason his eyebrows shot up one day and remained there, creating a look of surprise. This impression was strengthened by the narrow

curve of his lips and the way his head leaned to the right, as if he were listening to some sounds coming from his right shoulder. The thin, hook-
shaped nose on the almost flat surface of his face even looked somehow
warlike, not exactly like a beak, but something similar. Strictly speaking,
Shamil's appearance could be considered arrogant, jeering, and aggressive
but for the shadow of a smile which always seemed to hover around his
face, randomly touching his eyes or his lips, the smile of a man who is
always ready to admit defeat but with the kind of terms that would make a
victor think it better to give up the victory.

"It's a disgrace, they're pouring nothing but foam," Igor Ivanovich
lifted the mug to eye level.

"There's no beer without foam," said Shamil. "Here's a really strange
thing: it turns out that the earth isn't explored at all."

"In what sense?"

"In a direct sense. Do you remember Rakiya? She's the daughter of
Ashraf, Hakim's first wife." Shamil unhurriedly sipped some beer. "Rakiya
also has a daughter Nuriya. She's three years old. Makhuza collected some
clothes—we had some shoes left from our kids, I took it all to Leningrad
to give it to Rakiya. She lives on Kropotkin Street."

"Near the Evgeny Hospital?" specified Igor Ivanovich.

"It's Bakunin Street that's near the Evgeny, but this is Kropotkin near
the Sytny market. I went there, she wasn't there, I had to wait two or
three hours. You can't go to the movies with a big package. It was too
cold for the zoo nearby. So I went to the planetarium. It was very interesting. See those eggs?" Shamil pointed to the stack of hard-boiled eggs in
the showcase on the counter. "If you compare the earth with an egg, then
it's the shell that has been more or less explored."

"But there's nothing more to explore. It's all melted slush there.
Magma!"

Igor Ivanovich drained the last drops and firmly put down the mug.
Without looking at his friend, Shamil poured some beer in the mug he'd
put down. Igor Ivanovich picked it up again.

"It turns out that they don't know yet where this magma is. If it's only
where the yolk is or if it's also where the egg white is."

"Where the white is there's water and minerals, but where the yolk is,
there's magma," said Igor Ivanovich with the certainty of an eyewitness.

"They say 'the road to a better life'... After some five or six billion years
the solar system will turn into yet another uninhabited island in the universe..."

"Why an island?" asked Igor Ivanovich sternly without raising his eyes
to look at Shamil.

"That's what the lecturer said, he meant something specific. There were questions afterwards but no one asked about the island."

Igor Ivanovich was satisfied with the answer and nodded.

"Why am I bringing this up? If the sun sooner or later goes out, then how is it the 'road to a better life'?"

"You want life to stop?"

"That's impossible." Shamil smiled like a big boss who politely refuses some small request. "My thought is quite simple, I'm even embarrassed to tell you about it. If there's a beginning and end to everything, doesn't that mean that there must also be a middle?"

"Let's assume so," allowed Igor Ivanovich carefully, afraid that he was being led into a trap.

"So there is movement up and, whether we like it or not, down. That's how life is."

"I understand you." Igor Ivanovich regretted for a second that the drivers who were violently cursing the stupid management weren't listening to their conversation.

"If there's movement up, and then down, that means that this place, too, exists..." Shamil was describing flight and falling with his hand and his gesture could easily be understood. "We say, 'the top, the heights'... That's right, but is it worth striving for the top if the only road from there is down? I'm not against the top," Shamil clarified in an effort to keep the conversation in a loyal channel. "Don't think that I am against the top... I'm for the top."

"Do you see a way out?" Igor Ivanovich's voice was as stern as before, but an attentive ear could have definitely heard the flicker of a shadow of doubt.

"Just imagine—yes."

"What should be considered the top?"

"Exactly! I knew that you'd understand at once." Shamil burst out laughing happily, like third-graders laugh when they have solved an "impossible" problem. "What should be considered the top? For a tree it's one thing, for the sun, it's another, but for humans?.."

"Are you talking about children?" asked Igor Ivanovich who, after thinking hard, had regained his confidence.

"No. Is human life meaningless just because you don't have children? And there's no top? Humans are not just about children... You can love your children very much, and still be a real bastard under the guise of loving your children..."

"So you believe that this isn't the top here?"

"That's just what I'm saying! We've known each other for twelve years.

It's a long time. How far have you moved in twelve years as far as the top is concerned? You were a roofer? Or you moved twice—once to change apartments and once when the house was vacated for major repairs? So, is the conclusion that your life has no meaning? That's not how it is! That's not true. I don't know a single person in Gatchina who could say anything bad about you, and you know the sort of people here. I don't remember you ever offending anyone, and no one has seen your Anastasia Petrovna cry."

"And when Stalin died?" Igor Ivanovich reminded him.

"You've thrown me off the track with your Stalin. I'm losing the thread..." Shamil lifted his mug and looked at it as if he expected to see little fish in the transparent golden liquid. He saw none and took a sip. "Almost everybody cried then, and that has nothing to do with you. To what heights should a man go if his conscience is clean, if he never did anything mean, didn't provoke people, didn't torture or insult anyone?.."

"And who says that?" Igor Ivanovich asked carefully.

Shamil again burst out laughing and looked with surprise at the unruffled Nina—why wasn't she laughing?

"You've never tortured anyone either," said Igor Ivanovich.

"Well, Makhuza doesn't think so," Shamil grinned bitterly, "but you've done good."

"To whom?" said Igor Ivanovich with a start as though hearing about a lost purse. The word "good" in Russian has two meanings, and the very same letters can refer either to objects having exclusively material value—goods—which Igor Ivanovich couldn't deal with on his own, or to something positive in one's actions which has no material equivalent.

"And Marseillaise?"

Igor Ivanovich admitted that this reminder was convincing, although his smile and nod clearly protested that only a small effort had been expended by the hero in performing this good deed.

Here the heroine of the narrative finally enters, the meeting with whom was promised long ago, the first one of the neighbors to become acquainted with Igor Ivanovich when he moved into the house at the corner of Chkalov and Socialist Streets.

On that memorable evening Igor Ivanovich left the women to put things away in the chests and cabinets which had been moved to their proper places, and had gone outside for a smoke and to look around. He didn't hear Marseillaise Nikonovna approach from behind. Her voice, filled with that tormenting tenderness that had made more than one man's heart turn over, sang out confidently and passionately, "But how can anyone live with such short eyelashes?" Igor Ivanovich turned around at once and stopped, seeing before him a woman decidedly differing in every respect, as later became clear, from Yermolai Pavlovich's wife whom he also hadn't met yet. Marseillaise Nikonovna was embarrassed for some reason about her elegant name and instructed her friends to call her Mara or officially Margarita. And in fact, her eyelashes weren't anything like the whitish feathers of Yermolai Pavlovich's wife, but were thick and long, and with a light shadow they tamed the fatal shine of her gray eyes; she had a thin tall figure with dry, sinewy legs which had hardly any calves, but she possessed a bosom of magnificent splendor. No, we must stop, otherwise even a simple description of all the charms and accomplishments of Marseillaise Nikonovna will carry us oh so far away. It's odd, but behind her back people always referred to Mara by her full beautiful name, with a certain inexplicable touch of irony even. Yermolai Pavlovich's wife, generally envious of Marseillaise Nikonovna's success among the male population of Leningrad and its suburbs, continuously reproached her for her unmarried state, and pointed out sarcastically that if she were to have her passport stamped* like all *proper* women, she would have to write out a document as thick as the Gatchina Telephone Directory. Her eternally unmarried state hadn't prevented Marseillaise Nikonovna from bearing a daughter before the war and the boy Lyonya during the war—in 1942. This woman who was so generous with love could never understand why all her desires and considerable efforts in the direction of Igor Ivanovich were in vain. Several times when they encountered each other rather closely during holidays, especially at spring and summer holidays in the open air, particularly on May Day and on Trinity, Marseillaise Nikonovna would come up to him with agonizingly inviting questions. On one such holiday at a time when the most fragrant time of her life had not yet passed, she ardently spoke directly in his ear, "Why, Go-o-osha, why?... Why is it that I bring people unhappiness?!... It's so hard for me, Go-o-osha!..." In this way, looking within herself, listening to herself, and even seeing her listener only with the inner eye of her imagination, she would usually go to the edge of the precipice, and it was the rare man who didn't rush to rescue her... Then, as a rule, she'd start to punch her savior in the chest, but not for long. Although he was not sober because of the holiday, Igor Ivanovich said with sobering distinctness: "Just so there won't be any difficulties, Mara, call me Igor Ivanovich." This reply so impressed Marseillaise Nikonovna that she at once went around the cemetery—this was at Trinity—and started to tell everyone how Igor Ivanovich had

---

* That is, listing all her "husbands."

answered her. She flitted from one group of drinkers to the next, until a new feeling and a new passion swept her off her feet and helped her forget herself.

One recalls that the Empress had rebuked the Gatchina residents for not knowing Greek and Latin. It is certainly permissible to ask, why twist your tongue with *similia similibus* when you could quickly and easily say "diamond cut diamond." Exactly this method, well known both to those who speak Latin and to those who don't know any foreign languages, was resorted to by Marseillaise Nikonovna the next time.

Igor Ivanovich, of course, didn't know to what extent this unimportant incident, which had no witnesses, had elevated him in the eyes both of the people who knew him well and of those who hardly knew him at all. It was precisely after this incident that Igor Ivanovich's presence or even a reference to him allowed Marseillaise Nikonovna to feel like a proper lady, protected if need be, and even in a certain sense inaccessible. But Shamil's words about doing good reminded Igor Ivanovich of an entirely different story.

This second incident, as we'll call it, was not even connected so much with Marseillaise Nikonovna as with her son Lyonik, and it raised respect for Igor Ivanovich even higher. The fact was that Lyonik, who had worked in the dye shop of the Gatchina furniture factory since he was sixteen, was a nervous fellow and often caused scenes with his mother, especially when in an intoxicated state. All the various pretexts for these violent scenes were reduced in the end to the strongest of accusations, the one most impossible to refute: "You got me from whoring with a German!.." To those observing such a scene for the first time he always explained, "I was born in 1942. Isn't that a fact? And I have no father, isn't that a fact?" Marseillaise Nikonovna cried and tried to make up to her ferocious son. Once when a periodic fight spilled out from No. 3 on the first floor directly into the courtyard, it spilled out with shrieks, noise, tears, harsh words in a loud voice, with the neighbors separating them and threatening to call the police. Igor Ivanovich who had just finished giving his rabbits fresh grass and changing their water as though nothing was going on, walked up to the overheated booby and stood silently beside him. The fellow quieted down, the neighbors quieted down, too, and the tearful but still beautiful Marseillasie Nikonovna sniffed quietly and held on to the half torn-off sleeve of her blouse.

"If you were a German," Igor Ivanovich said softly but yet so that everyone could hear it in the silence that had fallen, "you'd be smart—but you're a fool."

Having said this, he went quietly to his apartment on the second floor. The violent unmasker of his mother's moral, but mostly political, inconstancy wanted to say something sharp, but immediately realized that any continuation of the brawl would only confirm the correctness of the strange neighbor, so he beat it to the apartment, and no one heard him ever make any more "German broadcasts," as they called it in the building.

"You bought the beer for dinner, or what?"

"I already told you, I'm expecting Nikolai, my nephew from Leningrad."

"It's nice here. It's nice in Gatchina, but nobody comes to see us. I call our relatives from Leningrad—Rakiya, Makhinur, Ganei, and Kerim—but nobody comes. Can anybody breathe the air in Leningrad? There's no air to breathe there."

"But the theaters..."

"Do you personally go to the theater much?"

"Not much. Very seldom. I don't like theaters because you have to dress, then undress. It's a waste of time."

Igor Ivanovich put his empty mug on the shelf and when Shamil made a move to pour some more, he covered the mug with his hand.

"The earth, you say." Igor Ivanovich started to button his coat and to bend back the fangs of his lapels. "At this point we ought to be interested in six feet of earth..."

"What are you saying? Now they don't dig that deep—you'll be lucky to get five feet."

"I like it in Gatchina. It's a nice place, dry... Is it true that Tatars are buried in a seated position?"

"Everyone is buried according to the law. Tatars too... Does our corpse belong to us, after all?"

Igor Ivanovich was in a hurry:

"Take care, Shamil. As they say, thanks for the company. I have to rush."

Shamil raised his mug with the rest of the beer in it.

The friends parted forever.

Since the relationship between Igor Ivanovich and Shamil will not be continued and will not be embellished by another word, gesture or event, it's possible to sum them up definitively and make a conclusive characterization of this irreconcilable friendship of many years.

The word "irreconcilable" isn't used here to darken, to place in the shadow of history the great number of gestures of friendship and good will, sympathy and support, concern and attention to each other which had accompanied their friendship during all these twelve years. Perhaps both of them so appreciated the company of the other because in this exchange each one could confirm every time his very own rightness and his very own view of the things and objects in the surrounding world. All who had witnessed or participated in their arguments, discussions or conversations—and that includes most of the people in Gatchina—were always amazed at the ease and unexpectedness with which either Shamil or Igor Ivanovich in the heat, at the very height of an irreconcilable conversation, suddenly agreed on some important point, but not the main point, and this very admission that the other was right was the pinnacle where their aspiring souls came together. The argument would seem to subside and both friends, finding themselves on the raft of friendship, suddenly stopped noticing the foaming unruly sea of irreconcilable contradictions around them. If among the observers of these moments there had been a witness to the meeting of the imperial personages on the raft at Tilsit,* who knows, perhaps this fortunate man might have been able to find similarities among people who are filled with magnanimity, nobility and justice.

Igor Ivanovich went out on the low flat front steps and looked over the area. The two-story row of houses led his eyes to the end of the street where a 130-foot high pile of red brick—the gigantic cathedral—stood alone, needed by no one.

Among the houses large and small that lined the former market square—which had become yet another city wasteland—it towered much like a fortress, affirming through its appearance its non-participation in the bustling and sleepy life which flowed by.

Igor Ivanovich decisively set out in the direction of the courthouse.

As usual his glance touched on the *Terek* street clock, as big as a drum, which had for years testified with its drooping hands to the senselessness of keeping time in a place like Gatchina.

Igor Ivanovich's intention was to drop by the courthouse and find out more precisely when the case was scheduled to be heard and whether Nikolai had arrived, or whether the case had been postponed to another day, which could happen. This intention was quite well-motivated and promised to be a small, but essentially necessary errand. But one would

---

*A reference to the meeting between Alexander I and Napoleon in 1807.

have to be very nearsighted not to notice that Igor Ivanovich simply couldn't deny himself the pleasure of entering a serious official institution on business and, moreover, completely without fear.

Igor Ivanovich's fate had been such that he hadn't had the slightest desire to get involved with a civil service job.

The very word "service," which was so applicable to Nastya's work in the trade organization, or for Igor Ivanovich's sister's job in the book-keeping division, and generally for many jobs, didn't describe the many-faceted activities of Igor Ivanovich himself. Although one could, of course, perhaps say that the navy and the army—where he had served in the mobile bath and laundry detachment during the war because of his heart trouble—could be called service, but not in the absolute sense: it seemed to him that service could only be voluntary, chosen by oneself, that is civil service. After the war, in which he was wounded, he spent five years in camps in the Svirsk area for having been a German prisoner of war, which happened to all the laundry workers, owing to the regimental comman-der's forgetfulness—he hadn't warned the "louse-killers" deployed in the forest of the tactical change of position. So after the war he worked in Borisoglebsk in a sausage plant, but the name "service" would be too ele-vated for "that kitchen," as Igor Ivanovich called the plant which featured emaciated frozen carcasses, bones, pus, and sausage almost liquid from an excess of starch. Nor would that name be suitable for his work in the car-pentry workshop at the city trade office or at the oil depot, or at other piddling institutions like them. Service consisting of official activity did not resemble at all the roles in which Igor Ivanovich had performed.

For instance, service implies a strict order, beginning with the need to show up punctually and to leave no earlier than prescribed. Even during the strictest of times, when you got time in prison for being late for work, Igor Ivanovich always had at his disposal some personal time, ranging from a few minutes to a few hours, which couldn't at all affect the pro-gressive motion of the state mechanism as far as further development went.

Never during his whole life had Igor Ivanovich been in a position which might have permitted him to say, "There are many of you but only one of me..."; "I won't receive (give out, give permission, examine, listen) any more today"; "You see, there's someone here, let me finish, then come in"; "So what's this you are trying to give me?"; "You've come to the wrong place"—and the things like this he had heard all his life when he had to move in the *service spheres*. He could never feel himself as an ele-ment, or as they used to say then, cog, of that gigantic, highly complex, beautiful and rational machine which embraced all of life in all its details, which is turned on at the same time (this is why people come to work on time), and is turned off at the same time, since there is no reason for some little cog to keep going if the entire machine is just resting and gathering strength for tomorrow's rotations.

And one more thing. In the civil service, as far as Igor Ivanovich knew, each person must prove himself, that is constantly prove to each and every one that he is worthy of his position and perhaps deserves a higher one. This is how the little cogs became wheels, the wheels became levers, the levers grew into driving belts, and these driving belts merge imperceptibly but very closely with the main flywheel...

But where Igor Ivanovich happened to work nobody expected or demanded any proof; just work and keep working.

When the time came for him to receive his pension there was real confusion. He collected almost all the essential documents with the greatest difficulty, and we have to consider that except for the documents about imprisonment and exile, all the others were really awfully difficult to collect; but it all proved to be futile, because in the end the social security office required a birth certificate or a legal copy from a church book, or at least some guarantee instead of them. And where Igor Ivanovich was born, what year, which month, in which books and in what language these corresponding entries appeared, this he himself couldn't guarantee, let alone find someone to certify it.

So that is the dreams of a comfortable 36 rubles, which had kept Igor Ivanovich and Nastya warm during the last years before their retirement, collapsed completely and irrevocably.

And perhaps it was because he hadn't worked in the civil service that Igor Ivanovich retained a deferential respect for office mysteries, for paperwork, for everything involving work with ink, pencils, abacuses and paper. Just observing that kind of work greatly impressed him and he saw only one way to express his respect and understanding of the complicated and important nature of the procedures he was observing—namely by his desire to disturb and distract the people engaged in civil service jobs as little as possible.

The walls of the building to which Igor Ivanovich Dikshtein was headed were famous for being the site of the first experiment in commemorating contemporary history. This first try at using marble didn't turn out too successfully. In 1917 the Gatchina City Soviet was housed in this building, barely differing from other city structures which had been erected under the supervision of the architects Shperer, Kharlamov, or Dmitriev. In memory of this event a plaque was put up in 1927 and unveiled, accompanied by music and speeches. The plaque informed the citizens: "Ten years

ago the first Gatchina City Soviet was located here..." In exactly one year what
had been inscribed for eternity had become obsolete, and the question came
up whether it would be necessary to renew the inscription every year or
whether they should at once cover up the ill-starred "Ten years ago..."

After the war the People's Court was housed on the second floor of the
building.

There are places which are indescribable. That's what people say, but
it's hard to agree. It's another thing to say that there exist some places
which are impossible to describe, and one could insist that the corridor in
the Gatchina court house as it looked when Igor Ivanovich was there is
one of those places.

The corridor is impossible on the strength of its extreme untypicality,
and rendering an account of it might easily lead one into historical error,
since it can't be asserted definitely that this impossible place continues on
to this day in its entirely impossible state.

Who knows, maybe it has become wider and a decisive hand may have
rooted out its acrid infusion of tobacco and wet felt boots, fur jackets
smelling of diesel oil, the sweetish smell of nursing breasts, the inescapable
smell of the men's toilet, since the door had been torn off during certain
memorable events and was at that time standing out in the corridor,
leaning against the wall, so that it was still possible, if one desired, to use it
to cover up the doorway.

Who knows, perhaps the Themis of Gatchina has already left these
walls and moved into a separate building in a toned-down Corbusier style,
a structure of glass and concrete, adding to the variety of architectural
forms and styles in the little town.

But meanwhile, the two weak lightbulbs could not fully reveal the
entire spacious ugliness of the rather long corridor with its shallow recesses
for stoves, nor could three little posters (about how to save drowning
people, the collection of taxes, and about some holiday or other), cover it
all. Most of the stoves were in the offices and in the two courtrooms. The
firewood that had been dumped here rather carelessly didn't attract the
visitors who were sitting on benches or simply standing along the walls.
The logs were damp, but any interference in the heating process, even
with the intention of somewhat decreasing the smoke which penetrated
into the corridor, was met by the sternest and most jealous objections of
the person whose job it was to see to the stoves.

To say that no laughter or mischievous children's voices were ever
heard in this corridor would be as unjust as not mentioning that people
often cried in this corridor.

Tears were seldom seen in the eyes of the people who had come here in groups or with companions or who had on the spot simply formed small parties of from two to twenty people. It was different for the individuals who had grabbed a comfortable corner of a bench with an unbroken arm rest or by a stove ledge, forming rather cozy little nooks; here they could give themselves over to profound sorrow in privacy, accompanied as a rule by quick movements of the hand with a crumpled handkerchief by the women and loud noseblowings by the men.

There are places that are impossible to describe!

But what does all this dense, blatant shame matter in comparison with the disgrace and pain, hope and fear, filth and pride, in comparison with the anguish and faith in miracles, with the thirst for truth and fear of truth which people bring here, inaccessibly hidden within themselves and even more often from themselves, this whole muddle of life's thorny complications, which only yesterday had been your own private business but now suddenly are torn away from you, like a play you have written which is being leafed through by a yawning director who knows that he has to stage it anyway...a piece of your life fallen into the hands of a lazy, untalented cast.

Why is this fellow with the head of a new recruit standing behind the low barrier, trying to make out something over there beyond the window when he can't hear anything, and only the peculiar pallor on his cheeks gives away the fact that he is involved in the sentencing?

The simple and pitiless truth, pronounced by the prosecutor, can't be diminished even by his inarticulateness, inconsistencies and incorrect stress on words of foreign origin.

Why doesn't this broken-hearted mother hear the words of the sentence, why is she thinking that everyone is looking at her accusingly because she at the last moment decided not to sell the television and give the lawyer more?

And only a slight, disinterested self-ennobling sympathy fills the souls of those who have crowded into the room, hoping to make the time seem shorter until their own case comes up.

Igor Ivanovich without trouble found Nikolai in the corridor and noisily greeted and kissed his nephew.

Nikolai was barely taller than Igor Ivanovich, and his warm Chinese coat with a belt and a mouton collar made his figure more solid. The open newspaper in his widespread hands gave him the appearance of an independent man who didn't expect troubles from fate: he looked more like a witness than anything else... And actually he was a witness to how in Leningrad, on Borovaya Street not far from Obvodny, a drunken driver from Gatchina had started before the green light changed and ran over a woman who was running across the street.

The nephew was looking through the open newspaper and in a rather coarse and playful masculine way salted his speech with such expressions as "slowdowns," "the devil knows why I did it," "they don't know what the hell they want." In Igor Ivanovich's opinion he looked splendid. Sitting down beside him on the bench, he also loudly, but with some restraint, cursed the procedures, the officials' inability to consider people's time and all the annoyances, and he sincerely stressed the fact that this case was extremely clear cut and it was simply ludicrous to fool with it for two months, remembering subconsciously that twice in his life his "cases," while much more complicated, had been resolved quickly and without any long, drawn out proceedings.

The people in the corridor quieted down and started to look at the vociferous Igor Ivanovich and his solid companion in the Chinese coat.

Igor Ivanovich even got a little excited. He was ready to go somewhere, tell somebody something if necessary, and point out and mention... But his nephew stopped him, remarking condescendingly and wisely that the officials cannot be rushed, that if they did piece work, then it would get moving, and he gave out a laugh... A crazy thought suddenly flashed through Igor Ivanovich's mind; perhaps they were getting paid by the piece *back then?*

"Don't wait here, Uncle Gosha... Why sit here and stew? As soon as I'm done I'll come over to your house."

"Don't even think of eating anywhere! We're expecting you for dinner. How do you like *Moskva* beer?" Igor Ivanovich held up the net bag with two fingers. The nephew expressed as much delight as if he had seen Mongolian vodka.

"We won't start without you, you hear!"

On this note they parted.

Life had directed its not inconsiderable efforts toward suppressing the feelings, wishes and needs of Igor Ivanovich since his youth, but this had not only failed to blunt his lust for life but had, on the contrary, sharpened it to such an extent that Igor Ivanovich could no longer allow himself to neglect even the slightest chance of gratification, and he tried to experience every such possibility to the fullest, expending his energy without concern. Therefore, instead of choosing the shortest way home, he took a roundabout way—past the cathedral.

Turning homeward Igor Ivanovich again began to contemplate that very skillful creation, as common as could be, actually—namely, the famous

Gatchina Cathedral of the Intercession—the whimsical translation of the Christian spirit into stone, which in appearance was a blend of church and barracks. No, this isn't the fruit of an artist's love, the kind of fruit which has, beyond the drawings and specifications, the secret aspiration of the artist to unite heaven and earth, to help the heart behold the light and harmony concealed in the inscrutable and the eternal.

The boarded-up windows and solidly shut doors imparted to the cathedral the appearance of a top security prison where, as everybody knows, the windows are not only traditionally covered with bars but also with those metal "muzzles," like gaping pockets, which let daylight in only from above.

Igor Ivanovich sometimes caught himself thinking, as he walked by the cathedral, that he was listening for something. His hearing really did get more acute by itself, not because Igor Ivanovich was hoping to discern a mysterious call, unheard by others, but because he simply couldn't believe that such an enormous building, with mighty walls and solid locks, didn't contain a single living soul. Perhaps it was that ancient instinct throbbing in his soul which doesn't let man accept uninhabited mountains, empty forests, the ocean depths or even the transparent empty sky, but insists on populating that world beyond human eyes with mysterious creatures and spirits, both good and evil—the capricious rulers of human destinies.

But there was no soul in this brick bastion meant to be the habitation of the spirit. Since 1904, when the cathedral was founded and the construction began, Gatchina had lived in proud expectation, hope and confidence, as if through the tall doors of the new temple everyone would enter a renewed life, cleansed of moral filth and even of poverty. They couldn't believe that so much labor, effort and money wouldn't add goodness and grace to life. The brickwork was excellent—now they don't even lay tile that well. They took their time building—working for ten years, but before they had finished the exterior, they threw all their efforts into finishing the interior, and consecrated the cathedral hurriedly as though foreseeing its short lifespan, and opened it to the parishioners in October of 1914. The war had started and they couldn't possibly count on a speedy completion of all the work.

The tent-shaped belfry soared upward at a height of 160 feet, placed on the top like a small chapel, and at 130 feet the helmet-like cupolas bubbled out in the canonical five-headed cluster.

And why did the Vokhonovsky Convent, nestling with its poor daughter church at the foot of the gigantic cathedral, need to raise such a temple when the buildings of the convent remained unplastered until its closing at the beginning of the thirties?

Born at the wrong time, the cathedral started to crumble after less than 30 years, as if it had been raised just for the purpose of amazing—either by the foolhardy conceit or by the limitless credulity of human beings, or perhaps just to become yet another example of the transitory nature of a body abandoned by its soul.

So it had stood there for almost 50 years—dead to heaven, dead to earth and dead to hope.

Just last year Igor Ivanovich was amazed to see workers attached to security ropes near the lopsided cupolas of which only the metal structures survived, making them look like huge cages for huge birds. But when only two of the four cupolas remained on their small drums everything was explained: the condition of the two others was considered dangerous, and they had only enough energy and means to guard against unnecessary misfortune.

Igor Ivanovich is no longer here and no one can say why he was attracted to this gloomy red brick colossus with cupolas broken right through, the steep inaccessible walls, the silenced bells in a belfry open to the winds.

Perhaps this most imposing edifice of the municipality of Gatchina, standing among the squat, two-story, ugly little houses reminded you of the gigantic battleship which had made even the large naval harbor in Ust-Rogatka seem small?..

And perhaps in a moment of spiritual weakness when you wanted a reasonable and just God to exist in this world, you would locate him right here, within the empty and cold walls, protecting his sorrowful wisdom from pagan fuss and incomprehensible verbosity, from flattery and cajoling in the unsteady candlelight and the glimmering gilt of the rich icon settings, from priestly importance and the competition of people in humble self-disparagement?..

Perhaps the wide flooring put together from sturdy planks, covering the roomy staircase at the main entrance, reminded you of one of those tiny Kronstadt piers where steam-powered cutters were moored, taking sailors on shore leave to flap their bell-bottoms all over the sidewalks of Petersburg and Gatchina, Strelnya and Oranienbaum—Rambov for short? This flooring was constructed to make it easy to roll barrels into the cathedral and drag crates and bags into the city trade warehouse, which had long since occupied the vacant premises.

All that's left is to conjecture that the cathedral exerted an attraction because of its fantastic combination of mundane features and details, reminding Igor Ivanovich each time of quite different aspects of his life, which had flashed by so quickly: the fortress, the battleship, the dungeon, the storage room, and the convent which in its day had gone unnoticed by the sailors, and the pulled-down cupolas which had until recently risen above the people. One can only console oneself with the fact that Igor Ivanovich himself was a rather fantastic man, and so you can rack your brains all you want, but you will never guess what exactly attracted him to this gloomy edifice which had grown old without ever having started to live.

Oh, Igor Ivanovich, Igor Ivanovich, my abyss... my still waters!.. No one will count the tears which life squeezed out of you, and who will hear the words which you didn't speak?.. Birth was your beginning and death your end. You were rejected at birth, and you couldn't hold on to anything in your life, either... Either you weren't needed or you didn't find a way to fit in, to hold on to anything, not malice, envy, or desperation... The earth ripples beneath you, but strictness is your support. All that you touched took you over completely, for you had no other life than that very minute... You are like the first man who ever felt the need to understand the sense and meaning of his every word, his every deed and action, who immediately turned this understanding into a rule and a law, not permitting yourself to retreat from this law and expecting the same from others, expecting it and demanding it for their own good. And every injustice and even outrage you put down to a failure to know these strict laws and regulations, each time wondering why people live according to hastily concocted provisional regulations when even the blind could see that the time had come to cancel them, but no, they won't do it. And what kind of power and good fortune do those people have who make up all these provisional regulations for their own advantage while others accept them and implement them without question?

Since in a way he essentially didn't exist, Igor Ivanovich was assigned no duties by anyone, no achievements were expected of him, and therefore, with full confidence he could consider that he had fulfilled his main duty in life as he understood it. What can be more important than to prepare oneself for the kind of life where changes and improvements will no longer be needed, where everything receives its own name and place, where it won't be necessary to stand guard over justice and honor since no one will encroach upon them? So it came about that Igor Ivanovich's thoughts and advice relating to rules and laws about the just and strict arrangement of life weren't needed by anyone and went almost entirely toward constructing and preparing for a better life the one man who was in part subservient to him, who had for more than 40 years borne the name of Igor Ivanovich Dikshtein.

Oh, Igor Ivanovich, Igor Ivanovich!.. Who will ever be so lucky as to know a man whose existence would be denied everywhere—about whom people would say that no such person could ever have existed! You don't exist, ask anybody! And no matter how your boots crunch on the snow, no matter how you clank your bottles in the net bag, slam doors and raise your voice at Nastya, you don't exist and you know this yourself better than anyone. And what kind of Igor Ivanovich can you be if even Nastya twice caught herself thinking she couldn't remember your real Christian name—she did remember it, of course, only not immediately.

Igor Ivanovich would probably be amazed to find out that his soul, filled to overflowing with strictness toward himself and with readiness to meet another, better life, because there was no room for him in this one, that his soul was perhaps that very abyss into which tens of states, hundreds of governments, thousands of little gods and tsars had vanished—an abyss that dissolves into itself century after century, saving from oblivion only those who were strict toward themselves and fervently yearned for another life.

Clanking the bottles, Igor Ivanovich passed the cathedral in a state of equality and independence, at this moment free from the burdens of concepts and of bodily sensitivity. And if it hadn't been for the excessive tension which was everpresent in Igor Ivanovich, he easily might have enjoyed in full measure a state conducive to bliss. Turning left, he disappeared behind a stone wall as though walking through it. And those few pedestrians who at that time were walking behind him along the former Constable Street couldn't see how the tall thin figure suddenly staggered, as though tripping or startled, like a man who suddenly wakes up and realizes that he has lost his way and, therefore, gazes all around him with a puzzled look, still trying to locate familiar objects, trying to understand how this happened and how he can get out of it... The net bag with the bottles slipped out of his hands and clattered down on the trampled snow... Here, 104 steps from the door to his house, the last merciful gift of fate awaited him—an easy death from a heart attack.

Igor Ivanovich staggered and fell sprawling in the snow. He was already dead as he fell.

———

The last thing that needs to be explained is the title *Captain* preceding Igor Ivanovich's name at the very beginning of the story.

Despite the fact that he went to the public baths only in the morning when it was almost empty and the steam was hot, it was impossible for Igor Ivanovich to conceal his naval background since he was covered with blue tattoos, like a medieval map of the night sky with Virgo, Lyra, and Aquarius. He firmly rebuffed all the efforts of his friends and acquaintances to find out the details of his service in the navy, which at first caused the concocting of legends, and later, no one knows how, led to the nickname Captain. The internal tension, sternness and categorical manner which were constant features of Igor Ivanovich also strongly supported the accuracy and correctness of the adopted title.

It is true that Igor Ivanovich was only called Captain behind his back out of respect for his serious and quick-tempered character, and for this reason he died without having an inkling of this—his third name, thought up by the friends and acquaintances with whom he had lived side by side for the last 15 years of his life. A woman screamed as she saw the old man fall.

A young man ran to stop a car. Brakes screeched. A car door banged.

Someone cried out when he recognized the fallen man as Igor Ivanovich.

The noise of the city entered the hollow body of the cathedral in muted echoes but didn't remain there, dissolving without participating in the particular life of this petrified cry of hope which stood forsaken by the people and by faith itself, an unrealized gateway to the kingdom of eternal bliss and recompense, a dwelling of the spirit abandoned by the spirit and condemned to abide.

1977-87

Translated by Margareta Thompson

Translated from *Kapitan Dikshtein* (Leningrad, 1989)

TATYANA TOLSTAYA
NIGHT

In the morning Alexei Petrovich's Mommy yawns very very loudly: hurrah, up and at 'em! The new morning sprays into the window; the cactuses shine, the curtain trembles; the gates of the nighttime kingdom have slammed shut; the dragons, toadstools, and terrifying dwarfs have vanished underground again, life triumphs and heralds trumpet: A new day! A new day! Too-roo-roo-roo-oo-oo-oo!

Mommy scratches her balding head very very fast and tosses her bluish feet off the high bedstead: let them dangle and think a while about having to drag around all day the two hundred and ninety pounds Mommy has amassed in her eighty years.

Alexei Petrovich's eyes are wide open by now. Sleep streams gently off his body; the last raven flies off dreamily into the gloom; the nighttime guests have finished gathering up their spectral, ambiguous props and interrupted their performance until the next time. A light draft sweetly fans Alexei Petrovich's bald spot, now and then unshaven stubble prickles his palms. Is it time to get up? Mommy will see to it. Mommy is such a big, booming, capacious woman, and Alexei Petrovich is little. Mommy knows the ropes and gets wherever she wants to. Mommy is all-powerful. What she says, goes. And he is a late child, a little lump, nature's blunder, a fallow patch, a soap sliver, a cockle, an empty husk destined for burning that by chance ended up among its sound brethren when the Sower lavishly broadcast the full-blooded seeds of life over the earth.

Can he get up yet or is it early? Don't give a peep. Mommy is completing her morning ritual: she trumpets into a handkerchief, pulls clinging stockings up the columns of her legs, and fastens them under her swollen knees with little ringlets of white rubberbands. She raises a linen frame with fifteen little buttons onto her enormous bosom; it's probably hard to fasten them from behind. A gray chignon is fixed to Mommy's zenith; refreshed teeth flutter out of the clean night glass and shake themselves off. Mommy's facade is covered by a white fluted dickey, and a coarse navy casing goes over the entire majestic edifice, concealing laces down the back, wrong sides, rear formations, service stairs and emergency exits. The palace is erected.

Everything you do is fine, Mommy. It's all right.

All the Men and Women in the communal apartment are already awake, bustling about and talking. Doors bang, water gurgles, tinkling noises come through the wall. The ship of morning has left the slip, it slices through the blue water, wind fills its sails, and well-dressed travelers laugh and exchange remarks on the deck. What lands lie ahead? Mommy is at the helm, Mommy is on the bridge; from the tip of the mast Mommy peers into the shining ripples.

"Alexei, get up! Shave, brush your teeth, and wash your ears! Take a clean towel. Screw the cap on the toothpaste! Don't forget to flush. And don't touch anything in there, do you hear me?"

Fine, fine, Mommy. That's how you always say the right thing. That's the way it all suddenly makes sense, the way the horizons are flung open and it's safe to sail with an experienced pilot! The ancient colored maps are unrolled, the route is drawn in a red dotted line and bright, easy-to-understand pictures mark all the dangers: here's a menacing lion, and on that shore there's a rhinoceros; here a whale spouts a toylike fountain, and over there is the most dangerous of all, the big-eyed, long-tailed Sea Maiden, slippery, deadly, and enticing.

Now Alexei Petrovich will wash and tidy himself; Mommy will come to check that he hasn't made a mess in there, or else the neighbors will make trouble again; and then something yummy to eat! What has Mommy made there today? You have to fight your way through the kitchen to get to the bathroom. Old women grumble over hot stoves, brewing poison in small buckets, adding the roots of frightful herbs and following Alexei Petrovich with their bad glances. Mommy! Don't let them hurt me!

He splashed a bit on the floor. Oy.

There's a crowd in the hall already: the Men and Women are leaving, they make noise, check their keys and purses.

The corner door with the frosted panes is wide open; the impudent Sea Maiden stands on the threshold, smirking and winking at Alexei Petrovich; she is all tilted; she blazes with Tobacco and has her leg thrust out; she has spread her net—wouldn't you like to get caught, eh? But Mommy will save him, she's already rushing up like a steam engine, red wheels clacking, hooting: Out of the way!

"Brazen hussy! Go away, I tell you! It's not enough that you... and to a sick man yet!"

"Ha-ha-ha!" The Sea Maiden isn't scared.

Quick—into the room. He's safe. Phoo-oo-oohh... Women—it's very frightening. It's not clear why, but it's very upsetting. They walk by—they smell so nice... and they have—Legs. There are lots of them on the street, and in every house, that one, and that one, and this one, behind every door; they're hiding, doing something, bending down, rummaging around, tittering behind their hands; they know, but they won't tell Alexei Petrovich. So he'll sit down at the table and think about Women. One day Mommy took him to a beach in the country where there were a lot of them. There was one there, kind of... a wavy kind of fairy... like a little dog... Alexei Petrovich liked her. He went up close and started looking.

"Well, anything you haven't seen?" cried the fairy. "Blow, get out of here, you retard!"

Mommy came in carrying a sizzling saucepan. He peeked. In it were rosy little nozzles of sausage. He was glad. Mommy loads up his plate, moves things around, wipes up. The knife breaks loose from his fingers and strikes sharply somewhere to one side, cutting the oilcloth.

"Your hand, pick up the sausage in your hand!"

Oh, Mommy, guiding star! You're pure gold! You'll take care of everything, wise woman, you'll untangle all the knots! You knock down all the dark corners, all the labyrinths of the incomprehensible, impassable world with your mighty arm; you sweep away all the barriers—now the ground is flat and level. Be bold, take another step! But farther on—there are more wind-fallen trees.

Alexei Petrovich has his world, the real one, in his head. There everything is possible. And this one, the outer one, is wicked and wrong. And it's very hard to keep in mind what's good and what's bad. Here they've made arrangements and come to agreements, they've written Rules, horribly complicated ones. They've learned them, they have good memories. But it's hard for him to live by other people's Rules.

Mommy poured coffee. Coffee has a Smell. Drink it, and it shifts to you. Why aren't you permitted to stick out your lips, squint your eyes to your mouth, and sniff yourself? Wait until Mommy turns her back!

"Alexei, behave yourself!"

After breakfast they cleared the table, set out glue and cardboard, laid out scissors, and tied a napkin around Alexei Petrovich: he was going to glue little boxes. When he finished a hundred, they took them to the pharmacy. That brought in a little money. Alexei Petrovich really loves the boxes, he's sorry to part with them. He wants to hide some unnoticed, to keep at least a few for himself, but Mommy keeps a sharp watch and takes them away.

And afterwards strangers carry them out of the pharmacy, eat little white globes from them, and tear up the boxes and throw them away! They throw them right in the wastebin, and not only there—in their own apartment, in the kitchen, in the garbage pail he sees a ripped and defiled little box with a cigarette butt inside! Then a terrible, black rage overwhelms Alexei Petrovich, his eyes glitter, he gushes saliva and forgets words, fiery spots jump before his eyes, and he's ready to strangle and tear someone to pieces. Who did it? Who dared to do it? Just get out! He rolls up his sleeves: where is he? Mommy comes running, placates and leads off the infuriated Alexei Petrovich, takes away the knife, and tears the hammer from his convulsively clutching fingers. The Men and Women are afraid then and sit quietly, taking refuge in their rooms.

The sun moved across to the other window. Alexei Petrovich's work is done. Mommy has fallen asleep in the armchair, she snores, her cheeks gurgling, and hisses: psht-sht-sht... Alexei Petrovich very very quietly takes two boxes and cau-autiously, on ti-iptoe, tup tup tuppity, goes over to the bed and car-r-refully puts them under the pillow. At night he will get them out and sniff. How nice the glue smells! Soft, sour, muffled, like the letter "f".

Mommy woke up, it was time for a walk. Down the stairs, never in the elevator—you couldn't shut Alexei Petrovich in the elevator, he would struggle and squeal like a rabbit. Why can't you understand—they pull, pull on your legs and drag you down!

Mommy sails out ahead, exchanging nods with acquaintances. Today we are delivering the boxes: it's unpleasant. Alexei Petrovich deliberately trips over his own feet: he doesn't want to go to the pharmacy.

"Alexei, put your tongue in!"

Sunset fell behind the tall buildings. Golden panes burned just under the roof. Special people live there, not like us: they fly like white doves, fluttering from balcony to balcony. A smooth feathery little breast, a human face—if a bird like that should land on your railing and bend its head and begin to coo, you would stare into its eyes, forget the human tongue, and begin to trill like a bird and jump with shaggy little legs along your iron perch.

Below the horizon, below the plate of the earth, gigantic wheels had begun to turn, monstrous belt drives revolved, and cogwheels drew the sun down and the moon up. The day was tired, he had folded his white wings and flown off westward; large in his roomy garments, he waved his sleeve and released the stars, he blessed those walking on the cooling earth: Until we meet again, until we meet again, I'll come back tomorrow.

On the corner they're selling ice cream. He really wants some! The Men and Women—but especially the Women—thrust bits of money into a square little window and receive a frozen crunchy goblet. They laugh, they throw the round sticky papers on the ground or stick them to the wall, they open their mouths wide and lick the sweet spiky cold with their red tongues.

"Mommy, ice cream!"

"You can't have any. You have a sore throat."

If he couldn't, then he couldn't. But he really wanted some! It was awful how much he wanted some! If only he had bits of money like the other Men and Women, silver and shiny; or a yellow paper that smelled of bread—they took those in the square window, too. Oy, oy, oy, how he wanted some, they all could have it, they all got it!

"Alexei, stop turning your head!"

Mommy knows best. I'll listen to Mommy. Only she knows the true path through the wilds of the world. But if Mommy were to turn her back... Pushkin Square.

"Mommy, is Pushkin a writer?"

"Yes."

"I'm going to be a writer, too."

"Of course you are. If you want to—you will be."

And why not? If he wants to—he will. He'll take a piece of paper and a pencil, and he'll be a writer. That's all, it's decided! He'll be a writer. That's fine.

In the evenings Mommy sits in her roomy armchair, lowers glasses onto her nose, and reads in a deep voice:

> Storm the sky with darkness cowls,
> Snow in eddies whirls and sweeps;
> Now like a feral beast it howls,
> Now like a little child it weeps...

Alexei Petrovich really likes that a lot! He laughs broadly, baring yellow teeth, he rejoices and stamps his feet.

> Now like a feral beast it howls,
> Now like a little child it weeps...

Just like that the words reach the end—and then turn back, and go on again—and then turn back again.

> Stor mthes kywi thdar knessc owls
> Sno win ed dies whir lsan dswe eps
> Nowl ikeaf er albea sti thowls
> Nowl ikeal itt lech il ditwe eps

That's great! Here's how it howls: oo-oo-oo-oo-oo!

"Hush, hush, Alexei, calm down!"

The sky is all covered with stars. Alexei Petrovich knows them: little shiny beads, suspended on their own in the black void. As Alexei Petrovich lies in bed trying to get to sleep, his legs start to grow down, down, all by themselves, and his head up, up to the black dome, always up, and it rocks back and forth like a treetop in a storm, and the stars scratch his skull. But the second Alexei Petrovich, the inner one, keeps shrinking and shrinking; he contracts, disappearing into a poppyseed, into the sharp end of a needle, into a little microbe, into nothing and, if he is not stopped, he will vanish into it altogether. But the outer, gigantic Alexei Petrovich sways like a lodgepole pine, grows, and strikes his bald spot sharply against the night dome—he won't let the little one disappear into a point. And these two Alexei Petroviches are one and the same. And that's sensible, that's right.

At home Mommy undresses, demolishes her daytime body, puts on a red robe, and becomes simpler, warmer, and easier to understand. Alexei Petrovich wants to jump into Mommy's arms! What nonsense! Mommy goes off to the kitchen. For some reason she's away for a long time. Alexei Petrovich checked that the little boxes were still in place, sniffed the glue, and took a risk—he went out into the hall. The corner door, where at night the Sea Maiden's guests titter, is ajar. He can see a white bed. But where's Mommy? Maybe she's there? Alexei Petrovich peeks cautiously through the crack. Nobody there. Maybe Mommy is hidden behind the wardrobe? Should he go in? The room is empty. On the Sea Maiden's table are open cans, bread, and a pickle with a bite out of it. And something else—a yellow paper and little round silver bits. Money! Take the money, rush down the dark stairs, into the labyrinths of the streets, search out the square window, there they'll give you a sweet cold little glass!

Alexei Petrovich snatches, jingles, overturns, runs, bangs the door, breathes noisily and hastily, stumbles. The street. Darkness. Which way? That way? Or this? What's that in his fist? Money! Somebody else's money! The money glows through his hairy fist. Put your hand in your pocket. No, it glows through anyway. Somebody else's money! He took somebody else's money! Passersby turn around and whisper to one another: "He took somebody else's money!" People pressed to the windows and nudged each other: let me see! Where is he? Over there! He's got money! Ah-ha, you took it? Alexei Petrovich runs into the darkness. Clink, clink, clink, clink—it's the money in his pocket. The entire city pours out into the street. Shutters are flung open. Arms jab from every window, eyes glitter, long red tongues are thrust out: "He took money! Loose the dogs!" Fire engines howl, hoses uncoil: where is he? Over there! Go get him! Alexei Petrovich thrashes about in panic! Throw it away, rip it from your hands, get rid of it, get rid of it, that's it, there! Use your foot, your foot! Tr-r-ram-m-ple the bits! That's the way... All of them... They aren't breathing. They're silent now. The glow's gone. He wipes his face. That's it. Which way now? Night. It smells. Where's Mommy? Night. In gateways wolves stand in black ranks, waiting. I'll walk backwards, that'll fool them. That's good. It's stifling. I'll undo my buttons. I'll unbutton everything. Good. Now? Women with Legs went past. They turned around. They chortled. Ah, so, so-o-o! Wh-a-at? Me? I'm a wolf! I'm walking backwards! Aha, that's scared you, has it? Now I'll catch up and pounce on you—we'll see what sort of Legs you have! He rushed at them. A scream. A-a-a-ah! A blow. Don't hit me! A blow. Men smelling of Tobacco hit him in the stomach, in the teeth! Don't!... Oh, leave him alone—can't you see... They walked away.

Alexei Petrovich propped himself against a downspout, spat black stuff, and whimpered. Poor little fellow, all alone, lost on the street, you came into this world by mistake! Get out of here, it's not for you! Alexei Petrovich cries with a loud barking noise, raising his disfigured face to the stars.

Mommy, Mommy, where are you? Mommy, the way is dark, the voices are silent, and the paths lead into trackless swamps! Mommy, your only, your best beloved, long awaited child, borne in suffering, is weeping, he's dying!...

Mommy comes running, Mommy gasps for breath, stretches out her arms, shouts, seizes him, clasps him to her breast, runs her hands over him, kisses him. Mommy sobs—I found him, I found him!

Mommy leads Alexei Petrovich by the bridle into the warm burrow, the soft nest, under her white wing.

His swollen face is washed! Alexei Petrovich sits snivelling at the table with a napkin tied around him.

"Do you want a nice soft-boiled egg? Soft, all runny?"

Alexei Petrovich nods: Yes, I do. The wall clock ticks. Peace. Delicious hot milk, mellow, like the letter "n." Something becomes clear in his head. Yes! He wanted...

"Mommy, give me paper and a pencil. Quick! I'm going to be a writer!"

"Oh, Lord! Misery mine! What on earth do you... Well, don't cry, calm down, I'll get them; hold on, you need to blow your nose."

White paper and a sharp pencil. Quick, quick, before he forgets! He knows it all, he's made sense of the world, made sense of the Rules, he's grasped the secret connection among events, grasped the laws that link millions of fragments of disparate things! Lightning flashes in Alexei Petrovich's brain! He frets, grumbles, snatches a sheet of paper, shoves glasses aside with his elbow, and, amazed himself at his joyful regeneration, hastily, in large letters, records his newly found truth: "Night. Night. Night. Night. Night. Night. Night. Night. Night. Night."

Translated by Mary Fleming Zirin

Originally published in *Oktiabr,* April 1987.

VLADIMIR MAKANIN
LEFT BEHIND

1

A dream haunts the old man—my father (Mother died, Father is lonely, and, when I visit him, he tells me about his haunting dream in great detail. If I don't visit, he calls me and tells me the dream over the telephone. Sometimes plaintively, sometimes angrily.)

I can't help him with his dreams—that's clear. But I can listen.

Father tells me how he runs out the gate, pulling his hat on his head, still in his undershirt (the undershirt isn't even tucked into his pants), the belt, not even buckled, swings back and forth as he runs. And, of course, the moment he runs out, Father already knows that the street is empty and he's fallen behind the rest. "As I was running out, I already knew everything for sure." "You felt it?" Yes, yes, he felt it ahead of time, he knew: the truck (a one and a half-ton truck from those times, banging noisily with its sides) had already left. He's all alone...

He dreams that the truck is already far away, and that the people there, in the car, in the back of the car, are also half-dressed, but they've managed to jump in, climb in, and they're shouting something to him and waving their arms while the car gathers more and more speed. And for some important reason, something unyielding, the truck can't stop for even an instant, or put its brakes on and pick up Father; and this calamity, this inevitability of lagging behind is seemingly the main feeling of this recurrent dream.

Is it excruciating, painful—undoubtedly so. But, in addition to the pain, is there at least the smoothness of a dream, the anesthesia of a slow glide through the air, and with it at least a smidgen of dignity, if he had to stay behind?.. Possibly not. There's absolutely nothing, just fear. He sees his little picture again and again: trucks roar off, speeding away one by one, people shout, drivers snarl back at them while pushing down on gas pedals and pressing against their steering wheels. The wheels of the trucks make grinding noises: one, then another, then a fifth truck; now the last truck roars off, and only now does my sleepy father, one of the very last people, run out of the house, slipping on the snow. "Guys!" he shouts, the freezing air burning his throat. "Guys!.." But the cars have a huge running start—he can see the last one—and that's why he's running after it, his shirt untucked and his hat hanging over one ear. Of course, he won't catch up with it. He simply can't, he's unable to catch up. At least he understands that, now that he's left behind; sleepy, half-dressed, he understands it more and more. Still he runs, tucking his white undershirt with his hand into what really is his underwear, tucking and running—not hoping and still hoping. By now he's been left behind. The frosty morning is sunless and gray. The truck is far away. He's alone in the middle of the road.

He'd complain that the dream was excruciating precisely because of its sameness, and that he certainly didn't deserve such a dream as a punishment. "I worked hard and honestly, I fought in the war honestly! I don't deserve this!" shouts Father, already gasping for breath in the middle of the day. He'd complain, insist on seeing doctors again. Because it's not simply a bad dream, because he suffers in the middle of the night, suffers in earnest, suddenly jumping off his bed and his mouth trying to catch some air. I won't even go into the palpitations—the pain, the pressing fear! How his poor heart knocks about in his rib cage!

(In the Moscow suburbs the absence of a phone is the usual. To call me Father leaves his house and walks about two hundred steps to a rickety phone booth near the post office.

He called at two in the morning. I could barely calm him down.)

I'm shaving, looking from time to time at my grizzled stubble in the mirror: when I'm unshaven, the gray makes me look older. The phone's ringing, I know that it's Father and I take my time because now he calls every day. The ringing's becoming frantic; I put my razor aside, step away from the mirror—but it's not my aging father, it's my daughter on the phone: "Dad!.. Dad, why didn't you answer? Can't you hear—I'm falling apart here!.." It turns out I'm needed. It turns out that her school friend, a young guy by the name of Vitya, has gotten himself into some sort of domestic trouble (something about getting a passport); the situation has been exacerbated by a mutually rude conversation at the police station; and now we have to help this young and hot-headed Vitya somehow—you can't manage without a passport.

"Dad, I'm waiting, I'm all nerves!" There are tears in her voice.

I begin to shave again, allowing this minor but, nevertheless, real concern to penetrate my consciousness. Father's call (from the previous generation) and my daughter's call (from the next generation) are like waves rolling in opposite directions, subduing each other. However, for a second both trills sound in my ears simultaneously, merging and locking in onto my "I" like the dates of a life trapped between them by some higher power. They overshadow me, as if "I" is a simple point of contact between these two mutually opposite signals from the past and the future.

I imagined how he (having gotten out of bed) goes to call me in the middle of the night, and my irritation immediately subsided. The phone booth is two hundred steps away from the house—not far—but you have to get dressed, adjust to the weather, decide whether you should drink tea first and then go to call, or go right away, quickly, while the dream is still fresh and beats and thumps in your heart, and your heart sinks, jumps, and can never return to normal; after tea—who knows—you might not want to go any more, and the two hundred steps might seem too far. Yes, yes, if you go right away, then you don't have to get over the embarrassment and awkwardness of a night call: you can do can do anything in a hurry.

He takes matches: he mustn't forget those. He remembers the number, but he has to see to dial in the dark booth. With a little help from the matches, a little by touch, he dials my number.

There he is, already old and stooped, standing in a suburban phone booth (the booth is dirty and smelly). The match lights and quickly burns out. Night surrounds him. A man stands there, and, after putting in fifteen kopecks, dials calmly and carefully. The old man is my father.

Who was Little Lyosha?.. He was a boy, at first a boy, then a teenager and a youth who trailed after an artel of gold prospectors and lived on their kindness. That was a long time ago. The prospectors walked a great deal—along mountains, valleys, and mountains again. Lyosha's feet were swift and his heart strong, but he lagged behind more and more—he was listless and young—and at times an extraordinary blueness would appear in his eyes, a childish blue mist which they called a quiet craziness. A boy like any other, but with this sudden something in his eyes. It was like a veil. Whenever they discovered that Little Lyosha had got lost again somewhere, Fedyaich, the eldest in the group, would just shrug it off. "So he's lost, that's fine, it's no skin off our neck!.."

Left all alone somewhere in a valley, Little Lyosha unfailingly would suddenly realize what had happened. He would immediately run after the group, hurrying and shouting:

"Hey!.. Hey-ey-ey!"

And they'd shout back if they were nearby.

But more often, Lyosha would come to this realization when he already lagged far behind. Then he'd walk alone. And spend the night alone. When it got dark, he'd use his eyes to track them down, he'd see the distant campfire of the prospectors who'd stopped for the night, and all night long he'd walk in the direction of that little light. But more often, he'd catch sight of Fedyaich and his companions' fire from a mountain so far away that suddenly he'd begin to whimper—he was still so little! And people had gotten to be so unfair, not like they used to be!—whimpering, he would start his own small campfire to protect himself from the cold, and would just sit there. He slept a little by the fire, but with the first cool of morning he had to walk on.

He would arrive on the scene by noon, when the prospectors' work was already going at full steam. He would sit near them and watch. But if he tried to work in his weakened state, he would collapse.

The prospectors were all strong fellows, real men, but he was only about twelve or thirteen. The prospectors did not stay put in any one place, but walked on and on, leaving shelters, huts, and dugouts here and there along their path.

Sometimes they'd find a bit of gold (usually only a little, but they did find it); and then, when they got to the point that there wasn't any left, Yegor Fedyaich would weigh the yellow sand, tie it in a tobacco pouch, and, after a quick meal, say: "Pack up, men! Let's get going!.." And they'd send somebody ahead and he'd find the old path. They followed and waited for the man with the cart or wagon. They'd sit on the grass by the road. Fedyaich would smoke. And the clouds would drift by unhurriedly. And it was only then that Little Lyosha would find them, catch up with them.

"Look at this, he didn't get lost!" Fedyaich would laugh.

But Fedyaich's assistant, the young and quick Shishov, all covered with the yellow gold-bearing clay, would say somewhat reproachfully:

"Lyosha, why didn't you conjure up a cart or two for us on the way? The timing would have been perfect!"

Lera—that was her name, the name of the girl I loved when I was a student.

Once the prospectors ordered Lyosha to guard (to stand by) an unusual boulder of malachite. They wanted to pick up the stone on the way back, break it into smaller pieces, and take it to the settlement's craftsmen: they wanted to make some money.

But when they returned from the stream, they simply couldn't find the boulder. They yelled for Lyosha, shouted, whistled with two fingers—but nothing. After wasting a lot of time, they finally formed a long line, and one of them, the last one in line, somehow chanced to find Lyosha. Lyosha was asleep. There was a large twisted crack in the boulder, and little by little Lyosha had slid down (apparently from the heat) to the bottom of the crack and fallen asleep there. Of course, he couldn't say anything to justify himself in response to the men's yells and bitter curses. And the men, worn out from work, were tired and hungry.

Fedyaich was so incensed that he ordered the men not to feed Lyosha; even before this happened Fedyaich couldn't stand anyone who slept during the day. Moreover, he'd gotten hoarse shouting for Lyosha (afraid of losing such a beauty of a boulder, one, moreover, with just a single, advantageous crack that made it easier to view the stone from the outside and inside, and made it easier to get to the design: to the natural play of the green veins). Hoarse and angry, he ordered the men not to feed Lyosha, and after lunch kicked him out altogether. But they brought Fedyaich around. They ran across some wretched beggar later that same day: disheveled, with gray matted hair and a huge cross around his neck, the poor beggar sat with them a bit while they rested, declined the kasha and hot water, had a piece of dry bread, then left. But first he interceded for Lyosha.

Fedyaich kicked Little Lyosha out several times.

There exists a peculiar temptation—to conflate time. I was probably searching for consoling words at that moment. And I couldn't find them. And on the phone I said to my aged father who was haunted by his dreams of falling behind: "Do you remember the old Ural story about Little Lyosha, the gold prospector? Do you?"

Most likely, the question required too much of an effort for my father's memory: Father wasn't delighted, nor did he express excitement, but our

usual conversation got off the track. Father got all tense: what's the connection between a youth who falls behind (yes, yes, there was some such
story!) and his dreams, in which he is so painfully left behind a truck?..
But there was no connection. Time merely shifted for an instant, but
didn't merge. And Father, justifiably nonplussed, asked: "And what is
there to remember, really?" He even repeated the question, as if trying to
pinpoint my meaning.

But I didn't know either what there was to remember—anybody could
get lost somewhere sometime. I laughed awkwardly into the receiver.

"Oh, I didn't mean anything in particular, just remembered it for some
reason."

But Father was already worried: Why this story? What's the connection?

"No connection whatsoever. None at all—I simply remembered! Some
time back I wanted to write a novel about it. When I was a student."

"A novel?.."

He finally believed that my words were in fact a coincidence, a fortu-
itous recollection that had drifted into our conversation, and he complained, saying that we often digress from our topic, and what for?.. But,
strangely enough, this brief sojourn into the past suddenly calmed him
down. Father sighed and said quietly:

"I'm going to bed. I'm sleepy."

2

Shishov was fast, young, and smart; he could understand things and
quickly take charge. Of course, they tried to steal an assistant like that
away, they tried to entice Shishov away and envied Fedyaich. Once some
strapping men from the Volga region doggedly followed the group for
several days (there were four of them; they were said to have been hired by
jealous rivals for a good sum of money). Taking advantage of Fedyaich
being sick, they attacked the prospectors and shot at them. The sleepy
prospectors hid in the bushes, while the Volga men dragged by the hair
those who hadn't run far: Little Lyosha and a new helper. In the end, they
broke both children's hands, threatening to do the same to the assistant
Shishov, hinting, as it were, that he shouldn't work so quickly and well. As
if to say, "The same's in store for you." They put a lot of their Volga experience into this business. Then they left, after they'd whistled and hooted
at the prospectors still hiding in the bushes, and after they'd broken one
of their pans and taken their food.

When they gathered together again, the prospectors cursed, accused one another, and, in the heat of the argument, didn't think to put splints on the boys' hands. They did take care of the young helper who, towards evening, began to moan loudly; but Little Lyosha had to wait for three days until Fedyaich, who was sick, finally splinted the boy's hands at home. This happened after the group returned to the settlement, when they came to Fedyaich, and (as they told their story) sat down to supper. Lyosha's wrists mended unevenly. And that's how they stayed.

Then Fedyaich kicked Lyosha out again, because now, with his hands all crooked, he could barely work or help in any way.

For some time after this, Little Lyosha hung about the settlement's church, swept up, took out the garbage, cleaned, and prayed; then he followed some horsemen around for half a year, then came back and again attached himself to Fedyaich's artel; and then it turned out that God had given him an extraordinary gift—the ability to find gold.

The prospectors' artel moved through the mountains, from stream to stream; and Lyosha followed them day after day, hurrying because he'd fallen behind. Usually he caught up with them only at the very end of a haul, by the stream where they had their last lengthy panning and their last stop. Then the artel would turn back home. On the way back they stopped (because they had to stop somewhere for the night) at the same spot where Lyosha spent his nights after he'd fallen behind; and they usually found gold there. Gold dust. And even nuggets. When they'd noticed it, they started making use of it. From time to time they'd even call their return trip "*Lyosha's way*," and on their way back they washed about four or five times more gold than on their initial search. So there wouldn't be any mistake, they put small pieces of mica in his pockets, so that the lagging Lyosha could inadvertently spill it here and there, leaving traces when he tossed about, dreaming, by his small campfire. The prospectors had a good chance of finding the place by the sparkles near the stream. Usually Lyosha himself remembered his night stops quite well, but occasionally (when he was trying to remember) he'd hesitate for a long time, walking along the stream and scratching his head in doubt: "Here?.." and then again: "Or here?"

With time they started to need him to lag behind. So it's not surprising that they walked quickly and easily, and that there was no way he could catch up with them; of course, on the way back the tired prospectors walked slowly, and would stop slowly and pan a certain amount of gold sand. It was almost a sure thing.

A rumor started that, of course, exaggerated and blew out of proportion his prospecting capabilities. He became famous. At first quietly, then openly, other artels started keeping track of Little Lyosha. He had no idea. He only noticed that they fed him better. This whole business led to arguments and clashes among the different artels. And while Lyosha dragged himself after his men through mountains and valleys, trailing behind more and more, prospectors from different artels fought more and more on account of him. And once after a fight some prospectors who were unwilling to give him up to some others—as happens in the world—killed him.

I was a student at one of Moscow's technical institutes, and, like everybody else who came from the Urals, I was homesick; it's not surprising that sometimes I felt like seeing mountains and the steppes leading to them all around me. When you find yourself in a big city, you at first tend to feel sorry for yourself (and for your hero). It touched my heart that Lyosha was little, that he ran around the mountains, and that he wasn't aware of his gift. The ambiguity of the finale was especially appealing in those old stories. Somehow nothing was said about the fate of Lyosha's murderers; but the murderers' children were cursed: they turned into stone. The fairy-tale nature of the story wasn't abruptly explained, nor was it obligingly whispered. Old women from the Urals can still point out the stones on the mountain slopes. Huge, ugly, twisted stones, protruding out of the ground—*come over here, I'll hand you over to them, I'll hand you over to them right now, for good, uhhhh, so scary... Now you'll listen to your granny, won't you?!*

In the dorm I shared a room with three math majors, and, leaving after classes for the public library, I justified my actions to them by saying that I worked better there than in our institute library. I'd say that I wasn't distracted by familiar faces there. Lera (who was a Muscovite) didn't live in the dorm and also came to the public library occasionally; she'd appear in the hall, and, the moment I saw her, I'd hide the notebook with my novel in a pile of books and lecture notes.

Often we'd immediately go for a walk, and I (notice the smoothness of the transition!) would tell her about some of my relatives in the Urals, about the beautiful green stones (which are scattered about right under your feet), about the mountains, and about the smells of the nearby steppe. Lera liked it, and she'd sigh: "I envy you. It's so interesting!"

But more often, in the spirit of the times, I, like many other students, talked about the consequences of Stalin's cult of personality, about the fact that there apparently had been many instances of the abuse of power, about Tukhachevsky, Yakir and many others, and how wonderful it was that everything was out in the open, and that justice had triumphed. I was passionate, impetuous, and talked with particular ardor about the simple people who had suffered:

"Just imagine, Lera, how bitter they must be!"

But Lera was silent. I noticed her silence when it was already present and would continue, but I didn't notice when it began. For some reason she was as guarded at these moments as she was sympathetic toward my stories about the Ural people: it was as if she weren't old enough to handle the boldness of these conversations. But, perhaps she didn't want to be able to handle them? We walked around the buildings of our institute, where fir trees, stretching their symmetrical branches with a rustle suddenly showered the ground with snow. Fresh snow crunched under our feet. A little farther stood our lane of snow-covered young poplars.

"Just think, Lera, to fight for the revolution for so many years, to give your youth to it, your best years, to give your thoughts and soul—and to be punished for nothing! That's true pain, that's true suffering!"

Lera was silent. She didn't voice any objections, no, no, but she didn't keep the conversation going either.

I would see her off to the subway station, sometimes to her house, and then would return to the dorm. In our room the students would be up late, talking, but there were times when all three were already asleep. I'd unload my notebooks and notes from my small gym bag (they were fashionable then instead of briefcases) into the desk. But I quietly hid the notebook with my novel (so that nobody would stumble upon it) on my shelf in the wardrobe, in that corner where my three T-shirts were folded in a pile.

No Name Mountain is more of a small plateau, a flat and gradually ascending hill that I remembered from my childhood. There were Mt. Snake, and Hare Mountain, and, simply, Mt. Stone, and there was also a famous mountain called Little Clay; its side was yellowish-white, and, after the rain dried up, they constantly scraped and trimmed the softened clay there. But of all those mountains only one, which stretched and ascended so high that it didn't even resemble a mountain, remained nameless. Nevertheless, it was a mountain, and if somebody tried to climb it, it took only half an hour for his feet and back to really appreciate that this wasn't a hill or a slope, but a mountain.

Once Little Lyosha, who had fallen behind, rejoiced suddenly when he saw a group of people climbing up the mountain; it was the artel, and he hurried after them.

But there weren't any people there. This mountain's deceptiveness was well known. The mountain not only sloped gently, but also undulated to such a degree that you were immediately and easily reminded of a bent, never-ending washboard. Bushes grew between the crests of these undulations, and when their sharp tops stirred they created the illusion of people walking. People seemed to be walking on and on, ascending No Name. The movement of a body in motion made the tops of the distant bushes peek out, and, having peeked, they'd immediately shift forward, move. A person would stop, not believing his eyes. Then the picture would freeze: there was nobody there. But then the haze would work on you. The undulations of the mountain probably forced an unevenly heated current of air; the warm air would curve, glance off the living tops of the bushes, and once again it would seem as if there were people there, the artel.

Lyosha would hurry on, but the artel would also be moving away, the men walking in single file. He stopped. The artel also stopped. He shouted to them: "Hey-ey-ey! Hey-ey-ey!.." and nobody even turned his head. They just stood there. But the moment he took a step, the artel immediately moved forward.

I described so painstakingly Little Lyosha's state as he hurried after the imagined artel, with the group mirage now freezing, now moving again and I felt such compassion that the state of mind of a person who's fallen behind and is trying to catch up imperceptibly entered into my consciousness, apparently entered it deeply and significantly. (And considerably earlier than I identified this feeling in myself. The feeling came first. That happens.)

He didn't understand that he had become needed. He didn't see himself either from his past or from the present; and with his wonderful gift he couldn't and wasn't capable of becoming rich, of course, or of determining his way of life (because of his childishness, because of his limited mind). But now they fed him better and dressed him pretty well: they gave him boots; Yegor Fedyaich eagerly took him into the artel, and, when the snow melted and the weather permitted, they would walk through mountains and make the rounds through valleys; they'd walk right beside him and even help him walk if they encountered a steep hill or a river crossing. But early in the morning, when he was drowsy in the warmth of the fire (he'd get really exhausted, tired from walking), they'd leave him and move on. He, poor soul, would be terrified waking up, because he was now one of them, because now they all seemed to be on good terms, and talked to him now so much more kindly—why were they leaving him behind now? What for?! Having found some peace and believing, as all weak people do, that now he was loved and would be loved forever, he'd suddenly wake up, look around the cold fire, and his heart would sink: they'd left him again, he was alone again!

He didn't know that they had to leave him behind: they thought that his rare (and still weak) gift came alive precisely in solitude, in his sleepy, shivering body. And jumping up from the ground, scared, and cursing his capricious fate, Lyosha would rush after them again. But he couldn't catch up with them the whole next day either; so he'd stay for the night somewhere, and start a fire, without connecting his stopover at all with the fact that on the way back they'd stop precisely in this spot and would almost always find some gold. Gold drew him, but he might not have realized that. It drew him by itself. Some people said that he could "hear" the gold with his crooked hands. With the scars of his crookedly mended wrists.

Although it wasn't hard to find where he stopped at night on account of his amateurish campfires, they nonetheless told him: "When you stop for the night, Lyosha, notice where you stop, or maybe, make a notch on a bush, or stick a branch or a stake in the ground by the stream to make it more visible." "But what for?" he would ask, raising his eyes, filled with blue mist. "Don't ask, Lyosha. Just do what we tell you!" And that's how it was. And they panned gold for themselves with the first easy sand. Occasionally, he also "heard" gold nuggets. In the old women's stories it was sometimes disclaimed, or at any rate doubted, that he could "hear" with his broken hands. For example, the famous Ural gold nugget *Deer* (353 grams; in the shape of a deer frozen in a high jump with its head turned to the left) was found by Little Lyosha even before the attack of the Volga men, when he was eleven, when he dug the yellow stone out with his stick at some stop after he'd become totally absorbed playing and walked down the stream away from the prospectors.

Other stories disputed Lyosha's murder. They lay in wait for him, but didn't kill him, just *broke his hands again* (that were already crooked?); he had new scars and after that couldn't "hear" gold anymore. But he could "hear." (He could understand adults' actions better now, but understood himself less and less. He "heard." That's all there was to it.) Incidentally, these stories also concluded more naturally. In the finale Lyosha, who kept lagging behind, fell behind for good. He got lost in the mountains at night and didn't find the artel. He was said to have gone over the ridge, crossed the woods, and come out at an Old Believers' farm. He lived there for a year. Then he seemed to have reappeared in the summer with the loggers near Listyugany. Then all traces of him vanish.

Having lost his men, he could have ended up with people who didn't know either about his sensitive hands or about looking for gold, and, understandably enough, rumors about him stopped of their own accord.

After his death (or his disappearance?), little by little they again began to look for the spots where he once stopped for the night, to check them as well as those paths along which he dragged himself after Fedyaich's artel when he was still a little boy. By that time gold-prospecting had acquired new gadgets and the technique of riddling. New enterprising people came into the business. They washed the panned-out sand again without any embarrassment and dug into places that had already been dug—just to dig deeper. They were thorough: they asked experienced prospectors (real silent types) about how many miles Lyosha could walk in a day, and how many in a night, and whether they remembered on which side of the fire the youth liked to sleep. Suddenly it became known that they found gold nuggets in the very place where the artel had taken a large malachite stone (in whose crack Lyosha had once fallen asleep), in the deep indentation left in the ground by the dug-out stone. And then the artel's "dregs" (the black, ferrous sand that had been left after panning) was reckoned to be worth something. Rumor spread that this youth, Lyosha, wasn't at all naturally lethargic, listless, and lazy; that he didn't fall behind Fedyaich and his men because he was weak or lazy. Gold beckoned him, it called him continuously, it attracted, drew, and beckoned him; it confused his brain and made him sleepy. That's why he fell asleep walking in the mountains, that's why he fell behind.

Years passed, but shrewd merchants and prospectors continued to seduce artel members, who'd really aged by now, with gifts, good drink, or money: Now, try to remember, old buddy, try to remember, grandpa, where did you go in your young days with the late Yegor Fedyaich when you and your young artel member Lyosha spent days and nights together?.. If they couldn't show them the places where they'd camped for the night, then at least they could show the path—even that was a lot, even that promised luck and success. And they'd lead some elder in his nineties, who was barely able to see or think straight, or, if his legs refused to obey him, they'd even carry him in their arms or on a stretcher roughly nailed together, through some impassable spot. And this is more than half a century later! The stream flows noisily; a group of ten to fifteen people is crossing the stream, and two of them, drenched in sweat, are carrying a half-blind old man. Like a tribal chief, the elder raises his arm and occasionally moves his finger weakly: let's go there, or maybe there—I'll remember in a second!..

Everyone stands still and waits. The stream flows noisily. And the old man lies on the hard stretcher, moaning. He's forgotten who he is and why he's here. He's thinking about his new hat with the ear-flaps. He doesn't understand why they're carrying and dragging him somewhere all the time; he begs to be taken home, says: "let me go," and cries.

I told Lera about the wonderful sturdy, rough, and spirited people who live in the Urals—in Rudyansk, Kaimyk, around Hedgehog Mountain. I transferred the stuff of legends into the present, and one moment populated the environs with daredevil reckless drivers, and the next (and even better) with the men in charge of explosives who, without hesitating, would sacrifice their lives for each other—who perished, burned, and suffocated in the shafts. Lera, a girl of that romantic time, would exclaim in her low voice: "How wonderful! How marvelous!"

Sometimes we'd visit her house, and Lera would say: Mommy, Mommy, listen to his story. And Anna Romanovna would turn to me with a stern look; and I'd start again about the Urals, and again with feeling. It was as if the blue contours of the mountains were right next door. But I was nervous because Lera's mother was listening to me, and as I told the story, I'd put together my words in a strange way, out of order, or, I'd flare up excessively and for no reason at all, and would become too emotional.

Anna Romanovna already had gray hair then; she was about fifty-five. She was a woman of few words. Sometimes we had supper together; it offered me the comfort of a small family when Anna Romanovna set the table, sat with us for about half an hour, and then left unobtrusively. But that time, however, she hadn't left yet and I went on talking about the wonderful people of the Urals (real characters!), how strong they are, how they go looking for ore and gold—and what pine trees, rocks and river bends you'd find there!.. The chicory with milk, which Anna Romanovna made so well, got cold. And the cheese sat untouched in front me—I was talking. And in spite of myself I was being swept away into unknown and uncharted waters. Yes, you know, they're real people, they're true working hands, whereas we are...

"Whereas we're just little students, all talk. What can we do?" And here I raised my arms just a bit, arms which in the evening light seemed thin and weak, if not pathetic. "What can we do?!"

I was overcome by homesickness and began to weep. I wept in earnest, wept tears, which was quite unexpected (for me, too). Of course, I didn't sob more than twice, but even two times was enough to make an impression. There was a pause. I sat at the table in the silence that followed, looking into my cup of cold chicory milk. Anna Romanovna said:

"You're a strange boy, Gena..." She understood that I needed help getting myself out of the silence.

"You haven't touched your cheese." She handed me a piece of cheese and some very fresh white bread, almost placing them in my hand. I chewed; tears of gratitude for her compassion, as often happens, welled up in my throat with new force, but this time I was able to control them and it went away. I gave a sigh of relief. Finally, I looked up. I even smiled as if to say: "See what can happen!.." Anna Romanovna repeated, with a different inflection in her intonation (but also soft): "You're a strange boy, Gena. And you're still such a funny boy."

She was reserved and kind.

Once Lera went to visit her girlfriend in the Moscow suburbs. She was supposed to return home late that night; I called once, then again—Anna Romanovna answered that Lera wasn't home yet. I kept calling every hour.

Shortly after midnight, my voice cracking from worry, Anna Romanovna said:

"Gena, don't worry. Lera probably stayed the night at Aunt Veronika's."

"How can I not worry?! She is so... so..." I couldn't find the words.

And Anna Romanovna calmly and with a mother's certainty completed the sentence:

"Lera is very independent."

I was astounded: I was convinced that Lera was fragile, tender, gentle, and shy in conversation—that's how I knew and saw her—it turns out, however, that with all that, she was also *independent*. Next morning at the institute I made my way through the entire row of students and, as usual, sat down next to Lera. The lecture had already started. But the students were still making noise and taking their seats. Lera touched me with her shoulder and whispered "hello," but her whisper and touch weren't enough for me. I asked her sternly: "Why didn't you call and let me know that you'd be staying the night at your aunt's?" Lera answered:

"I couldn't decide whether to go home or not. I called Mom after the last train had left."

"Wow, you're just so independent!" I said with irony. After this incident the remark became one of our favorites.

The remark also became popular with my roommates.

If one of us, quite innocently, said that he was going out for some fresh air, or, for example, to have dinner, I or one of my three roommates would get in the comment: "Wow, you're just so independent!" And all four of us, including the one going out for some fresh air, would laugh loudly and unrestrainedly, although I don't know what was so funny.

———

During the lecture breaks (and in a whisper during the lectures) the students were discussing a biting polemical article that had just come out in *Novy Mir.* Just like everybody else I became incredibly excited that day and hadn't calmed down that night when I left to walk Lera home. It was like a revelation: we knew the past now, but the past knew us now, too, and it seemed to be there. (We are given our due not for finding out something, but for a belated knowledge of ourselves.)

We were walking down some long alley. It was dark. I was talking about people who'd been repressed and about the rehabilitations that were continuing even now! I was summarizing the details of the resurrected post-camp fates for Lera, and passing on the rumors that were circulating all around; then my heart began to thump, I felt a pang, and I began talking about human suffering: hard bunk beds, searches, roll calls in the middle of the night; I talked, I was on fire, I wanted to make her a part of it, I wanted to draw her into the emotional experience, but Lera remained Lera—silent, as always.

That evening I suddenly got mad. And I asked her directly, demanding an answer:

"Why don't you say anything?.. It's one of two things: either you think that I'm insincere, or you don't care what I'm talking about... No, Lera, no, just answer me: do you care or not?" And she suddenly embraced me, pressing herself against me. It was dark in the alley. Then, standing close to me—I didn't see her face but I heard her—she whispered:

"Yes, I do."

And she moved away.

And we walked side by side again. I was shaken by our first embrace and I lost the power of speech.

People continued reading the *Novy Mir* article the next day too, during the lectures. I remember how, after arriving a bit late, I sat at the very top of the lecture auditorium; the view from there was excellent: I could see the volume with the blue cover being passed to Shitov on the left side of the room; a speed-reader, Shitov looked through it in five minutes, if not three, and sent it on to Kozlova; she and Mlynarova read it together, squinting their eyes; in addition, Gavrilets was craning his long neck and reading it over their shoulders. The journal moved down and then up again. Sometimes it was suddenly grabbed right out of people's hands. Outwardly however, their faces were inscrutable. It was passed on to Todolsky, then to Sergeev...

I didn't immediately notice the second copy of the journal on the right side of the auditorium; wrapped in ordinary lined paper, the journal was being passed around cautiously. Finally, I figured out the pattern: it was right below me, and the journal moved strictly diagonally through Ranenskaya, Kozhin, and Glukhovtsev. I even outlined its further movement in a dotted line: Rogov—Sychev—Olya Stavskaya. Even then this double movement appeared to represent two simplified destinies. The copy on the left fluttered here and there, like a blue moth, while the one on the right, unnoticed, seemed intent on crossing the whole sea of the student auditorium quietly and without witnesses, step by step, making inexorably for the opposite shore. The lecturer, meanwhile, was lecturing. Then another lecturer took over; there were six lecture hours that day, and four of them in the same auditorium, which was considered a great convenience.

Some of our more industrious fellow students—more precisely, female students—kept diaries, and held on to them. So now, retrospectively, I could try to recreate those days in a more expressive fashion (from a student's point of view), if not for fear that the chronological nature of the narrative and the very spirit of that significant time would crowd out Lera and my love for her. Because in fact it was just the other way around: love crowded out everything else.

I'll give just one typical detail.

Once I saw Tvardovsky leave the editorial office of *Novy Mir* and get into a car. We'd come there, to the editorial offices, with a big crowd of students and we saw him come out and get into the car. And he drove away. Admirers, we didn't need anything else: we just wanted to watch. He said something to his driver, and the car roared off immediately. We stood about five steps away. True, when Tvardovsky got into the car, he seemed preoccupied and a bit aloof. However, as I found out later, his somewhat heavy carriage and the way he almost threw his large body onto the seat cushions of the car were due to his bad legs.

He was ill then and probably pale. But because we were young, we thought his complexion very fair.

It happened during supper at their home. Lera was silent, I think. And Anna Romanovna left the room for a moment, then came back and handed me a photo of a man, not a very large photo, in a light blond wooden frame:

"That's Innokenty Sergeevich: my husband and Lera's father. He's dead now. He died *there*. He was just recently rehabilitated."

I remember blushing: my constant and obtrusive conversations about human suffering seemed so inappropriate (in comparison to the dignity of their silence). Now I turned the photo awkwardly in my hands. In my embarrassment I was going to put it on the table, on the crumbs of cheese and bread, when Anna Romanovna firmly and simply took it out of my hands and left the room with it. Still, I had time to say, even after the photo was taken out of my hands, and even though it was said to Anna Romanovna's back: "Forgive me..."

Anna Romanovna's husband and Lera's father had died about a year before. After the camp he lived in permanent exile in the small house of some railroad worker (they showed me another photo); and he died there. Lera didn't remember him. Anna Romanovna said that the process of rehabilitation wasn't simple, the archives were enormous (and in disarray), and cases were being carefully heard one after another; and it worked out that after Innokenty Sergeevich's case had been heard, he died. The rehabilitation papers arrived just before his death. And a nice letter arrived from the people where he lived, saying, we remember him and take care of his grave.

So this summer, the moment the weather settles down and Lera takes her finals, Anna Romanovna will go there; she wants to be where her husband lived and died. Lera will accompany her.

Anna Romanovna told her story...

I was probably shaken: in a few minutes, at a quiet and ordinary supper, all of my and my fellow students' emotional verbosity, lofty words and passionate conversations materialized and acquired concreteness. The guilt that had already burgeoned—a vague feeling of guilt that also was mine and yet not really mine—was now growing more distinct. It was late. I was going back to the dorm and my cheeks were burning.

I was unsettled for another, essentially unimportant, reason as well. The place where Lera's father lived and was buried was called Khonya-Desnovaya, after the name of the river. In the old women's stories and tales about Lyosha, who could "hear" gold sand, the Khonya River, among other places, was mentioned. Even if there are a lot of rivers and streams called Khonya, and particularly Desnovaya (which means the right-hand one, the one on the right), still the names coincided; and the places where Western Siberia borders on the Ural region were also close, one way or another they matched.

Little Lyosha and Lera—*everything that was mine*—had suddenly come together.

———

They had already fixed their departure date.

I was supposed to visit my parents during vacation, too. I was going to the Urals, they were headed beyond the Ural region. On different days, but nonetheless we were all going in the same direction.

Having fallen behind everybody else, yet at the same time able to sense and find gold faster than anybody, he (Lyosha) combined these extreme states. He mixed them up without realizing it. He lived a marvelous life without knowing that it was marvelous, and he envied the ordinary people who walked side by side in the artel and ate their well-earned kasha and bread on time.

But at first smells confused him. That morning (he remembered everything!) he was overtaken by the smell of a goat's path strewn with a goat's dark pellets. Lyosha's eyes couldn't make out anything yet, but though his eyes couldn't see, the smell of the path already oppressed and suffocated him. Lyosha moved to the left, but there the smell of the broken wild rose branches seeped through, and farther to the left his nose was attacked by the smell of a groundhog's distant burrow, with its first litter and the mother's chapped nipples.

Lyosha was blinded. He saw and he didn't see, completely absorbed in the smells. Finally, when his vision began to clear, he made out human figures in the distance—seven prospectors were climbing the mountain. One of them turned around. And for the first time shouted the words:

"Hey you, the one who's always falling behind!"

He didn't even scold him for slowing everybody down. He just shouted.

Once Lera formally invited me to come over. She was a little embarrassed and said:

"Come and visit my mother and me."

Usually I would walk her home and we'd stand at the entrance to her building for so long that we'd both get cold and go to their apartment for tea. But now she was suddenly inviting me. She didn't say "come over" or "come visit me at our house." She said—a little ungrammatically and in a very Muscovite way—"come see my mother and me". And, of course, it became clear that, no matter how many times I had visited them or had tea with them, now, for the first time, she and her mother had talked about me seriously. I wasn't ready for the conversation. The nearly two years of our quite innocent relationship could probably have been contained in this simple phrase: "come see my mother and me." I was nervous, and smoked nonstop on the way to their house. Then we sat down to tea, good tea, and not in the kitchen this time, but in their big room, at the round table covered with a good tablecloth, three cups and saucers set in advance and tasty homemade cookies in a bowl. A lamp with a big shade hung above the table. The lamp was hanging lower than usual—in a somewhat more intimate way—and I found the softness of the lighting pleasant. And then at tea Anna Romanovna asked: "Lera said you were from the Urals, Gena. Are you from the Urals?" I confirmed that I was and told them again where I was from, who my father and mother were; I'd talked about the Urals with them often enough—maybe she hadn't listened to my enthusiastic stories?..

"Gena, tell me about your part of the world," Anna Romanovna asked. "My husband, Lera's father, was repressed. He lived and died precisely on the border of Western Siberia and the Trans-Urals. I looked those places up on the map yesterday."

After a slight pause she said:

"He's been rehabilitated. But we learned about it too late."

She said it simply and calmly. She said it as if she were talking about the tea and cookies on the table. And I blushed then, feeling like a silly youth who had talked too much about human suffering (it was good that I hadn't said everything to her, but to Lera, Lera will forgive me). In the same even voice Anna Romanovna said, now about the tea:

"Is it cold?.. Shall I add some hot water, Gena?"

Afterwards she brought out her husband's picture.

As soon as she received the rehabilitation papers—"Now I have all the rights!"—Anna Romanovna went to Western Siberia, to the settlement of Novostroiny, which, according to knowledgeable people, was very close to Khonya-Desnovaya. She went "to take care of the grave and simply to be there." Lera went with her.

Lera didn't change at all during the days preceding the departure. She was the same sweet, modest, even taciturn girl with whom I'd been going to the theater and movies and whom I'd embraced sometimes on the way back in the darkness of an alley. I allowed myself to embrace her in the semi-darkness of the movie theater; this happened very rarely, and, because it was rare, we were both left breathless. Lera would start trembling quietly and I'd be infected by the tremors. We were together, as if swaddled, and we continued watching the screen together without really seeing anything.

Lera was given permission to take her finals early, and they left.

They left for two weeks; but after one month and already into the second (it was June, and by then I had already passed my exams) they still hadn't returned.

During the days preceding their departure I sympathized with them so much that the moment I saw Anna Romanovna and Lera off at the station, I ordered a phone call home, went to the phone station, and, when my five minute call was announced, immediately told my father that he shouldn't say anything to mother yet, but that I was going to tell him now that I was in love. I was in love with a sweet and wonderful girl, Lera—Valeriya—I loved her and was going to marry her because she loved me too. And only then did I feel a pang, pain.

In response my father (he was then also around fifty-five, but, in contrast to Anna Romanovna, a vigorous and strong man, confident of himself and his life) burst out laughing loudly and cheerfully. I didn't understand. For a moment I thought that there was interference on the line, but no, he was laughing, and I was deeply hurt by his laughter.

"OK, OK," he said. "Don't be offended. It's just that you're still a kid..."

The message was simple: "Come home, son, we'll talk then, if you and your Lera don't change your minds by then."

After passing my finals, I went home.

When I informed them that I was completely serious about getting married, and this time looking them straight in the eyes and not in the heat of the moment, Father did not say anything and went out for a smoke. And mother merely asked again the name of my fiancée.

Years passed, my mother died; and more and more years passed. Left alone now, my father moved to the suburbs of Moscow; he lives not far from me. We're on good terms; from time to time I visit him and cheer him up. Whenever I try to cheer him up and whenever I insist that a person shouldn't lose heart, he says to me: "Do you know how old I am? That's why!"

Yesterday I said to him again: "Do you remember when I was a student, a snivelling kid, and I wanted to write a novel. There was an old Ural legend—remember? It was about this boy, a prospector who, just like you, woke up in the middle of the night with his heart pounding and terrified that he had been abandoned, that he'd fallen behind..." But Father doesn't remember. What novel? What boy?

I remind him: "I wanted to get married then, I told you, but you laughed. You were good at laughing, Dad—remember?.."

"But you've been married for a long time now," my father says. "Your children are already grownup. You've had a wife for a long time."

He doesn't remember.

"Why the hell are you bringing up this legend! Do you mean an old wives' tale?" He's getting angry.

"Yes, of course. I just called it that out of politeness. I'm sorry. Of course, it's an old wives' tale."

(The doctors advised me to talk to him about his dreams as much as possible, to discuss them and eliminate their mystery.)

3

During the day he generally holds up fine. It's at night that he feels bad.

What can you do! We made the rounds of doctors again: we went everywhere, got a mountain of prescriptions, followed by a mountain of drugs: sedatives, sleeping pills and tonics. Father falls asleep, but in the middle of the night, at the very moment the sleeping pill stops working or wears off, the dream about being left behind lies in wait for him; it attacks him, bearing down on him and Father becomes instantly terrified, and drenched with sweat, shouts and calls. I suggested again that he should live with me for a while, but he refused again: he doesn't want to shout at night when my family is asleep.

A professor with a private practice whom my father consulted in secret, without me, advised him (just as this professor had advised me) to talk about his dream as much as possible with somebody close to him and to *talk it all out.* As a matter of fact, that's what we've been doing all along anyway. But now we talk on the phone for half an hour, or an hour, and any outsider would think that we are crazy.

The doctor thinks we're on the right track.

Father always lived, worked, and built (he's a builder) outside of the realm of dreams; he lived a life which never in any way came into contact with dreams. And when his life started drawing to a close, dreams simply had to make a mark on him one way or another. And they did.

"But I don't deserve these torments!" he said indignantly.

The spiritual aspect of every kind of "falling behind" probably suggests a norm; it suggests that somewhere there is defined and there exists a norm which doesn't allow any doubts, that the essence and the meaning lie in that norm and nowhere else. And the rightness of their special cases is so unconvincing. But to conform to the norm, to be like everybody else—is this what appeals and attracts us so?

As he fights off the dreams, he thinks only about one thing: he's been left behind, behind, behind... He may not like this nocturnal feature, he may think it accidental or not accidental, but it is already a part of him; and he is forever connected with these dreams.

And, if someone announced to him that from this night on, he'd be like everyone else again, that the dreams would stop tormenting and haunting him, he'd be glad, he'd raise his head for a while, but soon he'd begin to grieve, grow quiet, and perhaps would get depressed. "Where are my dreams," he'd say.

"What, then, is the truth of my life—is it that I was a builder my whole life? Or does the truth lie in the fact that in spite of all that building, I was overpowered by dreams after all?" asks Father, fervently and categorically.

However, there is no question here.

The house in Khonya-Desnovaya where the railroad worker's family—husband, wife, and grown children—lived, was large and solidly built; when the two-week visit was over, Anna Romanovna talked again to the mistress of the house, saying that she would like to stay longer if they didn't mind. After the death of Anna Romanovna's husband, his small room remained unoccupied, empty. For a while the railroad worker's second son lived there, but he then followed his older brother to a construction site—that's the way they left, one after another. Thus Anna Romanovna made her home where her husband had lived alone and then died. She tried not to move his belongings. His ashtray. His knife, suitcase, his books. She went to his grave and spent long hours there. She became taciturn. She didn't think about going away any more. And it turned out that she settled there.

Lera was afraid that some quiet calamity had befallen her mother. She tried to talk to her this way and that, and talked to the railroad worker and his wife; but, after sighing and moaning, they all decided together to let Anna Romanovna live as she was living. Her pension would be forwarded here, and she'd resign from her job by letter. Moreover, the railroad worker, in his frequent travels, would be in Moscow some day and would try to do the necessary paperwork to get her a small pension due her on account of her husband; she was entitled to it now and the papers were in order.

The only problem was the railroad worker's second son, a boy with a bad and noticeably aggressive disposition; once he got back and raged all night long: why had they taken his room? After he'd raged, however, he soon left. It's true, he wrote two threatening letters, one after another;

but then he found himself a job at some construction site, got completely wrapped up in it, and nothing was heard of him.

A month passed, then another. Lera wasn't living with her mother in Khonya-Desnovaya; she lived in the settlement of Novostroiny some forty to fifty miles away. She was trying to find a job there and had no intention of returning to the institute. And, as it turned out, not just because she wanted to be near her lonely, and suddenly aged mother.

I didn't worry when Lera didn't answer my letter, which I'd sent care of general delivery, Novostroiny. I calmly waited for the beginning of classes at the institute, so that I'd arrive in Moscow, and push my way through the rows of students, sit down next to Lera as usual, and there (in a whisper) ask her about everything. After the lectures, I'd walk Lera home, go up to their apartment, and then, at tea with cookies, Lera and Anna Romanovna would tell me about Innokenty Sergeevich in detail, about what they'd seen there and found out. I think that I even felt in advance how pleasant it would be to drink tea at their home at that hour of the day—to sit at the round table under the low-hanging, soft lamp, reaching for cookies in a small painted bowl again and again.

Then, suddenly, I received a letter from Lera, which was very short and seemed a bit rude to me. Lera wrote that she was finally "living a real life." And that I'd been absolutely right—one hundred percent right—when I told her that we were wimps, leading the life of pathetic specialists programmed in advance, while real life—with its smells, sounds and colors—was passing us by.

The letter ended with these words as if it had been torn off, but at the end there was an even shorter postscript which struck me very painfully: "And I fell in love here for real, too!" added Lera, with a clear and distinct exclamation mark.

That very night I rushed to our small railroad station and headed for Novostroiny. In terms of distance, and on the map as well (since I was going from the Urals to the Urals), it wasn't a long journey; but since I had to go to the Trans-Urals by local train, which meant a transfer and a layover, something that had to do with even and odd dates, it turned out to be far from close. It took me twice as long to get there as it would to Moscow, which was far away.

My heart ached; I tried to distract myself somehow, not to think, and, fighting the nagging pain, occupied myself (and already consoled myself, in a way) with the thought of connectedness: for better or worse, I'll be there now too; like Lera, I'll be connected with those people and with their life of suffering. The old railroad car clanked along, then reluctantly

made loud grinding noises as it speeded up, and once it had gained speed,
it hooted heavily and frighteningly. That's how it was: I was hurrying to
Lera, while Little Lyosha, whom I'd chosen to be my protagonist, hurried
to catch up with the prospectors' artel that had set out through the mountains. We were both hurrying—each in his own time.

On my very first day in Novostroiny I should have realized that Lera's
choice in love had to some degree been prepared for by my own excited
talk. Lera's choice was a noisy man of about thirty who had recently
served time in a camp and was now working as a driver in the settlement.
Even in her letter Lera seemed to have transgressed something, maybe her
own self. A rowdy young fellow, rough, with a weather-beaten face the
color of copper, he was even handsome. To us (to our student youthful-
ness and perceptions) he seemed like a man who was an adult, who had
really lived, and, of course, had suffered. To everybody else at the settlement he was simply the former prisoner Vasya.

We, of course, called him Vasily.
Lera was just a bit embarrassed when I arrived. She didn't hide anything; she was totally engrossed in her new infatuation and admiringly
described Vasily and his life to me. Of course, Vasily hadn't been repressed;
but he had spent several years in a camp, he suffered—right?.. Lera assured
me that I would understand her choice the moment I saw him. Her adoration was selfless, her feelings were sincere, and it was all over with the
past (our past).
"Ah, this is your friend," said Vasily. He got out of the truck and stomped
over to the washstand to wash his hands after several hours of driving.
And he added (from over there): "Friendship is a sacred thing."
And we stood by his truck, shifting from one foot to the other. And she
was right! I, too, was already seeing Vasily through her eyes. I was impressed
with his weather-beaten face, his neck, black from the sun, and especially
with his strong arms—huge knuckles, calluses, and deft hands. His whole
look of a trucker in boots and quilted jacket was beautiful. He smelled just
a little, either from drink, or from chain smoking cheap cigarettes. But he
was a man, a real man, and all of it put together only intensified his pic-
turesque quality.
Lera summarized for me her first conversation with Vasily, which took
place after he gave her a ride in his truck. It happened at night. A former
prisoner, and for the last six months now, a settler with travel restrictions,
Vasily gave Lera a ride and let her off near the barrack where he lived and
where he had to catch up on his sleep after the drive. Right then, feeling

enthusiastic and talkative, she wasn't even thinking of going to bed. Night. A dark barrack. Two people standing by a truck.

Lera: "And you slept on a bunk?"

"When I was doing time?.. Sure, on a bunk. Where else is there to sleep?"

Lera: "My God! I feel so sorry for you!.. You're a real man, Vasily!"

"I'm Vaska, a simple trucker."

She: "Don't. Please, don't act that way with me, Vasily."

He yawned from time to time, showing her that he was coarse, simple, and unbearably tired (the drive really was long and difficult):

"Why don't you push off to your capital cities, Missy. No use hanging around here."

Vasily talked the way a positive, handsome, and wholesome worker in a movie would talk to a young intelligent woman (to a literature teacher or a newspaper correspondent who'd decided to write an article about him).

He (repeats forcefully): "Get lost!"

Lera (smiling. Repeats his name tenderly): "Vasily..."

He: "Vaska."

She (even more softly and tenderly): "Vasily."

They're standing next to the dark barrack. Above them are the stars and the night sky. She doesn't want to leave. She doesn't want to part this way. But the engine is turned off. The door of the truck is shut. Vasily kicked the tires with his boots, looked everything over, and, without saying good-bye to the girl, without any sort of "good-bye," went into the barrack. He didn't give a damn about anything. He really could barely stand on his two feet.

"Vasily... You... Where are you going?"

"To bed."

She was left standing there all alone by the truck. He didn't even ask her where she was going to spend the night. Let her sleep wherever she wants. He left; he could hardly keep his eyes open.

Lera spent that night in the settlement's little office. For a long time she walked around the armed guard, kept looking at him and finally dolefully begged him to let her in. She slept there, sitting on a chair.

Lera talked about herself and Vasily enthusiastically; but something stood behind her, at her back, some shadow, and, as if I'd suddenly remembered something, I asked:

"And how is Anna Romanovna?"

"Mother?.. Mother is in Khonya-Desnovaya." And Lera (lowering her voice) told me that at first Anna Romanovna had taken a place in Khonya-

Desnovaya temporarily, but now she'd got settled in, and it was impossible to take her away: she was always going to his grave. Lera visited her there, sometimes staying over for a day or two, or even three in a row, but, actually, her mother didn't need her.

That same day Lera took me to Khonya-Desnovaya. At first we went to the house of the railroad worker, Khrapov, but Anna Romanovna wasn't in. Then, without hesitating, as if she were going to a familiar place, Lera immediately took me over the little bridge into the mountains. We walked for about half an hour. At the foot of an incline I saw four fenced-in graves and an old woman sitting on a newspaper that was spread out next to one of them. I saw her from afar. Then closer. The old woman was sitting there and whispering something (Anna Romanovna had aged a lot). When we approached her and came closer, she nodded—she recognized me, and said hello. But she didn't say another word.

Then Lera and I left, while the old woman remained sitting at the grave.

They had sunken eyes and skin ashen with fatigue. They weren't having any luck panning the sand; they panned it a second, third and fourth day—and found nothing, nothing. That's why, when they saw the little fool approaching them, mumbling and smiling with happiness at finding them, they began to push him around. Anger (as often happens) found an easy outlet. Someone pushed him in the back, so did someone else; they kicked and hit him, while he tried to dodge them, covering his face and head with his hands. "Guys! Guys!" he was no longer mumbling, but weeping, "Why are you doing this to me, guys?" They drove him off beyond the little knoll. But he sat down there, about fifty steps away from them, and whimpered quietly:

"Hey, guys, why are you doing this to me? I haven't done anything, I'm an orphan."

They worked, panning the sand. It was getting dark.

At sunset he was still sitting there, wailing (and driving them crazy). "I haven't done anything, I didn't do anything, I'll pan the sand like everybody else, Yegor Fedyaich, please forgive me, for God's sa-a-a-ke...," the wretched boy whimpered and wailed.

"Get outa here!" One of the young prospectors couldn't stand his wailing any longer and started chasing after Lyosha with a stick. Lyosha saw him approach, and he whimpered, whimpered and thought: "Let him hit me, let him kill me, it doesn't make any difference, the end is the same—the wolves will eat me." But when the prospector was about ten steps away, running with his stick raised high, Lyosha jumped up, yelled in terror, and started running.

He ran, his shoulder bag swinging; the bag got in the way, but he had food in it and couldn't drop it—he realized that. His pursuer slowed down, but Lyosha kept running, still covering his head with his crooked hands; he ran far, without realizing where he was going. He sobbed and cried, repeating: "Mommy, Mommy, let it be like this, let it be night, let the wolves eat me, I don't want to live anymore. Mommy, hear me in heaven, my kind Mommy, say something..." His shoulder hurt, and his tail bone, where the tarp boot had kicked him hurt, too. He knew that the pain would go away. He also knew that his mother wouldn't hear him. He just didn't know what he'd done wrong, couldn't understand, with his limited intelligence, that the prospectors only needed him when he fell behind and would start a fire somewhere, spend the night alone, and help them find the gold that they needed so badly for their livelihood.

Late at night shepherds would sit down around the fire that had just been started. The shepherds would rub their tired feet, put out their food by the fire, and then suddenly turn round at a rustle in the bushes, at a distant noise (like an animal passing close by—a wild hog? a wolf?), and they'd peer into the murky darkness of the valley. They'd search, then shift their gaze to the hill and see the silhouette of a boy moving away.

"A-aah. That's the one from the artel. The one who can 'hear!' Look, he got separated from his crew again!" the shepherds said. They followed him with their eyes. They felt sorry for him. And then they would settle down by the fire even more comfortably.

But he didn't get separated. He'd been following the prospectors for three days; he walked stubbornly and with determination, his shoulder bag swinging against his side. He wasn't a little boy anymore. He didn't react to insignificant snubs. At night he'd start a fire, make a bed out of fir-tree branches, and have supper; he always made a notch on a branch (or put a stick in the ground near a stream, or lined up three or four stones in the direction of the North star). Only then would he lie down to sleep. He'd be tired. But Lyosha slept restlessly, fitfully, yelling and desperately tossing his head in his sleep. And, all of a sudden, waking up in the middle of the night, he'd decide in a rush of fear that he was alone again (again, Lord!), he'd fallen behind, yes, yes, he'd freeze and starve. Because of some peculiar psychological quirk, he'd regress several years: he would turn from a youth who could "hear" into a little boy who'd fallen behind and perish. And although he usually had bread, lard, and pickles in his bag, in the middle of the night it seemed to him that he was hungry, very hungry; he'd find himself in his childhood, his early childhood, and that was why he'd jump up, put out his fire, grab his bag, and, starving and choking with loneliness and fear in the night, he'd run and run, hurrying to catch up with them. During this one anxious night (on the third or fourth night!) he ran up the mountain and finally saw their fire. He ran up close. The prospectors were asleep. It was just like any other night. Only the one in charge of the fire was dozing lightly.

As he approached the sleeping men, Lyosha's fear subsided, and he finally realized that he was no longer a boy, but a teenager, a youth, that he had food in his bag and that there was no reason to run and chase after them at night, choking with fear. He slowed down, pretending he'd simply found his crew. He walked up to them slowly. He said to the one who was sitting up, dozing:

"I saw the fire, thought it was our guys. What a warm night!"

"Do you want to eat?"

"Yes, all right. Give me some kasha..."

"It's millet today."

He had some millet and calmed down completely. He tried to find a place by the fire to lie down. It really wasn't cold: the night was warm. The fire smoldered away. The man in charge of the fire was hunched over again. The prospectors snored from time to time. For a moment Lyosha was suspended in the usual repetitiveness of existence, like a current of air. Lyosha thought to himself: "Should I lie over here to the side—here, maybe?" And in response his heart beat more and more strongly: *here, here.*

In the artel they treated Lyosha without any particular resentment or cruelty: they walked, above all they walked in search of their goal, they walked farther and farther; and because of the journey's hardships they didn't remember too well or think much about his luck—they walked and searched on their own, they dug the ground and picked the gold-bearing quartz out by themselves, they crushed, panned, and didn't complain about the work; maybe only towards sunset, towards the end of the day would they swear that the road was all clay and that the men were getting sick, and then begin to wonder about that sleepy fellow—he's disappeared again, fallen behind, perhaps he's been eaten by wolves—you feel sorry for the wretched cripple!.. Usually they wouldn't remember his gift until the way back, when everybody in the artel was suffering from back pains, when their bruised feet and hands ached, when they were eager to return home to their families, and suddenly they believed that pure untouched gold was waiting for them by a stream. And somebody would say: "Why *don't we try to pan* where Lyosha slept? We have to go back anyway, and they say that he can *hear* with his stumps."

———

The sleepy, warm tangle of bodies began to stir and turn, and you could hear angry voices and isolated shouts: "He's feeble-minded, he's a simple fool!.. He doesn't understand?.. But he understands where it's warm, doesn't he?" Displeased at having have been awakened in the middle of the night, they yelled at one another and, of course, at Lyosha, kicking and hitting him on the head. But Yegor Fedyaich made more noise than anybody else that night: "And I'm wondering, who's trying to get to my woman? He heads right for her like a shot, goes directly for her head first over everybody else." "I was looking for a warm place," Lyosha kept trying to justify himself. He hadn't even thought of waking them up. It was fall, the wind was whistling, and he kept crawling into the thicket of bodies until he found a warm place. "Sure, you can't find a warmer place than that spot in a woman," the prospectors burst out laughing, but he didn't understand: he was sleepy.

4

Anna Romanovna asked the mistress of the house—a fat and awkward railroad worker—whether there was anything she could hem or mend, and the latter, a soft-hearted woman, at first gave her something of her own or her husband's and then her sons' shirts and T-shirts. It all started when Anna Romanovna settled in the little room, visited the grave, and breathed the air which her husband had breathed there for many years, which was all more or less understandable, but then she began to sew, which was nothing unusual and understandable at first, but soon Anna Romanovna was sewing nonstop: she mended stockings and socks, sewed pockets on, and then, throwing her hands up in the air and saying that she hadn't done it right, took the pockets off, ripped the seams, and sewed it again.

In the meantime Lera was lovingly following Vasily around. "What's it to you?" she asked me. I didn't even try to reproach her, and it was typical that in full accord with the same love for the injured, I, like Lera, not only overlooked his shady sides, but began to respect and even admire him.

Meanwhile, Vasya was neither good nor bad. A former prisoner like any other, he sincerely repented at first, but then, at the settlement, he quickly realized that he was basically free now and that everything was behind him, so he straightened his shoulders and got a bit insolent—he certainly did.

Very little was being built in Novostroiny, despite its romantic name meaning New Building. There were quarries and jobs at the quarries, half a dozen barracks, and about fifty small private houses. And that was it. True, the settlement had a cafe with an old, hollow-sounding gramophone, but it was really a snack bar with the sign *Cafe* hung on it—badly run and poorly stocked—open to people from private houses but not, however, to barracks dwellers (meaning former prisoners). But even without the cafe Vasily could procure liquor, slipping by the checkpoint at the entrance to the settlement. When he was drunk he fought with the locals as well as the police (there were several of them—to provide supervision, so to speak). Vasily particularly disliked the police and called them "intellectuals," a word he had learned from Lera. This delighted Lera and me no end.

Instead of greeting them, he'd yell:

"Hey, you!.. Intellectuals!"

And, of course, Lera was afraid for him; she tried to soften his combative nature a bit. Shaking like a little rabbit, she pushed her way into the very thick of a fight. She hung on people's arms, dragged him away from a barrack or street brawl, and begged him: "Vasily, you're not like that at all. You're just *bitter*. Stop it, Vasily!" Or: "*You're bright and sensitive, Vasily. But you're too bitter, stop it!* To which he usually shouted: "Buzz off!"

Vasily would get involved in a quick affair with a cook or would suddenly disappear with a beefy representative from the consumer's union. Lera would find him, drag him, drunk, out of a smoke-filled little room, and take him away from these women, who in appearance were very simple and presented no competition; she'd pour tea down him and restore him to normal, all the while repeating: "Vasily. Are you bitter again? You should be kinder, Vasily..." Lera lived and breathed him. She managed not only to fall in love, but also to change.

If there were clouds of dust rolling down the road—that was Vasya! Even after several accidents, he still wouldn't slow down on the awful roads. Vasily seemed to rush about in a limited space without having the right to step out even for ten minutes beyond the borders of the settlement Novostroiny, beyond the quarries and the factory a hundred miles away. If the semi-steppe region was nothing but dust all the way to the horizon—the former prisoner Vasya was speeding along anyway. And Lera waited for him. I often waited for him with Lera, standing on an oval hillock overgrown with wild rose bushes.

"Hey, Gena," Vasily would say, jumping out of the truck. "How the fuck can you understand what a Saturday frisk means!"

His greasy right hand would shake mine. His left arm embraced Lera.

———

We especially liked it when Vasily would tell us about the bunks.

He told us how slowly the days go by and how a man on a bunk suffers intolerably. On a bunk a man clearly remembers his distant home town, his native land, the faces of his loved ones, a beer stand and close friends. But what can he do?.. Nothing—you have to work real hard. You look at the guard—the wind's howling—and the guard pitifully moves his rifle back and forth, back and forth: he's cold, too, and he huddles up, there's snow everywhere and if that weren't enough, guard dogs keep circling the zone...

Lera: "I felt it even in Moscow, Vasily. I knew you were on that bunk, and I didn't need the institute, the snivelling students, lectures, or Italian film festivals. I knew that it was snowing in the zone, and that you'd glanced outside the barracks and looked at the gray sky..."

He: "Sometimes I'd crawl down from my bunk. And I'd suddenly remember that song about a black raven. I'd be so depressed. And I'd think: 'Oh, raven, raven...'"

Vasily became a thief because of the booze, that is, by accident rather than by mercenary design. Back in his home town when he was drunk, he'd occasionally attack passersby at night and take their watches and rings. He got eight years. Four of those he served in a camp, and he was serving the remaining four at the settlement, without the right to leave Novostroiny.

Here, too, he liked to fight, yell and brandish his fists, none of which, actually, fell outside the settlement's norm of behavior.

"This is my friend," is how Lera introduced me to Vasily, and we shook hands as hard as we could.

Vasily said: "Friendship is fine. Friendship is a sacred thing."

He opened the hood and began to dig in the entrails of his dreadful, unbearably dirty and banged-up truck. He dreamed about getting rid of it. He dreamed about crashing hard into a telegraph pole, but to do it so that he'd be able to open the door and jump out at the last moment. "Will I get a new one in a strange case like that? If I'm not drunk at all, but crash right into a pole? Will I?" Vasily would ask, and I'd echo him in a deep voice: "You should."

In general my life then was an echo. Not just because I imitated Vasily, and not because the situation itself forced me not to oppose them but to get on well with them, if I wanted to be near both of them, as I'd been earlier. I was young and emotional. And why not admit it?—I was touched to the core by his stories of body searches and bunks.

———

There was a hillock that was a bit bare and covered with short wild rose bushes (about a ten-minute walk from the barracks). It offered a sweeping, clear view that enabled Lera to spot Vasily's speeding truck from far away. We'd wait for him there. We'd wander around the hillock near the wild rose bushes covered with small berries and keep an eye out for him.

I'd reason: "Of course, this is real life and real people. And of course we should try to live here. But we should also think about finishing our education since we've already finished two years."

She sniffed scornfully: "Don't be silly! Two years is plenty if I want to work as a weigher. It's probably even too much."

In fact Lera was already working part-time as a weigher (she was paid by the hour for the time being). She was making some money, was proud of it and generous with it, and once gave her entire pay, down to the last ruble, to Vasily to "blow" with his friends. Yes, yes, it wasn't a bad start. However, so far she had only a promise of a permanent job.

"...Wouldn't it be better to get an education and then come back here?" I said.

"Go ahead, get your education."

"And you?"

"I'll stay here as long as Vasily's here. I'll wait until his time's up, and we'll leave together. On the same train—no other way! And that's when we'll start thinking about textbooks and lectures—we may even remember you then, professor!"

The word "professor" was almost a swear word for us then.

I answered: "But it's possible that they won't *release* Vasily anytime soon." I meant that Vasya could get additional time for his uncontrollable temper and rash talk, and Lera understood my meaning only too well. I have to clarify something here: Vasily's actions and words seemed unbelievably bold to Lera and me then. We were delighted when "bunks," "screw," "stool pigeon" and "zone" were spoken out loud. We got intoxicated with these words and gasped for breath, as if we'd gotten too much oxygen, rather than too little. (And it was also a consequence of our own shaky courage, since we ourselves pronounced these words aloud, when we asked questions. Our hearts melted, our hearts were afloat. Once Lera and I spent a whole night on the subject, whispering: "Of course, Vasily has a stool pigeon watching him. A person like him can't be without a stool pigeon!" And then we tried to guess: "But who can it be?.. Can it really be old Mikheich?")

And then, with a glance back at the spindly wild rose and my voice lowered just in case, I repeated:

"It's possible they won't let Vasily out anytime soon."

"So what? Then we'll both go to Moscow later. By then you'll be a professor for sure and it will be easy for you to get us into the institute. You'll pull some strings and get us in."

The repeated word "professor" could be considered a deliberate insult. I didn't say anything. I became withdrawn.

We both fell silent for a while; not a word was said, silence surrounded us just like the wild rose bushes, and Lera suddenly asked in that sweet, astonishingly sweet voice of old, which she now used less and less frequently—she touched my sleeve and asked me:

"Go away, OK?"

A pure sound; after so many years my heart doesn't really remember much about that love or the loss of it, but it does remember the pure, pebbly, ringing sound of her voice.

One side of the hillock was overgrown with small shrubbery, the other three sides were bare and round and gave a view of the two receding roads, the crossroads where they met, and a twisting driveway in the distance. We walked around in small circles, waiting for the appearance of a dusty comet on the road. "Vasily! Vasily! It's him! I can feel him speeding, I know I'm right!" But Lera was occasionally wrong, since there were a lot of speeding cars around raising dust. When that happened, we'd continue circling the hillock, and each time I noticed some scrub pine and, in addition to the basic wild rose, an unusual small hazel bush standing all by itself. That hazel bush was special: on the left side it was broken and trampled, as if it had been slashed off, and the right side was also growing crooked, too—a crippled bush, unsure of itself. And I kept looking and looking at its unusual angle.

Now I wonder whether that was maybe Vasily's work, or, rather, the work of his truck. Once, in his joy at seeing Lera waiting for him, didn't he fly over the top of the hillock in his truck, fortunately trampling just one bush? He could do that with style. He flew up. He stopped the truck. Slowly and heavily, *wearily* he trod the ground in his tarp boots, moving toward Lera. "Wearily" was another word that Lera and I worshipped then. Lera stepped forward to greet him. But she didn't touch him, she just asked sternly, looking into his eyes:

"Was the drive difficult? Are you tired, Vasily?"

To which Vasily replied, spitting hot saliva, that yes, it wasn't easy and sweet, but in general that it was nothing, and of course it used to be much harder on a bunk.

It's obvious now that the feeling of compassion for people who'd suffered which captivated Lera and me then, sometimes filled us to the point of excessive overflow (precisely because of its fullness). This feeling permeated everything and everybody around us, just as air permeates space and all of its forms—the planes, volumes and shelters that still seemed to buzz from past deportations, the bars that were still on the barracks windows, the shabby barracks themselves, and, around them, hills and woods through which it was impossible to escape. The wish to confess your guilt to a person who has suffered, a subconscious wish (and by contemporary standards, a somewhat farcical one) to come here from the city and show compassion for the former prisoner Vasily was humane, no matter what you say.

The object of the feeling might not have been worth the feeling itself, the object might not have been suitable, but the feeling itself was sincere.

Where did Vasya live? (Or, to put it more crudely, where did he sleep? Because he lived all over the place within the confines of the quarries and roads around the factory.) Vasily was registered as one of the dwellers in barracks number one, where he slept in a room with three other former prisoners just like him. Two of them were young men (that is, around thirty or so), the third was a fifty-year-old man, Pyotr Mikheich, who at the time seemed to us a very old man and, sometimes, like an informer.

The four of them were on friendly terms and they liked to reminisce about the past; for the occasion they'd obtain some vodka on the quiet and also drink it on the quiet. They'd lock their door and sit there smoking for a long time.

These moments of reminiscing seemed supremely happy to the ex-prisoners, and Vasily wouldn't let Lera in if she wanted to be with him. "There isn't anything for you to do here"—he'd send her packing and close the door firmly behind her. Lera would walk around the barracks in agony. It's hard to say whether he was flattered by this or thought she was overdoing it. Then she'd scratch at the door again, dolefully trying to find out something, and then he'd come out and scare her, driving her away roughly: "Go away, go away, it's just men here, unless you want to be handed around from one to another! We know how!.." And Vasily would hem drunkenly, meaningfully, implying that you, sweetie-pie, have no idea how bad we can be. Lera would turn as white as chalk. Her heart would skip a beat; she was seriously afraid that she might end up in that room full of drunks. She'd heard about such things. There was a cafe at the settlement where there were women cooks and dishwashers; there weren't too many women, but there were some.

While the former prisoners talked about life and quietly clinked their thick glasses behind locked doors, Lera patiently waited somewhere at a distance. She tried not to cry, but sometimes she did; she tried to understand him.

In the same barracks number one, at the very end, there was a small room filled with old kettles (five), bedsprings and headboards for extra beds (three), broken bedstands (three), and all kinds of other attributes of dormitory life, including some broken old-fashioned round black speakers. In this small storage room old worn mattresses were stacked high up to the ceiling. Some of them were stuffed with straw instead of cotton. It was here, on top of these mattresses, that Lera slept, using one of the old bedstands as a ladder. Vasily would come to see her. He didn't spoil her too much, explaining that he was used to men's company, smelly male odor, and heartfelt swearing; he'd grown rough in the camp, he said, his soul had been crippled, he'd lost his sensitivity, and couldn't be tender with her all the time.

Lera tried not to cry: "I understand you, Vasily. I understand that it'll take a long time for you to forget those bunks."

She believed that. (She tried very hard to understand him.) It was possible that he believed it himself.

But now I think that maybe that's the way it really was.

Where did I sleep?.. But I was nobody, after all, recently arrived and, moreover, an uninvited guest.

There was no place to stay, but I was young, after all; there was a coal bin, an annex of sorts, which looked like a continuation of the barracks and was built on to the barracks' cross-beam. Lera slept right behind this bin, on top of twenty mattresses, moldy and smelly with age. In the annex there was some coal left over from recent times when they used to heat the barracks themselves (a small boiler-room had been put into operation just the year before). And there, on this petrified coal, on top of three mattresses filled with straw, I made my bed every night. The annex was small, no higher than my waist. So I entered it like a dog. It wasn't easy making my way inside. I'd crawl in. It's funny to remember now how once when I was frozen, I was crouched on all fours and took a dive and landed right in the torn upper mattress—right in the straw. I was shivering from the cold, and I didn't bother getting out of the mattress or changing my body's position; I just fell asleep the way I was. It didn't make any difference!

When you entered the barracks, you could see rooms on the left side, and on the right—a wall of tiny windows. As usual, the first room was a common washroom. Then followed the room of a "family man," that is, a former prisoner who'd acquired a family here. The next room was occupied by another "family man," the next, by invalids, the one after it by two extremely elderly white-haired former prisoners who were called "grandpa"; and only then followed that noisy room where Vasily lived with his three roommates. The last room was the former storage room or a pantry where they set up Lera on the mattresses. And half a meter away, but behind a wall (with an outside, street entrance) was the annex to the barrack—the bin where I slept.

Behind our barrack stood five more barracks with former prisoners, and beyond those, and surrounding them in a semi-circle, stood fifty or sixty small houses of free citizens. In the middle of the semi-circle there were a post office, a small movie theater and a police station. That was all there was to the settlement Novostroiny. In the distance you could see the boiler-room chimney. Still farther stretched a large overhead shelter where they temporarily kept their trucks; once I got caught there in a violent summer rainstorm, a real downpour that beat hard on the tin shelter.

At night I would think about Lera, while Lera thought about Vasily. To put our feelings in some kind of order (and to simplify things somewhat), you could say that in the middle of the night I dreamed about going into Lera's storage room, Lera fantasized about going to Vasily, while Vasily, as you know, sat with his buddies, drinking quietly and reminiscing about the past.

I visited Lera only in the morning; I talked to her standing in the doorway, since it was impossible to enter the storage room since it was crammed with bed stands and other junk. She'd answer from above, from the height of twenty flattened mattresses, that I'd come too early and no, no, she'd sleep a little longer, or, on the contrary, that yes, yes, she'd just woken up, she'd come down right away, change, and we'd go for a walk together. "Wait for me outside, Gena."

And then we walked for hours on the hillock by the wild rose bushes.

I didn't have anything to hope for. But the hours when Lera worked (she left for her weigh station every day) were absolutely unbearable for me. Lera would come back when it was already dark, immediately fall asleep and leave for the weigh station again early in the morning. And the former prisoners, without finishing their cigarettes and suddenly looking important, all hurried off somewhere. I killed time around the settlement. I was alone. The boredom made me miserable. I tried playing dominoes with the policemen on duty, but they were busy and I was killing time again. It was then that I ended up under the shelter for the trucks, caught

in a heavy drumming rain that turned into a downpour. The downpour
quickly died down.

Around the same time I had my first conversation with Kostik.

This Kostik was trying to talk me into an adventure. It was from him
that I heard about a barrack with former women prisoners who were set-
tlers now. Kostik described them in juicy detail, his eyes shining; he said
that they were middle-aged, devil-may-care, and that there were young
ones, too. Kostik was a wise guy and a lazy bum; day after day he loafed
about the settlement where he had to work for only a year. He invited me
to visit these women with him—"'cause it's more fun together"—but I
was embarrassed. Mine was a youthful (and very painful) hesitation, as I
tried to decide whether I should remain faithful to Lera and my love for
her if she was already living with Vasily. Kostik kept insisting, and I finally
agreed. But I didn't get the chance. While I was still struggling with
myself, the talkative Kostik, who was always poking his nose in everywhere, was murdered.

When he was drunk, he used to boast: "I hid at *their* place at the end of
the month: from the twenty-sixth to the first! Can you imagine—right to
the first!"

He tried to persuade me to hitch a ride in a truck to some village, and
there, he said, they had a bus that went to the crossroads, and from there
you had to walk for an hour, and then you'd have a whole barrack to yourself—and oh, what babes! And why not? We'll take off and go, why mope
around, right?

I immediately got excited and sweaty; and I tried to convince myself
that Lera was important, but I still had to find out about life, no matter
what it was like. And so I answered Kostik importantly: "OK.It's settled,"
and even grinned with satisfaction. "What did I tell you!" he also cheered
up. (But even after agreeing to it, I still kept trying to convince myself that
every experience is complex yet necessary.) Kostik was young, hardly older
than I was. From time to time we'd stop between the barracks to have a
smoke and talk over our scheme.

And then a truck pulled up. A policeman, who was sitting with his back
to me, got up, left his dominoes on the table, came up to the open side
(just opened a crack), and gave a shout. Men came up to the truck right
away, asking questions: "How?.. Where did it happen? Where did they
find him?" Two of them took the body out of the truck through the open
side and laid it down. I saw the murdered man: his skull was smashed, the
blood had already congealed; several people stood around and nobody
cried out any more—they talked little. Kostik lay there with a very fright-

ened expression on his face. And his look was quite clear—as if it had just frozen—and also frightened, not dead. I turned away and walked across the settlement and then somehow found myself on that hillock with the bushes; I walked around, waiting for Lera and Vasily. Two tiny trucks right on the horizon—first one and then another—dragged gray tails of dust behind them. I heard the voice of the murdered man: "From the end of the month, Gena, right until the first!.."

He used to say: "The most important thing is not to hurry, Gena. Remember that. It's important to concentrate. You should get there and be sure to have some tea, some chifir if she's nice, and act calm. Look around, but don't be too choosy, don't make them angry... It's best to arrive when they're at work, and only two or three of them are in the barrack," and he'd screw up his eyes sweetly.

I said to Lera: "...I see it so clearly: here's Vasily getting down from the bunk, the smell all around is awful, the prisoners are huddled together, crowded. And there's a shout: 'Get up!' and then the search begins. Everybody is lined up. In their long johns. They stand in the wind one after another and wait... I just realized now that Vasily has an astonishing face—it's both full of suffering and strong at the same time, unbroken. Is that true?"

Lera (lazily): "A genuinely weary face. He's really known life."

I (excitedly): "Yes, yes, he has! I sometimes think that..."

Lera (interrupting me: she doesn't like it when somebody else besides herself talks about Vasily): "What are you capable of thinking, you snivelling little student!"

I (confused): "But you're no better."

"Shut up!"

Lera was changing virtually in front of my eyes, becoming coarse, more and more noticeably feeling like a woman, but even more noticeably trying to purge any shyness or softness. She liked it when people referred to her as a broad. Vaska's broad. She liked living with him openly, without hiding. The next step was that she liked to talk about herself without restraint or shame.

She'd laugh: "If you want, I'll tell you about our lovemaking."

I was silent.

She: "Oh, you, my little boy! But do you know how wonderful it is (and seeing me blush deeply)... OK, OK, I won't!"

My sensuality even without this was at its peak, since I slept right next to the wooden wall of Lera's barrack, which was relatively sturdy and strong, but not soundproof. I couldn't sleep at all the first nights when Vasily visited Lera. I listened involuntarily, and it wasn't hard to identify the sounds. Once Vasily caught a cold and I heard his muffled cough, another time I could clearly make out his excuses, and, later, an angry cry, a racket, and the noise of Vasily accidentally tumbling down from the mattresses onto the speakers. But I never heard Lera's voice, even when their lovemaking reached its peak and Vasily would stay the night.

I remember how it suddenly dawned on me that he had spent the whole night there—he probably had done so before, too, but I suddenly realized it for the first time. My hearing involuntarily became acute. I experienced terrible palpitations, and then an unexpectedly prolonged weakness.

Here, too, Lera showed her increasingly strong character; her silence seemed emphatic and even more stern compared to Vasily's occasional, though infrequent, high-pitched yelp which I overheard in the middle of the night; it was more like a child's pathetic and weak cry rather than a sound made by a man. Afterwards I heard his voice, the slam of a closing door in the middle of the night, and distinctly heard his footsteps in the hall of the sleeping barrack. But it was clearly Vasily who talked and slammed the door as he left, and the resounding footsteps that receded were also his—Vasily's—whereas she didn't make a sound.

Lera's silence helped me make it through the night there in my dog shelter, permeated with the smells of petrified coal and nearly petrified mattress straw. I could pretend that Lera wasn't there. And I listened as the various barrack noises in the distance and other little noises of unclear origin started. It was just the first nights that I worried so much and so agonizingly, but later I'd try to comfort myself by deliberately convincing myself that Lera wasn't there—do you hear how quiet it is—she's not there, not there, not there; my eyes were wet with tears, but I did learn to fall asleep in the middle of the night.

And in the curve of the Khonya River, at the foot of a hill, an old woman sat by a grave. One day Lera and I visited Anna Romanovna again, and I remember how she lamented to Lera—as if complaining about herself—that here at the grave she sometimes talked to her husband as if he were alive, and that this wasn't good, because God knows what a stranger might think if he came up and heard her voice.

Summer came to an end, classes had started at the institute, but by then I'd gradually got stuck there, too. Lera and I seemed to walk endlessly around the wild rose, to have our conversations and were bogged

down, as if we were waiting for some turn in our common fate, but there
wasn't any. And there were no events. (Vasily was a reckless driver, but
even he crashed only once, knocking down two poles by the side of the
road and leaving the entire settlement without light for a week. He tried
to justify himself, claiming that he wanted to exceed his driving quota and
bag a bonus.)

But precisely the lack of events and the senselessness of staying any
longer at the settlement, painful idleness, and even the sameness of my
conversations with Lera kept me there. Because I was suffering not only
the torment of lost love. Yes, yes, I also envied Lera: I envied her finding a
new destiny and a new personality, finding, as it seemed, herself. Secretly I
hoped that I would luck out and perhaps by chance would suddenly meet
some rehabilitated person here (it could be a recent, belated rehabilitation—say, some last, forgotten man—things like that do happen!). This
would be a genuine, real person who'd suffered much more than this
quite ordinary former prisoner Vasya. He'd probably be an old man, very
old; I'd become friends with him—former thieves weren't the only ones
here, after all, Lera's father had lived here, as well as others!—I exclaimed
(silently), refusing to believe that I was late and had fallen behind the
times.

Once Lera said to me directly and brutally, as if she'd divined my secret
thoughts: "Get out of here, Genka. Go away..."

And added: "I want to live here alone, I want to be compassionate on
my own. You spoil everything for me."

And I left.

And that's all, really. That's how it all ended. Many years have passed,
and soon my daughter will be Lera's age, and she'll have a husband who
will love her and study with her at the institute. (And I will be quietly and
narrow-mindedly happy that they have something normal, good, and
understandable, and not at all like what Lera had, for example.)

...They didn't use to fence graves in then. Here it was important how
you looked: swells rolled down uniformly towards you from the mountain, or, maybe, in the opposite direction—one after another they retreated
from you upward, into the distance—and beyond the swells there were
only optical illusions in the shape of sparse bushes. No crosses, no stars,
only little mounds, as if huge artels on the way back from the mountains
left here those who had fallen behind. When the mountains ended, you
could feel the breath of the nearby steppes, and the people who came
down the mountains after burying their folk felt they had already returned

home, and they hurried to enter normal relations of exchange and sharing. Each year is different, however. The fates of the guards and the guarded
intertwined and unraveled again. It's a hill, but the slope is so unusually
even! And they carried their folk only as far as the hill, and there they felt
that they'd gone far enough and that the dead could easily be buried
there. The steepness of the swells made it impossible to carry the bodies
any farther. There were graves everywhere. And white landslides on the
left. Of course, they managed to bury people there, too; the swells are like
grave mounds—they can hide anything—and the earth isn't as hard as in
the mountains: you don't have to chisel it out, it isn't stone. And you see
there on the right?—a bald spot—the bushes break off and there isn't
even any grass; after the rain the earth slid down from several swells (they
hoed it too much) and all the small mounds poured down, down, down,
until they came together amidst the swells.

We talked to a neurologist yesterday. (Father's irritable. And I was like
a translator between him and the doctor, like a mediator, constantly adjust-
ing the contact and softening their words.)
    The neurologist was a bit arrogant: "What difference does it make
what kind of a dream you have! What's important is that it's a burden for
you. And people rid themselves of their dreams during the day, not at
night, my dear fellow."
    And my elderly and completely gray-haired father was full of indigna-
tion: "What do you mean 'not important what kind of dream'?!" (It
seemed to him that the doctor was inclined to forbid any discussion of
dreams!) "Listen to this. I'm lying quietly in my apartment; yes, I live
alone, my wife's dead... And, all of a sudden it's as if I'm not in my apartment, but in some hut. And outside, on the other side of the wall a truck
is leaving, honking like crazy..."
    The psychiatrist he saw in his office tells him the reverse: that it's very
important what kind of dream he has, and also important how often. But
the psychiatrist emphasized the subconscious and wanted to know certain
details about father's life, but father didn't have secrets, father didn't
understand and got vehemently angry: "What the hell do you mean—
details?!"

Today the weather's particularly bad. The sky is oppressive. In weather
like this dreams probably gather strength during the day, storing it up for
the night.
    Father called. He's envious of K. (his former colleague).

In the spring of this year Father got a garden plot. Father would never have gotten it, but they happened to have an undersized plot, a leftover plot which nobody wanted. Especially because there wasn't any chance of expansion: the plot was carved out on the very edge, and beyond it stood large and wealthy fenced-off summer cottages, about an acre or two each.

With seeming enthusiasm, Father began to dig up the ground, hoed a part, planted currants and buckthorn bushes on the sides, and… got bored.

Once, when he was standing there, bored, he saw on the opposite side, in the fence of a large (two-acre) summer cottage, somebody, probably a boy, quietly moving a wide board of the cottage fence aside. Father kept looking. Birds were chirping. Father said that at that moment he happened to be thinking about his childhood. The board, which was hanging on one nail, kept swinging, then it finally moved aside, and Father raised his eyebrows in surprise. Instead of a boy he saw an old man, slightly older than Father.

This little old man cautiously crawled through the newly made crack in the fence and looked around. He said with an amiable smile: "My God, what space!"

It was K. When he looked closely, Father recognized in the old man a very clever colleague of his, with whom he'd worked at one time and who afterwards had moved very high up in the world. Now K. was also retired, of course, highly thought of, with a summer cottage, a car, and other comforts. He didn't recognize Father. He probably didn't recognize anybody: his smile was so quiet and happy.

"Can you imagine being able to cheat like that!" Father was outraged. "I know, it's not hard to cheat people. But to be able to cheat nature itself: to receive childhood twice in one's life!" My aged father was outraged after he'd been tormented and harassed by dreams at night.

Why does a clever bureaucrat and charming schemer (Father doesn't begrudge the summer cottages or the status—forget that!—what he begrudges is precisely nature, woods, fields and stars), why does a clever bureaucrat even at the end of his life get serenity and peace, while he, an honest builder gets terrible dreams, palpitations, and the horror of falling behind that frightens him much more than the horror of bodily decay and death.

———

What a night!... Father called at four and again at five. Poor old man. My heart aches for him, but what can I do? It's already after six. If only he'd fall asleep.

K. He was smiling. K. was all clean, his little white head covered with soft silver hair. And his eyes were clear too, just a little discolored. And even the skin of his face was taut and soft, seemingly free of wrinkles. He was neatly dressed in a little blue shirt and shorts. Yes, that's what it was—a happy childhood.

"Have you noticed that there are a lot of swallows today?" he asked Father with a smile.

They kept building, having apparently lost both the purpose and the corresponding significance of building. They were prepared to lose everything except the ability to build. They held on to their construction sites with all their might; this consistency had become their primary and most noticeable feature.

They were surprising in their steadfastness and even propensity for sacrifice as they held on to their last ability—to build. (But why did it turn into a feeling of falling behind? But in general why does something turn into something else?) Remembering my youth, I, too, remember how my youthful conversations about sufferers and simple people, suddenly becoming embodied (materialized), were transformed into the image of the former prisoner Vasya. And when, perhaps out of professional habit, I attempt an analysis, a belated and not completely reliable reevaluation of my *transformed* relationship with Lera, I also remember (painfully! and sharply!) above all else how my own words turned against me. I remember, I think, searching not for the meaning—what's the use of that meaning now—but for the feeling of those days, although why do I need that feeling, anyway? What's the use, if the lesson is unnecessary and the relived feeling does nothing but tantalize and beckon with its marvelousness when I try to capture not so much that time, which is already past, as my failure to keep up with that time. I don't love Lera, Vasily, and myself as we were then (although I do love all *three of them*), as much as I love that time which I have left behind.

Of course, the idea is oversimplified. But that's precisely how, colliding with my youth, Vasya, appeared in the flesh out of nothing—with his truck and his everlasting bunks—and that's precisely how Lera stung me with my own words; and when I became unloved and wanted justice, that very justice may have already triumphed through the higher meaning of the words which turned into a boomerang.

I remember (already at the very end of my stay there) a guitar appearing in Vasily's hands. He began to sing. He had neither a good ear nor a voice. And I was so acutely sorry that he wasn't musical. I was upset and felt dejected. And I even turned away, I remember, and walked off. He was, after all, an image: to me he was a sufferer.

Lera (sharing with me): "...Vasily told me about his life. Hands—that's what a man needs there most of all. Strong and skillful hands."
I: "Work is work. And a man works his ass off as long as the rations keep coming."
Lera: "The rations kept coming, but camp officials didn't stop at pilfering packages, particularly the officials!"
And Lera again (and for some reason already arguing): "You're wrong: a man couldn't walk around there alone. Yes, yes, they were herded around in groups. It's easier and simpler to guard a group. The outhouse?.. But even there the prisoners were watched. They were always put in a group of three or four men and taken like that. Why?.. Because they were watched all the time, everywhere."
"But you don't necessarily want to be alone."
"You want nothing more than to be alone! You want solitude for five minutes even. Don't argue... Ask Vasily."
"I will!"
"Go ahead, ask him!"
Debates used to progress to that almost magical and very strained moment of "*ask Vasily*"... and, since Vasily wasn't there with us, we'd stare from our hill down at the curling thread of road in the distance. Oh, how white that road was. And our arguments seemed to us to be a matter of principle; of course, we failed to hear the naiveté of their old-fashioned tone or their parodic nature. As soon as Vasily arrives we'll settle it—find out everything or almost everything from the horse's mouth.
However, only a minute later we'd be at each other's throats again, arguing about how long a strong man could survive in a camp. Is individuality doomed on a bunk? If so, how can one save oneself?.. Yes, he's strong and willful, but there he's involved in a general deprivation of will. To remain in solitude is painful and frightening, but to be dissolved in common obedience is frightening as well. Unfortunately, he's not left alone. But a man knows how to be alone, by himself, even in a column, in the midst of everybody. That's why they smoke, by the way. Yes, yes,

smoking without interruption is a special intimate process. It's like a
book. "Do you know, Lera, no matter how triumphantly the movies
might spread (in those days there was no talk yet of the silver screen!),
reading books is indispensable precisely because it's intimate. It's both a
sermon and a confession in one..." "Come on, stop it! It's for you, the
show-offs (Lera immediately dissociated herself from me), that the book
is both a sermon and a confession, but, in fact, a book is just a surrogate
confession, while confession itself is a live voice." No, Lera, books, smoking and other common actions aren't invented for show-offs at all. Books
and smoking represent involvement in a process. Smoking is personal. It's
primarily detachment—yours and mine. Imagine: I'm in a column. They're
taking us to work. We arrive. But a guard (and here's the flaw in your rea-
soning, Lera) is also an individual. And a guard is also a person. Yes, an
evil one. Yes, they don't take good people there, I know. Yes, they turn
good people into evil ones, I know that too. But even an evil person
would grab a cigarette on the way to work. Yes, he wants to have a smoke.
Yes, him too. And before I take up a spade or a pickaxe I also, *also Lera,*
snatch a cigarette, roll it tighter, light up, and with the first gulps of smoke
the entire universe, all the continents and worlds, the whole sky and the
grasses, Tyutchev, Avvakum and Sartre immediately enter my consciousness. And nobody—nobody!—can interfere with this moment."
    Lera: "But it's not the crowd that kills. And you forgot again—*there*
they can't just simply light up. They don't have anything to smoke."
    "What do you mean they don't: they smoke!"
    "But maybe they're forced to work before smoking... and maybe they
limit the amount of tobacco they can have? Let's not try to guess—*we'd
better ask Vasily.*"
    And, afterwards, Lera and I finished our argument more or less calmly,
debating whether it was possible *there* to smoke to one's heart's content.
    "You're a rotten show-off. You smoke as much as you want and think
that Vasily and the other prisoners could also smoke without thinking
about it... Just imagine yourself on a bunk!"
    "Yes."
    "You've gotten off the bunk. You want to smoke—right? No, just wait!
Wait! But the first question is can you smoke in the barracks?"

    I didn't talk to Lera about love; when we were young that wasn't
done—we were embarrassed, ashamed of words—but I would suddenly
tell her that today I felt depressed, bad, that I didn't at all want to leave
here (I love you!); and she'd answer that Vasily had suffered a lot, that he
had scars on his back and a broken ear, that his ribs still hadn't healed

because they were so bruised and covered with bedsores from sleeping on bunks (I love him!). That's how we talked, talked as much as we wanted and a bit more than either of us wanted; we talked while a fine, warm drizzle spattered down onto the ground and the grass. We were walking in the direction of the hillock covered with the wild rose. And then, as a retreat from a painful topic, to soften things, Lera talked about her job at the weigh station in the second quarry, four miles away; she sat there in a small booth with a wide glass window, and under her stern gaze trucks drove from the quarry onto a mobile platform; after glancing at the arrow on the scale, Lera recorded the number of tons and hundreds of pounds and then subtracted the weight of an empty truck to get the net weight.

Words were inadequate; I couldn't convey to her that, having come here, loving her and being insulted every day and every night by her intimacy with Vasily, I, too, was in trouble and unhappy—just a step away from her in my little shelter on the hard lumps of coal. I also wanted compassion; and why wouldn't she, Lera, come to my rescue, why wouldn't she help me? Still, my feelings weren't that well defined, and, moreover, I already understood that my love, or another, or a third love, was nothing in comparison to the bunk that still prevented Vasily from putting flesh and muscle on his body.

A dog ran into my coal bin; he smelled everything, began sneezing from the dust of the worn mattress, and then jumped out in disgust.

We happened to be walking by.

"What's wrong with him?" asked Lera about the dog.

I kept quiet.

But Lera suddenly felt something herself, something like a reproach; after all, she wanted to suffer alone. And she said: "Leave, Genka. Enough..."

5

I left. But not before we had a tea that was so reminiscent of Moscow and the time of our love.

Languishing, I went once again, and for the last time, to that house on the River Khonya. I arrived early, in the first half of the day, and, learning that Anna Romanovna had already left for her husband's grave, I followed. Four fenced-in graves. Everything was the same as before. Inside one of the fences sat Anna Romanovna—she was sitting on the ground on a folded newspaper. She was silent. And what a heavenly warm day it was!

I didn't disturb her. I made myself comfortable nearby, about ten feet away. I sat on a stone, leisurely smoking. Bushes provided shade. Nearby was a stream next to which a tin cup was always placed on a stone. Swifts were flying overhead.

Half an hour passed. An ancient woman walked by; she was stooped and so old and decrepit that Anna Romanovna, who'd aged so much after coming here, still seemed relatively strong and lively by comparison. One thing stuck in my mind—the ancient woman, turning around, asked: "How do I get to No Name?" I shrugged my shoulders, while Anna Romanovna, who'd heard the question before, pointed into the distance, gesturing to the right.

I looked and saw the flat hills, as I had in childhood. Beyond the four neat fences (with Anna Romanovna inside one of them), beyond the wild rose, and farther, beyond the spring, began something surprising—a smoothly rising and seemingly empty spot. I didn't realize yet that it was a mountain.

High grasses and short shrubbery appeared to be moving their tops, merging; and it seemed to me that there, between the small hills, a small group of people was climbing—possibly, an artel. The mountain entered into me with its vivid clarity (through childhood); the mountain was already pressing down on me with its increasing enormity and heaviness—the mountain breathed and entered into me—I, however, was not conscious of it. I just sat there, my eyes following the stooped, ancient woman.

The old woman walked far away. She moved between the uniform small hills as if between small graves, as if she were searching among the small hills for the one which was close to her, her own. I had been watching her for so long that the flat hill was no longer a flat hill, but a grave mound of an enormous family who'd been buried God knows when—of people, pure and simple, people who'd died unknown, lost, forgotten, or half-forgotten. The mountain was common property—ours—and, therefore, the continuous rows of endless hills stretched by themselves equally for both the ordinary and extraordinary people. And there, in their midst, walked the ancient woman. She was searching for her own little hill; the farther she walked, the more attentively and slowly she searched, as if she were wearing herself out. I suddenly saw her little head, gray in a dark scarf; then her whole frail figure from the waist up appeared over the swell. One moment she'd disappear completely. The next, only her little head would reemerge. She had already considerably diminished in size. The dark spot of her scarf was barely discernible above the rippling haze of the innumerable grave mounds.

And more and more people seemed to be following her; some force was leading them, like the force of memory; and they came in families, broken families, handfuls of surviving relatives, in couples, or alone; for some reason all of them came here at the same time (as if for a wake). They emerged from the side of the road and they kept coming and coming in numbers; some wore hats, caps or scarves on their heads and others were bareheaded; there were men's faces and women's and small children's faces. A general flow, but without a crush. Some of them had walking sticks—old people's canes—others tried to sit down and rest at least for a moment. They were scattered all over the enormous flatness of the mountain; and it looked as if they would have more space if some of them moved to the left, others straight ahead of them and a trifle left, while the rest of them went to the right between the little hills; but more and more people kept arriving at the same time, so they had to walk in a crowd as before. But the moment they visited their loved ones, sat down by the mound in silence, and, after resting their feet, wanted to get up and go back, the mountain itself suddenly tilted, increasing its already considerable slope and, without distinguishing between their past guilt or involvement, spilled the people from its uniform swells, shook them off and pushed them back again into the present, not accepting their assurances or repentant words. Such a deceptive mountain. You look, and where you earlier had seen thousands upon thousands of people, there's nobody now.

Only an old woman. (Only the solitary spot of her dark scarf.)

And the warm day...

I had finished smoking another cigarette just as Anna Romanovna got up from the ground. She noticed me and gave a friendly nod. Her smile was cautious, blind: "Good day." And I answered, approaching her: "Good day, Anna Romanovna!"

We returned to the settlement together.

On the way back I wanted to say something and, to my surprise, I began talking about Lera; I'd kept silent so long, and here, right before going away, I suddenly said:

"Lera should go to school, Anna Romanovna. Why's she sticking around here—the school year has already begun."

I said it simply, the way a concerned relative would.

Anna Romanovna answered quietly: "Yes, yes, she should go to school."

When we entered the house, Lera was already there. She'd been waiting for us and had made the tea. There were rusks to go with it.

We sat down. And again everything at their home took place quietly, in a subdued way; and there was so much kindness in their quietness. Lera filled our cups. A round straw plate in the middle of the table held the rusks. I was silent; I thought that a conversation would start any moment. But no conversation started. We drank our tea, and when it got dark, Lera brought a candle in a low candlestick from the landlord. It was as if the Moscow apartment tea had repeated itself, only instead of the homemade cookies we had rusks, and I reached out to the straw plate in the middle of the table just as timidly and cautiously as before. The candle flame flickered slightly. Lera quietly told Anna Romanovna that while we were gone she'd washed the floors, brought some groceries for Anna Romanovna from Novostroiny, and put them away in various places. And the desire stirred in me again to remind her, even in a roundabout way, about the classes that had already begun in Moscow. But I watched Lera majestically pour the tea, I saw her calm hands and Anna Romanovna's calm, closed lips and her quiet, peaceful face and was ashamed. They were fine. And I shouldn't interfere. I asked for more tea. Lera poured more and asked whether I had a ticket and was going to leave soon. I answered: "Soon."

The landlady, a railroad worker, dropped in for a moment and said that the electricity was on now and that we didn't have to sit by candlelight. And she left. But Lera didn't turn on the light. And then I remembered what was missing in our get-together—the portrait that Anna Romanovna had shown me once. I whispered to Lera: "Do you want me to bring you your father's portrait sometime?" "You don't have to. We'll do it ourselves."

Dreams had probably been waiting timidly on the threshold of his consciousness for a long time (always? his entire life?); they stood there shyly, without trying to enter. Sometimes they looked through the door for a moment, they appeared, but father failed to pay attention to them, as all strong people tend to do ("What nonsense one dreams sometimes!.."). Father would laugh, he was the sole master of this large apartment then.

But suddenly, the moment he got old, they found their way in. And now Father is tormented night after night.

Of course, during the day he pulls himself together. And, moreover, he himself invites these bad thoughts: he would like to make sense of them, but they flatly refuse to recognize his pat day-time conversations; they just have to wait for night, to wait for his weakness, and then—burst in. Let him quiet down. Let him just lower his head on the pillow. And, once they burst in, they triumph, commit outrages and howl, yell, rush about, rage, rejoice in the middle of the night, and he can't do anything about them.

And if he ignored his dreams then, now his dreams ignore him. Yes, yes, he's already pondering the fact that this is some sort of revenge; but revenge begins only when you understand that *it's not for nothing.*

Father doesn't necessarily foreshadow me, my future, my old age—and yet I think about it. There's a shadow, a dark side to kinship: the recognition of self. I'd feel much sorrier for my father, I'd feel more compassion (and with more understanding), I'd love him more plainly, if he weren't so close to me, too close.

But on the other hand, my love for him has a face and a facial expression, and the face has eyes.

Once, after losing track of his artel, Little Lyosha tagged after some burglars at night. They were escaping, but Lyosha followed them all night long, not knowing whom he was chasing after, or with whom he was trying to catch up. He kept on walking. And they—burglars who had robbed a church (there were two of them)—decided that somebody had traced them and was following their tracks, that it was a pursuit, and the pursuer, as usual, was followed by angry men with cudgels from the settlement. They were moving faster and faster. But on the second night they were gripped with terrible fear; they couldn't believe that somebody was pursuing them—ordinary thieves—with such passion, such fierce persistence. On the second, and especially on the third night of the chase they decided that it was an avenging angel. A youth with streaming white hair was running after them from mountain to mountain with his arms outstretched. Being experienced, they managed to cover their tracks for a time. They hid in a secret lodge and lived there in the dark, feeding on dry bread and didn't light a fire. And the youthful-looking avenging angel kept circling, sensing that they were near. He also called to them louder and louder: "Wait for me! Wait for me!" Mystical terror overpowered them: they both went mad. Day and night they heard the voice calling. And at night Little Lyosha's small campfire appeared here and there: the fire that was looking for them.

They didn't even dare to think of escaping on Lyosha's side, and a mountain rose steeply on the other side. They decided to risk it: they climbed up, but then they had to descend a steep cliff, and of course, both of them perished during the descent. They fell, but even then they didn't hit the ground but landed on another cliff (located a bit lower), on a square ledge. It was so steep that the two of them, tied together with rope, went mad. They died a painful death, accepting it as punishment for desecrating the church, and crying from the pain of broken ribs, arms, and legs on that small rocky landing—on the ledge. To this day one can see two skeletons washed out by the rains, stuck in a crevice at that considerable height.

You can't get near the ledge, but it's possible to discern the skeletons from the upper mountain (it's higher but more accessible), which we often did in childhood to scare one another. And if today you take the shuttle helicopter in the direction of the grain elevator at the little Arakhovka River, near the pass where the cliffs become bare, the helicopter pilot, if he's in the mood, will draw your attention to the two piles of bones bleached by the winds. The pilot gladly points out this sight. However, a lot of passengers already know when to look out the window. A legend arose—a little self-perpetuating story—which claims that not everything is so plain and simple here, and that one of the skeletons is actually a woman's. Legends about love are the most tenacious, though not the most powerful. And somebody has already embroidered a heart-rending story about two loving hearts fleeing from either Siberian penal servitude or an Old Believers' farmstead. Love intercepts the deaths, reinterpreting and adapting them for its own purposes, and fills them out with sensual details (the triumph of life?!). Consequently, it's boring to listen to a story about some Little Lyosha who could find gold-bearing sand with his palms, elbows, and, particularly, with the scars of his crooked hands.

Here's a more prosaic variant. By mistake, Little Lyosha chased after a robber who was on horseback but couldn't escape far because the horse could barely move: it was completely emaciated, perhaps even sick, and with a colt. No one knows where the robber was rushing or what he had done. Little Lyosha caught up with him on the third day and only then, after he'd caught up with him, did he realize that he'd made a mistake, and that it wasn't members of his artel who were climbing the hill, noisily pushing their way through the brush at all. There was only one man walking, and, moreover, he was an evil man. He was in a hurry, he was fleeing from his pursuers on that hill. He suddenly attacked Lyosha in anger, intending to kill him; but Lyosha said to him: "Don't do it. God loves me. He torments me, but He loves me." That's what he said to the murderer. "God?" The fellow looked into Lyosha's eyes with a grin; however, what he saw there wasn't a pitiful tear (he didn't believe in tears) but that blue mist, a permanent bluish-white cloudiness, which so surprised and even frightened people. He refrained from hitting Lyosha. But the anger accumulated inside couldn't disappear that easily. So he went up to his poor downtrodden horse and hit it. He hit it two more times. And he killed it. The horse fell and couldn't get up again. And he went off on his own way somewhere. He carried his sack himself. The colt stayed with the horse. The horse was already wheezing and kicking the colt away and then, after a convulsion, became still. And the colt licked her sides, then her muzzle and lips. He licked her dead eyes, making them open for a moment, show blue, and then close again.

Lyosha squatted beside them; he looked at the horse, then at the colt. He had often seen death and wasn't afraid of it. He was just very tired, because after he'd fallen behind he ran for a long time, and then it turned out that he'd gone in the wrong direction.

Little Lyosha was of medium height. Maybe even a little bit on the tall side (a fast growing youth already), thin, with a handsome face, straight nose, light hair that fell forward, missing a lot of teeth, and he stuttered, although not badly. He stumbled over the first, initial words.

There exists a certain complacency, which consists of thinking that you belong to a detachment, a column or an artel, which, through adaptation within its ranks, marches correctly and at the right speed. And considers that the others have fallen behind.

"A dream is wearing him out because his memory is wearing him out? Are you sure? But what was so special in his memory that he wouldn't want to tell me about?" I asked again in a low voice.

"Oh! You don't know old men!" answered the psychiatrist, moving his lips and whispering to me as we left his office.

And just a little ahead of us walked my father—an old man who didn't hide or conceal anything, but who lacked something very important, something charitable—(maybe he had lost it a long time ago, but sensed what he had lost only in his old, feeble days).

And again he kept calling all night long. At two and at four. And then at half past five. He'll chase after that truck packed with people until the end of his days.

A wonderful evening! I arrived when father was cleaning fish—two little fish that he "caught himself." He'd sat there all morning with a fishing rod and caught more than his neighbor (the neighbor talked Father into going fishing, boasted on the way, and caught only one fish).

With these two fish—his hands and knife covered with fish scales, some little scales sticking to his neck even—Father was magnificent, kind, humane. He said that after he'd caught the second fish he couldn't fish any more, but just sat there remembering his wife, my mother. And there was mist over the river, mist...

"Do you at least understand? Do you understand me?" he kept asking, and at that moment I understood him so clearly and purely, so inexpressibly (in words), that I just kept nodding in silence. In the meantime he threw his two little fish into the frying pan. The smell of hot oil filled his little kitchen, we kept smiling silently, and all of this taken together was happiness; but for some reason it didn't seem like our present happiness, it seemed that these were our old happy days.

K. doesn't notice my father's currants. He thinks that there's a lot of empty land here. After his summer home everything around here seems empty. (There he has birch trees. There he has two full acres with plenty of garden flowers and arable land: vegetables, strawberries and dozens of apple trees.)

"What freedom you've got here!" K. says to my father.

I slept very lightly the nights before my departure from Novostroiny. The wind shifted and whistled quietly but audibly behind my annex; it moved in a draft on the floor of the barrack and skirted the round speakers in an air wave; a mouse scratched, and once, or sometimes twice in the night, Vasily let out a quiet and sensual cry.

I was leaving Novostroiny: first, I traveled for a long time by truck, then continued by train. I stood, subdued, by the window of the train car and gazed at the hills and pines flashing by; resting my chin on my hand, I sipped the railroad tea that smelled a bit of coal, while the clairvoyant Lyosha (in his time) hurried after the bearded gold prospectors. The train was going faster and faster. And, when I was already asleep on the top bunk, Lyosha finally caught up with the sleeping artel as well, and, frozen, without having had anything to eat, climbed into the huddle of warm bodies in the middle of the night.

It so happened that Fedyaich had a woman whom he'd brought along and kept there for himself, a woman with whom he'd made a deal one day and now was dragging around everywhere, feeding her on the artel's common money, of course. The artel wasn't too happy, but did not dare say anything to him directly, his enormous fists were really something! So the bearded, thickset men took special pleasure in paying him back for their enforced silence and quietly amusing themselves when they realized that the woman suddenly felt pity for the cripple. (There's no understanding women—she just felt sorry for him!) They chuckled with particular glee when Fedyaich discovered her in the middle of the night, just a short step away from him, sleeping in Little Lyosha's arms—he'd just arrived and was very cold. And Little Lyosha was already going on seventeen. Fedyaich was furious. He really yelled at him in the middle of the night. The sleepy artel members woke up and began to shout as well. Lyosha just blinked his eyes; he didn't understand. However, to beat him, a cripple whom they needed for their work, was, of course, sinful. Better to make him bleed a little, though, and Fedyaich hit him lightly with a cold fist.

He understood that the youth had crawled up next to her and pressed himself against her because he'd been cold and sleepy; he'd have crawled into a warm cattle shed as long as it was warm. Fedyaich understood that, but the artel members were making fun of him, and he thought he had to prove himself a bit.

"Tha-a-t hur-r-rts," Lyosha wiped his bloodied nose.

The majority of these people came from around the Volga region. Red-haired, broad-faced and energetic, they loved to have a good laugh, and their laughter was booming, loud, and sincere. "Ha-ha-ha-ha...," but their eyes didn't laugh at all; their mouths would open wide and beams of laughter would appear around their eyes, but there was only emptiness inside those light eyes. They walked around with pick-axes, spades and pans with only one question:

"Where?"

They were followed by the locals, our people, the worst of whom would sell their old mothers' bones for a nugget-rich spot.

But all of them, both the locals and the outsiders, were interested in the tall boy who chased after the artel. He was a fool, but he could "hear." They were frightened of his hands.

Three men came up to him in the mountains when he was sitting alone after he'd fallen behind. It was evening, but it was still light, and he was sitting on a hillock (he was tired) looking down on a winding road. It was warm. It was sunset. "God be with you, Alexei." "Hello." They sat down beside him to have supper, but he lay down, stretching out on the ground, having spent the entire day on his feet walking from one mountain to the next. They had a drink. They took some food out of their bags. "And how are things going with the gold?" they asked. "Are your wonderful hands searching for gold?" Lyosha had barely enough food, so they fed him. They gave him some smoked sturgeon and a bit of caviar. And then a rope suddenly appeared—he jumped up; but the one on the right managed to hold him by his feet; when they were tying him, Lyosha contrived to grab a rock and kept hitting and hitting with the rock; he bloodied the man's head and bloodied his ear, but the man still managed to hold Lyosha's thrashing feet down—he was enormous; drenched in blood as he was, he still held him down. "I don't have any gold, I don't have anything, broth-ers!" shouted Lyosha. "We know you don't." They tied him and then broke his "hearing" hands with a crowbar.

They were very practical, all three of them. To make sure, they kneaded and felt their work, they even felt his hands all the way through: were the bones broken?—those crookedly healed and "hearing" bones—were they broken? Once they were sure, they kept poking the soft tissue with a knife to cut the tendons in that spot. He lost consciousness. They untied him and left. They left some food. Smoked sturgeon. Some caviar. And water too. So he wouldn't die.

Some ancient woman gave him refuge for a time. And she nursed him back to life. Those three didn't want a sin on their conscience: they didn't want to kill him. They just didn't want him to search for gold, they wanted to search for it and find some themselves. But how can one find any after him? How can you find any if you follow the same path and ahead of you is a man who "hears"? They hoped that perhaps his bones would mend differently and, after healing would lose their ability to "hear." After all they wanted to find some gold dust too.

Lyosha was fortunate to find a Cossack village on the way. He suffered terribly and barely made it; the village was very small, somewhere near Kosyrt. But there was an ancient woman, a healer, standing right by the road. When Lyosha approached her house, the old woman got scared. Then he began smiling at her as best as he could. It was early morning. And the old woman saw that he was still very young and that he had child-like blue eyes. He could barely walk. He walked, holding his broken bones away from his body so that he wouldn't touch them as he moved. She asked:

"Who are you?"

And she also asked, for she hadn't made out what was what:

"What are you carrying?"

"My hands." And he kept smiling to put her at ease.

Vasily had a scornful expression he liked to use:

"Hey, you!" he'd say, berating the dominoes lovers. For some reason he particularly enjoyed bothering the players, and one of his amusements was to walk along the barrack towards the two tables that had been put together and yell threateningly at those who on a calm Saturday morning sat rivetted at those tables, playing quietly: "Hey, you!.."

It was precisely on a Saturday morning, when Vasily was unable to sit inside four walls, that he would emerge from the barrack and immediately begin pestering the players: he'd scramble the dominoes with a circular motion of his hand, and then someone would raise his hand at him (or swear at him), and Vasily in turn would threaten him and show his fist (and swear, too). But there wouldn't be any fight. They could get additional time for that, and who wants to fight if all he has left to serve, or, as they put it, "*to live out,* is a year or two, and then—home!

So Vasily got away with walking by the tables and bullying the players; and if there was a fight, then it was over quickly, almost instantaneously, and always at night, in the dark (on the side where the barrack's street lights—there were two of them—were out); and then Vasily would return with a huge black eye and spend half the night carrying on: "B-bastard! He kicked me in the ribs—a lowdown blow!... I'll find him tomorrow by his shiner—I gave him one too, uh-h-h, bastard!"

And all Saturday night and into Sunday the roughed-up Vasily couldn't calm down, and more than ever he wanted to talk about life, to reminisce about the past; all night long through the partially opened window of the barrack you could hear his drunken (and occasionally touching) pronouncements and sometimes even him singing with his roommates—the fairly simple former prisoners who probably were the ones who'd beaten him up in the first place. No different from life anywhere else. Perhaps Vasily had lost his head, not knowing where and how a marvel like Lera could have appeared out of the blue just for him. He didn't know what to do with this marvel. Whenever he held forth, he wouldn't spare Lera either: "Why do I need her—I'll give her to you, Seryoga, just like that, I'll give her to you myself, nothing simpler! What's a skirt compared to our friendship and years together! We gnawed on dry crusts! Shared cigarette butts! And what's so special about Lera-Lerochka, you won't even have to get her drunk—I'll tell her you're my pal—my buddy—and that you've suffered a lot, too. She's a good girl, she knows how to be sympathetic. And, my God, is she compassionate!.."

"We don't have any right to talk about his past transgressions!" I exclaimed.

"None whatsoever! He was on a bunk, do you understand, *on a bunk!*" exclaimed Lera.

With his jacket thrown over his shoulders, as was the fashion then, Vasily would approach the dominoes players and say: "Hey, you!.."

And our hearts (Lera's and mine) would sink. We watched Vasily's strong, muscular hand as it moved near the dominoes—will he really scramble them?! Ah! He shouldn't! The players are always angry! Still, he kept moving his hand in the air, circling above the dominoes, above the primitive game, honestly set up in a straight line, and one of the former prisoners (sometimes it was the policeman whiling away his time at dominoes) would say:

"Vaska, quit fooling around!"

Vasily's hand didn't always scramble their dominoes; after circling a bit in the air, threatening the players and making them nervous about the game, his hand would rise from the table, but not to finally leave the players in peace. Vasily suddenly (and now with both hands) would take off, snatch off the players' hats and switch them. Their heads were dissimilar; he'd stick a little vulgar cap on a huge head, while the small head of the prisoner sitting across would be drowning in the policeman's enormous service cap.

"Hey, you!.." Vasily would say and leave (for his truck), and this Saturday activity with the hats was the last thing I remember.

I left on a Saturday.

Early in the morning I got into the truck's cabin, Vasily got behind the steering wheel, and on my other side, holding my small suitcase in her lap, sat Lera. That's how the three of us rode, jumping up in unison whenever we hit potholes, our shoulders touching. And any former prisoner or local resident walking towards us in the settlement could see this standard final long-shot—three faces behind the windshield of a speeding truck. The truck kept jumping along the potholes, and the three faces behind the windshield would suddenly shift to one side; the three heads were simultaneously pressed down into shoulders, while one of the three (Vasily) turned the steering wheel.

From the window of my car when the train started, I saw them both, Lera and Vasily, still on the platform. ("Don't come again," Lera had whispered to me). Pines, hillocks, and a wonderful plateau-like mountain, which I saw half an hour later from the window, stayed there with them, stretched along the railroad tracks. I didn't feel as though I'd been driven away. It was more like I'd been sent on my way. And I was no longer in that time—the time of Lera, Vasily, and Anna Romanovna bent over the grave.

Upon my return to Moscow, filled with a residual bitterness and not knowing how to begin my life, I again started work on my novel. That's understandable. Day after day my sense of loss (and confusion) was a monotonous, dull torment. All of a sudden Little Lyosha grew to be much more in my notebook than simply a youth who used to fall behind. I lived through him. I was writing and it was going well, and I churned out page after page as if I were obsessed. I very rarely went to class; I wasn't living, but was almost gliding from one day to the next with my still weightless body. I couldn't think of anything except the moment when I'd bring my novel to *Novy Mir* and Tvardovsky himself would approve it.

Somehow I got through the winter exam period. (Yes, that's it, I'll take the novel to the prose section and, feeling resolute and maximalist, I'll say that I want Alexander Trifonovich to read it, since I've heard that he reads new authors himself. I know that he's very busy, I'll say, but I'm ready to wait as long as necessary.)

Like any beginning author who's in a hurry to take his first novel to a journal, I thought that my novel was certainly not bad, actually not bad at all, and that they'd understand, appreciate, and publish it. And then I, so-and-so, will be inducted into the constellation of *Novy Mir*'s writers of that time. I didn't know the hierarchy of those names, didn't know who was a bigger name and who was a lesser one—the luster of the names was equal, equally bright! Therefore I imagined, without any doubts or reservations, that I would be included in the world of such names as Yashin, Ovechkin, Ehrenburg, Syomin, Shukshin, Tendryakov, Abramov, and others.* The fact that others aren't named doesn't at all imply their disparagement but, rather, the impossibility of naming everybody. The world of names was enormous; the world was one.

"But this is unthinkable, this is delirium!" I'd tell myself—a very young man, just starting out, "this is unthinkable, this is such happiness!.. But why is it unthinkable, why is it delirium?" I'd say to myself—a very young man who'd written his first novel. "On the contrary, this is exactly how it happens, and a literary destiny is destiny, and participation and a debut have to start somewhere."

It was during that time that I called my father long-distance and talked at length about the prose in *Novy Mir* and about courageous, uncompromising art in general, so that father, who then was tough and strong, and knew how to laugh, asked: "Is this a free call?" And I remember answering indignantly: "Dad, how can you be talking about money now?.."

The novel was drawing to an end, the last pages were being written. At night I'd leave the dorm—I couldn't sleep. I'd roam the lane of young poplars (now they're monstrous spires, piercing the sky and intolerably clogging the highway and the entire surrounding area with their white down); I'd walk, tired and overwhelmed, and have mental conversations with Lera; I complained, reproached her for her unfaithfulness, and at the same time told her that it was she, she who gave me the strength to write my novel, because I saw my mountains, my No Name and my wild rose bushes in a new light, because only now had I discovered what I'd loved.

---

*Many writers and brilliant critics at that same *Novy Mir* continue to work actively today. The narrator names only those authors who are deceased, possibly to experience more strongly and relive his sense of having been left behind. (Author's note.)

I'd talk to her, tell her how my novel was gradually being written, how a youth who "heard" chased after a gold prospectors' artel from one mountain to the next, and Lera would answer me, that Lera of old, would answer: "Yes, my dear, yes, yes."

I hurried with my novel, as if I had a premonition that *Novy Mir* in its former capacity didn't have too much time left. In talking about those events, I won't force the feeling, or even increase it twofold: my task is simpler, narrower; but I will convey the sense of confusion and depression (rather typical for an excitable young man of that time) that I experienced upon finally bringing my novel to *Novy Mir* and learning that Tvardovsky was no longer there. "What do you mean—not here?.. But he was here." "Precisely," they answered. They explained the situation, and I left, holding the folder with the novel in my hands—I didn't even consider leaving it there. My sense of loss instantly coincided with the loss of Lera, the pain became sharp, personal—and I walked, walked, walked, and then, coming out of an alley and making a turn, I stood by a garbage can and began to tear up my first novel. I was at an age when you burn novels or tear them up right on the street, but it was hard to tear up: either my hands got suddenly weak or the paper was resistant, so I just threw it away.

6

After running around the mountains all day long, he'd just lain down by a stream to sleep. He'd started a fire and lain down—he hadn't even had time to dream—when some people, some other members of another artel jumped out from behind a hillock; sleepy as he was, he couldn't make out their bearded faces, he only saw that they were strangers. Lyosha was scared, but this time they didn't maim him, didn't even beat him up; they didn't need him—just the place where he was sleeping. They grabbed him and threw him aside. And then started to dig, wash and pan the sand. They started some large fires; they were in a hurry. At first Lyosha stood to the side, shivering from the cold. Then he lay down between two of the fires and fell asleep; it was warm with a fire in front and one in back. Something compelled him to sleep there, it kept him there and wouldn't let go!

They dug, crushed and panned, but he slept. Soon they moved, and chased him off again. Get lost! Get lost!.. Don't mess with our work!

In her sleep the woman heard him trying to push in here and there; then he cuddled up next to her—he was so cold—she put his head on her chest and caressed him with her hand: "Sleep, sleep..." His whole body shook and he thrashed about and wouldn't quiet down. Such a silly cripple; so, warming and caressing him, she, as happened with her at night, wanted to give him everything out of pity, but he shunned her, he didn't understand, he was still shivering from the cold; for a moment he relaxed, got warmer, but then he got cold again. She held him tighter by the shoulders then, pressing against him, she finally felt him—well, there, my dear, get your pleasure, my poor little boy—tormented by everybody, persecuted, always half-starved. She began rocking him a little, clasping him with her palms and lending him more strength with the rocking, although his eyes were closed and he himself didn't understand what was happening. However, her pleasure increased by the moment, and she wanted to cry out, she gave a weak cry, and immediately put her hand over her mouth: Lord, forgive me; all around everybody was asleep, it was quiet, they hadn't heard anything; but her unexpected pleasure didn't end, since Lyosha kept on sleeping. She found it sweet and unbearable that he was so young—just a boy—and, at the same time, already so grown-up; she didn't know what to do, and she began to wheeze quietly, putting pressure on her throat (which was convenient, since her measured wheezing blended with the others' snoring), she thought then how convenient it was and how skillfully she'd concealed and disguised it all, when, in spite of herself, she suddenly gave a shout, yelled at the top of her voice, so that all of them, sleeping and drowsy, jumped up. Fortunately, she had time to push Lyosha away, at least to give their nocturnal embrace a slightly different meaning. Still, those who woke up shouted at her: "Are you crazy, screaming in the middle of the night?" And the bearded Yegor Fedyaich, who had been sleeping a few feet away from her, began to yell: "What are you doing, putting the make on my woman?" he hit Lyosha, while she howled at Fedyaich:

"He's a cripple!.. He was cold!"

And Lyosha, cringing and deprived of warmth, was shivering again—his teeth were chattering and his whole body shook. But his eyes were closed; he was asleep and he didn't wake up.

The sun was already beating down.

"Here!" shouted Fedyaich, the chief man in the artel, whom they all respected, whether they liked it or not.

They surrounded him noisily near the stream. For a moment she was able to glimpse his gray head again (from the shelter). And his tense wry smile.

The assistant poured bucket after bucket of water on the pan.

"Here's more!" shouted Yegor Fedyaich.

And right away everybody started making a ruckus and talking, "Yes, you've convinced us, yes, yes, you're really lucky, Fedyaich!"

She heard Yegor Fedyaich say to them triumphantly: "Okay now—let's get to work!.." And, quieting down, they all went to take their positions—some going to the sand, others to the water. The assistant rinsed the sand with a wooden spade. They scooped the sand from the new ditch with a bucket and hauled it up on a rope. Yegor Fedyaich approached the first, lucky pan. He stood there for a minute, looking at the sky. A pouch was already dangling on his belt, similar to a tobacco-pouch, only heavy and rich as it swung there, a large pouch—dark and wet with the sweat of their toil, and full of wet, yellow, grainy sand.

"Ooh!" said Yegor Fedyaich and he wiped off the sweat and continued looking at the sky, happy and thankful.

He had a smoke...

And again there was an incessant noise as they riddled the sand. The woman looked back at Little Lyosha. He was still sleeping by the shelter. After running all night, he couldn't wake up, couldn't get up from his golden spot. He nestled right on the ground, a cripple, without a mother, without a home, how will he end his life?!... She called him in a low voice: "Lyosha, have some food, eh?" but he didn't hear her.

The woman had a potion from a monastery that was supposed to give long life and ward off illness. She hesitated: she seemed to part with it with difficulty, and then, after whispering something, she said a prayer and poured about two mouthfuls of it down his throat; but he was sleepy and coughed, and the precious liquid poured out of his mouth and flowed down his cheek into the hollow of his chest. She tried again—and again it didn't work. She didn't want to waste the potion and, pressing herself against him, noisily sucked the drops of liquid and air from the hollow of his chest—she swallowed all of it.

By evening when she'd finished cooking the kasha, Lyosha still hadn't awakened, but had already begun to be tormented by his daily malady: he'd suddenly wake up afraid. The woman had just finished adding wood to the fire and had returned to the shelter.

Lyosha jumped up, all dishevelled: "They haven't gone yet, have they?... I haven't fallen behind?"

"No, they haven't!" she said firmly.

"Is it night? Day? I haven't fallen behind?"

"It's daytime still, daytime. Sleep... There, see our men panning the gold? You can sleep."

And, shaking her head, the woman sighed again: what an unfortunate boy...

But after a while he jumped up again: "I haven't fallen behind?"

"Just lie down! Damned nuisance! Or I'll bash your head in!"

The woman pushed him down. She put him to bed. Finally, he began to breathe evenly. He'd fallen asleep.

She felt sorry for him again, and for some reason she took and held his broken, "hearing" hands. She looked at them. He suddenly unfolded one hand in his sleep and showed the palm. The woman softly cried out: "Oh!..," and let it go. His arm lay so strangely: it lay along his body in a straight line, but the broken wrist was twisted absurdly, as if even now, as he slept, the open hand was either searching or timidly asking God for something. It was as if the hand was frozen, as if it was reaching out. Cautiously and fearfully, the woman touched it again.

Father called and said that the night before had been very bad—he kept running in his dream, collapsing and stumbling in the snow with a sinking heart. He's certain that some night his heart will give out, because he's no longer up to it: let me just fall behind, let me die, but don't let me dream about it anymore.

Father related that there were new details in the dream: he was running up a gently sloping mountain, with rocks and snow-covered shrubbery everywhere, and the truck was already far away; and then Father stopped for a while to catch his breath and around him he saw several more people who'd fallen behind. Yes, he saw people! One of them sat beside a rock. Another lay on the ground right by the road. They were both calm and resigned now—they weren't running anymore.

"In my dream I thought: what if I could do the same thing..." And Father's voice trembled.

He said: "I keep talking about my dreams. And I don't say anything about your mother—how do you like such forgetfulness?"

"But you said that you sometimes cry about her. On your way to the store."

He nodded (there, in a Moscow suburb, in a telephone booth, he nodded): "Yes, yes..."

―――――

"On those bunks," Lera was relating Vasily's story, "life is completely different. A sense of camaraderie is especially important there. When you have to smuggle something... or avoid a search. Just give a shout and people come running. Without any fuss or a moment's hesitation (quickly as before an escape), each tells about what he knows and what he can do. He tells it concisely. Without boasting or exaggerating. But without underrating his abilities. Experience is a sacred thing. It's common property!"

"Yesterday Vasily and Eduard, his old pal from the camp, decided to smuggle a bottle in. Those are real men for you—I heard them talking. They didn't mince words, and the threats were bloody ones. They decided to smuggle four bottles at one shot. They said that they'd smuggle and hide them on their own. And I'd just provide a diversion. They gave me a bag (an empty one!) and said, 'We'll carry the bottles through while they're checking and doing a body search on you at the checkpoint, Lerka.' I got pretty scared. But then I thought: damn them, let them do a body search—you've got to do what you've got to do. But the guy at the gate was too embarrassed to search me—can you imagine!—his hands were dirty. He even glanced over at the washstand, wondering whether he should run over, wash his hands and then search me. But he got embarrassed... So Vasily and his bunk pal Eduard got through with no trouble at all. Afterwards we took the bottles to the grave of a third friend of theirs who had also spent time with them on the bunks and then died here later..."

When we used to walk down the narrow lane of poplars in Moscow and when I talked about unbroken (and broken) people, talked about the air that hits you in the back of the head when you fire a shot, talked about barbed wire, bunks, brotherhood and about a song at midnight, Lera walked beside me and listened quietly. And the young poplars also rustled quietly; come to think of it, they didn't rustle then; they just moved their scraggly foliage soundlessly.

Most often we used to walk along the lane of poplars near the dormitory of our institute before we ended up in Novostroiny and Khonya-Desnovaya, where the short and mighty range of the Urals starts to unfold, where Siberia begins and where, in the midst of other mountains, stands a marvelous, evenly rising mountain with longitudinal hills.

Lera used to say: "So what's wrong with you now?.. Why are you sulking, I (we!) have had it up to here with you! Your glum mug is spoiling the view—and you call yourself a man from the Urals!"

And again: "I wish you'd get lost—why are you hanging around here?!"
And deliberately coarsely: "Why the heck are you staring? Go away—I
have to pee. I'll go behind the hill, because I don't want to smell the john
in the barracks. Don't follow me! Are you deaf?!"

But I was truly deaf, at times I couldn't see or hear. And it hurt. And I
felt that it would be easier to submit to life, see its distorted features, illness, or even death, than to see this transformation. Her toughness and
rudeness seemed inexplicable. I was silent and just grew numb, I just felt
sudden stabs of pain in my chest and heart; I felt so much pity for her and
experienced a constant sensation of losing her, losing her.

"...A screw?!" said Lera. "Do you know how the word originated?"
The sort of argument in which people go through all the possible and
impossible interpretations of a word had already begun, and at first Lera
herself maintained that the meaning of the expression was obvious: the
guard, you know, turns around, as any guard would, on his tower. I agreed.
But I suggested that it's also a guard who shouts to the prisoners: "Don't
screw around!" Meaning, stand still, don't turn around, move in a straight
line, breathe evenly and don't look back. And because of this isolated
(constant?) shout the word stuck to the guard forever. Lera suddenly said
with passion that she had an idea, and that maybe a screw is actually a rifle,
handy to use at close range, a short rifle which turns easily (like a screw) in
his hands, the rifle he's armed with! Yes, yes, it's making a fetish, a fetish
out of a weapon, a cult out of a shot!... The idea was like any other idea, it
was speculative and homegrown, too, but for some reason Lera became
dreadfully attached to it—God forbid you disagree with her, her lips
began to tremble and she grew pale. And I, of course, was already constructing my own model: there was a moving searchlight on that tower, I
said, that lighted the barbed wire in a zigzag...

"*Oh, you!*" All of a sudden Lera completely blew her top. "There you
go again with your lights, you dumb show-off. Next you'll start going on
about some theorem about light refraction!"

"And you're no better with your cult of the shot. Your Vasily doesn't
know everything there is to know about prisons either..."

At this she grew pale: "How can you? He's not you—he was the one
who slept on a bunk for several years!"

"So what?"

"You!.. You!.. Go away!"

She was choking.

"Lera," I caught myself suddenly. "Lera, forgive me..."
"Get lost! Go away! I don't want to see you..."

All day long I tried to get back in her good graces, but Lera just kept shaking her head: no.

I repented, asked for forgiveness. "Lera, it just came out that way. Lera, my tongue's my enemy. Forgive me..." I tried to justify myself, I reminded her how long and what good friends we'd been—I'd loved her for a year and a half, almost two years, when we sat together at lectures, walked along the lane of young poplars, and there was nobody there, just the birds! My voice trembled.

Lera was inflexible: "OK, OK. I'm not angry... Just go away."

(Everything had to be left behind—the barrack and the brass washstand, No Name Mountain, the two policemen playing dominoes in the shade, and the wild rose bushes. And I had to continue experiencing this intimate unity for a long time afterwards. I had taken it in as something foreign, and left it behind as my own.) Lera kept repeating frankly and rudely:

"When will you split?.. Go away. We're sick of you."

And also: "I want to live here and show Vasily my compassion. I want to be alone with him—do you understand?"

But I didn't understand.

In this state of painful estrangement from each other we climbed the hillock; at that moment I was reproaching her, I think, and Lera was gazing at the sky—wide and blue. she looked at it for a long time, and then said: "Why do you keep whining all the time? OK, let's go, come on." And on that very spot, in a beautiful small clearing, beneath some young pine shoots on one side and a wild rose bush on the other, I received in ten minutes what I'd been so passionately and amorously expecting (but, wait, was that really what I'd been looking for?) and on which I'd spent so much of my youthful energy, thoughts, emotions and a countless number of words. Afterwards we continued walking on the hillock. Lera said:

"Well?.. Is everything all right now?.. Now you can get lost."

She had mastered their way of talking incredibly fast. Moreover, she had become much ruder than Vasily.

But I didn't understand. And was living again from day to day. But, still, something in me bent this way and that until it snapped very quietly, like a brittle wire. And somehow I all of a sudden said: "I'm leaving," and began to get packed. They saw me off quietly and kindly, as if I'd asked them. At first we went by truck. Then Lera carried my small, light gym bag, and Vasily and I shook hands. Vasily was carrying several bottles of home brew that he'd brought for the road—I walked between them by myself without any luggage.

The train started to move. I stood by the window. I was leaving, and outside on the lousy little platform, remained Lera's beautiful distant face and Vasily, who'd grown kinder and was waving now—Vasily with his truck, bunks, and bony ribs that refused to take on any flesh. The countryside, the wild rose hillock and barracks, and the Khonya River full of water remained behind.

And it seemed to me, as it does to anyone who looks out of a train window, that it was the countryside, the river, the barracks and the wild rose hillock that were running faster and faster, and running away, while I fell farther and farther behind.

Half an hour later, thirty-nine miles away from Novostroiny, the train crossed and quickly left behind the Khonya River, and with it the subdued Anna Romanovna and her husband's grave surrounded by other, nameless graves.

The Khonya is a small river but fairly deep and full of water right up to the brink. It seemed not to have any banks, but to flow on the same level as the ground.

I was falling behind in time, but not behind Lera, nor the wild rose hillock, nor the Khonya-Desnovaya graves, nor *Novy Mir*, nor from the recognition for a first novel.

Lyosha, who's fallen behind and is choking with his nighttime fears, is running in the dark. He's tired. He doesn't want to live anymore. He takes a few steps and, feeling weak, sits down and stays sitting on the ground; he puts his head in his hands, rubbing his cold ears. Should he die here? Will he be able to drown like that drunken prospector who drowned in a stream, for example? And what will happen then?.. He's cold sitting by the stream. It's pleasant to think that you'll die. His mother will pray for him there. It will all be over. He'll never have to wake up and jump, his hand clutching the linen bag, and run and run. He wants to fall asleep and wake up without fear at least once... He'll die—that'll be his peaceful and uninterrupted dream, and what then? And then the angels should know everything themselves and will take care of everything for him there.

This night sky is boundless. The number of stars there is inconceivable. But what if in the other world, too, in the sky where there's paradise and peace for everyone, what if there, too, he'll be disturbed by these stars, confused by them, because from a distance stars look so much like lights. He won't have peace, he'll keep running from star to star, and from that one to the next, mistaking them for campfires. Oh, Lord, Lord! How frightening!... He envisioned himself, a thin, starving youth, running across a field of stars in fear that he'd fallen behind. Will they yell at him there too, or not? "Oh, Lord, is it really true that death isn't the answer either, that it won't bring me peace—I want to have some rest—some rest," repeated Lyosha, and his small fist hit the stream, splashing the water.

Once Lyosha sat by a rock, looking at his own shadow. Then he shifted his eyes and saw another shadow. There were no people around—not a soul. Nobody. But there was a shadow. He was scared and thought: who is it? Is it my dead cousin Kolya?

They used to fall behind together, and if they were scolded, it was together, and they went hungry together, too.

Kolya, his little cousin, began to appear to him more often. He looked the same as he did when he was alive, only his lips were caked with blood. He would approach and sit down not far from Lyosha, and he seemed to be touching Lyosha's bag all the time. And he'd reproach him:

"You don't feel sorry for me, Lyosha, you don't weep for me."

Lyosha tried to justify himself: "I don't weep, but nobody will weep for me either."

His little cousin Kolya sighed heavily. He kept touching the bag. He sat by the fire and talked about his short life: so I spent my whole life chasing after people. And suffered. And didn't have a single restful night.

"And what about me?" Lyosha would ask. "Did I ever get any rest?"

"That's true. You didn't either." His little cousin Kolya was sad, and then he finally melted, melted away and disappeared.

Lyosha looked at the fire, his eyes wouldn't stay open. But he couldn't sleep, he had to get going; and he got up.

A campfire. Night. Shepherds are sitting around... Suddenly they hear somebody running. A shepherd picks up a gun, but puts it aside—the steps are too light: no, it's not a foal—they're even lighter—not a mountain she-goat either... Suddenly the thin youth Lyosha runs into the light of the fire.

"Oh!" He glances back, looks around, and realizes his mistake. And with a cry, runs away again.

The shepherds talk among themselves: "He's crazy..."

"That's how he runs around at night, poor soul. He's fallen behind and is trying to catch up with his crew."

Meanwhile Yegor Fedyaich and the other artel members picked up some other crippled boy: they took him to the banks that were rusty from digging, to the streams and valleys, but all for nothing. The cripple would wrinkle his forehead, pretend to search, and suddenly grow thoughtful for a long time: he was very good at imitating a completely blank look, as if he were communicating with higher powers; everything was right, everything looked the way it should, only he didn't find any gold-bearing sand. To say nothing of gold nuggets.

7

Every evening as I walked by the offices of *Novy Mir*, I thought anxiously about completing my wonderful novel and taking it to Tvardovsky and about how he'd read it. Pacing at some distance from the editorial offices of the journal, whose name alone made me tremble with excitement, I unwittingly began to narrow my circle around the square: I was getting closer.

To start with, I was receiving communion. (I was communing with the place.)

The first time I passed near the building of the editorial offices I moved quickly, without raising my head. At that moment I cautiously thought that if somebody would see me—one of the women editors who'll soon be accepting my novel—then there was nothing wrong in my circling, since I could be passing through by accident. Anyway, they won't remember my face. There are so many people around and there's a bakery and stores. And Pushkin's monument. Yes, yes, it's quite possible that I'm going to the movies and just turned the corner. Growing bolder, I'd come closer again. (I would come here after working on the novel: it was a respite, a kind of rest.)

As anyone could guess, there was still a lot of residual love in those walks around the journal's offices, a love that hadn't gone away yet, wasn't over yet. Lera wasn't there, and yet she was. A change of locale had occurred, but, in accordance with this change, one state of being was just making the attempt to be exchanged for another. And if when Lera and I walked together in the lane of young poplars, we were mostly surrounded by green foliage and branches, and could barely see any buildings and houses, then here, at the editorial offices, it was the other way around: the houses and buildings clung together, forming a wall, while the trees and foliage on Strastnoi Boulevard were hardly noticeable in the clear spaces between the buildings.

There was a building (it no longer exists) with lengthwise stripes on one wall: up close they looked reddish and broadly patterned, but from afar they looked dense, as if they were overgrown by dark creeping grass. I didn't raise my eyes and don't remember the top of the building, or how many floors it had, but I remember very well the stripes and the mould-ing, which were at eye level, and the roughness of the reddish plaster. And every time I saw somebody near this building walk towards me (from the editorial offices) and even casually raise his eyes to look at me, I'd explode in a shower of sweat, I'd be completely drenched in small beads of sweat, the way a bottle of Borzhomi mineral water fizzes when it's just been opened.

I probably didn't recognize the gradual substitution of feelings, and it tormented me. But, possibly, in my naiveté I even partly hoped that the publication of my novel would gradually exorcise Lera. How? In a very understandable and ordinary way. Because of my involvement with the renowned journal, Lera would be ousted by certain events, certain inter-esting people, and conversations about high art. Like cures like, and Lera would disappear of her own accord, she'd fly away into the far distance, into oblivion, like that frightened bird (a jay?) which, suddenly finding herself within the confines of the lane of young poplars, tried to fly back-wards, with little success; either it couldn't or didn't want to turn. Flapping its wings rapidly, the bird flew straight between the poplars, as if along air rails, and I glanced back and said to Lera: "Look!"

The Lera with whom I communicated then in my thoughts was the Lera who studied with me, who walked along the alley of poplars holding my hand, and who was quiet and thoughtful. She pronounced words as before. And, as before, was responsive in her silence. She was with me, which, of course, was the best testimony to the fact that that time was over and she was gone.

Step by step I was moving closer to the building—not from the side of the square, but from Chekhov Street—staying near the famous church on the left. The windows were dark—both on the first and the second floors. I assumed that Tvardovsky (his office) was located on the second floor and immediately saw a light—a dim light—in one of the second-floor windows. Most likely it was a sleepy night watchman sitting somewhere on the second floor there, with the windows of his room facing the other side (and I was getting just a glimmer of the light in the hall); nevertheless, like one bewitched, I couldn't tear myself away from the muted red glow in the window that had come to life. I went up close to the entrance, read the sign with the name of the journal and reached out and touched it with my palm. I looked around to make sure nobody was watching me.

I'm not sure whether my desire to publish the novel was so strong after all. I wanted to belong, as did hundreds or even thousands of young beginning writers who tried in vain to solve the math problem of combining time with time—their own time with the time of their society. But, of course, when I kept circling those houses at night, the essence of that emotional experience—perhaps unknown even to myself—could not have been reduced to a single and typically youthful desire of belonging to something that gives off a whiff of fame.

I wasn't aware of the latest events at all: I had shut myself off. The math majors (the circle to which I belonged then) didn't know much for certain: a lot of different and quite contradictory rumors were circulating; however, they did know the dynamics of the process, and had I communicated with my fellow students, as I'd done before, I would at least have realized in time that things were coming to an end. At any rate, students were already talking about an appeal (a letter) to Tvardovsky from one of his faithful readers and admirers, published in a newspaper, not a major one, but still something on the order of *Socialist Industry*. Letters like that were never accidental. The tone of the letter was suspicious. What is this, Alexander Trifonovich, what is happening? I knew you, I always loved you—the letter ran—I loved you and respected you for your "Tyorkin," but now the journal which you are in charge of is incomprehensible to me, a simple person. There's a lot of things that seem unclear and overly complex on the pages of your journal, and, forgive me for being frank, at times it appears strange and alien.

On one of those late evenings I finally allowed myself to approach the sleeping building of the editorial offices and stand there a little longer, to smoke right by the doors, in order to rid myself of the complex of a person who is crossing the threshold for the first time (and, I thought, to be psychologically more prepared for the initial conversation). I was afraid of appearing ridiculous and a beginner, although, of course, I was both—a beginner and a ridiculous one. And the next day, feeling bolder, I walked up to the editorial offices when there were still people there: I happened to get there at just that time which occurs in any lively institution at the end of a work day. The end of work. During that hour or half hour the staff and possibly the editorial board were all going home. But maybe they were off to some urgent meeting *at the top*, where they'd been summoned so late in the afternoon, to discuss the permission (or ban) of some controversial publication... God only knows what I imagined then! I was overwhelmed with excitement. I was watching the staff leave the office from a distance of five yards—I stood with my back to Strastnoi Boulevard. I heard bits and pieces of their conversations. In particular I was I stung by the bit of talk from which I understood that Tvardovsky was having trouble with his legs and might end up in a hospital soon, within the next few anxious days. "Is he in danger?" someone asked in alarm, and another member of the staff answered something about some connection between having bad legs and a bad heart, but the wind carried their words away.

There's no doubt that when I was walking around near the editorial offices, I was simultaneously walking and circling around my lost love. There's no doubt that I was trying to alleviate the pain. I tried, if unwillingly, to raise my belatedness in love to the height which could now be measured with an obviously higher measure, one more general or more universal. An attempt (that was partially conscious) to attach my own feeling to the feelings of others, and thereby to anesthetize myself, was concealed in the endeavor to elevate my despair, since universal pain is, perhaps, more distressing, but less sharp.

And, perhaps, the step that took me away from Lera, that is, the step away from love in the direction of writing a novel, was only the same method that has been used by people from time immemorial.

And the fact that I was walking around in circles and saw the buildings, bakery, trees and church cupolas, topped with crosses opposite the building of the editorial offices, was also understandable: my circling was the circling of any lover around his beloved; yes, yes, this was part of a method to achieve oblivion, pain's dissolution in the universal, since the lover, having devised (found!) a socially significant cause, roamed around the place where his beloved was obviously absent, trying, as if hypnotized, to convince himself that she was there.

And maybe this circling was in some way related to Little Lyosha's circling during his chase after the artel, when he'd wander near a copse and then run up a hill, where the glassy ribbon of a stream first sparkled, and Lyosha would freeze on the spot. He stopped. He cried: "Ah!" He realized that it wasn't at all necessary to chase and catch up with them; he could stay here for a while and sleep right there, on this spot to which he was drawn and where it would be so sweet to sink down to the ground. He'll neither search nor, more importantly, spade the ground. He'll simply lie down, he'll sleep, and the gold, from inside, from the ground, will lightly warm his sides and back. And he'll place his crippled hands, palms down, on the grass. Under the grass, under the sod there's yellow sand, warm yellow sand. And his hands will ache a little—here.

Once, having fallen behind, Lyosha and his cousin Kolya saw a wolf on a hill up close. It had a broad chest and strong, unblinking eyes. It stood there, looking. Both boys passed right by him as they crossed the mountain. And somewhat humorously Cousin Kolya kept saying to the wolf: "You're a good dog. You won't hurt us... Good dogs don't hurt little boys." He said "dog," as if he were unaware of who was looking at them from the hill, he said "good dog," deceiving himself, Lyosha, the wolf on the hill, the valley, the rocks around and the clouds.

As I walked from Naryshkin Drive to Strastnoi Boulevard, I couldn't avoid running into a fellow student who was going to the movies and who, figuring that there's nothing else to do on these streets, yelled at me without stopping: "Are you going to the 8:30 show, too?" meaning the next show, and I answered: "Yes, yes," and immediately waved to him as I moved away, as if I'd been swept aside by the crowds of people that were already visibly jostling hard during the rush hour.

I wasn't interested in joining the realm of lovers who'd failed in love: their number (enormous) didn't ease my suffering; being dissolved in them, in the enormous mass of unloved ones, had no attraction for me; however, belonging to those whose first novels had been rejected beckoned me much more, even warmed me. Secretly I probably expected that if they rejected my novel, then the addition of one rejection to the rest would consume me in some lulling anguish shared by all beginning authors—those plumes in the wind.

It's not surprising that things got superimposed externally as well: after walking down Strastnoi Boulevard for hours—to the point of complete exhaustion and shaking legs—I sat down on a bench to rest and, looking at the stream of Moscow cars, suddenly saw a truck—even its license plate number was similar to Vasily's; so right there and then Vasily stopped his beat-up truck, got out (I couldn't mistake his gait) and said to the policeman: "Hey, you!..," pulling the man's hat down over his ears. He then ambled over to my bench and said angrily: "So why are you sitting around like this? Come on, Lerka's waiting in the car!.."

In the editorial offices of the thick and thin journals, the department heads, as a rule, middle-aged women, smiled at all of us in a friendly way: they seemed to understand (and maybe they actually did understand) the whole age-old experience of rejected love: how it's transformed and, essentially, grows out of a rejected feeling into a non-rejected (or just initially rejected) manuscript of a beginning poet or prose writer. The affectionate and understanding look of these women was, unfailingly, gently relaxing and comforting: everything will pass, everything in this life does.

"What do you mean, 'not here'?.. But he was here, wasn't he?" I'd just asked again about the former editor-in-chief, and they answered: "Precisely."

After the shock I wanted to tear it up in some little street, but it wouldn't tear, and so I threw the manuscript away. I didn't know then that falling behind is a diverse phenomenon, but could already foresee its invariably personal and protracted nature; and I knew that I would feel worse and more disappointed if, as the curtain fell on the journal, the head of the prose department (a good-natured man or a nice middle-aged woman)—not yet replaced but no longer important—would turn down the manuscript.

For three years I didn't visit the house where Lera used to live with her mother, the house where I used to have tea under the low lampshade radiating such warm, cozy light. I was embarrassed to question the neighbors. (I thought that they'd remember perfectly well how Lera and I had stood for hours by the entrance to the house.) Nonetheless, after pulling myself together, I ran up to her floor and knocked on that same door.

Strangers were living there. The lamp with the large shade in the big room was still there and I don't think I took my eyes off it the whole time I was standing so awkwardly in the hallway. The people told me that Lera had come only once and, after quickly packing her things, had left again. She gave her furniture to various neighbors. She took only two suitcases and left. She dropped in to say good-bye.

On his infrequent visits to the settlement (as if halting for a moment in his eternal flight) Lyosha couldn't figure out the way of life there. Lyosha was especially puzzled by the settlement's women: they had undoubtedly something in common with that woman who'd pitied him; she was so affectionate and so sweet to him when she warmed him, rocked him lightly, and then began to moan a bit, or laugh softly, stuffing her mouth with her own hand (once, by mistake, she put his hand—his wrist—into her mouth, and he realized that she was biting it weakly, not at all painfully, a little more strongly one minute, a little more weakly the next, and when she pressed more weakly a quiet: nn-nny-ny-yy... escaped through her teeth and lips.)

———

Yesterday father said: "But I yell at you because I love you!"

In the past years I've heard this famous word in a variety of combinations and with all sorts of connotations; however, this word, when said to one's own son in a telephone booth with shattered windows, in a Moscow suburb, in the dark, at three in the morning, then this word still has meaning.

Father started to limp. So at night, when it drizzles (it's already fall), with his raincoat flapping at each step, he hurries to the telephone booth, limping and shaking his matchbox from time to time.

In the telephone booth he'll first light up his cigarette (invulnerable to the rain) and then call.

He's certain that he feels really good visiting his son—in his son's large apartment—that his heart feels really warm and tender. They had supper together and talked... his son, daughter-in-law and granddaughter. Moreover, before going to bed he was fortunate to catch the final scenes of a decent old movie on TV, a movie that before the war, in his youth, he and his (late) wife had watched together and that had brought them closer. He keeps holding on to this little bit of happiness inside. He'd been shocked by an explosion at a building site and had been irritable, but still, they'd been on good terms then; they had a good, long life together for a long time. His wife died before him. It just happened that way.

"Yes, I'm going to bed. Thank you, thank you," he says to his daughter-in-law.

And they all got into bed so quickly! They're young! He also went to bed in the room that they'd given him. He felt warm and comfortable. As he gazed at the night, he thought about his own former family happiness, and then thought about his son's present domestic happiness.

It's already dark in the room. Father lies there and it's as if he's taking private note of the moment when sleep overtakes him—they all have to go to work tomorrow and take care of business, but he'll be the first one up anyway. What a night! What pleasant peace... He turns off the night-light. The apartment is plunged into darkness.

He feels good. But suddenly he experiences something like a spasm under his heart. He's a bit frightened (not too much): what is it that alarmed him so?..

And now he's overwhelmed with a horrible, incomparable fear: this fear seems to wipe out, to strike out his entire life. Suddenly everything becomes revolting. The fear is unreasonable. And he's oppressed by the senselessness of life in general, in the face of death that comes to one sooner or later, the senselessness of any life, not just his own. It's so difficult. So wrong. Being a hardened man, he tries to distract himself with thoughts about his sons, his grandchildren, about the work he's done, about various construction sites in the past, even about his old feelings for a smiling young girl at the post office—his future wife—who hadn't put on weight yet and didn't have a single wrinkle; he manages to recall her, using her as a foil, moving her youth, her fresh appearance, her lips and blond hair toward this void; but no, no, neither his long experience as a construction worker, nor all of the former joy and freshness of the world have significance now, in the middle of the night, absolutely none, not even a distracting significance: what he's thinking about drowns out everything and everybody.

In order to shake off the delusion, he tries to fight fire with fire and to spite it, to think about the bad things, the dark things in life, but even the evil of the world, criminal cases, all manner of disasters, personal dead ends, total catastrophes and misfortunes don't distract him from the pain in his soul that is essentially so small, not really pain, but the original source of any pain, the original pain-horror, which paralyzes and numbs you, which makes life not worth living.

His bed is hard. He tosses and turns. He hears the voice of his dead wife: "Petrusha, Petya, what's the weather like there?" He suddenly hears her tender, compassionate voice, and then she asks something else, tormented by uncertainty about days and nights on earth—her voice is dark, and her words are dark, too. Father turns on the night-light. How can he sleep? And he turns it off again.

There's a knock at the door. It's one of the family: maybe his son or granddaughter are worried about his tossing and turning in bed and so they're knocking politely now. All right, I'll tell them I've got insomnia and would like a glass of cold water. Having banished some of his sense of fear, he gets up and turns on the night-light—now, that's just fine!..—but the knock is no longer a knock: someone is banging on the door. Well, this certainly isn't what your family is supposed to do. He walks towards the door with displeasure—why are they knocking like that?—he turns on the light and... and he doesn't recognize anything. It's a strange apartment, not even an apartment, but a hut. Why is he here? What for? Sleepily, he quickly pulls on his pants and, with nothing more than a shirt on, walks out, runs out to where nobody is knocking or banging any more, but, instead of people, it's a truck engine that's making such a resounding knocking noise. A truck speeds off... One truck after another! There's the last one. (There are a lot of people in the back of it.) He runs after it, gulping the freezing air. He tucks his shirt in. The road is slippery, the melted snow is frozen into a thin crust. It's so hard to run, the truck is so far away—it's impossible to catch up.

Translated by Nadezhda Peterson

Originally published in *Znamia*, September 1987

NIKOLAI SHMELYOV
THE VISIT

"Idiot! Good Lord, what an idiot! Gray hair and a mouth full of dentures—and you let yourself be taken in like that! Like a kid, like a green kid... You turned out to be a real baby, kid! One hundred thousand! God, one hundred thousand! In five minutes! The shame, the disgrace... They tricked this fool, wrapped him around their little fingers—they're probably laughing about it now—something to tell their grandchildren! And it serves you right for having your head in the clouds, it serves you right... Oh, the scoundrels, what scoundrels..."

It had already been five days since it happened, yet Gleb Borisovich Sukhanov, at one time a rank-and-file administrator of the Leningrad Philharmonic and now deputy director of a renowned Moscow theater, a distinguished, well-built and even handsome man in his own way, in the prime of life, as they say, still couldn't pull himself together.

In the semi-legal business world of Moscow, Sukhanov was somebody—not one of the most important players, true, but somebody all the same. He counted for something, his name was usually spoken with respect, people valued his word, and many were proud to know him—not just businessmen, but people who had nothing to do with business, who simply had contact with him in various everyday situations. Still, even for him it was a major sum, no doubt about it. You don't simply pull that kind of money out of your pocket, and he didn't print money. God is his witness, it didn't come easily to him. But that wasn't the shame of it—the shame was that they'd tricked him... And how! Like the biggest fool, like a drunken trader at the central farmers' market... But in the end traders didn't care where they threw around their money: raise a ruckus, smash a restaurant mirror three meters high, head off to Paris, or live well and lord it over everyone, toss a hundred thousand in some stranger's face—as if to say, here, that's the way we are, it won't hurt us—we'll only be stronger, a name is credit, too!.. But life is different now, and no matter what you do, the scale of things is different: if he could give free rein to his skills, if the regime hadn't bound him hand and foot—it would be a different matter. Then even one hundred thousand—what's a hundred thousand? Peanuts! You could make it in a week...

It must be said that Sukhanov was absolutely convinced (and not without grounds) that if he were given a chance, no Sol Hurok or Carlo Ponti could hold a candle to him. Damn, there was just no outlet for a man's abilities, no one needed them... It was fine for *them* there, in their own countries, but let them try to maneuver here: to set up any sort of serious deal you needed such caution, so much resourcefulness and brains and tact, and ultimately personal charm. And it's not enough to set it up—you have to run it so it doesn't fall apart, so that if something happens it won't expose you or anyone else, and no one will be caught. That damned regime lurks behind you like a wolfhound, breathing down your neck—at any moment it can suddenly bite off your head, and, all right, so you ruin yourself, but your family will have to live off handouts—that's what's so terrible, God save us all from that. It's only a myth that your partners will help you out and support you then: the hell they'll support you then, except for incidentals the first year—well, maybe two at most, but don't count on any more, they aren't fools—it's every man for himself, only God is for everyone... Well, so what, we're no slouches... The pity is that you try, you go all out—and for what? So that later they can strip you in five minutes and rob you in broad daylight—and who? A hood, the dregs, some punk you wouldn't shake hands with, but they've got you: they've got you by the neck in a death grip, how can you get away? You pay up, whether you want to or not.

For a long time afterwards he would remember that little dinner in the Warsaw restaurant which began so quietly and modestly, in solitude, in a half-empty hall; it was the closest restaurant to the recreation park, the food wasn't bad, and after playing pool in the park's poolroom, he usually dined there alone, and after dinner he would go to his office at the theater.

Gleb Borisovich was a gambler, a serious gambler—what you call no-nonsense. Despite his democratic nature, he usually knew precisely who to play with and who not to play with—that is, of course, if we're talking about a serious game, who to socialize with and, likewise, who, to keep a distance from so he wouldn't lose either his standing, which, to be frank, had not been easily won, or the respectability that so profitably distinguished him in the eyes of certain Moscow circles. Sukhanov had long maintained a reputation as a gentleman, and he liked to think that this reputation was solid; he prized it highly and maintained it skillfully, with an innate sense of measure and tact. If he departed from this image, he did so covertly, concealing it from all of his close friends so that no one would know a thing... Well, what of it? It was understandable—his nerves weren't made of steel, and from time to time a person needs a little excitement, some diversion—to get raucous, roll in the mud. You can't live without it, can't bear it otherwise, and in the end, what Russian doesn't love a fast ride? Smoke, a binge, champagne, young salesgirls or hairdressers, a restaurant on the edge of town, then someone's dacha, a two- or three-day spree, a hangover, a gray morning, empty bottles, a cigarette sticking out of a slice of sausage like a steamboat chimney, women's skirts tossed across the chairs... But gambling had an entirely different meaning in his life: it was his favorite pastime, his relaxation: a well-pressed suit, refinement, conversation with people you liked. And then the thrill of the game... Of course, there was passion—and how! But in his position he had to do everything in his power to curb his passion—other than allowing himself to take a card for laughs when the stage workers played "Twenty-One" while they waited for the performance to begin, or betting God knows what kind of money at the races... But even in these cases he never lost his head, and he'd stop in time when he started to have a really lucky run, or, on the contrary, when his luck really started to run out.

Sukhanov played pool and, of course, he played the horses—quite regularly, too—but most of all he loved and cherished the quiet evenings he spent by the fire playing cards a couple of times a week with an old group of friends in the apartment of a famous professor of urology. Sometimes they played bridge, less often poker, sometimes even canasta for the hell of it, but it was usually preference, good, old, sweet preference, where the important thing is the process of play—the sense of comfort, the mental concentration, the ever-changing composition of the game—and certainly not the win or loss at the end, which is rubbish, of course, if the partners are matched in skill and have known each other a long time. And they had known each other for a long time; their group was very respectable: a professor, a retired general, the director of a major stationery store, Gleb Borisovich, and sometimes also a rather famous playwright, who had an excellent command of socialist realist themes, but was a little greedy at cards, it must be admitted, and consequently was not a very reliable partner. So he was more of an alternate than a regular. To tell the truth, Sukhanov's character would have been better suited to poker—a game of chance, with high stakes—but first of all, he never dropped his guard, even here, in this group, choosing not to flaunt his money in front of the others, and second, he had to adjust to the circumstances, as they say: on his income the general was clearly not cut out for poker, the professor also seemed to have his limits, and the playwright took each loss so hard that it was clear he was not cut out for high stakes—he might even inform on someone so as not to pay up.

But, say what you will, so far his life had not turned out badly, not badly at all, especially if you looked back to where he began... An unsuccessful actor, a low-level administrator dashing around in a constant frenzy, killing himself for a paltry salary—not doing business, just running errands— Good Lord, how small-time it all was, in short—penny-ante stuff, shameful to recall now; a bat of a wife who didn't give a damn about him and cuckolded him right and left with the first taker. Once he even caught her with some punk black marketeer, the type who always hangs around the entrance to the Astoria Hotel or the airport... A ballerina... She was no ballerina, she was a slut... But now she was probably biting her nails out of chagrin: who needs you, you old hen, now that you're forty? Be thankful that at least you don't have any problems with money, and that's for our daughter's sake, not yours. I wouldn't have sent you a single ruble—hit the pavement, earn your keep, and if you can't—then starve to death. What's it to me? Thank God I'm through suffering with you. I did my time...

Everything changed—and changed radically—when he finally decided to leave that witch, got married to Regina, and moved from Leningrad to Moscow. Of course, it was difficult, it wrenched his heart, as they say... His daughter... He loved his daughter madly—a fluffy, affectionate creature, with mile-long eyelashes and eyes into which you could just gaze and gaze and forget, not remember, that there, beyond another door, begin filth, horror, shrieks, and the devil knows what else... But now his conscience was clean as far as she was concerned, considering she was taken care of for the rest of her life, there would even be enough for his grandchildren, and they had a wonderful relationship, even better than his relationship with Maxim, his son with Regina. It's true what they say about a daughter being dearer to a father than a son... How she throws her arms around his neck when he visits! And it isn't a matter of money, or gifts, or because he dresses her from head to toe, got her into the theater institute, introduced her to the right people and set her up for life, as long as she wasn't foolish, and she isn't foolish. No, it's because they are friends, they understand each other at a glance and they don't need anyone else when they're together: they can spend a whole day together strolling around Pavlovsk or Peterhof, just talking and talking... What do they talk about? It doesn't matter what they talk about—what matters is that they're happy together, effortlessly happy. What are words? Words are just words, smoke...

In Moscow, of course, he had also had to hustle at first—no avoiding it—but still it was easier. He seemed to immediately adopt the manner that best suited him: modest, virtuous, not too obvious, but not a push-over either, he met his obligations, he investigated and then carefully, gradually set up his contacts. When necessary he didn't scrimp, but nei-ther was he a fool—he didn't show off, he studied, he read, he gladly went out and just as gladly had people in. He often invested both time and money in people before the return was clear, even to Regina, not to men-tion others, but he saw it clearly, only it wasn't short term, but would emerge later, in the long run... So everything was as it should be: first the manager of a mediocre theater, then of a good one, now the deputy direc-tor of the same theater and its director any day, since clearly that wreck, that red-nosed drunkard, wouldn't last long—another year or two, and then he'd retire. When that happened, no one was going to search far and wide, and there he'd be, a ready replacement: young, forty-five years old, professional qualifications at just the right level, splendid relations with the collective as well as with the regional party committee. They knew him in the Ministry, where they listened to his opinion... Everything was set, everything was going along nicely. All he needed was patience, to keep from tripping up or taking even one false step. It's hard to build, but to mess things up—it doesn't take a great mind to mess things up—if you can't do it yourself, others will help, you won't have to wait—as they say, there's a sea full of volunteers...

The invaluable advantage of Sukhanov's current position was that he felt at home everywhere, whether he walked into a room alone or with his wife—a well-groomed, statuesque woman, always dressed simply and expensively, carefully coiffed, a pair of jewels on her ears and a ring on her finger, nothing else—into some club restaurant, the Theater Club, Cine-ma Club or the Literary Club. He always had a right to be there, and it would never even occur to anyone to question his presence, wonder why he was there and not some place else. If people saw him at a concert, at a dress rehearsal or the premiere of a new film, nobody was surprised to see him in his usual seat in the second row or in a box, but it was unusual not to see him or at least his wife there. If he sat on the presidium of an impor-tant conference—that made sense, too; after all, he was respected and dis-tinguished, a valuable colleague with great prospects for the future. Finally, if he showed up in a circle of business people or serious gamblers, there, too, he was always greeted with deference, and some even greeted him with outright envy—this guy has managed to set himself up, and they say he has a good bit of money, and a brilliant position, no chinks in the armor, as they say, and connections—everyone should have such connections, and he knows how to behave himself so that others can't help but feel embarrassed at being hopeless plebeians, or because they're wearing a poorly tailored, garish suit, or have an old hen of a wife they're ashamed to show in public.

He especially understood those people. He understood them perfectly and in his own way even sympathized with them. There was a time—and even now he often had occasion to observe something similar, only at a distance—when even he, no longer poor, not poor at all, would find himself in the home of some quiet, nondescript doctor—in a branch of science you can't even pronounce—or in the home of some disheveled writer in glasses, the type who isn't published and probably never will be. He also experienced that uncomfortable and seemingly unjustified sense of humiliation. Why? The devil knows why. The clothes on their backs were worthless, the odds and ends of furniture were junk, the stuff they served was pitiful, and no one would give a kopeck at the flea market for the host with the hostess thrown in—still, he was no match for the man, no two ways about it. Even if you screamed that you could buy them all, bag and baggage, with all their goblets, all of their books and all of their brains, they still wouldn't show you the door; they'd only shrug their shoulders and nothing more... But, look, all that was behind him now, and if he was still a little bit of an outsider, at least Regina always felt at home, even among these people: a beautiful woman's always a beautiful woman, even if you have ten Ph.D's, and besides, she wasn't a bad actress, not great, maybe, but she's got a name.

And as for businessmen—well, here he could hold his own without any bragging. Why not? He has everything, it's been ages since he had trouble getting something. His house is a storehouse of plenty—not even a house, but a museum; he has the latest model car, his own hair stylist, his own dentist, his own sauna, his own maitre d' in every restaurant, and the best tailor in town. Everything goes like clockwork, all it takes is a phone call, and he has nothing to worry about, they'll bring it right to his door without any bother at all—it just takes two or three complimentary tickets to a good show and the person he needs is on the line... A dacha? Why the hell does he need a dacha? It's much easier without one. He can get himself a room at any time at any hotel in the country; two or three calls—and he's in whatever professional art club he wants, even outside Moscow, even in the Baltic, and even in the south they are dying to see him, and, naturally, not alone but with his family, or without if need be... Foreign currency? No, not that, not under any circumstances—what is he, his own worst enemy? He still wants to live a while, and in that business the slightest mistake can be the end; you're lucky to escape with your life—it's bad to joke around with the KGB... So far they haven't abolished or aren't about to abolish the domestic currency, and he's got enough for a lifetime. Gems, porcelain, even books—that's another matter. Those things are reliable. Regina has good taste, she knows what to buy, and besides, there are specialists you can depend on. And it's good hedge against inflation, because those things certainly aren't getting any cheaper—they get more valuable every day... But: caution, caution, and more caution! As his card buddy, the director of the stationery store, once said, "Gleb, I could make five, or ten thousand a month. But I make two—and sleep better... " Of course, he's still not close to that blessed state... But he isn't that far, either... Two or three more years and he'll be director, and then he'll be able to walk away from business with a clean conscience. I'll buy a dacha in Peredelkino then, I'll raise tulips, visit the right people, play a few low-stake games, read books... I'll bring my daughter, Alyona, to Moscow, set her up in the movies—with what she's got, it's God's will, she can't spend her life vegetating in that hole... Maxim still needs to be brought into society—the kid is bright, he should get on the academic track; if it doesn't work out—it's no great shame, we'll find something else. We could send him to the Foreign Trade Department or the diplomatic corps. Let him travel around and see the world, give him a leg up so he doesn't have to knock himself out at first, maybe we can't do more, but at least we can do that much for him. After all, it's possible, it's really possible. There are such people, and he knows them personally, not from legend or from other people's stories— people who aren't afraid of anything now, who can't get caught, even though they flaunt everything they've got... like that Armenak, the old fox... He had a huge business in Baku, a million-ruble business, and now he's the quiet, modest manager of a clinic in Kuzminki, a pensioner. Where did it all come from? Just try to dig around and prove something. The business is all liquidated, he's left no tracks, he's been living the good life for a decade at his dacha, dabbling in the arts, interested in horses, raising his grandsons... And he—Sukhanov—what is he—worse than the others? He has everything figured out, he's double-checked everything that needed checking dozens of times. He has made arrangements, laid down the straw, so that if, God forbid, he's brought down, he'll have a soft fall. He's not likely to be shattered. At worst, they'll say he misused his influence. Money? There wasn't any money, you can drop that. A reprimand—I agree, go ahead and punish me. I made a blunder, live and learn. I ask you to let me

atone for my guilt, to justify people's trust in me. All these years without a
single wrong move, how could this have happened? I don't understand it
myself! Really, I just don't understand... . They deceived me, those sons
of bitches, I trusted them, I let down my guard.

Really, the danger could only come from three people—no one else had
direct contact with him. No, not even from three—two. What danger could
there be from the administrator of his own theater? He's no hot head—he
wouldn't try anything on his own. There really wasn't any danger. Gleb
Borisovich doesn't take part in any shady business any more, he's had
enough. He did his share of hustling in his time; let the other guy run
around and hustle now. He's young, he's still got some growing to do, all
those unofficial concerts—that's his problem. So what if he, Sukhanov,
gets an envelope with his share every month? Why, he could disassociate
himself from that in a minute—say he didn't know anything, the fellow
was paying back an old loan and that was all. Don't mix me up in your
business deals. You work it out as you like, me—I have, as you see, nothing to hide. You're saying I knew? I didn't know a thing—it's all dirt, slan-
der, a conspiracy. My enemies want to ruin me—they're trying to clear a
place for someone. How can you believe people like that? Swindlers, what
they wouldn't do for thirty pieces of silver! You can see for yourself what
kind of people they are.

But in his real life all that was nothing now—the serious business was
not carried out there, in the theater, of course, but somewhere else. That's
where there was a real risk. Sukhanov had invested all his capital in stock—
in a large manufacturing concern. His partner, Zakhar Grigorievich, an old
acquaintance, was someone dependable, tried and true. He ran the whole
business himself, and if something were to happen, he'd also agreed to
bear all the responsibility himself. But who could guarantee anything in
such matters? Of course, Sukhanov only financed the enterprise—and
who knows that, who saw anything, where's the evidence, where's even
one piece of paper? Other than that, he was only something like Zakhar
Grigorievich's consultant on communications. He introduced him to the
right people in the ministries and other organizations, helped formulate
the enterprise's overall policy, sometimes suggesting new opportunities, he
advised him on marketing, but he made sure he didn't know anyone else
in the business other than his partner—heaven help him, he saw to it that
he didn't know a single soul. And the transfer of the profits due Sukhanov
also seemed well thought-out: they were constantly checking, are there
any loose ends? It usually took place in his car, on an empty stretch of road
outside the city, or here, on a quiet sidestreet in the Arbat. Besides, the car
was outfitted with a clever little device—a trade secret—so that at any

moment the packet of money could be chucked out of the car. And in that case—just try to prove something. They both knew their business—they weren't fools. If Zakhar Grigorievich got in trouble, why should anyone suspect him, Sukhanov? An old pool buddy, a really nice guy, very smart, and, besides, a great admirer of my wife—we even got together at each other's house a couple of times—no, I wouldn't say often. We'd talk every now and again, sometimes he'd ask my opinion about some people, sometimes he'd ask for an introduction to someone... What for? Why shouldn't I introduce him? What business is it of mine? He could need them for any number of reasons. We all have to get by in the world, after all... Such a decent, respectable person, who'd have thought... Money? Me? What money? You must be kidding? He says that? He can say anything he wants... What a rat, I never would have expected this. Do you have some sort of evidence? No? Good-bye, then, we know our rights. And it wouldn't be such a bad thing either, by the way, to apologize before you go—all this hasn't been very nice of you... That's the way it would go, of course, just like that. And yet—a chill, a sickening chill had been gnawing at his stomach for a year now whenever he as much as thought about this other life of his, about which no one, not even Regina, really knew anything...

But that wasn't all. He may have been too clever in his caution. Why did he need to involve the theater cashier in this business? Well, he knew why—there was the very real danger that the money Zakhar gave him might be marked sooner or later, and it took a load off his mind to exchange it for the theater box office returns—that wrapped things up nicely. But to do this, first he had to sleep with the woman, and naturally he didn't want to—and she pouted and was hurt if the breaks were too long; and second, he had to nearly kill himself trying to come up with presents for her; as for the third, if something happened, how could he explain it all? No, he had to end it all before it was too late: ultimately there would be less risk in a packet of money, even if marked, concealed in a hiding place that only he knew instead of this woman. Who knows what she could come up with? She says she loves him, and everyone knows there's nothing worse than that: look into her heart and she'll blurt out whatever she wants, she'll end up in jail with you, and then she'll tell everyone she did it all out of love...

He had finished his appetizer when those two fellows walked up to his table. One of them, nicknamed Frigate, he knew. Like Sukhanov, he was a regular at the pool hall, and they had even played a few games together. He was a good player, no denying it, a strong player, but badly dressed, tall, skinny, with elbows sticking out and dandruff on his shoulders, as if he didn't have a home and there was no one to look after him—it was clear he lived alone, although that was even in his favor in a way—he was a professional, no mistaking it. The man lived just for the game and didn't give a damn about anything else. The other one was a rather imposing man of about thirty-five, in a leather jacket, carrying an attache case. Sukhanov had also seen him somewhere but couldn't remember where: probably at the track, where else—there aren't too many places in Moscow where you might run into the same stranger. Frigate said hello and asked if they could join him. The restaurant had already filled up—it was lunch time, and Moscow's professionals moved in droves, waiters darted like whirlwinds from table to table. There was nothing he could do. Sukhanov nodded amiably, although in principle he didn't approve or like the idiotic habit of being obliged to sit with someone: what if a person wanted to be alone because he was tired of company—didn't he have a right to that?

The waiter came to the table. Frigate and his friend ordered; they ordered generously from the full menu, not the lunch specials. That kind of order would take time, but, by the looks of them, they weren't in any hurry and were willing to wait: it was pleasant here—clean, warm, comfortable... Their table stood in the corner, by the window, and Sukhanov could see practically the entire restaurant, but the two who had joined him sat one with his back and the other with his side to the hall, and they'd moved their chairs close together to sit shoulder to shoulder. Sukhanov quickly realized what they were doing: they were playing a game, or rather continuing to play a game they had already begun before they joined him. They were playing *shtoss,* "beat the bank." So what if they were playing; they'd probably started and couldn't stop, they were so caught up in it and couldn't find another place to play. Big deal that it was at lunch! A game was a game, and it wasn't his place to judge.

Sukhanov sat and distractedly ate his soup, occasionally catching bits of conversation exchanged by the two players, but he wasn't paying close attention, because his thoughts were far away. Just a few days ago he'd been asked to make a serious decision, a very serious decision: Zakhar had proposed expanding the business to open a branch in Kaluga. After some hesitation, Sukhanov agreed, but naturally they needed money for this, some start-up capital. The terms were the same—shares, fifty-fifty. He had been forced to liquidate virtually all his personal resources, and now he was going to have to live more modestly for a while and wait until the branch began to turn a profit. But besides this, Zakhar had begun to worry recently; either he sensed something and was afraid, or it was just fatigue showing: he suggested they come up with another, more reliable way to transfer Sukhanov's share of the dividends to him without personal contact—in the car, without the car—he didn't care which. But what could they come up with? They couldn't very well put it under a stone. So he sat and racked his brains. Still, there was no point in getting angry at his partner—he was talking out of real concern, the man had his heart in the business, he was worried about both of them. But his head was empty, a vacuum inside—fit for nothing but reading mysteries. A grand gentleman, with his head in the clouds! Watch out, Sukhanov, if you stop taking care of the necessities, you'll eventually forget how to take care of yourself. All right, we'll think up something. He'd learned a lot in life, gone to a respectable school—the main thing was not to rush, not to jump at the first idea that came to his head...

"Gleb Borisovich," Frigate said suddenly, interrupting his thoughts, "Maybe you'd come in for one tenth, huh? For luck? For some reason I'm on a roll. It's just luck and my sins will catch up with me. But we all know that you—knock wood—have a light touch. Not just in cards, but in everything..."

The waiters had brought a carafe of vodka, appetizers, and a couple of bottles of mineral water. Without asking whether he wanted any, Frigate poured shots for all three of them. He had to drink—not drinking would have been a gaffe in his books. Besides, as they say, don't foul your own nest, you might need the person someday—anything might happen...

"God's blessing... So what do you think, Gleb Borisovich, one tenth? Are you in?"

"Do you insist? All right, I'm in... only don't go too high. I'm not flush these days."

"We play on a small scale. You know what we make. We're not in Monte Carlo..."

Why did he agree? Damned if he knew. Out of stupidity. He thought that if he turned them down they'd say he was disdainful, standing on ceremony, or thought he was too good for them. No, if you're in, you're in all the way; hold on, save face, it's better to lose a couple of tens. Sometimes you have to pay to maintain your reputation. So—he sat for a while with the common folk, showed a man respect—that was also capital, it counted for something, definitely counted, and somewhere in the ledgers life keeps strict balance—he had noticed that many times with himself and others. Sukhanov followed the game for a while and then, when he was convinced that the game was honest and the bidding wasn't out of the ordinary—a hundred here, a hundred there—his mind began to wander, he became distracted and stopped following what was going on.

Business was one thing...but his main worry now was something else. He had an enormous problem, greater than any business, and one that never left his thoughts now—not for a minute, a day, a night. He never thought, he never could have even imagined that he would have to solve a problem like this. Of course, he knew, he had heard, that recently people had tried or succeeded in setting things up that way. He even knew some of these people personally, but it had never concerned him. It had always been alien to him, alien to his habits, his convictions, his attachments, his plans for the future, and ultimately alien to everything that made up his life—forty-five solid years.

It hit him instantly, with no warning, like a bolt out of the blue, and, to be honest, it was almost the first time in his life he was at a loss. And the longer it went on, the more he felt that he was tied in a knot that he couldn't easily slip out of or cut without doing himself monstrous harm...

A month ago, in the evening, when they had both returned from the theater and were sitting in the kitchen drinking tea in peace and quiet, out of the blue, mid-word, Regina suddenly broke off her usual chatter about some social nonsense and pushed her cup away with her elbow so abruptly that the cup rattled. She looked him straight in the eye and said, "Gleb, that's it, I've had it. I want us to leave."

"Where?"

"Where? Switzerland, Holland, even America—wherever you want, I don't care."

"*Where??*"

"Don't play dumb. You understand perfectly well what I mean. We have to leave, Gleb. I can't bear it anymore and I don't want to."

"What's wrong—have you gone crazy?"

"I haven't gone anything. I've been thinking about this a long time. And I'm astonished that you haven't been thinking about it. You know we have a chance. I can get an invitation. Gleb, we have to leave, leave before it's too late. . . "

"What do you mean?"

"Everything."

"What's everything? My business?"

"Your business, and mine—everything. I don't want to stay anymore, Gleb. It's unbearable here, it makes me sick! I could just scream! Every time I put on my fur coat I feel like I'm doing something so obscene that I'll be taken in and arrested.... That I'll be stoned. Gleb, can't you see that we can't go one like this? In another five or ten years I'll be an old woman, Gleb."

That evening he had found the strength to cut off the conversation quite abruptly. But it proved to be only the beginning. Regina had clearly resolved to stand her ground and now she worked on him, using her feminine wiles every evening, using tears, persuasion, logic, tenderness, and threats, either in turn or all at once. It was hard to fight her, oh, so hard, and lately the battle had exhausted him. She had decided to wear him down, as they say. For each of his objections she had ammunition all ready, a precise, clear answer that was sometimes gentle, or sometimes laced with such venom, such vitriol, that he was dumbstruck: where did it all come from?

Slowly but surely he was backed into a corner.

"Birches? Oh yes, birches," she said. "Friends? What friends? Yours, I suppose? Since when do you have friends? Your interests? Your creativity? Gleb, don't make me laugh. Business? What business? Waiting till they put you away? You'll get what you're waiting for. No doubt about that. And what will happen to us then? Do you think about us? There? What will you do there? Do you think that with your brains you won't find work? We'll have enough to get started and besides, they'll help us, of course they'll help us, and there—do you really think you won't be able to make a living? What about me? Don't you think at all about me? Language? You'll learn it in a year. Connections? What the hell do you need your connections for? Everything you did here with those connections you can do there by yourself. Your holdings? Do you have to throw everything away? Why's that? Don't you think that with your experience you could gradually transfer everything there quietly, without any sudden moves? Other people have done it and so can you, if you just use your head. I don't need to teach you. Our son? Well, there's Harvard—do you think that's worse than the culinary institute? Better ask him yourself. Your daughter? Alyona? Alyona again? The world begins and ends with Alyona! Are you going to cling to her your whole life? She only needs you now, but as soon as she goes off and gets married, it'll be '*Attendez*, Papa, thanks for the gifts, but, you know, you've got your friends and we've got ours, so please stop getting underfoot. I'm sorry, but I just don't have time for you.'"

In the end, out of all those discussions he was left with only two arguments, but they were both quite compelling. The first was that he didn't want to, and the second—the second truly was Alyona. "I don't want to, can't you understand, you witch?! I don't want to! This is where I grew up, everything and everyone I have are here, I don't know anyone there and don't want to. I'm not a kid anymore, every street lamp here is dear to me, my folks have been lying side by side for years in the German Cemetery. Why should I uproot myself? I'm fine here. Dangerous? Yes, it's dangerous. So what? I knew what I was getting into. I'm careful, another couple of years and I'll lie low and settle down— I'll only have the theater, nothing else. Start all over again? Get to this position all over again—who'd let me? Who needs me over there? Break my back again, push my way up? All right, maybe it would be for different money and a different life—but who am I there? Nobody, nothing!.. And don't bring Alyona into this. I love you, I respect you, I'll be grateful to you my whole life, but don't touch her..." Everything will blow over, but Alyona will remain... Her little hands, her eyelashes, her nose—he trembled to think of how good, how painfully good it was to touch his lips to it... Her fingers, glancing over him rapidly like a net: tss—tss—tss with a light, barely perceptible touch on his temples, his eyes, his cheeks, stony from tension— he had to be careful not to scare her, not to give himself away, so she wouldn't catch a whiff of yesterday's drinking bout on his breath or something else... And that crunchy cartilage in her ear: when he pushes aside a strand of hair and nips her ear—she laughs: "Oh, that hurts, Papa, don't bite, you're not a dog..." Where would I go? I won't go anywhere! Go by yourself... And she will leave... clear as day... she'll go... she won't give a damn about me or anything else here—she's a smart lady, tough, that's why I love her. Divorce? Another divorce? How many times... And she'll take our son without a second thought.

"Gleb Borisovich," the same dull, wilted voice interrupted, "things don't look good... You and I haven't had any luck... He broke the bank, the bum... If we could have one hundred thousand from you..."

"Ho-ow much?" Sukhanov choked.

"One hundred thousand... and I'm putting in, you understand, nine hundred... "

"Th-th-thousand? What are you saying? Have you gone crazy?"

"No, thank God, I still have my senses. There was a million in the bank, Gleb Borisovich. You owe a tenth. We agreed."

"What? When?"

"You were sitting right here! Didn't you hear? There was a million, it went into the bank... Bad luck, of course...but what can you do—that's the way the game goes. Now I wouldn't mind changing places with that young man... Don't get upset, Gleb Borisovich. If you don't have it with you, you can give it to him later. He'll take your word for it. You're famous, everyone knows you..."

"What are you doing? You Judases! You might as well have shot me..."

"Now, now, Gleb Borisovich. That's really not becoming to you. Why such expressions? And what do you think I should do? Hang myself? Volodya, write down your telephone number on a piece of paper for Gleb Borisovich. Forgive us, my dear fellow, you'll have to wait a week. Gleb Borisovich and I can't pull together that kind of money in an evening. You'll wait? O.K.? Now that's smart."

"Gangsters, card sharks..." Sukhanov fumed. "What am I, some hick? What do you take me for, a sucker? Do you understand, Frigate, what you're doing? Who you're tangling with? Do you understand?"

"I do, Gleb Borisovich, I understand everything... What's so hard to understand? You're a big guy, and I'm little. But why are you getting mad at me? If there's someone to feel sorry for here, it's me, not you. It's nothing to you, but it's the end of me... Remember that for the rest of my life I'm in Volodya's debt..."

"Frigate, Frigate..." Sukhanov rasped, "You don't know me yet...you don't know me. I'll have your head, you slimy creep! You'll remember me. I promise you. I won't pay a thing, you rats! Nothing!"

"That's no way to behave, Gleb Borisovich, no way at all. Tsk-tsk-tsk... I didn't expect this. Never mind, you're just upset now. You'll come to your senses after you think it over... Good luck. But please be so kind as to let us know in a week."

The louse didn't even think it necessary to play his role to the end: he twisted his gloating, revolting mug and laughed rudely, baring his rotten teeth. Then he stood up and even winked at his partner as if to say, that's how it's done, guy, pay attention. They paid their bill and left, leaving Sukhanov gasping with rage and intense self-loathing—such a fortunate fellow, so smart, so prominent just five minutes ago, and this is what happened... The shame—what shame, humiliation, and ignominy... Crap! Absolute crap. Good God, what crap they were. They push my face to the table, hold me by the nape of the neck, shove my face in my food and push it around so I won't get too cocky or puffed up: maybe you're smart, but there are people smarter than you, and you're no match for them! You show off! You dimwit! The shame of it, Lord, the shame... I ought to be shot on the spot! Damn it, damn it to hell...

That night he suddenly remembered with incredible clarity, like a light flashing on in the darkness, where he had seen the fellow with the attaché case: of course, he was a hanger-on, one of Semyon's entourage. Semyon was a very famous professional gambler in Moscow who played everything there was to play—the races, pool, card games, backgammon, dominoes, bets on the winner—Spassky or Fischer, dice, lotto... This fellow was always showing up at the race track on Semyon's tail, a lackey. So that was it—Semyon took him in, and now it looks like he's matured and set up his own shop... Set up... That's what it's called, setting up your own shop... He's the type of bandit who belongs in a wild forest or on the highway with a knife hidden in his boot-top, but not here... That bastard ought to be picked up and kicked out beyond the city limits. Let them fight it out there, tear each other to pieces. But how do you do that—God knows where the authorities are looking and what they're doing, but they're not paying attention to what's under their noses.

At eight in the morning Sukhanov was already seated in a grill on the Arbat where they served a traditional Caucasian stew in the morning and where, he knew, the horse bettors usually had breakfast before heading off to the track. He was right—Semyon was there too: a miserable looking, scabby little guy of indeterminate age, with ears like two radars sticking out in opposite directions, a sharp little nose and tiny, lashless red eyes.

"Semyon," he began as he joined him.

"I know, Gleb Borisovich, I know everything. Please accept my most sincere condolences. What's there to say? You had bad luck."

"He's your man, Semyon."

"Mine?! What do you mean, Gleb Borisovich! Of course I know him, but to call him one of my men—no, Gleb Borisovich, that's going too far. He plays on his own, and I don't have anything to do with it."

"Semyon, I'm warning you. I'm not going to pay. And if your people start threatening me, I'll have to report them to the proper offices. I've always respected you, Semyon. I've considered you a gambler, a major player... But it turns out...it turns out that you're just a criminal, huh? A candidate for life behind bars? I'll help put you there, Semyon, you can count on me helping... You can bet on it."

"Stop it, Gleb Borisovich... Don't...don't talk nonsense—this crowd doesn't scare easily. You're a smart man and know perfectly well that you're in no position to dictate terms... What if the appropriate officials found out that a modest theater employee blew a hundred thousand in five minutes? Where does he get the money for a game like that? That would be the end of you, Gleb Borisovich. You don't need me to tell you that. And you know it's not hard for them to hear about it... And your reputation in the business world then? Have you thought about that? Sukhanov doesn't pay off his gambling debts—who would trust you for a kopeck after that? Come on, Gleb Borisovich, let's end this pointless conversation... A game is a game, and you have to pay up. I hear you still have another week, so don't waste it on these useless squabbles. If you can't spare the money, at least spare your nerves. These days they count for something, too..."

It was terrible, but the rat was right, absolutely right. There was no alternative—he had to pay. But where could he get the money? And so much? Unless he sold off something from his house, he didn't have much cash right now, altogether about ten thousand, no more—the Kaluga branch had put a serious dent in his resources, at least temporarily. Should he sell some of his paintings or antiques? He didn't want to, and in fact he couldn't. First, rumors would start up right away: Sukhanov has started to sell off his museum; what do you think that means, dear comrades? Second, there was no need for Regina to know about this whole affair. He'd never hear the end of it, she'd remember it her whole life, and it was impossible to sell an important piece without her noticing. She'd notice, she'd notice anything, the woman had sharp eyes, and there was no way in hell he could hide something from her. That meant there was just one alternative: borrow the money. But he had to use his head when he borrowed it, and not take from the first fellow that came along, and, of course, not borrow small amounts: the fewer people involved in this, the better. Semyon was right: he certainly didn't need to publicize this, and there was no sense in taking a spill on flat ground for no reason. There he was, minding his own business and suddenly—take that!—a banana peel under foot! You hit your head so hard you can't remember your own name—you can't even pick up the pieces, not yours or anyone else's... But I'll get those rats, I won't be myself if I don't get back at them sometime... Never mind—patience: the important thing is patience, and some day my turn will come.

Everything turned out the way he planned. Zakhar gave him thirty thousand, after first calling him a fool and threatening to break off relations if this sort of disreputable behavior continued in the future. He managed to wheedle twenty thousand from old Armenak. He had to tell him that he had seen a good house, a good plot of land, and the whole thing was of course very expensive and he had to go into debt, and who else could he turn to but him? The old man, a peasant at heart, valued real estate more than anything else on earth, and he was delighted when young and, so he believed, capable people ultimately came to the same conclusion he had reached: there are eternal truths on earth, and no matter how you squirm and balk at them, nothing will change them and life will run its course anyway. The stationery store manager gave twenty thousand without even asking what it was for: he truly sympathized with Sukhanov, you could say he loved him—"if you need it, you need it, for God's sake, Gleb, take it, especially since it's just a trifle to me—it would be absurd for serious men like us to even talk about it"... He only had to get another twenty, and that's why he had come to Leningrad: an old friend from those hungry years in the past still lived and worked here. He was now an important person who was involved in big business deals, and Sukhanov fervently hoped that he wouldn't refuse to help an old friend...

Where the devil was he? He called every possible phone number all day and still couldn't find him: he told his wife and all his friends and the people at work that he was here and waiting for him in such-and-such a room in the Evropeiskaya Hotel and that he urgently needed to see him. It was already getting dark, the street lights and the lights at the entrance to the Philharmonic were already on. The clamor of night life had started on the sidewalks along Nevsky Prospekt. If he'd just call, if he could just hear

his voice—he was going crazy waiting all day—pacing from one corner to
the other, one to the other, like in a cage. After all, he wasn't made of
steel... Should he call Alyona? Of course, it would be better not to call now,
it would be better to call her in a light-hearted mood, when all the misery
was over. But he could give her a call now, at least he'd hear her chatter a
bit into the receiver, and maybe they'd even have dinner together. It was
silly for him to sit here like a prisoner, glued to the phone all night. If
Savely was on a roll, on a binge, there was no hope of hearing from him
before tomorrow morning and bloodhounds wouldn't be able to find him
now...

"Alyona? It's me."

"Papa? You're here? How wonderful of you!"

"Yes, I'm here. I have to confess—I've missed you like crazy... What are
you doing tonight?"

"Papa, sweetheart, don't be hurt, but I can't tonight."

"Too bad. What about tomorrow?"

"Tomorrow? First thing in the morning if you want. Listen, it's already
autumn—let's head for Tsarskoe Selo, all right? Let's go to Tsarskoe Selo!
Free, light-headed, and drunk..."

"The *ulans* there smile as they mount their strong saddles..."

"Barracks, parks, and palaces..."

"And in the branches—wisps of cotton..."

"And the sunset 'salute' rings out to the cry of 'Well done, young men!'
Papa, you're so clever! So it's set, we'll go? When will you pick me up
tomorrow?"

"Wait, let me think... Probably about nine o'clock... That's a good idea,
we'll take a taxi for the whole day. Or at least until lunch for sure... "

Savely still hadn't called. The melancholy of the aimless evening and
the absurdity of the last few days were nearly unbearable. Should he go
out, run away? There was no place to go. Get drunk? There was no one to
drink with. Savely wasn't around, and in this state he didn't want to see
anyone else; to sit there, put on a good show, smile while your heart's
heavy and the only thing you want is to send them all, the whole world, to
the devil so you don't have to look at anything... There was, of course,
another antidote, but who could he find now? He'd gotten out of touch
with life here. He'd lost all those small-time connections from want of use.
He couldn't just pick up the phone like in the old days and say, "Come
over."

It was already eight when the telephone finally rang. "Savely? Is that you?
Where have you been, you old goat? You can't imagine how much I need you!"

"Sorry, Gleb, business. I got tied up—I haven't even had a chance to catch my breath. I'll see you tomorrow at three. At your spot in the Sadko."

"Tomorrow?! I need you now, today! What do you mean, tomorrow?!"

"Gleb, I can't. I really can't, believe me. I'll explain everything tomorrow. You're not dying, are you, I hope? And no one else is dying?"

"No, no one. It hasn't gotten that bad yet. But I need your help."

"Tomorrow, Gleb, tomorrow. I'll do everything I can, you know that—relax. Only I can't today. Please, forgive me, but, well, I just can't, even if you held a knife to my throat... And tomorrow before lunch I've got two lengthy meetings. No way to change them now—everyone was informed about them a long time ago, a week ago. "

"All right. The hell with you! You're leaving me in emotional chaos, as it were... You could at least send some little substitute so that I wouldn't have to sit here alone... "

"That's the thing! You should have said so right away. Otherwise—help! fire!—I'd feel like a heel: an old friend is in trouble and I... Age?"

"A beginner would be best."

"Color?"

"Doesn't matter. Besides—no, better on the dark side... After all, I'm getting on."

"Got it. What time?"

"Right away would be fine... By the way, what's your rate these days? The usual? Or is this something special?"

"No, the usual, like everywhere. And the rest is up to you. So this is the deal: sit in you room, relax, and I think I can arrange something in an hour. I have one specialist here: a clever guy, he's got everything worked out—you can't do better, I guarantee it, don't worry about anything. Anything at all. That's it, then, see you tomorrow, old man. Don't forget—at three. I'll be expecting you."

Sukhanov went down to the cafe to get a bottle of cognac, a couple of bottles of champagne, chocolate, and apples. He set it all out on the little table by the window, moved the armchairs in, drew the heavy hotel blinds tightly shut, got out a pack of good cigarettes from his suitcase, and turned on the radio, but softly, just so it purred in the corner... How's that, then? Good, cozy, only the overhead light is irritating. I should turn that off—the floor lamps are enough. To be frank, I'm not in the mood for lights. Hell, time is dragging. She should be getting here now. Actually, the whole thing might be pointless. What kind of lover could he be right now? Instead of brains his head was filled with some kind of rocks—or rather, cobblestones dug right out of the street, he only felt disgust in his heart, his legs were made of cotton, his hands were shaking. Oh, Gleb Borisovich, Gleb Borisovich... All right, that's enough now... What had really happened? They got him for a hundred thousand, and that was really too bad, of course, but they didn't kill him, did they? No? All kinds of things happen in life. You'll fill your glass with cognac now, a person will come in—one look and you'll feel better, at least you'll forget your troubles until morning. And then—then we'll see—then things will be clearer, things will fall into place. Savely won't let me down, he couldn't.

Sukhanov was sitting in the chair and smoking, flipping through some brochure left in the room by one of the previous guests, when someone finally knocked at the door—softly, cautiously—more of a scratch than a knock.

"Yes, yes, come on in," Gleb Borisovich said, his heart beating faster, "I'm expecting you."

Through the half-open glass door to the room he could see a figure in a white raincoat slip into the small, dark foyer. He heard the rustle of an umbrella being folded up, the clink of a hook on the coatstand—apparently in the dark the raincoat didn't catch where it should and kept slipping. Then the switch clicked in the bathroom: in the stream of light coming from there Sukhanov saw only a lock of thick hair falling below her shoulders, and the red patch of a blouse which tightly covered her breasts and upper back. An agonizing minute passed, water gurgled from the tap, and then he heard a familiar sound—she had probably put her hairbrush down on the shelf under the mirror. Light shone from the bathroom again and the girl came in—calmly, as if she lived there, as if she owned the place. One step, another, a third toward the chair... Then suddenly she stopped and froze.

"Papa?"

"Alyona? You?!"

Outside it was beginning to get light. The bottle of cognac, now empty, stood on the table; an apple with a bite out of it lay beside it. The ashtray was filled to the brim with cigarette butts, and the champagne had also been drunk—drunk, of course, by him alone: when Alyona had recognized him she dashed headlong out of the room. She even forgot her raincoat and umbrella. He made no move to stop her, and he was probably right not to try. What could he have said to her? And what could she have said to him? He couldn't get drunk: it's always like that with this damned cognac—all that happens is that his heart pounds and he shakes all over, and then, of course, the smoking—he'd gone through his second pack—just try to fall asleep. He'd like to drink some vodka now: one blow like an axe on the head and you're gone. He'd be out, everything would go up in blue flames—but where could he get vodka now? You couldn't buy it for all the money in the world... No, of course he could. Some cabby certainly had a bottle, but he'd have to go out, wander around the streets, hail a cab, ask for it, talk with him... And rain was pouring down outside. In the evening it had just been sprinkling, but now it was coming down in buckets and he'd get soaked to his skin. He didn't have an umbrella and he couldn't take Alyona's; actually, he couldn't bring himself to do a thing after everything that had happened.

What should he do now? What?! Lord, if you exist, teach me, help me. I don't have any strength left, I'm at my wit's end, I don't know what to do, where to go, what to say. I don't know why I've spent my life pounding away like a fish against the ice. I don't do anyone any harm, so what is this for, Lord? For what?! If you don't want to help—then at least explain it to me. You're silent? You're always silent when you're needed. That's probably why people don't believe in you. No, Regina is right: we have to go, get out of here right away, go to the devil, to hell, to New Zealand, to the Papuans, to the Bushmen, wherever. Anywhere but here, not here under any circumstances. I can't. I can't take it any more. Or if I could put my head under a tram and that would be the end! But you need strength for that, too, and I'm not fit even for that... Light... light... The light is still on in the bathroom, I should turn it off. What nonsense. It's bad enough that she left her raincoat and umbrella, she left her hairbrush too. You've got to give her credit, the girl was serious, thoroughly prepared for anything, for the whole night, it would appear. How disgusting: the brush is full of hair. Was she too lazy to clean it? Or didn't she have time? Get a move on, she said, a job's a job, and it's inconvenient, the customer's waiting... My God—this is her hair! Hers!! Her hair, which used to be so fair when she was born, like flax, and then gradually grew darker, turned chestnut. Once she cut it all off like a boy's. It looked good, but in the institute she grew it out again so it almost reached her toes. That's the only way they wear it, now, loose women, it's the fashion, damn it... I wonder if this is just a fashion with them too? Or didn't she have enough pocket money? But that's not a problem for her—pocket money? No? Or maybe it is? Does that mean I didn't send her enough? Is it my fault? I must talk with her, maybe she really didn't have enough money.

She could have told me, damn it! Have I ever turned her down, even once? And if I leave, what then? Will she walk the streets full-time? Other people put up with the sick and the maimed their whole lives. No, Gleb Borisovich, sit still, don't fight it. You're not going anywhere and don't even dream of it. You've taken up your cross—be so kind as to bear it.

There isn't going to be any New Zealand for you. You're going to spend your whole life now trembling, checking every woman you pass on the street—what if it's she? But Regina...there's no way to tell Regina anything about this, not a word, no matter what—she'd get too much satisfaction out of tormenting him with it, she'd be merciless, she'd get back at him for everything. Oh, yes, what about Regina... Regina will leave, for sure, if not in a month, then in a year. There's no stopping her. Another divorce, another court appearance. And she'll take our son with her. And he'll be left alone again. And there... What's there? Oh, Lord God, what?!

From the window to the door, from the door to the window. Back and forth, back and forth, along the long carpet that stretched out to the window. The rain had let up and a dismal gray overcast day was creeping into the room, and he might as well turn off the lamp. Sukhanov stopped in front of the big mirror, glanced at himself and instantly flinched and recoiled: a complete stranger looked back at him from the mirror—a stranger with thinning hair plastered to his forehead, a beefy, puffy, deep purple face, hunted eyes and a weak, slack chin that had once been heavy and powerful. The face of Mark Antony, it occurred to him. Mark Antony, who had lost everything in the end: both Cleopatra and the war.

Translated by Michele A. Berdy

Originally published in *Oktiabr'*, May 1988

VALERY POPOV
DREAMS FROM
THE TOP BERTH

What a train! Where did they get it? Looks like they dragged it through the mud for three days before they got it here. Strange, though, where could they have found the mud? There's been nothing but snow for a long time now. Apparently, it's left over from summer. However, there wasn't time to ponder such niceties—the crowd had rushed to the side of the platform, the numbers on the passenger cars hadn't turned out as expected—they ran from the caboose to the locomotive! My car No. 1 turned out to be the last one, the platform didn't extend that far, and I had to climb down and then pull myself up by the hand rail. The conductor, unshaven and sinister, dressed in some kind of woman's knitted sweater, was standing indifferently in the corridor. I hadn't expected to see him in a snow-white tunic, but still...

"Is this the sleeping car? The sleeper?" I asked uncertainly, as I looked over the gloomy platform and door leading to the boiler, a jumble of rusty pipes.

The conductor just stood there, looking at me for the longest time, then grinned morosely and didn't say anything... Very strange! I entered the car... Cars like this are good for going to prison in, because after you've done some time in one of them, the life to come won't seem so hard. The paint-chipped berths and the musty smell reminded me of the most difficult times of my life, not so much of past times, as of the ones ahead.

The compartments should at least have been designated for two people; I had paid for a sleeping car after all, but they were for four people!
Just what was going on here?! I dashed towards the conductor, but halfway
there I came to a dead stop. You know, it just wasn't worth it. He'd start
examining the ticket, and I'd only be asking for trouble, as they say. The
problem was that my ticket was stamped "free." A little old man with a
stick had procured it for me so that I didn't have to wait in line (the line
was enormous and there were no tickets), and it was only after he had
taken my money and disappeared that I noticed the stamp. I flinched, but
he had already gone. Being a distinguished railway worker, he was apparently entitled to a free ticket, but I, not being prominent... Well, better
not delve into the matter. We're not so much above reproach that we can
demand our rights... That's why they do with us as they please. We're a
double zero, an infinitesimal plus. I tried to wipe the windows, but most
of the dirt was on the outside. Oh, to be warm... an awfully complicated
antediluvian aggregate had materialized before me in the corridor. I blew
on my fingers. Our conductor's bulky woolen sweater inspired even greater
fear in me. He probably doesn't shave so as to retain body heat.

I pushed the creaking door, stepped out into the corridor, and immediately a passenger from the next compartment stepped out behind me, also
having decided to brave it.

"Excuse me, will you be serving tea?" he addressed the conductor amicably.

"No," grunted the conductor, without turning his head on his fat
neck. You could have carved the word in the cloud of breath coming out
of his mouth.

"What do you mean, no?"

"Just no! Can you heat without coal?"

"Don't tell me there's no coal!"

"Imagine that!" smirked the conductor.

"The railroad has no coal?" I exclaimed. "Go to the locomotive..."

"Come on! There haven't been any steam engines for a long time
now."

"And this car...is from those times!" I guessed.

The conductor, as though hearing something intelligent for the first
time, turned to me and said, "From those very times."

"Then why do they keep hooking them on?"

"Well, do you have anything better to suggest?" smirked the conductor
as he once again stared at the door opening onto the empty corridor.

"But we'll freeze to death!" declared my neighbor. "There's snow out
there." He nodded towards the outside.

"Well, that's your business," the conductor said indifferently.

"It's an outrage!" I exclaimed, unable to contain myself. "And in which compartment can we find the head conductor? Probably not in one like this."

The door from the staff compartment suddenly squeaked open, and a ruddy-complexioned sailor dressed in a sailor's T-shirt peeped out.

"For god's sake, why are you belittling yourself?" he declared. "We'll get there one way or another—after all, we're real men."

Shamefaced, my neighbor and I parted company and returned to our freezing compartments. Hmmm, it probably wasn't worth going to the head conductor—the matter of my questionable ticket might come up... With a screech the train finally started off slowly. Patches of light in the compartment kept lengthening and then disappearing. These changes came faster and faster, until suddenly the light was cut off. Everything was flooded in darkness.

Was there at least electricity in the compartment? The dim lightbulb on the ceiling lit up the orphaned, run-down berths and the cloud of breath coming out of my mouth.

I sat for a while, hugging myself and rocking back and forth. It was impossible to sit still, my blood was freezing, and my skin started stinging at frequent intervals, a symptom, as far as I knew, of hypothermia.

No, it was stupid to wait for death so complacently! I jumped up.

It couldn't be this cold in all of the cars—surely some of them were heated? The dining car must at least have a stove—they're probably cooking something there. Indeed, I remembered seeing the sign "Restaurant" right in the middle of the train! I opened the door, stooped forward, and made my way through the clanking, swaying coupling of the railroad cars... The next car was even colder. People had bundled themselves up in blankets and were sitting motionless in the dark compartments (for some reason no one felt like turning on the light, which I could really understand). Only the trickles of breath coming out of their mouths indicated that they were alive. It was exactly the same situation in the next car. What is this? What year is it?!

I went on ahead, not even bothering to look around, only mechanically opening doors—for the umpteenth time—onto the cold coupling. I stood there in the freezing cold, cautiously bent over until I managed to open the next door, and ended up in the next car, which was just as dark and cold.

Then suddenly I got stuck on the coupling between cars. I kept yanking at the door, but it wouldn't give; apparently it was locked. The iron joints forming the crossing clanked, criss-crossed into one another, and suddenly disappeared from under my feet. I was seized by panic from head to toe. I yanked and yanked at the door, but it wouldn't open. I looked back—the idea of going back was even more terrifying. I began to knock. Finally, a face appeared in the window, peered out into the darkness and began to shake no. I started pounding on the door again.

"What do you want?" screamed the face, opening the door just a crack.

"Is this the restaurant?" I bellowed.

"So it's the restaurant. What do you want?"

"What do you mean, what?" I tugged at the door. "Isn't it obvious?"

"That's impossible!" The face turned out to be female. "The restaurant is being inspected!"

She pulled the door shut. I managed to insert my hand—let her crush it!

"What kind of inspection can there be when there are no customers?" I shrieked.

She looked at me curiously; such a line of thought apparently had never occurred to her.

"Come in, then!" She opened the door just a bit more.

I rushed in. I had never had such difficulty getting into a restaurant—and, more importantly, at such risk! True, it wasn't any warmer here than in my own car, but it was warmer than the coupling between cars.

To my surprise, a man with his hair plastered into a side part, dressed in tails, with a starched shirt-front and a velvet bow tie, got up from behind a small table to greet me.

"Welcome!" He indicated a row of empty tables with a graceful movement of his hand. I sat down bewildered. Was it really me who just a few minutes ago had been bouncing up and down between cars?... Dignity, quiet... "They'll bring you a menu in just a second. The quality of the restaurant's service is being inspected. Inform me immediately of your complaints, no matter how insignificant they may be!"

"Well, of course," I answered in the same cordial tone.

The headwaiter withdrew with dignity and sat down at his table, his back ramrod straight. About twenty minutes later an unshaven waiter approached my table.

"Goulash," he declared, as though he had confused which one of us was supposed to order.

"And will that be all?" I made the standard waiter's response.

"It's cold!" he elucidated.

"And why is that?" I foolishly asked.

"The stove is out of order!" declared the waiter, shrugging his shoulders.

I looked at the headwaiter. He rose from behind his table, as he had before, his face immobile but joyful. He didn't even look in my direction.

"Well, all right," I gave in.

It was dim and cold in the restaurant. The only thing you could see in the dark window was a reflection.

The waiter finally appeared and banged a plate of noodles down in front of me. They were spread out like the crater of a volcano, but there was nothing in the crater itself. I sat for a while, stupefied, then dashed over to the headwaiter with his frozen smile.

"This is goulash?" I exclaimed. "Where's the meat?"

The headwaiter bowed his head with its impeccable part and went into the kitchen. A racket instantly ensued in which you could make out the voices of the waiter and the headwaiter. Then the latter appeared with the same smile.

"My apologies!" He took the plate from my table. "Your dish will be replaced right away. The waiter says that someone attacked him in the dark corridor near the kitchen and snatched the meat right out of the goulash!"

"Why are you telling me this?" I muttered and once again froze in front of the pitch-black window. Finally, after about forty minutes, I got the urge to move around.

"So where's the waiter?" I turned to the immobile headwaiter. Once again he politely bowed his head with its impeccable part and disappeared into the kitchen.

"Your waiter has been arrested!" he appeared, smiling happily.

"What do you mean, arrested?" I replied.

"He deserved it!" the headwaiter pronounced sternly, as though I had something to do with it. "It turns out that he was the one who snatched the meat out of the goulash and ate it!"

"Well, in that case, everything's clear." I declared. "And now what?"

"And now we will immediately send you another waiter!" he pronounced with dignity.

"Thank you!" I responded.

I waited a little over an hour for the second waiter after he had taken the order. Of course, he was probably honest, but where was he?

"Your waiter has been arrested!" the headwaiter informed me happily, not even waiting for my question.

"What do you mean? That one too?" My legs literally gave way.

"Well, of course!" he stated. "They all turned out to be members of the same gang. All we needed to do was make sure of it, and that we managed to do."

"Well, that's wonderful, of course," I muttered, "but where's my goulash?"

He looked at me with contempt: with such events going on, all I cared about was something so trivial!

"I'll try to find out!" he stated coldly, in not especially encouraging tones, and disappeared into the kitchen.

After an hour I lost my patience and peeked in.

"Can you at least tell me where the headwaiter is?" I asked a man dressed in a formal suit with a belt.

"The headwaiter has been arrested!" the man uttered with a tired but contented sigh. "He turned out to be the ringleader of the criminal gang operating here!"

"Wonderful!" I said. "But can't you find me something to eat?"

"Everything's been sealed!" the inspector answered sternly. "But if you want to be a witness, come in!"

"Thank you."

I sat in the employees' compartment. The waiters, in handcuffs, were being rounded up and led off somewhere, and so was the headwaiter... just as elegant as ever... I was dying for a bite to eat, but my desire was obviously out of place.

I wandered back through the cars.

"Is it possible to get anything at all done here?" I wondered in despair as I tugged savagely at the restroom door.

"It's locked," uttered my neighbor, who had appeared behind me like an apparition.

"What... permanently?" I uttered in a rage. "And that one?" I nodded towards the far end.

"That one too."

"But why?"

"The conductors are keeping chickens in there."

"In the restroom?"

"Well, where else can they keep them?"

"But why?"

"Well, apparently they wanted to sell them gradually to the restaurant, but they say they're having an inspection. So that's out of the question."

"And what are we supposed to do?"

"Nothing."

"And how do you know it's chickens?"

"You can hear them," my neighbor replied despondently.

In despair I sat in my compartment for a while, but that way I could easily turn into a snowman—I had to move, to do something at least! Once again I headed for the conductor's compartment. As I got near it, the door screeched open and out came the sailor—he was dull beet in color, dressed in a sleeveless sailor shirt, his arms naked and powerful. He brazenly winked at me, then turned to the window, darkened by the storm outside, and burst into song, his voice strained thick.

"Fare thee well, r-r-rocky mountains, the sea beckons us to high adventure!"

I listened attentively to the entire song, then pushed open the door into the conductor's compartment.

"What do you want?" asked the conductor, abruptly raising his head.

Maybe it wasn't very warm in their compartment, but it was at least festive, and the table was brimming over with the remains of a sumptuous feast. Blankets were keeping the walls warm, and another blanket was thrown over the window.

"Where is the head conductor?" I uttered, my lips frozen from the cold.

"I'm the head conductor. Do you have a problem?" asked the sailor jauntily as he walked into the compartment.

"No problems."

I returned to my compartment, climbed onto the top berth—the cold window didn't reach all the way up—wrapped myself up in a blanket (which didn't seem to me to make a difference), and started to freeze. Scenes of luxurious southern climates floated through my consciousness. It's true what they say about death by freezing being rather pleasant... Only one troubling thought (as it turned out later, my saving grace) kept me from sinking into bliss...

Hadn't I left the restaurant without paying the bill! Didn't I eat some bread and put mustard on it too! How do I know that these very kopecks won't play some kind of role in this whole business? Of course, now the question arises: do you have to be honest with petty thieves, but I think you do, for your own sake, if nothing else!...

Crunching like a snowman, I got down from the berth and once again made my way through the snow-swept clanking couplings, going from car to car.

The inspector of inspectors of inspectors—you could tell from the three bands on his sleeve—met me in the corridor of the railroad car.

I entered the car. Everyone was sitting at a table, singing. The inspectors sang treble, the inspector of inspectors baritone, and the inspector of inspectors of inspectors bass—the result was quite harmonious. The waiters in handcuffs and the headwaiter were also there, singing along timidly—for want of a stop they were all still there.

"What do you want?" asked the inspector of inspectors of inspectors quickly, giving me to understand that the pause between the lines of the song was short, so I'd better make the most of it.

"Here." I grabbed ten kopecks. "I had some bread and mustard. I want to pay up."

"They should erect monuments to people like him while they're still alive!" the headwaiter said earnestly, obviously trying to curry favor. He looked at the inspectors, as if offering to begin work immediately on such a noble endeavor.

"O.K. I agree to a monument... But only if it's in the restaurant!" I muttered and went back.

I noticed then that the train was braking, the cars started shaking and banging against one another, and it was becoming more complicated to get from one car to the next.

In the corridor I met the conductor, who was wearing something dirty and full of holes and had a bag on his back. He jumped down the steps and disappeared—probably gone in search of chicken feed...

That no longer irritated me. I had performed my duty to mankind. I could now lie down in my sarcophagus. I climbed on top and huddled up into a ball. The train stood there for a long time. It was quiet. My liberated consciousness was flying farther and farther away. Really, what was I doing trying to instill order into a railroad which I only had dealings with once a year when my own life was in total chaos, when I couldn't manage a semblance of order in my own house! Three years ago I had suddenly realized that there was a huge empty living space right next door, and I boldly started doing everything I could to get permission to take over that territory, to put in a living room, a study... then I estimated what it would cost me and I started doing everything I could to get it stopped. Any observer has a right to exclaim: "What an idiot!" I wrote a mountain of petitions: "I request that you deny my petition!" I penned a heap of anonymous letters against myself. Just so they don't take away what I have!

I was drifting off to sleep. Suddenly I saw myself in some courtyard... some dark figures had surrounded me... they were coming closer and closer... they were going to hit me... "A lot of good it'll do them," the jubilant thought flashed across my mind. "The idiots don't know this is only a dream!" The courtyard disappeared.

I found myself in the dining car, which for some reason was full of flowers; outside, the sultry south was floating by. My friend the headwaiter appeared, dressed in blinding white tails.

"Dinner... will not be served!" he proclaimed triumphantly.

He returned a minute later dressed in orange tails.

"Dinner... again will not be served!" he proclaimed.

"Perhaps something can be arranged?" I asked.

"Two watered-down coffees!" he commanded as he threw open the door into the sparkling kitchen.

I suddenly felt myself soaring blissfully through the air, stretched out full length on the berth, having kicked off the heavy blanket...Was it warm? You bet!

That must mean that when I had met the conductor at the stop, he was fetching coal, not chicken feed! Wonderful! It would be better not to wake up at all. I should start having fantastic dreams any moment now!

In my next dream I found myself in a wonderful toy store in the shape of an inflatable frog that was being blown up with a pipe...

Everything was implacably clear. It was time to get up!

In the corridor the conductor was sitting on an overturned pail, squinting blissfully at the orange flame in the furnace.

"So, what do you think?" He turned around as he saw me (after looking at the flame, he could not possibly have made out who I was).

"Wonderful!" I exclaimed. "Well, now that's settled, perhaps I could use the restroom too."

"Oh, all right." The heat had made him kinder. "Just don't hurt the chickens!"

He handed me the key.

"Why should I hurt the chickens?" I exclaimed sincerely.

I tore into the restroom. At first the chickens were quite ruffled, but they calmed down and perched in place, their cocked heads examining me with their beady eyes. I wondered what I looked like to those representatives of what is essentially another civilization. Did I represent the human race with dignity? Would they be insulted by the act I was planning to perform there? No, they weren't.

Utterly happy now, I climbed up on my berth and stretched out... What would my next dream be like? The sun was rising over the sea... I was flying on a chicken, getting closer to it. Up close the sun looked like a huge stove. The conductor was sitting next to it.

"Poor heating is a token of disrespect for the galaxy," he declared solemnly, wielding a poker.

Translated by Valentina Baslyk

Originally published in *Iunost'*, December 1987.

ANATOLY GENATULIN
ROUGH WEATHER

The elder girl was five years old. Her name was Gulnara. The little girls lived with their father—that winter their mother had fallen into the feed steamer on the farm and was scalded to death. The girls didn't see her dead; during their mother's funeral they sat on the stove shelf in Aunty Marziya's cottage, feeling very rich—Aunty had stuffed their pockets with caramels. Cut off from the adults' grief by the delicate screen of childish freedom from cares, they sucked the caramels and romped with their shabby dolls. Later, when they returned home, their own cottage, all scrubbed and tidied as if in preparation for a holiday, and for some reason strongly smelling of eau-de-cologne, seemed very roomy and cold as though something warm and cozy had disappeared from it. Their father, unusually quiet and slow, comforted his daughters clumsily, clapping them lightly on the back with his large, tough hands; his eyes were dull and he gazed somewhere beyond them. The little girls waited for their mother, but she didn't come. Their father told them that Mama had gone to town (a year ago she had gone there and brought back dolls for the girls), but the elder, Gulnara, heard the old women on the street pitying her younger sister ("Ay-ee, poor orphan!") and suddenly guessed that her mother was dead. The little girl had never seen anyone who had died and couldn't imagine her mother dead. In her short life she had only once seen a dying creature—a diseased chick. He ran after his mother hen with the other chicks, trying to keep up; he pecked something from under the hen's claws; sometimes he stopped and, closing his eyes, froze to the spot, as if he was going to sleep standing up; then he seemed to wake up and set out after the hen again. Next he suddenly swayed and fell, began to pant so fast that his little downy body shook, his eyes filmed over, his beak fell open, and the chick was left lying motionless in the middle of the littered yard with his thin little claws sticking up. But the hen didn't seem to notice. Clucking fussily, she scratched in the manure, and the cheeping chicks swarmed hurriedly around her claws, indifferent to their brother's death...

Gulnara took her mother's death like her absence, as if she had gone away for a long time, but the girl suspected that this absence would never end and Mama would not come home again. So when her father told her that Mama had gone to town, Gulnara objected, "She didn't. Mama's dead, I know that."

"Yes, daughter. You're a smart girl. She's dead," said her father quietly, staring at his daughter with strange eyes.

But the younger girl, Lilya, still a foolish little thing, really thought that Mama had gone to town and would come back soon, bringing her presents.

The girls' father, Faizulla, or as they still called him, herdsman Faizulla, in summer pastured the collective's cows. Sometimes he took his daughters with him to the summer farm. There they lived in a little wooden trailer, which reeked of saddle leather, horsesweat, and tobacco. While their father drove the cows into the mountains, the little girls were left alone. They played interesting games near the trailer and romped on the bank of the brook, erecting little dams; they modeled a toy house out of sand and clay and furnished it with colored pebbles, pretending they were various household utensils and dishes. When their father left for the mountains, he instructed his daughters to stay close to the trailer and out of the woods, because they could get lost and meet a wolf who would eat them, bones and all, or a bear who would drag them off into the forest.

But on the days when their father stayed in the village, he drank vodka. Drunk, he bawled songs or shouted piteously, "Galiya, why did you die and leave me alone with the girls, you bird-brained female, you so-and-so and such-and-such!" Faizulla would try to caress the girls, but they were scared of their father when he was drunk: his hands were calloused and he smelled of vodka and tobacco. Then he slept on the sofa right in his clothes, and the little girls, left to themselves, quiet in their orphaned state, rambled around close to the house. Longing for her mother, the younger one sometimes wept and called for Mama. "Don't bawl, I've told you before, you're a big girl now," said her elder sister and burst into tears herself.

The village of Kudashevo, the fourth brigade of the Beacon collective farm, was a small one, hidden away in a secluded hollow on the bank of a modest stream. There were forested mountains in the direction where the sun set every evening, and a road called the Tirlyan highway ran past the graveyard and across the stream. The girls drove down it with their father to the summer farm. Fields unfolded in the other direction, and far beyond the fields other mountains showed their hunched backs, but these were bald, stony, and yellowish green. There was a road extending that way, also, but the girls had never been down it and didn't know what lay in the distance. They didn't remember when they came into the world and from where, so it seemed or felt to them as if they had always been here, and the village was their entire world with its sky and sun, rains, stream, grass, winter blizzards and blue snowbanks and with its people, old men and women, little children, and all sorts of poultry. And the girls never stopped to wonder whether off in the distance there were other worlds and other villages. But then the elder girl already knew the surroundings of her village quite well. She had crossed the stream last year to pick currants with her mother; she knew the birch woods beyond the vegetable gardens; if you went a little deeper into the thicket, a large clearing opened out on the gentle slope of a hill. Last year she and Mama picked berries in that clearing.

It was a long summer day. Once again their father didn't go to the pasture. Yesterday he lay around drunk all day; this morning first thing he got drunk on sour wine and collapsed on the sofa once more. Aunty Marziya came and began scolding him: "You should think of the children, you boozer. Instead of lying around drunk, you'd do better to look for a wife!"

"Who'd take a man with two children? I'll put them in a children's home," their father answered.

Aunty Marziya scolded Faizulla some more, gave the girls their tea, and hurried off to work. The girls were left alone with their drunken father. Then Shakur-agai,* the farm manager, came and started pestering their father, demanding that he sober up and go to the pasture. Faizulla just bellowed and cursed. The little girls played outside under the awning until midday. They were hungry and wanted their tea, but their father didn't brew tea or cook anything. The girls each broke a slab off a dried

---

*Agai is an honorific form of address in Bashkir to an older man; apai is the equivalent for a woman.

heel of bread and ate it, washing it down with milk that Aunty Marziya
had left in a white saucepan. Then the elder, Gulnara, got the idea that it
would be nice, instead of hanging around the house, to cross the stream
and pick currants—the fruit must be ripe already.

"Let's go pick currants," she said to the younger girl. "But put on your
boots, or a snake will bite you."

Gulnara put on rubber boots. Both boots were for the same foot. This
was because one had worn out, and last month the younger girl forgot her
boots by the stream—she took them off and left them there, and when
they went back they found only the right one. Now Gulnara put her sister's boot on her left foot, although it was too small and pinched. And so,
taking a little toy bucket, the girls went to the stream, crossed it, and
began wandering through the trees looking for currants. But the fruit was
still completely green. Nothing else edible grew there, neither on the
ground nor on the bushes.

"Let's go pick berries in the birch woods," said Gulnara.

They walked around the village and headed for the birch grove. The
younger, as always, trudged silently behind the elder. But, before they
reached the woods, Lilya suddenly turned back and plodded off toward
the village.

"Where do you think you're going"?

The younger didn't turn around or answer.

"All right," said Gulnara, "Go, stay home, lazybones. I'll bring back a
bucketful of berries, and you won't get any of them."

She stood for a while watching her sister walk away and wavered for a
minute—go alone or turn back too—but the clearing, surrounded by
white birches and overgrown with grass and flowers, the fruit-filled clearing where she and her mother had picked strawberries last year, enticed
and invited her. Gulnara could see the ripe red berries hiding in the grass
so clearly and remembered their taste so well that she decided to go on
alone, imagining in advance picking a bucketful, bringing it home, and
telling her sister: "You wouldn't go, so there!"—and only afterward,
when her sister began to cry, would Gulnara spill a few berries into her
palm. She remembered that the clearing was very close to the village: the
vegetable gardens, the pasture beyond them, the edge of the forest, you
go a little way through the woods—and there's the clearing. Gulnara was
lighthearted as she entered the woods and wandered among the trees that
ran straight along the gentle slope of the hill. She had no fear of the forest,
because she had grown up there and been in it often and there was nothing in it she didn't know and understand, nothing to fear; here were the
birches in their white bark with black spots and leaves up to their very tips,

their crowns barely swaying and the little leaves rustling as if the trees were whispering to each other; here was the grass under her feet, stumps, and windfallen branches; and here was an anthill, the ants scurrying about in a rush on their reddish hill, too absorbed in their ant concerns to notice the giant of a girl. It was true that there was a wolf living in the woods who killed small sheep and ripped cows' udders and who might eat little girls. But Mama said that the wolf prowled only at night; in the daytime he was afraid of people and hid in a hollow. So she had nothing to fear in the woods.

Gulnara walked for a long time, expecting that any moment now the fruit-filled clearing would open out before her, but she didn't find it. Gulnara remembered it as being very close; true, a year was a long time to a little girl, and you might say that she had grown an entire lifetime and therefore had probably forgotten things. But Gulnara recalled exactly: she and Mama went out across their vegetable garden into the back lots, crossed the pasture, and entered the woods. But now she had come from the stream; she'd seen the back lot behind her house and the vegetable garden, and only then had set foot in the woods. That meant she'd gone the right way. Then why was there still no clearing? It couldn't have got overgrown with big trees in just one year. She'd go a little ways, and there would be the clearing and the berries. Just a little ways, and then a little farther. But there was still no clearing. Now the little girl noticed that the trees had gotten thicker and higher, the grass was up to her waist, and, besides, she remembered the clearing as being on a gentle slope, whereas now she seemed to be heading downhill. This puzzled Gulnara. Suddenly, not far ahead of her, something big and alive started up from the grass with an explosive noise, flew past, and fell like a brown clod into the depths of the thicket. The girl stopped in sudden fright, but it was just the noise of the wings that startled her and not the thing that rose from the grass. Gulnara guessed that it was a large bird taking off. And she wasn't scared of birds. The girl listened intently: the treetops made a soft noise, and somewhere in the distance a magpie chattered anxiously. "I must have gone the wrong way, I'll go a little farther and turn back," she thought. She walked a little farther. The trees stood dense and gloomy. She should turn back. But she kept on walking and walking. It was as if something were urging her on, as if something lured her that way, deep into the for-est; perhaps it was a childish hope for a miracle: I'll go just to those trees, and there'll be the clearing and it will be full of berries. "No, I'll go back," Gulnara decided at last and turned her back to the dense thicket, so that she was facing the edge of the forest and the village. And back she plod-ded. She was a little annoyed that she hadn't found the fruit-filled clearing and was returning empty-handed. Never mind, the little girl thought, tomorrow I'll go again and I'll find the clearing. Soon she would come out at the edge of the forest and see the vegetable gardens in the back lots, the red iron roof of the store, and her house...

The planning session or, as they called it, the "detail," began promptly at eight. At 7:45 Ilyasov, wearing his invariable navy blue gabardine suit and blue tie, entered his private office and sat down at his desk. The sun, already high above Three Colts Mountain, shone through the large window of the headquarters building. He sat alone, leafing through his notebook, reviewing yesterday's working notes, considering the problems of the coming day, thinking over impending business, and getting into a working mood. Nasima, his secretary, placed on the desk the typed reports on stockpiling of fodder throughout the Beacon collective farm on July 15. Old Khafiz, nicknamed Minister, dropped in. He was a pensioner, a war veteran (ribbons and medals gleamed on his shabby jacket), a heavily built, rather eccentric fellow. He often dropped by headquarters, although he had no obvious business there. Khafiz usually sat to one side and strained his deaf ears to catch the conversation. In the village they said that he sniffed around everywhere, looked for flaws and irregularities on the collective farm, and scribbled letters to the ministry, the regional committee, the district committee, and the newspaper. When Ilyasov took over the farm, at first the old man irritated him. Khafiz would look at him as if he were thinking slyly: "We'll see, we'll see what sort of chairman you are." Then Ilyasov got used to the old man and stopped paying attention to him when he dropped by his office. Today, however, he was out of sorts and asked sharply, "What're you doing here? Did I send for you?"

"I'm just trying to figure things out," the old man responded placidly.

By and large Ilyasov could guess what the old man was trying to figure out. Stung, he waited a minute before answering loudly: "You won't succeed, agai! To figure it out, you'd have to be in my place!"

"They won't put me there. I'm an old man. And my head's got a hole in it."

"Yes, agai, here you need a sound head and iron nerves," Ilyasov said in a slightly milder tone.

Then the specialists arrived. Except for the farm manager Islamov and the head mechanic Saifullin, they were all young men, barely over thirty, close to the chairman's age. They sat down in chairs against the wall. Their faces wore a glum, concentrated look, and there was a tense expression in their eyes. Nail, the secretary of the party committee, came in and took his usual seat at the long table covered with red cloth that adjoined the chairman's desk. The session lasted half an hour. Ilyasov glowered at his advisors and, following the customary procedure, spoke to each in turn. He began with the head engineer Atnabaev. The day's agenda was as follows: the granulator at the vitamin-meal plant had broken down; until it was repaired, the vitamin meal had to be poured into sacks, but they were low on them. Rudnik had promised them some, and somebody should go there right away. There was a shortage of trucks, two of them needed a change of bearings, but where could they get them? The Ural was waiting to be unloaded, they had brought a new feed mixer for the fourth brigade, but there was no crane to unload it. They couldn't send the farm mechanic, the cranes at the other farms were busy, and somebody had to go to town and make an arrangement with the service station. There weren't enough Belarus trucks to transport the silage. The two K-700 tractors hadn't been repaired since last spring; there were no spare parts. They'd gone to Kazakhstan, to the Turgai steppe, to beg for parts, but would they get them? It was already July sixteenth, and there wasn't a single haystack in the meadows. The annual grass crops hadn't been gathered yet. The herdsmen at the second farm were letting their calves run over the hayfields at Black River; the calves didn't eat the grass, but just trampled it. Also, at the second farm, half of the milking machines were out of order, and they were milking the cows by hand. The fourth farm had no herdsmen, one was on a binge and the other had broken his leg on his motorcycle. That was how it always went: one thing after another, this or that—in short, as Ilyasov liked to say in moments of despair: "Nothing's going right, boys!"

After the session, the specialists took from the desk the statistics on stockpiling of fodder and, shoving the papers in their pockets as they went, left quickly and to all appearances energetically; they gave the impression that as soon as they left headquarters they would immediately set to work feverishly. But Ilyasov knew that first they would drink their tea at leisure at home, and by the time the chairman's instructions reached the brigades and farms, they'd be watered down and late. Everyone—the chief agronomer, the chief livestock specialist, and the others—would immediately be mired in routine, in everyday squabbles, irregularities, and shortages, and their subordinates, of course, would not get all their work done: some because they were incompetent or negligent, others simply because they couldn't get one thing or another done because something had not been supplied in time, something had not arrived, or someone had missed work altogether, goofing off or on a spree. The collective farm was large, no matter how hard you tried or checked up on everything yourself, you couldn't keep everything under control, and you couldn't totally trust the specialists either. Ilyasov felt that they led a day-to-day, routine way of life and didn't want to rise any higher, to the level of social, state interests. He could handle everything himself, if various windbag bureaucrats didn't keep tearing him away from his main work, but they kept on calling him to the agricultural directorate, the regional council, the district party office, or to a conference. Today he had to get to the fourth brigade and sort out on the spot what was going on with the herdsmen, and from there he should drop in at the second farm to find out about the milking machines and the crop damage.

After the planning session Ilyasov spent an hour on telephone calls, drawing up various papers, and signing applications and orders. Then a woman came in asking for a truck to pick up the groom's family in a neighboring village where her daughter was getting married. Barely glancing at her, Ilyasov growled rudely that he had no free truck to give her. After the woman left, he asked his secretary Nasima who she was. It turned out that she was the best milkmaid in the collective, a woman who had been decorated twice. But how could Ilyasov be expected to recognize her when he hadn't been in the village very long? He still didn't always get the names of his chief specialists right. The chairman was unnerved. He couldn't have given her a truck in any case, but he could have spoken to her like a human being.

At ten o'clock Ilyasov went home for a bite to eat. There was nobody at home. His wife, who was a teacher, had gone to a seminar in Ufa, and his daughter was at Pioneer camp. He fried some eggs, had tea, and then took the wheel of his Gazik, or Rover as they called the chairman's speedy, ubiquitous little jeep, and took off for the fourth brigade, ten kilometers away from the farm center. He was escaping on the sly, one might say, without telling his secretary and avoiding a meeting with Nail, the party organizer—he didn't want to get stuck with him. Ilyasov didn't like traveling with the party organizer. Nail was a local man, he knew everybody and everybody knew him, and therefore people were more likely to take up all their problems with him than with the chairman. This stung Ilyasov—it made him feel that he lacked authority and independence.

When he reached the fourth brigade, he didn't stop in the village, but tore down the street and immediately drove up the hill to the summer farm. He had to go and see for himself first, and then on the way back he would talk to the farm chief about the herdsmen. The collective farm just didn't have enough herdsmen. Widespread mechanization and technology had supplanted workers, but in the pastures old-timers with long whips were still whooping out obscenities just the way they always had. The older, established herdsmen retired on their pensions or died, but young people didn't replace them. They were no fools; give them cars every time. Young people lived now with one eye on the town and, as soon as they got out of school or the army, they took the first opportunity to settle there. They had to work harder and were crammed into dormitories, but on the other hand they walked on asphalt; they didn't have an easy life, but they'd left the soil and manure behind.

Ilyasov drove without haste. The track with its deep bitten bumpy ruts dodged through the pass; woods stood thick on the slopes—birch, aspen, an occasional pine—and sometimes the desolation left by lumbering or the new plantations could be seen. To the left a brown gloomy cliff loomed in the distance, above the curly silhouette of the woods. Ilyasov was born far from the crest of the Urals, in a place where there were no more spurs, and steep treeless slopes extended, gradually giving way to the steppes east of the Urals. He was used to open spaces and the wormwood-scented wind of the nearby steppe. In the mountains, however, he always felt melancholy, ill-at-ease, and depressed; he always thought that mountains were the most useless part of the earth, a pile of stone, land that couldn't be plowed—there were spots where you couldn't even mow hay or pasture cattle. Ilyasov didn't like mountains... The narrow road passed through a ravine and went on climbing. As he approached the farm, he noticed the irregularities right away: by this time the cows should be pastured on the grassy mountain slopes, but here they were languishing at the farm, standing and lying about, chewing their cud, on a black, slimy mash of dirt mixed with manure and urine. Milk cans and pails—they still milked by hand here—hung on stakes; rags and cheesecloth were drying. A plank trailer with a stovepipe stood beside a little stream, which had been dammed for a watering pond. It looked as if the herdsman had not driven the cows to pasture after the morning milking. Ilyasov thought that tomorrow the report on the milk yield at the Beacon collective would end up on the desk of the first secretary of the regional committee, and it was quite possible that during the morning detail Latypov would phone him to ask why the yield was down. They could tell him again about the herdsmen, the bad weather, and the broken machinery. But tomorrow the district committee would also get a summary of the yield by district, and they didn't give a damn about a farm lost somewhere in the mountains or the existence of some fellow named Ilyasov, the chairman of the backward collective farm; for them it was statistics, just statistics, results—they had a plan, and the plan had to be fulfilled even when it was impossible. "Why the low results in that region? Take measures, buckle down!" "The low yields are Ilyasov's, he's the one who's dragging down the region." "Send for this Ilyasov! How many reprimands has he got?"

The chairman honked his horn, climbed out of the jeep, and walked over to the trailer. The herdsman, a sleepy, unshaven old fellow, came out the door to meet him, prepared in advance for a disagreeable talk—his face was downcast and guarded. Ilyasov shook his hand and asked what was going on.

"There's no secret about what's going on," answered the herdsman, averting his eyes. There was a frown on his lightly pockmarked, broad face.

"Nothing's going on, agai!" Ilyasov glanced at his watch. "It's one o'clock, and all your cows are still lying in the mud. What kind of order is that, do you think?"

"It's not order at all, that's clear," agreed the herdsman and suddenly took offence. "But you'd have done better to ask me first how many days I've been working with no relief."

"Who are your relief men?"

"Who? There's no secret about it. Mavlit and Faizulla. Mavlit broke his leg, and Faizulla hasn't dried out for a week now. I said to the farm chief: if you don't relieve me by tomorrow morning, I'll let the herd go to the devil! Last month it was the same: Mavlit and I pastured them without help, and they paid us peanuts! Does that make any sense?"

"O.K., agai. I'll talk to the farm chief; we'll relieve you."

"You should come more often," the herdsman spoke in a slightly milder, more conciliatory tone. "The party organizer came by a month ago, but since then they've forgotten all about us. Nobody cares how we live here; it's all: give us the milk, fulfill the plan..."

Ilyasov had no answer for that and remained silent. The herdsman went over to the trailer, took his whip off a nail, and with whoops and curses began urging the cows to their feet. The unnerved Ilyasov drove back to the village, having decided in a fit of temper to have a stiff talk with the farm chief and Faizulla the herdsman. He recalled that Faizulla was the husband of the milkmaid who perished last winter when she fell into the feed-steamer at the farm. The steamer, a deep pit one-and-a-half meters in diameter located in a dark and crowded spot in the feed plant, wouldn't cool down for days at a time. Such dense steam rolled from the pit that you couldn't see a thing around it, as in a fog. The woman stumbled, fell, was scalded, and died in the hospital from her burns. She left behind two children. Who was to blame? That was clear enough: the livestock specialist. He had failed to observe safety precautions: he hadn't erected a barrier around the pit or even covered it with boards. But he got off lightly: he just lost his job. In the other brigades they'd installed mechanical feed mixers in the plants a year ago. They had brought a unit for the fourth brigade too, but the truck carrying it was still standing in the mechanics' shop; there was no crane to unload it.

As he approached the village, Ilyasov saw the houses far off, prosperous center-walled structures with built-on wings and porches. They all had plank gates painted blue and green and high fences. Everything about the homesteads was solid—these people lived near the woods. The chairman turned off down the lane to the farm and the silage trench, where he could hear a tractor rumbling. There he found only the brigade leader Nazhib, who was still a young man, tall, rosy-cheeked and, like everybody in the village, absolutely calm and deliberate. It was hard to imagine him rushed or preoccupied: from time immemorial these people were used to living in this out-of-the-way spot at the foot of quiet mountains, far from the highway and fast-paced, bustling life. Nazhib shook the chairman's hand and attempted to put a respectful look on his ruddy visage, although his whole appearance, his leisurely movements, and his mocking eyes betrayed the ironic condescension of a healthy, placid man toward the preoccupied, harassed Ilyasov. After they talked about the silage and repairs to the feed plant and the boilers, Ilyasov asked about the herdsmen. Nazhib said that they would have to speak to the farm chief Shakur, because that was his direct responsibility. They got into the jeep, drove to Shakur's house, and honked under his window. Shakur, who was just as healthy and ruddy as the brigade leader, looked out the open window. He was sitting around drinking tea.

"Come on into the house, we'll have tea," shouted the farm chief.

"There's no time for tea. Come on out, we have business."

Shakur put on his leather cap, came out to the street, and shook hands with the chairman.

"What's going on here? The herdsman's working without relief, and the cows are lying around in the mud all morning."

"That's just the way it goes.... One man broke his leg on his motorcycle, he's in the hospital, and the other's on a binge. Whenever you go to see him, he's lying around drunk and cussing a blue streak. Who can I replace him with? Nobody will go. That's how it goes, you know, I'll have to replace him myself. There was some talk about transferring the cows to the second farm, maybe that would be best."

"There was talk, but we're not going to do it!" snapped the chairman. "You'd like to take it easy, eh? Where does the herdsman live?"

Faizulla lived far away, on a little street that began at the store. They got into the jeep, drove to the other end of the village, and stopped at the gates of an old house with a double-pitch roof. It was already timeworn, subsiding and patched with clay between the logs, but the gate, which was painted green, looked like new. They went into the yard. Under the awning a little girl with a grubby face and a dirty dress was playing among the woodchips, blocks, and rubbish. Seeing the men entering, she tore herself away from her dolls and said in a hoarse voice, "Uncle, Papa's lying drunk, and Gulnara went to pick berries."

The door into the house was wide open, and chickens were wandering about the entry; inside the cottage, in the kitchen, flies droned as they ran across the old, cracked oilcloth on the table, swarmed in the unwashed dishes, and landed on the whitewashed stove. A quilt with its stuffing falling out lay on the floor. In the main room of the cottage Faizulla lay on a sofa, his feet in their dirty socks tucked under him. Pillows, bedclothes, and rags were scattered about the floor and the bed; the room smelled of neglect and orphanhood, and there was a whiff of potato spirits. Nazhib shook the herdsman, who was lying with his face to the wall.

"Faizulla, get up now. The chairman's here, he wants to speak to you."

Faizulla mumbled, struggled into a sitting position on the couch, and lowered his feet to the floor. "Ah, the boss has come to see us." He formed his lips into the semblance of a smile; his eyes, lackluster and sleepy, the yellowish whites bloodshot, gazed dully and senselessly at the chairman; a sparse black growth bristled on his swollen cheeks, chin, and upper lip.

"Why don't you show up for work? Why are you on a binge?!"

Faizulla was slow to answer; he peered vacantly at the chairman for a while before saying: "Can't you see I've got trouble? My little girls ask me where their mama is. And I don't know what to tell them. I tell them Mama died, the older one seems to understand, but the little one is still waiting for Mama..."

"You'd be better off thinking of them than going on a binge!"

"Don't shout at me! Next thing every stovemender, forester, and horse doctor will be shouting at me!"

"There's a man out in the pasture five days without relief, and you loll around drunk. You should be ashamed!"

Faizulla kept silent for a while again, as if trying to make sense of the chairman's words, and stared at him in vacant perplexity. Then suddenly he spoke soberly and angrily: "I'll replace him, I'll do it today. You thought that... You thought that Faizulla was out of it? Faizulla has been a herdsman for twenty years, and every year he gets a bonus. Just look, my wall is covered with citations for good work. I'll be there! Once I've said I'll go, I'll be there for sure!"

Outside Ilyasov asked the brigade leader, "You think he'll go to work?"

"He's angry now, he'll be sure to. He's a good herdsman when he's sober. He's been hitting the bottle for a week now, maybe longer."

Ilyasov knew better than anyone what it was like to hit the bottle; he had suffered from the same malady not all that long ago. But now, as is usually the case with reformed alcoholics, he despised drunkards.

Nazhib invited the chairman in for a cup of tea, but Ilyasov refused, although he certainly could have used a bite to eat. He refused because he knew that wherever there was tea, there was bound to be something stronger, and even if he got away without drinking, after he'd shared tea with the farm chief and the brigade leader, they would no longer have the same strictly formal relationship. In general, you had to keep your guard up with these people who were used to their peaceful life in an out-of-the-way spot in the mountains and liked their idle hours over tea. Moreover, the chairman was unnerved as he drove off. "Every stovemender, forester, and horse doctor." Ilyasov didn't know who mended the stoves, but the forester was, of course, Nail, the secretary of the party committee: before graduating from the agricultural institute, he had worked as a forester in the local section. The horse doctor was undoubtedly himself, Ilyasov, because he was a livestock technician, a specialist in horse breeding. "Every stovemender, forester, and horsedoctor"—the phrase kept turning obsessively in his mind all the way.

... But the woods never ended. They stood high, thick and gloomy. The birches had coarse black bark on thick butts at the bottom and farther up became white and slender, with spreading branches, and at the very top, green waves of foliage rolled back and forth with a steady noise; above the treetops the wind roamed, and higher still, the sun was shining. The little girl kept on walking through the trees. She stumbled over wind-fallen branches, fell, and went on again, all the time peering with hope into the thickets—any minute now a shaft of light would appear before her, the birches would give way, and she would come out on the edge of the forest. But the birches didn't end, and the edge seemed to be moving farther and farther off.

Gulnara was hot in her outgrown yellow kapron jacket, and she unbuttoned it. Her sister's left boot pinched her foot—she would have taken it off and gone barefoot, but she couldn't: you might step on a thorn or a snake might bite you.

Now and then she grew pensive. Short, simple little thoughts crossed her mind; she remembered Aunty Marziya scolding her father, "Instead of lying around drunk, you'd do better to look for a wife!" A wife—that meant, another Mama. She tried to imagine that other Mama, but only the dim, familiar image of her mother, which had already started fading, came to mind. It wasn't even her face she remembered, but her voice

when she called her fondly: "Gulnara, daughter!" Then suddenly she saw
her unshaven father with his growing stubble of beard lying on the sofa
drunk, and Gulnara mentally scolded him in Mama's words: "Oo-oo,
you're nasty when you slosh down vodka!" Then she recalled the way the
tiny downy chick had died: his beak was wide open as if he were asking for
something to drink, his eyes were filmed over, his little legs stuck up, and
beside him the hen scratched away, as if nothing was wrong, and the
cheeping chicks bustled about beside her claws. Then Gulnara thought of
the stupid little boy who lived five cottages away from them but came into
their yard and, without asking, started playing with their toys as if they
were his own; green snot constantly dripped from his nose and he sniffed
and sucked it back in (Aunty Marziya said that the boy was so stupid
because his father guzzled vodka). And then, with special pleasure and
tenderness, she recalled her doll, for whom she would make a new dress.
She imagined a playhouse outside under the awning, and in that house a
toy-sized sofa, table, mirror, and mats on the floor; she and the doll are
living there together, and her sister comes for a visit. "Wipe your feet, I
just washed the floors. Come in, be my guest; we'll have tea right away."
And then one day that same stupid little boy, whose name was Gadib,
comes and starts living in her playhouse. "O.K. then, stay and live here,
since you're here already and have nowhere else to live, and are always
wandering around other people's yards. Just blow your nose and give
yourself a good wash with soap." The girl was still carrying her toy bucket;
she loved the bucket, which they had bought at the store; when Mama
was alive, she took it to pick berries and currants. "When Papa sobers up
and shaves his beard, I'll tell him to buy me another bucket and make a
yoke. I'll fetch water and do the housework." Gulnara was getting tired.
She kept stopping and catching her breath, and her heart pounded very
fast in her breast: pom-pom-pom; when she stood still and the grass
wasn't rustling and dry branches weren't snapping underfoot, the little
girl could hear the quiet of the woods and make out various distinct
sounds in that quiet: the rustle of a small forest creature in the grass, the
noise made by the wings of a large bird, and some little birds warbling
back and forth. The only thing she couldn't hear anywhere were the
sounds of village life: neither dogs barking, nor roosters crowing, nor the
chirring of a tractor working in the field. But the little girl still went on
believing that the village was nearby and that any minute she would come
out on the edge of the forest. After a rest, Gulnara moved on, now in a
great hurry; over there stood some birches, she would reach them, and
that would be the end. She got to the birches, and beyond them stood the
same unbroken, dense woods. Sometimes her path was barred by fallen

dried trees lying flat on the ground in the grass. The little girl stepped over them, but sometimes she came across such large, thick ones, with dense dry branches wedged into the ground below and looming up in an impenetrable hedge, that she had to make a detour around them. The farther she went, the more often she stumbled onto these toppled trees, beside which the grass grew high and dense. Gulnara gradually began noticing that she was walking through an unfamiliar forest, one she had never seen before—there were no big trees and fallen birches like these where she had gone with Mama. And the grass that grew here seemed different, it looked strange, even hostile. But she hadn't guessed yet that she had strayed into a large wild forest. Gulnara had no doubt that she was headed in the right direction, but she couldn't and didn't know how to explain the fact that the woods around her were strange and there was no end to them.

Gradually the sky over the trees darkened. It grew gloomy below too, on the very bottom of the thick green layer of forest life; coolness wafted from the grass. Flies came flitting; they had swarmed around her earlier, but now in the stifling lull before evening they hung over the little girl in a dense swirling cloud. There were flies at home, too, in the cottage, but those were the large domestic flies, they settled insistently on the bread, ran across the table, and tickled your cheek and swarmed on your lips while you slept, but they didn't bite. But these tiny caustic forest flies not only bit very painfully but also flew into your eyes, nose, and mouth. They made Gulnara angry, and she kept brushing them off, crying out loud in pain. Then she noticed that she was going uphill, and the farther she went, the steeper the ground under her feet became. This made her suspicious. She had gone uphill out of the village, after all, because the berry clearing was on the gentle slope of a wooded hill. For the first time the little girl was disturbed as she guessed that she was going the wrong way. She walked on a little farther—the slope got even steeper, the woods reached up to the sky, closer to the clouds. "I shouldn't be going uphill, I should go down, the village is that way," she suddenly realized and turned back. For a while longer the girl went on walking, crawling across fallen trees or going around them, always hoping to come out of the woods, but as before only wild forest, with no glimmer of light in it, surrounded her. In the meantime the sky had grown completely dim, and the wavering semidarkness of late evening sank into the woods. Gulnara became frightened. She remembered that when she entered the woods the sun was still high, and now it had already sunk behind the mountains. But when she had gone with her father to the farm, which was a good distance from the village—Gulnara always found the ride very long—the sun just barely shifted position in the sky. And for the first time it occurred to her that she was lost. Gulnara knew the word "lost." Her father would say, "Don't go far into the woods, you'll get lost." And then he would often tell her and her little sister, "You'll get lost and a wolf will eat you up." That's why the words "lost" and "wolf" now came simultaneously to the little girl's mind. She knew what a wolf was, she had a picture book with a drawing of a wolf—a wild beast like a dog but with a big head on a short neck and fierce eyes. Last winter in the village a wolf killed a calf belonging to their neighbor Ishbulata, and just this spring one had ripped open the udder of a cow in Papa's herd. Once she realized she was lost and thought of the wolf, the girl became frightened, and a chill of terror shook her frail little body and her legs turned to water. It was then that she began to cry and to shout desperately, and then plaintively, without stopping, to wail at the top of her voice and call in entreaty, "Ma-ma-a-a." Then she remembered that Mama could not come to help her anyway, because she was dead, and she began to shout, "Pa-pa!" Then even that seemed hopeless to her, Papa was far away and couldn't hear her, and she simply began to wail out loud—from indignation, despair and fear. Now Gulnara's steps became unsteady and sluggish, and she could barely drag her tired, numb feet; she stumbled, fell, got up, plodded farther and, after she had gone some distance, suddenly discovered that she was no longer carrying her bucket. She must have dropped it when she fell. She was afraid to retrace her steps, although she regretted losing the bucket so much that grief was now added to her fear. "O-o-o, ah-ah, ah, oo-oo-oo!" she kept crying out loud.

Slowly but inevitably it grew dark. Darkness crept closer and nestled at first in the grass, in the low shrubbery, and then in the treetops. In daylight the surroundings were recognizable, familiar, and therefore not at all frightening. Birches were birches, Gulnara had long been familiar with them: like all trees, they grew, turned green in summer and stood naked in winter; they were felled, sawed into firewood, split with an axe into blocks, and stacked in neat piles. Although she wasn't familiar with the grass under her feet, the flowers, and the low bushes, they still resembled plants that Gulnara knew well: the nettles, burdock, tall weeds, white willows and bird-cherries which grew beside the stream. They were all just bushes and trees. But now, in the dusk of the creeping night, those grasses and trees that were so easy to recognize in the daytime became strange and frightening: each bush was a clot of darkness, and two paces away from Gulnara black gaps yawned in the grass. When it grew completely dark, she saw phantoms closing in around her, and the place swarmed and teemed with shadows and wisps of light; in front of her, behind the trees, some sort of creatures, small and large beasts, probably wolves, darted in and out; and from behind Gulnara felt something huge, black and woolly breathing a deadly cold down her back and on the nape of her neck. But for some reason they, these beasts, didn't attack yet; they ran beside her, rustling in the grass and clashing their teeth; her cries must have scared them off. The little girl was still moving, but she went very slowly now, constantly stumbling and falling, getting up, running into trees in the dark, stepping on downed branches, and falling again. She was no longer thinking, she didn't remember about the edge of the woods, and she had no hope of making her way out of the dark depths of the wild forest. Only fear, fear of the big, black, woolly thing that was stalking her, preparing to spring on her at any moment, drove her on, forcing her somehow to keep her feeble legs moving. But now there was no place to run: the frightening black phantoms of the night clustered around her in front and on both sides, from all directions. The little girl stumbled and fell—and didn't get up again. With her head clasped in her little arms and her legs tucked under her, she lay on the ground, curled up in a ball with her eyes closed, and kept crying out loud. The wild beasts were coming closer and closer, rustling through the grass right beside her; the breath of their stinking jaws and the clash of their bloodthirsty fangs was directly above her....

They didn't miss Gulnara until evening—or rather, it was Aunty Marziya who missed her when she came to milk the cow and feed the little girls. She shook the sleeping Faizulla, and he woke up hung over and, finding everything disgusting, goggled dazedly at his cousin and couldn't understand a thing. When at last he realized that Gulnara hadn't come home, he mumbled indifferently: "She'll come. Where could she get to? She's probably still playing in the neighbors' yards."

But the little girl didn't come home. Night was falling, and there was still no Gulnara. By then Faizulla had begun to worry; he went outside, walked back and forth calling his daughter, and then returned home and, waking the younger girl who was curled up on the sofa, asked her where her sister was.

"She went to pick berries," Lilya answered, half-awake.

"Where did she go, which way?"

"There."

"Where? Into the woods?" Faizulla pointed out the window through which the mountains could be seen, black against the gloom of night.

"There."

Since he couldn't get anything sensible out of his daughter, Faizulla ran to Marziya's house.

"Maybe she's spending the night with Zakira's children in the loft," said Marziya.

They went to the Khilazhevs. Gulnara hadn't shown up at their house. They returned home and roused Lilya again.

"Tell us where you and your sister were today," said Marziya.

"We crossed the stream to pick currants."

"And where did you leave Gulnara?"

"She went to pick berries."

"Where?"

"In the woods."

"The girl's lost." Marziya became alarmed. "We've got to search for her."

"Where should we search?" asked Faizulla.

"Across the stream. She told us they crossed the stream."

She rushed outside and ran to the stream. The mountains and the forested slopes, fused into an unbroken blackness, were mysterious, wild and frightening. Faizulla and Marziya followed the Tirlyan road to the stream, forded it, and started shouting, "Gulnara, Gulnara!" They listened: it was quiet. All they could hear was music in the village, probably from the open windows of the club, and the sound of voices—they were showing a movie. They went down the road, shouting into the nocturnal silence, and then returned home, unable to bring themselves to dive into the dark thickets. Marziya upbraided Faizulla the whole way, "That's your vodka for you! It never leads to any good. I knew things would turn out badly!"

"Don't yell!"

"Why shouldn't I yell? Just use that drunken gourd of yours to think what it's like now for the child in the woods, in the darkness! Her heart could burst from fear."

Faizulla kept a gloomy silence. When he got home, he fell into bed, but he couldn't sleep for thinking of his daughter. There was hope: Gulnara might have played late with some of the neighbors' children and stayed overnight—they might have just taken pity on the orphan, fed her, and put her to bed—or, deciding for some reason that her father was at the farm, she might have followed the road that way. Nevertheless, Faizulla couldn't sleep. When the dawn roosters started crowing, he got up, took his bridle, and went to the meadow where his bay gelding had been pastured for the last week. He saddled the horse and rode to the farm. From time to time he veered off the road, going first to the left and then to the right, and shouted "Gul-na-ra!" The only answer was his echo. He arrived at the farm. It was early yet, but herdsman Safuan, Faizulla's relief, had either already brought in the cattle or not driven them out to pasture at all. Safuan was sleeping in the trailer. Faizulla shook him.

"What, you've come to relieve me?" Safuan asked, half-awake.

"My daughter's not here?"

"Why should she be here? Is she missing?" asked Safuan, getting up.

"Yesterday she went into the woods and never came back."

"And here I thought you'd come to relieve me. I told the brigade leader already: relieve me today or I'll leave the herd. Am I so special, eh? I haven't been home for a week. I can't even get to the bathhouse—my whole body itches. You've got no conscience at all, Faizulla!"

"Don't yell! I'll relieve you this evening. I'll work off the time I owe you, and you'll get a rest. I have to find my daughter. She's just a kid. What's it like for her now if she's gotten lost in the woods?"

"You shouldn't drink so much."

"O.K., you know where you can go!"

Faizulla left the trailer, mounted his gelding, and rode back, going slowly. Once again he kept leaving the road and shouting "Gul-na-ra!" at the top of his voice. He still had hopes of finding his daughter at home when he got back to the village. At the store he met old Yumabika and said hello to her.

"Did you see a calf on your way?" asked the old woman. "Yesterday morning we put it out to pasture; in the evening it didn't come back, and I thought that maybe the warden caught it in the wheat and locked it up at the farm, but no. I'm afraid a wolf got it."

"Your calf will show up, but now my daughter's disappeared. Yesterday she crossed the stream to pick currants and never came back. I've been searching since yesterday—she's nowhere to be found."

"Maybe somebody drove off with her. They say that in one village a girl was carried off," said the old woman in a puzzled way. "Yesterday a car drove through the village. It stopped at the store and then went off toward Tirlyan. Maybe the man in the car drove off with your daughter. He saw her, lured her, put her in the car, and drove off."

"Why would a stranger take my daughter?"

"God knows. It takes all sorts. Some folks are childless. You'd better go to Tirlyan right away and file a report with the police."

The old woman totally unnerved Faizulla. As he approached his house, he still had a faint hope that Gulnara had turned up, but when he went in the house and didn't find his daughter there, he lost heart altogether. He took the little one to Marziya, had tea with her, and rode into Tirlyan, a town some twenty kilometers away across the mountains.

He rode without haste. From time to time he left the road to shout "Gulnara!", returned to the highway, and then rode on, thinking his melancholy thoughts. When he was sober, Faizulla was always melancholy and thought aggrievedly that he was a luckless, unsuccessful man, a loser, that nobody respected him and that all the woes of the world were piled on his shoulders. Now here was another misfortune—his daughter was missing.

But the way Faizulla figured it, he'd never had any luck from birth. He was still sucking his mama's tit, rocking in his cradle, and soiling his diapers when the war broke out. His father, a brigade leader on the collective farm and, according to his mother's stories, a competent, active man, was called up immediately. He held his son in his arms for the last time and, drowning his sorrows in bitter vodka, went off to the distant war to the sobbing sounds of a harmonica. His mother received just one letter, and then there were neither letters nor a death notice—he was swallowed up in Russia's vast expanses. It wasn't until '46 that the regional military command sent a notice: missing in action.

Overtaxed by men's work, cursing her fate and weeping a flood of widow's tears, his mother raised her son alone. Faizulla somehow made it through fourth grade and, with a feeling of relief, left school forever and the books that were so hateful they made his head ache. Maybe he would have gone on halfheartedly, passing from class to class, but they only had an elementary school in their little village, and for the seven-year school you had to go to the bigger town ten kilometers away. Food was still hard to come by, and in those years he was shoeless and poorly dressed, too. So Faizulla went to work on the collective farm, at first driving the hay sweep during the harvest and then riding the rake and even plowing. Afterwards he started pasturing calves and, before his time in the army, as a full-grown boy, he started herding cows.

He came back from the army a fine eligible fellow, although he had never been in love because he was bashful—perhaps because he was an orphan; in the club he always stood to the side, too shy to approach the girls. Now, after the army, he and his mother should have had a chance to live like other people, but once again they had unexpected bad luck: his mother's health failed. The strain of the war years, the heavy loads she had lifted—in short, the men's work beyond her strength—it all began to tell on her, everything went wrong. The diagnosis was a hemorrhage, his mother was in the hospital for a long time and she aged rapidly. It was one thing after another or, as they say, misfortunes never come singly: in the winter his mother slipped and fell off the porch and broke her right arm. The arm mended crooked and she had trouble moving it. Now Faizulla had no choice: he needed a wife. His mother even began nagging him about it. And she found him a bride. A teacher, the daughter of brigade leader Sirai. Well, what of it, why shouldn't he marry a teacher? He was a young, healthy lad with black hair tumbling over his forehead, a broad chest, and strong arms. But would she, an educated girl, marry him, a herdsman? Maybe if he drove a truck or a tractor or was a brigade leader or an accountant at headquarters. No, the teacher wouldn't marry him. Before that Faizulla hadn't so much as looked at her, but now, with his mother nagging him to marry, he sized her up more closely and saw that she had painted nails and hair cut short and curled in ringlets. Was that someone who would live with him and bear him children? No, he needed a simpler sort of wife, someone as uneducated as he was—cut the cloth to fit you, as the saying goes. But life plays funny tricks! Only later did Faizulla find out that the teacher had been willing to marry him, that she liked him. How he regretted it, how he regretted it afterwards, but by then it was too late: Sirai's daughter married someone else. And Faizulla got married, he had to get married by the time he was pushing thirty and his mother couldn't manage the house alone and stayed for months at a time in the hospital. He got married when he didn't give a damn about anything anymore because he had acquired a passion for vodka and grown indifferent to the female sex besides. Here's how it happened: his mother was back in the hospital, and the house was a mess, not fit to live in, though, it's true, Marziya did milk the cow. Faizulla put up with it all for a while and then decided to marry. An eligible girl from the next village, no longer in the bloom of youth, was working as a milkmaid on the second farm. She was an orphan too: her father had been killed in the war, and her mother died young. The girl's name was Galiya. As the eldest child, she raised her younger sister and brother; they grew up orphans and had more than their share of deprivation and hunger. The girl was no beauty, but you couldn't call her ugly either, particularly when she was all dressed up. Faizulla had known her earlier during the year she spent herding cows on the second farm before transferring to his, the fourth. One day the drunken Faizulla went up to Galiya at a meeting of cattlebreeders and without preliminaries brought up the subject of marriage. "O.K., I'm willing," she answered simply. So he took her home with him right from the meeting. When his mother came home from the hospital, his new wife was already running the house.

His mother hadn't forgiven Faizulla for not marrying the teacher. She took a dislike to her daughter-in-law from the first. "You refused to marry a nice, educated girl and brought home a slut!" His mother was used to running the house her way; she was stingy and had a bug about cleanliness to boot. And now she thought that his bride was ruining them, taking food to her brother and sister in her own village. His mother found fault with everything: Galiya couldn't bake bread, didn't get the laundry clean, and went around looking like a beggar. The two women began quarreling. Galiya had a rough side to her tongue, too. Sober, Faizulla kept silent, but, when he was drunk, he sided with his mother and took his wife to task, although most of the time he liked her—she was healthy and a hard worker. Afterwards, when his mother took to her bed, Galiya took care of her as if she were her own mother, but, be that as it may, one day she wounded her with the reproachful words: "You rubbed me in shit, and now you're on your deathbed and can't do without me!"

After his mother's death they settled down to apparent peace, but Faizulla was always off on a binge, he went downhill. He tormented his wife and he tormented himself, and his children grew up like orphans even though their father was alive. Life went from bad to worse, and it was clear that it wasn't going to get any better. Then misfortune struck—his wife died, and now his daughter was missing.

Thinking about his luckless life and picking at his emotional scabs, Faizulla rode into Tirlyan. First he went to the police station and told them about his daughter. They took down her description, asked her age and name, and promised to inform him if anything turned up. Then Faizulla went to see a man from the village who had been living in Tirlyan for a long time now; he had tea with him, told him his troubles, and set out for home. All the way he thought about his daughter, blaming himself and cursing vodka and his fate. "If my daughter is found, I'll give up drinking, I swear it. I won't put the girls in a home, I'll raise them myself," he thought in a burst of lucidity. "Allah, maybe you really do exist. Give me back my daughter, let her be found, let her be there when I get home now. I swear to you, Allah, if you exist, I'll give up drinking, I won't take another drop of that poison, I'll be the soberest man in the world. All-a-ah!..."

He approached the village, still hoping that his daughter had been found. But Gulnara was not at home. Faizulla rested a bit, watered the horse, gave him grain to eat, and then once more set out for the woods. He rode down the Tirlyan road again, making wider detours, riding into the mountains and deep into forest thickets and again kept shouting, "Gul-na-ra, Gul-na-ra!" His anguished call echoed and re-echoed across the wild mountains and swampy woods....

Salakhov Nail, the secretary of the party committee at the Beacon collective farm, would have been happy, of course, to be like the ideal party organizers he had read about in books and seen in films about life on collective farms. To the farmers they were almost like their own fathers and carried great authority, and the chairman never took a step without asking their advice and help. But life isn't the movies; you have to live it. He, party organizer Nail, was one of the folks here, a village boy, and they knew him, as the saying goes, inside out; they remembered the time not so long ago when he was a snotty kid—as children some of them had played knucklebones with him, stolen turnips from other people's gardens, and gone to school with him; in their dissolute youth others had gotten drunk with him and tried their luck with the girls. Besides, half the village were kinfolk, some close, some distant, and then there were all the in-laws and close relatives. People knew all about his minor transgressions during the time he worked as a forester; for instance, they remembered that his cousin took the institute qualifying exam in mathematics for him. (What else could he do? Math was Nail's weak subject.) In short, he wouldn't always be the party organizer and boss; he'd finish his days in his native village, among close relatives, in-laws, cousins, and other family members. Maybe that was why he didn't stick his neck out to gain authority, didn't play the boss and wasn't anything like the ideal party organizer in the movies. And most of the time he thought that he was out of place and could have done more good working as a livestock specialist. But when the regional committee bureau slapped him with a stiff reprimand for unsatisfactory political and educational work on the collective farm and for the bad sanitary condition of the village, he gave up altogether.

Ilyasov's predecessor Shakirov had let the collective farm's affairs drift—or, rather, he had shifted them to the shoulders of the party organizer and brigade leaders. Shakirov was an inveterate hunter and fisherman: he would pick out two spirited horses and disappear for weeks at a time in the mountains, going after graylings in the upper reaches of the White River and killing roe deer; once he even wounded a crane, although nobody could recall that free bird ever being hunted in these parts. They said that Shakirov's wife had a yen to taste crane flesh.

Finally Shakirov was removed as chairman and appointed manager of a state farm. As might be expected, the regional committee once again nominated an outsider to the collective farm, a "Varangian" as Nail called all the alien chairmen. Yes, the collective had bad luck with its management cadres. Since the start of collectivization more than ten chairmen had come and gone, and only one of them had been a local man, a fellow from their village. The first was the estimable Khudaibirdin, now deceased:

he organized the collective farm and was its permanent chairman until the war started and he was promoted to chief of the region. But later he came back to his own collective farm and, sparing neither himself nor other people, cursing and swearing shamelessly, he rescued its utterly ruined economy from poverty and inertia. The bosses disliked him for his insubordination and independent obstinacy; in the third and fourth brigades he was simply hated, particularly by those who lived in remote parts and were used to stealing and slipping away from work on the collective. The chairman made no allowance for folk like that and gave them no peace. They sent complaints, saying that Khudaibirdin was rude, swore foully at them, and made their lives impossible, and at that point the bosses discovered certain illegalities in the chairman's managerial zeal—and kicked Khudaibirdin out in disgrace.... After that came a series of outside chairmen, people just passing through, unsuited to management, some of them drunkards and windbags, who lasted less than a year on the collective farm. Of these ten chairman only the last, Ilyasov Marat, had a higher education; he was a graduate of the agricultural academy. On his own collective farm, forty kilometers away, Ilyasov first worked as a livestock specialist and then became chairman. He made a mess of managing it, drank himself silly (he had kinfolk everywhere, and they were always "honoring" him and seating him at the head of the table), drank himself into delirium tremens, and was treated for it. After the cure they sent him to the Beacon, as far from close relatives and in-laws as possible. It was clear that he had no intention of putting down roots here either: he lived in official quarters and kept his suitcases handy.

Party organizer Nail was firmly convinced that a chairman should be chosen from his own collective; he should be a local man, with roots in the soil, who knew good land, who had run over it barefoot as a boy. Nail was convinced that the only man who could be that type of manager was the present chairman of the town council Iskhakov Rais, a wily, businesslike fellow who carried authority in the village. A few years back he had said to Nail, as if joking, but you could hear the badly concealed grievance behind the joke: "They've stuck the collective with an outsider again. What's wrong with me for chairman? I've been a brigade leader for fifteen years, I know how to manage. Never mind, this one won't last long either. You'll see, I'll be the next chairman." But the regional council evidently had its own ideas about the matter and sent the usual Varangian; as they say, the bosses know best.

Nail didn't get on with the new chairman from the start. Ilyasov reinstated all the people who had been removed from their jobs in recent years. O.K., the party organizer didn't object, he recalled what Latypov, the first secretary of the regional committee, used to say: "There's nothing simpler than removing somebody, firing him, but you'd do better to train a person and teach him to work." But when Ilyasov tried to put Akhmetshin Yulai in charge of the second farm, Nail was indignant. Yulai was an irresponsible fellow, a drunkard and a loafer; when he was boss of the warehouse, he was caught stealing; they made him beekeeper, and he froze the collective's bees in a brick shed. And the mess in the beeyard! "As long as I'm secretary of the party committee here, Yulai will never have a responsible job!" Nail said at the time, feeling his heart pound and knowing that his face had become tense and pale. Since then every time he caught sight of the chairman's short stocky figure, his head cocked stubbornly on his bull neck (privately Nail called Ilyasov "the bull"), his puffy face and constantly guarded gray eyes, the party organizer grew tense and gloomy and turned pale.

After the planning session Nail went to his own office on the second floor, sat down at his desk, and began to reread the text of a report he had drafted yesterday for presentation at the open party meeting on Saturday. Rais, the chairman of the village council, came in, as always brisk and clean-shaven, wearing a tie and smelling of eau-de-cologne. He shook hands and reported, "The fourth brigade called. There's an MP alert there—a girl's missing, herdsman Faizulla's daughter. Yesterday she went off into the woods and never came back. Faizulla looked for her all night with no luck.

"The last thing we need is an MP alert!" thought Nail aggrievedly.

There was a moment of anxious silence.

"I understand, of course it's hard to organize a search right now," said Rais, as if he guessed the party organizer's thoughts, "but we'll have to. She's a child, she'll die in the woods alone."

They went to see the chairman. Ilyasov heard them out, frowned, and said viciously, "He should drink less! I was at his house yesterday: he was lolling about drunk, and the children were left on their own." He drummed his fingers on the desk in silence and added in a different tone, "I don't have the men or the transport." He opened his notebook. "Two trucks, the GAZ-51 and the ZIL-103, are in the shop, the Ural has a load in it and there's no crane, one truck is in Kazakhstan, one is carrying fertilizer to the supply depot, the Belarus are all being used for silage, and the Magafurov carries the milkmaids, and silage in between. That's everything."

"We could send the youth brigade out to search," said Nail diffidently, knowing in advance that the chairman wouldn't agree. He was thinking of the youth brigade that was harvesting hay in the mountains seven kilometers from the village.

"I won't give you the young folk," pronounced Ilyasov stubbornly, glowering at the party organizer. "It took a lot of effort to organize the brigade. If we turn them loose, we'll never collect them again. They're forecasting rain east of the Urals, to lose a day now would be tantamount to a crime. And where would we get the transport? They can't cover ten kilometers on foot! And, by the way, we've received another phonogram, reading us the riot act. All the figures show us under the quota."

The chairman was right, of course. All the work they'd gotten going somehow would come to a standstill for the entire day. The spring had been cold and dry, and the grass came up late. It was already the middle of July, yet there wasn't a single haystack on the collective farm. The annual grass wasn't ready for mowing; when the grass did come up, there were the usual persistent rains, the ground got soggy, and then neither the Whirlwind nor the Belarus could get into the fields. Of course, had the last chairman been there, Nail wouldn't have hesitated a minute, he would have sent people out to search for the girl at once. After all, spending the night alone in the woods was dreadful enough for an adult, let alone a child.

"You mean, to hell with the girl?" said Nail, turning pale.

"Who said to hell with her? We have to search. It's not as if there aren't plenty of people in the village! Organize the teenagers. There are plenty of those loafers hanging around the streets or by the stream or dashing around on motorcycles. They've got their share of idlers in the fourth brigade, too.

"Still, that's not very many."

"It's enough. She won't have gotten far in a single night; she's wandering around near the village somewhere or lying in the bushes."

You could round up some people, of course. Nail had thought of that himself, but how would you get them there? His jeep could take five at most. They could pick up ten more or so in the fourth brigade. Not many.

Still, by noon they managed to collect eight teenagers. Two of the boys were older, they had finished high school and were at home slogging away at their school books, studying for the institute. Eduard, the son of tractor-driver Sabrai, had a motorcycle; the son of the fireman, Shaikhislam Ural, rode pillion and his younger brother sat in the sidecar. Five boys piled into the jeep. They drove to the fourth brigade in Kudashevo, a quiet, secluded village standing in an out-of-the-way spot in the foothills of the Ural crest that seemed to have frozen in happy peace and drowsy unconcern. Only the magpies on the fence stakes chattered excitedly about something, and the laying hens clucked in the cattlesheds. Nazhib, the bulky and sluggish brigade leader, responded to the question, "Well, how's it going?" by pushing his small leather cap to the back of his head, scratching his black wiry hair thoughtfully, and saying that he had already sent the local boys into the woods along the Tirlyan road. But nobody knew for sure where to search for the girl; the little one said her sister had gone to pick berries, but when you asked where, all she kept saying was, "She went into the woods," and which woods she didn't know. And there was forest on all sides. The brigade leader's wife, Nazhib Zakiya, said that someone claimed to have seen a car of some kind passing through the village heading for Tirlyan, and that made them wonder if the man in the car hadn't grabbed the little girl; they heard that there had been cases like that in some villages, little children were carried off God knows where.

They left the jeep and the motorcycle in the village by the gate outside the brigade leader's house, walked over to the stream, crossed it, and divided up into two groups. Nazhib and Rais led one group along the left side of the road; they couldn't bring themselves to let the boys go off alone—they were just kids, after all, and didn't know the area. If they got lost, you'd just have to look for them too. Nail led the other teenagers. The high-school graduates, Eduard and Ural, and two of the school boys went with him. They spread out to a distance approximately ten paces apart and plodded slowly though the woods. They shouted "Gul-na-ra!" and listened for an answer or the sound of a child crying, but all they heard was the double echo of their own voices. Then they started fooling around and amusing themselves by yelling at the top of their lungs, "Ah-oo! O-ho-ho!" They climbed mountain slopes, went through dense thickets, came out into lumbered clearings and cuttings, and once again forced their way through a thick palisade of birches. Nail found it hard to keep up with the boys and maintain their youthful pace; in recent years he had gained weight and gotten fat, he wasn't used to long hikes, and his paunch made itself felt. He took off his jacket and carried it carefully in his hand to keep his comb, wallet, and pen from falling out. In an hour Nail was completely worn out. He lost heart and started thinking that searching for a mite of a girl in these great mountain forests was as hopeless as looking for a needle in a haystack. Besides, the little girl had probably lost her voice long ago from constant crying and shouting, so they wouldn't hear her even if they passed right by; it was all just a useless waste of time and effort. The boys had also had enough and clustered together and stopped yelling. They sat down to rest in a small glade.

"We should be searching with a dog, we won't ever find her this way," said Eduard.

Nail had thought of that himself. But that morning they hadn't even had sense enough to call the police right away. They thought they could manage on their own; they would go into the woods and find the little girl right away or, better still, she would have been found before they even got to Kudashevo.

They sat for a while, caught their breath, and then set out downhill heading for the road. They came out at the summer farm and met Nazhib's group there, together with the boys from the fourth brigade. Of course, they hadn't found the girl. Nail asked brigade leader Nazhib about the situation with the herdsmen and whether they'd had any luck getting a relief man. Nazhib answered that the farm chief, Shakur himself, had replaced old Safuan, while Faizulla had saddled his horse and been out since early morning searching the surrounding forests for his daughter.

"What a business! So there's nobody in the village who can do the herding," said Nail derisively.

"Well, who is there? The young people won't hear of it, and among the old fellows—Ibatulla is beyond it already, and Idris is sick," said Nazhib guiltily. "Faizulla's a good herdsman when he isn't drinking."

"And when's that?"

"His wife kept him in hand before; now he's gone completely to pieces."

The boys went higher up the stream and started fooling around, splashing each other and yelling. Nail squatted beside the clean, fresh water flowing over the yellow pebbles, drank his fill from cupped hands, washed his face and neck, and wiped himself with his handkerchief; Rais and Nazhib drank some water and rinsed their hands, too. Then Nail glanced in the open door of the trailer and began cursing. The posters and charts he had sent a week ago had been tossed into a corner, the box with drawing-pins lay scattered on the floor, there were crumpled padded jackets, a greasy straw mattress, and rags of some sort on the bunks, a swarm of flies hovered over a dirty pan and spoon on the stove, and empty bottles of jug wine stood in the corner. No matter how often Nail berated the farm chief for the mess and dirt in the trailer, he never got anywhere. He stepped inside now and, swearing, pinned the posters to the trailer's board walls, then came out and sat down on the steps beside Rais and Nazhib.

They sat for a while, talking idly about one thing and another, and then headed back to the village in a group. As they walked down the street, people, old men and women, looked out from their gates and asked, "Did you find her?"

"No."

"Where did you look?"

"We went along the Tirlyan road to the farm."

"But the little one said that Gulnara went to pick berries. And we don't pick berries along the Tirlyan road. The berry patches are over there, in the birch groves beyond the vegetable gardens," said one old woman and pointed. "Maybe she went that way."

Brigade leader Nazhib's wife said the same thing. Faizulla's cousin Marziya brought it up, too; all morning she'd been running around the woods beyond the garden plots, keeping close to the edge of the forest— she didn't dare go farther on her own. They should search there, of course. The local boys had immediately dispersed to their houses, and Eduard and the other teenagers were standing around the jeep waiting to set out for home. Nail consulted Nazhib, who said that he would try to round up the local boys right away. Rais also thought that evening was still far off and they should continue the search.

"Here's the situation, boys. We're going to move into the woods over there and comb them as deep as we can," Nail announced to the teenagers. "I understand that you're tired and you're ready to eat, but be patient a little longer; the little girl in there hasn't eaten for a day now."

The boys, who had clearly had enough, kept silent and glanced away. Eduard finally said, "We can't. We've got to go home."

"Why can't you?"

"At seven the fourth episode of 'Stirlitz' is on," Eduard answered.

Nail glanced at his watch; it was ten minutes to six.

"So what? You'll see it some other time."

"What other time? We want to see it today."

"My sainted aunt!" Nail swore to himself. "Hey, fellows, come on now!" he started again reproachfully. "You're grown-ups now, educated, Young Communists. Are we really going to abandon a little girl in trouble for a TV show?"

The young men maintained their sullen silence. They were healthy boys who had never gone hungry. They wore jeans from the department store in town and had hair down to their shoulders. On the whole, they were good kids, smart, they knew their abc's and had learned math and physics, but their hearts had barely learned the alphabet.

"I'm watching the show, too, you know." Nail actually did enjoy watching television. "Well, so we miss the fourth episode, that's no great loss, they'll tell us about it later," he said, without losing hope yet, but he saw only a stubborn sullenness on the boys' faces.

"Listen, fellows—I'm not begging you, I'm speaking to you officially as the chairman of the village council," said Rais, as always quietly but impressively. "Bear in mind that this is a serious matter. If the little girl perishes, you'll share the guilt."

The boys smiled in insolent condescension, as if to say, "You're taking a lot on yourself, mister; you can't scare us."

"But Uncle Rais, we've searched already, and what good did it do? Maybe somebody really did carry her off in a car," said Eduard.

"O.K. then, rush off to your TV sets," Rais pronounced softly and apparently calmly and, turning away from the boys, said through clenched teeth, "Where on earth do boys like these come from?"

"What d'you mean, where?" growled Nail. "We raised them ourselves."

The boys started the motorcycle, settled on the pillion and in the side-car, and rode off.

"What about us?" said one of the remaining teenagers.

"Oh, are you in a hurry to see 'Stirlitz,' too?" Nail feigned surprise. "Well then, of course, we'll just have to go, won't we?"

He climbed into the jeep and said to brigade leader Nazhib, "Collect the local kids and keep searching the woods until dark. First thing tomor-row organize more people and search all day. Keep me posted. I'll phone the police today and have them send a dog."

The boys crowded into the back seat and the jeep hurtled out of the village. Nail was in a bad mood, not at the thought of the little girl now blundering about the woods, hungry and out of her wits with loneliness and fear, but rather from self-reproach: he hadn't managed to organize a search, he couldn't convince or even force those brats to go into the woods. As always when he felt bad, he looked for some soothing thought in which to take refuge. And it occurred to him—he hadn't given the idea any attention earlier—that perhaps the girl really had been carried off in a car, although it was not clear why anyone would carry off a strange child, but nevertheless he now admitted the possibility. The thought seemed to lift some share of the guilt off his shoulders, and off the others as well: it wasn't because they'd searched badly that they hadn't found her, but because they'd looked where the girl wasn't and couldn't be. Let the police do the searching, let them launch an investigation and put a notice in the newspaper.

When they got back to the village, he and Rais immediately telephoned the police in town from the council office.

"When did the girl disappear?"

"Yesterday."

"Yesterday she disappeared, and you don't call until this evening!" the angry voice boomed in the receiver. "We can't go out now, all our trained dogs are busy."

"When will you come?"

"Wait," and they hung up.

———

... Later she was roused by the cold, an earthy forest cold that lashed and battered her thin small body unmercifully. There were no wolves, and she was alive. It was getting light, morning wasn't far off. Gulnara now knew that she had spent the night alone in the woods, lying on the cold ground and damp grass. All at once she recalled yesterday's wandering in the forest thickets and her fear of the dark, and she saw how hopelessly alone she was in that wild green desert, how small and helpless in the cold dusk of the close-pressing throng of huge trees. She remembered everything and again started weeping and bawling out loud. Then the girl calmed down slightly, for hope arrived with the dawn, and soon she would come out on the edge of the forest, today they would be sure to find her, her father would find her, or Aunty Marziya. The girl got up and plodded on. The morning light filtered down from above, at first casting a dim light on the upper foliage and then flying downward, to the very bottom of the forest depths, and chasing away the dusk of night, driving it out of the bushes and grass. A breeze came running and whispered lightly in the tops of the birches, some kind of bird twittered, and the familiar sounds and voices of life raised the little girl's spirits. Besides, she imagined Papa sobering up by evening and asking her sister, "Where's Gulnara?" "She went to the woods to pick berries." Papa became anxious and ran into the woods, but it was already dark and in the dusk he couldn't find her among the trees; but now it was light and Papa ran into the woods again. He was searching for her, and Aunty Marziya was searching, and brigade leader Nazhib was searching too: they were all searching for her, and soon they'd find her. She stopped, no longer weeping, stood stockstill, and listened: leaves rustled, a bird clucked, rustling noises raced past her, and far off a magpie chattered and a crow cawed, but there were still no human voices to be heard. And the little girl started crying again or, rather, moaning, softly and monotonously: "Aah-aah-aah!" And again she started walking; she took short steps, her little legs moving slowly and unsteadily as they caught on the grass and fallen branches, and she kept stumbling and falling.

Her whole little body, her whole being, felt hunger the way she felt pain. Gulnara had never been hungry before; sometimes she had simply been ready to eat when Papa hadn't made anything, and then she broke a heel off a round loaf and ate that. The girl began looking carefully at the grass beneath her feet; maybe she would find something edible. She knew for sure that everything edible grew only on the ground: grain ripened in the fields, and there were potatoes in the vegetable plots, wild garlic grew on the hill on the other side of the village, and sorrel showed green on the slopes running down to the water meadow. Across the stream, if you climbed farther into the alder and bird-cherry thickets, you might find a small black or red currant bush; ripe berries hid in the thick grass of little clearings among the birches. In the spring oxalis grew in the plowed fields; and her father sometimes dug up a turk's-cap in the forest and brought it to the girls. It was all edible and delicious. Here, in the wild forest, there were also many different plants, but Gulnara wasn't familiar with them and therefore she didn't know whether they could be eaten; they were probably all inedible and bitter.

Looking around to the sides, under her feet, in the grass, and at the bushes and the tree trunks, the girl saw life everywhere: ants swarmed on their ruddy mounds and ran up and down the white trunks of the birches; some sort of beetle crawled along a blade of grass, and again, as it had yesterday, a large bird rose from the grass and flew off, startling the girl with the explosive noise of its wings. Around her there were probably many other different forest dwellers concealed in the thick grass; there was food here for all of them, and, indeed, the flies swarming around the little girl had drunk her blood all night, so that her face was swollen from their bites and itched unbearably.

The welcome sun now lit the treetops; it was probably broad daylight now. The little girl didn't know how much time had passed since she had awoken and how long she had wandered in the depths of the forest. At times she fancied that she had been roaming the woods for a very long time, perhaps she had always roamed them, and her life as a child in the village, her father and sister belonged to another world, one that she had already begun to forget or that she had only dreamed, although rationally she understood that she had spent only one night in the forest, and therefore it was the second day since had she left home. Her legs kept giving way from the weakness brought on by hunger and fatigue, everything grew dark before her eyes, things began whirling around her, and she fell in the grass. She would have lain that way without moving, she would have stayed there, resigned to her bitter fate, if hope had not gleamed before her through the dull fog of her stunned consciousness—the edge of the forest was just over there, soon... Her father was already searching for her in the forest, soon she would hear his voice, "Gul-na-ra!" Aunty Marziya was also searching, everybody in the village was searching for her, they were going through the forest and calling, it was just that they were still far, far off. The little girl got up and, stumbling and falling, moaning constantly and monotonously, "Aah-aah-aah," she moved on a bit farther. And again she fell, facedown in the aromatic grass, and then turned slowly over onto her back. The bright sky glimmered and wavered far overhead; it seemed to Gulnara that she was lying at the bottom of a deep pit, and all of life, the village and its people—everything—was there overhead, in the sunlight, and from there nobody could see her in that pit, nobody could find her and pull her out. If only she could rise up there, if she could just fly out of the ravine and see the edge of the forest from above, the village, all the surroundings… She lay there for some time, breathing through her open mouth, feeling the quick throb of her little heart, and looking in anguish at the green dusk hanging over her. She no longer wanted to get up, her strength was gone, but the hope that the edge of the forest and open expanses were not far away brought her to her feet once more and again impelled her forward… When the hunger pangs became unbearable, the little girl tried to eat some of the grass: she started chewing on an unpalatable, tasteless stalk, but it tasted bitter and her saliva was thick and sticky. The grass was probably inedible. Gulnara spat it out and did not try again to eat the inedible greens.

Once she thought she heard her name. A woman's voice called "Gulnara!" She heard the shout through the rustle of the grass under her feet and stopped stockstill as hope flared up in her, but the shout was not repeated. She plodded on and, as soon as the grass began rustling under her feet, again she heard, "Gulnara!" The shouts came from quite nearby, in the direction she was going, just beyond the trees. The girl stopped again—and once more all was quiet. All that reached her ears was the distant chatter of a magpie and the faint murmur of the foliage. She started shouting, shrieking very loudly so that they could hear her. And she headed towards the spot from which the woman's voice had called to her. It took Gulnara a long, long time to take those few dozen steps, treading on the high grass, crawling across fallen trees and forcing her way through the low underbrush. But there was nobody there. She went farther and once more heard the woman's voice ahead calling "Gulnara!" Again she began shouting loudly in response and dragged herself in that direction.

The sun was already directly over the forest. Its rays penetrated the foliage to the very bottom of the green dusk, and spots of sunlight stirred on the grass and the trunks of the birches. Sometimes a warm ray fell onto Gulnara's dishevelled blonde head and gently touched her face; the girl sensed it as something alive and good, a soothing touch, as if someone large and merciful was tenderly encouraging her helpless child and whispering words of hope…

———

That same day everybody in the three other villages of the Beacon collective farm knew that a little girl, the daughter of herdsman Faizulla, was missing; they thought about the misfortune and, among other concerns and affairs, discussed what had happened.

"A five-year-old girl's lost over in the village of Kudashevo. They say she went into the woods and never came back," some old woman would begin a conversation over evening tea, feeling a faint excitement at this grievous event which overrode her daily, ordinary problems and emotions. And, as if ashamed to be talking about it so calmly, without heartfelt grief, she added with a sigh, "The poor little thing—she might collapse and die."

"They'll find her. Where can she have got to? They're searching, I daresay she didn't go far, and it's not winter now," rejoined her husband, who had long since forgotten the constant fears he had had for his own small children.

"They say they searched all day today and didn't find her."

"They must have gone about it wrong then."

Or a young mother said to her five- or six-year-old children, "There's a little girl just like you who's lost in the woods. And you, too, spend whole days off somewhere on the other side of the stream!" And, not so much grieving as glad that, thank heaven, all was safe and sound at her house, she sighed, "God save her!"

And in the late twilight, as always on clear summer days, people gathered on the bench at somebody's gate, gossiping about this or that and, among the talk of brigade affairs, haymaking, politics, or simple scandal, they also discussed the missing girl.

"She didn't get lost, she was carried off," said one of those for whom a little girl lost in the forest seemed too ordinary an occurrence, and who saw in all the vicissitudes of life an insidious play of fate or evil intent on the part of human beings. "They say a car passed through their village."

Many agreed and even found an explanation, "He's probably childless. Childless people take kids from children's homes. He saw a little girl roving around with nobody to watch her; he lured her, put her in the car, and drove off."

"They say that nursing babies are taken right out of the maternity ward now. So the child never knows his parents aren't really his. Some little goose fools around and has a baby and then she gives it up and leaves it at the maternity ward."

"It's a mystery to me how anyone can give up her own baby, born in pain. It must take a heart of stone!"

"What's so mysterious about it? That's how young folks are now. Why, they say that in those huge apartment buildings in the city people keep a dog instead of a child."

"You don't say! And we each gave birth to five or six children."

The old women and the younger ones debated a while and decided that if the man in the car had really taken the child in order to adopt her, it wasn't such a disaster—they'd heard the father was getting ready to take his daughter to a children's home anyway...

Cool darkness crept up on the village from the direction of the mountains and the damp meadows across the river. The night fog spilled there like a gray flood over water meadows, tussocks, and swamps; the silence of the July night thickly covered the sleepy earth. On the village street, in the yards, and at the gates—right alongside the dwellings of people— something lifeless, inhospitable, and wild came to rest, as if it had crawled there along with the darkness from the deserted fields, mountain valleys, and black nocturnal forests. The talk on the benches died out, people went into their warm cottages, got into their soft goosedown beds, hid their lives under quilted blankets, and left daytime affairs, problems, anxieties, and fears behind. Only a few of them took a minute to imagine the fragile life of the tiny girl far from houses and people, on the wild ground, in the infernal darkness of the forest, in the fog and cold and, imagining themselves in her place, whispered in distress, "God keep her!"

Minister hadn't heard yet that a little girl from the village of Kudashevo was lost. Perhaps Minister was the only one not to know. He didn't know not just because he lived in a remote spot beyond Fire Mountain, in the very last cabin, but because he had no woman in his house, no street newspaper on two legs, so to speak, to bring him various daily items of village news. Besides, he was hard of hearing and couldn't catch random conversation on the street. If news of the girl's misfortune had reached his ears, he would certainly have become extremely upset; he would have lost his peace of mind, as he did every time he saw anything out of order in the village or heard that somebody was in trouble.

Minister was his nickname, but the old man's name was Khafiz or, as they call honored fellow villagers, Khafiz-agai. Even his own sister called him Minister. ("Have you seen my Minister?") And the young people didn't know his real name at all; they called him Minister-agai or even just Minister without the honorific agai—that was how close the nickname stuck to him.

Nobody could really explain why his fellow villagers had started calling old Khafiz Minister. Some said that once when he spoke up at a meeting he was supposed to have said that every collective farmer should think like a minister; others said that Khafiz spent his whole life scribbling letters to various ministries about irregularities in the village and the region; still others claimed that he was just crazy and thought in complete seriousness that he was a minister just like the ones who sat in a big city in a big office behind a big desk with telephones and decided all questions and problems.

The war had passed through Khafiz's life and fate like a fiery whirlwind, crippling his body and searing his heart. In his youth he was a very healthy lad and had another nickname—Khafiz the hero, or Khafiz-palvan, because he was the strongest man in the region, an invincible wrestler at the *saban-tui*.* How many people had tried to beat him! Wrestlers from other regions came to the sabantui; once even palvan Tashbaev, who was unbeaten in his own lands, came from the Kazakh steppe and Khafiz pinned him flat, to the enthusiastic roars of his fellow villagers. In those years a legend circulated that Tashbaev, in revenge for his defeat at the sabantui, ambushed Khafiz on the upper Ural highway and attacked him with a knife as he was returning from the bazaar. But Khafiz the hero hit Tashbaev so hard on the jaw that he crashed unconscious to the ground; Khafiz tied him up, binding him with his own reins, put him in his saddle, and chased his horse off in the direction of the Kazakh steppes.

After he did his stretch in the army in 1940, Khafiz enjoyed a bachelor life a while and then married Saniya, Rakhmatulla's daughter. The war broke out before seventeen-year-old Saniya could bear him a child, and Khafiz went to the bathhouse with his young bride for the last time and rode off to the war without any particular hope of coming back alive. Near Smolensk he was surrounded and managed to escape; during the winter, near Moscow, he was wounded in the leg, spent some time in the hospital—and went back to his unit. Khafiz went back to the front from a reserve regiment, riding in a jolting heated cattlecar full of soldiers. In Stalingrad he was wounded for the second time, again in the leg and again, as if on purpose, in the left leg. But the wound only grazed the bone, and a month later he was once more on the march in the gray ranks of the infantry, wolfing down battlefield rations from a soldier's mess kit.

Suddenly his wife's letters stopped coming. Khafiz became worried and depressed and, although he was a non-smoker, took to rolling his own tobacco and inhaling the smoke. He kept writing, sending one military triangular-shaped letter after another asking why there was no answer, what was happening at home? At last a letter came. His mother wrote, or rather his sister wrote to her dictation: "I didn't want to inform you. But

---

*A traditional Bashkir spring festival

why should you remain in ignorance, you'll grieve and somehow bear the grief. Our beautiful daughter-in-law is no longer with us. She died this spring. They sent her to the transport station to learn to run a tractor. She finished the course and drove her tractor from the station to the village. The other women got safely across the steep slope alongside Magpie Wood, but Saniya's tractor rolled downhill and turned over. Our beauty lay beside her tractor looking just as she always did. Not a single bruise or a single scratch on her. Perhaps her dear heart burst from fear..."

The light in Khafiz's eyes dimmed, his face instantly grew dour, and gray streaks appeared in his coal-black hair. He gritted his teeth and kept his grief to himself. He didn't care whether he lived or died. He may have even consciously sought death, exposing his robust body to German bullets and shrapnel, but the enemy's iron missed him. Khafiz seemed to have a charmed life.

A German mortar finally caught him in the battle for the Dnieper. A splinter pierced his skull, and black blood gushed from his head. Khafiz passed countless months flat on his back, at times sinking into sweet delirium with strange visions, at times returning to the desolation of the hospital ward. He was finally discharged on medical grounds and sent home. The wound healed with a hairless film of skin that gleamed in a lustrous pink bald patch on his shaven bluish skull. He suffered from headaches; any trifling upset set his head throbbing, and everything around him would grow dim and turn upside down.

Khafiz came home to an orphaned and hungry village, which had grown depressed and quiet without its men. His mother again told him the story of Saniya's death and how she lay like a living beauty beside her overturned tractor. Khafiz visited his wife's grave, shed a few tears, drowned his sorrows in bitter home-brewed beer, and resumed his wretched life.

He still had a mighty body; with his shaved head and bull neck he looked like the same hero who had wrestled at the sabantui. But now the festivals were not celebrated, and even if one had been arranged Khafiz could hardly have appeared on the public square. He felt as if his life beat and pulsed unprotected now, under the thin layer of glossy pink skin. Children sometimes asked him, "Khafiz-agai, show us your wound." He took off his cap and bent his head. "Can we touch it?" The children cautiously fingered the quivering bald spot in joyful amazement.

His father was a clever carpenter. Even before the war Khafiz had helped him build log cottages and put up plank "Russian" gates. Now Khafiz took to the axe, saw and chisel again, realizing that they would earn him his daily bread for life. He and his father worked together. They repaired cowsheds and calfbarns that had grown dilapidated during the war and built new ones. The work was measured and tranquil, although far from easy. But Khafiz still had the strength to handle an axe and saw and lift logs and blocks.

Time flowed just the way the river Yaik flowed beyond the village. The war ended and, after the destruction and hunger, life in the village returned to normal. True, things went slowly, shakily, and unsteadily; true, the women went on bending their backs in the fields and on the farm, but now there was bread. In the fifties the village began to build. Men back from the war who were able to work and young fellows who had grown up and finished their army service raised amber-colored center-walled cottages to replace their bleary pre-war hovels and adorned their yards with high plank gates. Master carpenter Mavlitbaev Khafiz was in demand. He started making money, took a drink now and then and, when he was tight, bawled a song that the boys who marched with him from the Volga to the Dnieper had sung during the war: "Oh, Galiya, you dear young Galiya..." or, recalling his late wife, he wept bitterly... His mother hinted at marriage: there were lots of eligible girls in the village after the war—he could take his pick. His mother had already chosen Khalida, Kamalitdin's daughter, a girl as sturdy as a firearm and bold—as they say in the village, she struck fire wherever she went. But Khafiz's heart wasn't free for another woman, and his body seemed to have become indifferent to female caresses and reciprocal tenderness; and he kept thinking: why should I, with a hole in my skull, set up my own family; I'm getting along all right living with my father and mother.

The river flowed and time passed. Time, like the river, had its quiet sandbars, quick and sunny shallows, and black backwaters. His sister got married, his father died, his mother aged, and Khafiz himself grew older. In 1971 his mother passed away too. Time went by, Khafiz lived alone, and people began to notice his eccentricities. When a neighbor or his sister dropped in, he would pay no attention to whoever entered, but would sit motionless, staring at a single point as if deep in contemplation about something or other. Or he would walk down the street talking to himself. He would mutter, "Where are we going? Where? No, we're not on the right road." He gave up carpentry, sold his cow, and began to live on his veteran's pension. His sister Zukhra planted potatoes for him, and she also brought him milk for his tea. That strange contemplative streak and the muttering under his breath lasted for a few years, and then suddenly he changed completely. It was as if a new heart had lodged in his large wrestler's and carpenter's body. Khafiz pinned the ribbons and medals that had been lying neglected in a tea canister to a jacket he had once bought to wear on holidays and for visits and which was still as good as new; he slung an old, shabby, leatherette satchel across his shoulder, shoved a notepad, pen, and pencils into it, and set out on foot to make the rounds of the collective farm and the brigades. He dropped in at the farms, the summer pastures, the camps in the fields, and other people's yards, and, looking for something and muttering constantly to himself under his breath, he kept making notes in his little pad.

"What are you looking for?" people would ask.

"It's not a matter for your mind, understood?" he answered (he had a habit of inserting the Russian word "understood" after every second or third word, accenting it on the wrong syllable).

"Instead of roaming around wasting time, you'd do better to build me a nice bathhouse."

"There are affairs more important than your bathhouse, understood?

"Understood, understood!"

"Understood your ass!" Khafiz cursed. "The counter-revolutionaries are back, there's sabotage everywhere!"

Khafiz got in the habit of speaking out at meetings. He never failed to demand the floor. They let him speak and listened to him. He didn't speak from his seat, but went up to the platform. He began every speech with the words, "Brothers and sisters!" And, glancing at his tattered notepad, he would start leveling criticism. He reported that herdsman Faizulla got drunk and fell out of his saddle and, while he was sleeping it off, the cows trampled the oatfield; that Salikha, the woman in charge of the dairy, took cream and butter home every day; that yesterday at Whiterocks the unwatered calves were bawling at noon; that DDT was poisoning the collective's bees and destroying the trees; that when you went to the first-aid post, the girl paramedic had a dirty coat and there was no medicine; that they should give some thought to the question of why, at the height of the summer harvest when one day's work meant a year's food, vodka was being delivered to the village—wasn't that sabotage? "Brothers, sisters, you all know old Asiya. She's in her seventies, her husband and only son laid down their lives during the war. All her life she worked for the collective farm; she plowed, harrowed, and sowed, from early spring to white-fly season she went barefoot, and all winter she rushed about in ragged soft boots and a torn sweater, working at threshing or at the farm. And now that she's old, you've forgotten her! Which one of you has looked in on her at least once or taken an interest in the way she's living in her hovel? The roof will cave in and crush her. Is the collective really not in position to put up a new cottage for her? Brothers and sisters, we must all think like a minister, and answer for everything like a minister..."

"That's right!" exclamations rang out from the hall. "What you say is right, Khafiz-agai."

Time passed. Khafiz went around the collective, making notes, speaking out, cursing the disorder, stirring up things at headquarters, and sometimes looking in at the yards of farmers who were clearly well off and muttering to himself, "The kulaks are back. They're kulaks." Some considered him a simpleton, others made hints about his head wound—in short, they got used to Khafiz, as one gets used to eccentrics and other unworldly people, and the main thing was that his fellow villagers agreed with everything he said: "What you say is right, agai, that's right." His jacket wore thin, his ribbons and medals became tarnished, his cap faded, his closely cropped hair and the stubble on his cheeks turned white, and he even seemed to diminish in size. And in all those years the only thing he accomplished was to get a cottage built for old Asiya.

Then Minister started calling on the regional bosses. At first the secretaries wouldn't let him in to see "the man"; he was busy, they said, he's holding an important meeting. But in time, as he got bolder or more desperate, Minister started brushing past the secretaries to the various bosses and had his say, reporting on everything. And surprisingly, they agreed with him, too: "What you say is right, agai, we'll take measures." When he saw that nothing changed, Minister started writing letters to the district center, to the ministries and newspapers. But he never got an answer; it was as if the letters got no farther than the bottom of the blue mailbox. True, one letter—in which he wrote that the head mechanic Saifullin was living beyond his means, buying a car and building a concrete garage on heaven knows whose money—that letter was answered or, rather, a commission of some sort came from town. But the head mechanic wriggled out of it by showing documents: the car had been bought legally, he had saved money from his pay and sold meat at the bazaar; everything was in order at the garage also—in short, he got off with a scare.

On the day when Minister found out that the daughter of herdsman Faizulla in the fourth brigade was missing, he had spent the morning writing two letters to the district center. One was about the fact that some people in the village fed livestock on bread bought at the store, and the second, that the farmers were assigned the worst pasture for their own cattle—the grass was trampled and eaten down to the bare earth. Minister put the letters in the mailbox and went to check on two women, old Asiya and the milkmaid Sabira, a chronic alcoholic from a mountain village. Although the collective had put up a cottage for old Asiya, they had roofed it with tarpaper, and since then the roof had deteriorated and started leaking in the rain. Minister's first business was to drop in on Asiya, who had recently gotten feeble-minded and believed once again that her son had survived the war and would soon come home. Minister questioned her about her daily life and her health, promised to beg a piece of tarpaper from the warehouse and patch the roof, and was ready to leave when Asiya suddenly asked him, "Do you know what direction England's in?"

"England's across the sea. Far from here. Why do you care?"

"I keep thinking sometimes: maybe my son's there in that England."

"Sure, anything's possible. I'll write a letter to England."

"Write, dear heart, write!..."

Minister brought the old woman two buckets of water from the pump down the street and strode off to Sabira's house.

Sabira's story was the age-old one of a girl whose future husband fell during the war years somewhere in the broad expanse of land between the Volga and the Elbe. A fine, strapping milkmaid, she spent her life squeezing the milk needed by the state from the cows' scraggy udders; winter and summer she went around in rubber boots, wading through kilometers of mud; she shifted mountains of manure and silage, contracted polyarthritis, and in her old age took to drink. Perhaps at first Sabira found consolation in vodka and escape from loneliness and depression, but afterwards she couldn't live without it...

There were no curtains hanging and no flowers standing in the windows of the relatively new cottage that the collective farm had built for her. From the door came a stink of something sour and musty. Old rags were scattered about the dirty floor; an empty vodka bottle stood among unwashed cups and plates on a table covered with worn oilcloth. Flies were buzzing over the dishes. The drunken Sabira lolled on the crumpled bed on top of a greasy blanket. Her dress was hitched above knees swollen with polyarthritis. She must have drawn her pension yesterday and gotten drunk, and she had already managed to take a drop or two today as well. She would drink up her pension and then go around the village begging for more sour wine. Minister pulled her dress down over her legs and shook the sleeping woman.

"Get up, what's all this snoozing in broad daylight!"

Sabira mumbled, turned onto her side, opened her eyes, and looked dully at Khafiz. "What do you want?"

"You're drunk again! We'll have to send you for compulsory treatment again."

"So? Send me. I've been there before," she answered indifferently.

She got up and sat on the bed, her legs dangling to the floor. Her uncombed gray hair, braided in a straggly plait, was tangled on her head like dusty old wool. She reeked of alcohol.

"You could at least clean up your room!" grumbled Minister.

He put the dirty dishes away in the cupboard, brought water from the pump, and began washing the floor with a piece of burlap he himself had brought not long ago.

"Don't come and see me any more, Minister" said Sabira after a period of silence. "Or else folks'll begin to think you're my lover."

"You're all I need. What love could I get from you?"

"So, why do you come then?"

"I'm just sorry for you, you fool."

"Why be sorry for me? I'm a lost cause. I'll kick off soon. It's the little girl I'm sorry for, if they don't find her..."

"What little girl?"

"What, you haven't heard? Women at the store were saying that herdsman Faizulla's five-year-old daughter went off into the woods and got lost, they can't find her now..."

That was how Minister heard about the missing girl and lost his peace of mind...

The whole day, until darkness fell, the little girl kept walking through the woods, or rather she kept moving from place to place. She was no longer strong enough to walk. True, she stayed upright for a time, but after a few steps she fell and then went on crawling on all fours. She was driven by that same hope that the edge of the forest was near and the boundary close by; an unquestioned belief that they were searching for her spurred her on. The little girl cried all the time, or she thought she was crying: actually she had lost her voice, only a forced wheeze broke from her throat, and her dry, inflamed tongue no longer fitted in her mouth. Above all, Gulnara wanted a drink. Now she heard the purling of a brook all the time—it was somewhere nearby, just beyond the birches; she crawled doggedly toward it, but the same birches stood there, and the same waterless wooded terrain, extended, overgrown with grass, and the purling of the brook had moved farther off. But the girl kept hearing it, so distinctly that again she crawled in the direction where she heard the brook purling. Again, as so often before, she tried eating grass, but her swollen tongue got in her way, and she was no longer strong enough to force her sagging lower jaw to chew.

When it began to grow dark, and the little girl realized that night, the cold, dark, frightening night, was coming on once more and she hadn't been found, a sudden deduction penetrated her weakening reason, and her hope of rescue seemed to hit against a blank wall: nobody was searching for her, Papa was lying around drunk, and Aunty Marziya didn't know where she'd gotten to. She, Gulnara, herdsman Faizulla's daughter, was going to die in the woods, die like her mother had died, like the little chick had died. She remembered the chick's lonely death; she remembered how his tiny life, which nobody needed, had failed, and his eyes filmed over; he tumbled over and again got up in a flickering thirst for life, and once again fell. He took a long time to die, his little downy body quivering and finally growing still, his thin little twiglike claws sticking up. And beside him his mother hen, clucking fussily, scratched diligently in the manure and rubbish in front of her greedily cheeping brood and failed to notice the dying chick, just as if he were not her own chick patiently hatched in the stuffy chicken coop. And now when the little girl realized that she was abandoned, nobody needed her, and she would once again be left alone in the nocturnal forest, her frail child's heart broke completely. She fell down, closed her eyes, curled up in a ball, and didn't get up again. She had become a chick rejected by all living things, a dying chick...

The next day Nazhib, the chief of the fourth brigade, had no chance to organize a search for the girl. In the morning they called and informed him that his wife's father had died. His father-in-law lived at the farm center; he was old and had been sick for a long time. Lingering on, racked with internal pain, he would shout at night, "Old lady, I'm dying, call the doctor woman!" His wife fetched the nurse, an injection seemed to give the old man some peace, but some time later he would start shouting again, "I'm dying!" Now at last his torment was over.

In this world death is an ordinary affair. Once born you can't escape death. But the birth of a baby is a joy. They sever and tie the umbilical cord, wash and swaddle him, and put him to the teat—and that's it, live! But a man dies in torment, conscious of his nothingness, and leaves grief and troubles to the living.

It took all morning to dig the grave and knock together a coffin. After the funeral Nazhib went to the shop to negotiate with the welder for an enclosure and a little pyramid for his father-in-law's grave and then, before he went home (his wife was staying with her mother), he decided to look in at headquarters. It wasn't that he had business there, but he thought he should show himself to the bosses; maybe they had some instructions. Although, to tell the truth, Nazhib didn't like going to see the bosses very much. He always went into the two-story headquarters feeling tense and with a premonition of unpleasantness and failure. Downstairs, in the vestibule, there was a smell of tobacco, dust and paper, and to Nazhib those official clerical smells were a sign of a different, business-like, anxious, gloomy life, the life of institutions, waiting rooms, long corridors, and offices with plaques on the doors upholstered in leatherette felt and, on those plaques, the names and initials of the bosses who inspired respect and trembling, with typewriters rapping away, the constant ringing of telephones, the impenetrable authoritarian faces above desks covered with telephones, and the voices, hoarse from smoking, of men, bosses and their deputies—in short, a life which always seemed incomprehensible and foreign to Nazhib and which always made him feel timid, submissive, and guilty. He entered headquarters his normal self—big, unhurried, and self-confident—but as he went upstairs to the second floor, walked down the corridor, and saw the door to the chairman's office, he seemed to shrink in size and his heart somehow timidly contracted; as he saw himself through the bosses' eyes, he saw the leader of the fourth brigade, a man whose work was so full of shortcomings, accounting errors, and omissions that they would berate him non-stop. He had gotten used to waiting for the reprimand and the superior tone of the talk. However, Chairman Ilyasov, whom Nazhib had dreaded meeting, was not at headquarters. That cheered him up. But Nail, the party organizer, was in his office; Nazhib felt freer and more comfortable with the party organizer, who was a local man, and a talk with him, no matter how touchy, never seemed offensive, and the party organizer had never cursed anyone in his life; he just spoke sarcastically, carpingly, and made you feel ashamed. That old fool Minister, as the Russians say, with a the spigot to every barrel, was sitting in the party organizer's office. Nazhib shook hands first with Nail and then with Minister, took off his leather cap, and sat down.

"Well, how are things going there?" asked the party organizer.

"I just buried my father-in-law," answered Nazhib.

"I know, my condolences." Nail assumed an expression of sympathetic grief. "And the girl, of course, hasn't been found?"

"Who's had time to search? It's been one thing after another. Yesterday evening we ran around the forest, shouted and shouted, and came back. Now it'll be hard to find her, it's the third day, after all. Not every adult could hold out, let alone a child. She's lost her voice and can't shout anymore; she can't walk either, she's lying somewhere in the grass..."

"Eh, fellows, fellows!" The party organizer shook his head in vexation. "It's all like a song they broadcast on television not long ago: 'The house burns, and here I stand.' Our only hope now is the police dog."

"Why haven't they come yet?"

"They're catching criminals. Day before yesterday somebody robbed a store in Buidy—by crawling across the roof and dismantling the stovepipe. And yesterday someone in town cleaned out an apartment in broad daylight. The police promised to come today, but for some reason they still haven't shown up. Yes, the poor little thing's had no luck, nothing's worked out in her favor... Today, of course, you've had quite a day ... Just the same, see if you can talk the boys into making another trip into the forest; it's still light."

"I'll try. But there's something else... Maybe we're turning people out for nothing? Nobody believes the girl got lost, they all say that some man carried her off in a car. An old woman claims to have seen it. And Faizulla isn't even searching anymore..."

"And if she wasn't carried off, if she's there in the forest—what then?" Minister suddenly interjected.

During the talk Nazhib had forgotten that the old man was there; now he looked more attentively at him. They said that when he was young he was a wrestler; even now, old and gray, Minister looked like a palvan. He'd come back disabled from the war; for a while he'd been a carpenter, but then he'd turned peculiar—perhaps he'd gotten a bit touched—and stopped working, and now he hung around the collective farm, criticizing everybody, teaching everybody how to live, writing denunciations of everybody, although it had been a long time since anyone took him seriously. Two ribbons and tarnished medals gleamed on Minister's worn jacket—that inspired respect; a rosy bald spot quivered and pulsed in the middle of the white stubble on his close-cropped head—the stretched skin over the hole left by a splinter wound.

"Well, we're searching..."

"You're searching badly! Did you ever go on the attack? You didn't. But I did. You have to search the way you attack, the way you go into battle, understood?"

"Understood, Khafiz-agai, what you say is right," agreed Nazhib.

"Understood your ass!" cursed Minister. "Whose fault is it the girl got lost? Yours!"

"Well, can you beat that!" Nazhib was surprised. "A girl accidentally gets lost in the woods, and I'm to blame!"

"Right! Understood now? Here's how I, with a hole in my head, think: if the child dies in the woods, we're all to blame, starting with the brigade leader and ending with the minister himself who sits there in the center. Understood?"

"You are correct, Khafiz-agai," agreed the party organizer with a smile. "Golden words."

"Well, I'm off. I'll phone if I have news."

Nazhib put on his leather cap, said good-bye, and left, upset by the attack from that old fool Minister, although deep in his heart just the same he felt that the old man was somehow right. As he left headquarters, Nazhib as usual looked at the sky. The afternoon sun was shining, but in the sky, which was clear overall, a change was going on: something was breaking up and shifting in the azure heights. Eddying air currents stretched out, long filaments of white clouds that looked carelessly smeared against the blue background began to coil and fold, and in the west an alarming dark shroud was visible behind the distant craggy peaks. Nazhib didn't like that sky. "I hope it doesn't rain," he thought.

She lay all night without sleeping. Or rather it was only her body that remained awake, wasted to the bones, curled up tight on the bare ground, and trembling incessantly in the short jacket that gave no warmth. But she was loosing consciousness. When the little girl woke from her oblivion for a few short minutes, she was alive only insofar as she felt the unbearable cold and the raw earthy dampness. But in the morning, when the sunlight reached her through the foliage, she opened her eyes and saw the same green abyss from which she would probably never escape. She warmed up and then passed out again and suddenly came to with a definite sensation of lying right at the edge of the forest and feeling the free wind of the open fields on her face; she forced her sticky lids open and once more saw the same endless palisade of white birches retreating into green dusk and the quiet green vault above her. She closed her eyes and, after her weak agitation, again fell into oblivion....

Then thunder stirred her into awareness. She opened her eyes and saw that the sky had darkened; evening had set in again. But the approaching darkness no longer brought fear with it, or maybe she simply no longer had the strength to be afraid. It rumbled once more, so close that she felt the earth shudder beneath her. She guessed that it was a thunderstorm; she knew and feared thunderstorms. Panic-stricken, she convulsively tensed her whole body in an attempt to stand up and run, to hide somewhere, but she had no strength left to stand and there was nowhere to run. All she could do was shut her eyes tightly and curl herself into a tighter ball. Suddenly there was a booming crash right above her head like a crack in the vault of heaven, and it was as if the fissure released the dense deluge that now poured over the earth. Heavy cold lashes of water battered and flogged the little girl unmercifully and thoroughly soaked her jacket. The thunder was incessant. Through her closed eyelids she perceived the lightning as crimson flashes, as if a huge fire were raging around her. When it made a deafening crash and blazed close beside her, the little girl started and, propping herself up on one arm, held her swollen face to the rain; in a momentary dead flash of lightning she saw luminous and apparently motionless withes of rain among the white trees; then the dark, damp blackness banged shut over her again, she fell backwards and, with all feeling of life gone, remained lying there...

The thunderstorm started in the evening. Rain fell to earth in an unbroken stream, and the earth, as if choking with the abundance of moisture, couldn't manage to absorb and drink it all in; hollows drowned in the stagnant overflow from the flood, and seething torrents rushed down to the river from the mountain slopes and narrow valleys, the slanting roads and village street, and both sides of Fire Mountain. Violet flashes of lightning flogged the ceaselessly rumbling stormy blackness; they blazed overhead, blazed on all sides, and glittered even on the ground. The air began to smell of sulphur. Human life seemed paltry and helpless in the fiery eddies of the electrical avalanche rolling across the earth. God knows where the free dumb children of nature hid and kept safe on nights like this, where the forest birds spent such nights, but people hid in their houses, closed the dampers of their stoves, slammed the shutters over their windows, and recalled words of prayer. Lightning struck the substation, and the electricity went off. Without bright electric light, the cottages began to seem like caves, dark and scary; some folks had kept kerosene lamps with three-quarter-inch wicks, others had candles; when they were lit, in the weak light to which their eyes had long since grown unaccustomed (the young people had never gotten used to weak light), in the dim light of those antediluvian lanterns, human life seemed to revert to fifty, to a hundred years ago. Gloomy shadows swayed on the walls; a spidery semidarkness wavered under the ceiling and in far corners, and in the yellow kerosene light, people's faces, with their sharp shadows and dark eyesockets, seemed changed beyond recognition; they looked timid and dim. The torrent of water roared beyond the cottage walls; amid the dense deluge the cottages stood like isolated islets remote from one another; and beyond the villages, just like a hundred years ago, there were wild forests, deserted fields, and distant mountains, and you couldn't imagine a living soul out there. But somewhere in their forest cabins or plank wagons the herdsmen were not asleep, and someone on horseback was riding down the road late, afraid of the lightning and thinking dark thoughts about the uncertainty of human life. Somewhere in the mountains young boys and girls, harvest workers, huddled close to each other in their wet tents and, drowning their terror in affected gaiety or perhaps roused to a joyous

excitement by the sharp, shivery sensation of the riot of the heavenly elements, sang songs and told funny stories. And somewhere in the forest
the lost girl strayed. Many people had troubled thoughts; in their hearts
many of them felt something like pangs of conscience (here I am, where
it's warm, and she's out there in the storm; what's it like for her?), but
only for a short time, because they didn't have the strength to imagine the
girl in the woods at that hour—it seemed incredible, unthinkable; therefore they clung eagerly to the same easy thought, "She must have been
carried off."

The most disagreeable and annoying part of it, especially for the
young, was the lack of television. After all, today they were broadcasting
the sixth episode of "Stirlitz"; it had left off at a very interesting place. No
movie was showing at the club, there were no dances. A few youngsters,
driven out into the rain by the boredom of the evening, gathered at the
club that night; they passed the time under cover on the porch and swapped
jokes as they waited for the lights to come on—then they gave up and
went their separate ways home.

On this troubled stormy night, shaken out of their customary way of life
with electric lights and the television screen that for them was like a window on the world, people marveled that there was a time, just twenty years
ago, when they had managed without electricity, without television, and
even without radio. And now the storm damaged the thin line that brought
to their village the force called current and light, which nobody understood but everybody had long since gotten used to, and life seemed to
have reverted to the troubled dusk of the past. So they never learned what
happened to Stirlitz that night, and Aunty Khalima went to bed without
her evening tea—she was out of gas, and the electric hotplate wouldn't
work without current, of course; she would have heated up the samovar
that was standing forgotten in the hall, but it turned out that there was no
coal in the stove. The storm raged all night, shaking the cottages with a
brittle crackling and disturbing people's dreams with flashes of white fire
which reached the brain even through closed eyelids. By morning it had
moved east to the steppe regions and a quiet, dreary rain, as cold as autumn,
began pattering. In the morning the chilled, waterlogged world looked
gray and sad. Old folks said they couldn't recall such a storm. People with
learning explained that there were flares on the sun right now; that was
why, they said, electricity was raging on earth. But the old folk had their
own explanation. The sun had nothing to do with it, they said; it's the fault
of the atom because that very atom ruined the whole sky, there was a dry
spell for two years running and rain poured all summer because of the
atom, so the atom has caused all our woes, it's getting us into a real fix.

As usual Ilyasov was at headquarters by eight o'clock. The chairman of the village council, Iskhakov Rais, was waiting for him on the porch. They shook hands, and Rais began by saying that he'd called the police again; they promised to come today, but they couldn't guarantee results because the dog wouldn't be able to find a trail after such a rain; a good dog, it turns out, finds the trail eight hours afterwards at most if, of course, the trail hasn't been trampled or washed out by rain, and the little girl had been in the woods for three days already.

To tell the truth, due to the bad weather and the problems connected with it, the girl wasn't so much forgotten as somehow relegated to second place. Besides, Ilyasov was comforted by the convenient thought that the little girl must have been carried off anyway.

They went upstairs to the second floor as they talked.

"So why are they coming if they can't guarantee results?"

"They say that it's necessary to know the exact direction the little girl took. After all, she's probably worn out by now, she can't shout and is lying in the grass somewhere, if she's still alive after the storm. So a person could walk past her and not spot her, but a dog might run across her. But in any case there's not much hope for the dog; we need to organize people for a search, we need a truck."

Party organizer Nail was waiting for them in the chairman's office. He was sitting sullen and pale (for some reason he always turned pale when he went to see Ilyasov), prepared for some tough talk. About the little girl, of course, and about the truck. He was, you see, the only one whose heart ached for the girl, and that despot Ilyasov Marat, who was an outsider, didn't give a damn. "As if I needed the trucks for myself! I'll give you trucks today; I can give them because the trucks are free today, and I have the right to give them," thought Ilyasov, shaking the party organizer's hand heartily and, turning to Rais, said, "Will two trucks do?"

"I think so. In this weather we'll do well to round up enough people to fill two trucks," answered Rais.

"Then here's how we'll do it: we'll give you the high-sided truck that carries fertilizer to the supply depot and the Syrtlan truck," said Ilyasov, looking at Nail as if he were seeking his advice. Then he turned back to Rais: "Pick up tarps at the warehouse, or people will be soaked to the skin." He sat down at his desk and asked Nail, but in a different tone now, "Did you phone about the lights?"

"I called the substation. Lightning struck the post between Sovkhoz and Rudnik, and lines are broken at other points as well," Nail answered calmly; his face had softened and regained its color. But Ilyasov guessed that the party organizer was not very happy that a clash had been avoided and he hadn't had to do battle for justice. Be that as it may, they would be working together for some years, and they would have to adapt and learn to work well together, and overall Nail wasn't a bad fellow. "They promised light by afternoon."

"They always promise light by afternoon," Ilyasov grinned.

"I won't stay for the planning meeting then, I'll go and round up some people."

"Find the time to stop by the fodder plant and see if they've finished the foundation for the feed mixer."

After Rais and the party organizer left, the specialists arrived for the planning session, although there wouldn't be much to plan today. Even those who rarely showed up at headquarters on clear days—mechanics and sawmill workers—looked in; Ilyasov didn't know many of them. Minister honored them as always with all his decorations and his field satchel at his side. They sat and considered what could be done without electricity in the gloomy rough weather. The supply depot was at a standstill, and the garage, too. And then, either from the boredom and exasperation provoked by the weather or from idleness, they began to talk about various shortcomings and shifted to criticism. They recalled everything that was wrong and mismanaged, which on ordinary days they didn't give a thought to or were silent about altogether. Things are out of whack on the collective farm; life is haywire, our work is slipshod, we don't take care of our machinery. We should build a shed to store the combines. Never mind the shed, there's no garage for the tractors. We abandon our machines in the fields, that's what! The seed drill is standing in one spot, and the harrows are rusting in another. A steel hay sweep's been lying around the chicken farm since last year, right out on the road; everybody goes by and sees it, and nobody picks it up, but next winter we'll be out searching for it under the snow. They say it used to be considered sabotage if a collective-farm horse got its neck chafed; you paid a fine, and they could even put you in jail, but now any drunken fool can get on the tractor and break the machinery—and nobody touches him.

Bit by bit they recalled another story which had become a joke on the collective farm. Big bosses were supposed to pass through the region, and preparations were underway to receive them. People were taken off work and things were being cleaned up, especially along the road that they assumed the bosses would take. God forbid that there should be a broken or discarded piece of machinery standing anywhere or any ironmongery and junk lying around. Last spring they had left a four-base plow at the foot of Maximov Mountain, on the shoulder of the road; the rains came, the plow was covered with mud washed down from the plowed land, and then the mud dried out and hardened and grass grew over it, but the upper part of the plow was still in plain sight. That would never do, the bosses would see it. It had to be pulled out. But how? It was awkward hooking the plow to a tractor, they started pulling it on a cable, the cable broke, and the plow never budged. Then Chairman Shakirov, Ilyasov's predecessor, said, "We'll bury it—and that'll take care of it; afterwards we'll find a way to dig it out." They brought in a bulldozer and buried it, the bosses took another road, and it was autumn before they remembered the plow...

Or take electricity. Every storm means an outage. For three days the collective goes without light. The shop comes to a halt, the farms stop, the milking is done by hand. And in winter? Every icy spell means another outage. On the farm the cows go hungry, calves kick off, piglets freeze, heating batteries burst in the school, and the bosses at headquarters sit around in sheepskin coats.

"This is already the seventh outage this year!" Minister, who had long been straining his deaf ears and listening attentively to the speeches at the spontaneous meeting, suddenly interjected, slapping his satchel: "I've noted it all down." And concluded, "There's nobody in charge, that's the problem."

"The Rural Energy Trust is in charge of the electricity," said head engineer Atnabaev, without even a glance at Minister.

"And who's in charge here? You should be in charge. Just go and make your demands of the trust like a real man in charge, understood?"

"Understood, understood."

"Understood your ass!"

"The line must be twenty years old already, it's all rusty, rotted, and rickety, there's a short circuit if the wind barely shakes the wire, never mind lightning," Atnabaev went on, not at all offended by Minister's curses.

"You think we don't make demands?" intervened Ilyasov. "We've done so much talking on that score at the bureau, at plenums, we've written so many papers..."

"Then you've made your demands badly. You're only bold with the women here—and there you probably sit and breathe out your ass or read from your little piece of paper! Or am I wrong?"

"What you say is right, Khafiz-agai; you're right. Just save some of it for the meeting," agreed Ilyasov.

"I have enough left for the meeting, enough for ten meetings; I've noted it all down," Minister slapped his field satchel again. "Only we shouldn't be wagging our tongues here, but going about our business.

Here we sit, preaching to the wind, and there's a little girl perishing in the woods!"

"We're searching... We're organizing people now... I already allotted two trucks. And the police are coming with a dog..."

"A lot you'll carry on two trucks! You should organize all available transport, you should raise the entire village, everybody, big and little. That swampy forest is tens of kilometers across; a child there is like a grain of sand. You should comb every inch of the woods and search day and night. And don't pin your hopes on the dog. It's the third day already, so it won't be able to pick up the trail."

"We already combed the area; we didn't find her."

"You searched the wrong spot then. If you drop a coin on the floor, where do you search? It'll roll off to the side without fail. It's the same with a person in the woods. He gets turned around; if he isn't following a road, he keeps heading to one side. Did you ever go on the attack? You didn't. But I did. You have to search the way you attack. You have to rouse everybody as if for war! Understood?"

"There's no war now. That was another time, another way of thinking," objected Atnabaev.

"I don't agree," Minister's face had turned crimson from excitement, and the stubble on his cheeks became even whiter. "For us every day is war!"

"O.K. now, comrades!" Ilyasov interrupted loudly, letting it be understood that he didn't want to hear any more of Minister's eloquence, which he, like many others in the village, didn't take seriously. "Let's get down to talking about work."

They came to this decision. The third and fourth brigades would continue laying in silage; a truck would be sent to the mountains for the youth brigade, to keep them from getting soaked while there was nothing to do. The builders would keep on working. As soon as the lights came on, the mechanics would be back in the shops.

You could cut the smoke in the room with a knife. On ordinary days Ilyasov didn't allow smoking in his office, but today everything was haywire, and again it began to seem to him that the collective had become unmanageable, that once again, "Nothing goes right, boys!"

They dispersed about ten o'clock. Afterwards from his window Ilyasov saw the police arrive in their jeep. One of them went into the village council, and half an hour later two high-sided trucks stopped at headquarters. People were sitting in the back under a long tarp. Nail jumped out of the cab, Rais and the policeman left the council, and the party organizer got into the police truck. The trucks moved off, and Rais stood for a while on the porch and then, making his way around puddles, strode off toward his house.

Minister went around the village. He decided to cover the entire village, visit every house, and rouse people to search for the little girl. His first stop was at the house of his neighbor Akhmatvali, the veterinarian, who had a horse to ride and a motorcycle. If he was busy, he could send his youngest son. An old Zaporozhets was standing in the veterinarian's yard, a sign that his brother-in-law had come from the state farm. It turned out to be right—the two, with sweat pouring off them and well mellowed, sat at the table dragging out a leisurely chat; Akhmatvali's wife, also red in the face, was pouring tea. Akhmatvali, who was a gentle, jolly man of forty, treated Minister amicably with just a touch of mockery. He was a good neighbor; he rushed to help whenever needed, and never refused requests for help...

"Come join us, Khafiz-agai." His bright gray eyes tipsy, he invited Minister to join them. His neighbor Khatizha set another cup on the tray.

"No, no thanks. I can't stay," Minister had already realized that he wouldn't get anything sensible out of the veterinarian. "Is your son home?"

"He and the boys went on a vacation to Iremel. Why do you want him?" Khatizha was curious.

"What do you mean, why? We have to search for herdsman Faizulla's daughter. I want to round up as many people as I can and go into the woods."

"You're on a wild-goose chase, Khafiz-agai. Let the bosses worry about it," said Akhmatvali. "Besides, who'll go into the woods in this rain?"

"They searched already and didn't find her. They say she was carried off in a car," said Khatizha. "Join us, why are you standing by the door?"

Without a word Minister left and turned in at the next house. Vakkas, a mechanic, also had a motorcycle. Vakkas had just finished steaming to his heart's content in the bath and lay on his featherbed with a towel across his chest.

"That's a good one, Khafiz-agai! How can I go off into the woods after a bath?" said Vakkas, panting. "It's a lost cause. The army's what they need, they should appeal to the soldiers stationed in the mountains. A regiment of soldiers—and you could comb every inch of the woods, if, of course, the little girl is really lost and didn't drive off with some stranger."

The next man, the young peasant Yulai, was hacking away with an ax in his backyard, building a bathhouse. He wouldn't even stop to talk to Minister.

"What's that? Don't bother me. You can see I'm busy."

Minister skipped the house of two pensioners. He went to see herdsman Fuat. Fuat himself was in the pasture, but his son Rifat was sitting in the main room.

"No, no, he has no time! He's studying for the institute. He's slogging away at his textbooks day and night; how can I send him out in the woods in the rain," Rifat's mother, Zakiya, clucked. "I'm sorry for the girl, of course, but what can we do? We can't abandon everything and rush off into the woods, can we?"

After he'd been to a dozen more houses, Minister realized that he wasn't going to rouse anybody. They were all good people, everybody was sorry for the girl, but nobody wanted to go out and search, or rather they couldn't go. Maybe some sort of order or directive was needed? And then Minister decided to go to regional headquarters, to the boss, to Latypov himself. "We'll have to rouse the region," he thought.

Until eleven Ilyasov kept busy with various papers and made phone calls; then he went home for lunch. It was still raining—at times a fine watery powder, at others a dense noisy deluge, during which the thick lines of large drops falling vertically intersected the spidery threads of the slanting drizzle and formed what looked like a watery net hanging from the sky to the earth. Wet gray-black clouds hung so low that their tousled tresses covered not only the spine of Uraltau, but the tops of the lower mountains around it as well. The street was soggy, and a large pool of water was spreading by the headquarters building.

Ilyasov lived in a brick building that had two apartments built by the collective farm to house visiting specialists. At home he hurriedly drank his tea and then made his way through the sticky mud to his dilapidated jeep and drove out to the brigades and farms. There was the telephone, of course, but Ilyasov never trusted phone conversations; if you weren't on the spot to plague and goad people, they'd use the rain as an excuse to take the day off, heat their baths, and start in on the liquor. Besides, he'd gotten the idea of trying to run the milking machines off the Belarus tractor. When he arrived at the third brigade, everything was as dead as if a universal disaster had occurred instead of rain and a power outage. He went to see Amirkhanov, the chief of the third farm, and consulted him about the Belarus. Amirkhanov scratched the back of his head and said, "Let's give it a try." They hunted down the tractor driver and brought the tractor back to the farm. They connected it to the milking unit, but the tractor didn't generate enough power. In short, nothing goes right, boys.

Totally unnerved, Ilyasov returned to the farm center, sat for a while at headquarters waiting for a call from the bosses, and then called the substation himself. They were fixing the line and promised that the current would be back on any time now. It was midday already, and "any time" would probably be evening—in short, the day was already wasted. Exhausted and hungry, he went home, to the solitude in which his preoccupation and constant nervous strain turned into depression and impotent rancor. When his wife and daughter were at Ilyasov's side, they had ways of distracting and reassuring him, but now he could only languish in an empty apartment, and in the gloomy rough weather besides!

He lit the gas in the kitchen, put a pan full of water on the burner, and found some macaroni in the cupboard. Just then there was a knock at the door, and someone stamped his feet in the entry.

"Is the master at home?" said Rais loudly, coming into the room.

Rais lived in the next apartment. He had turned his house over to his married son and had moved into an empty official apartment while he was building himself a new place.

"He's at home, he's at home, come right in," responded Ilyasov, wondering why the chairman of the village council was honoring him with his presence.

Ilyasov had long taken a guarded interest in Rais. At times Rais struck him as being expansive, genial, and a bit simple, but at other times he seemed like a man with an eye to his own interests who adroitly played the simpleton, ingratiating himself with the new chairman almost as a friend, but in secret actually having a far from flattering opinion of him. "We'll live to see what kind of chairman you make," the amused eyes of the village-council chairman sometimes seemed to say.

"Come join us, neighbor. My brother's here from town," said Rais.

Ilyasov didn't want to go; going meant drinking with the guest. After his cure he had promised himself and sworn to his wife that he would never take even a drop of liquor, whether he was on holiday, out visiting, or at home. And especially here, in a new place, a strange village.

"Thanks, but I won't. I don't drink, you know."

"Who says you're obliged to drink? You'll keep us company and have a talk with my brother. We're not great drunkards either," insisted Rais. "Or is it the custom in your village to turn down invitations?"

No, in his native village, as in other Bashkir villages, refusing an invitation was not acceptable. It was taken for lack of respect; it might be thought that the person being invited disdained those who invited him. If he didn't go, Rais would think that the new chairman scorned his company, and he, Ilyasov, had to live and work with Iskhakov. Besides at home he would have a fit of the blues and have to fix himself a meal as well. "I'll go and be sociable for a while," thought Ilyasov. "At least I'll eat. And maybe by then the current will be back on." He turned off the gas and went to Rais's apartment.

Iskhakov's brother was just as big-boned and fat-faced as Rais himself. Eyes that were just as black and had the same sly squint glanced at Ilyasov in curiosity and appraisal as they shook hands and muttered their names. The brother wore a nice suit, so it was hard to tell from his appearance whether he was a boss, engineer, or worker.

Rais opened a bottle and, tipping it over the glass standing in front of Ilyasov, said, "I'll pour you a hundred grams anyway, neighbor. Whether you drink it or not is up to you."

Rais's wife, Saniya-apai, put a large skillet of fried fish on the table. The brothers drank up and started eating. The talk at the table as always began with trifling matters. Rais said that here they were living by a river, and yet they ate fish bought at the store. Nobody knew where it was caught, all they knew was that it was called "hake," and yet, there was a time when they caught pike, ide, bream, and chub in their own river. Whatever happened to them? Even the gudgeon were gone now. Gradually the talk switched to the collective farm and management matters. Rais's brother wanted to know why the collective farm didn't turn a profit; he insisted, even demanded, that they explain it to him understandably and without wasting words.

"I don't know," Ilyasov avoided a direct answer. He had his own opinion about the collective farm's unprofitability. "You'd do better to talk to our economist; he could explain to you what our purchase prices are, how much we pay the state for a kilogram of forage grain, what the land structure of the collective is, how many head of cattle we have, how many 'menials' "...

"What menials?"

"Menials are our name for head of cattle that are not on the books," Ilyasov answered, thinking rancorously: What the hell possessed me to start jabbering with you! "For instance, there are 400 cows on forage at the farm, but only 300 on the books, and the plan takes only those 300 into account. Well, you can see for yourself, that raises the figures for milk yield. You don't get it? Well, how can I explain it... After all, we can't go on increasing the number of cattle forever, our resources are limited. And there's no milk without fodder, so that's how we keep out of the hole."

"That means, you chisel on the figures."

"Why is it chiseling? We fulfill the plan," said Ilyasov, glancing belligerently at Rais's brother. "You don't get it?"

"I asked you why the collective doesn't turn a profit, and you go on at me about some menials or other." The guest wouldn't let up.

"Azat, leave the man alone," intervened Rais. "I'll give you an answer, and it's a simple one: our collective farm doesn't turn a profit because we work badly. That's all there is to it."

"What your brother says is right: we work badly. People don't take a responsible attitude to work; it's as if they weren't farmers but daylaborers," Ilyasov agreed. "Now I remember my father. He used to gulp down some leftover sour noodles, belch, and go to work. No complaints, no demands, and not a word about getting his kilograms in the fall. Some years he did, some years he sweated and only got chaff. Old Minister was right when he said that we used to sing when we worked on the collective farm. And now? Two days ago I went to visit the youth brigade: some of them were working halfheartedly, and the others were busy with a hot card game. Yesterday I met a healthy lad on the street and I asked him why he wasn't at work. And he set a condition to me: "When there's koumiss in the fields, then I'll go." Ilyasov thought of telling them about Faizulla the herdsman and his missing daughter, but he kept silent; he didn't want to get started on that disagreeable story. "So that's the way we work."

"It all depends on leadership," muttered Rais, chewing his fish. "Someone has to take charge."

"Eh, if everything were only that simple! That's at the heart of it: it doesn't all depend on leadership. They talk about it all the time now, the newspapers keep writing about the boss, the boss, but there are a lot of bosses above that boss. With big briefcases. They give him directions and orders, they flay him alive: 'Fulfill the plan,' 'produce,' but he can't expect help from anyone. For instance, we have an endless problem with spare parts. The regional committee doesn't give us any, nor does the Agricultural Directorate or the Agricultural Machinery Trust. You have to jump around like a flea on a hot skillet to get even a bearing. We go to Kazakhstan, we take them lumber and boards, and in return we get a few measly gears..."

"Just the same, ninety percent of it depends on leadership," interrupted Rais. "The late Khudaibirdin was a peasant without much education, but he did great things for the collective farm after the war, because he was a real boss. But you've had five years of learning—to teach you to use your wits instead of complaining."

That came very close to a direct attack. Rais was telling him to his face that he was a bad chairman. Something in Ilyasov's mood broke and disintegrated: they invite you over and then start badgering you. He thought about leaving, but that would offend his host, and he didn't want to quarrel with him. In his rancor and depression, with a feeling like despair in his heart, he unexpectedly, even for himself, picked up the glass, drank, and instantly got drunk, as if he'd fallen into a pit. And they went on talking drunkenly and chaotically. Ilyasov abjectly tried to prove to Rais and his brother that it didn't all depend on him, the chairman; it wasn't his fault that the collective farm had no electricity, the Agricultural Machinery Trust wouldn't give him a crane to unload the feed mixer, and there were no spare parts and the granulator at the supply depot hadn't been repaired.

Then somebody else arrived. It turned out to be Rais's brother-in-law from the Yaik Collective Farm. He'd driven over in his Zhiguli to ask them to his house.

"I've come to pick you up, get ready. Farida has made stuffed meat pastries and expects you."

Ilyasov tried to make his escape, but they wouldn't hear of it.

"Rais's guest is my guest," declared the brother-in-law. "What's a man to do in this weather? Pay visits and drink vodka, that's all."

The five of them piled into the car and drove to the next village, part of the Yaik Collective Farm, ten kilometers away from the Beacon. Ilyasov and Rais's brother went on quarreling about the same things: the collective farm, its unprofitability and shortcomings. Rais and his brother-in-law took the side of their guest from town. And the guest turned out to be altogether addled, he wouldn't let up on Ilyasov and, fixing his lackluster, crazed eyes on him, kept repeating: "Menials, you say, figures, you say, and it's all because of people like you that I have to feed on margarine."

"From your paunch nobody would guess you feed on margarine," parried Ilyasov.

"You leave my paunch alone!" Rais's brother grabbed Ilyasov by the lapels and stared dully at him.

"Azat, you're at it again! Leave the man alone," shouted Rais and said to Ilyasov, "Don't be offended, he's a good fellow, but as soon as he's had a drink he has to pick on somebody."

But Ilyasov was offended, offended by everyone he'd talked with around the table; he tore loose from Azat's hands, pushed him aside forcefully, and walked off down the street heading home on foot right then and there. He dimly remembered walking in the rain, tramping through puddles, scooping up mud into his ankle boots, shuffling down the street of the strange village, and trying to find the road that led back home; then he blacked out, and when he came to, he found himself, damp and chilled, lying on a bench outside somebody's gate. He had sobered up somewhat, but his whole body was seized by unbearable shivering, a disgusting nausea rose in his throat, the calves of his legs cramped spasmodically, his heart would throb fiercely and then suddenly stop as if it had got stuck, and Ilyasov felt that if he didn't have another drop right away, he'd die on the spot. He couldn't go back to the house of Rais's brother-in-law; they could all go to hell, all those Raises and their brothers! Ilyasov glanced around and saw a brick building with large windows across the street. Ah, it was the grocery store. Behind the glass something white stirred in the dark depths—it was the saleswoman in her white coat. Ilyasov fumbled in his pockets—not a ruble. He tramped through the puddles to the store and went in. The saleswoman, stout and ruddy cheeked, was weighing rice for an old woman. Bright bottles stood on the shelves. Ilyasov marked time at the counter, pretending to search for money and, when the old woman finally left, he appealed timidly to the saleswoman, "Apai, can you give me vodka on credit until tomorrow? I'll bring the money in the morning.... I'm the chairman of the Beacon."

"We don't sell on credit!" the saleswoman replied categorically, scrutinizing the damp, rumpled, wretched stranger with mocking contempt. "How come the chairman of the Beacon suddenly takes a notion to buy vodka from us on credit?"

"You don't believe me?"

Of course, the question was idiotic: why should she believe him when she didn't know him? Was she supposed to be able to tell by his dark blue jacket and skewed tie that he was a chairman? And even if the saleswoman did know Ilyasov, she still wouldn't have given him credit. She told him so, "It doesn't make any difference whether I believe you or not, I don't give credit anyway."

"What's wrong with you, for God's sake! I'll leave you my jacket and tomorrow morning..."

"I have no use for your jacket."

"You won't give me any then?"

"No, I won't!"

Ilyasov left the store. It was still pouring. The soggy road and its muddy puddles had a doleful appearance. If only somebody would come by, if only some loser would come to the store, he could flog his jacket for a three-spot, have a drink, warm up, and deaden his nausea, and he didn't even want to think about what he would do after that. He was in a dreary, vile mood from the realization that he, Ilyasov Marat, had fallen off the wagon, that he was a mediocre man with no willpower—as his wife said, a weak character. That was why he was a bad chairman; after all Iskhakov Rais thought he was a bad chairman, and that meant everyone else did too. It all made him want to die somewhere in a deserted field and let the ravens peck his eyes out....

Ilyasov plodded down the street. He kept walking, not caring where he went, slipping and sliding, scooping liquid mud into his boots and getting his trousers dirty. He wondered in passing when there would finally be clean asphalt on the village streets, which looked like a swampy marsh whenever it rained, but at that moment the thought seemed vain and futile to him, and he began thinking instead about how worthless he was and what a failure.

Outside the village a black Volga came up behind him. Ilyasov stopped, turned toward the car, and even started to raise his hand, but then he changed his mind: the bosses usually rode in a black Volga. The car braked as it came abreast of him. Through the rain-fogged windshield, across which the wipers crawled, Ilyasov made out a heavy face under the hard brim of a hat pulled down over the forehead, and it looked very familiar to him. When the car stepped on the gas and, instead of stopping, drove on, Ilyasov caught sight through the side window of the back of a solid authoritative head.

"Latypov," he guessed, hoping that it wasn't so. "Was it really him? It was, it was! Rushing somewhere. Did he recognize me or didn't he? Of course, he did. He didn't stop because he saw I was drunk. That's all we need—for the first secretary of the regional committee to start picking up drunken chairmen along the road."

In ten years the regional boss had changed three times. Yulaev replaced Gadelev, and then Latypov replaced Yulaev. Local wits said that Gadelev made a mess, Yulaev fidgeted, and Latypov was patching things up.*

"I'm done for!" thought Ilyasov, shuffling in the rain down the muddy road toward his village. "Done for!"

On Akbai hill a mini-Zhiguli picked him up—Saifullin, the son of the garage chief, was coming from town to visit his family. With a sense of catastrophe and a feeling that his whole life was crashing down around him, Ilyasov arrived home, went inside, threw off his damp, muddy clothes, lay down on the sofa, and stayed there all evening. He didn't think or wish for anything; he just had the sensation, resembling a critical illness, that he was done for. Then he dozed off, falling into a restless sleep, and woke only towards morning. Before him arose first secretary Latypov's heavy face and the authoritarian back of his head—Ilyasov no longer doubted that it was Latypov he had met on the road. The morning to come was going to be very disagreeable. He drank some water from the teapot and lay down again.

---

*Puns in Russian: Gadelev made a mess [gadil], Yulaev fidgeted [iulil], and Latypov was patching things up [lataet].

Yes, he had bad luck, all his life he had had bad luck. When he was a student at the agricultural academy, he nursed naive dreams of getting his diploma, returning to his native village and showing them what he, Ilyasov Marat, was capable of. After all, you'd think that as young specialists with higher education replaced the semi-literate old chairmen, things could be managed scientifically, risks could be taken. Yet he became instantly bogged down in daily squabbles; he was caught up and carried along by the customary routine of the old life in all its laxity, fiscal irresponsibility, indolence, and indifference. When he tried to be independent and enterprising, the comrades with big briefcases told him, "You're still young, don't take so much on yourself" or "You think you're the only smart one, and we're all sitting here like fools?" Besides, half the village were relatives and friends; everybody asked him to visit, made him welcome, sat him in the place of honor, and waited on him. It was a while before Ilyasov caught on that it wasn't him, Ilyasov Marat, they loved, but the boss, and that the people around him were not friends, but toadies, and not relatives, but rogues, unexposed crooks and pilferers. And by the time he began to realize, it was too late. So they transferred him here, to the Beacon Collective Farm. A strange village where you didn't know the people and you didn't know the resources. Everybody looked at you with an expression that as much as said, "We'll see what kind of big shot you are." Or it was "every stovemender, forester and horse doctor." Party organizer Nail and chairman of the village council Iskhakov Rais seemed to be working in harness with you, but you had no way of knowing what went on in their hearts and minds. He was a foreigner to them, a "Varangian." And most distressing of all—everything went wrong, one thing after another. You finished slapping a half-assed patch over one hole, and another spot opened up. It was harvest time, they should be going all out to finish mowing, and now there was the bad weather and the breakdown of the transmission lines. They had to get the farms ready for winter; a feed mixer had been brought at last for the fourth brigade, but there was no crane to unload it. And there was the little girl... Who knows, if the collective farm had gotten that feed mixer two years earlier, the little girl's mother would probably be alive today, and the girl wouldn't be an orphan and might not have gotten lost in the woods. Ilyasov tried to comfort himself, however, with the thought that there was no link between his life and work and the fact that the little girl was missing, but all the same... And one way or another he always fell down on the job and ended up in disgrace. What would happen now? Would they transfer him again? What was he going he tell his wife?

In the morning, suffering from a headache and depression, Ilyasov drank some strong tea and went to headquarters anyway. He came into his office like a stranger. In his thoughts and emotions he was no longer chairman; it was useless and foolish to think of work and plunge into the problems of the new day. Nail the party organizer came in and as always shook his hand. Ilyasov didn't need to ask whether they'd found the little girl—it was clear from Nail's face that they hadn't; and in general it was only a fleeting, momentary thought. Worrying about the girl had become a secondary consideration to Ilyasov. He got through the planning session somehow, glowering at the specialists; he talked about work, but it was all like a dream. He was waiting for the thunderclap, for disgrace.

At ten o'clock the phone rang. With a sinking heart Ilyasov picked up the receiver and heard Latypov's heavy bass: "Latypov. How's it going there?"

Ilyasov said that they had been idle all day yesterday due to the bad weather and the power outage.

"I know!" Latypov interrupted him in exasperation. "Let's not be so quick to blame the weather. And another thing: what's this about a little girl? Why am I the last to hear about it from your Minister?"

Ilyasov was silent for a minute, feeling his face burning, before replying: "Well, we searched for two days straight and didn't find her..."

"Didn't find her and forgot all about it. Organize the young people and the schoolchildren. I've made arrangements here to send the older kids from the Pioneer camp."

And he hung up.

For some time Ilyasov sat in a daze, digesting and analyzing the talk with Latypov. The last straw was that the man had talked to him without a single word about yesterday. Ilyasov was well acquainted with the first secretary's character. If he went for you immediately and tore you to shreds, you'd get off easy, there wouldn't be any further complications or official follow-up. But if he kept silent, you could expect no mercy. If he hadn't shouted at Ilyasov now and brought up yesterday, the question would be decided at the bureau...

Ilyasov went to see the party organizer. He had never gone into the party organizer's office before, but now he went. And he told Nail about Latypov's call. They thought about it and decided to take the older schoolchildren off the job of weeding beets. They were living in a work camp seven kilometers from the village; right now on account of the bad weather, they were moping in their tents, of course. The bus that carried milkmaids to the summer farm would be sent after them, and today the milkmaids would go to work in the high-sided truck.

An hour later Pioneers arrived from regional headquarters and, joining forces with the kids from the work camp, drove to the fourth brigade. As they were leaving, Ilyasov went over to the window and, through the windows of the city bus, dulled by rain, he made out Minister's red face with its white stubble...

They found the little girl. They found her only a month later, after they had lost all hope. To be more precise, they found her bones, five kilometers away from the village, not far from the second farm. Herdsman Sabit was picking raspberries and stumbled across the little girl's remains. She had crawled as far as some old mining slag heaps that lay along Dry Creek, but had evidently already been too weak to scrabble over them. If she had made it across those low hills, which were overgrown with an impenetrable thicket of alder and bird-cherry, she would have come out right where the herdsmen were. They identified her by her yellow jacket and rubber boots. Both boots were for the same foot.

Translated by Mary Fleming Zirin

Originally published in *Oktiabr*, April 1987.

VIKTOR EROFEYEV
THE PARAKEET

In response to your inquiry, most esteemed Spiridon Yermolaevich, to wit: what fate has been determined for your son, Yermolai Spiridonovich Spirkin, who compelled a dead bird to undertake unnatural flight, I shall not respond immediately. And why not? Because, my dear sir, I must admit I would be ashamed to do so. My bosom was rent with emotion as I read your petition, written in the blood of paternal feeling. You have disquieted me, Spiridon Yermolaevich, shattered me! Words cannot render the anguish you have unleashed upon me, only the howl of the beast. However, I harbor no complaint against you. I sensed in my heart your paternal urge to defend your son, Yermolai Spiridonovich, before legal authority, implying in obscure words that your son, Yermolai Spiridonovich, was since his earliest youth possessed, as it were, of a mighty love for those of God's creatures capable of flight. I allow as to the correctness of your implication. I shall say even more. Every child is subject to a weakness for birds, capturing them in groves and forests, as well as in open fields and in gardens with snares, or buying them with their coppers at the bird market, in order to lock the bird in a cage, especially if it be a songbird. In such actions the law discerns nothing blameworthy and thus indulges them in their innocent amusements. And so, of course, it must be—there is a time and place for amusements, but world culture, most esteemed Spiridon Yermolaevich, is, in my most humble opinion, wont rather to think in *symbols,* the interpretation of which is a matter for learned men. Since ancient times, for example, there has been a fashion for divination by the entrails of birds that fly by. If, on the other hand, some living bird were to fly into a room of your house, be it no more than a goldfinch, would you be pleased at such a circumstance, Spiridon Yermolaevich? No, you would not be pleased at such a circumstance. And why not? You would not, I reply, because you would see that as a terrible *symbol.* I am prepared to recount any number of such scenes of human benightedness, but I strive, however, toward a conclusion that has direct bearing on your son, Yermolai Spiridonovich: the bird is a creature which disturbs the soul, the bird is a mysterious creature, not subject to our whims, and so any pranks with it are a bad business. And indeed, what sort of shenanigans is your little boy up to? He plays pranks! Yermolai Spiridonovich pleases to play pranks with a dead parakeet—an especially suspicious bird. The parakeet is a *symbol* in and of itself, and the devil himself couldn't figure out how to interpret it, inasmuch as all of world culture since its inception hasn't managed to do anything more than gossip about it as about some beloved idol. Moreover, it is an overseas bird. And you, Spiridon Yermolaevich, with such frivolousness as had better been applied elsewhere, scribble in your inquiry that your boy's amusement, so you say, was of an utterly innocent nature. Of small matter, you think! My son, you say, Yermolai Spiridonovich, took the eternally departed parakeet, nicknamed Semyon, climbed nimbly to the roof of your own home, which is located on Swan Street, and began tossing it upward, like Ivanushka the Fool, reckoning that the dead creature would, in its airy native venue, find a second breath, take wing and give a chirp, that is, in a certain sense, even be resurrected. Judging from your hasty words, there was in this deed of Yermolai Spiridonovich's more a want of consideration than any base design, more a surfeit of morbid fantasy, a weakening of nerves and trembling throughout the body, than any tidy plan and intrigue. Whereupon you, understandably indignant over his actions, volunteer to flog your boy, Yermolai Spiridonovich, with a lash and without any leniency. It's a clear case of paternal feelings! I repeat once again: we have no complaint against you, Spiridon Yermolaevich, on this account. You are an honorable man and for the time being you remain as such. But deign to understand us as well, we who have likewise served the fatherland all these many years, place yourself in my position, for example. Why, if such experiments were to become more frequent, what then? And what if the overseas trash were to ascend? According to the assurance of your mad son, Yermolai Spiridonovich, the bird did indeed flap its unclean wings a couple of times—that is, displayed a certain attempt at resurrection! Well, what if all of a sudden, contrary to our expectations, it up and actually was resurrected? In what terms would we explain this particular circumstance to our countrymen, so trusting in our best intentions? I become lost in fatal conjecture ...

WOULDN'T WE BE FINE FOOLS!

Eh! What's there to say! Your boy, Yermolai Spiridonovich, turned out to be of a delicate, one might even say frail, build. We were amazed. What had he become? Well, young man, I inquired of Yermolai Spiridonovich, having given him a good looking over, answer the question: with what intent did you dig the bird up from its place of interment, or, in other words, from the cesspool? Whatever in hell possessed you, we must ask, to exhume it? He answered meekly, but hurriedly and with undeniable courtesy, aiding himself in his answer with his little white hand, with his little hand, don't you know, he aided himself so that it would come out more accessibly. I went on the alert observing manners like these. I saw that not only his build, but his manners, too, are alien, mere civility and nothing more. You don't have a Yiddle in the woodpile with that one, do you Spiridon Yermolaevich? He kept trying to get me to understand, he aided himself, you see, with his little hand—a pretty sight, you might say. But the trick didn't work—this is not a circus! And I sit and note to myself: this pickle's not from our brine! And what did his words add up to? What sort of picture was taking shape? Tell the story, I say, from the very beginning, and don't wave your little white hand in front of my nose, I won't stand for it! He broke down into a profusion of excuses, as if I needed excuses from him, as if in offering these excuses of his he somehow came forward as my benefactor! But I keep silent. However, in the meantime, I ask him: so you, Yermolai Spiridonovich, wished to resurrect the bird, but this bird, according to competent witnesses, was already sorely afflicted by worms of the earth, didn't you notice? Worms as white as your little fingers? They clung all over it, just as the ants did, they partook of that feast... And could such a bird be resurrected? And how did you not recoil at taking it into your pampered hands? He answers, hanging his head: what about the Phoenix bird? I see, my dear sir, Spiridon Yermolaevich, that your boy, Yermolai Spiridonovich, is clever beyond his years. The Phoenix bird, indeed! From where, we ask, do you have knowledge about such a Phoenix bird; what is it, I ask? It, says he, was a certain red-feathered eagle that flew from Arabia to ancient Egypt; there it burned itself up alive after it had lived to the venerable age of five hundred years, and then it was reborn from its ashes, young and hale, hence worms are no obstacle here... He's managed that cleverly, I see. What, I ask, is the point of this fable about the red-feathered eagle? How, I continue the question, have you fallen into a life in which

you believe in heathen lore? He answers once again evasively: a fable, he
says, is meant to be wondrous. Don't you try to wriggle out of it, I tell him,
don't you keep denying it or, I'm telling you, I'll give you a fable you'll
never forget! Now, out with the whole truth, you hooligan! But, he
screamed with emotion, I'm telling you the pure and honest truth! And
again he fluttered his little hand. Well, God bless you, then: you talk, and we
shall sit and listen. Only don't get excited, don't scream. At whom, I say, are
you screaming? At whom, so to speak, are you raising your voice?! I,
Yermolai, could be your father, and you have taken it into your head to
scream at me! He is silent. He flushed. Could I, I ask, be your father, or
couldn't I? Why, he answers, couldn't you be? I am appealing to you just as
if you were my own father... See that, I think to myself, he is already calling
me his own father, squirming like a horny wench... There is more here than
meets the eye. I am curious: and this parakeet of yours, turquoise in hue,
nicknamed Semyon—is he, as I suspect, also some kind of *symbol,* or what?
Everything in world culture, Spiridon Yermolaevich, is *symbols,* nothing but
symbols, wherever you cast your glance, especially parakeets. And he, your
son, Yermolai Spiridonovich, in answer takes recourse to a childish lament,
relates the story, well known to us, of the death of the parakeet called
Semyon in the family of the physician to the boyars, Agafon Yelistratovich,
your neighbor on Swan Street, who purchased the overseas bird for the
amusement of his two small children: five-year-old Tatyana Agafonovna and
the three-year-old sniveler Ezdra Agafonovich; he purchased it, as was customary, at the bird market, from the Dutch merchant Van Zaam, or, as we
call him, Timofei Ignatievich. That merchant, Timofei Ignatievich, is in no
way remarkable, mild as he is of manner, except for a scar on his Dutch nose
which he received in our climes as a result of a minor scuffle with his wife. I
initiate you into these particulars so that you, Spiridon Yermolaevich, might
know that I work for the bread I eat: without the particulars you won't get
the picture, the more so if there is foul play. And so your neighbor, Agafon
Yelistratovich, purchased an overseas parakeet of diminutive stature, perhaps
for the sake of thrift, and it was christened Semyon. The bird was locked, as
was customary, in a cage. It was fed, from what Tatyana Agafonovna says,
with wheat. But that parakeet, known mournfully for its, thank God, unsuccessful resurrection, resolutely refused to eat the wheat or other sundry
feed, flouted its overseas airs, and, despite the children's ministrations,
started to die, by reason of a voluntary hunger strike. On the third day
Semyon died to the general lament of Tatyana Agafonovna and Ezdra
Agafonovich, the three-year-old sniveler: which villain still does not talk, or
pretends not to. The agony lasted three and a half hours, during the afternoon, and ended with the natural death of the bird.

In such terms does your son, Yermolai Spiridonovich, relate this story, whereupon he turns into its principal personage. But not all at once. As was cutomary, after the bird's death, its burial service was conducted in the cesspool, in order that infection not be spread. At the burial there gathered a small crowd of twenty-six snouts, drawn by the yelps of the physician's juvenile spawn. As was related by Yermolai Spiridonovich, who himself took part in the funeral procession in the capacity of an observer, he passed the night before the procession in auditory hallucinations, in spite of the boyar physician Agafon Yelistratovich's having pledged to his children to buy them as replacement for the defunct parakeet something even more amusing, such as a goat. In the morning Yermolai Spiridon-ovich left home with the firmly set intention of rescuing the bird from its cold grave when it was drizzling, increasing the amount of mud on the streets, and Mam'selle Shchelgunov from the window of her parental home, during a break between her harp-playing lessons, distinctly saw your son, Yermolai Spiridonovich, scrabbling with his fingernails to take the parakeet from the cesspool, his appearance recalling nothing so much as a mangy cat, she said, with a hankering to treat itself to some dainty morsels of carrion. The following disgrace is somewhat familiar to you, my dear Spiridon Yermolaevich, judging by your thoughtless question, one surprising coming from a man in the service. How ever did you con-trive to raise a madman, and one who subsequently came to be a real trou-blemaker into the bargain! How? About this you keep silent, supplicating for your son, but I would like to know, as a lesson for others. For I imme-diately grasped, as soon as he came before me, that he was not at all our sort, however much he might pretend, and I said to him, when he fin-ished: and now, boy, let's have the whole truth. And he lips back at me that that's it, he says, that *is* the whole truth! Shall we then make a wager, I say, that that is not all? My young stalwarts are standing in the doorway, in their red caps, grinning. Hey, I say, don't be so quick, you jokers, to bare your teeth, maybe the young man will change his mind, will even win a hundred rubles from me with an honorable discharge thrown in. Uh-uh, my stalwarts shake their heads, he won't win, he's an out-and-out pre-varicator, wherever he came from. Shut up, I say, don't give me your pre-mature judgments!—and I turn to your son, the dear youth, moving up close: Have the guts for this, Yermolayushka? Yermolai says to me, recoil-ing: I have nothing more to say. I told you everything. But, believe me, I did nothing wrong... It turns out, then, that it was some sort of childish tantrum that made you decide to dig up the bird, is that so, Yer-molayushka? You dug up the bird and nimbly hopped up onto the roof. And whispered tenderly: Fly, my Semyon! Fly, my little pigeon! And Semyon the worm-eaten turquoise parakeet flapped his turquoise wings, flapped a couple of times in blind hope of returning to his former life... "And here," I said then, angry now, "here you are, Yermolayushka, here you have a *SYMBOL!*" "There's no *symbol* here!" wailed your son, that silly goose, Yermolai Spiridonovich, "there's none!" "Now you just go and tell that story to somebody else..." "Why is it," Yermolai Spiridonovich replies to me, "that you imagine *symbols* appearing everywhere?" I fell silent and stared piercingly at that youngster of yours, Spiridon Yermolaevich, and after wiping my bald spot with a napkin, I answered, "They appear to me, my fine Yermolai Spiridonovich, because world culture, may the Lord forgive me, since its very birth, as the wisest of men assure us, has been stuffed with *symbols,* and there's no way for us, no matter how hard we try, to spring ourselves from that cage!" And I struck him, your brown-eyed boy, right in the teeth with all my soul, because I'd grown weary, I took preventive measures, but my fist...well, you, Yermolaich, know. And so his teeth spattered in various directions, just like pearls from a broken string— they spattered and tumbled. We were silent for a while... When our beloved Yermolai Spiridonovich came to, he looked at me with his gap-toothed mouth in surprise. Why, says he, such unkindness? It's all right, I assure him, don't cry, new ones will grow in! My stalwarts stand in the doorway, in red caps, ready to bust a gut. But Yermolai Spiridonovich himself is cheerless, counting his losses, and he doesn't even smile at the joke. It is proper to smile, I admonish him, when your elders joke with you and could be your father. You were the one, I exclaim, who taught us to laugh at jokes when you did the trick with the parakeet!

We tormented and tortured your son, Yermolai Spiridonovich, we couldn't have done otherwise, we've not been taught any other way. We marveled at his frailness of build. A gallant little thing! We tormented him for the most part in ways that would gladden the soul. We plunged him, for example, into manure muck over his head: we told him to wallow; we impaled him, blindfolded, on purpose, you understand, using in place of a spike the manly tool of our sturdy Fedka, known as The Veteran. Do you remember him, Spiridon Yermolaevich? He remembers you well, he says that as lads you once went at it in a game of lapta, together with Sashka Shcherbakov, who drowned last winter in a hole in the ice. We also let ants loose into his prong; we blew him up through his shitter like a frog with the aid of an English pump; we tore his nostrils and fingernails with pliers; we called some women of shame and bade him, Yermolai Spiridonovich, lick their shameful ulcers that they might be healed. He licked. Well, what else is there to tell you? Finally we tore off his knackers—as useless. We threw them to the dogs. At least they got some use out of them. What

good would they do him? Do we, my dear Spiridon Yermolaevich, need
an heir of his? I don't think we do. And the way in which he suffered this
loss was again painfully intemperate, he was angered and became abusive
upon returning to consciousness. He called us beasts and barbarians,
which is even unfair. Screaming while on the rack is, of course, not forbidden, they all scream on it, but why the insults? We are not independent
people, our duties demand that we execute serious orders, and he tells us
that for this we are, as he says, barbarians. No, my dear friend, by and
large it's you who turns out to be an utter barbarian, it's you who went
against the natural order of things, not we, and when he's on the rack,
what's on a man's mind is on his tongue as well, as is observed of drunken
people, and consequently my supposition regarding his not being our
sort, my good sir, has been confirmed with every passing hour. I, thank
God, know my business, I earn my bread, and therefore I have an idea of
how our kind of people scream on the rack and how those who aren't our
kind do. One of ours would never call me an barbarian, because he doesn't
think that way, but your scoundrel admitted that he did. He behaved, I
regret to inform you, rather cowardly. After the manure muck, when he'd
had a good puke, he begged for mercy and, like a little child, promised
that he wouldn't do it any more, and said that in the future he wouldn't
put on airs, that he'd behave quietly and would eagerly serve the state.
That's all fine—but who needs his contrition? Still, we asked him anyway:
dispel our doubts, we said, concerning the resurrection of the parakeet
nicknamed Semyon. Perhaps there was some discord between you and
your neighbor Agafon Yelistratovich? In his denunciation of Agafon Yelistratovich he said that there didn't seem to be any discord, but this physician, he said, was a drunken sot, which is why he doctored people with a
shaky hand. We, to be sure, know Agafon Yelistratovich as a man of excellent record, and we responded to the denunciation regarding sottish
drunkenness with total indignation. However, how could you explain that
not even three days had passed since the moment of purchase of the parakeet when the parakeet keeled over in horrible convulsions, as if someone
had poisoned it, and even earlier had seemed sick, did not chirp, and went
off its feed? Wait, wait, I thought, let me figure this out. I wiped my rasp-
berry bald patch with a napkin and, subsequently, I ask Yermolai Spiridonovich, your son, having previously squeezed his scrotum (which at that
time continued as yet to depend from his person), as a preventive measure: in case of deception. Wait, wait, weren't you, I asked, the scum who
himself poisoned the overseas bird with the desire to vex your neighbor,
the boyars' physician Agafon Yelistratovich, and his despondent children
as well, Tatyana Agafonovna and Ezdra Agafonovich? No, answered your

son, Yermolai Spiridonovich, bug-eyed from pain, no, no-o-o!!!—and his pretty little eyes turned white, and we bit our little lip, didn't we, because it hurt us, didn't it. "No-o-o!.. I mean Ye-e-e-e-s!!!" We squeezed harder, we were trying to understand: did he say yes or no? "Yes! yes! It was me!" Yermolai Spiridonovich screams at me, as if he took me for somebody deaf. "Me! I did it," he said, "to vex them!!!" "Well fine, then. To vex them—but why?" Ow, he screams, it hurts! let me go! and he is twitching all over, the poor thing. Let me go! I can't think like this! Then don't think, we say, just answer—but we loosened up a bit, for we were afraid he'd bite his tongue, and how would he be able to have a conversation then? "I wanted to vex him," he explains, "because I didn't like him..." "Why didn't you?" we squeezed again a little more... "Because," he screamed, "he served the fatherland honorably!" "So that's it!" I say. "You should have said that in the beginning! Well, rest, dear boy..." And when he had rested, I say: but didn't you want to poison Agafon Yelistrat- ovich as well as the bird? He keeps mum, he's thinking. I was just getting ready to squeeze when he answers: yes! Well, you can see for yourself what kind of story we have here, my esteemed Spiridon Yermolaevich, but we decided, all the same, not to rush: we are mistrustful people, pardon the expression. Next day we took him for a little jaunt on the rack, he could use that, he's a bit stooped, don't you think, Spiridon Yermolaevich, it wouldn't hurt to straighten him up while we're at it. It's an excruciatingly funny line of work, I warrant, especially if it's a wench, but let me tell you, your son is a delicate fruit, just like a wench, if not better... But I don't dare weary you any more with details, allow me to make just one digres- sion of a purely physiological sort. You and I, Spiridon, would be as use- less as philosophers and con artists had we not noted mankind's great pas- sion for torture. How come the state protects its loyal citizens by law from arbitrary rule and petty tyranny? It protects them because otherwise the people in the state would die out after destroying and torturing each other. . . For example, the wenches don't do anything for my prong, it lies motionless, doesn't sense any distinction between their minimal particu- larities, having sampled quite a few of them, but when I get ready to really put the screws hard to a man, with all the authority vested in me by the state, I can't help it, it looks up to the sky, and sometimes I get so worked up that I spatter my britches all over, and my old lady thinks that I've been getting a little something on the side, but she's wrong, I'm just returning home from work... This passion is a profound mystery, and philosophers are in the main silent about it, burying their heads in their shoulders like ostriches; it's a mystery more significant than rolling your finger around in your sixth hole, Spiridon, you turn your insides out and still don't know something from nothing. But, at the same time, I like the humble sufferers, the ones who only fart and quack when they're on the rack, I respect them, and I wouldn't ever swap a sufferer like that for a hundred Englishmen, because torture and suffering are a thing pleasing unto God, and what's an Englishman?—shit and nothing more! Or let's say we take the prophet Elisha, who some children mocked one day for being bald. Look, baldy!.. A minor insult: it's proper for any man of worth to have a bald spot. And Elisha didn't say a mean word to the children, he set two she-bears on them, and they tore forty-two children to pieces... And there, brother Spiridon, you and I have food for thought: an edifying picture!— and here you go writing inquiries, besmirching paper all for naught. I have no doubt that a man will sell out anyone and anything, you just have to approach him slowly, don't scare him—just give us time! But we're not given time, we're hurried, pressed, rushed. That's why things get bungled up in our business, and because of that, Spiridon, the screwups multiply . . .

And now you be the judge, Spiridon Yermolaevich, what would have happened if that worm-ravaged parakeet had ascended? WOULDN'T WE BE FINE FOOLS! And, according to your troublemaker's words, it did flap its wings a couple of times, although later on the rack he recanted his careless words. But, you know, that louse got all tangled up in his words towards the end! You see, either he himself poisoned the bird, or, he says, it was together with Agafon Yelistratovich, in order to test the poison, or—it even came to this, I'll tell you in confidence—he made a denunciation to the effect that you, his own father, Spiridon Yermolaevich, goaded him into exhuming the dead creature. At this point (or was it, perhaps, earlier?) we tore off his knackers to teach him not to shoot his mouth off like that about his father for no good reason, tore them off and tossed them right to the dogs: let them have a little treat... And now he's agreeable to everything, ready to sign everything, to confirm anything we say, he responds affirmatively to every question. What good does that do, you be the judge? We see that he wants to undermine the investigation, set it onto a false trail, conceal the shameful truth. But we came, via a roundabout way, to the truth, arrived, in the bitter end, at the shared opinion that your boy, Yermolai Spiridonovich, wanted to resurrect the parakeet in order to prove the superiority of the overseas bird over our own sparrows and thereby to diminish our pride, to hold us up to the world in a ridiculous and incorrect light. When Yermolai Spiridonovich and I came to share that common opinion, we embraced in our joy: a job well done, I say, is its own reward, bring us, my stalwarts, wine and viands, we shall make merry! And my stalwarts bring us white salmon, suckling pigs and lambs, sundry souffles and a wine that has the playful name, Madonna's Milk. We ate and then shot the breeze...

However, I dimly suspect that you, Spiridon, inflamed by paternal feeling, which we cannot hold against you, are further interested in the matter of what became of your son, the unforgettable, fondly remembered, Yermolayushka. And what could become of him? Nothing became of him. Everything, thank God, turned out for the best. Early the next morning, at about five, when the sun's brilliant orb gilded the poppy-head domes of our holy churches, he and I went up slowly, arm in arm, to the bell tower. We feasted our eyes. All around lay our capital city in mellow morning sleep and fog, the cocks were crowing and the orchards resounding. The granaries, the thoroughfares, the locomotive whistles, the university—all was in its place. The river ran like a silvery serpent through the city, and on the far bank, high up, there stood a pinewood—a sight to behold! And what an aroma, Spiridon, wafted up from the grasses. The scent of clover, Spiridon, and a heavy scent it was! "Glorious!" I uttered, looking about. "Glorious!" uttered Yermolai Spiridonovich. I looked at him from the side. I'll say just one word about him: gorgeous! Even his hungover pallor, shading into a delicate blueness, enhanced his appearance. Unwittingly beguiled by lascivious demons, he had arrived at the hour of his deliverance, and, foretasting his new life, he was beatified in advance. "Well, Godspeed!" I said, and I led him by the arm to the ledge of the belfry. "Fly, Yermolayushka! Fly, my pigeon!" Spreading his arms out to form a cross, he stepped into the emptiness. For just a minute I was almost seized by the torment of doubt: what if he were to ascend like a turquoise parakeet, to the demons' delight? With a certain disquiet I leaned over the railing and glanced below. Thank God! Smashed! Flopped down nicely, I could see, with his brains splattered like a ripe melon all over the pavement. My stalwarts in red hats ran to cover Yermolai Spiridonovich with a piece of state-issue cloth. I crossed myself.

Don't grieve, Spiridon Yermolaevich! Forget it, don't grieve! As if he were worth grieving over! Don't pine for the scoundrel! He testified against you, too, but I hid that document, didn't let it go any further. When your paternal feelings have cooled down, pay me a call: we'll go to the bathhouse, steam ourselves, drink some beer. My old lady brews a good strong beer, it really hits the spot! Drop by whenever you feel like it, forget the formalities. You'll still father a few more kids, you seem to be a real man, still in good working shape, even if you are getting a bit on up there. And if you don't father any more—it's no big deal, you'll do just fine. There are plenty as it is! And your boy, Yermolai Spiridonovich, he's gone straight up to heaven for sure: a martyr will always get to heaven, even if his cause is wrong. And he looks down on us tenderly from there, plays with his turquoise parakeet, strokes its little feathers—and gives thanks. When you think about it, when you picture that, you even get jealous, Spiridon, honest to God you do... Well, fine, then, to hell with him, let him rejoice!

Translated by Leonard J. Stanton from the author's manuscript

VIKTOR EROFEYEV
ANNA'S BODY,
OR THE END OF
THE RUSSIAN AVANT GARDE

Anna! Anna! Anna!—her heart jumped.

Anna Ioanna! Anna Ioanna!—resounded in her ears.

An-na-Ioan-na...—her stomach announced, like a distant locomotive, and, instead of steam, it sent the shot of a belch into her nose.

Anna awoke from the shot. Like a great fish, like a whale tossed up onto the shore of a stupefied ocean, Anna lay in her bed in the middle of the night. Pensively she sucked her thick chapped lips, then reached for a cigarette. Something flopped from the night table onto the floor. Probably a book. Probably Borges. Anna kept fumbling in the darkness. An ashtray fell, but didn't break. But everything probably spilled out of it. Anna breathed audibly and fumbled.

Anna! Anna! Anna!—her heart jumped.

Anna raised herself up on an elbow and started fumbling for something else: she fumbled on to it. The yellow bedside light went on.

Among the creams, the medicines, the saucers, the evening papers with half-finished crossword puzzles, she found a crumpled pack. With violently shaking wet hands Anna lit up and sat upright in bed.

Anna's body had somehow become possessed lately. Anna's body would fatten, then abruptly thin, then fatten again, then abruptly thin again, then fatten, then thin, then thin, then fatten. And besides that, her ears were dripping. Drip-drip. Liquid on lobes. Droplet and bolls. And the grocery store. Anna was glad she knew how to talk with waiters. And, just for laughs, what's your name? And they would always answer honestly: Volodya, or Tolya, or Slava. Drip-drip, her ears dripped, and her ears itched. In desperation Anna stuck her fingers in her ears. At times she was seized by a powerful desire to tear them off. Tonight Anna's body was already quite fat, it still hadn't reached its apogee, but it was already as pleasingly slick as salmon, and, with her eyes lowered, Anna could contemplate the ovals of her burgeoning cheeks—the inflamed buttocks of her face, in the grip of an allergy—between which a cigarette billowed. In the corner of the room a New Year's tree with rust-red, needleless boughs held toy tree ornaments here and there on the very tips of the sere boughs. Broken spheres of different colors shimmered on the floor. It was almost the end of February. In October they had celebrated her fortieth birthday. Drip-drip,—her ears dripped. Lenochka, a student, wan of face, had flirted with mature men.

Anna's right eye had gone out of control, too. If she closed the left one, then instead of the world there'd be French painting, a lilac Rouen, a frog's pond, pointillism. If she closed the right one, there'd be Russian realism. The right eye saw a maximum of 15 percent. The left one saw everything, our entire reality.

Sometimes Anna felt that she was Anna Karenina, sometimes—Anna Akhmatova, sometimes just an Anna on the neck.* Depending on this, her relationships would change; sometimes she would fall in love, sometimes she would emigrate to Paris, sometimes she would burn the snow with tears until she experienced her latest love. Some Jews would come, bringing first hundreds, then thousands of faded rubles, her husband abroad would compose anti-patriotic pamphlets, would summon her, but what was the point? Sometimes the police inspector would drop in, look sidelong at the empty bottles: he'd stand a while, stand a while, then leave...

Anna reached for the bottle of cognac, splashing as she poured, and took a look at the tree.

"I'll throw it out by Women's Day," thought Anna, and drank it down.

She felt warmer. Anna took a deep drag and settled back on to the pillow. Then she drank one more shot, grew flushed, and her legs stirred. Anna's right leg bent at the knee and went way off to the right, so that all five of her toes with their long-neglected untrimmed nails stuck out from under the sheet. Anna's left leg, which was also bent at the knee, slid off

*The title of a story by Anton Chekhov. "Anna" was a medal awarded by the tsarist government.

to the left and bumped into something alive.

Anna's whole body shuddered, she cowered, gripped in mortal dread.

To her left lay a man. He lay with his back to Anna, facing the window. Anna recognized him from the back of his head and almost screamed. It was the man she loved, the one she loved most, the very most, who had jilted her two months earlier, after they had returned from a winter resort in the Caucasus. He had driven her home from the airport, tanned and gray-eyed, and told her that he'd call and drop by the next morning, he kissed her on the temple with an easy nonchalance all his own, but he didn't call and he didn't drop by, never-ever.

He'd been skiing off cliffs—and she'd been sleeping.

He'd been splashing around, convivial and frail, in the pool—and she'd been sleeping.

He'd come from the sauna, flushed and abashed—and she'd be sleeping.

Rousing her fat body, he'd say: "Moscow girls go to the steam room nude; but Leningrad girls—all of them!—wear swimsuits."

She'd answer, half-asleep: "That's all so boring!"

In the evenings he would get drunk with the Leningrad girls, black marketeers, and Circassians, and she would also get up and get drunk.

Every day, when the un-Russian sun was at its height, she'd awake with the thought of getting a pool pass from the local woman doctor. Finally, on the eve of her departure, Anna appeared before her fastidious, ugly puss. Anna stood, like a clash of two worlds, like a fatal contest between Picasso and Botticelli, generously displaying her Slavic breasts to the woman doctor, and that woman of another faith, dumbstruck by such beauty, involuntarily issued the required pass.

How did you get in, my boy, without keys, without clothes? How did you penetrate my warm, dark burrow here?

The man she loved—the smartest and handsomest man in the world, and very, very talented—the very sight of whom at times was enough to send her into a spasm of love, something that hadn't happened to her even once before—slept, curled up like a pretzel, in a familiar, mud-brown shirt, and without any shorts. Anna stretched her trembling hand toward him, but pulled the hand back. She sat up, took a comb from the table and quickly started combing her blond hair. Then she glanced at the mirror and leisurely began to make up her eyes, applying green eye shadow...

And now, and now... but first, unnerved as she was, she'd take another drink. Anna had her drink and smiled. She knew what she'd do. She wouldn't wake him up. Let him sleep, let him sleep till morning! He's probably tired, let him sleep, and I'll caress you softly, slowly, the whole night through. You sleep, and I'll come to you in your dream and eat you up, my boy! You sleep, and I'll come to you: yum-yum!

Anna laughed, covering her mouth with her hand. Anna snuggled into euphemisms as if they were second-hand furs.

Anna! Anna! Anna!—her heart trumpeted.

"I knew that you'd come," whispered Anna. "I knew! I knew! I knew!"

"How wrong you are, my joy!" Anna smiled. "Why waste yourself on trash? Why do you need sluts when you've got me? You keep writing and writing and writing, but none of it's any good! You can't show that smut to a child or to decent people. You write abominable stuff," she shook her finger warningly at him, "and you'd do better to write about us, about how you came back to me, about the love you and I have, about the snow that falls in quiet flakes on a tired city, about a lilac branch in the garden, about what's inside every one of us, however mixed up he may be... You'd do better to write about how much I missed you, longed for your touch and your eyes, how my breast aches from the loss... You sleep, and do you know what, I'll turn my little boy into—I'm not going to tell!" Anna laughed again. "You'd do better to write about the purl of scarlet blood beneath your cold iron shield, pity cripples and raise the dead—go on and raise the dead, go on—raise them!"

"And here you are asleep," murmured Anna, stroking the man's sleeping belly, "and you have no way of knowing how you rise above the world, how you grow for me like the Eiffel Tower or the Leaning Tower of Pisa, or some other winged monument... And God—surely he is in every one of us, in every house and in every apartment, and in this tree, and in this cognac, and even my mother, who spent her whole life teaching materialism... and even in materialism!"

Anna used her teeth to tighten the loose knots of the bandages on her wrists.

"White cuffs...," she sobbed, "Yes, I'm a fool... I was a fool— Forgive me! But now you're mine again, you've come, you're all mine!"

Anna! Anna! Anna!—her loving heart was being torn to pieces.

Anna turned out the bedside light, made herself comfortable, passed her dry tongue over her lips, and, as in an old fairy tale, gobbled up the man she loved. And that's how on this night the history of the Russian avant garde came to an end.

Translated by Leonard J. Stanton from the author's manuscript

GENNADY GOLOVIN
ANNA PETROVNA

You have probably seen them, these tiny milky-pink flowers, in parks or backyards in late fall, when it's already almost winter.

A bit dirty, with a timeworn rosette of petals nicely singed around the edges by the rust of the first frosts, they aren't, of course, really in bloom at this time of year—they just look as if they are. They seem to be dozing under the dirty, damp leaves, under the rusty, clinging dead grass. So at first you can't tell whether these untended little daisies are still alive, or whether they died long ago. If you pick them up in your hands, they'll crumble into a delicate, sorrowful dust...

Even in autumn, these poor flowers do not evoke either tenderness or pleasure. Quite the contrary—one feels a coarse grief or even annoyance at the sight of them: they have too strong an aura of malevolent oblivion, of bitter orphanhood, of some poor abandoned graveyard.

You'll see them while walking by, and suddenly you'll catch yourself hurrying to get past.

With just such a godforsaken little daisy would I compare Anna Petrovna, the heroine of this story. She was living out her last days, quietly, patiently, anonymously and uselessly, in a dusky little room in an enormous gloomy brick apartment house in Krasnaya Presnya.

———

Anna Petrovna was already in her eighties, and from all her once-numer-
ous relatives she had only one granddaughter left—Marina—of whom
Anna Petrovna was not terribly fond, because the granddaughter had
grown up to be a rather strange individual (although Anna Petrovna herself had brought her up from the age of four until her first marriage)—with
cheap bright-red hair, masculine and athletic-looking, a spirited bitch,
who cared about nothing in the whole, wide world except her own person.

And it was Marina who was to blame for the situation in which Anna
Petrovna found herself in her declining years, for the fact that she was not
living in her two well-lit rooms on Bolshaya Polyanka Street, where she
had previously lived for forty years, but in nine square meters, in this disgusting, I would say Dostoevskian, little room, which more than anything
resembled a narrow, disproportionately high box, or more precisely, a
crevice—two meters wide and three and a half high—whose long-unwashed
window, tall and skinny like a church window, stared out at a crowded
depressing little asphalt courtyard where sickly saplings withered in little
squares of petrified earth, blocked off by railings and replanted every year;
where beside sandless sandboxes, unfortunate children killed time, list-
lessly scratching the asphalt with shovels of various colors; where an abandoned old car, without wheels, slowly disintegrated day by day, getting
covered, every day it seemed, with more bright and triumphant sores of
rust; and where from morning till evening people lined up at the glass-
recycling station. Meek and oppressed by many sorrows, they sat on old
rickety crates beside a peeling wall totally covered with feeble-minded
graffiti.

The view from the window was not a cheerful one, for sure.

But this didn't bother Anna Petrovna very much. And it wasn't only
because it hadn't been all that nice in the courtyard on Bolshaya Polyanka
either. It was just that she was at that quiet, almost semi-comatose, stage
of life, when practically nothing—except, maybe, how they themselves are
feeling—seriously bothers people, and all the weak energy of their imagination is spent solely in submissive (yet strange to say, chilling!) expectation of their last day on earth.

Two or three years ago, Anna Petrovna had finally come to believe that
she had only a very short time left, and ever since she sincerely thought
that each fall would be her last. (For some reason she was sure that she
would die in the fall, at the very beginning of winter.) And in the year of
our story, she was almost *certain* that her end was near, and that was why
a lofty dignified indifference, like a disdainful wall, had cut her off almost
completely from the world around her.

...Here, inside, behind that wall, it was very quiet, very peaceful, and generally quite pleasant, though also sad, while life, which had bustled so busily and boisterously around her, now bustled somewhere out there, off to the side, and already scarcely touched Anna Petrovna's imagination. Well, approximately the same way as she was not touched by the fuzzy silvery aquarium movements of the shadows on her black-and-white TV screen, where the sound had not worked for a long time, but which she sometimes absentmindedly turned on: she would gaze fixedly at the screen, guiltily and anxiously, straining to understand, but she no longer could understand what these people were worrying about, or why...

Nowadays she liked most of all to look at the line of people below her window.

She felt an affectionate, though faint, sympathy for these poor people as they sat tiredly and patiently for whole days at a stretch on the battered, rickety crates, moving from time to time, as if at someone's command, from one crate to another. How carefully, as if they were something very valuable, they would move their bags with the shining cleanly-washed empty bottles, how deeply saddened they were, these people, how submissive they seemed, how meek.

That isn't to say that she felt anything symbolic in this endless daily line of people. It was just that everything she saw here somehow strongly affected her. After all, essentially, she, too, was sitting in a patient, black line, and the mysterious window, toward which all these people were so abjectly and submissively leaning, was no longer all that distant from her either.

On Tuesdays, when the recycling station was closed and, consequently, there was no line and only the pathetic crates, covered in places with bits of torn newspapers, leaned against the deserted wall—on Tuesdays Anna Petrovna experienced a kind of irritating gap in her life, a vexation, a strong sense of unease, and she even seriously feared, that if she should die, she would certainly die on Tuesday, because nothing occupied her leisure time on that day, and her soul, languishing in idleness, was especially defenseless and submissive to anything.

She was a proud woman, and she tried never to ask her granddaughter for anything, but one day she couldn't help it: painfully and without looking at her, she asked Marina, if, since she came to visit her anyway, she couldn't, whenever possible, visit her on Tuesdays. Marina, naturally, agreed quickly and easily, "Tuesdays? Fine. I'll come on Tuesdays." And immediately, of course, asked, "And, what, Granny, is special about Tuesdays?"

Anna Petrovna didn't feel she needed to answer that question, and everything remained as before: Marina would drive up in her dark coffee-colored Zhiguli on Monday, Thursday or Friday—whenever she took a notion. And she took such a notion, it might be noted, never more frequently than once a month.

Anna Petrovna waited for these visits and, at the same time, she was terribly upset by them.

After her granddaughter came, for two days she would always have a buzzing in her head, a rippling in her eyes and a sharp, painful ache in her eardrums from Marina's blaring (she was a kindergarten teacher), drill sergeant's voice.

After Marina left and the door closed behind her, Anna Petrovna would feel like someone who had just had a heavy, rumbling, infinitely and painfully long, cast-iron train roll past them for a very long time.

Anna Petrovna had long since ceased passing judgment on people , but everything inside her would clench in protest and hostility when this woman would noisily, and always unexpectedly, burst into her home, crudely trying to look young, false through and through in her cheerfulness, in every gesture and in every intonation of her voice, which always seemed on the verge of some coarse remark.

With her Santa Claus shriek of joy: "Hey, Granny! See what I've brought you!", she would plop her bag on the table and begin to extract her "goodies," as she called them—any kind of worthless trash, the first sight of which would distinctly turn Anna Petrovna's stomach: some sort of ominously gray, limp franks; packages of cheese, half dried up, crushed out of shape and smelling like vinegar; smoked sausage, with ends that were black and soggy from age and a casing which was covered with a creeping layer of blue mold—in general, everything that Marina discovered, with surprise and irritation, in the bowels of her refrigerator when she defrosted it once a month, and that caution did not permit her to eat herself and stinginess prevented her from tossing in the garbage.

I dare say Anna Petrovna guessed the source of these goodies. However, it would have been hard to read even a hint of this in her face.

With the years, especially the recent years—years no longer just of old age, but of decrepitude—Anna Petrovna's face had become all but immobile and revealed almost nothing, except that this was the face of a very old and very tired person, and even the mask of arrogant tranquility, unwittingly formed by the wrinkles and folds of skin, no longer had any real meaning.

The displeasure, for instance, at having to put up with Marina's company was, in general, barely perceptible: it showed in a certain confusion in Anna Petrovna's glance and also in the way that, every now and then, she would, for no apparent reason, shift her hands around on the table— Oh! still very beautiful hands, although, of course, also very old—with cleanly washed, dry, rough skin, like bluish marble, with delicate, very feminine fingers, which had escaped anile rheumatism. From one of these fingers peered a strange and even ugly, heavy, crudely-made ring of tarnished silver with a transparent bluish stone, too large and too transparent not to be a fake.

Nothing would change in Anna Petrovna's face, even when her granddaughter would start "cleaning up" the apartment—wiping imaginary dust from the television set, sweeping the spotlessly clean floor, making a loud racket as she moved chairs from one place to another... But sometimes Anna Petrovna would look around distractedly in bewilderment: it always seemed to her that Marina must be putting on her act for a third person: just look at her, she may be a bit crude, but she's solicitous, she may be terribly busy, but she doesn't forget Granny... It all smelled like a farce, a cheap farce. And only someone like Marina would fail to see this.

For a long time now Anna Petrovna had had no illusions about her only living relative.

There was no mystery for her, either in these visits or in this ostentatious attention.

Anna Petrovna was tranquilly aware that her granddaughter, even after exchanging both of Anna Petrovna's old rooms in her scheme to get an apartment for herself, even after "borrowing," as she and her husband expressed it, all of Anna Petrovna's savings (and these savings were considerable, almost eight thousand rubles, which, as a matter of fact, made possible the acquisition of Marina's dark, coffee-colored, dumpy little car)—Anna Petrovna was tranquilly aware that the young couple had no intention of dropping their solicitude, since they were certain that she was still rich.

Lord knows how they came to this pathetic, greedy certainty! The reason was, most likely, that they were terribly shocked (Anna Petrovna noticed this) at how easily and even carelessly she had parted with those miserable thousands. Marina, she recalled, had barely started her moaning (clearly calculated to last more than one day) about how tight their finances were—and Anna Petrovna was already up, getting her coat off the hook so she could go to the bank!

"No-o, people don't let go of their *last* money so easily!," the young couple must have thought. "A sensible person" (and even in their view

Anna Petrovna was a sensible person) "doesn't so cheerfully and casually hand over that kind of money to outsiders!" (and that they were outsiders, they realized all too well...), "hand it over without a receipt, without witnesses !.."

"There's only one situation where that's possible," they must have thought, "if those eight thousand are only a small part, an insignificantly small part of such a sum, of su-u-u-ch a sum...!" And here Anna Petrovna would always giggle to herself rather maliciously, vividly imagining Marina's excited, greedy eyes, and her smile, drooling with anticipation, as she secretly discussed her grandmother's mythical fortune with her husband.

It should be noted that Anna Petrovna never, not by a single word, tried to disillusion them.

This was, of course, a matter of quite simple craftiness.

"Let at least this motive, not the purest, of course, bind them to me for the time being," was approximately what the old woman thought. "What can be done if the times are such that even a young couple dreams only of being rich, and family feeling, to judge by Marina, nowadays is worth precisely as much as my present bank account."

Her fear of finding herself entirely alone, without anyone to help during her final illness, and her aversion to thinking that she might be buried poorly and without respect were stronger than the dislike, or rather, fastidious disgust, that she had felt for some time toward her granddaughter and her new husband.

And this was exactly why she didn't respond, with almost mysterious significance didn't respond when Marina, clumsily beating about the bush, from time to time would start talking about some money that would be left after "who knows what might happen..." and, as a result, Anna Petrovna ended up almost consciously misleading her granddaughter, virtually hinting to her by her silence that there was some hitherto concealed fortune, and this realization troubled the old woman constantly, if only vaguely, and this was one more reason that Marina's visits were unpleasant.

And, nevertheless, each time she looked forward to Marina's visit.

These visits were agonizing for Anna Petrovna, no doubt about it, yet they (a strange, but accurate comparison) were like a disgusting, but absolutely necessary medicine, which one *must* take, even though each time one had to put up with the nasty taste.

It was a horrible medicine, but when Marina would finally disappear and Anna Petrovna would exhaustedly make it to bed, groaning in self-pity and feeling completely worn out—almost battered—then the strange effect of this barbaric drug would begin; then the incomparable bliss of *rediscovered peace* would descend upon her, for the sake of which, without knowing it herself, she allowed in her home from time to time this alien and unpleasant creature named Marina.

It was such a strong, sweet and youthful feeling, and, best of all, it so marvelously generated a congenial and drowsy multitude of desires and quasi-desires, and memories and quasi-memories—let's put it this way, of desires embodied in the form of certain memories—and they were so narcotically real, these memories, and already so transparently clear and pictorial, as if they were color photographs in the glossy pages of some expensive magazine, that a festive shiver of *life* again began to drench Anna Petrovna's soul, inducing rapture, rapture almost devoid of bitterness—a respectful delight in everything that had happened to her on this earth. And what had happened to her on this earth was—life.

It's not true when people say that old people do not need much, that their desires are few and insignificant. Anna Petrovna wanted many things, craved them voraciously, many different kinds of things. And—a fortunate aspect of her old age—the things she seemed to crave most of all often appeared to her in these waking dreams.

And after spending some time in the past, Anna Petrovna would return to her present colorless life, and though she would completely forget what she had seen, she would somehow be reassured by it, be given a vague, but persistent sense of the *significance,* both of what had happened to her then and of what was happening to her now.

...Very often she wanted a sunny summer morning and a flag-blowing breeze, still fresh from the previous night and even a bit chilly, to blow evenly from the Moscow River, from the Crimean Bridge, whose impudent new silhouette was still strange to her eye—she wanted it to excite her, to give her goose bumps, and to persuade her, better than any slogans, of the marvelous Future that awaited everyone; she wanted the breeze to play with the multicolored flags up high—each of which, fluttering and vying with one another, devotedly stretched out with the wind toward the green, fluffy depths of Gorky Park—and the brass band to be playing deep inside the park, but very far away, so that you couldn't make out the tune but only hear the amusing, distinct and apparently offended voice of the big bass drum which grumpily beat out: boom... boom-boom-boom... boom...

Where had she been going then? Who had been waiting for her there, on the smooth, neatly rolled, red crushed-brick paths of Gorky Park?... She could no longer remember. And it wasn't a memory about that, but about how steadily and freshly happiness was blowing from the Moscow

River, from the Crimean Bridge, how the cheery flags were streaming in the azure heights—just like Deineka's frescoes—a whole naive forest of multicolored flags!—and how the corners of her eyelids stung from the crinkle of the smile which had been on her face all morning, how happy and energetic her cheerful, tanned body felt under the thin cotton blue and white T-shirt with the carefree turned-back collar still smelling faintly from ironing, and how, every now and again, as she walked, the poor, worn, gentle cloth would caress her slightly chilled, firm nipples with a shamefully ticklish, gentle touch.

Something unbearably happy, morning-like and sunny was waiting for her ahead. She was in a hurry, but she had to stop at the edge of the sidewalk because all of a sudden some bicyclists began to flash past in a long continuous line—coming from somewhere and headed for somewhere—in faded, worn tank tops with unashamedly plebeian swirls of black sweat under the armpits and down the spine; stern, worried faces; the bronzed calves of their legs, as if carved from stone, turning the pedals so rapidly and easily, that it seemed their only task was keeping up with the pedals, which were turning by themselves.

She quickly got very excited at the sight of this mass of wild, angry male power rushing past, and—at that very instant—with a sudden fearful thrill, she noticed what an attentive and kind look one of the racers had managed to cast her way. He was blond, with a simple, very Russian, very Northern face, which lightly and trustingly shone with that glance through the stony, petrified mask of his concentrated, sullen and difficult pursuit.

And in a single instant they managed to sense and understand everything about each other. And to be happy for each other.

She was happy that it was so enjoyable for him, and most important, so *necessary* to dash right now along the Sadovoye Ring—coming from somewhere and headed for somewhere—always expecting to feel tired, but not tiring, and with ever-increasing pride, feeling not the slightest, not the least bit tired...

And he was happy that it was probably so nice and enjoyable for her, so tanned, so blue and white, so young and bright-eyed, to be walking on such a wonderful morning to Gorky Park, where a brass band was already playing, though no one knew why (just playing, just for fun...), and the linden trees were blooming, and the red paths were neatly swept and deserted and where there awaited her something unbearably happy, sunny and pure, like everything else that morning...

They just had time to sense all this, and be tenderly happy for each other, and to be sorry that they had to part, and—they parted.

The race flashed by and was gone, it dashed off into the distance, and the wind, rushing after it—the carefree bicycle wind of youth—was blowing on Anna Petrovna's face, tickling her forehead lightly as it blew across her light, sun-bleached, closely cropped hair, which she had washed with painstaking enjoyment the night before in the gloomy silence of their enormous communal kitchen, and which that morning still had the cheerful, almost caramel smell of strawberry soap.

Anna Petrovna was quite fond of this memory, although she always experienced a certain degree of embarrassment: after all, how could this really have happened to her? This had been either in the late thirties (most probably), or after the war, and either way she would no longer have been so young.

But as a matter of fact—and somehow Anna Petrovna had completely forgotten about this, as she had completely forgotten about many other things—all this hadn't happened to her, but to her daughter, as a teenager, when, one marvelous Sunday morning, the two of them had set out for Gorky Park just for fun, and the flags were flapping in the blue sky and they could hear the music from somewhere, and everything was clean, deserted and fresh, as on a holiday morning... And on that morning during some searingly happy, deeply thrilling moments, suddenly, by some miracle she, the mother, merged completely with her daughter—a pitifully long-legged, sassy and already terribly lonely sixteen-year-old girl with a soul that was already troubled—a fragile, helpless little boat, already quietly casting off from the maternal shipside, already beginning to feel, timidly and joyously, the powerful, masterful current of the River of Life.

It was strange, but her daughter almost never appeared in her other memories.

Sometimes an image would come to her of some quiet, infinitely sad morning in the crowded little room in the dormitory on Golyanovka, with its disproportionately huge windows from floor to ceiling, which made the room chilly and uncomfortable, and its thin plywood door, which opened, as if onto the street, onto an echoing, eternally dark hallway, without end or limits. Just like the street, it was always packed and crowded with casual, noisy students, but that morning even the hallway was deserted and quiet, just as the whole, wide world was deserted and quiet—the world at whose very center Anna Petrovna was sitting on a cheap stool and nursing her newborn daughter. She was suffering immeasurably because there was no place to lean her badly aching back, she was having a difficult time unsticking her clinging, stinging eyelids and every so often, she dropped off, as if fainting, into a dark thicket of sleep.

Even now, after many years, she could see, as if it were real, the Buddhist mask of that little face, the size of a fist, all flushed and arrogant (it still didn't evoke any tender feelings—only worry and, of course, compassion). This wasn't a memory about her daughter though, but about how sad and funereally silent the world was, about how her back ached from the uncomfortable position (which she had assumed almost intentionally, so that she wouldn't accidentally fall asleep and drop the baby), about how drunkenly her eyes rolled from her terrible need for sleep, and what a wondrous thing it was—to feel the milk leaving your body, to feel the easing of your breast, and how sweet it was to know that this sweet little leech would get its fill, would empty the breast, let go of the nipple and be quiet and at last she could, stiff-backed like an old woman, drop the little bundle in its basket, and then herself hobble over and fall!—face down onto her bed, wildly rumpled, long unwashed and still preserving the warm body heat of the night! And fly, fainting from the sweet, soundless shriek at the back of her eyeballs, into the black, bottomless shaft of sleep.

She was sorry for herself to the point of tears: she was so completely exhausted, deserted by everyone, had so completely let herself go. She was sorry for this little caterpillar of a daughter, so trustingly helpless, so defenseless against all the iron misfortunes of the world that it made her poor heart shudder...

And she was also sorry—solemnly, mournfully sorry—for everything that might have happened to her, Anna Petrovna, in this world, but which now would never happen, because with the appearance of this little leech, smacking her lips so greedily, enormous layers, whole continents of the Possible had split off, had floated off, leaving her, as if on a tiny ice block in this drab little room. And it would be like that all the rest of her life.

She felt so heartbreakingly, unrelievedly, sorry for herself, and there was no end to her grief, but at that moment something suddenly happened outdoors, something moved in the heavens—the sun peeked through. And a dusty square of this reluctant autumn sun fell into the room, breaking in two at a drunken slant along the corners of the walls, ceiling and floor, and with its edge—as if by chance—it covered her shoulders and aching back, like the corner of a mother's sad shawl.

She felt the gentle, quiet weight settle on her shoulders—her daughter let go of her nipple and started to breathe heavily, and Anna Petrovna suddenly started to cry with happiness.

And this memory was about these mysterious happy tears, about the weight of the sun on her shoulder, but not at all about her daughter, who left this world when she was barely thirty years old and whom Anna Petrovna had resolved, once and for all, to try never to think about, for these thoughts brought a sharp, stabbing pang of guilt that she, so old, could keep on living and living, while her daughter, so young, had so sadly and horribly been killed, dying along with her lover, an Arctic airplane pilot, in a train accident after the war at Moscow Station No. 3.

She used to be a draftsman—as they said, a "great" draftsman, to whom people brought work from the far ends of Moscow and for whom people signed up on a waiting list, the way you do for a famous seamstress or hairdresser.

But for the last fifteen years, she hadn't taken any work, not even the simplest, drafting jobs and, as she had been used to working day in and day out, the loss was very painful.

That was probably the reason that during this whole fifteen years she often saw a vision of some late winter evening with yellow dandelions of street lights modestly shining along a dozing street, and she would be looking down onto the street, which, just as in the provinces, was softly filled with high drifts of violet-colored snow, and on the far side of these snow drifts—so unlike Moscow!—the windows flickered with a cozy, orange light in the ancient, black, little wooden houses of the old district of Zamoskvorechye.

At this time silence would reign in the world.

Silence, at this time, would also fill Anna Petrovna's room with a heavy peace, like gloomy water. It was a very comfortable room in a well-built, pre-Revolutionary apartment house—with ceilings which were high, but well-proportioned for the building, with dependable brick walls, with old-fashioned ribbed radiators along these walls, from which there always issued such a dense, excessive current of dry, iron heat that even in the fiercest cold spells (and at that time there were some really fierce cold spells) she had to keep the external transoms constantly open, and so some tattered, passionately melting fibers of delicious, exciting cold floating in from outside always seemed to be hovering in the room's well-warmed air...

On such evenings working was a delight.

It was a delight, after impatiently dashing off the tiresome household chores, to finally stand in the doorway, triumphantly raise her hand and—click off the light switch, eliminating the chandelier's overhead light, and again, feeling in her soul something akin to rapture, see a previously unremarkable corner of her room suddenly, as if on a stage, become cozily spotlighted, become the center of everything. This was the corner where she had set up her drafting machine, which, with the wall-like surface of its drafting board, blocked off her so anxiously beloved work space from the rest of the world. This work space would now be efficiently filled with the swing-arm lamp's bright light, reflecting off the refined shining surface of the drawing paper that she had prepared for work.

It was a delight to pick up and feel in her fingers the elegant hovering weightlessness of the pointed and wickedly sharpened Koh-i-noor pencil, whose golden edges gleamed so nobly and modestly, to feel it in her hand and begin working on a painstaking, detailed penciled draft, covering the whole zealously shining flatness of paper firmly pinned to the board with a spider web of very fine lines and barely marked arcs and linkages, so that, after a while, it seemed to be an indistinct, blurry haze, and only Anna Petrovna, of all the people in the world, could see the shape of the future blueprint glimmering ever more definitely and clearly in this graphite conglomeration.

And her joy was already quite boundless, when, after putting India ink in the drafting pen (it would be more exact to say: "after feeding the bulging steel beak of the drafting pen a small drop of India ink—heavy like black mercury..."), she drew the very first line—taut, ideal, like a guitar string, and which, just like the string, immediately began to *resonate*...

Being rather vain, like all Master Craftsmen, she loved the moment when she had to show her work to the client.

Her clients were for the most part engineers—not very successful people, tormented by the demon of inventiveness—simultaneously both proud and timid, both arrogant and insecure.

And for her it was a delight, a delight she could never get used to, to see with what amazement their grayish faces, as a rule badly shaven and exhausted from insomnia, would light up when she unpinned the newspaper covering the drawing paper and showed them the draft, to see how with almost childish enthusiasm, scarcely able to believe their eyes, they would begin gazing at their progeny, brought to life by Anna Petrovna's genius; their instantly beaming eyes would scan the page hurriedly, greedily and insatiably, and it was an ineffable joy to *feel* the joy pouring into these insecure souls, rubbed raw by unjust failures, as they would go over and over the draft in greedy adoration and then start admiring it once more. It was so beautiful and ideal that what the draft represented also seemed, at that moment, beautiful and ideal, and it was a joy to see these people regain a proud dignity and a belief that they were needed.

For some reason her clients would always hurry off after that to be alone, to bask in the warmth of this inspired, reignited flame—and Anna Petrovna, after seeing them to the door, would return and, with an offhand, slightly theatrical gesture, toss the money into an old cardboard petit-four box—a gesture that grated even on her, but which was repeated every time, as was the momentary displeasure it brought. Then she would turn off the lamp on the drafting machine and walk over to the mirror—to be alone for a bit with someone just like herself, a slightly tired and, alas, already aging, but, nevertheless (you could see right off), happy woman, on whose face a soft maternal smile of kindly condescension kept trying to fade out, but was unable to.

...The mousy twilight would float into her little room like quiet smoke through the long unwashed, dingy, church-like window.

Almost completely invisible in this darkness, her breathing barely audible, pitifully curled up like some insignificant heap of dirty old rags and just trying to keep one bony knee from rubbing against the other, feeling all the tender decrepitude of her body, each shrunken bone of it, each dried-up muscle and sinew, there lay an old woman named Anna Petrovna on a cheerfully springy bed, which no longer even bent down under her weight and, either sleeping or day-dreaming, she kept one hand under her cheek, like an obedient child, and the other would touch the pillow, which she would occasionally caress with her still amazingly beautiful fingers, at times as if gratefully, at other times apparently in encouragement. And on one of her fingers the absurdly heavy ring of old, tarnished silver flaunted its mysterious vulgarity...

...and some half-forgotten showers would again be splattering on the ground—good-natured summer showers, making the water in the river turn gray and hiss amusingly, like a carbonated drink, and which it was so much fun to hide from, panting, under the safe, parental cover of some squat, old spruce trees, and quietly sit there, hidden: listening to the rain, listening to the remote, sweet memory-voices inside her of unsheltered distant ancestors...

...and then came fierce, lead-colored dawns—pouring down dull gray water to flood the deserted parade ground in front of the enormous, drab, yellow barracks, with their little squares of windows. And the camp bugle's call, time after time tiresomely soaring upward and flitting above the parade ground with inappropriate gaiety, as if skipping there, seemed to leave in the ominous, gloomy sky some precise little black angular curlicues, which did not immediately dissolve and, more than anything, resembled a quick flourish with a soft pencil on flat, lead-gray paper.

The biting cold of iron in her hand, as she squeezed the rough rusty spike of the fence grating—like despair, that cold pierced everything that was sadly occurring at that moment in Anna Petrovna's soul:

the urgent, hungry hope of seeing once more, of *finding some way to save*, among that multitudinous throng of frighteningly identical people who had suddenly filled the courtyard, the only face in the world for her, the face she loved to the point of adoration,

and the degrading, humiliating despondency at the obvious impossibility of doing this,

and the searing joy which suddenly flared up, when, finally, she saw and recognized him!

and the dismay because it was so hard to recognize him, more like a lucky guess,

and the horror—because his beloved face was already the face of a stranger, of a man forcibly estranged from her, and like all the other faces in the column, it already seemed to be sprinkled with the leaden, deathly dust of this July dawn.

...A command was given, and with good-natured awkwardness they lined up single file and started thumping their loose-fitting boots, first in place, and then toward the exit from the parade ground. And they walked, our near and dear ones, quietly walked to their death, and a terrible weight seemed to lie in the beggarly pack that each one wore strapped to his shoulders...

To her own spiteful amazement, Anna Petrovna howled like a wolf under her breath. She was afraid to even imagine what her face must look like now—it had to be horrible, because the most horrible thing that could possibly happen had happened: her beloved had been led away to his death (*to his death*—she knew that for certain), and there was no way whatsoever that she could stop this routine little crime.

...and she would hear some long forgotten tunes, switching, racing ahead and interrupting one another:

sometimes in the semi-dusk of their dacha (outside the thriving, gloomy greenery of summer foliage was flush against the open windows, almost bursting in over the window sills...), someone—Sister? Mama?—would be rapidly playing, with condescending chic, some children's piece of Schubert's.

This bright, pure little melody would seem terribly sad—like a lonely child, dancing alone in an enormous half-dark, empty house, because... because this light-heartedly skipping little polka was already too *little* for

everyone—for the one who was playing, of course, and even for Anna
Petrovna, the little girl Anya, who like a grown-up at this moment was
shivering under Mama's plaid wrap, crunched up like a gloomy little
squirrel in a corner of the enormous, cozily sagging sofa. Tucking her legs
beneath her like a grown-up, pale and nervous, with a somewhat hostile
attentiveness, but almost without fear, she was acutely aware of the mysterious and new processes that were unhurriedly and obscurely taking place
within her... And Schubert's little polka, leaping up and jumping around,
kept rushing around on the shadowy parquet floor, and something like
dismay could already be felt in the magical little bells of this carefree pup-
pet song...

...sometimes—"Eins, zwei, drei!"—some violins, frightened half to
death, would suddenly start sobbing and laughing convulsively and loudly,
even shrieking in wild gaiety, in some dirty Ukrainian farm hut, packed
tight with fantastically frightening peasants, trying to outlaugh, outeat
and outdrink each other.

She smelled a nauseating stench of kerosene from a dozen lamps, mag-
nanimously lit on each table for the festive occasion; she gasped and felt a
sharp scratching in her throat from the rank, home-grown-tobacco smoke,
which hung almost motionless in a thick, bluish layer throughout the
house; and an icy railway station draft blew on her feet along the floor—
from the door, which, it seemed, people were opening every minute directly
out into the black winter night.

People kept coming in and going out through the doorway. Bulkily
dressed, laden with weapons, they kept drunkenly catching their sides on
the door lintels, rattling their sabers and laughing with well-fed guffaws,
and the three or four musicians, dressed in black and looking very strange
here in their long, Jewish coats, looking more than anything else like
frozen crows, huddled together tightly and were pushed farther and farther back into the corner.

With false recklessness, they ran their bows at terrible speed over their
shabby, little toy-like violins and, at the same time, in a studiedly varied
manner, they made some strange movements with their bodies (probably
also to show gaiety) and some awful grimaces which gave their faces a
sourly sweet expression. From time to time, first one of them and then
another would glance servilely but attentively at the groom, who towered
threateningly and drunkenly beside his bride, who sat there already half
dead from horror, from the endless nausea of this horror; barely a teenager,
the girl was afraid to look up at what was happening around her and

squeezed her icy fingers as tightly as she could between her knees, and soundlessly whispered through her bloodless, bluish lips, "... not me... don't let it happen to me... not me..."

As if stung by a whip, from time to time one of the fiddlers would shout out, "Ein, zwei, drei !" and the mockingly gay music, baring its teeth and seeming to giggle maliciously, would start galloping off on a new round. And nothing could express better than this music all the horror, all the nightmarish improbability of what life was doing to her, Anna Petrovna, on that endless night, which stretched on and on, like some exhaustive torture...

...and sometimes—she would suddenly clearly hear the friendly provincial hiss of some phonograph record, so worn out that through the hissing she could barely hear the mossily plush, marmalade tenor, singing so carefully (probably raising up on his toes, off of the lacquered, ladies' heels of his shoes...). He sang so very sweetly, slightly slobbering the words: "rose ... shadowy garden... silhouette...," that it wasn't even disgusting any more, but simply made you laugh. And it was amusing to hear how sweetly and seductively this tango tried so seriously to deceive her, and it was amusing to notice what beauty—and oh! how beautiful it was!—had been stashed all around for this amorous drama: here is the steamy southern night, and the moon, and the silvery sea, and the silvery cypresses ... and she was completely reduced to giggly embarrassment by this fellow, who like Turkish candy, cautiously insolent and imperviously stupid, every now and then would appear over her shoulder with the operetta-like part in his greasy, curly hair, startling her with the vulgar manners of a lower-class servant, and at the same time of a leading man from the silent films. All this was rather discouraging—could something like this really be serious?!—but this strange, delicious situation somehow kept enticing her to play up to his lead coquettishly, to make "mysterious" eyes, to smile enticing smiles ... and it was sweet to feel her dizzy little head, with the heavily flaming blush on her cheeks, tipsily moving on the thin stem of her neck from one bare shoulder to the other bare shoulder, and every second know, remember, try not to forget, that all this wasn't serious, wasn't serious, well, of course not, it wasn't serious...

* * *

The old woman would look—in equal measure greedily, curiously and tenderly—would look at all these women, so unlike each other, and only occasionally would there float through a confused: "How strange that all these women—are me..."

...and this one, with her face thrown back blissfully, smiling automatically, but a bit tensely, looking into the blue airport sky and feeling the warm airport wind, like a gentle powder puff, teasingly tickle her neck, open for everyone to see, excitedly watching a little red snub-nosed plane performing some incomprehensible, and apparently very complicated maneuvers up there: first, inspiredly, motor whining with the last ounce of effort, flying up at a steep angle invisible to the eye, and then, suddenly, catastrophically silent, starting to fall, whimsically turning somersaults, so that through the bleachers there instantly spread a single sigh of bewildered horror, everyone's breath sticking in their throat and a wild fear growing bigger and bigger, as if flying down from a mountain top... always, however, replaced in time by a happy sigh of relief, as the motor again began to beat, and the little red plane, skillfully and dashingly extricating itself from the intricate loops of its fall, would again soar up along a steep victorious arc toward the zenith and once more would do something exciting and risky there, and again would fall, so that it could, in circus style, shake its little wings in farewell and victoriously fly off past the edge of the field, instantly disappearing from view...

And then the blue space above the flying field at Tushino—it would be more exact to say a certain theoretical blue cube in which the representation of an air parade had been shown—for a minute or two would be deserted, it would be easier to hear the breeze, somehow a very carefree one, like a sea breeze, and—

and it was a delight to be aware that by turning your head just a little—to the left and a bit up—your eyes would meet the same even, wise, abundant tenderness that they met in the eyes of your beloved...

...and this pathetic woman was also Anna Petrovna—the one who was trudging along, after escaping, against all probability, from the cruel jumble of refugee wanderings—crowded, tightly-packed railway cars, dirt, shame, hunger, the humiliating feeling that you were a rag, floating down a muddy current...—trudging along, no longer feeling anything except pitch-black exhaustion, senilely dragging across the floor boards her monstrous soldier boots, laced up with pieces of telephone wire, trudging along—

and her relatives were staring over at her, and everything was written on their faces in that clear moment: the repulsion, and the resentment, and the pity, and the fear of infection—and she, trudging along, afraid she

wouldn't have the strength for these last few, most difficult steps, no longer
feeling either joy, or relief, or salvation—she suddenly stopped in sleepy surprise, seeing a mirror for the first time in the last month and a half.

A gray old beggar woman cautiously glanced at her from the mirror. The
beggar's face was strangely alive.

Anna Petrovna took a step closer, bent over and saw that her own eyebrows were moving, gray with crawling lice. And—she lost consciousness
for a while from the pitiless self-loathing, which had hit her like a blow in
the face.

Then somehow she cried out: "Please don't touch me!"—and a little
later, with her head already shaved bare by the crudely domineering hands
of one of her aunts, the bravest and most compassionate of all her relatives,
who, nevertheless, had not been able to keep an expression of revulsion off
her face while she wielded the scissors—a little later Anna Petrovna, once
more hysterical, almost howling, and sobbing with humiliation and happiness, was locked in the threshing shed alone with a fifteen-bucket tank of
hot water, a sheep trough and an enormous piece of squishy soap screwed
on a stick and tossed to her along with the stick from behind the door by
someone's frightened hand.

At first she sobbed and shouted and laughed, all at the top of her voice,
unable to control this horribly vulgar animal voice of hers, but later on she
moaned exhaustedly and voluptuously, whined blissfully, and toward the
end, with no strength left, just wept quietly, continuously, sweetly, lying on
the bottom of the chiseled trough, which was like a shallow coffin. She tried
not to move and to lie as flat as possible, so that the water in the brim-full
trough would cover her completely, like the blanket her mother used to
tuck in right under her chin when she was a little girl.

...and this woman, strange as it may seem, was also Anna Petrovna.

She was sitting alone in a friendly, lazy rookery on an Odessa beach
which the sultry heat had drained of life. She was sitting on a light blue
woven bedspread like a little raft, patiently and painstakingly fussing with
her abundant reddish hair, gathering it into a knot—and at the same time
holding a few hairpins between her lips, frowning, and slyly looking around,
stopping from time to time to patiently rearrange the skirts of her light cal-
ico robe, which kept coming open at the knees.

Finally, she finished with her hair, got up and—seeing some small red
spots in her eyes because she had gotten up too fast and because the sun,
which was pouring its bright mass down on everything all around, had
struck her pupils too violently—started unhurriedly, as if absentmindedly, to
undo the buttons at her breast, with each unbuttoned button overcoming

an instantaneous protest, equally instantaneously overruled, because, of course, it was immodest, taking off her dress in front of everybody...

Finally she nevertheless took off her robe—or rather, let it drop to the ground, like a colorful, insignificant rag—and straightened up, sighing deeply, but also a bit apprehensively.

She felt the cold, the sun and the male glances.

By habit she gave her hair knot a toss, threw back her head and started walking toward the water with the special gait that she privately called the "royal heron," but after just a few steps, she completely forgot about such nonsense—because the sand on the beach was so excitedly, inquisitively, almost unbearably, burning her tender feet—

because her whole body, almost completely bare, was breathing with such enjoyment and contentment—

because, with each step, ever closer and higher, the sea rose up in front of her, gloomy and slate gray from the sun, high in the sky—the sea, which in a very offhand manner was hanging out along the beach, jerkily chasing along the sand all kinds of petty trash, worthless, but not at all offensive to the eye.

She stepped lightly across a border of scum and strode into the sea, happily amazed at how warm the water seemed here on the sandbank, and walked in deeper, cautiously feeling her way along the unpleasantly silted bottom with the soles of her feet

After a few steps, not wanting to wait until the water, already up to the top of her hips, stung her with an unpleasant chill, she got up her nerve and squatted down, plunging in up to her shoulders, then quickly stood up and, now already a part of the sea, waded on in deeper, somnambulistically smiling in expectation of that one blissfully swooning moment, which was, really, what always drew her to the sea, the moment when the sea, with a sigh, would finally swallow her up *completely,* lifting her up and holding her weightless in itself, rocking her cautiously and tenderly... And in an instant her sinful soul would suddenly forget its body and soar!—soar with blissful liberation, with jubilant relief—into the heights! and, it seemed, into the expanse of sea!..

* * *

Anna Petrovna could never tell when these visions changed into dreams. And, actually, weren't they really dreams—dreams of her youth, dreams of the life, which irrevocably and indifferently had flowed through her, as sand flows through an hourglass?

And maybe, on the contrary, the dream was what began when she opened her eyes every morning—her patient vegetating beside the boring window? And life, her real life, still remained only in those nocturnal memories about herself?

* * *

She hadn't felt any pain for a long time. Life simply seemed to be expiring out of her.

She guessed that these were, evidently, her last days, because it kept requiring greater and greater efforts to live.

Strange, but she felt no fear. Only there was an ever-increasing bitter tenderness in the way she gazed at the pathetic human line under the window in the courtyard. And for the first time in many years, she felt like crying: for them, for herself, for them.

Once she dozed off with her head resting on the windowsill—dozed off so deliciously, so gratefully, so exhaustedly!—and for the first time without any sort of protest, she thought through her drowsy haze that she really was going this time—slowly, but really going—and how wonderful it was that *this* was happening this way, with no suffering, as if it were all just drowsiness on the sun-warmed windowsill.

After that she would often let herself doze off in the daytime beside the window, whenever weakness got to be just too much for her.

From time to time the moments of drowsiness would get longer and darker. She felt this. She would notice her face muscles involuntarily relaxing as soon as she had barely closed her eyes and her face would become unfamiliar, alien. Her jaw would slacken and, as if from outside herself, she would look with contempt on the frightening grin which bared her dead plastic teeth.

But she didn't have the energy to make her face presentable.

One day Marina, bursting into Anna Petrovna's room, saw her in just such a state.

The unexpectedness of it threw her into a tizzy; however, noticing that Grandma was still breathing, she managed, with a lot of grunting and groaning, to drag her over onto the bed.

Anna Petrovna woke up, of course. But she really didn't have any strength at all, not even enough to get herself into bed.

Uncomplainingly she let herself be put into bed and covered with a blanket.

And all this time she was steadily, intently, quietly looking at Marina; she didn't know her granddaughter in this role.

And somehow, she felt terribly sorry for Marina. She wasn't pretty, wasn't nice, wasn't intelligent, but still, she wanted to seem pretty and nice and intelligent...

Anna Petrovna sighed mournfully and suddenly—very much to her own surprise, parting with her trivial little secret with unexpected ease— almost without expression, she uttered, "I have nothing left at all, dear Marina. Don't be upset—but there's *absolutely nothing* left."

It was as if Marina had been caught in the act. She started bustling around. She found something that needed to be moved on the table. She kept her face turned away.

"...you two, I know, it seems, were hoping. But—please don't be angry, if you can help it—there just isn't anything *at all*."

"What were we hoping for?" Marina yelled rudely and falsely. "Why should we hope for something?! What's the matter, Granny? Have you completely flipped?!"

Anna Petrovna, however, was hardly listening.

Suddenly overflowing with ineffable pleasure from this little scene, feeling with spiteful irony the completely false theatricality of what was going on (and, at the same time, being glad of this: "So, I'm still not being serious ... That means it won't be too soon, if I'm so amused..."). And Anna Petrovna did this:

she reached out her hand to Marina, theatrically bending it at the wrist, and said, with more than a bit of surprise, hearing how affected and theatrically exhausted her voice sounded:

"Take this anyway, granddaughter... You can, at least, keep this to remember me by."

(What farcical devil had suddenly got into Anna Petrovna? What mischievous need had made this her time for a theatrical performance at the very brink of death?)

Marina gaped uncomprehendingly at her grandma.

A certain semblance of anxiety could even be seen on her face.

But when she realized what Anna Petrovna was talking about—the ring with the crude bauble—she blurted out with relief, not bothering to conceal either her scorn or the fact that she felt insulted: "Huh! What would I want that for? Go flaunt it yourself!"

"Take it," Anna Petrovna insisted.

And Marina took it. Whether she didn't want to go against a dying person, or (most likely) because she was simply unable to refuse any free gift, she suddenly bent down nimbly, sort of pounced on Anna Petrovna's outstretched hand, and began to pull it off.

"That hurts..." Anna Petrovna wrinkled her forehead in irritation, adjusted her head on the pillow and suddenly—went back to sleep.

She dropped off to sleep—like a log in thick black water—and it was a pity she couldn't see how her granddaughter, sitting there at the table, at first just sat there thinking, then started sobbing resentfully, and then cried convulsively, though softly, sticking out her lip like a little girl.

And she kept tracing, tracing some hurried little squares on the table-cloth with the ring, which lay forgotten in her hand, and with her other hand from time to time she seemed to be neatly brushing the squares off to one side ...

And it didn't seem that she was crying about her lost hopes for Grandma's wealth at all, but about something quite different and peripheral—about her own life, perhaps.

* * *

...And a day later, Marina again burst noisily into Anna Petrovna's quiet habitation, breathing hard from anger.

The old woman, as usual, was sitting there beside the window with the lights off, peering mournfully down into the courtyard... —

—suddenly! the door burst open with a horrible crash, Marina flew in, and—it began!

Something so incomprehensible, disgusting, shameful and terrifying began that at the sight of her granddaughter Anna Petrovna's heart shrunk up into a dry, weak little fist and did not relax again.

Hastily, as if in a panic, her poor little heart started to chatter in half-beats, and a nauseating, gay swing began, alternately elevating Anna Petrovna up to a ringing height, where her eyes widened in terror, and then flinging her, mercilessly, brutally, briefly, into the despairing darkness of death...

Marina was shaking in rage and hate. She was even bobbing up and down, baring her teeth in agony because she couldn't yell at the top of her lungs or make any substantial movement in this narrow, hateful space.

"What have you foisted off on me? *What* have you foisted off on me?" Marina was yelling in a strangled whisper. "What's the matter, couldn't you say, like a human being, what you were giving me?! So you decided to get me for good this time? Well, this is what I've come to tell you: if anything bad *happens* to us because of your little ring, I swear it!!—I'll, I'll... I'll choke you to death with my own two little hands!"

Anna Petrovna looked at Marina without understanding a word she was saying and couldn't recognize her at all. Sometimes there seemed to be a flash of something familiar, but instantly—as if with the wide swing of a dirty, tattered paint brush, it would blur away! And again some unknown, dangerous unruly animal would be raging in front of her.

"You've always hated me! You think I don't know that? I was in your way! Always in your way! And now—have you gotten even?"

"Oh, Lord!" the old woman was shaking. "Who is this? What's this all about?"

She didn't understand a word that Marina was screaming. She didn't understand anything—except this violent hate directed *against her*. And she didn't feel hurt or angry either (how could she!), only terrified...

"You begrudged it..." Marina, her eyes half closed, was shaking her head from side to side in slow torment. "You resented giving it to your only close (!) relative... Would it have been hard to tell me what kind of a ring you were giving me?"—

and suddenly she shrieked wildly, as if inspired, "You wanted to frame me, to get me sent to prison?!"

Here something tinkled pathetically, falling over on the table. Marina, startled, turned to look and then—suddenly—with malicious glee, brushed off onto the floor everything that was on it!

The sound of breaking glass—like throwing gasoline onto a fire—made her flare up again...

Screaming in ecstatic malevolence, "Well, this'll show you good! This'll show you!"—she nimbly started knocking down off the walls all the little shelves with their pathetic little vases and statuettes. (She didn't miss a single one, and where she couldn't reach, she didn't mind jumping up on the table or on the bed.)

Suddenly she rushed over and, tearing it off its hook, with greedy pleasure ripped Anna Petrovna's old dressing gown to shreds. Then immediately, jerking out the bureau drawer, she started grabbing the underwear in it and—clearly already out of her mind—hastily ripped it up, lifting each piece up in her arms, as if demonstrating to Anna Petrovna: "This'll show you! It's not seventy thousand! But you'll remember me!"

Everything seemed to be ripping easily: it was all old and had been washed and rewashed... But then she got some old bedspread in her hands and, even straining and groaning, she wasn't able to break apart its crudely stitched edge. And—it was as if she herself had broken apart! She tossed it aside.

Her hands were shaking badly.

She looked around once more, inspired (the inspiration, however, was fading: she couldn't see anything else that she might be able to tear up, rip apart or destroy...) and quickly, as if suddenly coming to her senses, she dashed out, smashing the door behind her with such force that the key flew out of the keyhole and skidded along the floor with a pathetic tinkling sound.*

And then there was silence.

Anna Petrovna sat with her eyes half closed, leaning the back of her head against the wall, and the wild swing kept swinging her: up—with a shriek, down—with a moan, and the weak life trembled inside her during these moments, on the verge of extinction—like the flame of a thin little candle in a nasty, black draft...

* * *

Anna Petrovna saw a strange fish: in dead sluggish water—in the gloomily flowing depths, near the very bottom—a pallid fish, which had come alongside a coal-black petrified tree stump, and was tinnily thinking about something,

—was tinnily thinking about how strange it was that she had to keep swimming, swimming, swimming (her whole life!)—overcoming the lightless dull force of the current (her whole life!)—eternally striving to be on the go, eternally resisting the opposing dense flow of water, like temptation—

—like the temptation to flip over recklessly on her side! to yield recklessly to the current! to let herself experience (at long last!) that fantastic feeling of poignant, sweet rest, *Rest*, that she had dreamed of all her life, this fish, as a reward, there at the end of this monotonous heroism, which she did not really understand: to keep swimming, swimming, swimming—her whole life!—upstream, against the current, to the upper reaches.

---

* ...She dashed out, smashing the door behind her, flew down the stairs at a run and jumped in her car.

The ignition key was dancing in her fingers, just wouldn't go into the keyhole. She fought it for a long time, breathing furiously; finally she got the key in, but didn't start the motor. Like a little girl, she sat on her own hands: she couldn't drive in this condition; she had to calm down...

...And no sooner had she thought, this fish, about that tempting rest, than she really did, easily and deftly, turn over on her side!—

and instantly she was malevolently and furiously whirled, dashed and overturned, mortally and shamefully exposing her white belly! And only that second did it suddenly become clear: how strong, how brave and beautiful this fish had been, resisting *such a dangerous* river her whole life.

"I probably almost died just now," thought Anna Petrovna.

It was late evening. Maybe even early morning.

She got up and, cautiously testing the floor with her feet before taking a step, and holding on to the wall and the furniture, began making her way to her bed.

She was shivering violently, but it was a strange shivering. Not the shivering of illness, but not stopping and not stoppable; it seemed that all her internal organs without exception—every cell, every sinew, every fiber—were jerking, beating, pulsating and dancing in a wild uncoordinated jumble.

She had to calm down. But, Lord God Almighty, how could she calm down, when *that kind of money*—seventy thousand!—had been snatched right out of her pocket?!

"And it's all her fault, all her fault... Are you giving somebody a present? Well then, give it to them like a human being! At least give them a hint that you're giving them something valuable! But she just poked it at me—'to remember me by!'—like some trinket from a tobacco stand!..." Again Marina was shaken by a frustrated, violent trembling.

And again—although already she didn't want to—she started to remember how she and her husband had gone yesterday evening to see Lev Yakovlevich Kuznetsov, a jeweler who had the parking space next to theirs—so they could show him Grandma's present. They just up and went, for lack of anything better to do... "Even from a mangy sheep, you might get a tuft of wool"—that's what they were thinking, idiots!—maybe it would be worth a hundred rubles?... The silver ought to be worth quite a bit anyway?...

Lev Yakovlevich took the ring—disdainfully, almost with a smirk. He took it—and was instantly, in the twinkling of an eye—*transformed!* Even seemed to be—frightened!

Right then!—right then, it still wouldn't have been too late to catch on, to grab it out of his hands and hide it somewhere safe! And, in case of trouble, later on you could laugh right in Lev Yakovlevich's face: "What do you mean, my dear sir? You off your rocker? What ring are you talking about?.." After all, everything had been instantly obvious in Kuznetsov's eyes: his eyes had turned lustful and calculating. He couldn't hold back his ecstasy, even started to click his tongue...

Lev Yakovlevich examined the ring for a long time—thinking, calculating. Finally he got it all figured and computed and, apparently, came out with this: it was too great a risk. On the other hand, it would be much more advantageous to do something else: inform the proper authorities, inform them honestly and nicely. And, the main thing, he wouldn't have to be envious of anyone, and he'd have a clear conscience, and, where it counted, God willing, they'd give him proper credit for this deed!

"Yes," Lev Yakovlevich said and gave back the ring. "It's quite valuable. But exactly how valuable, I can't tell you right now ... If you want to know precisely, come see me tomorrow at eleven thirty, at the shop.

As if she really had been the one who had just been mercilessly dashed, overturned, hurled about and beaten in that murderous river...

Finally she made it to the bed. She lay down—covering her head with her arm, as if to fend off a beating. She wanted very badly to fall asleep; she felt ill. But sleep did not admit her until dawn.

"In regard to the questions presented to her, Citizeness Zakharova-Kochubei, Anna Petrovna, Russian, born 1901 in the city of Murom, testified as follows:

"The ring until recently belonged to her, and more precisely, until September 29 of this year, when she gave the ring to her granddaughter, M. N. Novosyolova. The ring was not given to M. N. Novosyolova for the purpose of selling the ring. The ring was given to M. N. Novosyolova as a keepsake, because of Citizeness Zakharova-Kochubei's poor health and possible death in the near future. She cannot testify to anything definite about the origin of the ring. It was given to Citizeness Zakharova-

---

Marina and her husband went out the door. And he—reached for the phone.

"Knock-knock." "Who's there?" "Police informer so-and-so. I want to give you information about the Two-Faced Janus—a premier diamond, sought since the Civil War, a national treasure, which I, Lev Yakovlevich Kuznetsov, have now found."

The next morning Marina was just ready to leave for the store, when the doorbell rang. Two men. Young—athletic. Red ID cards. A polite conversation. A half-hour ride in an official Volga.

Well, and at the end of the ride—three aged jewelry experts, a jovial Lev Yakovlevich, a couple of police colonels and three men in civilian clothes.

"Sign here, Marina Nikolaevna. Here, and here, and here..."

Expropriated! That's a word they have, a special one; when they pick your pocket—that's expropriating.

"Thank you," they say. "We sincerely thank you, Marina Nikolaevna! You have helped return to our Motherland (unintentionally, it's true) our national treasure, the world-famous Two-Faced Janus!—and in every word they spoke and in every glance there seemed to be hidden a sneer: "You're a fool, Marina Nikolaevna! You're an ignorant fool!"

And Lev Yakovlevich (the louse! I'll puncture his tires!) smiling sweetly and continually looking around at the policemen, as if at home here among equals, says at the end, "Marina Nikolaevna, yesterday you wanted to know how much this ring is worth ... Now, of course, it doesn't make any difference to you, but if you're interested—seventy thousand is the price of your little stone! Naturally, a crude approximation..."

...Marina sat there, remembering all this, just as she had several hours earlier in that office—her eyes half closed, biting her lip—feeling as if somebody was slowly pulling her insides out of her...

Finally she sighed with a groan, shook her head once and pushed on the starter button. Zhiguli Baby immediately started to coo devotedly. Marina thought something indistinct, but mournfully affectionate about the car, something like: "...you're the only good thing in my life..."

Slowly she started driving.

Kochubei in the spring (February-March) of 1919 or 1920 by a man
whose surname or nickname was Kochet and whom she calls her first husband; the marriage was not registered, but there was a wedding. As to this
person, Kochet, she cannot testify to anything definite. He was a military
man, one of the detachment officers. The commanding officer in the
detachment was a man whose surname was Perebiynos. As to the question, on whose side the detachment was fighting, she cannot testify to
anything definite, explaining this by her extreme youth and lack of understanding of what was going on in the world, who was fighting whom and
for what reasons.

"The ring was given to Citizeness Zakharova-Kochubei, as she thinks, at
the moment when she was left, ill and unconscious, in the village of
Vasilievka in the Yekaterinoslav District of [crossed out] Province. When
she recovered consciousness, the ring had been placed on the ring finger of
her right hand with the stone in, toward the palm. Citizeness Zakharova-
Kochubei never again saw the detachment of Perebiynos or the man named

---

"...I don't care (although, of course, it would be awfully interesting to know) what
kind of millionaire you lay under or what kind of tricks you showed him, that he would
compensate you so generously!.."

Marina drove out of the courtyard and again, again without wanting to, and again
getting all worked up, started mentally shouting at Anna Petrovna: "I don't care! But just
why, you bitch, did you decide to play your dirty trick on me?! Why didn't you even hint
what kind of a stone the ring had?! Do you think I would have hauled it off to the jewelry
store? Do you think I couldn't have found a buyer—a quiet, honest one? Why, I would
have sawed it up into pieces, that premier diamond, I wouldn't have cared that it is, you
know, a *treasure!!* 'It belongs in the State Diamond Collection'... We still don't know
whose 'diamond collection' it'll show up in now!.. But me! Good Lord! Like a simple-
minded fool! Just think! I handed it over with my own two hands!!."

And once more she started trembling violently, and, naturally, at the very first traffic
light, noticing too late that the light had turned red, she slammed on the brakes so angrily
that a dump truck, driving behind her, didn't have time to avoid her and, without any pity
or leniency, rammed into her trunk.

The windows shattered. A terrible pain flared up in the back of her head from the blow.
She screamed. But not just from the pain. She screamed more because of the unimaginable suffering which her darling Zhiguli Baby must be experiencing after the heavy,
blunt-nosed, cement-splattered truck rammed at high speed into Baby's shiny rear end,
mashing it into an ugly accordion...

But even this didn't end the nightmares of that horrible day.

...It was already late in the afternoon when Marina finally dragged herself home. (She
had been towed home with a rope by the very same dump truck that had mutilated her.
And he had ripped her off for an extra ten, the lout.)

She climbed up the stairs, barely dragging one foot after the other. Bruises had ripened
under her eyes. On the whole, a pretty sight!

Her husband opened the door. Politely took her coat from her shoulders. Escorted her
into the living room ahead of him. But in the living room—he couldn't hold out any

Kochet, who probably placed the ring on her finger as a farewell gift. As to the circumstances of her presence in the detachment: she was forcibly removed from a train. As to the value of the ring, Citizeness Zakharova-Kochubei definitely testifies that she knew nothing. All her life she wore it as a good-luck charm. This is the first time she has heard the name 'Two-Faced Janus'. She makes no claims on the ring in regard to anyone.

"This report of my testimony is accurate. A. Zakharova-Kochubei."

When the very young, thick-lipped, little lieutenant finished suffering over the report and handed it to Anna Petrovna ("Sign here, please"), she revived. She was somehow almost enjoyably worried.

She took the proffered sheet alertly, but instantly, barely glancing at it, felt distinctly nauseous at the sight of this cheap greenish paper upon which some lazy curlicues of a dirty lilac color were cavorting freely—sometimes tripping and piling up on each other, sometimes crawling off every which way. Just the way they looked immediately made her think of some sort of *degeneracy*. And these lines reeked of such a hopeless and dejected incompetence that Anna Petrovna couldn't help glancing curiously once more at the little lieutenant and, quickly feeling sorry for him, became even more firmly convinced of her feeling: "A real loser, of course... His whole life, in any place—a loser."

The lieutenant offered her his pen for the signature—a ball-point, the kind they sell at newsstands.

Anna Petrovna, with a disdainful smirk, making a surprisingly aristocratic gesture with her fingers, rejected it: "Oh, no, young man. You write with *that one* yourself. And for me (be so kind), look there in that little box on the dresser."

In the little box—in a narrow flat case made of formerly very expensive dull soft black leather, she kept... No, it should be expressed this way: Her

---

longer. "You," he says, stupid cow! And all because of your stinking relatives!.."

It turned out that *they* had visited him today too. They had questioned him: "What kind of stone, where was the stone from, by what right did the stone..."

And after all the questions and interrogations, the main thing—his own boss also had called him in. "I don't know," he says, "and I don't want to know just what you are accused of. With your White Guard relatives," he says, "sort things out somehow by yourself. But I just wanted to tell you that, after what just happened—don't ever even think about any business trips abroad."

"Do you even understand, you idiot," Marina's husband was yelling as if through a megaphone, "what your grandma has done with her little present?! I've been crawling up this ladder for ten years! I've had to lick off every rung, before I could step up onto it! I went ahead and married you, you imbecile, so that no problems would arise there! And now?.. And now—what?!.."

favorite, still pre-war, Parker *lived there*—at ease, reclining grandly in its fluffy and silvery velvet nest.

Black and gold, a bit heavy for her hand, with an old-fashioned, but amazingly sensitive point, it looked rather unpretentious and plebeian; actually, however, it was extraordinarily comfortable in her hand, reliable and in a most amazing manner always instilled in Anna Petrovna a feeling of competent strength and a serene confidence in this strength, even when she was only taking it out to sign for her pension.

Slowly, with pleasure, she unscrewed the massive cap with the clip in the form of a golden arrow; she opened up her Parker and her face even brightened up when she felt its fullness and weightiness in her hand.

She told the lieutenant to give her something solid—to put under the paper. He looked around in obedient perplexity and asked indecisively, "Maybe my briefcase will do?"

She graciously acceded: "All right."

She tried out the ink in the pen.

Once or twice she waved her elbow, making a loosening-up movement. Then she firmly placed the pen on the paper and unhurriedly, but without stopping, signed distinctly:

A. ZAKHAROVA-KOCHUBEI

...The ink turned glassy as it dried. Anna Petrovna watched it quietly.

The thought that this, perhaps, was the last time she would ever sign her name came and went, without making her especially sad or upset.

She just looked at the dozen and a half letters she had drawn and seemed to be pleased.

Thousands of people live, feeling a vague discontent and dissatisfaction with the way their signature looks on paper. From childhood all the way until their death they keep putting off until later its final polishing. And most often they never do get around to it...

Anna Petrovna had nothing to be ashamed of. The image formed by the letters of her signature was pleasant and flattering to the eye, even to an eye as particular as hers.

The capital "A", drawn narrowly and steeply, was raised like the steeple of a Gothic cathedral. It could have seemed too high, this "A", and even skinny, but the energetic cuneiform cross stroke, placed with amazing precision, instantly made the whole structure very harmonious (and, besides, sticking out a bit on the left side, it also balanced the rather risky slant of the whole letter to the right).

The capital "Z" was also both high and narrow. I dare say, it was also a bit arrogant and cold, but definitely exquisitely done. The haughtily upraised head of the letter, when carefully examined, consisted of a number of very fine lines, like jewel facets, and because of this, in spite of its smallness, it did not by any means seem insubstantial, nor did it at all remind us of a snake's head, as is often the case when contemplating the letter "z" in the most varied handwritings... And the letter's lower part was drawn decisively and vigorously and finished with a loop—angular and abrupt—which immediately changed into a tiny "a", which lived, pressed tightly against its capital letter, like a bud to its branch.

The "kh"* was artistic and delicate. But only in that part which came down from the right and to the left. It was done with a carefree flourish, with a bold sweep and even with recklessness, which was, however, curtly and categorically interrupted by another cuneiform line (clearly rhyming with the crossbar of the first capital "A").

This anarchic streak in the "kh" naturally gave birth to its neighboring (on the other side of the tiny, neatly drawn "a", which modestly stood alone) consonant "r", a luxurious, slightly Bohemian, full-blooded letter with baroque embellishments, after which it would have been unthinkable to write the "...ov", which followed it, either feebly or austerely. And it really did seem to have been drawn in one merry, long breath, this "...ov"... (Although we couldn't help mentioning here that the "v" suffers from some hard-to-grasp lack of taste in the way it is written. Maybe it was some uncertainty in the stroke, maybe a lack of freedom in the transitions... Anna Petrovna, by the way, always felt this herself, but—she had learned to accept it. As people learn to accept certain of the less desirable traits of their character.)

And after the luxurious, generous, vivacious "...rov", the name concluded with an unexpected, small, neatly closed, carefully drawn little nun "a", which stood a bit apart from all the others.

Then came her lighthearted second surname—Kochubei.

When she pronounced this name she always imagined some hot steppe, with Cossack scalplocks and horsetail banners waving in the wind—spaciousness, gaiety and lavishness,

As if suddenly, for an instant, oxygen was being added to her blood.

And it, this name, could, of course, only be written in one way: with this striking, double-wedged, broad and severe "u",** with this gay "b", which had to have its little curl fluttering in the wind, with this capital "K", which seemed to have been made with three saber strokes, with this breve mark cap-

---

*   The Cyrillic letter which resembles the English "x" is transliterated as "kh" here.
**   Looks like an English "y".

ping the "...ei"—which, like a bird, was flying upward, and, also like a bird, but now a dead bird, was falling earthward.*

These letters vividly reminded her of the man who once bore this name and who had given it to her.

And even now it gave her great pleasure to write: KOCHUBEI.

The ink had dried. Anna Petrovna was reluctant to let go of the paper. As if for the first time, as if for the last time, she peered at her signature.

Yes, it was a complete little country.

It was an energetically living, beautiful and proud city—on the shore of a melancholy lilac sea, which extended, as to the horizon, to the top edge of the paper. Word-waves, pushing in confusion, climbing upon and mashing each other, were pressing right up against the walls of this citadel, and it seemed that any second now and they would inundate it.

The lieutenant took the paper and he too seemed to see something.

He scrutinized the signature for a long time. And at that moment he resembled a little boy—an unfortunate little boy, who, alas, had long passed the time to become wiser.

And Anna Petrovna again felt sorry for him.

Solicitously—as if, for example, it were an etching sheet — the lieutenant placed the paper in his briefcase. He kept shifting from one foot to the other.

It was time to go, but it seemed that he wanted to say something else, unofficial, to this old woman, who had obviously somehow made quite an impression on him. Stupidly, as if waiting for something, he peered at Anna Petrovna; he suddenly mysteriously blushed—his cheeks and even his neck turned completely crimson— angrily blurted out "good-bye!' and, banging against every possible obstacle, started to pick his way out of the room, embarrassedly muttering profanities under his breath...

But, without meaning to, he made *such* a screech with his boots on the broken glass in the doorway, such a horrible screech that it was as if Anna Petrovna, who had been watching him good-naturedly and a bit sardonically, had been hit—as if she had been hit in some unimaginably tender nerve plexus! And instantly she was convulsed—from revulsion and pain—into a tight knot!

The pupils of her eyes immediately were sharply constricted. And—unconsciousness—for the umpteenth time these last few days!—overtook her.

---

*The "i" is written like an English "u" with a breve mark over it.

....

....

....

A broom was rustling along the floor.

The glass slivers that someone was sweeping up cautiously jingled along the floor boards—they were sliding with a brief scandalous tinkle onto the metal floor of the dustpan.

Someone was tidying up her room.

Anna Petrovna was listening with her eyes closed, and she was in no hurry to open them.

For some reason these noises made her feel amazingly calm and comfortable.

...The person doing the sweeping went out into the hallway to dump the dustpan, and there (evidently he had suppressed a cough in her room, so as not to awaken her...) freely cleared his throat.

Anna Petrovna heard in surprise that it was a man.

"Who could it be?"

She tried to answer that question, but she couldn't even think of anyone—she had been alone for so very, very long.

The only person who came to see her occasionally—to clean the apartment, to bring some milk products from the store, to borrow "three rubles for my lord and master"—was her neighbor, Faina. But— a man?!

He was gone for a long time.

He was gone for so long that it might seem he had gone away for good.

However, Anna Petrovna somehow wasn't at all worried by his absence. He would come again soon—she knew that. Simply knew it, and that was that.

But the main thing—the room, even though he had gone, was still *filled* with him: it exuded a kind of good-natured calmness, and a slightly mocking belief in something wonderful and good, which was definitely going to happen—if not today, then tomorrow, if not tomorrow, then the day after.

That was something Anna Petrovna had not felt for an infinitely long time—neither in herself nor in anyone else—and she, evidently, so passionately, so hungrily needed just such a feeling of life (for it, with unmistakable delight, provided evidence of the *Harmony,* which, despite the obvious, nevertheless did exist in the world, and it was precisely Harmony that she, in her last days, was subconsciously and greedily seeking in everything that occurred in these last days; for the absence of Harmony would signify with cruel regret, above all, the waste, the insignificance and fortuitousness of her, Anna Petrovna's, stay on this earth...)—and she, evidently, so vitally needed this peace in her whole view of what was occurring, that, sensing this in her mysterious guest, God knows how she sensed it, she suddenly was childishly elated, as, perhaps, someone dying of asphyxiation is elated when his bronchial tubes blessedly catch the cool tenderness of oxygen, and she *began to breathe*—so peacefully, luxuriantly! and so gratefully yielded herself *completely* to this wondrous feeling! and— as if a strong, cool hand had been placed on her feverish brow—floated off slowly, floated off, without ever having opened her eyes, into a new drowsy state—now ineffably pleasant—almost golden—like the sun through your eyelashes...

...And a skinny, light-haired girl looked at her furtively— a nine-year-old girl in a worn and faded, short little dress, which hung down dilapidatedly from her scrawny shoulders, uncovering the tops of her stringy legs, still like a little chicken's, with the knees sticking out and tanned to a dirty dark-blue shade... She was standing a bit behind and off to the side from her mother, and Anna Petrovna could feel the girl's quiet attentive gaze the whole time she was drinking that thick, cold milk from a cloudy liter jar, unable to even pause for breath, barely able to keep from groaning out loud with the ecstasy and delight which poured out along with every unhurried, delicious swallow.

Finally—"oo-ooh!"—she joyfully emptied the jar and could now look at the little girl—and immediately her heart melted with tender pity when she saw the ecstatic adoration, the timid delight with which this skinny little thing looked her over from head to toe, with her little grayish-blue eyes open wide, as if in amazement.

The girl, caught staring, instantly blinked, lowered her eyes, almost ready to cry, then again glanced at her distrustfully, almost even resentfully, and then again—devotion and ecstasy irrepressibly blazed up in her eyes at the sight of this fantastically beautiful, graceful woman, terribly happy, terribly free in every single movement. Something even trembled pitifully in the girl's face because the emotions affecting her were so strong.

And Anna Petrovna—so suddenly, intimately!—sensing the girl's soul, quickly squatted down in front of her, almost jumping down, and with an amusing, hurried desire to teach her, too, this skinny little thing, the happiness that she herself had fully possessed these last few days, quickly hugged the girl, caressing her head and spine, skinny like a kitten's, and said, immediately feeling how inadequate the words were for what she felt and wanted to say: "You'll grow up... you'll be beautiful! You're sure to be very beautiful—with light hair and blue eyes. Be sure and be kind, all right? What's your name?" ("Lilia," the girl answered in a thin, sad voice)—and already feeling that words were useless, but still just as tormented by the burning desire to communicate the secret of happiness to this poor little towheaded girl, Anna Petrovna hugged her deeply and tightly, hoping and believing that this secret, perhaps, would be communicated to her in some other way, without words, and would enter the girl's memory along with the smell of her perfume, of her tender, grateful body, which her lover loved so much, along with the feeling of the victorious and fruitful strength which her whole being calmly radiated these last few days.

She sensed that the girl was furtively glancing at her mother. Anna Petrovna pushed Lilia back a little way, again carefully caressed her flaxen hair, rather thick and long unwashed, and said again, "You'll be beautiful and grown up, and you'll do this with your eyes..." and she showed what regal and somewhat theatrical eyes would be made by the beautiful lady that this Cinderella would become, and Lilia laughed, sincerely happy, and Anna Petrovna started laughing and the mother also smiled, with an effort reshaping the wrinkles on her face, which were habitually frozen in an expression of gloom and worried weariness.

"She's Mother's little helper..," the mother uttered almost reluctantly what was probably her highest praise. "May God give her..."

And this whole scene was lit up—as if by the dim autumn sun—by the tranquil presence of a man who was waiting for her, in no hurry and with no desire to hurry her, Anna Petrovna. He sat, completely relaxed, on some logs, gray from age and rain, absentmindedly tapping a twig against his canvas boot and from time to time, with contented curiosity, glancing all around, as if trying to remember everything firmly and permanently.

He was somewhere nearby in the room again.

Anna Petrovna finally opened her eyes, eager to see her mysterious visitor.

Her first feeling was sharp disappointment at how boring he seemed: she saw an ordinary gray-striped suit jacket, a hunched-over spine and some not very neat hair, so neglected that it was hanging out over his collar in large ringlets.

He was sitting half turned away, almost with his back to Anna Petrovna, and doing something—apparently cutting something—on the table.

Anna Petrovna looked unhappily, almost hostilely, at her uninvited visitor's spine. But then he turned his head a little bit to the side—and Anna Petrovna with relief and pleasure sort of snorted to herself: wha-at a nose he had!

He had such a remarkably large, good-natured, soft nose, that, by this fact alone, its possessor could not but be a good man.

He immediately reminded her of some old caricature of Kornei Chukovsky.*

...But civility required that she inquire who he was and what he was doing in her home. So, without feeling any real need to do so, she asked, "And who are you?" having, strangely enough, a distinct feeling of embarrassment from this question, asked in such a point-blank and tactless manner.

He quickly and gaily turned toward her. "Me?.." and he wiggled his nose, "I told them," he nodded toward the door, "that I was your nephew."

He waited to see how Anna Petrovna would react to such a statement, and getting no reaction, said with obvious relief, "Why don't I get you some tea? I have the unpleasant feeling that you haven't drunk any tea for two days. And by the way, I'm your neighbor. From another apartment building, it's true... Right now, for lack of anything better to do, I've thrown together some sandwiches; so for a start, why don't I get you something to eat and drink?"

He also had a scraggly beard—not very attractive, like a peasant's somehow. But his whole appearance, Anna Petrovna decided, was, more than anything else, like a peasant's—one with no land, a "sharecropper" as they used to say in the Ukraine. If he were wearing an old homespun coat, with a piece of twine for a belt, bast shoes with cloth wrappings for socks and a rabbit-fur "three-eared" hat, you would have a ready-made illustration for a nineteenth-century story of peasant life.

In his eyes though—in spite of their being placed much too close to his enormous nose and in spite of their seeming, as a result, rather too small and simple-minded—in his eyes she could see a considerable "bookish" intelligence, patient, calm, not deceitful, which, however, did not, let us repeat, did not keep his face from resembling an uneducated person's face, and to be even more precise, the face of a wise old gnome from a children's play in which helpless, innocent good is persecuted by crude, stupid evil, and he, this gnome, has to philosophically bide his time as he watches this scandal people have paid to see.

He was right: Anna Petrovna was terribly hungry. The last time she had eaten must have been just before Marina raised that ruckus here. And how long ago had that been?

---

*(1882-1969), critic, translator, author of children's books and works on child psychology.

She ate as if somebody was chasing her: dropping crumbs, rushing, not taking time to chew. It was embarrassing to eat that way in front of a stranger, but she couldn't control herself!

And, really, the tea that he poured for her from his thermos bottle was first rate: excellently brewed and both sweet and hot. And the sandwiches were wonderful: the bread (her favorite, twenty-two kopecks) in proper thin slices, the butter spread on not too stintingly, but not too thick either. And then the ham for these sandwiches (as if he had known)—the ham was *just* her favorite kind, for which in still quite recent times she would take the trouble to ride the bus out by herself—always to Yeliseyev's, so that she could stand there in line (but not, of course, a disgracefully long line like the ones nowadays), and buy exactly three hundred grams (neither two hundred nor four hundred) and have it sliced, because for some mysterious reason this ham lost a lot of its flavor if it was sliced at home instead of at the store by the clean young hands of the neat little doll of a salesgirl, with her long and, obviously, terribly sharp knife—with its thin evil edge, which had almost dissolved from an innumerable multitude of sharpenings, and which seemed especially dangerous in the vicinity of the heavy pine handle, whose wood over the years had acquired the exact appearance of bone, maybe even of ivory...

Her visitor was tactful. During her whole meal he pensively sipped tea from his thermos cap and with exaggerated attention studied the picture on some postcard that he found on her desk.

"There!" Anna Petrovna said at last and placed the empty cup on her clean plate. And sort of thoughtfully, sadly, "It's terrible to have an appetite like that. I've eaten everything. I wanted to stop for decency's sake, but I couldn't. I'm sorry."

"I'm glad you liked it," her visitor said promptly, laughing. "When I finally do get up my nerve and change professions, I'm going to go work in a restaurant as a sandwich specialist. I'll make sandwiches, buttered bread slices, canapes!"

"And why..," Anna Petrovna handed him the plate, "and why must you change your profession? What are you?"

"Me!" repeated the visitor again and he again repeated his recent humorous gesture with his nose. "I"m... even saying the word makes me ashamed... I'm an historian."

"Why, is that very bad?"

"That depends. It's not good for me."

Anna Petrovna was silent.

She didn't have anything to say on the subject, but mainly a feeling of satiety had irresistibly and triumphantly started floating through her whole body in a friendly, sleepy wave.

She was embarrassed, but her eyelids were again sticking together.

It was boring to talk.

It was so much nicer to know that right now she could freely drowse off and that in her drowsy state she could quietly enjoy to her heart's content her thoughts about this young man who had turned up so strangely and who was so tactful and thoughtful—that she could, now consciously, recall once more that wonderful feeling of *discovery,* which smelled so tenderly of warmth, which she had suddenly briefly felt within her and which had excited her like a little girl and which her whole soul rushed after so!

She managed to open her eyes a bit. "It's embarrassing, but I'm going to go to sleep again. I'm sorry. I'm so afraid that you'll leave me. Do me a favor. There's some money there in a little box on the dresser. Buy something for me to eat. It doesn't matter what. I eat everything. And do forgive me..," she again closed her eyelids and went away, beginning with relief to sink into oblivion, as into water, like golden-honey, and she kept waiting for that recent blissful feeling to return to her soul, serenely confident that any minute now... there was sure to be something wonderful, summery, quiet and joyous. But by some inconceivably perverse quirk of memory it was a nasty February day that appeared to her—depressingly spacious, terrifying with the corrosive boredom of the gray snow-covered fields, stretching on endlessly and limitlessly in all directions...

...Anna Petrovna—apparently in fear and horror—from time to time was tossed upward in the sleigh. Throwing off the sheepskin coat and the horse blankets, which had been piled on her because she was sick, she would suddenly spring up on her knees, look around and again fall wildly headfirst into the straw, when she saw only the same thing, frightening and boring: a gray sky, a gray field and the black long snake of the wagon train, crawling along, weaving, from one sloping hill to the next.

They would again cover her up. She could feel how heavy the pile of clothing was on her, but there would be no heat. Only an annoying weight and always the same continual exhausting, biting shivering, which seemed to gnaw every cell in her body from the inside.

Every now and then Kochet would come by—the man whose name she had recently had such a hard time remembering. He would walk along beside the sleigh, always apologetically asking the same thing: "You're awfully sick, Annie, aren't you?" no longer in the least a conqueror, a conquered conqueror...

She would close her eyes and answer distantly, hoarsely: "It's all right. Please don't worry..."—and again the sleigh would be shaking, the snow would whisper, the harness would squeak.

And suddenly: "Hey, you son of a..!" someone shouted wildly and loudly with insane gaiety.

Anna Petrovna again was tossed up as they went over a big bump.

From the sleigh directly behind her a prisoner was running away through the snow right into the steppe, yelling shrilly like a drunken man.

In a shirt top with no belt, barefoot—some dirty gray rag unwinding from one foot as he ran—he looked exactly like a drunk, stupidly and senselessly waving his arms.

They yelled after him, mockingly—there was no place for him to run to. The empty steppe stretched all the way to the horizon.

Kochet was already on horseback. A snub-nosed handy carbine was dancing impatiently in his hands.

Happily he cocked the carbine and suddenly noticed Anna Petrovna looking at him. He squinted at her lustfully.

He frowned in irritation and lowered the weapon. With obvious reluctance he shouted off to one side, addressing no one in particular, "Hey, men! Somebody go get him!"

The driver of her sleigh—a kindly strawberry-pink old man with the merry nose of a drunkard and a thick gray beard—with unexpected gusto pulled a rifle out from under the hay. "Why go get him?" he muttered, clearing his throat and pulling off his mittens. "A bullet will get him..."

Guns started to merrily bang away on all sides.

The man, like a clown, desperately waving his arms, sliding on the snow crust, kept running and running down a slope in the steppe.

Someone's young voice uttered obscenities in merry irritation after every one of his shots. It was all like a big joke ...

And suddenly—everything was quiet.

Now there was nobody running, energetically sliding along there, in that snowy steppe.

And everyone, as if on command, suddenly turned to look at her driver, who at that moment was slowly lowering his dilapidated .375 rifle: then he thoughtfully and seriously opened the bolt and a merry empty cartridge flashed, spinning in the air, and quietly vanished in the straw.

He raised his head, and immediately everyone quickly turned away.

"Thirsty..." Anna Petrovna groaned through her clenched teeth, remembering the brook, glittering black and fat at the bottom of the slope in the steppe. "He was just thirsty, he wanted a drink..."—and a feeling of nauseous disgust with life struck her in the face like a splash of black blood.

* * *

"Did you want a drink?"

Anna Petrovna opened her eyes.

She saw the cup, the face of her gentleman. She understand absolutely nothing.

"Did you want a drink?" repeated the stranger.

"...he was running to the brook, and they shot at him..," Anna Petrovna was babbling like a little girl, still not quite awake. "Probably he was just thirsty." And then she was wide awake.

She reached out her hand, but not for the water. She timidly laid her fingers on his hand. She suddenly felt quiet and calm.

Good Lord! How long it had been since she had touched anyone with her hand!

"True old age, true loneliness," she thought vaguely, "is when you don't have anyone, like this, to touch..."

She slightly prolonged this moment and, noticing that he had also noticed it, was embarrassed. And then she said, in honest self pity, "You don't know, thank God... How horrible it is when you have no one to touch hands with, like this."

After a while, watching him unpack what he had bought (almost entirely milk products—as if he knew her tastes), she asked indecisively and even with a kind of ingratiating giggle, "I'm almost afraid to ask—what if it frightens you off?—but how did you turn up here? That is, I mean, what brought you here? Please excuse the..."

"No, *you* excuse me!" he responded energetically. "I just came in, you know! No hello, not even a visiting card."

"...and right away started sweeping..." Anna Petrovna tried to match his tone.

"Exactly! And right away started sweeping..," he repeated and suddenly became serious, almost solemn. "My name is Victor. And my surname is Poluektov, although all my ancestors in my father's line—I checked it myself for five generations—were named Kukishev.* But my father, you know, in his younger days was a bit embarrassed by it and registered (not, I think, without some pressure on the part of my mother) under this

---

*From "kukish," slang for "fig," a gesture of contempt, consisting of an extended clenched fist with the thumb placed between the index and middle fingers.

indubitably stylish name: Poluektov. In my own defense I might say that, since I feel quite guilty toward my ancestors (after all they were hard-working, decent people—from the middle class, one was even a merchant in the third guild), if I manage to get an article printed somewhere, then I always sign it proudly: Kukishev! For which, by the way, the administra-tion looks at me askance, for it sees signs of disrespect and also all kinds of impermissible allusions to God knows what. Yes. And I was brought to you, Anna Pavlovna by—*Greed*. By her alone, the hussy!.. I think I already told you that I'm an historian. And the topic of my current research is "The Working Peasantry of the Southern Ukraine during the Civil War." There's more. I was just leaving my apartment building to go to the insti-tute, when I ran into my old school buddy, Yuri Ryumin (the lieutenant who came to see you today). One thing led to another and he told me all about you. By the way, you completely captivated him. Yes. This sounds like fiction, but I— literally a week ago!—was reading about your Perebiynos in the archives!.. Well, since I am at least some sort of historian and, consequently, am obliged to believe in all sorts of coincidences, I had to come see you."

She obviously had understood nothing. "Well, and what about me? What am I... to you?"

He gave a very forced laugh, hiding his embarrassment. "Well, maybe you can tell me something interesting. Don't worry, I can use anything! And if you can't remember anything at all—that's no disaster either, I won't be offended."

Anna Petrovna was very seriously distressed. "I'm afraid that you won't get anything useful from me. My memory (you're young, you can't under-stand)—my memory... is like a spider web: you see something, you see it very clearly, and you try to touch it—and it breaks! And in your hand...—and here she made a gesture, very precise, with her thumb and forefinger as if she were picking the spider web off her fingers.

And suddenly horror was written across her face.

A grayish blue individual was standing silently in the doorway.

He was wearing something on the order of a military dress coat, but with civilian buttons, and also uniform-like trousers, but, strangely enough, he was not wearing boots. Although boots were simply begging to be included in the picture, for this man's whole appearance crudely and sim-ply hinted of some special *service* (or maybe, even more simply: of a fierce, ineradicable desire for this service), connected with defective human nature and with his daily, boring efforts, if not to improve the human race, at least to make it toe the line...

And it should also be mentioned that the cheap grayish blue cloth of his homemade uniform in some strange way instantly brought to mind the official gray boredom of some orphanage— or more precisely the identically and indifferently dressed children of this orphanage, silent, sleepy and unhappy...

His face, which could also be called courageous—the medallion face of some recruiting commander, slightly frightening in its mindless enthusiasm—was at that moment amazingly nervous, like a child's, and very pale from tension (Anna Petrovna was even worried: that's the way people look when they're about to faint). It, his face, also exuded some kind of bluish gray tone, which all but concealed the sclerotic pinkness of his cheeks and the sides of his nose.

The stranger said "Hello!" in an unsteady voice, and tried to get rid of his nervousness by coughing a few times. However, he didn't get rid of it, but only drove it deeper inside him, whence it immediately started bursting out in strange inappropriate puffs and pants and in a poorly controlled, almost galloping, sentence intonation.

"Hello!" he repeated. "I don't know if you know me or not, but I'm Shchitovidov. Vice-Chairman of the Housing Committee Council."

Here Anna Petrovna twitched, startled. Poluektov brusquely stood up, almost jumped up, and uttered a rapacious, relishingly ominous sound: "So-o-o!"

"I have come in order to officially," here Shchitovidov literally gasped for breath and lost his train of thought. "...to the meeting of the housing committee in regard to rumors, which have been circulating," he once more made a mouth like a fish, "in regard to you, Citizeness Zakharova-Kochubei!"

"So that's how it is," Poluektov said cheerfully and energetically and, taking a step forward, moved up unpleasantly close to Shchitovidov, who was forced to take a step backward and found himself almost outside the doorway.

"In regard to the 'which have been circulating,' I'll explain to the housing committee right now myself. I'm her nephew and Anna Petrovna is not altogether well, but I know all about it, so let's not bother her, and let's hurry, all right? Everyone, I imagine, is already at the meeting?"

And, tactfully pushing the vice-chairman out into the hallway, he himself disappeared behind him.

Everything had happened in such a ridiculous rush that Anna Petrovna smiled. And then laughed quietly.

She felt fine.

...And later on, while she was walking down the hallway at a slow patient pace, slowly scuffing along in her wornout slippers and from time to time touching the wall with her finger, as if holding on to it, and obediently stopping after every two steps to rest on the third and let her heart calm down; and while she meticulously performed her pathetic old woman's beauty ritual in the badly lit bathroom, splattered with slop, with great effort enduring the filth and poverty of her surroundings; and while she was walking back—already both a tiny bit refreshed and a tiny bit more cheerful—never taking her reverent eyes off the honey glow of the sunlit strip pouring out of the partially open door of her room across the narrow hallway...—during this whole time Anna Petrovna never stopped feeling that recent newly returned sense of discovery, of the proud possession of something—a sensation, almost childish and a little ridiculous, but one which gave her a lot of pleasure and comfort.

As she herself noticed with surprise, she felt distinctly more cheerful.

She put the bedspread on the bed. She laid out the things Victor had bought on the table in some semblance of order. She folded up his shopping bag with especial care, almost tenderly, and quietly hung it on the back of the chair.

She was drawn to the window. The sun was enthusiastically pouring through the window aperture, partitioning the room like a dull, reddish wall.

She stepped over there, into this light (for some strange reason feeling very tense), and was instantly bathed in such a nice, friendly warmth of strength that her kind visitor immediately came to mind, and a feeling of peace, of blessed quiet briefly rang anew in her... sort of the way a beat or two of crystal bright music suddenly rings out when someone accidentally, for a moment, opens the lid of a music box...

The white window sill was hot from the sun, and with her marvelous young fingers Anna Petrovna absentmindedly caressed its smooth surface, which felt as if it were covered with a smooth pottery glaze and she peered out into the courtyard—already automatically dividing her attention in half between the strange line of people frozen along the peeling, dilapidated wall, and this vividly warm, almost sensuous, passionate heat, which spread through the ends of her caressing fingers.

Some little boys were persistently jumping and horsing around under her window, trying very hard to get into her field of vision (the way they would jump around somewhere outdoors or in the stands at a ball game, if they noticed a movie camera pointing in their direction), but Anna Petrovna didn't notice the little boys.

Something—not necessarily anything unpleasant—was distracting her right now.

"Yes! After all, now I've got a *problem!*" she finally remembered. "He said he needed for me to remember something interesting and special from those times. But—Good Lord!—what can I remember? What kind of thing?"

and suddenly, in a single instant, her heart started beating excitedly, because she was afraid, seriously afraid that she wouldn't be able to remember anything. And in her busy imagination she began to grasp at some reflected past events dimly visible through the blackness of her memory, but, as if frightened by her sudden brusque interest in them, they instantly started to fade, those vague reflections, or else like capricious sun dogs, they would flash somewhere off to the side of her attention—and almost nothing, just worthless garbage, would be left in the net, which she was hastily dragging up onto the beach.

Anna Petrovna was living her ninth decade of existence on this planet. And the unsteady fabric of her memory was already completely worn out—so it would unravel even from just a steady effort...

She was in despair. She felt her own worthlessness. The sharp pain of loss.

She felt a dejected, nauseous shame at the disappointment that Victor was bound to experience as soon as he realized her senile mental incompetence.

"But what is this?" she suddenly thought in confused surprise. "So many things?! This shame... and this pity... and the fear of losing... And all these things are—me??"

He came in, alert, happy, cheerful. But strangely enough, neither his cheerfulness, nor his alertness offended her elderly ego. Quite the contrary, a meek, almost maternal joy fluttered in her heart when he came in like that—alert, cheerful, and immediately filling the room with the good-natured calmness of a solid, strong person.

She saw some flowers in his hands.

"For you!" he said, handing her a little bouquet of rather faded chrysanthemums, clearly embarrassed, as many men are embarrassed when they perform this, to their mind, rather strange ritual.

"For you! For the ineffable pleasure, which—thanks to you! — I have received from meeting with your marvelous housing committee. A panopticon like that," he continued, all in the same overly cheerful tone "is something I never in my life expected to see. Believe it or not, they have a slogan hanging on their wall: 'The people are the eyes and ears of Soviet power!'"

and Anna Petrovna meanwhile, painfully enduring the crunching and crackling of the cellophane, so icy to her touch, was liberating the flowers, slowly and a bit surprised, reliving the feelings she always had when she fussed with flowers that someone had just brought her (Oh! How many bouquets she had been presented in her lifetime!)—that strange, anxiously tender, slightly compassionate and always somehow hurried desire to *rescue* them—as if they were children in trouble—to give them shelter and something to drink and eat as quickly as possible.

She lifted them out, and the flowers lay dejectedly in her palm, exhaustedly and fearfully dangling their stems, whose bottoms were already slightly wilted and crudely smashed.

One flower was dying. Its head was drooping, already completely doomed and dejected. Anna Petrovna examined it carefully and found the place where the stalk—like a faceted tube, covered with stiff fur—had been almost imperceptibly broken and squashed. The flower's capillaries were tightly pinched together here, it was suffocating and the bright juice of despair had started to dry on this barely noticeable, but undoubtedly fatal, wound.

Her compassion caused her to get upset. She tenderly laid the flower's head down and barely awaiting a pause in Victor's monologue—("...with the last name, I swear to God, of Schizophredinov... He jumps up! 'I propose,' he says, 'freezing all her goddamn bank accounts!' Yours, that is...")—and awaiting a pause she mournfully requested, "Could you bring me some water? Maybe in that jar over there."

Carefully and nervously, she cut off each stem at a long slant and, feeling at that moment compassionate relief and joy, immersed the flowers in the water. She arranged them evenly around the perimeter of the jar neck (she wanted each of them to have enough room), put the bouquet up on the television set and...

—and instantly had the strange feeling that there were now *three* of them in the room.

"Well! And then, following all the rules for a gentlemanly discussion," Poluektov merrily continued his report, "I accused them of criminal ignorance of their national history, and specifically, the history of the Civil War. For, if they had known their history, they would not have dared accuse you of belonging to one of Makhno's counter-revolutionary bands, because precisely in the spring of that year Perebiynos's Makhno unit was part of the Red Army's Southern Front, and, consequently, you, living with them, not only were not implicated in counter-revolutionary activity, but, on the contrary, it may be said, you were heroically fighting against the White hydra for today's indubitably bright future."

"Good Lord!" said Anna Petrovna, very condescendingly and calmly, "What nonsense..."

"It may be nonsense..." Victor started to say, but then suddenly agreed, "But yes, it is indeed nonsense. And that's why it really wore me out, talking to them."

She glanced at his face and saw how exhausted he actually was. Or, more precisely, tiredly saddened... And suddenly she pitied him so strongly and maternally, as only one who is leaving for good can pity those who are remaining behind.

"You've gone to so much trouble for me," she said guiltily, "and, of course, you have your own things to do." ("And, of course, you have your own things to do," carried a tone of bitter dismay.) "You go now. Why should you sit here with an old woman?"

"But I'll come back! Do I have your permission? This evening?" And, nevertheless, she heard the relief in his words.

"Of course..."

"...I'll finish up my miserable chores and come back."

"Do come. I'll be waiting."

And he suddenly realized that she really would be waiting. And he also realized that *very* few people had had the honor to hear this woman say: "I'll be waiting..." And, strangely, for a moment he felt very proud.

Anna Petrovna was waiting.

Thin as a rail, the meek little old woman was sitting motionless, as if even afraid to move a muscle, her hands diligently folded in her lap, her glance resting on the floor, somewhere beside her feet; and it was evident that she was attentively listening for something that was going to pop up any second, that was approaching (she felt that!) from the unbelievably remote far-offness of her memory—something important, majestic, full of meaning and significance—clearly worthy of being told to Victor—and she was already exulting softly in her mind, imagining how she would tell Victor about this, and ever more impatiently increasing her concentration ... And then, when *it* already should have at last appeared—

there appeared before her gaze only this: first the floor boards, covered with gloomy red paint, then her hands, diligently lying in her lap, the thin cotton flannel of her dressing gown, and then also the reminder of her own dry and emaciated body, sitting on a chair, beside the window, in this emotionless waiting pose.

Again nothing was left in the net, which she was so laboriously dragging up from the black depths of her memory.

And again, briefly, black despair scraped across her soul.

"It's so horrible, so shameful, so desperately hopeless," Anna Petrovna thought slowly, vaguely and bitterly, "to live until you're in such a state that there's *nothing,* not even the smallest trifle, that you can *give* to anyone."

But both the bitterness and the desperation passed and were gone. An anticipatory calm took possession of her.

...It was the calm of an autumn forest, at the time of year when the leaves have already fallen and, deadened by the rains, lie densely underfoot like a damp, slightly springy, multi-layered carpet; when the winds and rains grow calmer—those winds and rains that have been frolicking wildly, with merry vengeful malice among the poor helpless trees; when suddenly a bitter frost strikes, and the skies instantly seem to raise up and—

with a clear, pitiless, icy eye, Winter, unsociable and a bit frightening, glances down at the earth, still far away and in no hurry to come in.

Anna Petrovna loved and admired the forest at this time of year.

There is neither despair nor sadness then in the way the forest's iron trees stand, sternly and silently, on the deserted land, in cold formality. In the way they wait for the inevitable: with dignity, steadfastly and simply.

In such a forest one must not talk. One must walk, gloomily pulling one's collar around one's face, with bitter lips closed uncompromisingly tight, and alertly, with compassionate intensity, and quickly look around, seeing very far and very clearly, as humans are never allowed to see either in the coldly magnificent wintertime, or in the fidgety springtime, or in the festive, senselessly bustling summertime.

In nature there is no sorrow in this pitiless hour of dying: just the *peace* of waiting. Just infinite, like the world, patience and undying, like the world, hope.

Just patience. Just hope.

Patience and hope.

...She repeated these words to herself, but, as usual, losing the thread which connected them to her previous thoughts, felt in them neither meaning nor solemnity.

Something was pleasantly disturbing her today.

Anna Petrovna concentrated on her thoughts, uncertainly cast a glance around the room and—well, of course!—her heart jerked affectionately when she saw her bouquet. Although the chrysanthemum leaves still looked as exhausted as ever and the petals still reminded one of a strip of paper that someone had disdainfully crumpled in their fist, the bouquet clearly seemed more vigorous. She could distinctly feel life cautiously awakening within the flowers and there was suddenly a delicate tremor of understanding between the old woman and the debilitated pale flowers, gazing at her across this whole room, which was already starting to fill up with its normal dusky twilight.

Something emitting a calamitous sharp sound burst into the room from behind her head, just beside Anna Petrovna's gaze. And then she glimpsed an awkwardly somersaulting uneven piece of glass, which flashed briefly a couple of times—and immediately disintegrated into powdery frosty dust. Something splattered behind her—all this at the same time, everything blurring together in her mind—and then a fine rowdy hail beat on her back like a drum.

The woman squeezed her eyes tightly shut and bent over. And from behind her and over her head something started to break completely apart, collapsing in a scandalous tinkling of freedom.

And trying to escape, feeling a heavy, shameful pain in her spine, and deeply ashamed of her animal fear, which, as if in mockery, was bending her to the floor, pushing her under the bed to hide in her den, Anna Petrovna fell like a sack of flour off her chair onto her knees, hurting them badly. She pressed her head up against the barred metal headrest of the bed, desperately hanging on to its flimsy metal bars and pleading with herself to *endure* both this horror and this beastly howling of her badly humiliated pride, and with icy amazement realizing that this *had happened once before*—

...in that railroad car, after the window had maliciously deafened everyone, bursting like a black star, something had struck—a bullet—with such a terrible, serious, *murderous* force that the wall of the car shook and something splattered in all directions, and all the people, so tightly packed in their seats, instantly experienced the same nauseous terror, so that immediately (a peasant, the nearest to the window—some glass had cut his face—suddenly let out a shameful squeal like a little pig), immediately, they threw themselves down onto the floor, speechless and breathing heavily, banging against each other's heads, all of them for some reason thinking they had to get under the bench to save themselves, and all the time pushing each other away, stubbornly, and generally without any bad feeling.

A disrespectful bristle from someone's coat was squirming around on her face. She felt a piercing fear. But even while pushing her head further into the darkness, scratching her tender face against the dirty sandpaper of someone's clothing, and stupefied with fear, she also felt:

a miserable revulsion, lasting a miserably long time, at what was happening to her right now, a nasty misery of humiliation and a burning shame because she *couldn't keep from being* just like all the rest—and she pleaded with herself to endure all this, because it was so easy, it would have been so easy to just die at that moment from both the revulsion and the shame.

And then a rude hand jerked her out from that little knot of tightly herded people, and started pulling her down the aisle of the car, causing an unbearable pain in her shoulder blade. The aisle was crowded with tense, silent peasants, who were hurriedly and agilely roaming from compartment to compartment, hauling along suitcases, packages which were falling apart, and people who didn't want to be hauled along. When this overwhelming, rude, impetuous force started dragging her along, she first of all, of course, heard a deathly wail inside her, but she also felt *relief*, a strange relief, because she was being dragged perhaps to even greater humiliation, and maybe, even to her death...

Beside the train, which had stopped right in the middle of the steppe, there was a rapid, thievish commotion, the more incomprehensible in that dusk had already fallen, and it seemed that with every passing minute all around it kept getting more definitely and rapidly darker.

The sleigh, the riders bouncing up and down in their saddles, the restless horses tearing the reins from their riders' hands, the mishmash of figures running, crawling, rolling, scrambling in different directions—she managed to notice all this in a flash, because the man who was pulling her along had jumped down from the step without worrying at all about her, and Anna Petrovna was immediately also pulled off of the train.

Grabbing her arm, he jerked her out of the snowbank and again started pulling her along—this time, thank God, at least he didn't dislocate her shoulder blade.

Anna Petrovna, who had been mainly preoccupied with keeping her feet under her, had somehow still not managed to look at her abductor's face—to find there at least some hint about her immediate future.

Finally, he looked back at her (she had tripped over something and accidentally fallen on her knees), he looked back and she almost fainted from nausea and horror!

A vampire from her most frightening children's stories—a wiry little peasant, a debauched brat, with hardened blue knots of unpopped boils on his face, with wet lips and flaring nostrils on his small nose, which looked as if it had been broken at the bridge—that's who was pulling her!

And she couldn't run any more—because of the nauseous hopeless disgust which had overcome her.

But he kept on dragging her along behind him, maliciously and relentlessly, although he himself was already visibly tiring, both from her passive resistance and from the weight of two black leather suitcases which he was carrying, holding them both miraculously in one hand and helping himself along at each step with a desperate push of the knee.

One of the suitcases finally started falling apart. Pink and white lacy things pushed out, clinging to his leg.

He let go of Anna Petrovna's arm and, quickly getting down on his knees, set about stuffing the underwear back into the suitcase. But it seemed to keep bursting out stubbornly, like rising dough from a pan, ever more profusely and persistently.

Someone, running past, banged her painfully on the shoulder. Anna Petrovna screamed and was pushed away a couple of steps, where she was again shoved by someone who didn't see her, and only then did she finally come to her senses and start running.

Anna Petrovna ran, half blind from fear, avoiding the horses' heads, and jumping away in panic from people she met, tearing loose from someone's lazily shameless hands, pawing her as they ran past. She ran, not knowing where she was headed, with only one single clear feeling, "Get away!" and already she icily felt that her brain was going mad from the feverish feeling that she was a chip of wood which was being tossed around in a wildly seething kettle.

And suddenly: "*Girl! Stop!*"

Out of the blue, he jumped off his horse, youthfully and gracefully planting his feet in the snow in front of her, and at the same time grabbed her quickly and adroitly by the arm, almost breaking her slender wrist, even through her coat sleeve.

"Stop! So, have I got you, my dear?"

He was, strangely enough, both calm and good-natured, and even, for some reason, in a good mood, and maybe he was the only one there not at all worried by the pitiful commotion of banditry going on all around. There seemed to be a magic circle around him—a quiet space, surprising in this evil Sodom—from which, she immediately realized, she no longer had the strength to flee or try to escape.

And, surrendering, she let her arm drop.

* * *

A brickbat, almost half a brick in size, had been carefully wrapped in paper and thickly and clumsily wound round with black thread.

Victor broke the thread apart, squeamishly frowning with the effort.

On the paper had been drawn a skinny degenerate skull, two enormous, crooked crossbones under it, and a flaunting inscription: "ANARCHY IS THE MOTHER OF ORDER!"

"Uh-huh..," Poluektov said, without any special expression, although gloomily. "I would guess that these are young Tamerlanians, that is followers of Timur,* who have clearly misperceived their civic duty."

Anna Petrovna did not immediately respond. Victor had her sitting on a chair, wrapped up in a blanket almost to the top of her head, but she just couldn't get warm. And how could she expect to get warm in a room where almost half the window yawned vacantly out into space and where the wind from outdoors frolicked freely in merry, insolent enjoyment.

"What was that?" she finally asked.

Victor looked at her and, after a noticeable hesitation, answered energetically and incoherently, "A natural, one might say, disaster. But since there are neither casualties nor collapsed buildings, as is often the case, there is no need to get upset: I'll figure out something right away to take care of the window."

He went out into the hallway.

She heard him walk around quickly out there, move something heavy, swear in irritation. Then everything was quiet.

The silence went on and on.

At first Anna Petrovna didn't pay any particular attention, sure that if she just pricked up her ears she would definitely and immediately hear him. Then she began to worry, already suspecting, but still refusing to believe that he had gone and deserted her, but when she nevertheless realized this, became convinced of it—

suddenly such a desperate, such an extreme, howling *loneliness* took hold of her that, momentarily losing her sanity, she suddenly stood up, dropping the blanket which was keeping her from freezing to death, and started moving toward the door like a blind woman, hands stretched out in front of her, trying to utter his name and at that instant completely forgetting it!

The hallway, cluttered with dead, dark angular things, was barely lit by a worthless little yellow light bulb.

There was no one in the hallway.

Anna Petrovna, desperately expending her last bit of strength, kept walking farther and farther down this endless hallway, ever more clearly

---

*A pun on the name variations of the 14-15th century Turkestan conqueror Tamerlane—Timur, in Turkic. In the 1940s a popular children's novel *Timur and His Team* spanned the playfully patriotic nickname "Timurovets"—a follower of Timur.

realizing the self-destructive folly of what she was doing—she no longer would have the strength to get back—and a miserable mortal terror tormented her.

For a long time now she had not feared death. But now, for the first time, she felt really nauseous: to end her life here, in this musty hallway, in a scrap heap of dead things that nobody needs, of squashed suitcases overgrown with thick dust, torn boxes held together with rough wire, broken bicycles, sacks and trunks filled with boring trash?!..

And she *saw* clearly how she would die: like a sick, homeless dog, crawling up to the threshold of some stranger's silent door.

She could hear steps.

Victor hurriedly rushed out from behind a turn in the hallway. He had a big box in his arms, some pieces of cardboard and some packages.

"Is that you?—here?" he asked in surprise, almost running into Anna Petrovna and not immediately recognizing her in the darkness. "I had to run home."

Anna Petrovna sighed convulsively, childishly, nodded, took a step and pathetically grabbed hold of his coat sleeve.

He looked around—the bathroom door was nearby. Visibly embarrassed, he couldn't think of anything better to say than: "You probably want to go in here? Let me help you." He laid the things in his arms down on the floor and slowly escorted her, formally supporting her under the arm.

She did not resist.

"This is it, the moment of my shame..," Anna Petrovna finally said and laughed, with a happy lilt to her voice.

Hurriedly, working very efficiently, he nailed up the broken window with the cardboard he had brought.

An electric heater was in the big box he had brought. Victor turned it on and this awkward-looking contraption immediately captured the old woman's heart, not so much by its heat (in the frozen room the heat couldn't be felt for a long time) as by its glow, which imitated the restlessly crimson color of a hearth. Anna Petrovna immediately involuntarily stretched out her hands in front of it and instantly felt the incomparable bliss of someone safeguarded by fire on a freezing night.

"How nice... Oh, how really, really nice!" she kept repeating, unable to stop, and wiggling her beautiful fingers, which were sultrily illuminated by the heater, and it seemed she really did feel the fire almost unbearably burning her hands and the heat moving with a sweet pain along her frozen veins.

She looked happily around at Victor.

Smiling, he looked at her from the window, still holding the hammer and some scraps of cardboard in his hands, and she could see from his smile what a nice man he was.

And right then she started to cry unrestrainedly. Bending over the heater and never pulling her greedy hands away from it, she looked up at Poluektov from below, turning her face a little toward him and crying bitterly, and in bitter haste said, "But I... nothing... It's so awful! But I—can give you nothing. Nothing at all! It's so awful, Victor, so awful!"

He was alarmed. "Now, now, please! What are you talking about, my dear Anna Petrovna?" He walked over and sat down on the bed beside her, and she kept on weeping: "Nothing... absolutely nothing..." He patted her on the head like a little girl: "Now, now, calm down... Now, now, what's the matter, Anna Petrovna?"

And Anna Petrovna—with some childish, long forgotten motion suddenly cuddled up against his side trustingly, this little old woman, all dried up like a chip—she cuddled up under his shoulder and obediently quieted down, sort of hiding herself.

And—at that moment she needed nothing else, absolutely nothing else in this life!

....

....

....

"Up there..," answered the elderly bearded peasant, who was down on his knees putting together some concrete forms. He answered her gloomily and carelessly, but then immediately did a double take and took another look at her face, and this look became admiringly affectionate, even a bit embarrassed. "He's up there... Up those plank stairs—all the way up to the top..," he said slowly and with unconcealed pleasure, but also with some effort to fix her in his memory, he looked her over carefully, his eyes warming in delight. "Only don't fall: they're rickety..," he added suddenly with concerned anxiety, and started to return to his axe, but immediately again raised his eyes, now already looking at her *for future reference.*

She smiled generously at him: "Thank you!"—the most pitilessly youthful smile she had, which even caused the peasant to sort of grunt. He was flustered and embarrassed and mumbled something unintelligible to himself under his breath, with the intonation of an affectionate obscenity: "Why you're the icon lamp of the Lord God!"—and once more, this time it seemed fearfully, he turned to watch her leave.

But she, hopping with respectful caution from one dried-up clump of clay to another, feeling his gaze on her and also dozens of other gazes (but not at all trying to walk in any way differently, for that morning, from the moment she woke up, everything that she did, she did precisely, to her surprise and joy, as she should)— with this natural, unforced hopping she quickly and merrily covered the boring, petrified space of ugly, badly mutilated reddish earth which lay at the foot of the construction project. She ran up onto the first planks, surprised to catch briefly the sweet pine scent, so strange here, but which was exuded, of course, by the boards of the scaffolding and which couldn't be drowned out even by the tomb-like, slightly rotten, raw breath of the slowly and powerfully hardening concrete which was wrapped around this whole enormous, crude structure—the largest, they said, grain elevator in the Soviet Union, which was being built in the middle of this steppe.

The rickety stairs started trembling, irritatedly and dangerously, instantly making her moderate her speed, and she obediently started moving differently (but almost as fast), easily catching the new tempo and, as before, feeling a distinct pleasure in everything she was experiencing: in her light, carefree running; and in the mathematical monotony with which the wooden stairways sent her first in one direction and then in another, taking her higher and higher; and in the fact that the height was not at all frightening to her, just exciting—with each flight up thrilling her anew, on a new note; and in the way the wind up high was playing so protectively and furiously with her weightless little dress and was generously blowing all over her, bathing her whole strong body from head to toe in a merry, shameless boldness...

She kept going up higher and higher and with each new flight she felt a more exhilarating thrill as she tried in vain to get a complete view of this great dusty steppe, so immense and inscrutably mysterious in its immensity and poetic melancholy.

At this early hour, without raising much dust, some lazy carts were already moving along the steppe toward the construction site, and people were flowing there in unhurried rivulets—from the ugly randomly scattered workers' barracks with their crudely patched corrugated plastic roofs, and from the Kalmyk yurts which surrounded the construction site in a sparse ring, keeping a timidly respectful distance, and from above resembled the tops of wasps' nests, and people were flowing from the multicolored roofs, closely grouped and clinging to the river, of the "old" settlement, where she had still never once been in her year and a half of work here, but which she immediately recognized by the pathetic tatters of gardens, the dusty short saplings squeezed up tight against the houses and by the little steeple on the tiny church, with its cross dejectedly tilted over on its side...

A truck gaily sped along, dragging behind it a still not particularly magnificent foxtail of dust.

Some saiga herds skirted the settlement in a wide arc, rushing off to the south. Dusty yellow on dusty yellow, they resembled little islands of faded feather-grass, blown along by the wind.

The sheep flocks stood motionless—three or four pinches of poppy seed, meagerly strewn on a faded red plush tablecloth.

And farther off—along the hazy horizon, promising still another murderously scorching day, shimmering mercurial pools of mirages were starting to spread here and there with their inescapable silhouettes of some sort of pyramidal trees, ghostly gray and apparently shivering with some secret fever.

She kept going up higher and higher, and feelings of happiness, precision, immortality and merriment were singing inside her in various voices, crazily and resoundingly; her strong, sun-tanned feet in their white canvas tennis shoes flashed tirelessly; without being aware of it, she never stopped smiling, because this impetuous ascent was like an irresistible Attraction, and with each flight upward a mysterious joy swelled crescendo in her—mysterious...

...because there was no way she could have known ahead of time that there on the top platform of scaffolding, having dropped out for half a minute from a politely meaningless verbal free-for-all which the construction engineers were having with some commission which had inopportunely descended on them—apparently suddenly saddened by some casual thought which had struck him, blindly and somewhat bewilderedly gazing out at the steppe which stretched before him in a defiant, deserted semicircle all the way to the hot, gloomy horizon, a bit irritatedly rolling a dead "Delhi" cigarette from one side of his mouth to the other, unthinkingly and dangerously leaning his elbows heavily on the flimsy post of the stair railing—stood a man who...

"Hello! I think you must be Kochubei!" she blurted out boldly.

She couldn't help smiling. A timely breeze with girlish chic scattered her sunbleached, modishly bobbed hair along her tanned forehead. Her eyes (she sensed this) were shining.

"I think you must be Kochubei," she blurted out boldly.

"I think so, too..," he said, unbending and turning around toward her—and suddenly irrresistibly, with the release of a long-awaited, maybe even agonizingly awaited, climax, he smiled, and as a result his strange, rather unpleasant face of a brown-haired Indian, tanned to a kind of dusty murkiness, with merciless wicked scars of wrinkles at the wings of his nose and at the corners of his mouth—this whole coldly, economically, sternly constructed face of a Great Lord suddenly lit up so marvelously and vulnerably and with such child-like clarity that at once somewhere near her heart something quivered fatally: "I'm *lost!..*"

"...then this is for you," she said, still with a smile, but an already anxiously departing smile, "then this is for—you!" and she timidly handed him...

* * *

She woke up in a terrible fright.

"What time is it? Are you here? They'll be worried about you! You must go! Why is the light on?.. Put it out! It's so cold..."

Victor looked at her carefully. Anna Petrovna's eyes glittered unhealthily. He thought she had probably caught a cold, no telling how long she had sat on the floor under that broken window.

"Do you have any medicine?" he asked.

"Medicine?" she obviously didn't realize what he meant. "God forbid! No medicines help me any more." She uttered these words rapidly and more and more her speech called to mind delirium.

"For old people like me there is only one medicine. But why don't you go home?! They'll be worried about you! Your wife—or who do you live with?" (contempt and even hostility jingled unpleasantly in these words of hers)—"she'll say that you... *have gone off to another woman!*" And suddenly she started laughing uncontrollably, unpleasantly baring her wet plastic teeth and drooling saliva. But right away she cut short her laughter and confessed to someone, "Good Lord, how terrible this is! How awful! If you only knew *how* awful! But I'm not going to lie down. God forbid! Somehow or other I'm going to sit it out like this..."

and she tried to move over to the corner of the bed so she could sit there, but she wasn't able to move and she stopped talking, bewildered.

Victor said, "May I?" put down some pillows in the corner, covered them with a plaid, so that later, after she sat down, she could cover her shoulders. Rather unceremoniously, but of course, not rudely, he picked her up from behind under the armpits and with hospital-style intonations: "All right, let's go, one two, let's move!" he easily pulled Anna Petrovna over into the corner and seated her there, covering her with the plaid, a blanket, and then his raincoat on top of everything.

She looked at him helplessly and submissively. "Please don't think that I'm trying to drive you away..," she said after a brief hesitation. "But why are you risking trouble with your wife?"

"No trouble," Victor answered reluctantly. "I'm temporarily a free man, so that..."

"And you know!" Anna Petrovna irrelevantly, clearly listening only to herself, declared with the joy of some unexpected revelation. "You'll be a good historian! Because you are so good with people."

"I'm *already* a good historian," Poluektov snapped in an unexpectedly offended tone.

"It will all pass!" Anna Petrovna spoke out in hasty assurance, feeling with surprise that the fog which usually clouded her thoughts was thinning out. "It will all pass—whatever it is that's bothering you now: some failures, unpleasantnesses, some misunderstanding! Tomorrow you'll look around—and just smile, because it will all seem so unimportant!"

Anna Petrovna even felt in her chest a little moan of tenderness for this painstakingly private, thoughtful, patient, nice man.

With frightening clarity she *saw*, in a single moment, both him and his whole future: Oh! a future not very full of successes, more often cloaked in the gloom of a mild sorrow than happy, filled to the end with that even, sullen stubbornness with which his whole life he was fated to defend his concept of what Life is.

He was wonderfully and horrifyingly like her son—the son, which, alas, Anna Petrovna had never had, but who, it turns out, she *knew*.

And a kindred spasm—painless, but leaving a terribly bitter aftertaste—contracted her heart when she gazed unabashedly at his narrow, and for that reason, unpleasantly attentive, eyes, dark in the dim light, and suddenly read there the most sincere bereaved suffering, pain and orphaned bewilderment!..

And also: a stubbornly smoldering *expectation* of something important from her.

"How very much, Victor!" she again started to speak rapidly. "If you only knew how much I want to protect you and, don't be offended, to teach you something!! But, no matter how hard I try... and I really am trying... but no matter how hard I try!"

He began to say something soothing, and she again felt tears flowing down her face.

"Patience..," she suddenly uttered with ironic bitterness, vaguely recalling something recent. "Patience and hope. Isn't that what I should teach you?"

———

However, he repeated these two words in a different way—very respectfully and carefully. And they had a solemn ring.

"That is worthy," he said, "of being inscribed on the family coat of arms: 'Patience and Hope.'"

But Anna Petrovna couldn't tell whether he was talking that way seriously, jokingly or simply to soothe her.

Her tears had tired her. "I've never cried so much in my whole life as I have today," she said with an apologetic intonation and she closed her eyes.

Her condition had obviously deteriorated.

Poluektov noticed a crude shadow of exhaustion and light irritation on her face. And her face momentarily looked the way it probably would look (Poluektov noted coldly) when death occurred.

Suddenly she started breathing rapidly and agitatedly. Victor was frightened.

Her hand started flopping back and forth on the bed, as if in panic. And only when they touched Victor's outstretched palm, did her fingers suddenly relax in relief. Instantly Anna Petrovna's breathing also became calm and even.

Poluektov was awakened by some strange sounds—like some piteous groans or maybe somebody whimpering.

"........?!" he asked, quickly waking up and discovering to his surprise that he had been asleep, sitting on the edge of the bed and holding Anna Petrovna's hand in his.

"...Tenderly bending over the brook," the woman recited distinctly without opening her eyes. "The weeping willows doze, tenderly bending over the brook..," she smiled dreamily, but also ironically. "It's a very old song. I'm sorry. I didn't realize I was speaking aloud."

She fell silent for a long while, and then again mumbled, "Where art thou, Dearly Beloved.., wafting sad dreams to me..." And she opened her eyes. "I've forgotten it! Why don't you tell me instead about your..," she paused, slowly seeking the right word, "about your beloved. If that's all right. Is it all right? I'm sure she must be a nice person."

Victor grunted something humorous. He boringly creaked his chair for a long time. After a while, though, he did speak, and not unwillingly...

"I really don't know what to tell you. Well, her name is Valya. She graduated this year in library science..."

—but Anna Petrovna instantly felt suddenly bored and spitefully lonely. She just couldn't, much as she might want to (and it turned out that she didn't really very much want to...) imagine what she was really like.

Even so it was clear to her, Anna Petrovna, with complete, irrational, crudely maternal clarity, that this unknown Valya—*was not the one for him!* And in her there energetically flared up a strong dislike for this little gray mouse from the library stacks who was trying to sneak her way into Victor's life and take the place of that one and only woman who...

was trudging down a white graveled country road beyond the Oka River on an early summer morning, dipping her bare feet with enjoyment in the already warm, fluffy dust—between fields of low scraggly rye, through which the gray earth, numb from the heat, peered up worriedly—under the clearest light-blue skies, spread so extravagantly over and around her that sometimes she was even slightly shaken by this immense expanse—was walking with her head down, apparently deep in thought, but as a matter of fact not thinking about anything in particular, just feeling a smile wander across her face, feeling the gloomily sweet heaviness of her eyelids after an almost sleepless night, feeling the ever more persistent warmth, already stinging her cheekbones and forehead, of the sun, which by this hour had already risen a fair distance and become like a small, but furiously and frenziedly shining, eroded hole in the sky, one glance at which would clog the eyes with ashy darkness, and then for a long time afterwards some reluctantly melting coal-black tatters, vaguely reminiscent of clouds, would shimmy around in front of your gaze, and the figure of a wheel, which seemed to have been drawn with a quick black marking pencil, kept coming back, now vanishing, now reappearing clearly...

The road almost imperceptibly sloped down toward the still distant river.

It—the road—was itself like a river—with its long sleepy bend—in the middle of this peaceful, smoothly, lightly sighing plain, which seemed at this early hour completely unpopulated, but, of course, it only *seemed* that way: you could look around and see the poor, shingled roofs of the village they had just left; and not far away a closely bunched herd of sheep was visible in vivid black and white contrast and beside them the black, sleepily motionless figure of their shepherd, and from a far-off, very distant field some rapid flashes, one after the other, unbearably white, dazzled the eyes—from the flashing blades of a horse-drawn mowing machine, which had already come out for the day's work...

The sun was still shining slantwise along the earth and everything all around was lushly cratered with shadows. Every narrow gully, and every ravine and boundary strip was filled with islands of transparent, greenish coolness. Every separate blade of grass was festively, fervently, exuding green, and beside each grass blade was clearly printed its tiny, little new shadow.

The crowns of some trees ahead curled moistly, appearing slightly silvery. Their uneven broken line marked the banks of the Oka, still not visible to the eye.

Off to one side a leafy grove gazed somberly—like a steep, strong cloud which had sat down heavily on the steppe. And a nocturnally damp, blue shadow lay bleakly beside it.

Some birds in the grain fields were joyously calling back and forth.

On a bare mound a powerful large thistle was fearlessly resplendent, bathed profusely in dew, all covered with a multitude of silvery shining beads, which made it look like a crudely over-decorated Christmas tree.

Every so often a young breeze from the river would gust briskly, but instantly die down and then gust again, not at all discouraged...

Everything around, not yet wilted by the heat, was wide awake in a quietly merry mood and full of that resplendent active happiness that occurs only in nature, and only on an early summer morning just before a scorching hot day.

The road was like a river, and the woman walked down this road as if she were floating, as if someone were pulling her—so that she didn't seem to be exerting herself even slightly in order to walk. And from this rather strange dreamy feeling which made her head swim, and, mostly, from the happiness at everything that was happening—both to her and around her—there were moments when she would experience something distinctly akin to despair, and at that time an ecstatic cry would push against her larynx, trying to burst out, and a slow, blood-curdling chill would crawl along her backbone, stopping her breathing for a moment and making her heart beat erratically, but not dangerously.

The sun was baking down ever more attentively, the scorching heat was beginning, and the woman unbuttoned first one, and after that, more impatiently, two more buttons, and then, completely (her whole being simply ached with an overwhelming, incomprehensible desire *to get even closer*)—and then, completely roguishly and briskly, slipped out of her blouse, leaving it to hang freely around her hips, and kept on walking, now naked from the waist up, but not, strangely enough, feeling any kind of confusion or embarrassment, or on the other hand, any kind of bravado— just a feeling of deep relief, like a sigh after a fit of choking, and a dazzling *simplicity*.

Her companion, who had managed to get far ahead, had stopped and was waiting for the woman beside a footpath which ran off to the side, away from the road. He watched her walk toward him.

He watched her simply, almost without any expression on his face. And there was a slightly condescending tenderness in his eyes, squinting bitterly from the sun, which fell slantwise on his face.

She walked up in front of him; he continued looking, savoring the moment. Then he took a short stiff step toward her and respectfully inclining his face, which was very serious at that moment, even sad, softly touched his lips to her breast, near her heart, and lingered a little longer in that intentionally submissive pose.

And the woman... and the woman at that instant, struck by fate, lifted her face heavenward, suddenly blinded by happiness, and almost fainting from the overpowering poignancy and terrifying sweetness of the emotions tearing at her, throwing her arms behind her back with some strange tension as if she were getting ready to fly, and even, it seemed, raising up on her tiptoes...—and the woman at that instant was imploring herself to do just one thing: to hold on, not to die, to remember—with every cell, every nerve fiber, every drop of blood!—*to remember this forever.*

* * *

In bewildered consternation Anna Petrovna looked around her and could not recognize herself in her present life!

Some strange man, all hunched over in a chair, was killing time beside her bed. He was sorrowfully illuminated from below by a crimson light and you couldn't tell whether he was dozing or simply staring meditatively at the heater.

A terrifying cave-like shadow fell from him on the walls and ceiling.

Anna Petrovna peered at him for a long time without recognizing him. Then suddenly she remembered *everything.*

"Why, I know who you are!" she exclaimed, and she herself caught in surprise the sly intonation of a madwoman. "I know who you are!"

She felt a malicious satisfaction when she saw the man give a start at the sound of her voice.

"They Sent You To Me!" she declared solemnly. "To check up on me. Because... because..."

and suddenly heard with horror that she was talking *nonsense!*

Suddenly she had the nightmarish feeling that she was very, very rapidly, inexorably sliding toward the edge of some cliff, and then—she was already falling!—into the abyss, black from despair and burning shame!

"...because the ring... You know, the one I gave Marina! You must know, because..."

"My God!" she thought, helplessly and miserably. "*Who* must know? Know what?"

Some angry devil was wobbling around inside her.

She screamed out something terribly insulting and unfair to Victor—taking pains that it should be as insulting—and unfair—and hurtful!—as possible—so that she could still have this one last caustic pleasure: the pleasure of cutting off, of killing the last meaningful living tie to this world—so that she would finally be left alone, completely alone, deserted for good by everyone, never again to be needed by anyone, because...

"Because for you the ring..." she began with extraordinary contempt, "because on account of this miserable ring you all are ready..."

"Good God! Stop this," she thought.

She was already feeling faint because of this conflict with herself. She was already convulsed in shame from what was going on. She knew the words which she, right now, this very second, *must* say: "Don't listen to me!"—but she kept on saying something maliciously angry and disgusting...

"Well at least give me something to help me!!" she suddenly cried out. "Some water, at least! Medicine! Smelling salts! I realize that's not what they put you here for, but doesn't this torture have to end sometime?!"

He handed her a cup of water and said, "We ought to take your temperature now too..."

She glanced at his face in amazement, almost jerked away, hearing that good-natured, calm, clear voice.

And only now did it strike her: he hadn't said a single word back to her in answer to all her insane ravings...

She could have died from shame!

She squeezed her eyes shut in annoyance. She hurriedly felt for a tablet, swallowed it with the water, and lay down, turning her face to the wall.

It felt like she really did have a fever. Her joints ached. She felt like curling up into a ball. But this wasn't, this wasn't at all what was tormenting her most of all right now.

A tedious stench was left hanging in her soul after her scandalous hysterics, it just wouldn't dissolve, and she hadn't even managed to tell him not to believe these words that she had used like a whip, as if across the face!—and he had listened without a word of his own...

And now this insult, inflicted on another, began to torment Anna Petrovna as if she had herself been insulted, but a hundred times worse!

And so now she was lying on the bottom of a drowsy stupor and gazing, face to face, at this terrible insult-guilt of hers, and this insult and guilt, neither increasing nor decreasing, hung in front of her, motionless and emo-

tionless—like that tinny fish of her dreams that swam near the very bottom
and stopped with its cruelly scratched side alongside the coal-black petrified
tree stump, and the disturbed silt around it, like a stench, just would not settle, it just hung there like a cloud of smoke, making it ever more difficult, more
painful and more of an effort to breathe...

...and suddenly very frightened that she would just depart with this
agonizingly tedious stench in her soul, she rubbed her eyes hard and sat
up suddenly against her pillows and, not seeing Victor beside her—with a
sense of absolute catastrophe because Victor was no longer beside her—
shouted hastily, "Victor! Victor!"

already knowing for a certainty that he would Never appear again,
because she had been so irreparably unjust to this man, and the black poison of repentance started flowing triumphantly, spreading and stinging,
inside her breast...

"Victor! Victor!" she shouted pitifully and bitterly, instantly feeling
herself to be exactly what she probably really was right then—a pathetic,
feeble old woman, deserted by everybody and staring in confusion at her
empty hands.

He came in quickly, almost ran in from the hall, quite worried—obviously by her shout.

"...I was seeing the doctor out..."

She looked at him, finding it hard to believe, finding it hard to see his
face clearly through the film of tears blurring her eyes.

Then she leaned her head back against the pillows in relief and completely submerging herself in the ineffable pleasure of salvation and peace,
asked dispassionately, "Why, was the doctor here?"

immediately, however, recalling some faceless figures in white, pene-
trating through her recent stupor, and a husky female voice, peevishly
telling someone, "Well, you just try and hit a vein like that! You call that a
vein? It's not a real vein, it's just a tiny thread,"—and some kind of fussing
around with her body, futile and unnecessary fussing (and judging by how
much contempt and routine boredom there was in *the way* they fussed,
turning her over from one side to the other, never leaving her body alone,
she guessed that they too, these people in white, understood perfectly the
complete futility of all this fuss...), and she felt terribly ashamed that she
(God knows, without wanting to!) was taking them away from *living*
beings, who, maybe at that very moment, needed their help much more
than she did, and it was annoying that these people in white just refused
to understand this and wouldn't leave her alone and continued to inter-

fere, not allowing to happen *properly* what must happen and was already happening to her.

"Make them leave me alone," she rasped. "You tell them."

"They found pneumonia," Victor answered. "They won't leave you alone."

"They won't have time..." She grinned regally and immediately remembered, "Another thing. I was afraid that I wouldn't see you again: *Forgive me!* I said a lot of dreadful things to you—they're not true. Don't believe them."

Pleased, but also relieved, he laughed.

He cautiously touched her hand. "You needn't have worried, Anna Petrovna. I didn't believe you anyway." And continuing to look at her with that same slightly sentimental smile of satisfaction, he added, "You know, if I'd have met you some fifty years ago, I don't doubt that I'd have fallen head over heels in love with you!"

"Yes, I don't think you would have missed out on that," the woman agreed in an unexpectedly dry tone and suddenly became gloomily pensive.

After a while as some sort of regretful apology she said, "You must have had a hard time with me... So, they're not offended, are they?" she asked Victor for some reason, and boldly looked him in the eye for an answer. And suddenly an unbelievably sly imp flashed for a tiny moment in her lemon-black eye sockets, already funereal, already terrible. Suddenly such a merry, young blueness flared in them, that Poluektov even groaned slightly in delight and fidgeted a bit and felt a momentary sharp respectful pang of envy for those upon whom such blueness had once been lavishly bestowed.

"...not offended. And I'm not offended. And that's that. And the main thing, I did get to apologize to you. Outside there's probably snow on the ground?

"Not yet."

"And those... poor souls... still stand out there every day with their bottles?"

"What else can they do?"

"I feel terribly sorry for them when it rains, or when it's just about to snow... There's some money up there on my dresser; give it to my neighbor Faina. Let her... But, you know, I've probably completely let myself go?"

"But in general..," she said after a short pause in an unexpectedly clear, strong voice, but with her eyes already closed. "But in general, it's a lot like when it's just about to snow."

And Poluektov understood that Anna Petrovna had said this just for him—with a simultaneously soothing and parting intonation: "Don't worry too much..."

When she once more opened her eyes, she was startled to see how far down she was lying—as if on the very bottom of a long, narrow and terribly high box, which only after a long, hard effort did she recognize as her living quarters.

And more than ever before this room reminded Anna Petrovna of a crevice.

She even briefly imagined some enormous floor—stretching to the horizon. Or rather, some wooden plain, carefully nailed down, with floorboards running off straight into the distance and merging there, at the juncture with the sky, in a tight geometric bundle. And here, in one of the crevices between the floorboards, in the dusky, fluffy, cobwebby dust, which had accumulated and reminded her of some very light musty felt, lay her body—the dry, empty husk of her body, looking slightly charred, no longer good for anything and no longer needed by anyone.

The feeling was humiliating, and she immediately tried to stop it, attempting to at least sit up. But right away she nearly died from the pain, which latched tenaciously onto the back of the neck as soon as she made an effort to lift her head.

She remained lying the way she was, but now, thank God, she at least realized that she was lying on her bed in her miserable little room, and there wasn't any floor, and it wasn't a crevice that she was sprawled in, forgotten by everyone, although the room as always did horribly remind her of a dusty crevice, where she was sprawled out and dying, forgotten by everyone.

She rolled her head to the side and saw a man, sleeplessly and obediently sitting at her table.

Again the feeling of irritable strangeness that she had felt when she regained consciousness returned. Again she couldn't understand where she was, what she was, or what was wrong with her.

She lay there helpless (again it seemed that she was down very low, nearly on the floor...), and at her desk some man—she peered carefully at him in consternation—was painstakingly and clumsily wielding a needle, with amusing solemnity pulling out and upward a nearly half-meter-long length of thread: he was mending her robe!

A caustic, biting peevishness, like acid, began eating at her.

Everything was *wrong*! Everything was somehow out of joint. Everything seemed somehow to be arranged to spite her and make her uncomfortable!

And her blanket was suffocating her, scorching her, but she wasn't able, she didn't have the strength, to fling it back and let her body cool off.

And the wall that she was lying beside kept (she could *feel* this) continually swaying and tilting slightly, ready to fall on her at any second, and she couldn't crawl off even a little ways toward the edge of the bed! How could she crawl away!— she couldn't even wiggle her finger, literally: mentally she sent an order to her fingers, but they remained immobile, because the signal (she could see this) was instantly extinguished as if it were stuck in the murk of her decaying body...

She felt cramped.

She felt cross and irritable.

She felt peevish and nauseated.

Then it was as if someone somewhere had closed a valve. The cramped feeling and the crossness and the offended irritation and the biting peevishness—like swirling water, all very rapidly started piling up and filling up too fast... Finally it overflowed in a flood and—

—and Anna Petrovna, with a sudden violent jerk, rolled over on the bed and fell—sort of threw herself—down on the floor, but without feeling either any pain from the fall or any fear, her attention latching solely onto the briefly flashing sense of pride that she had been able to make even that kind of movement.

...And someone instantly called out—desperately, with gleeful terror, as the very last hope, "A-a-anya-a-a!!"

and she immediately saw a ball flying straight at her—a gloomily gray artificial leather volleyball, not very well pumped up, and so, more angular than round. It had been hit sharply at her in a masculine and distinctly mean manner diagonally across the court by the untalkative military aviator with fiery red, stiff, curly hair, who for some reason always came from the nearby sanatorium ("Now why would he do that?" the local girls would smirk, glancing expressively at Anna Petrovna) to play volleyball on their court, although everyone knew that the sanatorium had a much better court, and a new net, and a leather ball, and the players were incomparably better... Not better, of course, than this fiery redhead, who they said had played on the Air Force national team and whose championship caliber was indeed shown in literally every movement of his on the court:

in the way he served—with such an incredible "hook," that the ball, spinning in a short low arc over the net, would drop almost perpendicularly onto the second line to the helpless and pitifully frantic motions of the defenders;

and in the way he softly, with an impressive open respect for his teammates (who clearly did not at all deserve this respect) set the ball up for them;

and, of course, in the way he attacked when there was a good pass above the net—leaping for the ball even from the back line, greedily, joyously, rapaciously and instantly hitting the ball nearly straight down right under the net, as if making some victorious exclamation mark in honor of a Genuine Volleyball Player, of whom here, of course, people had not the least notion.

...In such moments he would tower above the net, menacing and implacable—nearly up to his waist!—his body leaning slightly back, his arm bent threateningly, and pause briefly in mid flight, as if surveying his opponents' court... and then his movement would be heard—yes, be heard like a shot—the lightning, saber movement of the blow with which this redhead hit the ball as if he were killing it.

It was unthinkable to successfully defend one of his hits—one of his *real* hits. This had long been clear to everyone;

this was also clear to everyone that time, too, when desperately, and with gleeful terror, and as the very last hope, everyone suddenly shouted, "A-a-anya-a-a," and she saw the gray angular rock of a ball flying at her face, hit with such stupendous force, that it wasn't even spinning at all, but seemed to be standing in the air, merely yawing slightly from side to side.

And beside and behind the ball—the mocking gaze of the military aviator, seeming a bit insane and irritated at something, glowed coldly—a gaze which offended and shocked and angered her greatly,

because she alone *knew* what others only guessed—that he really did come to their court to play volleyball only because of her,

because she alone *saw* what others did not notice and would never be capable of noticing: how his face, morbidly expressionless, and apparently always ready to take offense, how this face would shine in happy relief and even a bit stupidly, when he would arrive at the court and finally see her and their eyes would accidentally meet.

because she alone *felt*, with sympathy and condescension, what others could not feel: how the flustered agitation, pitiful delight and completely juvenile excitement overcame this grown man whenever they happened to be on the same team, and how absolutely boundlessly happy he was in such moments—to be on the same team with her.

And when they found themselves on opposite sides of the net, sparing her pride to the point of ridiculousness, he would not play to her side at all! Or if he did, then he would tap the ball so softly, with such careful solicitousness, that she was the only one who never had any trouble returning a ball hit by the intimidating military aviator.

But now he had hit—really hit—without the slightest mercy—something had happened—vengefully—the way people pushed to the limit free themselves from their tormentors.

God knows she had never tried to torment him!—but there was no longer any point in thinking about that, for this ferocious ball was already coming right at her face, murderously and terrifyingly, and in her imagination—for the millionth fraction of the blinking of an eye—there had already flashed something wild and terrifying: some bloody splashes, some bloody smear—what would be left of her face. And terrible pain. And stinging humiliation. And the nauseating anguish of complete helplessness... But...

...but—in the very same fraction of an eyeblink that she saw all this—her body was already performing its miraculous miracle:

arching her back so incredibly far that from the side it looked as though the woman was sadly toppling over on her back, her body, was already flying, impelled by a precise springy push of her strong extended legs, in the same direction that the ball was speeding—as if to get away from the ball—simultaneously performing one more amazingly complicated—corkscrew—movement, so that as a result she found herself with her back to the oncoming ball, her back to it and a bit below it...

and her arms at the very same time were performing another action of their own, dictated by God knows what instinct: prayerfully crossed at the wrists, they stretched frenziedly up as far as they could, apparently into emptiness, but actually—to that one, single point of space, where their motion and the path of the ball, flashing above her shoulder, were destined to intersect and where the ball—crudely searing the skin of her tightly closed wrists, instantly losing its crushing force, was destined (she *knew* this!), meek and peaceful, to bounce back to the net...

And that was what happened.

Searing her skin like sandpaper, visibly jolting her freely swinging arms downward, the ball bounced back to the net, accompanied by a collective "Oo-oo-h!" from the amazed spectators, and she happily slammed to the ground, feeling with a smile the insignificant pain in her elbows and knee, still all shaken from the fantastic relief which *exploded* inside her as soon as she felt the body of the ball solidly and truly land on her wrists, and its dark, heavy contents—as if briefly overflowing, very strongly, but not at all viciously or brutally—jolt her arms downward: she could barely realize that a miracle had happened—she had returned the ball and returned it accurately!

And instantly—on the heels of this thought—she remembered that desperate, very last hope, which mischievously, but still sincerely, shrieked in that desperate cry: "A-a-an-ya-a-a!!" ("Save us! There's no one else, A-a-an-ya-a-a!").

and she nearly cried with sudden gratitude to those who, in spite of everything, had still believed in her so strongly.

She ran her happy glance along the blobs of faces turned toward her from all sides of the volleyball court, seeking out the one single face in the whole wide world that she needed to exchange glances with—right then, that very minute...

but horror overwhelmed her.

She found that she could no longer remember his face! Not a single feature!

A blurry, foggy blind spot appeared whenever she tried to remember that dearest of all faces.

And sickened by this horrifying loss, she again cried out something quite different than she had intended—a doomed, pathetic: "Victor!"

he came and leaned over her and she, so pathetically worshipful, thirstily *drank* in his face with her eyes. As if, dying of thirst, she had started drinking with her eyes. And urgently: she wanted to keep drinking and drinking...

Poluektov, appearing to realize what was happening to her, did not move, subjecting himself to her gaze, and his face maintained an expression of tense embarrassment—as if a blind person were running rapid fingers over his face.

Finally she tiredly closed her eyes and when she opened them again, they were portentously vacant.

Turning her face away from him toward the faded wallpaper where some little woven baskets of flowers, all monotonously overturned with their bottoms up, kept flying and flying off somewhere, she uttered apologetically, though also already almost indifferently, "I just didn't reali..." And life ended inside her.

"Anna Petrovna!" he called in a cautious voice, as if awakening her from sleep. His answer was silence. He sighed, got up and walked off to look out the window.

The little asphalt courtyard was empty. There were just some rickety broken-down crates, covered in places with wet, torn newspapers, standing in some semblance of a line along the dilapidated, peeling wall.

It was dark, and, judging by all the signs, it was about to start snowing at any minute.

* * *

...When it was just beginning to snow, when it was about to start snowing at any minute, and all around everything was filling up with inky, gloomy darkness—filling up so apprehensively and precipitously that it seemed that the sky had suddenly very, very quickly come down to earth, squeezing out and strangling the light—when from this sudden darkness your eyes would suddenly begin to sting viciously, and whatever these eyes would glance at, would instantly seem to turn sour in caustic, hopeless sorrow; when the puddles, previously undistinguished, would suddenly begin to shine like insidious, vengeful silver and the trees would turn black as coal, funereal, and people's pale, white faces would apprehensively appear here and there in the dark burrows of the windows, anxiously peering out; when everything dejectedly stopped stock-still and only some rumpled crow, sort of blown sideways by the wind, would swiftly float across the sky from east to west, where the icy crevice of the sunset, with a yellowish inflammation around the edges, was already shining terrifyingly behind the black cubes of the apartment houses...

—at this time she would be so depressed, so inconsolably lonely, standing in the gray dusk by the window, from whose invisible crevices a draft blew so mordantly and clearly, feeling the dismal poison of this unfriendly evening crawling along her veins, feeling a savage longing for vanished light, joy and merriment fill everything around her, no longer leaving even the slightest hope. It was so depressing, so lonely and at the same time so sweet to stand there, feeling the little lump of her heart tenderly aching for the man, who at that very minute, under those lowering skies—enduring, obstinate and more and more bitter—still (she knew this!) was on his way to see her...

The darkness would reach its furthest limits, and then at this last edge, beyond which, it seemed, there was already nothing except despair, she would fill herself with sympathy and compassion, would suddenly concentrate her sorrow on him, her whole being even sort of howling with the fierce hunger to *help him!..*

and, wonder of wonders—a moment always came, when, triumphant, she would begin to feel a link stretching between them, warm and alive, and then he—was not alone, and she—was not alone.

And for some reason it always seemed that it was through their efforts that the world would suddenly brighten up in relief: finally the skies would open up and thickly, hastily, one after the other, the snowflakes would start streaming down.

And for some reason it always seemed that the white excited murmur of the snowfall was like the hurried story told by someone to someone about how disaster had come close, how disaster had already been at the door and how disaster had spared them.

* * *

"Marina is in a sanatorium; it's completely out of the question to upset her," Novosyolov announced when he heard Poluektov's news.

The conversation took place in the entrance hallway, where both of them were standing.

"I don't think I even dare inform her about this sad (here he smiled thinly) event: after all, my dear Marina is so delicate." His smile was completely unrestrained.

Poluektov looked at him without speaking, curious.

"If you had any material assistance in mind, then, alas, we don't have any money right now. Marina had to bribe right and left, you realize, in order to get into the sanatorium and then to obtain imported medicine."

Poluektov was observing him very attentively and minutely. Probably the gaze of his narrow, stubbornly sardonic eyes unpleasantly disturbed Novosyolov.

"To make a long story short," he said almost rudely, "Marina is not going to have anything to do with this business. And she won't give you any money. If you were hoping—who knows what you are thinking?—for help from *me*, then I also pass. I don't like this sort of thing, and besides I never in my life got anything from that old creep except unpleasantness. Do you know," (here one could hear truly touching sincerity and echoes of hurt feelings)—"do you know what they say about me now at work? 'Novosyolov? Oh! Is he the one who got stuck with the ring?..'"

Poluektov grunted, apparently with enjoyment.

"And you, personally—who are you?" (Alarm could be heard in his belated question. He, of course, was thinking of some possible official problems and the consequences they might cause him.)

"Her nephew," Victor said as usual and turned toward the door.

Novosyolov was exultant.

"That's really remarkable—that you're her nephew," he whispered, warmly and happily inspecting his visitor and pulling back the locks and bolts to let him out of the entrance hallway. "The spade's in your hands now, as they say. You take care of the funeral. Good-bye, nephew. You've made us very, *very* sad with your sorrowful news."

At these words Poluektov turned abruptly around.

But looking once more at Novosyolov's face, he turned away wearily, and without saying another word, walked to the elevator.

There were three two-kopeck coins in his pocket.

He phoned three of his friends, and the next day—a marvelous farewell-to-autumn day—they buried Anna Petrovna, after taking a simple and thoughtful last look at her tallow-colored face, already insignificant and disdainfully crumpled by death.

"And, by the way, chief, the ground here is hard as a rock..," he was informed by one of the gravediggers, who had just finished tamping down the burial mound—a cheerful, bright-eyed, student type.

"It is?" Victor absentmindedly asked back and more or less expectantly started staring at his face with his persistent, overly attentive gaze.

Then he reached in his pocket and, without looking at it, gave him a five-ruble bill.

"Too little, chief!" the fellow yelled in mock reproach.

Poluektov smiled sullenly. "Well, chew on it awhile—maybe it'll swell up and get bigger," and he patted the student on the shoulder and set out to catch up with his three friends, who, striding leisurely along, had already managed to get far ahead on the cemetery walkway, and like true friends were enjoying questioning each other about life.

Translated by John Beebe

Originally published in *Znamia*, February 1987

ABOUT THE AUTHORS

VIKTOR EROFEYEV
(b. 1947, Moscow)

The son of diplomats who spent three years in France (1956-58), Viktor Erofeyev in 1965 enrolled in the Department of Languages and Literatures at Moscow University. After graduating in 1970, he embarked on his graduate studies at the Gorky Institute of World Literature (IMLI), which culminated in his dissertation on Dostoevsky and French Existentialism (1975). Since his first review in 1968, Erofeyev has published articles and books on de Sade, Camus, Fyodor Sologub, and such thinkers as Nikolai Berdyaev, Lev Shestov, and Vasily Rozanov.

Best known as a critic and scholar at IMLI specializing in French and contemporary Existentialist literature, in 1978 Erofeyev gained acceptance into the Writers' Union as a critic. Less than a year later, however, the much publicized Metropole affair (to which Erofeyev contributed two stories and a novella) led the Union to expel him as a writer. For a while after the scandal, Erofeyev experienced difficulties publishing his scholarly pieces and especially his fiction. Despite Erofeyev's reinstatement in the Union, his prose has met official resistance. It has been disseminated unofficially through circulation of his manuscripts and through public and private readings. Owing to the current relaxation of Soviet controls, in the last two years Erofeyev has traveled throughout the United States, lectured at universities, and negotiated contracts with American publishers for works that have yet to appear in the Soviet Union.

Apart from his as yet unpublished novel, *A Russian Beauty* (Russkaia krasavitsa), Erofeyev favors the short form and a linguistically suggestive style of unexpected juxtapositions. Antiquated elevated lexicon jostles with slang and vulgarisms, the poetic consorts with the vulgar, and lyricism alternates with low naturalism. Scenes of murder, beatings, onanism, excretion, myriad forms of uncontrolled violence, and the like (which recall the underbelly of Existentialism and Jarry's Theater of Cruelty) occur with almost compulsive frequency in Erofeyev's fiction, often interspersed with echoes from classics of Russian literature. His is a Postmodernist prose that bespeaks fragmentation, relativism, and alienation— and voluptuously enjoys violating its readers' sensibilities in the process. The two stories included here, which have been translated from copies of Erofeyev's original manuscript, show him at his characteristic best.

Clearly, the year 1988 marked a turn in Erofeyev's fortune as a prosaist: a bowdlerized Russian version of "The Parakeet" (Popugaichik) appeared in *Ogonyok*, which also awarded the story a prize; the emigre Russian almanac *Panorama* printed "Anna's Body"; and Erofeyev made his debut in the Soviet journal *Youth* (Iunost') with two stories entitled "A Letter to Mother" (Pis'mo k materi) and "Galoshes" (Galoshi). His series of interviews with writers such as Vasily Aksyonov that have started appearing regularly in *Ogonyok* display his astuteness and skill as an interviewer.

H. G.

ANATOLY GENATULIN
(b. 1925, Bashkiria)

Genatulin's official biographical sketch reads like a McGuffey's primer on how to become a well-published Soviet writer of his generation: "Participant in the Great Patriotic War (World War II). Awarded Order of Glory, Third Degree, and medals. After demobilization worked on the construction of the Sochi hydro-electric station, then in a Moscow factory until 1975. Member of the Union of Writers since 1978." This model biography would lend itself to socialist realism of the old-fashioned variety, but what distinguishes his work from that discredited literary doctrine is the raw moral energy with which Genatulin attacks social and political irresponsibility.

Both in theme and style Genatulin is perhaps the most traditional writer in this collection. Typical of his generation, Genatulin first wrote about the war, but has recently turned to the contemporary village for his themes. His late-blooming, Bashkirian variety of village prose as represented by *Rough Weather* powerfully combines realistic detail with moral analysis. Genatulin communicates a sure grasp of his fictional terrain and leaves no doubt that he cares about it passionately. This sense of passion not only overcomes the conventional genre and stylistic simplicity, but also makes them technical assets: the moral message is paramount and the reader should not be distracted by trivial literary devices. His broadly humanistic concern carries over to contemporary literary politics. When an open meeting of the reformist April Group of the Writers' Union was disrupted in January 1990 by a small band of anti-Semites shouting "Russia for the Russians, the Jews to Israel," Genatulin noted his dismay (*Moscow News*, 4, 1990): "I fought against fascism on the front and now I have encountered it in the center of Moscow. I am a Bashkir, my wife is a Tatar, and we have lived all of our lives in Russia, but never have we encounterd anything like this." His most recent collection of short works is *The War Is Almost Over* (Vot konchitsia voina, 1988).

B. L.

GENNADY GOLOVIN
(b. 1941, New York)

Golovin's biography normally lists Moscow as his birthplace, but in an interview related to this first American publication of his work he revealed that he was in fact born in New York City, where his Muscovite parents worked for a few years in the Soviet Consulate. The long years of official xenophobia led him to cite Moscow as his birthplace.

Golovin was a travel journalist before quite recently devoting himself entirely to fiction, and his short list of favorite places in the Soviet Union are suitably far-flung—Kamchatka, the Kalmyk steppe, the north near Vologda, and especially the village near Moscow where he spends the summers with his young family. Similiarly, a sense of geographical-philosophical diaspora pervades the narrative structure of his works, in which a good, but simple, protagonist finds himself struggling through a violently or arbitrarily interrupted journey to reach home—a place of strong human relationships and spiritual values—from a remote, peripheral, unfriendly locale.

Golovin has strong affinities with the Russian classical traditions of realism in a context of moral and historical analysis. In his psychological portraiture of the "little" person cut adrift in a callous, complex society, he is akin to Chekhov; in his predilection for borrowings from the detective genre he establishes links to Dostoevsky; and his belief in a didactic role for literature in building a just society reminds the reader of Tolstoy, among others. "Literature is a lifesaver that I want to toss to people," he has said.

Anna Petrovna is the tale of a sensitive woman's survival through civil war, displacement, family loss, poverty, and, in her old age—violent abuse and death. Golovin does not allow either history or sociology to dominate his heroine and his own focus on her courage to remember. He renders Anna Petrovna's inner voice through a complex, convincing construct of modernistic devices. *Patience and Hope* (Terpenie i nadezhda, 1988), his first collection of stories, takes its name from the central theme of the story. Despite the shattered expectations and random reprisals of his fictional world, these voices resonate in a polyphony of memory, need, and consciously chosen risk for the sake of love, exemplified by the patience and hope of his character, Anna Petrovna. While in most ways Golovin is a traditionalist, a spirit of literary exploration pervades his work. His literary innovation and ventures into the blank spots of such previously taboo themes as Soviet social injustice and historical chance, have established him as a genuine voice of glasnost—and one of its freshest, most promising ones.

B. L.

FAZIL ISKANDER
(b. 1929, Sukhumi)

Like Gogol, Turgenev, Bunin, and Nabokov, Fazil Iskander made his literary debut as a poet. With four volumes of verse published, Iskander continues to write poetry, though fiction has gradually become his dominant mode and is what attracts his wide audience among Russians and Westerners. A resident of Moscow for over two decades, Iskander differs from all of his contemporaries for his unique, singlehanded creation of a fictional history of his native Abkhazia. This autonomous republic in the Caucasus, whose exotic traditions and colorful characters Iskander presents in a humorous, leisurely, epic manner, serves as the setting for many of his stories.

Iskander's first published stories, *Forbidden Fruit* (Zapretnyi plod, 1966), revealed his gift for sly, gentle satire. His satirical skills as well as his predilection for first-person narration and loosely-structured, digressive forms that could be extended indefinitely characterize most of his prose, whatever the subject of his irony. Most memorable among his many collections are his *Goatibex Constellation* (Sozvezdie kozlotura, written in 1966, translated into English in 1975), a sardonic depiction of Soviet genetics and journalism that thematically prefigures such current best-sellers of perestroika as V. Dudintsev's *White Robes* (Belye odezhdy, 1987) and D. Granin's *Bison* (Zubr, 1987) and his *Time of Happy Discoveries* (Vremia schastlivykh nakhodok, 1973). A hilarious dystopia entitled *Rabbits and Boa Constrictors* (Kroliki i udavy, 1982), also published abroad, and a collection of non-satirical stories, *Under the Sign of the Walnut* (Pod sen'iu gretskovo orekha, 1979) spotlight, respectively, Iskander's capacity for allegorizing and his flair for plangent lyricism.

Critics and readers concur, however, that Iskander's major achievement is his artistic monument to Abkhazia: the potentially infinite series of narratives revolving around the larger-than-life figure of the toastmaster Sandro and around the boy Chik—Iskander's fictionalized self-portrait. These include the volumes *Sandro of Chegem* (Sandro iz Chegema, 1979) and *The Defense of Chik* (Zashchita Chika, 1983). Because these picaresque chronicles, full of humor and zest, touch on such sensitive subjects as nationalities, repression of minorities, and the absurdity of political slogans that are manifestly at odds with lived reality, Iskander had to wait until glasnost for their publication in the Soviet Union. Early this year, however, the journal *Youth* (Iunost') awarded Iskander one of its prizes for the stories printed in the journal during 1988. Other tales of Abkhazian life doubtless will follow and eventually comprise yet another volume of that republic's fictional history.

H. G.

MIKHAIL KURAEV
(b. 1939, Leningrad)

What really happened in Soviet history? How did ordinary men view the catastrophic events they took part in? These are the questions Mikhail Kuraev sets for himself in two long tales widely recognized as among the most impressive new writing to appear during glasnost—*Captain Dikshtein: A Fantastic Narrative* (translated here from the book version) and *The*

Night Watch: A Nocturne for Two Voices with the Participation of VOKhR Rifleman Comrade Polubolotov (Nochnoi dozor: Noktiurn na dva golosa pri uchastii strelka VOKhR tov. Polubolotov, *Novyi mir*, 12, 1989). Both employ sharply ironic fictional tools to analyze crucial times: *Captain Dikshtein*—the Kronstadt uprising of 1921; *The Night Watch*— Stalinist terror. Essentially Kuraev stands history on its head and then presents it from the perspective of ordinary men with their small passions, large fears, and remarkable gifts for survival. The result is a kind of anti-history with few certainties or reliable landmarks.

The reader finds an unmistakably Russian human landscape and in the background a peculiar, eclectic edifice made from history's fragments— pieces that are simultaneously valuable and unreliable from being almost constantly under demolition and reconstruction. His super-ordinary protagonists are men whose identities, both internal and external, have been transformed by the cruel forces of Soviet political history.

Two aspects of Kuraev's biographical profile seem important for understanding his sensibility as a writer. First, he was born to a family of pre-revolutionary intelligentsia, and his early childhood was ringed by World War II and the seige of Leningrad, from which he was evacuated with his mother and brothers in 1942. Second, he graduated from the Leningrad Institute of the Arts in cinematography and went on to work as a scenarist in Lenfilm Studios (1961-68). A childhood dominated by war and Stalinist repression provided a natural incentive to study Soviet history—and rewrite and reconstruct it from new sources and perspectives—and so far this is Kuraev's favored material. The narrative point of view changes frequently, sometimes even abruptly, as if the narrator is alternating his lenses for dramatic, visual purposes. A broad, sweeping scan is followed by a detailed close-up, often with an ironic montage of images.

The Russian literary tradition reverberates in Kuraev. His preference for a phantasmagorical realism reveals ties with Gogol, Veltman and Dostoevsky. In an interview for this anthology—his first publication in English— he pays eloquent tribute to them as cartographers of the delusory territory of Petersburg-Leningrad, but disclaims any direct literary ties: "I myself cannot determine what in my writing is from Kuraev and what is from the writers I love and the writers I dislike. I don't have anything concrete in mind when I write, but nevertheless I see enemies in front of me."

Kuraev is now writing a film script on the life of Socrates—a joint project with his wife, the writer Olga Trifonova-Miroshnichenko. But he leaves little doubt that he will return to another chapter of Russian history. "A bitter happiness has fallen to us contemporary Russian writers. We're obligated to write about what our predecessors had to remain silent or to whisper about. It's only now that strong and honest works can be written about the year 1947, about what happened in 1957, 1960, 1970, and 1987."

B. L.

VLADIMIR MAKANIN
(b. 1937, Orsk)

A member of the Gorky Institute of World Literature, Makanin joined the ranks of the literati in the 1960s, but until recently attracted relatively little attention. Although his reputation among Soviet readers has grown recently, he still remains unknown and untranslated in the West. Makanin's tendency after the appearance of his first novel, *A Straight Line* (Priamaia liniia, 1965), in the journal *Moscow* (Moskva), to publish the majority of his subsequent narratives in book form may explain the deferred recognition by Soviet critics and public alike. Since Soviet commentators rarely react to literary works printed outside of journals, Makanin's fiction throughout the 1970s was virtually ignored.

Two constants unite all of Makanin's fiction: his preference for novels and novellas over the short story and a fascination with shifts in time and place. In other respects his work falls roughly into three periods that reflect a steady process of maturation: that of apprenticeship until the early 1970s; of wide-ranging experimentation from the mid-70s until the mid-80s; of self-assured artistry since 1987. Some critics discerned in Makanin's first novel affinities with Young Prose, but with time he became pigeonholed as a member of the "Moscow School." The prose of this group, which emerged in 1979 and unites such talents as Anatoly Kim, Vladimir Orlov, and Ruslan Kireyev, typically engages in moderate formal experimentation, largely with time, space, and narrative, and focuses primarily on the average man newly transplanted to the metropolis. Now critics acknowledge Makanin as a *sui generis* writer belonging to no identifiable literary movement or circle.

Makanin's fiction of the second period offers an unvarnished, often impersonalized depiction of the crass materialism and spiritual indigence rampant among Moscow dwellers: e.g., *The Safety Valve* (Otdushina), *Old Books* (Starye knigi, 1976), *Portrait in the Round* (Portret i vokrug, 1978). Uneven in quality and occasionally heavyhanded, these records of moral bankruptcy invite comparison with Trifonov's Moscow novellas. During the late 1970s and early 1980s, Makanin with increasing skill and subtlety explored the possibility of temporal and spatial recuperation in the interests of integrating both the self and the manifold aspects of one's culture, as evidenced in the novella *Voices* (Golosa, 1978) and the novel *Where the Sky Merged with the Hills* (Gde skhodilos' nebo s kholmami, 1984).

The categories of time and space play an even weightier role in Makanin's most recent publications: *A Man and a Woman* (Odin i odna, 1987), *The Loss* (Utrata, 1987), and *Left Behind* (Otstavshii, 1987). In these works Makanin achieves nuanced effects through parallel and intersecting plot-lines and characters who ring subtle variations on the same themes. Ruled by a multi-leveled, interfused Time, Makanin's fictional world is propelled by the Forsterian imperative: "Connect!"

H. G.

LYUDMILA PETRUSHEVSKAYA
(b. 1938, Moscow)

Although Lyudmila Petrushevskaya came to literature in 1963, and subsequently attracted a small but enthusiastic group of devotees in theater circles, her growing international reputation today as a masterful playwright is unquestionably a cultural benefit of glasnost. A married mother of three children who has translated from Polish to make ends meet, Petrushevskaya graduated from Moscow University and worked as a radio reporter and an editor at a television studio before making her initial foray into literature—as a prosaist. Although Soviet and Western critics now emphasize her contribution to drama, she has continued to write short stories throughout her long career.

For a quarter century the Soviet literary establishment refused to publish Petrushevskaya, with the exception of occasional stories and individual plays, because her works confront volatile topics in forbidden areas: they expose the moral indifference, psychological disintegration, and social corruption of the urban intelligentsia, especially during the Brezhnev years. Long before glasnost rendered such subjects *de rigueur*, Petrushevskaya's fiction and drama treated prostitution, alcoholism, physical violence, existential dislocation, and acute psychological alienation in aesthetically complex and uncompromising terms. Convened in such externally nondescript settings as poorly furnished apartments and decrepit housing, her spiritually disenfranchised urbanites articulate, inflict, or come to terms with pain as they struggle with the cruelty, betrayal, and compromise perpetrated by life and family, or resulting from their own actions. Virtually all of Petrushevskaya's characters live on the brink of disaster, of a despair that finds expression in verbose, deflective outpourings of linguistically idiosyncratic chatter that mingles colloquialisms, bureaucratese, poetic diction, malapropisms, slang, and folksy speech. These logorrheic passages, however, camouflage as much as they reveal, for the telling omission plays a key role in Petrushevskaya's fiction and drama.

With the advent of glasnost, Petrushevskaya has finally seen the publication of her collected stories, *Immortal Love* (Bessmertnaia liubov', 1989) and her drama, *Songs of the Twentieth Century* (Pesni dvadtsatogo veka, 1989). Her plays, which formerly were associated almost exclusively with small theatrical groups, such as the studio Chelovek (known above all for its brilliant staging of her one-act play "Cinzano") now enjoy regular performances in Moscow, and have been staged abroad: in Amsterdam, New York, and Louisville.

Despite these symptoms of success, Petrushevskaya leaves many of her spectators and readers uneasy, at least in part because of the hard-hitting grimness of her vision. Many Muscovites, for instance, found "Our Crowd" "extreme," "frightening," and "full of unnecessarily revolting details." Her grotesque humor, her matter-of-fact depiction of untarnished, often repulsive, physiological specifics, and her unflinching recognition of the brutal, rarely acknowledged actions motivated by human desperation tend to overshadow the love and strength that sustain her characters in the face of overwhelming odds. Survival is no mean feat in Petrushevskaya's created world, and, as "Our Crowd" illustrates, it triumphs at a chilling price. But, like Petrushevskaya's oeuvre, her survivors may yet live to experience better times.

H. G.

VALERY POPOV
(b. 1939, Kazan)

"Wait! This can't be happening!" Popov's narrator often says in a variety of ways as he confronts a new round of absurdities in the rountine of contemporary daily life. The author of more than a dozen books for adolescents, Popov during glasnost has become a satirist whose adult readership values him for his deft grasp of the outrages of ordinary Soviet existence, his wistful wit, and in a time prone to verbosity and amplification, his brevity. His stories have appeared especially frequently in the literary journals *Yunost* and *Avrora*, and his recent book of collected stories, *A New Scheherazade* (Novaya Shekherezada, 1988), has attracted the kind of critical attention often slow in coming to a satirist. Beneath his characters' stoical grin one finds a seasoned connoisseur of the grotesque.

The much abused train passenger in "Dreams from the Top Berth" uses a formula typical in Popov's satire for coping: through humorous fantasy he invents a place for himself in the very real and ridiculous world of the everyday. "How much longer can we endure the absurd without losing our very selves to it?" his small city folk seem to mutter. Somewhere between the wit in the early stories of Anton Chekhov and the deadpan, devastating observations of Mikhail Zoshchenko, Popov's humor seems perfectly suited to the period of glasnost—its shortages, contradictions, and manifest tribulations of change or promises of change. Dialogue and respect for diversity are the most crucial ingredients for dealing with the complex sources of the daily nightmares, Popov argues in a recent article on the new intellectual freedom in the Soviet Union. "New dogmas are in no way better than old ones. Authentic literature must preserve a personal, living and unconstrained view of people—a literature free at all times from political arguments and 'special assignments'" (*Literaturnaya gazeta*, November 8, 1989). Currently the head of the prose section of the Leningrad Writers' Union, Popov's first-priority now is editing a volume of contemporary literature by Leningrad writers and poets, including those living abroad, such as Joseph Brodsky and Sergei Dovlatov.

B. L.

NIKOLAI SHMELYOV
(b. 1936, Moscow)

Nikolai Shmelyov combines two careers: those of writer and economist. Since graduating from Moscow State University in 1958, he has worked in various economic institutes in the Soviet Academy of Sciences, gaining considerable national fame as a professor and author of books on problems in world economy. His fate as a writer, however, has suffered the vagaries common to many literati in the Soviet Union.

After the publication of Shmelyov's first story (Odoviannye soldatiki, 1961) in the journal *Moscow* (Moskva), none of his fiction appeared for over two decades. This long silence ended in 1987 with his novella *The Pashkov House* (Pashkov dom), which attracted considerable attention from critics and readers. So did subsequent pieces, notably his novel *A Performance in Honor of Mr. First Minister* (Spektakl' v chest' gospodina pervogo ministra, 1988).

Shmelyov's fiction is firmly grounded in the tradition of realism, favors rather simple plots, a straightforward style, and characters caught in crises arising in part from their own weaknesses and mistakes. In tracing the circumstances that have led to their moment of reckoning, Shmelyov reveals the psychology of acquisitiveness, accommodation and fear. His flawed protagonists customarily experience a degree of self-awareness through the soul-searching naturally prompted by personal catastrophe, as demonstrated in "The Visit" and "The Case of the Fur Coat." Shmelyov occupies a middle position on the contemporary literary scene, somewhere between the neo-modernism of alternative prose and the fatigued realism of more conservative exposé fiction. His preference is for clarity, simplicity and immediacy of effect.

A similar clear-headed directness marks his publicistic writings, e.g., the articles "Advances and Debts" (Avansy i dolgi, 1987), "New Worries" (Novye trevogi, 1988) and *The Turning Point: Revitalizing the Soviet Economy* (New York, 1989). In his capacity as economist and publicist, Shmelyov has visited the United States and consulted with American specialists, many of whom consider him one of the foremost economists within Gorbachev's program for economic change.

H. G.

TATYANA TOLSTAYA
(b. 1951, Leningrad)

A granddaughter of Alexei N. Tolstoi, a graduate of Leningrad State University's Department of Classical Languages and Literatures, and now a Moscow resident, Tatyana Tolstaya worked for a publisher before making her literary debut in 1983 with the story "On the Golden Porch." Hailed at once as a fresh talent, Tolstaya nonetheless was not launched on her meteoric career until the publication of "Peters" in 1986. Her collection of thirteen stories, *On the Golden Porch* (1987), appeared in translation two years later (Knopf). Joseph Brodsky and others have acclaimed her verbal mastery, vivid imagination, and profound originality.

An educated, energetic woman of extraordinary independence and vitality, Tolstaya has traveled widely in the West, partly to promote translations of her work in the United States, France, England, Italy, and elsewhere. Her outspoken interviews, conducted in Russian, English, and French (she also knows Greek), have bred controversy, especially among Soviet conservatives and Western feminists. Wherever she appears, Tolstaya fulfills the role of eloquent, fearless spokeswoman for writers' freedom from official proscriptions and constraints; she openly and consistently criticizes the network of repressive, bureaucratic mechanisms that for decades have coerced literary life in the Soviet Union.

If Tolstaya's vigorous public activity leads one to anticipate ideological confrontation in her fiction, any one of her stories quickly dispels those expectations. Her highly condensed narratives offer meditations on the elusive significance of the individual life; the conflicting claims of spirit and matter; the complex nature of perception, language, and human interaction; and the transforming power of memory and the imagination. Of the nineteen stories Tolstaya has authored so far, "Night" remains her favorite. Although the Soviet publishing house that brought out her collection neither altered nor censored her texts, it nonetheless excluded "Night" from the volume, presumably because of a reluctance to admit that retarded adults may be found among Soviet citizens. This compact narrative contains all the features that comprise Tolstaya's distinct authorial signature: a luxurious, sonorous prose saturated with expressive metaphors and metonyms that enable radical condensation—a prose rich in rhetorical devices, intertexts, echoes from folklore, and erratic shifts in mood, tone, perspective, and diction that is marked by irregular rhythms and intense poetic energy. Isolated stylistically from other writers brought into the limelight during glasnost, Tolstaya has closest links with Gogol, Bely, Bunin, Nabokov, and such creative innovators of the 1920s as Olesha and Babel. Hence Brodsky's deserved recognition of Tolstaya as "the most original, tactile, luminous voice in Russian prose today."

H. G.